Policing in
Modern Society

Policing in Modern Society

Bruce L. Berg

BUTTERWORTH
HEINEMANN

Boston Oxford Auckland Johannesburg Melbourne New Delhi

Butterworth–Heinemann supports the efforts of American Forests and the
Global ReLeaf program in its campaign for the betterment of trees, forests,
and our environment.

Library of Congress Cataloging-in-Publication Data
Berg, Bruce L.
  Policing in modern society / Bruce L. Berg.
      p.   cm.
  Includes bibliographical references and index.
  ISBN 0-7506-9867-5 (pbk. : alk. paper)
  1. Police—History.   2. Law enforcement—History.   3. Police
administration—History.   4. Criminal investigation—History.
5. Social control—History.   I. Title.
HV7903.B47   1999
363.2'09—dc21   98–48869
                                                           CIP

British Library Cataloguing-in-Publication Data
A catalogue record for this book is available from the British Library.

The publisher offers special discounts on bulk orders of this book.
For information, please contact:
Manager of Special Sales
Butterworth–Heinemann
225 Wildwood Avenue
Woburn, MA 01801-2041
Tel: 781-904-2500
Fax: 781-904-2620

For information on all Butterworth–Heinemann publications available, go to our
World Wide Web home page at: http://www.bh.com

10 9 8 7 6 5 4 3 2 1

Printed in the United States of America

Table of Contents

Part I   **The History of Policing**   **1**

Chapter 1   Social Control and Social Order   3

Police Officers, Crime, and the Law   3
Human Nature and Social Control   4
Deviance Versus Crime   7
Crimes and the Law   9
Types of Crimes   10
Felony Versus Misdemeanor Crime   11
Mala In Se and *Mala Prohibita* Crimes   11
Summary   12
References   12
Questions For Review   13

Chapter 2   The Historical Evolution of Policing   15

Governing Human Behavior   15
Law Enforcement in Antiquity   16
The Kin Police   16
The Code of Hammurabi   17
Mosaic Law   18
Greek and Roman Influences and Contributions   19
Early English Contributions   20
The Development of Markets and Cities   23
Crime and the Industrial Revolution   25
Henry Fielding and the Bow Street Runners   26
Sir Robert Peel and the Peelers   27
The Development of Policing in the United States   29
The American Hue and Cry   30
The Rattle Watch and Other Early Systems   30
The Modern Police   32
The Political Influence Stage   32
The Reform Stage   33
The Professional Stage   33
The Police and Community Relations   34
Summary   37
References   37
Questions For Review   39

Chapter 3   The Organization of American Law
                Enforcement Agencies   41

        Police Jurisdictions   41
        Policing the City   42
        County Law Enforcement   45
        State Law Enforcement Agencies   46
        Other Early State Level Agencies   49
        Modern State Police and Highway Patrols   50
        Federal Law Enforcement Agencies   52
        The Department of Justice   52
        The Treasury Department   57
        Summary   62
        References   63
        Questions for Review   64

Part II   **Police Operations   67**

Chapter 4   Police Patrol and Traffic Functions   69

        Police Organization   69
        Patrol Work   70
        Protecting and Serving the Public   70
        Securing Scenes and Beginning Investigations   73
        Allocation and Deployment of Patrol Officers   75
        Distribution of the Patrol   76
        Temporal Distribution   76
        Geographic Distribution   78
        Types of Police Patrol   82
        Foot Patrol   82
        Mobile Patrol   84
        Proactive Versus Reactive Policing Strategies   92
        The Kansas City Preventive Patrol   93
        Community-Oriented Policing Efforts   97
        Team Policing   98
        Storefront Policing   99
        Citizen Academies   100
        Reducing the Fear of Crime   101
        The "Big Three" Community Crime Prevention Strategies   102
        Police and the Traffic Function   104
        Traffic Control   105
        Accident Investigation   106
        Summary   106
        References   107
        Questions For Review   109

Chapter 5   Investigations, Juveniles, and Special Units   113

Divisions of Labor in the Police Organization   113
The Investigations Division   115
The Police Detective   115
Investigation   121
Clearing Cases   124
Vice and Narcotics Squads   125
Undercover Police Work   126
Internal Affairs: Policing the Police   129
Juvenile Division   130
Juvenile Gangs   131
Juveniles and Drugs   132
Special Weapons and Tactics (SWAT) Teams   133
Summary   134
References   135
Questions for Review   136

Chapter 6   Criminal Investigation   139

Scientific Detection   139
Inductive Reasoning   140
Deductive Reasoning   141
The Preliminary Investigation   141
Procedures in a Preliminary Investigation   142
Modus Operandi   144
Sources of Information About Crimes   145
Complaints and Complainants   146
Information from Witnesses   147
Reports and Report Writing   147
Guidelines for Writing Reports   148
The Elements of Who, What, Where, When,
    How, and Why   149
Summary   151
References   151
Questions For Review   152

Chapter 7   Interviews and Interrogations   153

Gathering Information   153
General Guidelines for Interviews   155
Interview Preparations   155
Interviewing Witnesses and Victims   156
Types of Witnesses   157
Interrogating Suspects   159

Interrogation Preparation   161
Arranging Interrogations   162
Interrogation Approaches   162
The Logical Approach   162
The Emotional Approach   163
Indirect and Direct Line Approaches   163
Deflating or Inflating Ego Approaches   164
Understating or Overstating Facts Approaches   164
Confessions and Admissions   164
The Polygraph   165
Summary   166
References   166
Review Questions   167

Chapter 8   Constitutional Regulations and the Police: Life, Liberty, and the Pursuit of Criminals   169

The American Peace Officer and Constitutional Protections   169
Arrests by Police   174
Probable Cause: Searches, Seizures, and Arrests   177
The Exclusionary Rule   178
Vehicle Searches   183
Stop and Frisk   186
Field Search Techniques   190
Voluntary Consent Searches   191
The Open Field Doctrine   192
Summary   194
References   194
Questions for Review   195

Chapter 9   Criminalistics and the Police   197

Forensic Science and Scientific Investigation   197
The Origin of American Forensic Laboratories   198
Evidence   200
Collecting Physical Evidence   203
Documenting the Crime Scene   203
Locating and Identifying Evidence   204
Fingerprint Evidence   204
Types of Fingerprints   206
Lifting and Preserving Fingerprints   208
Photographing Fingerprints   208
Development Techniques   209
Fingerprint Files and Searches   210
Automated Fingerprint Identification Systems (AFIS)   211
Live Digital Fingerprinting   211

Shoe and Tire Impressions   212
Other Kinds of Physical Evidence   215
Blood as Evidence   215
Blood Typing   216
Biological Specimens and DNA Typing   216
DNA Profiling or Fingerprinting   218
Other Biological Specimens as Evidence   219
Non-Biological Specimens as Evidence   219
Odontology as a Forensic Investigative Technique   221
Guns, Bullets, and Barrels   222
Summary   223
References   223
Questions for Review   225

Chapter 10   Computers and the Police   227

The Computer as a Double-Edged Sword   227
Computer Applications in Policing   229
Computers and Communications   229
Large Databases   231
Computers and Suspect Identification   231
Programs for Criminal Investigation   232
Computer Programs and Forensics   234
Crimes Involving Computers   235
Cyberpunks and Cyber-Criminals   238
Internal Computer Crimes   240
Computer Manipulation Crimes   243
Support of Criminal Enterprises   244
Hardware and Software Thefts   244
Investigation of Computer Crime   245
Securing a Computer as Evidence   246
Summary   249
References   249
Questions for Review   250

Chapter 11   Police Discretion   253

Discretion and Decision-Making   253
Discretionary Situations   254
To Arrest or Not to Arrest?   260
Factors Affecting the Myth of Full Enforcement   263
Use of Force   266
Excessive Force   266
Decision-Making and Police Liability   267
Non-Deadly Force   269
Managing the Use of Force   270

Progressive Stages of Permissible Force   270
Deadly Force   273
Fleeing Felons   274
Firearms Training   277
Predicting Misuse of Deadly Force   278
Summary   279
References   280
Questions For Review   283

Part III   Police Culture   285

Chapter 12   Women and Minorities in Law Enforcement   287

Women and Law Enforcement   287
From Matron to Police Officer   288
How Do Female Officers Compare to Male Officers?   291
Promotion of Policewomen: Moving Up through the Ranks   293
Defeminization of Policewomen   294
The Police Personality and Policewomen   297
Institutionalized Discrimination in Policing   298
Cultural Diversity in American Policing   299
A Closer Look at the Black Police Officer   301
Cultural Diversity Training   302
Summary   302
References   303
Questions for Review   306

Chapter 13   Police Subculture   309

Two Myths About Police Behavior   309
The Need For Group Support   310
Culture   312
Subculture   312
The Police Academy   315
Inside the Academy   317
Field Training   319
The Academy Classroom Experience   320
Cynicism and Authoritarianism   320
Acquiring a Police Personality   323
Formulating the Police Working Personality Concept   323
Esprit de Corps   325
The Occupational Role of the Police Officer   327
Police Officer Styles   329
Typologies of Policing Styles   330
Modern Policing Styles   333
Summary   334

References   335
Questions for Review   338

Chapter 14   Police Ethics   341

Ethical Standards   341
Police and Ethical Standards   344
The Social Contract of Policing   345
Fair Access to Law Enforcement   346
Support of the Public Trust   346
Maintenance of the Peace, Safety, and Security   346
Justice System Teamwork   347
Unbiased and Objective Police Work   347
Authority Versus Power   348
Organizational Ethics for Police   350
Summary   352
References   352
Questions for Review   353

Chapter 15   Police Deviance and Corruption   355

The Line Between Deviance and Corruption   355
What Is Police Corruption?   358
An Unintentional Effect of Enforcement Priorities   365
Corruption of Individual Officers   366
Corruption of Departments   368
External Factors that Explain Corruption   369
The Occupational Opportunity Explanation   369
Controlling Police Corruption   372
Summary   373
References   374
Questions for Review   376

Part IV   **The Forecast for Policing**   **379**

Chapter 16   Hazards of Policing: Danger, Stress, and AIDS   381

Dangers in the Police Environment   381
Police Work and Stress   387
Eustress and its Effects on the Police Organization   390
Stress and the Officer's Family   390
Stress, Coping, and Alcoholism   391
Role Conflict and Stress   393
Police Stress and Suicide   394
AIDS: A New Police Stressor   395
The Need for AIDS Training for Police   396
AIDS Defined   397

Transmission of AIDS   397
Implications for Law Enforcement   399
Stress from Perceptions of AIDS   400
Handling People with AIDS: Agency Procedures   401
Police Officers with AIDS   402
AIDS and the Law   403
Summary   404
References   405
Questions for Review   408

Chapter 17   Police Professionalism   411

Professional Police Officers or Police Professionals?   411
Profession Versus the Professional   412
Shadow-Box Professionalism   413
Police Unions   416
Police Agency Accreditation   421
Suggested Benefits of Accreditation   422
Detractions of Accreditation   423
Summary   425
References   426
Questions for Review   427

Chapter 18   The Future: Education, Training, and Privatization
in Policing   429

Policing as a Career   429
Higher Education and Police Officers   430
Experience as the Officer's Best Teacher   435
The Value of College-Educated Police   436
From Man-at-Arms to Police Scholar   438
Is High School Preparation Enough?   439
Educational Directions for the Future   440
The Privatization of Policing   441
A Glimpse into the Future of Policing   443
Summary   443
References   444
Questions for Review   447

Index   449

Part 1

The History of Policing

1 Social Control and Social Order

CHAPTER OBJECTIVES

After reading this chapter you should be able to:

1. Understand the role of the law enforcement officer in today's society.
2. Discuss the nature of norms in society.
3. Explain deviance.
4. Differentiate between informal and formal social control.
5. Define crime.
6. Delineate various bodies of law.
7. Explain the difference between a felony and a misdemeanor.
8. Identify *mala in se* and *mala prohibita* crimes.

POLICE OFFICERS, CRIME, AND THE LAW

The phrase "law enforcement" officer typically conveys the notion of one who enforces the laws. In fact, some might argue that the primary purpose for the existence of law enforcement officers is to enforce the formal and codified rules of a society; in short, to enforce the law. If one were asked to close one's eyes and picture a law enforcement officer, the average person would likely envision a man wearing a dark blue uniform, wearing a gun on his hip, and a silver badge of some sort on his chest. In effect, some sort of municipal police officer. Although this media-enhanced stereotype is not entirely incorrect, it is not entirely accurate. Law enforcement officers are not limited to the level of the municipality. Nor, for that matter, are law enforcement officers restricted to males or any particular racial or ethnic type.

KEY TERMS	informal social control	statutory law
	laws	regulatory law
norms	case law	mala in se crimes
deviance	precedent	mala prohibita crimes
social control	common law	

In this book, as in the real world, law enforcement officers are presented in a broader context. As several chapters will detail, law enforcement encompasses a wide variety of functions and may exist at different levels and branches of government.

This book will, however, focus heavily upon various types of uniformed police officers and agencies. In any context, the uniformed police officer is much more than an enforcer of laws. The uniformed police officer represents a personification of American social order. The officer is the front-line representative of the U.S. government at the local community level. To be colloquial, the police officer is "The Man."

For some, the police officer is the symbolic banner of the criminal justice system. For many others, the police *are* the criminal justice system. It is a uniformed officer who must often make the split-second decision to draw a service weapon and shoot a fleeing, violent felon or simply to pursue the criminal on foot. It is the patrol officer who, upon seeing a suspicious person lurking in shadows late at night, must decide whether further investigation is warranted. It is the line officer who, upon discovering a store's open door after closing time, must enter the darkened building and perhaps confront an armed intruder.

It is also frequently the uniformed line officer who must free the 3-year-old boy whose mother has frantically, but unsuccessfully, tried to extricate him from the locked bathroom, or who must rescue the fabled kitten up a tree. Sometimes, the police officer must locate the appropriate social service agency when an aged community member telephones the precinct to report that the utility company has turned off the gas. It may also be a uniformed officer who saves the life of a traffic accident victim who lies bleeding on the ground as the officer arrives on the scene before an ambulance.

The uniformed police officer carries a heavy burden, a friend to some, an enemy to others, a social worker to many, and a life preserver to all. In addition, members of society expect police officers to enforce criminal laws, maintain traffic laws, be knowledgeable on various regulatory laws, building and health codes, and maintain the peace throughout the community. How police officers accomplish all of these functions unfolds in the remainder of this book.

Before considering the various functions of police officers, it is important to understand several basic ideas, theories, and concepts of policing. Let us begin with an examination of the need for social order and control in society.

HUMAN NATURE AND SOCIAL CONTROL

Humans are social beings. From the earliest cave-dwellers to modern apartment-dwellers, people seek the support and company of other people. Throughout history a tension has existed among humans between their need and dependence upon one another and their feelings of personal safety. A similar social tension exists between an individual's personal sense of freedom (liberty) and society's need for social order and control. These social tensions represent a balance between total freedom leading to anarchy on the one hand, and total control leading to tyranny on the other hand (Critchley 1972; Berg 1992). The police as the social institution charged with representing the interests of the community, hold these elements of total freedom versus total control in harmony.

Words such as order, control, constraint, and conformity tend to conjure images of bland, robotic people moving around under the governance of some Orwellian Big Brother. Yet, the essence of social cohesion or solidarity, which are much less affected words than "control," "constraint," and "conformity," are a consensual sharing of certain ways of doing things. In short, it is an agreement upon some set of rules. Unadministered, uncontrolled free activity ceases at once from being liberty and instead becomes anarchy.

Thus, without social controls, people could recklessly drive their cars, assault and steal from one another, or even rape, kill, or mutilate others. In this instance, unbridled activity ceases being freedom and becomes chaos. Free societies depend upon a balance between a person's ability to act independently and without fear of official repression or reprisal and a person's responsibility not to infringe upon others' abilities to act independently as well.

In today's fast-paced, Internet-driven, and technologically advanced society, one still witnesses many systems of social rules. These are rules of dress for certain occupations, rules of conduct in and out of the classroom, rules for different games, rules for the safe operation of motorized vehicles, rules of decorum in talk rooms of the Internet, rules of etiquette, rules for certain religious rituals, rules of proper behavior on first dates, and the lists go on. Interestingly, each system of rules varies both in its degree of formal articulation and when violated, its censures by society. Social scientists describe norms as the elemental units in social rules.

Briefly defined, **norms** are guidelines for conduct or basic social expectations for acceptable behavior. Knowledge of certain norms, therefore, provides one with the specifics of how one should behave in various social situations, especially social settings. Norms are sufficiently elastic to allow for some limited range of adherence and even violation.

For example, in the United States when one enters an elevator, the usual expectation is that one will turn around and face the door. If, however, one were to enter and remain standing facing the rear of the elevator car, one would violate a social norm (an elevator ritual). Although this norm violation might receive some puzzled or even pained expressions from other passengers, very little formal sanctioning is likely to occur. If on the other hand, this same elevator-norm violator were to enter the elevator car, stand facing the rear, and curse or spit at another elevator rider, some greater sanctions might result. In the first case, the norms were stretched, but not to the limit. In the second case, the elevator rider moved beyond the limits of social tolerance: beyond the limits where the other elevator riders were willing to be permissive.

Most people in society follow norms more or less like the elevator rider. The adherence to social norms is not rigid, unyielding, or unchangeable. Norms adjust and adapt to such other fluid social contours in society as religious values, technology, social needs, and the law. Violating norms beyond the social limits of a given society is called **deviance**. The process of responding to norm violation, enforcing rules and sanctions, and returning the group to a state of norm conformity is called **social control**. In later chapters, these terms are more fully examined.

Social controls are ever-present and powerful limitations on certain socially undesirable behaviors. Usually, social control manifests itself as a highly informal, frequently unwritten and unspoken, system of rules and norms. Yet people in society operate in their daily lives both by adhering to various rules and norms and by assuming that others will share in and follow these norms.

For instance, when one goes shopping in a supermarket and is ready to pay a cashier, one queues up behind the last person waiting to be checked out on a given line. Similarly, each person on line expects that other shoppers will queue up according to this general understanding of queuing rituals. If, however, someone pushes into the line ahead of those already waiting, that person is violating queuing norms. There are no statutes in any state's penal code on cutting into a supermarket checkout line. In spite of this, angry patrons on line may impose serious sanctions on the norm violator who cut in ahead of them. In this particular situation, the invoking of what are essentially informal social controls. **Informal social controls** involve sanctions such as angry words, nasty looks, grimaces, and insults intended to reestablish social order, in this case, the queuing ritual. There are no queuing police, and I doubt very much that anyone has ever done jail time for line jumping. Yet, in supermarkets, banks, libraries, concerts, and any other place where lines form, people tend to act appropriately. Unfortunately, the maintenance of social order of society in general cannot always be as neatly or effectively accomplished through these informal social controls and sanctions.

To afford protection that preserves liberty in society, certain norms and rules have been established formally. These formal rules, called laws, create required guidelines for behavior, rather than merely expected ones. Thus, **laws** are formal codified written rules for behavior. In order to assure adherence to these required rules or laws, society has developed various formal sanctions that can be invoked whenever someone violates these laws. These formal laws, in contrast to informal norms, seek to assure safety and security for members of society, as well as to provide guidelines for ownership of personal property.

Laws, then, are a kind of backup system that clarify and strengthen the importance of certain norms already supported by society. Unlike social norms, however, laws are politically legitimated rather than culturally or socially accepted. So, a person who violates a law in society enters a system that possesses the political backing of the entire society. It is on the basis of this political support that various institutions of society are empowered to apprehend, detain, adjudicate, and remand the law violator either out of or back into society.

The maintenance of liberty in our society requires that members be constrained from unbridled behavior. Although most members of society do follow appropriate norms of social behavior, many others do not. As a result, laws and politically backed methods for administering and enforcing them are necessary.

Laws, then, are a formalized system of rules. In turn, laws are intended to complement and buttress the informal system of socially appropriate behavior represented by social norms.

The U.S. Constitution guarantees under law one's freedom to choose a particular lifestyle, manner of speech, religious preferences, level of education, and occupation. Thus, one's freedom depends on provisions under law. Law as described above, is a formal mechanism of social control. If members of society feel the need for greater constraint, they may enact more stringent or numerous laws. Conversely, if members of society believe that existing laws have outlined their usefulness or have not effected the kind of control anticipated, these laws may be repealed.

DEVIANCE VERSUS CRIME

Deviant behavior refers to a very wide range of social activity. If one could witness the vast range of social conduct as a continuum, as illustrated in Box 1.1, it would be possible to see that annoying, bizarre, eccentric, gross, bad, and good behaviors all can exceed the acceptable range of social tolerance.

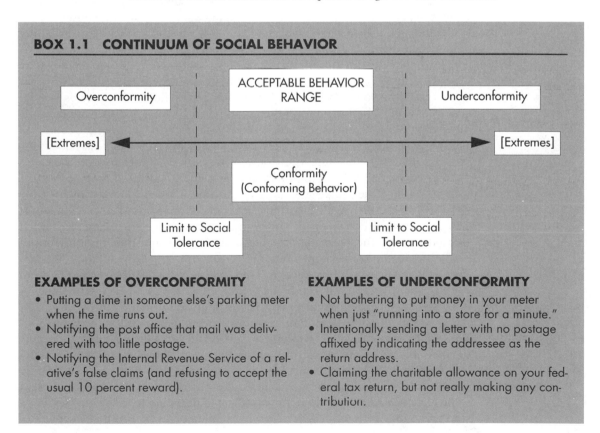

BOX 1.1 CONTINUUM OF SOCIAL BEHAVIOR

Overconformity   ACCEPTABLE BEHAVIOR RANGE   Underconformity

[Extremes] ◄————————————————————————► [Extremes]

Conformity (Conforming Behavior)

Limit to Social Tolerance   Limit to Social Tolerance

EXAMPLES OF OVERCONFORMITY
- Putting a dime in someone else's parking meter when the time runs out.
- Notifying the post office that mail was delivered with too little postage.
- Notifying the Internal Revenue Service of a relative's false claims (and refusing to accept the usual 10 percent reward).

EXAMPLES OF UNDERCONFORMITY
- Not bothering to put money in your meter when just "running into a store for a minute."
- Intentionally sending a letter with no postage affixed by indicating the addressee as the return address.
- Claiming the charitable allowance on your federal tax return, but not really making any contribution.

As Box 1.1 shows, within the range of acceptable behavior are slight stretches in social tolerance. In the direction of overconformity, there are "ideal values." These involve various altruistic actions such as putting a dime in someone's parking meter. Conversely, there are "practical norms," which move in the direction of underconformity, but are not usually seen by society as serious violations of social norms or the law. Still, these may be viewed by many citizens as violations. In essence, these practical norms are how most people in society govern their daily lives. It is common, for example, to see someone stop by a parking meter, run into a store for a minute, and never put money in the meter. Although technically this is a violation of law, it is not one that most people will view as terribly serious. Similarly, more serious excesses of social tolerance than practical norms, while not criminal, may nonetheless be viewed as deviant.

Jerry Simmons (1969) interviewed a cross-section of Americans, and asked them to list which type of people they classified as deviant. Simmons (1969:3) found that most lists included expected categories such as homosexuals, prostitutes, drug addicts, and criminals. He additionally found: . . . it also included liars, career women, Democrats, reckless drivers, atheists, Christians, suburbanites, the retired, young folks, card players, bearded men, artists, pacifists, priests, prudes, hippies, straights, girls who wear makeup, the president, conservatives, integrationists, executives, divorcees, perverts, motorcycle gangs, smart-alec students, know-it-all professors, modern people, and Americans.

In short, how one defines an act or actors as deviant relates to a given time and place, and the person(s) making such an assessment (Siegel 1995). Naturally, certain behaviors are defined more frequently than others are as beyond the limits of social tolerance and therefore deviant. Vulgar words were not only viewed as deviant and a stretch of social tolerance in 1961 when comedian Lenny Bruce uttered them, but they got him 90 days in a county jail for being obscene. In 1979, the Supreme Court of the United States in *United States v. George Carlin* ruled for Carlin. Carlin had brought suit when his record, "Class Clown," was banned in several cities as obscene. Carlin's album contained the routine "The Seven Words You Can Never Say on Television," including words that got Lenny Bruce arrested. The high court ruled that such language, when uttered during a theatrical performance, is acceptable and should not be considered obscene. For some people, comedy performances by George Carlin, Richard Pryor, Eddie Murphy, Chris Rock, Adam Sandler, and others are seen as deviant, even by today's standards. For other people, however, the comedy monologues of these performers fall squarely within the limits of social tolerance.

Deviant behavior, then, amounts to a range of activities that does not conform to the expectations of a given group of people. Within the array of possible deviant acts are behaviors of overconformity, such as feeding coins into someone else's parking meter, social stretches of accepted behavior, such as profanity used during a comedy routine; and underconformity, which may represent minor law violations such as not putting a coin in the meter and running into a store, or more serious violations such as theft or even murder. People frequently confuse the concepts of crime and deviance. These terms are not, however always one and the same.

For instance, smoking marijuana is illegal for use in most states, but is it actually deviant? According to several research studies, a significant number of Americans have used or are using drugs such as marijuana. Even a U.S. President admitted to having once tried marijuana while in college.

In 1986, the state of Oregon's legislature narrowly defeated a bill that would have legalized marijuana. The bill lost by a single vote. In 1996, the state of California ratified a bill (Proposition 215) making it legal to use marijuana for medical reasons under the direction of a physician (Manning 1997). That same year, Arizona ratified a similar bill (Peterson 1997). It would be incorrect to argue that all crimes are acts that significantly depart from social norms of society. It would also be inaccurate to assume that most deviant acts are crimes. For example, if one were to observe somebody shoplifting in a department store, but did nothing to stop it, one has not likely broken any law. Some people might view this non-action by the observer as underconformity or perhaps even deviance. This ambivalent behavior, when involving a misdemeanor, however, is not a crime in any jurisdiction.

On the other hand, if one were to observe the assault and rape of a young woman in a bar, and did not at least report this crime to the police, in many states, this failure to act would constitute a crime. The question, then, may be what exactly are crimes?

CRIMES AND THE LAW

One can certainly find slightly different definitions for crime in various textbooks. A fairly stark legalistic view might suggest that it is simply a violation of criminal law (Hagan 1986). From this legalistic perspective, regardless of how reprehensible, morally outrageous, or deviant an individual's act, it is not technically a crime unless specifically defined as such in a criminal law. Sutherland and Cressey (1974) offer four factors that for some provides the classic definition for crime:

1. Political authority assumes it. The state assumes the role of plaintiff or the party bringing forth charges. Murder, for example, is no longer an offense against an individual, but against the state.
2. It must be **specific**, defining both the offense as well as the prescribed punishment.
3. The law is **uniformly applied**, that is, equal punishment and fairness to all, regardless of an individual's social position.
4. The law **contains penal sanctions enforced by punishments** administered by the state.

In effect, these elements suggested by Sutherland and Cressey link the definition for crime with criminal law.

At one time, most people considered crime a private matter. When one person was injured or offended by another, that person sought compensation in the form of revenge. In some instances, these led to blood feuds and the destruction of entire families (Chapter 2 will consider this in greater length). As time progressed, crimes became offenses committed against the Crown (a king, queen, or thane) and later, against subjects of the Crown (Lee 1971). Eventually, fines levied on behalf of the Crown (or the state) evolved, and the connotation of the state as plaintiff emerged (Hagan 1986). Today, a common definition for crime is "a specific act or commission or omission in violation of the law, for which a punishment is prescribed" (Cole and Smith 1998:6).

TYPES OF CRIMES

Legislative statute or statutory law defines one type of crime. Crime additionally is determined on the basis of case law or common law. **Case law** is the use of judicial decisions from previous and similar adjudication to determine the outcome of a subsequent case possessing similar facts. Hence, case law's determinations are significantly influenced by previous decisions called **precedents**.

Common law originated, and continues to be the main body of law in England. In early colonial America, residents were subjects to the law handed down by English judges and hence, to English common law. After the American Revolution, the colonies in America adapted and changed the English law to fit their particular needs. In many states, legislatures standardized many common-law crimes such as murder, burglary, arson, and rape by putting them into statutory form or **statutory law**. In other words, the legislatures created formal statutes. In other states extensive penal codes were passed, thereby abrogating the common-law crimes (Ferdico 1996; Samaha 1996).

In addition to common law, statutory law, and case law, administrative or regulatory law defines crimes. Typically **regulatory laws** administer civil privileges, such as the privilege to own a handgun or drive a car and other licensed activities. Regulatory laws, however, may also encompass criminal charges. An example of a regulatory law that includes criminal charges would be mailing cocaine to someone. This activity certainly constitutes a misuse of the mail as governed by federal mail regulations. It is also a criminal offense to have or distribute cocaine. Another example might be a bartender selling alcohol to minors. The Department of the Treasury's Bureau of Alcohol, Tobacco, and Firearms also governs such illegal sale of alcohol. Thus, provisions contained in statutory law, case law, or common law, and administrative law establishes crimes. Taken together, these various bodies of law are often referred to simply as "the law." In a general sense one can consider law a formal and binding set of rules that regulate conduct of members of a society. In addition to offering descriptions of appropriate behavior, the law provides sanctions for violations of its provisions. Dean Champion (1990) suggests that the law serves four primary functions, which include:

- Legitimate the existing social structure.
- Regulate social conduct in society.
- Regulate/maintain freedom.
- Resolve disputes between members of society.

FELONY VERSUS MISDEMEANOR CRIME

Usually, crimes committed in the United States are classified by the justice system as either felonies or misdemeanors. Originally, this distinction was a critical one. Under medieval English common law, felonies were crimes for which a person could be required to forfeit all property and often his or her life. Distinctions between felonies and misdemeanors are not always clear-cut. Often, the distinction is made on the basis of the length of sentence imposed for the crime. Although sentences, even for the same crime, vary from state to state, felonies typically are among the more serious and usually carry lengthier sentences than misdemeanors. Felonies, then, contain capital crimes—those for which the death sentence may be imposed—as well as crimes for which the sentence includes imprisonment in a state prison for more than one (or in some states two) years. Misdemeanors are less serious crimes for which fines and shorter county jail time may be imposed. Usually, misdemeanors carry no more jail time than one year. The distinction between types of crimes is important. Later in this book it will become clear that police discretion, what represents permissible force, rules of evidence, and other police issues frequently revolve around whether the crime was a felony or a misdemeanor. In a manner similar to dichotomizing between serious and not serious crimes (felonies and misdemeanors) another distinction can be drawn between natural crimes, and *mala in se* crimes, and crimes created by people or *mala prohibita* crimes.

MALA IN SE AND *MALA PROHIBITA* CRIMES

Mala in se **crimes** are inherently bad acts. These involve forbidden behaviors that members of society agree need to be outlawed. These behaviors include serious crimes such as rape, assault, murder, robbery, and similarly heinous offenses. *Mala in se* crimes are sometimes referred to as violations of natural law.

In contrast to these natural law violations, **mala prohibita crimes** are the breaking of laws created by humans, or the breaking of laws and ordinances passed by legislative bodies. Unlike the universal and timeless *mala in se* crimes, *mala prohibita* crimes reflect a society's current moral temper and values. *Mala prohibita* crimes periodically are created to control a behavior during a given time, but later removed or modified to reflect changing values and attitudes predominant in society. The change in legal drinking age to 21 across the nation represents an example of *mala prohibita*. Similarly, the recent elimination of a national maximum driving speed of 55 miles per hour exemplifies a *mala prohibita* crime.

Other examples include laws and ordinances associated with hand gun owner-ship, prostitution, abortion, and even smoking ordinances.

SUMMARY

This chapter conveys the idea that social order and freedom require certain ele-ments of control and constraint. One simply cannot have liberty and personal freedom in the absence of rules, laws, and order. All societies provide an elastic range of acceptable behavior. Behavior that society sees as overconformity, and behavior society sees as underconformity is deviant. Yet, even when behavior may be so odd, bizarre, or repugnant that it stretches the limits of social toler-ance, it may not be illegal. Crime is conduct that society classifies as illegal. To qualify as crime, behavior must be specifically defined in the law, be enforced by some political body, and associated with prescribed penalties.

Laws themselves are divided between those that are *mala in se*, or inher-ently evil in nature (e.g., rape, murder, and assault), and *mala prohibita*, or those established strictly by statute or ordinance.

The task of the law enforcement officer, which will be more comprehen-sively detailed in future chapters, is to enforce the criminal laws (as well as other types) and to provide certain necessary community services. The uni-formed police officer serves the important symbolic function or personifying the American criminal justice system.

REFERENCES

Berg, Bruce L. *Law Enforcement: An Introduction to Police in Society.* Boston: Allyn and Bacon, Inc., 1992.

Champion, Dean. *Criminal Justice in the United States.* Columbus, Oh.: Merrill Publish-ing, 1990.

Cole, George F., and Christopher E. Smith. *The American System of Criminal Justice.* 8th ed. Belmont, Calif.: West/Wadsworth, 1998.

Critchley, Thomas A. *A History of Police in England and Wales.* 2d ed. Montclair, N.J.: Patterson Smith, 1972.

Ferdico, John N. *Criminal Procedure for the Criminal Justice Professional.* 6th ed. Minne-apolis/St. Paul: West Publishing Co., 1996.

Hagan, Frank E. *Introduction to Criminology: Theories, Methods and Criminal Behavior.* Chicago: Nelson-Hall, 1986.

Lee, William L. Melvill. *A History of Police in England.* Montclair, N.J.: Patterson Smith, [1901] 1971.

Manning, Anita. "Medical Use of Pot Raises Legal Concerns." *USA Today,* Wednesday, January 15, 1997:1.

Peterson, Karen S. "Boomers Hash Out Merits of Therapeutic Marijuana." *USA Today,* Wednesday, January 15, 1997:12D.

Samaha, Joel. *Criminal Law.* 5th ed. Minneapolis/St. Paul: West Publishing Co., 1996.

Siegel, Larry J. *Criminology.* 5th ed. New York: West Publishing Co., 1995.

Simmons, Jerry L. *Deviants.* Berkeley, Calif.: Glendesary, 1969.

Sutherland, Edwin H., and Donald Cressey. *Criminology.* 9th ed. Philadelphia: Lippin-
    cott, 1974.

QUESTIONS FOR REVIEW

Objective #1:

- How do most people stereotypically envision police officers?
- Why can it be said that uniformed police symbolically represent the criminal justice system?

Objective #2:

- How might one define a norm?

Objective #3:

- Would informing on another student who was cheating on a test be considered a crime? Explain your answer.
- Why is putting a dime in a stranger's parking meter a form of deviance?

Objective #4:

- When people shout angry words at a line jumper, is this a form of formal or
  informal social control? Explain your answer.
- When a police officer arrests a shoplifter, is this a form of formal or informal
  social control? Explain your answer.

Objective #5:

- How might you define crime, from a legalistic perspective?

Objective #6:

- What is meant by case law?
- What body of law governs fishing licenses?

Objective #7:

- Would you classify intentionally shooting someone as a felony or a misdemeanor?
- What is the main difference between a felony and a misdemeanor?

Objective #8:

- Would the act of smoking in a non-smoking building be a *mala in se* or *mala
  prohibita* crime?

2 The Historical Evolution of Policing

CHAPTER OBJECTIVES

After reading this chapter, you should be able to:

1. Discuss law enforcement during antiquity.
2. Define kin policing and blood feuds.
3. Describe the Code of Hammurabi.
4. Outline the rational aspects of Mosaic Law.
5. List several contributions to law enforcement from Greek and Roman times.
6. Explain the tithing system from medieval England.
7. Describe the importance of the Magna Carta and the Statute of Westminster.
8. Discuss the contributions to policing from Henry Fielding and Robert Peel.
9. Consider the American watch and ward system.
10. Detail the early political influences on American policing.
11. Speak about issues relevant to the Reform era in American policing.
12. Communicate the historical problems that have plagued police community relations.

GOVERNING HUMAN BEHAVIOR

The enforcement of law may be accomplished by brute military force, by some form of less rigorous public censure, police activity, or some combination thereof. As this chapter details, the evolution of policing is marked by elements of each. The literal beginning of formal law enforcement is shrouded in a cloak of mystery, mysticism, superstition, and historical romanticism. When one

KEY TERMS	rational law	assize of arms
	Praetorian guard	fences
kin policing	urban cohort	Bow street runners
blood feuds	vigiles	Peelers
Code of Hammurabi	tuns	pay scot
lex talionis	tithing system	rattle watch
Mosaic law	parish constables	political patronage

attempts to trace the evolution of law enforcement from antiquity to modern times, it becomes impossible either to completely or absolutely identify the origins of this practice.

During ancient times, social order was chiefly patriarchal—a father figure governed the social organization of the group. This individual was responsible for determining the guilt or innocence of an errant family or clan member and administering any punishments. Tribal customs gradually developed as the basis for behavioral guidelines and evolved into informal modes of conduct. Laws, as one might think about them today, do not appear until considerably later. Let us turn to the past and consider some of the ancient versions of the police function and their implications for modern policing.

LAW ENFORCEMENT IN ANTIQUITY

During ancient times members of the clan and tribe themselves provided the police function. The head of the tribe or clan had executive, legislative, and judicial control. Although the head of the clan might appoint members of the tribe or clan to special tasks, such as assisting in the enforcement of his rulings or activity as his personal bodyguard, these appointees still were essentially members of the local community. In other words, these individuals did not represent an organized policing system.

During ancient times, the enforcement of a group's norms and customs was handled primarily by the injured party or by one's family and kin. In turn, crimes committed against the group, such as an attack, typically were handled by the entire clan or tribe. As time progressed, what began to arise was a kind of rule enforcement system based upon individual and kin responsibility. Textbooks frequently refer to this sort of system as a kin-police system.

THE KIN POLICE

In **kin policing**, the family, clan, or tribe assumes the responsibility for administering justice. During these ancient tribal periods, justice usually operated under the philosophy of retaliation. For example, let's say a member of one's family were stopped and the chicken he or she was carrying taken. The family of this victim might handle this by hunting down the thief, retrieving the chicken, and perhaps beating the bandit. Consequently, justice was harsh, brutal, crude, and frequently disproportionate to the offense. Branding or mutilation of apprehended offender was common. In some areas, one could expect to have a hand cutoff for stealing something. Or, one might be branded on the forehead as a criminal. Under kin policing, each member of the group possessed a rudimentary type of official authority and was therefore empowered to enforce the group's customs and code of laws. Unfortunately, this would sometimes lead to bloody battles or **blood feuds** between families that might destroy entire clans.

THE CODE OF HAMMURABI

Around 2100 B.C., informal and customary codes of law fell away. Groups began to establish codified (written) and thus more rational and formal systems of law. Among the earliest was the Code of Hammurabi, the king of Babylon (around 1750 B.C.). **The Code of Hammurabi** was written on a column of stone and discovered by a French government expedition exploring the Persian Gulf in 1901. The code contained 282 sections that described the responsibilities of each individual to every other individual in the society. It outlined rules for private dealings between individuals, methods for dealing with runaway slaves, reclaiming stolen property, inheritances, return of purchased slaves if they were ill, and a vast array of other circumstances (see Box 2.1). In addition, the code detailed penalties for violations.

BOX 2.1 SAMPLE SECTIONS FROM THE CODE OF HAMURABI

The Code of Hammurabi is believed to be the oldest set of codified laws. It contains 282 sections and provides comprehensive guidelines for most social and civil interactions between people. A small sampling from the code:

1. If a man weaves a spell about another man and throws a curse on him, and cannot prove it, the one who wove the spell shall be put to death.
2. If a man weaves a spell about another man, and has not proved it, he on whom suspicion was thrown shall go to the river, shall plunge into the river. If the river seizes hold of him, he who wove the spell shall take his home. If the river shows him to be innocent, and he is uninjured, he who threw suspicion on him shall be put to death. He who plunged into the river shall take the house of him who wove the spell on him.
3. If a man has accused the witnesses in a lawsuit of malice and has not proved what he said, if the suit was one life (and death), that man shall be put to death.
4. If he has sent corn and silver to the witnesses, he shall bear the penalty of the suit.

5. If anyone harbors in his house a runaway male or female slave from the place or the house of a noble, and does not bring them out at the command of the majordomo, the master of the house shall be put to death.
6. If anyone has committed a robbery and is caught, he shall be killed.
23. If the robber is not caught, the man who has been robbed shall make claim before God to everything stolen from him, and the town and its governor within the territory and limits of which the robbery took place shall give back to him everything he has lost.
185. If a man has taken a small child as a son, in his own name and has brought him up, that foster child shall not be reclaimed.
186. If a man has taken a small child for his son, and if when he took him his father and his mother he offended, that foster child shall return to the house of his father.

continued

BOX 2.1 *continued*

229. If a builder has built a house for someone and has not made his work firm, and if the house he built has fallen and has killed the owner of the house, that builder shall be put to death.
230. If it has killed the son of the house-owner, one shall kill the son of the builder.
231. If it has killed the slave of the house-owner he (the builder) shall give to the owner of the house slave for slave.

Source: Vern L. Foley. *American Law Enforcement: Police, Courts, and Corrections.* 3rd edition. Boston: Allyn and Bacon, Inc., 1980, Appendix C.

As many of the sample sections of the Code of Hammurabi suggest, a major contribution of this set of laws was the concept of *lex talionis* (an eye for an eye). This notion of retributive justice exacts as remedy a sum equal to, but not greater than, the loss or injury. The Code of Hammurabi marked the symbolic end of blood feuds characteristic of previous centuries.

Also found in the text of the Code of Hammurabi was what may have been the first recorded representation of the principle of *lex talionis*. Roughly translated, *lex talionis* means "an eye for an eye and a tooth for a tooth" (Seagle 1947). The code was quite brutal. Many crimes such as robbery, were punished by death. Nonetheless, many scholars believe that this retributive philosophy was intended to limit the kinds of rampant blood feuds that often resulted under kin policing systems. Philosophically, under the provisions of *lex talionis*, one could exact no greater penalty than the worth of that which had been lost. This ancient principle can be seen as a forerunner of at least two major modern notions of law and justice. First, it suggests the concept of a uniform and prescriptive social reaction to violations of society's laws. Second, it implies a system in which, theoretically, the penalty was intended to fit the crime: the more serious the nature of the crime, the more serious the punishment.

In addition to regulating a wide variety of criminal and civil law violations, the Code of Hammurabi made special provisions for the protection of children. For instance, if one received certain property from a child without parental consent, one might be guilty of a capital offense (Ludwig 1955:12). Even family relationships were regulated by the code. In fact, the code specified several punishments for rebellion and disloyalty among family members. While the code clearly articulated a number of civil and criminal matters, it provided no special treatment of children who violated public law. It is unclear whether children who violated the law were punished by the family or were subject to the same harsh punishment as adults.

MOSAIC LAW

Mosaic law (ca. 1000 B.C.) emerged approximately one thousand years after the Code of Hammurabi. Like the code **Mosaic law** was intended to provide a formal and rational system of law. The notion of a **rational law**, in this context, suggests the ability for one to know in advance what behaviors are prohibited, and what are the penalties for their commission. For the ancient Hebrews, the Torah and the interpretative supplementary sacred traditions served as a normative system that governed behaviors in all areas of life. Unlike other legal systems emerging across the Mediterranean during this period, the bearers of this legal system were not a ruling class. In fact, the ancient Hebrews were a pariah people (Weber 1978:824), a nomadic guest culture within other, larger cultures. Consequently, interactions and dealings with outsiders was a kind of foreign commerce. Because of this, transactions were governed by slightly different ethical norms than those that applied to deal with insiders (other Jews).

Mosaic law, like the Code of Hammurabi, represented important moves toward formalizing and standardizing law into a rational system of enforceable rules of conduct. It was not until the early Greek city-states developed that major innovations in policing and law enforcement arose.

GREEK AND ROMAN INFLUENCES AND CONTRIBUTIONS

It was during the development of early Greek city-states that clan or tribal policing (kin policing) fully gave way to community or city policing. Peisistratus (605–527 B.C.) the ruler of Athens, often is credited with creating the first formal system of policing. Peisistratus developed a guard system charged with the responsibilities of protecting the ruler, the watchtower, and the highways (Germann et al. 1976). In contrast to the more democratic legal system of Athens, the Greek city-state of Sparta developed a ruler-appointed police force. Since Sparta is sometimes characterized as having had an authoritarian regime, this early police system often is described as the first secret service (Germann et al. 1976).

The ancient Roman era had considerable influence on modern day policing as well. Under Augustus Caesar, the first emperor of Rome (27 B.C.), the **Praetorian Guard** was created. This guard unit was composed of handpicked members of Augustus' army and was charged with the responsibility of protecting the person and property of the emperor. It was also during the reign of Augustus that history saw the creation of a rudimentary city police force, commonly referred to as the urban cohort. The **urban cohort** was a less select military unit of men than the Praetorian Guard but also chosen from Augustus' army. This guard unit originally preserved the peace of the city. Later, and in the wake of considerable civilian unrest and several major fires in Rome, Augustus formed the *vigiles* (watchmen) of Rome. The *vigiles* were a non-military unit of several thousand men whose duties included both fire fighting and keeping the peace in the city. The vigiles were armed with staves (clubs) and traditional short-swords and were assigned to various geographic precincts throughout the city. The vigiles were empowered to arrest lawbreakers, signifying the first formal civilian police force.

EARLY ENGLISH CONTRIBUTIONS

After the fall of Rome around A.D. 395, Europe witnessed several centuries of turbulent warfare and successive conquests. It was not until around the seventh century A.D. that the history of policing again began to make meaningful strides forward. During this early period of England's history, concepts of community and mutual responsibility became more sophisticated than those practiced by primitive styles of kin policing. It was largely during England's feudal period that small self-governing villages, or **tuns,** began to emerge. It is within the tun that history witnesses the strengthening of individual and mutual responsibility for personal and group security, police enforcement, and justice.

Superstition and magic, as methods of determining one's guilt or innocence of a crime, began to yield to more efficient and rational organized systems of justice and law. Borrowing from the *frankpledge*, developed by France during the seventh century, England created the tithing system. The **tithing system** established the responsibility of each tun member for his neighbor and provided an organized peacekeeping mechanism for the safety and protection of the tun.

Tithings were composed of groups of ten families belonging to freemen. All men over the age of 12 were required to be in a tithing. Each member of a tithing was responsible for his own good behavior, the behavior of his family, and that of his fellow tithing members. The tithing itself was responsible (as a group) socially and financially for the behavior of its membership. Thus, if a tithing failed to apprehend an errant member, the entire tithing might be made to pay restitution to the injured party (Reynolds 1984). As part of their self-government, members of the tun elected a chief tithingman. The chief tithingman was responsible for raising the hue and cry, or call to arms, which mobilized every able-bodied man to pursue an offender. The chief tithingman was further responsible for dispensing punishment to the offender.

As the small villages began to increase in population and geographic size, so too did their policing needs. Eventually, groupings of ten adjacent tithings evolved into what were called a hundred. Within the hundred, people elected a headman called a reeve or headborough. The reeve presided over monthly meetings in which members of the hundred discussed their various needs and problems. While the reeve administered the hundred, a constable (from the French *comes stabuli*, meaning officer of the stable) was placed in charge of supervising and maintaining the hundred's equipment. This position was similar to the modern quartermaster. Interestingly, the early French *comes stablis* also were charged with the task of raising and maintaining armies.

Given the connotation of the French, and the importance attached to hose soldiers (cavalry) during the medieval period, the concept of a constable becomes somewhat clearer. The advent of the warhorse significantly altered not only styles of military battle, but society in general.

As time passed, high constables emerged and administered both hundreds and petty constables who had begun to take on the more traditional role of peace officer in the towns and parishes of the English countryside. Shires, or

Figures 2.1–2.3
Superstition and magic gave way to various trials by battle, and eventually to more rational organized systems of justice and law.

geographic areas analogous to a modern county, developed as several adjacent hundreds began to come together. These shires were governed by a shire-reeve, appointed by either a nobleman or the king. Shire-reeves were freemen, not vassals. This meant they were not the chattel of a lord. The position of shire-reeve had both quasi-military and judicial authority. A number of contemporary historians suggest that both the title and office of the modern sheriff derive from these early shire-reeve.

The tithing system arose and flourished chiefly between the seventh and ninth centuries. During the later part of the ninth century, Alfred the Great consolidated England and found the tithing system useful in his attempt to unify the people and the nation. The tithing system was further refined under the later rule of William the Conqueror. He established a series of 55 individual military districts and placed an official in charge of each. These officials were responsible directly to the Crown, unlike the more autonomous shire-reeves. The shire-reeves, in fact, soon found themselves replaced. While the position of shire-reeve remained, its role and authority changed. No longer, for example, did the position possess the judicial powers of the earlier office. In place of this, William the Conqueror installed the *vice comites*, predecessor of the circuit judge (see Barlow 1970; Reynolds 1984).

The simple tithing style of mutual responsibility for its members soon gave way to the frankpledge. In many ways the frankpledge was a system of compulsory collective bail fixed for individuals. However, this bail or pledge of property and possession, was not set after arrest for crime. Instead, it was established as a safeguard in anticipation of it (Critchley 1972). The early history after the Norman conquest of Saxon England in 1066 found two alien cultures living side by side in one land. However, one culture was the conqueror, while the other was a defeated and oppressed people. The Normans increased the restrictions of mutual responsibility remnant in the old Saxon tithing system. They required the newly appointed royal shire-reeve to supervise a specially held biannual hundred court called the sheriff's tourn (see Morris 1968; Critchley 1972). The purpose of this court was to ensure that all eligible men were enrolled in a tithing and had thus pledged their good behavior and that of one another. This view of frankpledge and sheriff's tourn, also was used to maintain brutal repression. Although the Norman sheriffs were royal officers and thus men of great power, they were also often men of few scruples. In addition to extorting the payments of fines at the least opportunity, they were very brutal in their dispensing of justice. Several sheriffs were notorious for gouging out eyes, in other ways mutilating, or hanging thieves. These sheriffs were brutal even for the twelfth century!

As a form of citizen-based policing, the tithing system worked reasonably effectively during the feudal period of England. During this time England was chiefly an agrarian society. By the thirteenth century, tuns had grown into small towns chiefly populated by people still living in manors with strong community life, but weak resources. English society was dominated by a hierarchic, wealthy, and militaristic aristocracy. The majority of England's population was illiterate peasantry.

Throughout the thirteenth century, farming was the staple occupation of English peasantry. As English society became more urban and populations more geographically mobile, the tithings became increasingly unable to maintain control over the growing numbers of transients, beggars, and vagabonds who were not bound to any local tithing. Gradually, the entire basis of medieval society shifted from agrarian to urban and from a military aristocracy to an elite aristocracy of wealth.

THE DEVELOPMENT OF MARKETS AND CITIES

By the thirteenth century, earlier temporary markets and bazaars had begun to become permanent towns and cities. As England's export and domestic cloth market developed so too did the populations of towns. Soon small towns began to bulge at the seams, giving way to new towns and eventually large crowded cities. Urban centers began to sweep across what had previously been empty space, and suburbs crawled increasingly further into the English countryside. Along with increasing populations and urban development came major changes in forms of government. These arose in the shape of mayors, councils, and explicit rules set forth in the Magna Carta.

The Magna Carta

The Magna Carta, or "Great Charter" as it is sometimes called, is a cornerstone of both democracy and law enforcement. Under pressure by angry nobles, clergymen, and an increasingly organized citizenry, King John of England signed the Magna Carta in 1215. Similar to the Bill of Rights, the Magna Carta gave the common Englishman due process, the right to a trial by jury, and local governmental control. In short, the Magna Carta eliminated arbitrary edicts by lords and established both the responsibilities of the state and the supremacy of formal law (Critchley 1972).

As previously suggested, the tithing system was better suited for agrarian life than for an urban setting. In an attempt to reaffirm the old tithing traditions of local mutual responsibility, King Edward I issued the Statute of Winchester in 1285.

The Statute of Winchester

The Statute of Winchester sought to replace the weakened tithing system with the **parish constable** system. In effect, however, the statute simply replaced a failing and inadequate system with another ineffective system. The statute ordered that one man from each parish serve a entire year as an unpaid constable. In addition to general peacekeeping activities during the day, the parish constables were expected to work in the evenings with groups of citizen watchmen (also unpaid) to guard the city streets and the town's gates.

The statute also reestablished the hue and cry of ancient Saxon England (Lee 1971; Germann et al. 1976). As in the past, this required that all able-bodied men in the area immediately cease their work when they heard the call,

Figure 2.4
In 1285 King Edward I issued the Statute of Winchester, which replaced the weakened tithing system with the Parish Constable System.

and go to the constable's aid in pursuing and capturing an offender. In order to ensure that the hue and cry could be enforced the statute further established the assize of arms. The **assize of arms** required that every male between the ages of 15 and 60 to keep a weapon in his home as a means for keeping the peace. Thus, while the Statute of Winchester shifted the formal responsibilities for policing from the community to the parish constables, in effect, every man continued to be responsible for policing his community.

It is not difficult to understand why few men were anxious to become constables. The position was unrewarding both personally and financially. Thus, men usually were forced to maintain their regular job while taking on the added responsibilities of the constable. Yet, men actually had little choice but to serve since the alternative was punishment, usually being sent to the pillory. While the parish constable system was a considerable hardship, and not terribly effective, it remained the primary policing system in England for the next six hundred years.

Throughout the fourteenth and fifteenth centuries, policing gained in size and sophistication. These changes came as an unavoidable consequence of a rapidly growing and increasingly transient industrial society. By the early 1500s, England had become an active participant in world commerce. America had been discovered and England was quickly rising as a leader in the production of wool. Throughout the English countryside, farmers had begun to put down their plows and give up farming. In place of large planting fields, farmers began developing pastures for grazing sheep. As land owners began converting their farms into sheep ranches, fewer and fewer farm-hands were needed. This enclosure system resulted in a mass migration of one-time farmers into the more urban centers. Since farmers had been largely a peasant class while in the countryside, they quickly developed into a volatile horde of poor but angry city dwellers. Crime inevitably increased as these dispossessed and unskilled farm folk arrived in what were already overcrowded cities. Crime in cities soared; places such as London and Liverpool grew almost overnight from small towns to cascading harbors of deviance and iniquity.

CRIME AND THE INDUSTRIAL REVOLUTION

By the beginning of the Industrial Revolution during the eighteenth century, England found itself faced with mass poverty, unemployment, overcrowding, and serious crime problems. The cities began to transform into huge slums. In the absence of child labor laws many children worked alongside their parents for up to 16 hours a day. Much of the literary work of Charles Dickens and the socio-economic observations of Karl Marx (Marx & Engels 1906) quite accurately portrayed the squalor, deprivation, and crime of eighteenth-century England.

The cities, which had originally attracted the displaced agrarians seeking jobs as unskilled laborers, changed into hordes of unemployed marauding gangs. Machines such as the steam engine and the power loom further devalued the need for unskilled factory workers. Crime in the streets of England was rampant. The crowded cities attracted thousands of pickpockets who plied their trade with enormous agility—and vigor. Cities also offered an effective and speedy way to dispose of ill-gotten goods. **Fences**, people who deal in stolen property, began to surface in most large cities throughout England. Counterfeiting, a longstanding problem for the English, became so prevalent that at one point estimates suggest there was more phony money than real in circulation.

Prostitution, like counterfeiting and pickpocketing, developed as an alternative to unemployment. Numbers of prostitutes grew so rapidly that at one point, 25,000 were believed to be active in London alone. These lawless conditions led to a variety of attempts to restore order. Among these law enforcement innovations were rewards for the apprehension of criminals, harsh penalties for even minor crimes (at one point death could be imposed for more than 160 different offenses), and citizen groups known as vigilantes to combat crime.

Unfortunately, many of these innovations backfired. Criminals began both to inform on one another and to frame innocent people, either for the reward or as blackmail. In short, the reward system created a new, institutionalized form of criminal activity.

In hindsight, it seems obvious that the kinds of obligatory and part-time avocational policing systems of the time simply were ineffective for such largescale criminal activity. The various policing systems used had neither the proper training or desire to combat crime on a large scale. Carl Klockars (1985: 28) has similarly observed:

> The deterioration and demise of the parish constable system illustrates the central flaw in all systems of obligatory avocational police. As the work becomes more difficult, demanding, or time consuming, obligatory

avocational policing takes on the characteristics of forced labor. Unpaid, it has to compete with earning a living. Motivated only by the threat of punishment, it becomes unwilling and resistant, Offering no one any reason to learn to cultivate the skills necessary to do it well, it becomes undependable, uneconomic, and of poor quality. In short, the more we expect police to do, the less we can expect obligatory avocational police to do it. For all of these very good reasons, obligatory avocational systems cannot serve as a basis for a satisfactory modern police.

HENRY FIELDING AND THE BOW STREET RUNNERS

It was not until 1748, when Henry Fielding became chief magistrate of Bow Street in lawless London, that any meaningful police enforcement strategies arose. Henry Fielding was assisted by his blind half-brother John, who later succeeded Henry as magistrate. Henry Fielding eventually established a mounted officers patrol of Bow Street. This patrol rode the crime-infested roads leading into the city. He further innovated a foot patrol to sweep through the congested and heavily populated residential and business areas of the city. In many ways, these patrols were precursors of modern mobile patrols (discussed in greater detail in Chapter 4 of this text).

The Bow Street Horse and Foot Patrol was certainly the most cohesive and effective policing force of its time when it began 1805. By 1828 it had grown to a mounted unit of 2 inspectors, 4 deputy inspectors, 100 mounted patrol officers, and 127 street patrol officers (Rumbelow 1971). Unfortunately, London's population during this time had grown to more than one million. Excluding the parish watchmen—a motley and unreliable crew—and the Thames police, whose patrol was limited chiefly to the river, fewer than 400 men were involved in enforcing the laws of England and preserving the peace and safety of the streets of England.

For the most part, Fielding is remembered for having created the **Bow Street Runners**. Henry Fielding strongly believed that in order to ensure crime prevention, private citizens should join forces with the municipal patrol force he was creating. He suggested that these citizen-volunteers could swiftly move to the scene of a crime, diffuse any angry crowd, and begin gathering information and facts about the crime. These "running civilian volunteers," then, became the Bow Street Runners. The Bow Street Runners, or Thief-Takers, as they came to be called, initially numbered only eight and were attached to the court at Bow Street in Westminster. Their numbers were later increased to 12. These runners were markedly different from the other avocational police systems of the time. The work of these Thief-Takers seriously altered the contest between professional thieves and the wealthy citizens of London. The Bow Street Runners made a serious study of investigations and locating criminals and quickly became experts skilled in this area. Unlike their more amateur peacekeeping predecessors (such as watchmen, parish constables, and some of the privately employed police officers of the period), the Thief-Takers did not offer reluctant or only perfunctory police service. Thief-Takers actively pursued and captured criminals, motivated by the prospects of reward money (Lee 1971).

The Bow Street Runners certainly accomplished a considerable amount of good by apprehending a number of predatory gangs and various infamous criminals. However, they were also a source of considerable crime themselves. Stimulated by the hope of financial reward more than any sense of civic duty, their methods were often questionable, to say the least. They were only concerned with apprehending those criminals who would bring the largest rewards. In other words, the Bow Street Runners were not particularly interested in pursuing fugitives from justice whose capture was chiefly for the good of the community. Furthermore, prevention of crime was never a concern of the Thief-Takers. Obviously, such a concern would run contrary to their primary interest in securing rewards for capturing criminals. As a consequence, the services of the Bow Street Runners were actually available only to people wealthy enough to post a sizable reward. Additionally, several of the Thief-Takers were later found to have been involved in the commission of crime in order to obtain rewards. It has been supposed that this spawned the expression, "It takes a thief to catch a thief." In spite of their questionable methods, the Bow Street Runners were, in many ways, the prototype for both private investigators and detective divisions in modern municipal police departments.

SIR ROBERT PEEL AND THE PEELERS

Sir Robert Peel, who served as Britain's home secretary in 1829, had been impressed and inspired by the work of Henry Fielding. Like Fielding, Peel believed that one contributing factor to London's severe problems was poorly trained, undermanned, and overworked police personnel. Peel also believed that if any crime control was to work, it would require both the backing of a strong body of law and the support and respect of the public. Because of this attitude, Peel worked toward improving the harsh, vague, and frequently arbitrary nature of the laws during his time. Peel managed to have the death penalty abolished for many of the 160 assorted offenses for which it could be imposed. He also believed that agents of the law needed to be a nonavocational unified body of well-selected, and well-trained men. Additionally, Peel adhered to a rigorous use of a probationary period for his officers.

In 1829, shortly after Peel had introduced a "Bill for improving the Police in and near the Metropolis" to Parliament, his Metropolitan Police of London were organized. The primary organizational purpose of this police agency was the prevention of crime (see Box 2.2).

The police constable who made his appearance on the streets of London in 1829 was a very different kind of officer from his predecessors. Peel had recruited his new police force from the best men he could locate. Individuals who sought entrance into the new police force were expected to be in good

BOX 2.2   THE PEELIAN REFORMS

"I SPY BLUE, I SPY BLACK, I SPY A PEELER IN A SHINY HAT" [Anonymous]

Sir Robert Peel desired to establish a body of noble law enforcement officers, a group of men responsible for safeguarding life and property in London's corrupt and lawless metropolitan area. To assure an effective, organized operation, Peel set forth a 12-point guideline, sometimes referred to as "Peelian Reform":

1. The police must be stable, efficient, and organized along military lines.
2. The police must be under governmental control.
3. The absence of crime will best prove the efficiency of the police.
4. The distribution of crime news is essential.
5. The deployment of police strength by *time* and *area* is essential.
6. No quality is more indispensable to a policeman than a perfect command of temper; a quiet, determined manner has more effect than violent action.
7. Good apperance commands respect.
8. The securing and training of proper persons is at the root of efficiency.
9. Public security demands that every police officer be given a number.
10. Police headquarters should be centrally located and easily accessible to the people.
11. Policemen should be hired on a probationary basis.
12. Police records are necessary to the correct distribution of police strength.

Source: Bruce L. Berg. *Law Enforcement.* Boston: Allyn and Bacon, Inc., 1992:25.

To a large extent, the essence of policing in modern America and England continues to reflect these basic elements offered 170 years ago by Sir Robert Peel. His orientation was for a consolidated municipal force to overtly patrol the streets of London. His "great experiment" was intended to prevent as well as intervene in crime.

---

physical condition, possess above-average intelligence, and be of high moral character (Lee 1971; Miller 1977).

Peel was sufficiently committed to his dream of an effective municipal police force that he personally participated in the interviewing of more than 12,000 applicants in order to locate 1,000 suitable officers. Sadly, Peel's desire to orient the police toward crime prevention failed to last very long. Owing to the potential for financial rewards, these public police officers became more and more active in crime investigations and less concerned with crime prevention. During the initial two years of its operation, the Metropolitan Police force fired (or through resignation) nearly 500 of the original 1,000 officers. But the concept of personal integrity and high moral character among officers has been firmly implanted in police organizations ever since.

Unfortunately for Peel, all of his efforts to demonstrate the moral fortitude of his Metropolitan Police force personnel continued to meet with doubt and trepidations from Parliament and the public (see Browne 1973). During the first several years of its operation, most citizens viewed members of the force, or **Peelers**, with disrespect. Even law-abiding citizens of London continued to view the Peelers as disreputable and referred to them as crushers and blue devils (referring to the familiar blue coats of the Day Police, who preceded Peel's Metropolitan Police). Some of the original officers were beaten and thrown into the Thames (Rumbelow 1971). Such public disdain and rigid internal organizational discipline were certainly factors that affected the high rate of attrition during the early years of the agency's operation.

Undaunted by the problems, the Metropolitan Police succeeded in only ten years in winning the approval and respect of the public—and the criminals. The catcalls and derogatory names used for the officers during the earlier years were soon replaced with the more affectionate one of bobbies (after Sir Robert).

In 1939, legislation was passed making it possible for communities outside London to create their own police forces. Laws that created tax-supported police agencies throughout England were passed in 1856. Sir Robert Peel's great experiment had become an overwhelming success.

THE DEVELOPMENT OF POLICING IN THE UNITED STATES

The concepts and law enforcement practices that form the core orientation of modern American policing can be easily traced back to their ancient Saxon roots. When the early colonists arrived on the shores of the New World, they carried with them their household goods, their crafts, and their seventeenth-century English policing traditions. While there were several sizable pockets of New World colonists from countries other than England (e.g., the French in Louisiana), it is the overwhelming influences of the English that have left the most indelible impression on modern policing.

At first, colonists naturally banded together for safety and security in small towns similar to those of their Anglo-Saxon ancestors. Until the colonies gained their independence from England, the protection of early settlers was chiefly the responsibility of the king's representatives. Typically, these were town constables and sheriffs. Colonists also used a night-watch system borrowed from their English past.

Because of the northern climate and soil were less conducive to farming than southern regions of colonial America, and in part because more of the early settlers of New England came from more urban than agricultural backgrounds, towns became the principal governmental unit across most of the north.

As northern towns, counties, and cities developed, early law enforcement styles reflected urban English traditions. In many of the early northeastern colonial settlements, the constable and sheriff were frequently augmented by an avocational watchman system. Watchmen patrolled the settlement's streets at night, again following the traditions of late medieval English policing styles. The watchmen, in fact, remained the principal form of nighttime security in America until the mid-1800s when the first full-time formal (vocational, municipal) police forces were started.

The flat, fertile expanse of southern colonial America naturally attracted settlers with more agrarian backgrounds. These individuals brought with them attitudes, beliefs, and law enforcement styles that had grown up in the peasant-filled countryside of England. This included the county sheriff. Perhaps the earliest of these county sheriffs appeared around 1634 in Virginia. From this early seed grew a tradition of the American sheriff as the most powerful and significant law enforcement figure across the southern United States. In many ways, the distinctive southern and northern law enforcement practices that originated in colonial days continue today.

The northeastern and southern regions of the United States were settled much earlier than most of the western and southwestern regions of the country. The West can be characterized by its adaptation of various orientations from both northern and southern policing traditions. Perhaps by virtue of its more rural and isolated geographic location, the West initially adopted the southern sheriff as its primary law enforcement agent.

In northern colonial America, policing interests and techniques typically maintained pace with the rapid growth and industrialization. Nonetheless, public concern for safety and increasing pressure by citizens for improved protection led first to a daytime watch intended to supplement the night watchmen and, finally, to a municipal police system.

THE AMERICAN HUE AND CRY

The principal policing strategy practiced by early watchmen, like their earlier English counterparts, was to raise a kind of hue and cry if they saw a crime being committed. Criminal sightings were fairly rare, and the number of colonial watchmen was usually small. Serving as a watchmen was a civic responsibility, and like its English avocational predecessor, the system was replete with problems.

Boston organized the first official night watch in 1636. This watch was organized in a military fashion with a single commanding officer and six watchmen. Boston's official night watch was augmented by a volunteer citizen patrol (Lane 1967). While the citizen patrol was voluntary, it was expected that members of the community would either serve or **pay scot**. Paying scot meant to hire a surrogate to serve in one's place. A colonist who failed either to serve or to hire a surrogate was fined a stiff penalty. In some instances, the colonial courts used watchmen service as a punishment and a misdemeanant might be sentenced to serve on night watch (Costello 1972).

THE RATTLE WATCH AND OTHER EARLY SYSTEMS

The police problems that faced New Amsterdam (New York) during the seventeenth century, under both Dutch and English rule, were less serious than those afflicting London and other English cities of the same period. Like the other early colonial towns, New Amsterdam, owing to its small population, did not experience widespread or organized vice and crime (Richardson 1970). Nonetheless, there were problems related to public order. As a seaport town, sailors on shore leave frequently created disorder in drunken tavern brawls. Occasionally a runaway servant from New England or Virginia would reach New Amsterdam and may well have constituted the colony's first criminals.

New Amsterdam remained under Dutch control until 1664 when, following the English conquest, it became New York (Costello 1972). While still influenced by the Dutch, in 1658 a paid night-watch patrol emerged. This night-watch force, known as the **rattle watch**, had its members carry wooden rattles to announce their presence. The idea was to allow a lawbreaker time to flee before a confrontation with the watchman. These wooden rattles allowed watchmen to communicate with one another while on patrol (Crump and Newton 1935). Duty on this paid eight-man force was imposed upon each citizen by turn, and every household was taxed for its support. In an attempt to ensure that citizens took their turns in the watch, fines were levied for neatness, sleeping on the watch, failure to do a watch, and negligence while on watch.

In 1700 Philadelphia created its own night-watch system, followed in 1712 by Boston with a paid, full-time night watch, (Bopp and Schultz 1972). Boston's paid watchmen received approximately 50 cents a night. In 1803 Cincinnati started a night watch, in 1804 New Orleans began its nighttime vigil, and in 1808 St. Louis established a night-watch constabulary (Kappeler 1995).

As implied throughout, these watch and rattle systems were far from effective. Germann et al. (1976:66) describes the effectiveness of these systems:

> These early watchmen, like their counterparts in England at the time, were very lazy and inept. Minor offenders were sometimes sentenced to serve the watch as punishment. Often called leather heads, these guards were so dull that the towns sometimes had to formalize even the most simplest duties. New Haven, in 1722, had a regulation that "no watchman will have the liberty to sleep"; and a 1750 Boston rule stipulated that "watchmen will walk their rounds slowly and now and then stand and listen."

Night-watch policing continued to the exclusion of daytime patrols until 1833 when Philadelphia began a 23-man daytime force. Philadelphia expanded its night watch to 120 men and began to fashion a paramilitary organization by appointing a captain to command both day and night forces (Fosdick 1969).

The first full-time (vocational), salaried, consolidated day- and nighttime police force in the United States developed in New York City in 1844. A number of cities combined their day and night watches throughout the late 1800s. Baltimore and Newark combined their watches around 1847. Boston followed suit in 1850, as did Providence in 1864. Full-time municipal police forces took a bit longer to emerge.

By 1856, eight cities had full-time municipal police departments (New York, Detroit, Cincinnati, Chicago, San Francisco, Los Angeles, Philadelphia, and Dallas). These early police departments were often corrupt and manned by poorly trained personnel. In spite of serious detriments, these early police agencies represented a significant organizational advancement over earlier avocational and watchmen systems.

By the 1870s, most American cities had a police department even if this was a one-person department. In the more rural and southern regions of America, the county sheriff was the dominant law enforcement officer. In the vast and scarcely populated territories of the western United States, federal marshals were primarily responsible for law enforcement activities.

THE MODERN POLICE

The metamorphosis of American policing has gone through a number of stages. For the most part, there is general agreement in the literature regarding these stages. However, there are some distinct differences as well (Strecher 1991; Williams and Murphy 1991). Below, the police will be examined in terms of the following stages: The political influence stage, the reform stage, the professional stage, and the public and community relations stage. These evolutionary stages suggest how policing in America has advanced to where it is today.

THE POLITICAL INFLUENCE STAGE

From about the middle of the eighteenth century until about the 1920s, municipal government and policing were dominated by big-city political machines. Politics influenced every aspect of American life, and policing was no exception. The decision about who would be hired, who would be promoted, and even who would be in command were all decided by the political machine (Kappeler, Sluder, and Alpert 1994). To some measure, even arrest practices and what services the department provided to the community were determined by backstage political bargains.

Political and economic corruption became a serious problem in police agencies during this period. Many politicians saw the police as a mechanism for intensify their control and power. The police department was not only responsible for keeping the peace and enforcing various laws, but in many ways was the chief social service agency of the time. To get elected to public office, many politicians had to make promises to their constituents. Among the more powerful promises was the assurance of employment, and the provision of various social services. Police jobs became an important part of the political patronage system. **Political patronage** involves promising a job to someone in exchange for their assistance in getting a political candidate elected. Under political patronage, however, the individual promised a position need not have any of the necessary skills or prerequisites required by that position. Naturally these jobs were popular, since they required no skill and usually paid fairly well.

During the 1800s, many police departments were actually involved in a wide range of social services. The Boston and New York police departments provided lodging for thousands of homeless people during the mid-1850s. In addition, these early police agencies provided various health service activities, and social service functions (see Gaines, Kappeler, and Vaughn 1997:52–53).

Many politicians and police leaders were genuinely interested in social services and pushed their police departments towards these activities in earnest. Some, however, were simply part of the political machine, and corrupted these activities as well as inhibited justice. For these disreputable politicians, the police represented an extremely useful tool used to secure election results, reward those who helped them, and even to punish those who might stand in their way. In many cities police were used to enforce various election laws and to monitor the polls. This would also sometimes include discouraging people from voting against a certain candidate, and encouraging them to vote—sometimes more than once—for *the right candidate*.

THE REFORM STAGE

By the 1890s, politically dominated and corrupted police agencies began to come under growing public criticism. The public concern was directed not exclusively towards police, but at all social agencies. American cities faced similar problems related to increased crime, population density, inadequate health, sanitation, and housing problems. Many historians refer to the period from about the mid-1890s through the mid-1920s as the Progressive Era in the United States because these various social problems began to be seriously addressed.

Pressure to reform the police and local government came from both the private and public sectors. Reformers often included religious leaders and civic-minded upper- and middle-class business and professional people. Police reform, however, was not to occur quickly. To a large extent, police reform seemed to peak and valley over time. In some cases the reforms to police activities was especially distinctive and resulted in investigative commissions. At other times, the changes may have been more subtle and initiated by individual police administrators. At still other times, public pressure forced political reform that resulted in changes in police activities. For many critics of police reform, the necessary changes have not yet all been accomplished.

THE PROFESSIONAL STAGE

By the 1920s, the reform efforts had gained momentum and were having an increasingly effective impact on police agencies. Along similar lines to the already occurring general reforms in policing, the period from about the late 1920s through the 1960s, saw important changes in the role of law enforcement, its organizational structure, and the contribution to policing by science and technology. The professional stage in policing is sometimes described as a shift from what had ostensibly been a social service emphasis, to a more law enforcement and crime fighting one (Moore 1978; Johnson 1981). During this period, police begin to demonstrate a greater use of standards of law and organizational policy as a basis for decision making in the field. This more formal approach tended to replace undue influence by politicians, personal considerations, and underworld figures.

The campaign by police agencies to reduce the influence of political machines, and the desire to direct police agency efforts towards more objective law enforcement goals, meant changing the organizational and administrative structure of police agencies. By the 1950s, there had been numerous and meaningful changes in American police agencies. The organizational structure had become more bureaucratic and authority more centralized. Police agencies had formally adopted the military model first suggested in 1829 by Sir Robert Peel for his Metropolitan Police Department.

Police professionalism soon was swept up with the growing American emphasis on bureaucracy in business and industry. From this orientation, a professional police department was one that operated with a high degree of efficiency and effectiveness. Efficiency and effectiveness were measured by how well the department operated to objectively enforce the law and maintain the peace. Old styled foot patrol officers were replaced with faster more effective mobile patrols. Training requirements and standards of training began to arise. Police departments soon adopted other bureaucratic organizational principles of centralized organization, chain of command and communications, educational requirements, standards for training, spheres of competence, and so forth.

These objective organizational concerns also lead to developments in scientific criminal investigation. The underlying concern in scientific criminal investigation was a systematic, rational and detached approach to law enforcement. This scientific approach contrasted dramatically with earlier politically influenced approaches (Berg and Horgan 1998).

Police officials soon sought technological and scientific innovations on a variety of fronts. These included filing and indexing of reports, fingerprints, modus operandi files, radio communications, forensic sciences, and computers. Police organizations increasingly depended upon physical traces and evidence found at crime scenes in order to investigate crimes. In general, this stage of the professionalization of police resulted in more efficient and objective police organizations.

THE POLICE AND COMMUNITY RELATIONS

Throughout the turbulent years of the 1960s, anti-war and civil rights protests, street crime, union strikes, and unrest on college campuses intensified problems facing the police in America. These activities, along with changes in the welfare system, revelations about poverty in the United States, and a growing feeling of helplessness among residents of big city ghettos, created an atmosphere of tension and civil unrest that was nearly tangible. Riots in major U.S. cities such as

New York, Los Angeles, Chicago, Detroit, Washington, and Pittsburgh were common to read about in the newspapers throughout the 1960s (Gaines et al. 1997). Most of these riots involved police-citizen confrontations, and have been attributed to the volatile conditions of the times.

It was also in the 1960s that America suffered through a number of demoralizing politically prompted assassinations. In 1963, President John F. Kennedy was killed in Dallas—as was his alleged assassin Lee Harvey Oswald. In 1968, Dr. Martin Luther King Jr., one of the leading civil rights leader of his day, and Robert F. Kennedy, the U.S. Attorney General and brother of John F. Kennedy, were both slain. Assassination became an unfortunate method of voicing one's discontent with the political order.

History has demonstrated that the police in the United States were largely unprepared to deal with the civil and political unrest that raged throughout the 1960s. In fact, it has been suggested by some sources that police may well have contributed to creating the atmospheres that were conducive to riots (National Advisory Commission on Civil Disorder 1968).

During the early 1970s, a number of investigative commissions reported considerable corruption and illegal behavior among police in several large city forces (see for example the Knapp Commission Report 1973; Pennsylvania Crime Commission 1974). These reports served to add fuel to an already burning conflict between citizens and their police.

A new group of reformers seemed to emerge during the 1960s and 1970s. Even the federal government took measures to improve the police problems in the country. In 1968, the Omnibus Crime Control and Safe Street Act was passed. This act, along with subsequent legislation, provided various types of financial resources for state and local police and criminal justice agencies. Substantial portions of these grants were spent on new and improved equipment, modern training materials, and various other programs for police. Among these programs were many attempts by larger local level police agencies to improve police community relations. These programs included various in-school officer friendly programs, the development of the Police Athletic League (PAL) to work with inner-city youths, and even the development of various street-corner or storefront substations, in order to be closer and more accessible to neighborhood residents.

Throughout the 1960s, many departments also used crime prevention as a public relations strategy to improve their faded image with the public. Throughout the 1970s and into the 1980s, efforts included a variety of educational programs designed to instruct the community how to protect themselves. Some police departments would even provide an electric etching device for local resident to mark their possessions for identification.

A large number of police departments across the nation also established "block watch," or "neighborhood watch" programs, which encouraged residents to work in cooperation with local police. Police explained that residents could serve as an extension to local departments by serving as their "eyes and ears" in the community (Rosenbaum 1988).

By the early 1980s, the police-community relations movement had evolved in to a police response model. Throughout the 1980s crime remained a serious problem, and its reduction was a central campaign issue in a number of state level political campaigns. Even the presidential campaigns of Ronald Reagan—and later George Bush—were built on platforms of law, order and drug reduction. Many police departments adopted programs that generically had come to be called *community-oriented policing* (COP). By the late 1980s and early 1990s, COP programs began to shift to a new acronym, *problem-oriented policing* (POP). Both COP and POP programs involved local police departments analyzing crime problems in their communities in an individualized way. Custom-tailored solutions, then, could be developed for problems specific to a given community. Thus contrasts dramatically with earlier styles of policing where officers responded to calls and tried to apply some sort of universal solution to various problems. The emphasis, in many ways shifted from handling a given problem for the moment, to one of attempting to resolve a problem more completely.

Figure 2.5
Throughout the 1970s and 1980s, neighborhood watch programs encouraged residents to work with their local police.

SUMMARY

This chapter began with an outline of the original forms of policing. As suggested this may well have been little more than family members banding together in order to protect themselves against rival families or marauding groups. This early style of protection is sometimes referred to as kin policing. As society evolved and became more complex, informal norms gave rise to codes and loose configurations of laws. In turn, these laws evolved into more sophisticated and better organized systems, and groups to administered them.

Although primitive and rudimentary by today's standards, the Peissistratus guards and the urban cohort of the early Greek city-state were major organizational advances in the ancient history of policing. In fact, significant changes in policing were rather slow to emerge during much of England's early history after the fall of Rome.

As England changed from a largely agrarian to a largely industrial society, however, there were concurrent changes in policing. Small villages, markets, and towns gave way to large sprawling cities. As populations grew, so too did the crime and health problems in them. Eventually Sir Robert Peel established the first truly modern police with the founding of the London Metropolitan Police force. This police organization, and the training and ethical standards Peel insisted upon for his officers, remains an important idea for policing even today.

This chapter also described several leading colonial law enforcement carryovers from the English tradition. Perhaps chief among these was the watch and ward system of patrolling the colonial settlements. This watchman system provided a cornerstone upon which modern policing was built.

As outlined in this chapter, certain geographic and climatic aspects of colonial America influenced early policing styles and practices. For example, the South offered a more rural and agrarian style of life than the North. As in England's countryside, southern sections of colonial America established law enforcement organizations centering around sheriffs. Conversely, northern sections of America, like the urban centers throughout England, developed municipal police organizations.

Additionally, this chapter considered several critical law enforcement innovations as avocational voluntary watch systems in America evolved into more vocational policing systems. This included an examination of three major evolutionary stages in police history: The political influence stage, the reform stage, the professional stage, and the public and community relations stage.

REFERENCES

Barlow, Frank. *Edward the Confessor*. London: Eyre & Spottiswood, 1970.

Berg, Bruce L. *Law Enforcement*. Boston: Allyn and Bacon, Inc., 1992.

Berg, Bruce L., and John Horgan. *Criminal Investigation*. 3d ed. Westonville, Oh.: Glencoe/McGraw Hill, 1998.

Browne, Douglas G. *The Rise of Scotland Yard*. New York: Greenwood, 1973.

Bopp, William J., and Donald O. Schultz. *A Short History of American Law Enforcement*. Springfield, Ill.: Thomas, 1972.

Costello, Augustine E. *Our Police Protectors: A History of New York Police*. Montclair, N.J.: Patterson Smith, [1885] 1972.

Critchley, Thomas A. *A History of Police in England and Wales*. 2d ed. Montclair, N.J.: Patterson Smith, 1972.

Crump, Irving, and John W. Newton. *Our Police*. New York: Dodd, Mead, 1935.

Fosdick, Raymond B. *American Police Systems*. Reprinted, p.669. Montclair, N.J.: Patterson-Smith, 1969.

Gaines, Larry K., Victor E. Kappeler, and Joseph B. Vaughn. *Policing in America*. 2d ed. Cincinnati, Oh.: Anderson Publishing Co., 1997.

Germann, A. C., Frank D. Day, and R. R. H. Gallati. *Introduction to Law Enforcement and Criminal Justice*. Springfield, Ill.: Thomas, 1976.

Johnson, D. R. *American Law Enforcement: A History*. St. Louis: Forum Press, 1981.

Kappeler, V. E. "The St. Louis Police Department." In *The Encyclopedia of Police Science*. William G. Bailey (ed.) 2d ed. New York: Garland Press, 1995:701–704.

Kappeler, V. E., R. Sluder, and G. P. Alpert. *Forces of Deviance: Understanding the Dark Side of Policing*. Prospect Heights, Ill.: Waveland Press, 1994.

Klockars, Carl. *The Idea of Police*. Beverly Hills, Calif.: Sage Publications, 1985.

Knapp Commission Report. *The Knapp Commission Report on Police Corruption*. New York: Braziller, 1973.

Lane, Roger. *Policing the City: Boston 1822–1885*. Cambridge, Mass.: Harvard University Press, 1967.

Lee, William L. Melville. *A History of Police in England*. Montclair, N.J.: Patterson Smith, 1971.

Ludwig, Frederick J. *Youth and the Law: Handbook of Laws Affecting Youth*. Brooklyn, New York: Foundation Press, 1955.

Marx, Karl, and Friedrich Engels. *Capital: A Critique of Political Economy*, translated by E. Aveling. Chicago: Charles Kern, 1906.

Miller, Wilbur R. *Cops and Bobbies*. Chicago and London: University of Chicago Press, 1977.

Moore, M. "The Police: In Search of Direction." In *Managing the Police Organization*. L. Gaines and T. Ricks (eds.) Minneapolis/St. Paul: West Publishing Co., 1978:50–72.

Morris, William A. *The Medieval English Sheriff to 1300*. New York: Barnes and Noble, 1968.

National Advisory Commission on Civil Disorder. *Report of the National Advisory Commissions on Civil Disorder*. New York: Bantam Books, 1968.

Pennsylvania Crime Commission. "Report on Police Corruption and the Quality of Law Enforcement in Philadelphia." St. Davids, Penn.: Pennsylvania Crime Commission, 1974.

Reynolds, Susan. *Kingdoms and Communities in Western Europe, 900–1300*. Oxford, England: Clarendon.

Richardson, James F. *The New York Police: Colonial Times to 1901*. New York: Oxford, 1970.

Rosenbaum, D. P. "Community Crime Prevention: A Review and Synthesis of the Literature." *Justice Quarterly,* 5(1988):323–396.

Rumbelow, Donald. *I Spy Blue: The Police and Crime in the City of London from Elizabeth I to Victoria*. New York: St. Martin's Press, 1971.

Seagle, William. "Hammurabi: King of Babylon." In William Seagle (ed.) *Men of Law: From Hammurabi to Homes*. New York: Macmillan, 1947.

Strecher, V. "Revising the Histories and Futures of Policing." In *Police and Society: Touchstone Readings*. V. E. Kappeler (ed.) Prospect Heights, Ill.: Waveland Press, 1991:69–82.

Weber, Max. *Economy and Society II*. Berkeley, Calif.: University of California Press, [1920] 1978.

Williams, H. and P. V. Murphy. "The Evolving Strategy of Police; A Minority View." In *Police and Society: Touchstone Readings*. V. E. Kappeler (ed.) Prospect Heights, Ill.: Waveland Press, 1991:29–52.

QUESTIONS FOR REVIEW

Objective #1:

- During ancient times who governed the social order of the group?

Objective #2:

- What is meant by kin policing?
- What were blood feuds?

Objective #3:

- What was important about the Code of Hammurabi?
- What is meant by *lex talionis*?
- In what year was the Code of Hammurabi discovered?

Objective #4:

- Why is the Mosaic law considered rational?

Objective #5:

- What was the Praetorian guard?
- What were the duties of the urban cohort?

Objective #6:

- What was the purpose of the tithing system of medieval England?
- Who was required to be a tithing member?

Objective #7:

- What rights for citizens did the Magna Carta provide to Englishmen?
- In what year was the Magna Carta signed?

Objective #8:

- What police patrols are attributed to Henry Fielding?
- What did the Bow Street Runners do?

- What police agency did Robert Peel establish?
- Why were Peel's officers originally called "blue devils"?

Objective #9:

- Why did colonial settlements choose to develop watch and ward systems?
- Who served in colonial watch and ward patrols?

Objective #10:

- What is meant by political patronage?
- Why did many political machines use police jobs as payment for assistance in their political campaigns?

Objective #11:

- Who were the people largely involved in the reform stage of police in America?
- Why was there a need for police reform?

Objective #12:

- What sort of political unrest caused clashes between police and civilians?
- What is the intention of problem-oriented policing activities?

3 The Organization of American Law Enforcement Agencies

CHAPTER OBJECTIVES

After reading this chapter you should be able to:

1. Describe law enforcement at the county level.
2. Explain municipal policing.
3. Discuss the origins of state police agencies.
4. Speak about highway patrols in America.
5. Draw out the history of the U.S. Marshal Service.
6. Examine the historical roots of the Federal Bureau of Investigation.
7. Explain the duties of the Drug Enforcement Administration.
8. Detail the central purposes of the Immigration and Naturalization Service.
9. Describe the history and duties of Federal Postal Inspectors.
10. Distinguish between the plain clothes and the uniformed division of the Internal Revenue Service.
11. Discuss the responsibilities of The Bureau of Alcohol, Tobacco, and Firearms.
12. Outline the divisions and duties of the Internal Revenue Service.

POLICE JURISDICTIONS

Law enforcement may occur at a variety of governmental levels. It may occur at the county, state, federal, and even international levels. While the law

KEY TERMS

jurisdiction
municipal police departments
county sheriff's departments
county police
state police
Texas Rangers
Arizona Rangers
New Mexico Mounted Police
highway patrols
federal law enforcement agencies

U.S. Department of Justice
U.S. Marshal Service
Federal Marshals Service
FIST (Fugitive Investigative Strike Teams)
Bureau of Investigation
Federal Bureau of Investigation (FBI)
Unified Crime Reports (UCR)
National Crime Information Center (NCIC)
Harrison Act

Volstead Act
Drug Enforcement Administration (DEA)
Immigration and Naturalization Service (INS)
Department of Treasury
postal inspectors
Secret Service
counterfeiting
Tariff Act

enforcement agencies are similar at different levels, they may also differ in their types of responsibilities and activities. This variation in activities and functions are determined in part, by the agency's *jurisdiction* and mission. **Jurisdiction** usually refers to the area or issue over which the authority of a law enforcement organization extends. Typically, *area* literally refers to the geographic location where the agency operates and has authority. For example, municipal police agencies typically have jurisdiction within a city's municipally incorporated area. A sheriff's department generally has jurisdiction in townships, and in unincorporated areas of a municipal district.

The *issues* aspect of jurisdiction is given to represent the subject matter and class or area of law or crimes the agency is responsible for enforcing and investigating. These legal perimeters help to outline an agency's goal or mission. For example, the Drug Enforcement Agency's jurisdiction, relative to subject matter, is directed toward federal drug laws, money laundering, and related crimes. Marine patrols are frequently divisions of sheriff's departments whose issues involve safety and criminal activities on the waterways of the community. There are, of course, occasions when two or more levels of government will simultaneously have jurisdiction in legal matters. In these cases, the agencies strive to work together harmoniously and with the sense of mutual cooperation. Sometimes, there are disputes between agencies regarding who should be in charge, and which agency should perform various activities. More often than not, however, cooperation between agencies eventually prevails.

Policing may occur in small rural areas or in large, complex metropolitan areas. In 1993, there were nearly three-quarters of a million (746,736) full-time, sworn officers representing all levels of law enforcement in the United States. In addition, best estimates indicate there were an additional 53,723 part-time personnel working in police protection capacities (Maguire and Pastore 1994). This chapter examines each of these governmental levels of law enforcement to draw out the basic structure of policing in America.

POLICING THE CITY

As indicated in Chapter 1, when one thinks about a police officer, what typically comes to mind is a dark blue uniformed city police officer. Municipal police organizations are, in fact, among the primary types of policing organizations in the nation and include the majority of sworn officers. Nearly 58 percent of all sworn officers in the United States work in municipal police organizations. **Municipal police departments** differ from their county law enforcement colleagues in several ways. First, most municipal agencies employ a greater number of personnel (both sworn and ancillary) and offer more extensive law enforcement services than county agencies. Second, because of the added complexities associated with a large work force, municipal agencies frequently have larger financial and equipment resources than county organizations. Third, large metropolitan municipal police organizations may share local law enforcement responsibilities with other municipal agencies. For example, arson investigations in many large cities are investigated jointly by the municipal police agency and an investigative branch of the local fire department. In some cities, such as Boston, one finds a "Registry Police Department, a Massachusetts Bay Transit Police," force, the "Metropolitan District Commission," an agency similar to other large city parks and recreations police, and the "Boston Metropolitan Police." In fact, Boston may have as many as 26 separate agencies responsible for various aspects of municipal policing. Other cities commonly have, in additional to a municipal police, separate housing, transit, parks, or port authority police organizations.

The size of municipal police departments varies immensely across the nation. The largest municipal police department, by far, is the New York City Police Department (NYPD). The NYPD employs nearly 31,135 police officers (UCR 1995). A list of the 12 largest municipal police departments is shown in Table 3.1. This list includes all municipal police departments with at least 2,000 employees. The smallest departments contain only a single sworn officer. In fact, according to the *Uniform Crime Reports*, in 1994 there were approximately 426 municipal police departments with only one sworn officer (UCR 1995). The majority of municipal police agencies in the United States operate with ten or fewer sworn officers.

There are a number of differences between policing a large city and a small town. In most small towns across the United States, crime is not as serious a problem as it is in large cities. In many small towns, the leading crimes involve larceny—thefts, under-aged drinking, driving under the influence, and to a

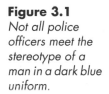

Figure 3.1
Not all police officers meet the stereotype of a man in a dark blue uniform.

Table 3.1 *Twelve Largest Municipal Police Departments*

Total # of	Department Employees	Sworn Officers
New York City	39,953	30,135
Chicago	15,226	12,971
Los Angeles	10,744	7,869
Houston	6,992	4,935
Philadelphia	6,977	6,101
Washington, D.C.	4,760	4,106
Detroit	4,381	3,855
Baltimore	3,635	3,065
Dallas	3,435	2,777
Phoenix	2,844	2,088
Boston	2,653	1,978
Milwaukee	2,511	2,055

Source: Adapted from *Uniform Crime Reports for the United States, 1994*. Washington, D.C.: USGPO, 1995, Table 78, pp. 297–356.

considerably lesser degree than in large cities, drug-related crimes. Small towns typically are less likely to have violent crimes such as murder and rape occur frequently or with any regularity—although small college towns do sometimes sustain a disproportionate number of sexual assault reports. Conversely, many large cities are likely to have more violent crimes occur in a single week than most small towns will endure in a year.

In addition to levels of crime in small towns differing from large cities, so too does geographic size make a distinction. City size has bearing on salary, fringe benefits, job advancement possibilities, available types of assignments, administrative styles, organizational structure, and police community relations (LaGrange 1993). City size may even impact the amount of media attention a department receives. Both the electronic and print media seem to keep the police departments of large cities in America under a constant microscope. For example, when was the last time you saw a story in a national news magazine about the police in Yell, Arkansas, or Zolfo Springs, Florida. Yet, it is not uncommon to see magazine stories about police from New York City, Los Angeles, Boston, Dallas, and even Miami. Scholarly research has also shown a marked preference in studying large-city police departments. This may reflect a tendency among may researchers to stress widespread generalizability, and the need to have large aggregate numbers in their sample size to accomplish this task. Whatever the reasoning, the result is that a far greater amount of information is available on large police departments than small ones.

Stated directly, there are many differences between large and small police departments, as well as between large city and small town policing requirements. Throughout this book, it is important to recognize that statements offered may not always fit every department in the nation. However, generalization offered in this book should fit most large departments, and efforts will be made to discuss variations that might occur in smaller departments.

COUNTY LAW ENFORCEMENT

Rolling down the highway with your C.B. radio set to Channel 19, you suddenly hear, "county mounty on the move one mile south of the five-mile marker." That "county mounty," of course, is likely to be a deputy sheriff. Although the duties of the **county sheriff's department** may vary from one jurisdiction to the next, their chief officer remains the traditional law enforcement agent, the sheriff. Among the several ways to distinguish the various activities of the sheriff's department is to consider the region in which it is located. In the South and major portions of the Mid- and Southwest, sheriff's departments often serve as the principal law enforcement agency in the area. In many smaller communities the sheriff's department also may be responsible for tax assessing and tax collection, patrolling the local bridges and highway extensions, serving as jail attendants and courtroom bailiffs, as well as the execution of both criminal and civil processes (i.e., the serving of warrants, subpoenas, and eviction notices). Conversely, in the Northeast the local sheriff's departments do little active law enforcement and considerably more of jail, courtroom, and process-serving tasks (Brown 1978; Berg 1992).

The position of sheriff holds a unique slot in the American policing system. With the exception of sheriffs in Rhode Island and Hawaii who are appointed, the position is an elected one. There are, in fact, approximately 3,100 elected sheriffs in the United States, with the largest department residing in Los Angeles County, California (Reaves 1992).

Some **county police** organizations report to a county commission or other form of county government and operate independent of the sheriff's department. These may include county detectives who are typically responsible to the state's attorney office and who operate autonomously, and are not usually part of the sheriff's department or other police organizations in the county. Counties usually create county police when the population and workload in the county becomes too large for the sheriff's department to effectively handle. In some cases, county police organizations are established when county officials desire to exercise more control over local law enforcement operations. Since the majority of sheriffs are elected, they frequently have substantial autonomy to operate their departments as they see fit. In other words, sheriffs have total control over the agency and consequently wield considerable local political power in their own right. On the other hand, county governments usually have nothing more than budgetary control. County police organizations are typically

Figure 3.2
In many jurisdictions the sheriff's office is the main local policing organization.

managed by a chief hired by the county commission or a similar governmental board.

STATE LAW ENFORCEMENT AGENCIES

State police agencies have fairly recent origins in the evolution of policing in America. While corruption and ineffectiveness within municipal police agencies may have been motivating factors in establishing state police divisions, these are not the only reasons. Before the existence of **state police**, each state was forced to rely upon its municipal forces to administer and enforce all of its state regulations in addition to all local ordinances. When a local sheriff or municipal police chief saw a particular state law as inappropriate, unjust, or just unnecessary, this law was not likely to be enforced. Since local law enforcement agents were drawn from the communities in which they worked, they sympathized more with their fellow community residents than with residents of the state.

Among the earliest state policing agencies were the Texas Rangers. As Samora and his associates (1979) suggest, with the possible exception of the Royal Canadian Mounted Police, there is no police agency more famous the world over than the Texas Rangers. During the 1990s, a television program entitled *Walker Texas Ranger* further popularized this state-level, range-riding police agency. As well, the program's catchy opening statement, "One riot one ranger" nicely captured the basic romanticized public image of the Texas Rangers that has evolved.

The Texas Rangers were established by the Republic of Texas' provisional government in 1835. Originally, the Texas Rangers included three companies of men and began as a paramilitary force to defend settlers against marauding Indians and to maintain the border between Mexico and Texas. What is particularly interesting about the Texas Rangers is that, while they are frequently pointed to as forerunners of state police forces, they were not originally designed as such. In fact, during the early period of "ranging men" (as they were known from 1823–35), the rangers did little investigating and no community service. This contrasts with police agencies both of that time and today

Figure 3.3
Chuck Norris has brought the Texas Rangers into the homes of many Americans on a weekly basis.
Printed by permission of CBS.

where officers are responsible to their communities. The concept of range men being public servants simply did not fit their highly independent and semi-autonomous activities.

Rangers companies did not police any given community of colonists as municipal forces did. Texas created the Rangers to secure and maintain the frontier of the Republic of Texas (Samora et al. 1979). Order maintenance and peace-keeping were the principal tasks of the Rangers. Their functions were to repel Indians and Mexican revolutionaries bent on overthrowing the government of the Republic and retaliating for the cattle-rustling undertaken in Mexico by Anglo-Texas cowboys (Samora et al. 1979).

After 1835 the Texas Rangers began refining their activities—although always slightly maverick, they soon came to investigate crimes that occurred in the state. Today, the principal task of the Texas Rangers, in addition to border patrolling, is crime investigation.

On May 16, 1865, Governor John A. Andrews announced that the state of Massachusetts would open the door at 50 Broomfield Street in Boston as the first headquarters for a "state constabulary." The chief constable would direct the statewide activities of the state police force from this Boston-based office (Powers 1979). Police historians recognize this early state constabulary as the first state police force.

In 1875 the Massachusetts State Constabulary became the State Detective Force. After posting a bond of $5,000, each of the newly appointed 15 detectives was granted statewide powers. The central purpose of this new state police was to assist the attorney general and various district attorneys in evidentiary matters and the pursuit of felons. In addition, the governor had the right to call upon the State Detective Force to suppress riots or in other ways preserve the peace (Powers 1979).

In 1876 the responsibilities and policing powers of the Massachusetts State Detective Force were significantly expanded. Their duties then included inspecting public buildings and factories throughout the Commonwealth of Massachusetts. Their mission was primarily to assess conditions that might lead to accidents or fires. In addition, the force was expected to ensure that all laws pertaining to child labor and working hours were adequately enforced.

Originally, Massachusetts State Police officers were unarmed. In fact, the force existed, in one form or another for over 50 years before officers were permitted to carry either badges or weapons. The laws of the Commonwealth were enforced largely on the personal integrity and reputation of the organization. In 1906 the Massachussetts legislature passed a law that prohibited the unlicensed carrying of a loaded pistol or revolver. The statute also outlawed the carrying of an assortment of other concealed weapons. In 1908 the Commonwealth authorized state detectives to carry badges, revolvers, truncheons (short clubs), and handcuffs. Soon the state police organization emerged as the District police, which in 1920 became the Massachussetts State Police.

While Massachussetts was busy arming its state officers, another significant development emerged in state policing history. In 1905 the Pennsylvania state

Figure 3.4
In 1865, Boston opened the doors at 50 Broomfield Street as the first headquarters for a State Constabulary. This agency later became the Massachusetts State Police.

legislature enacted a bill that established America's first uniformed state police organization (Powers 1979). Earlier state police organizations had focused their attention on limited frontier problems and enforcement of unpopular vice laws. The Pennsylvania State Police, however, founded with three clear purposes in mind: to establish an executive enforcement arm to assist the governor in carrying out his duties; to restore order in coal mining regions of the state, where labor disputes had led to a series of riots and terrorist attacks; and to strengthen law enforcement in the rural areas of the Commonwealth, where county police had been unable to provide adequate police services.

OTHER EARLY STATE LEVEL AGENCIES

Other forerunners of state policing organizations developing around this time were the **Arizona Rangers** (see Box 3.1) in 1901 and the **New Mexico Mounted Police** in 1905. Like the Texas Rangers before them, both of these agencies were essentially border-patrolling organizations, not policing as in Pennsylvania and Massachusetts.

BOX 3.1   BLAZE FORTH A NEW STAR: THE ARIZONA RANGERS

Texas was not the only state with ranging men. In 1901, 11 years before it became a state, Arizona established the Arizona Rangers. During its territorial days, like other western border territories, Arizona faced tremendous problems related to growth and development. Hostility raged as homeless settlers drifted across the land, and outlaws terrorized railroads and settlements and then holed up in stony crags rising from the vast, desolate desert of Arizona (Arizona Highway Patrol 1987).

Under the shade of tall pine trees, outlaws camped and planned their crimes. It was common for them to attack emerging settlement towns and raid livestock from the nearby ranches that were developing with the prospering of Arizona's cattle industry (Wagoner 1970). To establish order and safety, a group of Arizona men donned silver stars and rode the range. Like the Texas Rangers, this Arizona company of men was somewhat unorthodox in its policing style. They wore no uniforms, carried no banners, but did wear five-pointed stars that signified their authority within the territory of Arizona.

Because of the efforts of the Arizona range men, the cattle industry was able to flourish. As ranches and towns became better established, agricultural and technological strides were also made. Soon, Arizona had established a copper mining industry and, with the development of water pumping and irrigation technology, Arizona joined the ranks of the nation's leading cotton producers.

The five-pointed star and a blue-barreled revolver (to prevent any glint from the sun or moon when chasing down desperadoes) became the trademarks of the Arizona Rangers. Today, the tradition of the five-pointed star lives on, but now is worn by the sheriffs in each of Arizona's 14 counties.

MODERN STATE POLICE AND HIGHWAY PATROLS

Today, the most common state policing organizations are the state police and the highway patrol. Every state, with the exception of Hawaii, has some sort of state constabulary. In addition to state police and/or highway patrol organizations, most states have various state warranted police organizations with limited jurisdiction or limited purpose.

Twenty-six states have developed state **highway patrols** whose duties are focused on traffic enforcement and accident investigations along the highways and byways of their state. The legal authority and jurisdiction of highway patrol officers extends across the entire state. State police organizations can be found in 23 states. While state highway patrols are generally focused extensively on traffic enforcement on state roads, state police usually have expanded enforcement authority. State police have legal jurisdiction that extends across the state, and are authorized to make arrests for any violation of state statutes (LaGrange 1993). Table 3.2 shows which states have highway patrols, and which have state police agencies. As well, this table indicates the size of each organization.

There are also 35 states that have investigative agencies that are independent of either a state police or highway patrol organization. These organizations usually are part of the state's Department of Public Safety or a Justice Department within the state government. Examples of these include the Florida Department of Law Enforcement and the Georgia Bureau of Investigation.

Table 3.2 *Types and Size of State Law Enforcement Organizations*

State	Type	Officers	State	Type	Officers
Alabama	HP	637	Nebraska	HP	453
Alaska	SP	330	Nevada	HP	349
Arizona	SP	840	New Hampshire	SP	248
Arkansas	SP	476	New Jersey	SP	2,674
California	HP	5,686	New Mexico	SP	412
Colorado	SP	512	New York	SP	4,071
Connecticut	SP	977	North Carolina	HP	1,284
Delaware	SP	590	North Dakota	HP	118
Florida	HP	1,545	Ohio	HP	1,435
Georgia	HP	891	Oklahoma	HP	717
Idaho	SP	170	Oregon	SP	805
Illinois	SP	1,898	Pennsylvania	SP	4,307
Indiana	SP	1,059	Rhode Island	SP	207
Iowa	HP	608	South Carolina	HP	943
Kansas	HP	602	South Dakota	HP	152
Kentucky	SP	902	Tennessee	HP	744
Louisiana	SP	723	Texas	HP	2,626
Maine	SP	313	Utah	HP	379
Maryland	SP	1,552	Vermont	SP	280
Massachusetts	SP	2,452	Virginia	SP	539
Michigan	SP	1,991	Washington	SP	972
Minnesota	HP	*	West Virginia	SP	539
Mississippi	HP	508	Wisconsin	SP	466
Missouri	HP	865	Wyoming	HP	153
Montana	HP	195			

* No information available
Source: Adapted from *Uniform Crime Reports for the United States, 1994.* Washington, D.C.: USGPO, 1995, Table 76, p. 295.

Additionally, many states have developed various limited-authority, state-warranted police or law enforcement agencies. These include investigators attached to state attorneys' and public defenders' offices, some departments of motor vehicles, alcohol control bureaus, state gaming and revenue commissions, and even fish and wildlife wardens.

FEDERAL LAW ENFORCEMENT AGENCIES

Unlike local police agencies, which originally were given broad policing powers, **federal law enforcement agencies**, owing to their highly specific functions, were given much more narrow powers. Americans feared becoming a police state, or developing a national police force. Consequently, Congress did not create a systematic centralized federal law enforcement agency. The emergence of federal law enforcement agencies was, in fact, relatively slow and deliberate. Typically, a federal law enforcement agency was not congressionally mandated until the flagrant disregard of law grew so great as to endanger the welfare of the nation.

Within the jurisdiction of the federal government are approximately 60 different law enforcement and regulatory agencies and more than 69,000 employees (Reaves 1994). For the most part, federal law enforcement responsibilities reside with the Treasury Department and the Justice Department, although other federal agencies do have policing and law enforcement authority. The following section discusses a number of the major federal investigative and law enforcement agencies.

THE DEPARTMENT OF JUSTICE

The U.S. Department of Justice is sometimes called the legal arm of the government. The **U.S. Department of Justice** is headed by the attorney general, who is empowered to enforce federal law, represent the U.S. government in federal court actions, and to conduct law enforcement investigations. The Department of Justice was created in 1870 and includes the following major law enforcement agencies:

- The U.S. Marshal Service
- The Federal Bureau of Investigation
- The Drug Enforcement Administration
- The Immigration and Naturalization Service

Each of these agencies is discussed below.

U.S. Marshal Service

The first federal law enforcement agency established was the federal marshal organization created by President George Washington in 1789.[1] In its original form, the **Federal Marshals Service** more resembled a national sheriff's organization than a federal law enforcement agency. The first appointment of 13 marshals corresponded to each of the first eleven states and one each for the districts of Kentucky and Maine (Morris 1995). Each marshal represented a judicial district. Each marshal was empowered to hire deputies to assist as needed. As new states and territories were added to the United States, the U.S. Marshal Service expanded.

When first created in 1789 with the passage of the Judiciary Act, federal marshals were charged with two basic responsibilities: (1) Attending to the needs of the federal courts in each of the 13 judicial districts; and (2) executing all lawful precepts issued to them under the authority of the U.S. government (*The National Sheriff* 1982; Berg 1985). Typically, marshals were responsible for discharging many of the law enforcement duties traditionally associated with early American sheriffs in each of the districts.

Like many early policing organizations, the marshals have operated under the auspices of several different federal agencies during their lengthy history. Marshals have served the presidency, the federal court system, the Department of Justice, as well as the departments of Treasury, War, State, and the Interior (*The National Sheriff* 1982). In 1969 the **U.S. Marshal Service** was established; in 1974 it was elevated to the status of a federal bureau. Although modern marshals continue their tradition as presidential appointees, deputies are now hired under competitive civil service procedures. Currently there are 94 U.S. marshals and approximately 2,153 deputy marshals representing all 50 states and American territories.

Contemporary marshals continue to focus their energies principally towards servicing the federal court system. First, they service the civil and criminal process and execution of arrest warrants. This includes seizing property to satisfy judgments issued by the federal courts. Second, the marshals provide physical security for federal courts and for the protection of federal judges, attorneys, and jurors. Third, they transport and protect federal prisoners and witnesses.

During the early 1980s, the marshals service took over responsibility for the Federal Witness protection and relocation program. This program previously had been operated by the Federal Bureau of Investigation (to be discussed later). The marshals also developed a sting operation called "FIST" (Fugitive Investigative Strike Teams). Under a **FIST** operation, U.S. marshals and their deputies saturate a single geographic area with warrants and subpoenas. Although these projects last only about 90 days, they average 3,000 warrants each (Safir 1983).

With the exception of a few highly publicized incidents, like the problems occurring at Ruby Ridge in 1992, the U.S. Marshal Service remains largely out of the public's eye. Yet, they were the primary law enforcement agency across western America during the mid-1800s and were responsible for capturing many desperados.

Federal Bureau of Investigation (FBI)

The need for a Justice Department, created in 1870, is sometimes attributed to the chaos and lawlessness that followed the American Civil War during the country's period of reconstruction. The need for some type of centralized federal law enforcement agency seemed apparent to many, but abhorrent to others. On July 1, 1908, U.S. Attorney General Charles J. Bonaparte quietly established the **Bureau of Investigation**, renamed in 1935 the **Federal Bureau of Investigation**. The Bureau of Investigation was chiefly a detective force that operated under the direction of the attorney general.

In 1924, Attorney General Harlan F. Stone placed J. Edgar Hoover in charge of the Bureau of Investigation, making him its director. Hoover set about the task of professionalizing the Bureau of Investigation which was suffering from weak leadership and increasing amounts of internal corruption. Under Hoover's leadership, the bureau changed its public image and enhanced its ability to investigate crimes and apprehend law breakers. Hoover established rigid entrance requirements including requirements that agents possess college degrees.

Also under the direction of Hoover, in 1924, the bureau opened its identification division, which served as a national clearinghouse for information on criminals. The identification division began with about 810,188 fingerprint cards obtained from the Federal Penitentiary at Leavenworth, Kansas, and from the International Association of Chiefs of Police (Peak 1993). Today, the identification division has nearly 200 million fingerprints electronically filed and processes thousands of inquires each day. In 1998, access to this computer base of fingerprint files will be made possible for law enforcement agencies through a simple computer telephone hook-up.

Throughout its history, the FBI has been portrayed as one of the most colorful and romanticized law enforcement agencies in the country. The exploits of FBI agents have been portrayed in television series, movies, books, and magazines. In fact, during the prohibition era, the FBI was instrumental in capturing a number of notable gangsters who themselves have become romanticized over time. Some of the more notable include John Dillinger, Charles "Pretty Boy" Floyd, and George "Machine Gun" Kelly. The FBI's reputation, however is not entirely unsullied. For example, it has been well established that during the anti-Vietnam protests of the 1960s, J. Edgar Hoover maintained private dossiers on many political leaders, and many Americans he declared "subversives." In fact, from 1962 through 1968, the FBI planted numerous wiretaps and hidden microphones in order to monitor civil rights leader Dr. Martin Luther King, Jr. In 1973, President Richard Nixon revealed that the FBI had also been involved in a number of illegal burglaries in order to gather intelligence information. These various revelations resulted in numerous investigations into the activities of the FBI.

More recently, in 1993, the judgment of the FBI was called into question because of their handling of a raid on the Branch Davidians' compound in Waco, Texas. The situation was originally handled by Alcohol, Tobacco, and Firearms agents (to be discussed later) but was taken over by the FBI when ATF's efforts failed. The FBI was then confronted with one of the longest stand-offs in law enforcement history. For 51 days, agents of the FBI tried to convince members of the Branch Davidians to peacefully leave the compound. Finally, the compound was stormed with tanks and tear gas. Almost immediately, the compound was engulfed by fire and 85 residents, including many children, were killed—some by their own hands, and others apparently as a result of the fires (Department of the Treasury 1993). In 1995, the FBI's involvement in the shooting of civilians at Ruby Ridge sparked additional questions about the bureau. However, in 1996, the FBI successfully negotiated with a "patriot group" calling themselves the Freemen who, like the Branch Davidians, had barricaded themselves in a compound, this time a farm house in Montana. After another lengthy stand-off, the Freemen peacefully surrendered.

The FBI operates 59 field offices throughout the United States and has approximately 10,120 special agents (Reaves 1994). The bureau's investigative priorities include white-collar crime, political crime, organized crime and racketeering, drug operations, espionage, domestic terrorism, and terroristic crimes committed against Americans in foreign countries. In addition, the FBI is responsible for coordinating and publishing the **Uniform Crime Reports** (UCR) for the United States, which collects national statistics on crime, criminals, and criminal justice agencies. The FBI also is responsible for maintaining the **National Crime Information Center** (NCIC), which serves as a national clearinghouse and database for wanted persons, wanted and stolen vehicles, and stolen property. Beyond these services, the FBI crime labs provide scientific analysis services to local and state agencies across the country. Finally, the FBI provides both training classes at its training facility in Quantico, Virginia, for local and state policing agents, and frequently, training officers on loan to these local and state agencies.

Figure 3.5
The Uniform Crime Reports are produced through the efforts of the FBI.

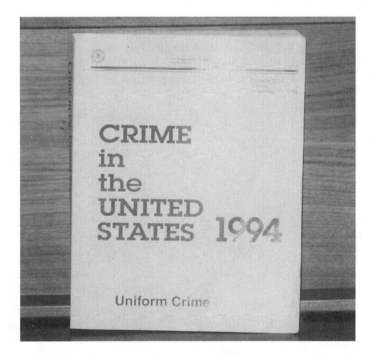

Drug Enforcement Administration (DEA)

Federal interest in drug enforcement can be traced to the Harrison Act (1914), which established federal jurisdiction over the distribution and use of controlled substances. The **Harrison Act** was primarily a tax law, but Section 8 made it unlawful for any nonregistered personnel to possess heroin, cocaine, opium, morphine, or any of their products. Originally, the Bureau of Internal Revenue Service was given jurisdiction over enforcing the provisions of this act. The Internal Revenue Service created a division containing about 162 agents who were responsible for enforcing the law (Lyman and Potter 1996; Bailey 1995).

During the 1920s, federal narcotics agents focused most of their energies on organized gangs of Chinese immigrants suspected of importing opium. In 1920, the **Volstead Act** brought Prohibition to America, and the Narcotics Division of the Prohibition Unit of the Revenue Bureau was created.

In 1930, under the directorship of Harry Anslinger, the newly created Federal Bureau of Narcotics (FBN) increased its authority and expanded its enforcement powers. For the most part, the FBN concentrated its efforts on the illegal importation of drugs into the United States.

In 1968, the FBN was removed from the Treasury Department and combined with the Bureau of Drug Abuse Control from the Department of Health, Education, and Welfare. This blending of agencies created the Bureau of Narcotics and Dangerous Drugs (BNDD) housed under the control of the Justice Department. This actually was the first time in American history that the Justice Department was given jurisdiction over the enforcement of drug laws. The **Drug Enforcement Administration** was actually created by President Richard Nixon in 1973, when he reorganized the nation's drug enforcement system. The director of the DEA reported directly to the Attorney General. Nixon hoped that the combining of several drug enforcement related agencies into a unified DEA would result in a stronger attack on both drug suppliers and drug users.

Figure 3.6
The Drug Enforcement Administration has approximately 2,813 agents placed in 19 domestic field offices in the United States.

The attorney general turned over control of the DEA to the FBI in 1982, providing both agencies with concurrent jurisdiction over drug enforcement. Today, the DEA has approximately 2,813 agents placed in 19 domestic field offices in the United States (Gaines et al. 1997). In addition, the DEA has 72 field offices located throughout 49 foreign countries.

Immigration and Naturalization Service (INS)

Although not directly an investigative and enforcement agency, the Immigration and Naturalization Service does fall under the Department of Justice. The **Immigration and Naturalization Service** (INS) was established under Article I, Section 8, of the U.S. Constitution which gave Congress the power to establish such a service. In 1798, the Alien Act gave the president the power to expel aliens who were considered a threat to national security. In 1864, the office of the Commissioner of Immigration of the Bureau of Immigration was created. In 1903, this bureau was placed under the control of the Department of Commerce and Labor. Later, this evolved into the Immigration and Naturalization Service, and was placed under the Department of Justice in 1940.

The central purpose of the INS is to control the entrance of aliens into the United States. In terms of law enforcement, the major INS unit is the border patrol who are used to dissuade illegal aliens from entering the United States. INS is also responsible for monitoring those aliens who have already entered (both legally and illegally). The border patrol was established in 1924 with a staff of about 450 officers. Today, the border patrol employs more than 3,920 agents (Reaves 1994) responsible for patrolling more than 8,000 miles of border.

THE TREASURY DEPARTMENT

The **Department of Treasury** was one of the two original cabinet-level departments created in 1789. Its primary responsibility centers around the fiscal affairs of the federal government. The Treasury Department also maintains several enforcement branches among its regulatory agencies. These include:

- Federal Postal Inspectors
- The United States Secret Service
- The Bureau of Alcohol, Tobacco, and Firearms
- The U.S. Customs Service
- The Internal Revenue Service

Federal Postal Inspectors

Postal inspectors, or "silent investigators," actually owe their creation to America's first postmaster general, Benjamin Franklin, who in 1775 who hired a postal surveyor. But it was not until 44 years later that the federal postal inspection agency formally came into existence. The problems of mail fraud and misuse of the federal mail service prompted the creation of a Post Office Inspection system in 1829. It was not until 1936 that the postmaster general was authorized to actually employ postal investigators. These **postal inspectors** were meant to pursue all regulatory matters related to the Post Office Department.

During the 1960s and 1970s, the postal inspectors directed much of their effort to curtailing the use of the mail for transporting illegal drugs and explosives. Following the passage of the Child Protection Act of 1984, considerable energy on the part of the postal inspectors was directed at apprehending child pornographers, who frequently send their wares through the U.S. mail (Ball 1987). Although chiefly a regulatory agency, criminal laws related to the mail and covering postal inspectors are covered in Title 18 and Title 39 of the U.S. Code. These laws include mail-conducted lotteries and pyramid schemes, burglary or robbery of the mail, and use of the mail to distribute obscene or crime-inciting materials. A list of some of the principal crimes enforced by the Postal Inspection Service are shown below:

- Blackmail and threatening communications
- Child pornography
- Counterfeiting and related crimes (counterfeiting stamps and money orders)
- Destruction, obstruction, and delay of mails
- Employee theft/embezzlement
- Lotteries (importing or transporting lottery tickets, mailing lottery tickets, making false representation of lotteries)
- Mail box destruction
- Mail fraud and misrepresentation (use of the mails for frauds or swindles, use of fictitious names or addresses)
- Contraband and non-mailables (firearms, explosives, drugs, injurious items)
- Obscenity and sexually oriented advertising
- Theft (including theft of mail matter, credit cards, and keys, or locks stolen or reproduced; theft or damage to mail bags)

Among the interesting aspects connected with the various operations aspects of the postal inspectors is that they are, as mentioned, a regulatory service with police powers. What this actually means is that certain latitudes are permitted them than more traditional law enforcement agencies could not undertake. A partial explanation for this is that use of the mail system is a privilege, not a constitutional right.

Federal postal inspectors have two major divisions. One division is primarily responsible for internal crime. This includes thefts or frauds committed by employees of the U.S. Postal Service. The other division is primarily responsible for external crimes. This group of postal inspectors work with local and other federal agents to apprehend people who commit crimes using the postal service.

This may include people sending contraband through the mail, or who use the mails to perpetrate frauds such as chain-letters or similar pyramid schemes, or mail order sale swindles.

U.S. Secret Service

The **Secret Service** was established on July 5, 1865, when William P. Wood was sworn into office as the first chief of the U.S. Secret Service Division. The primary mission of the Secret Service Division was to combat counterfeiting and counterfeiters. **Counterfeiting** has long been a weapon used in war to destroy the confidence of a people in their government. During the American Revolution, the British dumped huge quantities of fake continental currency into the American economy—effectively destroying public confidence in these private bank notes (Bowen and Neal 1960). Similarly during the American Civil War, it was estimated that as much as a full third of all money in circulation was counterfeit. While Congress had passed a counterfeiting law in 1842, this legislation had few teeth since local law enforcement seemed unable to contend with rampant counterfeiting. Since the private banks producing paper money across the country were not restricted to any real standards of production or uniformity in design, counterfeiters enjoyed almost unrestrained prosperity.

In 1863, the federal government authorized production of the first national currency, commonly referred to as "greenbacks." Unfortunately, this effort did nothing to inhibit counterfeiting. Two years later, however, with the establishment of the U.S. Secret Service, the manufacturers of phony money did have something to fear about their chosen vocation.

After the assassination of President McKinley in 1909, Congress ordered the Secret Service Division to provide security for the president. Before this congressional order, there was no federal agency formally responsible for protecting the president. Today, while still responsible for thwarting counterfeiters, the Secret Service's principal responsibility is directed towards executive protection of the president, the vice president, and their immediate families. In 1965, after the assassination of President John F. Kennedy, the division was renamed the U.S. Secret Service. The Secret Service employs approximately 2,186 agents (Reaves 1994).

While many people are aware of the plainclothes division of the Secret Service and their executive protection duties, in fact, there is also a uniformed division. The uniformed division of the Secret Service was established in 1922 at the request of President Warren G. Harding. The duties of this uniformed division is to provide security for the White House, the treasury building, presidential offices, the vice president's residence, and foreign diplomatic missions.

In addition to executive protection and protection of certain official buildings, the Secret Service is additionally authorized to investigate credit card and debit card frauds, or frauds relating to electronic funds transfers, such as those involving money transfers between banks, and automatic teller machines.

Bureau of Alcohol, Tobacco, and Firearms (ATF)

The Bureau of Alcohol, Tobacco, and Firearms originated as a unit within the Internal Revenue Service in 1862. Their duties, at that time, were to enforce certain alcohol and tobacco tax statutes. In 1972, the Bureau of Alcohol, Tobacco, and Firearms was created by order of the Treasury Department. ATF was now mandated to enforce all laws relating to alcohol, tobacco, firearms, and explosives. In 1976, the ATF was given additional responsibilities concerning violations of federal wagering and gambling laws.

ATF, like several other federal agencies, has a colorful early history. At one time, ATF agents were better recognized as "the revenuers." Revenuers were depicted in films as ax-wielding G-Men (government men) running through backwoods hills ripping up illegal moonshining stills. Although it is true that the regulation of liquor production and taxation continue to be a function of ATF, its tasks have been significantly expanded. In addition to regulatory responsibilities associated with sale, transport, and distribution of firearms and explosives, ATF also provides ancillary assistance to state and local agencies investigating cases involving explosives, bombs, and certain incendiary devices. In fact, in recent years, much of the ATF's attention has been directed towards controlling guns and explosives, and away from regulating alcohol. The particular activities of the ATF are spelled out in its mission statement:

- Suppress and prevent crime violence through enforcement, regulation, and community outreach.
- Ensure fair and proper revenue collection.
- Provide fair and effective industry regulation.
- Support and assist federal, state, local, and international law enforcement.
- Provide innovative training programs in support of criminal and regulatory enforcement functions.

In 1993, agents of the ATF sought to investigate firearms charges against members of a commune known as the Branch Davidians, residing in Waco, Texas. As a consequence of careless planning, the simple serving of warrants became a heated battle that resulted in the death of four agents and the wounding of 20 others (Treasury Department Report 1993). As well, a 51-day standoff occurred during which time, the FBI was called in to take charge of the situation. Following the incident at Waco, Texas, it was learned that Congress had been considering abolishing the agency. Many people speculated that the ATF's grandstand play at the compound in Waco, Texas, was undertaken in an attempt to demonstrate the need for the agency. In 1995, following the bombing of the Murrah Building in Oklahoma City, the ATF was effective in their investigation. From their efforts and those of the FBI, evidence was located that lead to the arrest of several suspects in this bombing which killed 150 people—many of whom were children.

U.S. Customs Service

When America declared its independence in 1776, the young country was struggling at the brink of bankruptcy. On July 4, 1789, the first Congress passed and President George Washington signed the **Tariff Act** which authorized the collection of duties on imported goods. This Tariff Act was called "the second Declaration of Independence" by the news media of the time. Four weeks later, on July 31, 1789, the fifth act of Congress created the original customs districts and ports of entry.

For the next 125 years, virtually all of the government's bills were paid by revenue collected by customs. The Customs Service still is responsible for a significant source of income for the federal government.

The U.S. Customs Service is empowered to assure that all imports and exports comply with U.S. laws and regulations. The service focuses upon collection and protection of revenue, guards against smuggling and is also responsible for the following:

- Assessing and collecting customs duties, excise taxes, fees and penalties due on imported merchandise.
- Interdicting and seizing contraband, including narcotics and illegal drugs.
- Processing persons, baggage, cargo and mail, and administering certain navigation laws.
- Detecting and apprehending persons engaged in fraudulent practices designed to circumvent customs and related laws.
- Protecting American business and labor and intellectual property rights by enforcing U.S. laws intended to prevent illegal trade practices, including provisions related to quotas and the marking of important merchandise; the Anti-Dumping Act; and, by providing customs recordations for copyrights, patents, and trademarks.
- Protecting the general welfare and security of the United States by enforcing important and export restrictions and prohibitions, including the export of critical technology used to develop weapons of mass destruction, and money laundering.

In addition to enforcing various specific customs laws, the U.S. Customs Service enforces more than 400 other provisions of law for at least 40 agencies. These include laws prohibiting drugs form entering the United States, certain white-collar crimes, and the illegal export or importation of high technology and munitions.

Internal Revenue Service (IRS)

Perhaps one of the greatest fears in the hearts and minds of many Americans is finding a letter in their mailbox from the IRS asking them to come in for an audit. Yet, the IRS is not exclusively composed of dozens of beady-eyed, white-sleeved accountants wearing horned-rimmed glasses and poking calculators with the eraser ends of pencils.

Established in 1862, the **Internal Revenue Service** has three principal divisions. These include an investigative division, and audit division, and a collection division. The investigative intelligence division, the smallest of the three, investigates violations of tax law that come to the attention of the IRS. In addition to cases that specifically correspond to income frauds (tax evasions), the investigative unit may also look into cases concerning citizens who own certain types of automatic weapons and machine guns. Several statutes require that owners of automatic weapons and machine guns pay taxes and obtain licenses for these weapons to be lawfully owned. Among several federally coordinated drug enforcement and interdiction programs developed during recent years are those engaged in by the IRS audit and intelligence divisions. In 1985 a federal banking law was implemented that required that all banks formally notify IRS whenever a patron makes a deposit or withdrawal amounting to $10,000 or more. Bankers refer to this as IRS Form 4789. The intention of this law is to assist in identifying potential large-scale drug trafficking or money laundering schemes. The IRS is also involved with various other federal agencies in confiscating money and property obtained by drug traffickers under federal forfeiture laws. In addition to the above, the IRS is, of course, also involved in disseminating various pieces of information about tax regulations to the American public.

Federal Law Enforcement Training Center (FLETC)

In 1970 Congress established the Federal Law Enforcement Training Center in Glynco, Georgia. Many law enforcement practitioners affectionately refer to FLETC as the "Disneyland" of law enforcement training. FLETC offers extensive training for 60 federal agencies and an assortment of semi- or quasi-governmental agencies at both its Glynco campus and its Tucson, Arizona, campus. Training at the Tucson campus includes instruction for the security forces used at many of the nations nuclear power plants; contract security guards hired to protect the federal courts through the U.S. Marshal Service; the Indian Police for the Bureau of Indian Affairs, and a number of other agencies.

SUMMARY

Chapter 3 outlined law enforcement at a variety of levels. The intention was to indicate how modern policing has evolved into a highly organized operation with numerous branches and specializations. While none of the brief descriptions offered was sufficient to completely describe each agency, they did provide a sense of the basic organizational structure of the American system of policing. It should be noted, however, that the majority of activities undertaken in the realm of policing occur at the local level. Municipal police and county sheriff's departments remain the heart and soul of policing in America. While state and federal agencies provide important and necessary police services, it is the municipal police and sheriff's departments that provide basic police services to the average citizen.

REFERENCES

Ball, Joanne. "Child Pornography Probe Targeted 12 New England Residents." *The Boston Globe*, September 15, 1987:17, 19.

Bailey, William G. "Drug Enforcement Administration." In *The Encyclopedia of Police Science*. William G. Bailey (ed.) 2d ed. New York: Garland Press, 1995:241–244.

Berg, Bruce L. *Law Enforcement: An Introduction to Police in Society*. Boston: Allyn and Bacon, Inc., 1992.

Berg, Bruce L. "Private Security in the Public Sector: The U.S. Marshals Service as a Case Example." Paper presented at the annual meeting of the American Society of Public Administrator. Cincinnati, Ohio, November 1985.

Bowen, Walter S., and Harry Edward Neal. *The U.S. Secret Service*. New York: Chilton, 1960.

Brown, Lee. "The Roles of the Sheriff." In *The Future of Policing*. Alvin Cohen (ed.) Beverly Hills, Calif.: Sage, 1978.

Department of the Treasury. *Report of the Department of the Treasury on the Bureau of Alcohol, Tobacco, and Firearms Investigation of Vernon Wayne Howell also known as David Koresh*. Washington, D.C.: GPO, 1993.

Gaines, Larry K., Victor E. Kappeler, and Joseph B. Vaughn. *Policing in America*. Cincinnati, Oh.: Anderson Publishing Co., 1997.

LaGrange, Randy. *Policing American Society*. Chicago: Nelson-Hall Publishers, 1993.

Lyman, M.D., and G. W. Potter. *Drugs in Society: Causes, Concept and Control*. 2d ed. Cincinnati, Oh.: Anderson Publishing Co., 1996.

Maguire, Kathleen, and Ann L. Pastore. *Sourcebook 1993*. Washington, D.C.: U.S. Department of Justice, Office of Justice Programs, 1994.

Morris, S. E. "The U.S. Marshals." In *The Encyclopedia of Police Science*. William G. Bailey (ed.) 2d ed. New York: Garland Press, 1995:796–798.

Peak, Kenneth J. *Policing America*. Englewood Cliffs, N.J.: Regents/Prentice Hall, 1993.

Powers, William F. *French and Electric Blue: The Massachusetts State Police*. Lowell, Mass.: Sullivan, 1979.

Reaves, B. A. *Sheriff's Departments 1990*. Bureau of Justice Statistics. Washington, D.C.: U.S. Department of Justice, Office of Justice Programs, 1992.

Reaves, B. A. *Federal Law Enforcement Officers, 1993*. Bureau of Justice Statistics. Washington, D.C.: U.S. Department of Justice, Office of Justice Programs, GPO, 1994.

Safir, Howard. "United States Marshals Service Fugitive Investigative Strike Teams." *Police Chief*, 1983:34–37.

Samora, Julian, Joe Bernal, and Albert Pena. *Gunpowder Justice: A Reassessment of the Texas Rangers*. South Bend, Ind.: University of Notre Dame Press, 1979.

Uniform Crime Reports for the United States, 1994. Washington, D.C.: GPO, 1995, Table 78, pp. 296–356.

"United States Marshals Service." *The National Sheriff*, April/May (1982):28.

NOTE

[1] In 1789 the Revenue Cutter Service was also created in order to respond to problems of smuggling. Later, these tasks were absorbed by other federal agencies. As well, the Customs Service was created in 1789, but was originally ostensibly a revenue collecting agency, and not an investigative law enforcement one.

QUESTIONS FOR REVIEW

Objective #1:
- Why do some communities have county detectives?
- What are the central duties of sheriff's departments in the southern region of the country?

Objective #2:
- What are some of the ways that municipal police agencies differ from county ones?

Objective #3:
- Who are the Texas Rangers?
- In what year did Massachusetts establish their State Constabulary?
- In 1905, where was the nation's first uniformed state police organization created?

Objective #4:
- What is the principal jurisdiction of a highway patrol?

Objective #5:
- What president established the Federal Marshals Service?
- What are the principal duties of the U.S. Marshal Service?

Objective #6:
- What were some of the reasons behind the creation of the Bureau of Investigation?
- In what year was the name of the Bureau of Investigation changed to the Federal Bureau of Investigation?

Objective #7:
- What are the chief responsibilities of the Drug Enforcement Administration?

Objective #8:
- What activities are under the authority of the Immigration and Naturalization Service?

Objective #9:

- Who is credited with having established the Federal Postal Inspectors Service?
- What types of crimes do postal inspectors investigate?

Objective #10:

- When first established, what were the principal duties of the Secret Service Division?
- What are the principal duties of the Uniformed Secret Service?
- Who, in the Secret Service, is responsible for Executive Protection?

Objective #11:

- In what ways is The Bureau of Alcohol, Tobacco, and Firearms involved in revenue collection?
- What are some of the chief crimes that The Bureau of Alcohol, Tobacco, and Firearms investigates?

Objective #12:

- In addition to auditing taxpayers, what are some of the activities of the Internal Revenue Service?

Part 2

Police
Operations

4 Police Patrol and Traffic Functions

CHAPTER OBJECTIVES

After reading this chapter you should be able to:

1. Identify patrol as the basic field operation for police departments.
2. Distinguish between calls for service and law enforcement calls.
3. Describe what is meant by order maintenance.
4. List elements basic to patrol operations.
5. Detail activities associated with the preliminary investigation.
6. Discuss elements of patrol deployment.
7. Explain differences in various types of shift structure.
8. Delineate categories or labels used to describe geographic distributions of patrol forces.
9. List various types of mobile and specialty patrols.
10. Explain proactive and reactive police models.
11. Consider the reasons behind community policing efforts.
12. Discuss the purpose of the traffic function for police agencies.

POLICE ORGANIZATION

Most American police departments are organized in a military, or quasi-military hierarchical arrangement. In other words, as highly structured bureaucratic organizations with well-developed divisions of labor and authority-based ranking

KEY TERMS

calls for service
law enforcement calls
order maintenance
victimization surveys
preliminary investigation
allocation of patrol
deployment of patrol

temporal distribution
watches
tours of duty
geographic distribution
the beat
patrol sectors
the precinct
proactive police model
reactive police model

citizen academies
Officer Friendly programs
block watches
operation I.D.
home security surveys
selective enforcement
accident investigation

structures (see Figure 4.1). This militaristic nature is visible in several ways. First, officers typically wear uniforms that resemble military uniforms. Second, police officers are divided into ranks whose titles sound like military rankings and establish a chain of command: captain, lieutenant, sergeant, corporal, and patrol officer. Finally, police operations are organized around a team effort with careful strategic planning, not unlike military operations.

The military image of police departments serves as an adequate means for understanding the outward appearance and formal organization of the police. However, it is not completely accurate for describing the day-to-day decision making and activities of the average police officer. Soldiers, in the military, must wait for orders before they can legitimately undertake any action. When actions are taken, they are guided by clear and exacting orders and instructions. For instance, soldiers cannot change their positions without orders, they cannot fire their weapons without orders, and they cannot even rest on marches without permission. Police officers, on the other hand, are given a slightly wider berth in which to operate. In most situations they are permitted a wide variety of lawful decisions and can choose from an array of optional actions. They can, for example, decide whether or not to issue a traffic citation; to arrest or take home a teenager drinking beer on the corner; to talk to or arrest a rowdy bar patron; and so forth.

PATROL WORK

Police patrol typically accounts for at least 60 percent of a department's personnel. While 80 percent of American police departments employ fewer than 20 officers—and more than half fewer than 10—the principal activity among officers is patrol work (Adams 1994; UCR 1995). Many of us have grown up watching Andy Taylor, at least in reruns, the fictional sheriff of the little North Carolina town of Mayberry (played by Andy Griffith), and his one deputy, Barney Fife (played by Don Knotts). Andy was the sheriff, chief law enforcement officer in the area, and a patrol officer. Like Andy Taylor, in the real world, small police agencies frequently require their chiefs to serve as the local juvenile officers, records clerks, traffic officers, criminal investigators, and patrol officers. The greatest amount of time, however, will be spent in the activity of patrol.

In this chapter, the central focus is on law enforcement's basic field unit and operation, patrol. To understand fully the objectives of patrol, it is important to consider the primary orientations of police officers in general. Let us consider the watchwords of most municipal police agencies: "To Protect and Serve."

PROTECTING AND SERVING THE PUBLIC

While a fairly grandiose and encompassing statement, the principal objectives of policing are succinctly summed up by the phrase "to protect and serve." To be sure, the public expects patrol officers to be crime fighters and crusaders for good and fair justice regardless of how successful they may be at it. Patrol officers are also expected to serve the community. In other words, patrol officers function as social service, community relations, and public relations agents in addition to law enforcement agents. Officers must give directions to lost tourists, help children find runaway pets, educate community members through speeches and public appearances at civic, school, and church or synagogue functions, maintain lines of communication between residents and the police, and so forth.

As research repeatedly demonstrates, a large majority of calls to the police are service calls. In his study of the Syracuse police, James Q. Wilson (1968) found that only about one-tenth of all calls received by the department during an average week were law enforcement related. In 1980, Richard J. Lundman found that while police activities may vary in different police agencies, law enforcement calls among departments he studied never exceeded a third of any single agency's calls. According to Harry W. More and Fred Wegener (1997), police officers spend no more than 10 or 15 percent of their on duty time actually enforcing criminal law. The majority of their time is spent providing essential, but non-police, calls for service.

Figure 4.1   *The dispatcher is an essential aspect of any police agency.*

In 1997 the numbers of service, but non-emergency, 911 police calls became so burdensome to many police agencies that a second number, 311, was added nationally. Now when citizens need to contact police for various non-emergency police related activities they may do so on a separate number. Experimental use of this 311 number in Baltimore, Maryland, reduced the number of non-emergency police calls to 911 by 30 percent.

Calls for service are distinguished from **law enforcement calls** in that the former does not lead to situations in which a summary arrest (an arrest made on the spot) can be made. For example, when a teenager is playing his or her stereo too loudly at 2 or 3 A.M., and the neighbors complain to the police. An officer will be dispatched to the home of the teen, but is not likely to make an arrest. Instead, the teen is more likely to be given notice that he or she must lower the music. Assuming the teen responds appropriately and does lower the music, it is possible that the situation will end there.

Calls for service commonly require little more of an officer than to get a cat out of a tree, remind the participants in an argument that their problem is a civil one and that they should try to resolve their differences calmly and amicably. In some instances, of course, an individual may be arrested during a service call.

The local police officer is often expected to be an information resource for the area. Because officers are trusted sources of information, they are frequently called upon to give directions to specific business or residential addresses, local community events, the best place in town for chops or lobster, where to buy tropical fish, how to get into a car when someone locks the keys inside, where the local shopping malls are, where to find a place where one can have film developed in an hour or where one can locate access to the beach. As the most visible representative of local government, uniformed officers of local police and sheriff's departments must be prepared to answer such non-law enforcement related questions.

In addition to the direct crime intervention and service function of patrol officers, there is a broader notion associated with patrol. This notion is order maintenance. **Order maintenance** has become a kind of catchall for activities that are legally the responsibility of the force, and also for those tasks that have become traditionally associated with them.

It is impossible to determine precisely how many crimes are committed each year. It is generally agreed, however, that a far greater number of crimes are committed than those that are reported. **Victimization surveys**, which ask members of households if anyone in the family has been the victim of a crime (regardless of whether it was reported), demonstrate the disparate rates between officially reported and actually occurring crimes. The inference here, of course, is that whatever it is that patrol forces are doing, it is never enough. Traditionally, police agencies are charged with the responsibility of preventing, repressing, and solving crimes. These responsibilities are hampered by the realities of limited funds and personnel and increasing sophistication among professional law violators.

Geoffrey Alpert and Roger Dunham (1992:135) list 11 basic activities taken care of by patrol operations. These include:

- Deterring crime through routine patrol.
- Enforcing the laws.
- Investigating criminal behavior.
- Apprehending offenders.
- Writing reports.
- Coordinating efforts with prosecutors.
- Assisting individuals in danger or in need of assistance.
- Conflict resolution.
- Keeping the peace.
- Maintaining order.
- Keeping pedestrian and automobile traffic moving.

This list, however, largely reflects a fairly traditional nuts-and-bolts policing position. With many police agencies today, it is necessary to expand this list to include various issues related to community policing (Cordner 1995). These might include, but may not be limited to, issues such as:

- Community safety education.
- Community involvement/relations.
- Problem-oriented policing.
- Coordination of recreational activities for youths.
- Coordination of programs to reduce fear of crime among community members.

As suggested here, and as will be drawn out later in this text, contemporary efforts in community policing expands patrol activities well beyond traditional limits. Further, many of these activities previously have been delegated to the non-patrol unit in police departments. Modern police patrol work has become more participatory. In other words, teamwork between the public and the police is no longer mere rhetoric; it is a necessity if police are to perform their activities effectively (Adams 1994).

SECURING SCENES AND BEGINNING INVESTIGATIONS

Patrol officers are constantly available and patrolling the streets, ready to respond to whatever situation occurs. Often, this will include performing preliminary investigations of crimes or traffic accidents. The activities that take place at the scene of a crime immediately following its report to or discovery by police officers are all part of the **preliminary investigation**. In most cases, many of these activities are initially undertaken by members of the uniformed patrol unit of the police agency responding to the call for assistance.

Patrol officers responding to a criminal event typically are responsible for certain important aspects of the eventual investigation. For example, the

Figure 4.2 *When an officer arrives at a possible crime scene, he or she needs to gather information in order to determine if a crime has been committed.*

officers arriving on the scene of a crime must immediately determine what has happened and whether anyone is injured. The officer must also determine whether a criminal act has been committed and, if so, the type of crime. Should the initial facts prove unfounded or of a non-criminal nature, the matter can be closed with the first report. If, on the other hand, the officer determines that a crime has been committed, the officer will have to make a number of additional decisions regarding the need for medical assistance, additional personnel, equipment, and so forth.

When police arrive at a crime scene, they often find a situation filled with confusion. A bank robbery may include frightened or injured customers and workers. At an assault or rape one may find a number of well-meaning people watching or assisting the victim. A burglary may cause family members to feel unsafe and violated in their own home, and distrustful of people. In any of these situations, the officer must remain calm and take charge.

A preliminary investigation may be the prelude to an in-depth or follow-up investigation. In larger departments, the follow-up investigation is usually made by detectives. They are responsible for investigating the crime, potentially apprehending the offender, and preparing the case for court. In smaller departments, the responding officer may also be responsible for the follow-up investigation.

The roles and responsibilities of patrol officers and detectives, therefore, are not always distinguishable. Much of what a patrol officer or detective will do at a crime scene is determined by the size of the agency undertaking the preliminary investigation.

The initial information, regardless of who collects it, provides the foundation for the eventual criminal case against a suspect. If all of the available information is not collected, accurately recorded, and reasonably processed, much of the follow-up investigation will proceed without the benefit of all the existing facts. This may necessitate repeating much of the preliminary investigation, and can lead to the potential loss of valuable evidence.

Uniformed officers arriving on the scene of a crime must call upon their powers of observation to assess what is going on. They must protect the scene while attempting to locate witnesses and identifying possible pieces of evidence. The more effectively the responding officers manage the scene the better this will assist the investigation.

Certainly, it is clear that every criminal incident contains unique elements. Yet, it should be equally clear that there are also many similar activities that must be undertaken at all crime scenes regardless of the specific crime involved. A list of the kinds of questions a responding officer should ask him or herself when responding to a crime call might include the following:

- Does the officer understand what is actually happening at the scene?
- Is a suspect present?
- Could there be more than a single suspect?
- Does the situation require backup?
- Does the situation require specialists?
- Are there injured parties?
- Do the injured parties require medical professionals or transport to medical facilities?
- Is there evidence apparent?
- Are there any witnesses?

ALLOCATION AND DEPLOYMENT OF PATROL OFFICERS

The phrase **allocation of patrol** refers to the proportion of the agency's officers assigned to patrol or other departmental duties. Some large American police departments may allocate as much as 60 percent of their full complement of officers to patrol duties. **Deployment of patrol**, on the other hand, refers to the proper distribution of the patrol force in order to accomplish four primary activities. These include:

1. An equitable distribution of the workload across the patrol unit.
2. Assurance that an acceptable level of calls for service will be handled by the patrol unit.

3. Sufficient personnel coverage to respond to variations in police calls during different hours of the day or night, or day of the week.
4. A flexible work schedule that can accommodate the needs of the department, the community, and the officers.

These goals for deployment are rather idealized, and are likely never to be completely achieved. However, they serve as a good target towards which departments should aim. In the real world one finds considerable variation in the proportion of officers assigned to patrol and other duties in agencies across the country.

DISTRIBUTION OF THE PATROL

To operate efficiently, the patrol must be distributed effectively both temporally (throughout the day), and spatially (geographic distribution). Different patterns of distribution may be used, but all must cover a full 24-hour period every day. Personnel and equipment must be assigned to different geographic areas in order to carry out the day to day patrol duties of the agency. The traditional geographic breakdowns are called the beat, sector, and precinct, or in some parts of the country, division, parish, or reporting district. The following section considers some temporal allocation concerns.

TEMPORAL DISTRIBUTION

The **temporal distribution** of officers or the time schedule of departments, is not always the most obvious ingredient in good policing. Nonetheless, time is a very important element in law enforcement. Some types of crime, for example, are more likely to occur at certain times than at others. For instance, most industrial and commercial burglaries occur during the late-night hours when these establishments are closed and when darkness can provide cover for the intruders. Consequently, these areas require increased police patrol during the nighttime hours. Or, in police management terms, these areas at night represent an increased workload. Conversely, residential burglaries, although certainly occurring at night, tend often to happen during the daytime, when residents are out of their homes at work, school, or shopping.

Traditionally, the 24-hour day is divided into three major shifts, or **watches** or **tours of duty**. These include:

Day shift	8 A.M. through 4 P.M.
Evening shift	4 P.M. through midnight
Night shift	Midnight through 8 A.M.

Well-designed patrols will have an unequal number of officers assigned to different shifts, in order to more appropriately cover a given jurisdiction's crime problems. For example, during evening and night shifts, one would intuitively expect a slightly higher number of patrol cars in commercial areas than during day shift. In some departments, shifts are rotated on a regular basis (typically on a monthly basis) among most of the officers. In other jurisdictions, many of the officers are assigned to permanent shifts. Interestingly, night shifts are often sought by new officers because they believe these will offer a greater likelihood of police activity than day or evening shifts.

There has been considerable concern about the physical, psychological, and emotional effects upon people who work rotating shifts. To be sure, permanent shifts allow an officer to establish more regular eating, sleeping, family, and social, and educational activities. Unfortunately, not all jurisdictions can afford the luxury of hiring enough officers to provide extensive coverage during all shifts on a permanent basis. However, increased coverage may occur during special events or in case of emergency.

To accommodate a slightly more regular lifestyle for officers and in keeping with trends in other occupational groups where shift work predominates (e.g., nursing), innovative shifts have arisen. For instance, in some departments, the four-ten schedule has become popular (Moore and Morrow 1987). In this shift pattern, officers are scheduled to work a 4-day schedule of 10-hour shifts in place of the more traditional 5-day 8-hour schedule. In jurisdictions where this schedule has been used, officer job satisfaction and morale have gone up. Explanations for why officer satisfaction increases are related to the additional time off and their ability to catch up with sleep, family activities, and life patterns.

From an administration perspective, the four-ten schedule allows for an overlap of shift coverage simply impossible with the traditional 8-hour shift. So, departments are able to increase their street forces during peak hours of crime activity (8 P.M. through 3 A.M.). In addition, because the patrol force is better rested and more satisfied with its working conditions, its job performance improves as well. A typical four-ten work schedule is set up as follows:

First shift (replacing day shift)	7 A.M. through 5 P.M.
Second shift (replacing evening shift)	4 P.M. through 2 A.M.
Third shift (replacing night shift)	9 P.M. through 7 A.M.

Another benefit of the overlap in shifts under the four-ten plan is that command, administrative, and specialty officers can flexibly alter their schedules to be available to more than one shift during a given workday (Moore and Morrow 1987).

In some departments, a third shift structure has been used. This shift structure is known as the four-two schedule. In this scheduling format officers are assigned to work 8 1/2-hour shifts 4 days a week, followed by 2 days off. The seventh day of each week is used as a kind of pivot to move the schedule ahead, thereby alternating which days each week an officer receives off. Over the course of the month, the pattern that emerges is one that allows the officer to have the same days off for two consecutive weeks. These 8 1/2-hour tours typically are:

Day shift	7:30 A.M. through 4 P.M.
Evening shift	3:30 P.M. through midnight
Night shift	11:30 P.M. through 8 A.M.

The four-two scheduling scheme also allows for a slight overlap in patrol. For the most part, this extra half hour is designed for paperwork and a smooth transition from one shift to the next. As a result, unlike the four-ten schedule, personnel on the streets is not meaningfully altered.

In recent years a fourth scheduling format has developed involving 12-hour shifts worked thrice weekly. In this scheduling structure, the officers work 3 days of 12-hour shifts and are off for 4 days. This scheduling plan allows for considerable overlap and coverage on the streets. In addition, it provide officers with considerable regular time off to pursue family relations, educational goals, and recreational activities. Some departments use the 12-hour shift structure and a half-hour overlap during three duty tours daily:

Day shift	6:30 A.M. through 7:00 P.M.
Mid shift	1:30 A.M.through 2:00 A.M.
Evening shift	6:30 P.M. through 7:00 A.M.

Other departments structure four 12 hour duty tours daily:

Day shift	6:00 A.M. through 6:10 P.M.
First mid shift	10:00 A.M. through 10:10 P.M.
Second mid shift	3:00 P.M. through 3:10 A.M.
Night shift	6:30 P.M. through 6:40 A.M.

The decision to use two or three 12-hour shifts each day is largely a product of department size and complexity. In larger departments that operate in larger more active jurisdictions, the three-twelve shift structure may be necessary. In smaller and less active areas, the two-twelve format may be sufficient to provide the department, the community and the officers sufficient flexibility. These 12-hour shifts leave officers short 4 hours weekly from full-time status. These additional hours are made up through a variety of methods. In some cases, an extra day (a fourth 12-hour shift) is added and worked into the schedule periodically. In other cases, the time is made up through special duty activities, in-service training, or other department business. The various scheduling plans suggested here, along with other experimental types, all attempt to balance safety on the streets with the cost of providing the best police services possible.

GEOGRAPHIC DISTRIBUTION

In addition to the temporal distributional concerns, police administrators place considerable emphasis on **geographic distribution** or physically where officers should be deployed through the community area. Let us begin examining this aspect of police deployment by considering the basic unit, the beat.

The Beat

The basic geographic unit of patrol is **the beat**. Speaking generally, this encompasses the patrol officers' assigned area of movement or surveillance. Whether the officer is on foot or uses some kind of motorized vehicle, the officer assigned to a beat is responsible for all events and activities—service and criminal ones—that occur in this area during the officer's tour of duty.

The beat is a fundamental element of police patrol. In fact, the effectiveness of the entire police organization can be linked to a properly developed and implemented patrol force. Unfortunately, many police agencies tend to simply assign patrols in an ad hoc and somewhat arbitrary fashion. Frequently, patrol assignments are made on the basis of data complied in the department from police activity reports of the past. The mistake some departments make is failing to recognize that police calls and incidents do not occur in a vacuum. Calls for police services are affected by a variety of factors including, the time of day, the day of the week, the weather, and even the season of the year. For example, in communities where there is a university present, rapes tend to increase, on campus, during the months of September and late January and early February. The explanation for this involves changes in residence in dormitories because of the changes in semesters. Because new people are moving into dorms, strangers and would-be rapists can enter buildings with a certain amount of immunity and anonymity. It is likely, then, that calls for service, or assistance to the campus police, will occur at a higher level in these months.

On a more regular basis, many towns have strips where bars, restaurants, and movie theaters are located in close proximity. It is likely that during weekend evening hours, these areas will have more calls for service than during weekdays or weekday evening hours. It is important, therefore, to recognize that not only levels of activity, but more discrete elements such as when these levels of activity occur, should dictate patrol deployment.

Thus, demand for police services fluctuates in many departments, and may influence the type of scheduling format as well as the configuration of officers during each shift. In other words, the boundaries for day shift, and hence, the number of officers assigned, will be different from that of evening, or night shift. The effectiveness of a department's crime prevention efforts and criminal apprehension is effected by the deployment of the agency's officers. When carefully designed, beats will vary in size and numbers of officers, reflecting consideration of such factors as population density at different times during the day, types of areas (residential, commercial, entertainment), previous records of police activity, and even the environmental (topographical) aspects of the areas.

Figure 4.3
Rape rates on college campuses sometimes increase at the beginning of academic semesters. Women on campuses need to be particularly careful.

A

B

The Sector

Patrol sectors consist of a number of beats combined ostensibly for administrative purposes. Each sector has a supervisor, usually a corporal or sergeant who

Figure 4.4
Areas where bars, restaurants, and movie theaters are located in close proximity frequently need more patrol at night than during the daytime.

A

B

is called the line supervisor. The line supervisor's function is to coordinate the various activities of officers on the beats in the sector. The line supervisor is also charged with the responsibility of assisting patrol officers in the sector and managing a crime scene when necessary. In addition, line supervisors observe officers in order to assess their performances, and correct errors in police technique (Adams 1994).

The Precinct

In many of the larger cities of the United States, the geography requires that sectors contain many beats or that many sectors be created. To handle such large settings, a larger division of the work area is necessary. The **precinct** refers to this larger area, which consists of several patrol sectors. In a manner similar to the sector, precincts are geographical divisions intended to improve administration, coordination, communications, and supervision of the officers on patrol.

TYPES OF POLICE PATROL

Modern policing strategies include both fairly traditional and advanced innovative attacks on crime. Regardless of the variations in styles of allocation and deployment, there are principally two major types of patrol: walking (foot patrol) and riding (mobile patrol). Historically, the foot patrol or "walking a beat" is certainly the older of the two. Early mobile patrols were accomplished on horseback. The advances made in automobiles, motorcycles, electric cars, as well as the changes in community lifestyles, have necessitated alterations in modern patrolling. Let us consider the various kinds and styles of patrolling.

FOOT PATROL

A vestige, perhaps, of the watchman style of policing, the foot patrol is probably the original type of patrol. Although significantly reduced during the 1960s and 1970s, the foot patrol has experienced a resurgence during the past 20 years or so. Skolnick and Bailey (1986) suggest that police agencies in a growing number of cities are again returning to walking beats in an attempt to work more closely with their communities in reducing crime and fear of crime. In what has become a highly regarded article titled "Broken Windows: The Police and Neighborhood Safety," James Q. Wilson and George Kelling (1982) called for the police to leave the shells of their patrol cars and take to the streets. Wilson and Kelling suggested that walking the beats allows officers and citizens to better come to know and support one another. Wilson and Kelling also suggested that primary emphasis should be placed on deploying patrol officers in locations where they can best instill public confidence and inspire feelings of safety—even if these locations are not in the areas that receive the highest number of calls for police services. Ensuring a sense of community, public safety, and maintaining the order, and not crime fighting, according to Wilson and Kelling, should be the mandate for police officers on patrol:

> Just as physicians now recognize the importance of fostering health rather than simply treating illness, so the police—and the rest of us—ought to recognize the importance of maintaining intact communities without broken windows (Wilson and Kelling 1982:37).

While walking limits the officer to relatively small area of geography, foot patrol is still the most effective form of patrol. Patrol officers walking their beats can deal with special problems associated with preventing and repressing crimes. Two subcategories of foot patrol can be identified: fixed post foot patrol and moving foot patrol (Adams 1994).

Fixed Post Foot Patrol

As implied by the language, fixed post foot patrol involves a stationary type of activity. Fixed foot patrols are ideally suited for such activities as traffic direction, surveillance, crowd control at special events, and a showing of police presence. When major events, such as the Super Bowl, major boxing events, or even movie premieres occur, it is not uncommon to post officers in fixed positions. These officers provide a physical showing of police presence, as well as placing officers in positions where they can assist tourists, monitor traffic, and observe crowds.

Moving Foot Patrol

Moving foot patrol allows the officer to walk a limited area of space (a beat). It is particularly useful in high-density pedestrian areas such as business and shopping areas, near bars and taverns, in high crime neighborhoods, by theater and restaurant areas, hospital zones, and where there are many multiple-family housing or apartment complexes.

Figure 4.5
Fixed foot patrol may include directing traffic.

MOBILE PATROL

Typically, mobile patrols are associated with the black and white units made famous in such television shows as *Adam 12* and *Brooklyn South*. Actually, cruisers come in a variety of colors, but in most jurisdictions they remain two-tone (two shades of blue and brown, black and white, orange and yellow, and so forth). In part, the idea behind these distinctively colored vehicles, like the distinctive uniforms worn by officers, is to draw attention to them. Uniformed police officers and their vehicles are not intended to blend into the background.

Police cruisers are likely the most extensively used and, in many ways, the most effective means of transportation for police patrol. Cruisers are well marked with lights, sirens, and distinctive insignias identifying them as police vehicles. In most cities these patrol cars are late-model vehicles. In typical police use, these vehicles have life expectancies of about 2 or 3 years (60,000 to 100,000 miles).

The average patrol car is designed as a kind of mobile police station. It is equipped with the latest in radio and computer gear, various types of rescue and restraining devices, including in many cases first-aid kits and oxygen tanks. As a consequence of the public concern over AIDS, many patrol cars now additionally carry surgical masks, airways, and protective rubber or latex gloves.

In many of the larger or more modern police departments (city size is not always an accurate indicator of the level of its police department's technological sophistication), computer terminals, mobile fax machines, and even laptop computers are being added as standard equipment in police patrol cars.

The use of computers and related communications technology is growing rapidly in law enforcement. Some of the innovations that are becoming standard in many police communications systems include the following: automatic fleet monitoring systems, significantly improved handheld transceivers, computerized logging and recording of dispatch operations, voice-activated call in report recording devices, radio scramblers to ensure security during police communications, and a variety of computer supported dispatching and deployment programs (Sharp 1991; Barker et al. 1994). The combination of links of computer networks such as the FBI's National Crime Information Center (NCIC) and dispatchers and mobile patrols may prove to be enormously useful. Also, as detailed in Chapter 9, computer technology has advanced to a stage where fingerprints can be electronically scanned, transmitted to a fingerprint base computer, and a suspect identified in minutes.

Although the marked police car is an ideal vehicle for urban and some rural areas, other types of vehicles are sometimes required for patrol. For example, beach patrols in some West Coast areas and in certain seacoast locations in the Northeast are accomplished with four-wheel-drive vehicles such as Jeeps or police dune buggies. Regardless of its outward appearance, a police vehicle provides a fast, safe, and effective means for rapidly moving to a crime scene or transporting suspects or victims in a crime to the police station.

Another important issue related to the delivery of patrol services involves the question of one- or two-officer cars. For the most part, there are two central views on this. From the point of view of police administrators, the one-officer car is the most fiscally effective. It is the least expensive way to obtain the greatest coverage of a geographic area. Certainly, two one-officer cars can traverse more physical space than one two-officer car. Thus, patrol and surveillance of a neighborhood or community is increased. Moreover, police cars, (even when replaced at regular intervals) tend to be less expensive than officers' salaries. As a result, many police administrators view one-officer cars as a way to increase departmental mobility and surveillance capabilities while not appreciably increasing their budgets.

The other major viewpoint is that of the officers in the field. From their vantage, one-officer cars enormously reduce safety during a potentially dangerous situation. Although research on one- versus two-officer cars does not indicate greater safety is always afforded by two-officer cars, officers' perceptions tend to persist. As Chapter 16 will detail, police officers' perceptions of risk and

Figure 4.6 *Police cruisers permit officers to move quickly and transport people and equipment.*

danger create a number of somatic problems. Their perceptions should not be discounted.

In spite of many police union and benevolent organization arguments against the use of one-officer cars, their implementation continues to prevail, especially in smaller departments. The use of two-officer cars (as well as two-officer walking patrols) has been limited during recent years to areas of demonstrated high crime and/or high risk.

Beyond foot patrol and mobile units there are several other, less conventional types of patrols. These include mounted patrol, motorcycle, bicycle, and small vehicle patrol, helicopter and fixed-wing airplane, marine patrol, and K-9 patrol.

Horse Patrol

Mounted patrols have a long history in American policing. It has been suggested that the San Francisco Police may have had one of the earliest horse patrols, beginning in 1874 (Gaines et al. 1997). Under certain circumstances, horse patrols are especially useful in patrol work. In areas of large expanses of land that automobiles cannot easily travel (or may be restricted from traveling),

Figure 4.7   *Horse patrol is effective in some areas, but limits storage space.*

horse patrols may prove useful. For example, one would not expect to see a motorized officer racing across the wooded paths in Central Park in New York City or through pedestrian malls in certain parts of Providence, Rhode Island; Columbus, Ohio; Long Beach or San Jose, California; or similar areas. Horse patrols are also very useful when it is necessary to move or control large crowds such as might congregate during a parade or protest. During the evening hours in New Orleans, and especially during Mardi Gras, horse-mounted police patrols are common on Bourbon street where crowds of hundreds of people congregate.

There are, however, significant limitations related to the use of horse patrols. First, they have limited storage space. Unlike patrol cars, horses simply do not have a trunk or even a back seat. While they are quite agile, and useful in pursuing a suspect who is on foot, a horse-mounted patrol officer is no match for a speeding automobile. Finally, horses are fairly expensive to purchase, and even more expensive to maintain. For example, in 1997, the New York Police force sought to increase the number of horses they had in their mounted patrol. Unfortunately, there was no money to purchase additional horses. Instead, the police appealed to the public and asked that people consider donating a horse to the patrol.

Motorcycle Patrols

Motorcycle patrols have traditionally been associated with traffic control and enforcement. Motorcycles have also been used by some jurisdictions, however, as a general fair-weather patrol vehicle. The motorcycle's speed and maneuverability are outstanding features of its pursuit abilities on the highways, making it an extremely valuable police vehicle.

Bicycles and Other Small Vehicles

The bicycle has long been used by police officers in other countries. In China, for example, where streets are heavily congested with both cars and pedestrians, bicycles provide an effective mode of transportation for patrol officers. In England and Ireland it is fairly common to see an officer riding along on a bicycle. American law enforcement, especially departments located in densely populated urban areas, increasingly have begun using bicycle patrols. Bicycles allow officers to travel greater distances in less time than walking. Unlike the enclosed cruiser, a bicycle provides a somewhat more personal interaction between community residents and the police officer riding it. While bicycles have similar storage limitations to horse-mounted patrols, they do have the advantage of having a lower maintenance cost than horses.

In addition to bicycles, other types of small motorized, golf-cart-like vehicles have been successfully used by police agencies. These small carts allow officers to patrol regular beats either in addition to foot and/or automobile

Figure 4.8   *During recent years police bike patrols have increased enormously across the nation.*

patrol or in place of them. These carts provide shelter for officers during inclement weather, can be loaded with radio and rescue equipment, and offer a relatively speedy form of transportation. In many ways, these carts are similar to patrol cars, but may be more practical under certain circumstances. During local county or state fairs, such carts allow considerable mobility and effective transportation, whereas a large cruiser would be impractical.

Helicopters and Fixed-Wing Aircraft

Among the many technological innovations that have been adapted to police patrol during the past several decades is the use of aircraft, both fixed-wing and helicopters. A number of police and sheriff's departments as well as highway patrols make regular use of aircraft as part of their patrol divisions. Aviation patrols provide a number of functions including the ability to observe long stretches of highway or inaccessible land masses, search and rescue, transportation of prisoners and personnel, pursuit of suspects fleeing on foot, and coordination of ground and air pursuits of suspects fleeing in automobiles. Furthermore, aircraft are finding increased use in drug enforcement activities both to pursue drug smugglers, and to locate fields of marijuana.

Figure 4.9 *Helicopters have become necessary and effective tools for many police agencies.*

The first airborne police unit was created in New York City around 1930. Its creation came in response to daredevil pilots who had begun to fly all around the city, frequently buzzing or crashing onto homes in densely populated areas (Potter 1979). The original unit began with a single amphibious plane and three biplanes. This air patrol unit operated until the mid-1950s, when it was upgraded to a fleet of helicopters.

The Los Angeles Sheriff's Department was another early user of an airborne police unit, experimenting early with the use of helicopters. Several police aviation units have incorporated the use of thermal infrared technology in their arsenal of equipment. The Forward Looking INFRARED device (FLIR) is rapidly becoming and essential tool of police aviation units when searching the ground, even at night, for suspects. Because the device uses heat to locate and image objects, a suspect hiding under a vehicle—or inside of a shed—will still be illuminated on the device's screen (McLean 1988). Like aviation units themselves, this device is extremely expensive and costs approximately $100,000.

In 1996, the Miami police department, the Dade County sheriff's department, and the Broward County Sheriff's department jointly began using a helicopter-mounted version of LoJack. LoJack is an electronic car-theft detection device. By taking it airborne, the agencies were able to cover a greater amount of area in a very short period of time.

Marine and River Patrols

Because many cities have large harbors or waterways, the use of boats to patrol these areas may be necessary. In some instances, this may prove a relatively simple task. In New York, for example, the coast is fairly short and straight and offers little need for extensive patrolling outside of the immediate harbor area. North Carolina, Florida, and other Gulf Coast jurisdictions, however, prove more difficult to patrol. Florida is estimated to have more than 300 clandestine coves and bays where smugglers can land and unload contraband, chiefly drugs. North Carolina's riverways provide similar concealment and numerous places for smugglers to navigate, hide, and unload cargo. Additionally, recreational waters such as those of the three rivers surrounding Pittsburgh are patrolled to assure boating safety, as well as other possible law infractions.

Canine (K-9) Patrols

One of the most valuable tools ever enlisted in the law enforcement profession is the canine. Dogs have long been used by law enforcement agencies to search for lost children and to locate jail or prison escapees. In recent years, dogs have additionally found their way into more proactive policing activities such as searching for explosives and drugs. In some jurisdictions, foot patrol officers are accompanied by a canine partner. This serves to augment what would otherwise be a one-officer patrol car. These teams typically have trained extensively together, live and play together, and developed extremely strong ties.

The canine's superior sense of smell and acute hearing enables the canine handler to conduct thorough and complete searches with a minimum of time and other personnel. When a building or dwelling needs to be investigated, the canine usually will enter first, followed by the handler (International Association of Chiefs of Police 1977).

Dogs also have been used quite successfully during searches of suspicious vehicles to locate drugs being smuggled in hidden compartments. Federal customs agents, state police, and a variety of other federal agencies have used dogs to search locations, packages, vehicles and even people for suspected narcotics. During recent years, canines have also been used to search airports, public building, bus terminals and railway stations for hidden explosive devices (Kaplan 1997).

Some observers are concerned that dogs employed in various patrol activities are really being used as decoys or as expendable and replaceable tools. This is not, however, the intention or purpose of canine members of a K-9 team. Trained dogs, in addition to their relationship with their partners, cost large sums of money to purchase, and require months to learn their tasks and become certified for patrol of search activities. No police agency intentionally sends dogs into dangerous situations because they are seen as more expendable than a person. In most cases, it is simply safer for the dog to enter (see Box 4.1).

Figure 4.10
K-9 patrols pair highly trained dogs with officers/handlers.

A

B

BOX 4.1   THE GLENS FALLS CITY POLICE DEPARTMENT CANINE DIVISION

The officers in Glens Falls, New York, always recognized the benefits of having a canine patrol. Unfortunately, as a small police agency, they had other department priorities that took precedence over the purchase and training of a patrol dog. That is, until Thanksgiving of 1993. On that fateful afternoon, a 3-year-old stray purebred German shepard wandered in and out of traffic on Warren Street, a main drag in Glens Falls. The dog, named J.D., was saved by alert patrol officers. They located J.D.'s owner, but the owner lived in a small apartment and told officers he did not have room to keep the dog.

Patrolman Joe Affinito decided that he would adopt J.D. Together, Officer Affinito and J.D. trained and completed a 400-hour course that certified J.D. as a patrol-trained dog. J.D. now accompanies Affinito on Patrol, as his partner.

Dogs are more agile, swifter, lower to the ground, and can see better in the dark than their human partners. Additionally, a screaming police officer is far less likely to get the attention of an armed felon than a growling or barking trained police canine.

Regardless of the kind of patrol one is involved with, field officers must be constantly available, vigilant, and on the street in order to perform certain routine police activities. These include preliminary investigations of traffic accidents, criminal law violations, civil disturbances, and other types of emergencies. Policing agencies can no longer indulge themselves in what has proven to be rather unproductive, watchman-like patrols. The cost of vehicles and their upkeep, along with general operational expenses, simply cannot be justified by a passive or haphazard style of police patrolling. The days when a good patrol unit was one that could demonstrate that half its time was spent physically on patrol, cruising and searching for the unexpected to happen, can no longer be defended as appropriate police work (Adams 1994).

PROACTIVE VERSUS REACTIVE POLICING STRATEGIES

In the face of austerity cuts and budget streamlining in many police agencies, a debate over proactive versus reactive policing has been raging for nearly two decades. Essentially the problem rests on police organizations' inability to afford the luxury of measuring patrol time by the quantity of time logged by patrolling officers while reacting to calls for police. The **proactive police model** includes such activities as selective coverage of roadways during holidays in order to check on the sobriety of drivers, increased patrol coverage of high-hazard collision locations, and increased monitoring of selected high-risk robbery locations. The **reactive police model**, involves generalized patrolling activities, and quick response to calls for police services after crimes have occurred.

Many people believe that the major role of police officers is enforcement of laws. But research undertaken throughout the 1960s, 1970s, and 1980s demonstrates that only a fraction of an officer's time on the beat is devoted to "crime fighting." Albert Reiss (1971), for example, examined patrol practices in a number of American cities in an attempt to characterize a typical day's work. He found that patrol work defies all efforts of typification "except in the sense that the modal tour of duty does not involve an arrest of any person" (Reiss 1971:19). Using statistics reported in *Uniform Crime Reports*, Egon Bittner (1980:127) found that patrol officers average only a single arrest of any kind each month and only three index crimes (a category of crime) during an average year.

Mark Moore, Robert Trojanowicz, and George Kelling (1988:6) reported that police "fight serious crime" by developing a capacity to intercept it, to be in the right place at the right time during a given patrol, or to arrive so quickly after a crime is committed that the offender is captured. Although this kind of reactive policing may be appealing, it remains unclear how effective it actually is at reducing crime. During the past several decades, confidence in a reactive approach to policing has waned in the face of growing empirical evidence suggesting its effectiveness is limited.

It is inaccurate to suggest that the sole role of the police officer is crime-busting. In fact, crime reduction often results from a heightened awareness of safety and security needs in one's home, place of business, and community. Additionally, law enforcement tasks are not exclusively directed toward strict enforcement of laws and apprehension of criminals. In modern police organizations throughout the 1980s and 1990s, strategies for combating crime have turned to an examination of precipitating causes (Moore et al. 1988) and community interventions. This approach has required police departments to build closer relationships with their communities and to enhance the communities' self-defense efforts. The underlying theory is that existing police strategies can be strengthened through increased contact with citizens. This includes both individuals residing in the community and various neighborhood groups.

THE KANSAS CITY PREVENTIVE PATROL

Among one of the earliest studies designed to measure the effectiveness of high-visibility random patrol by uniformed officers was the Kansas City Preventive Patrol Project.

The study arose within the Kansas City Police Department in 1971. Under the administrative guidance of Chief Clarence M. Kelley, the Kansas City Police Department had already developed considerable sophistication in various aspects of police technology (Kelling et al. 1985). The department included a number of young, professionally motivated officers, and the concept of both short and long-range planning had become institutionalized in the agency's organizational style. Kelley also was quick to explore the utility of various new police methods and procedures. Kelley was open, therefore, to the idea of conducting a study to determine the effectiveness of one such new procedure. The basic strategy of the Kansas City project has been outlined by Kelling and his associates (1974). Briefly, the project began in 1972 and concluded in 1973. The project identified 15 beats and matched them for such items as crime rates, calls for service, ethnicity, and income levels. All 15 beats were located in the South Patrol Division of Kansas City and were subdivided into three groups of five beats each and labeled as follows:

1. *Reactive*—No preventive patrols (i.e., no randomly assigned marked cars patrolling the area). Instead, officers entered these areas only when responding to calls for service.
2. *Proactive*—Assigned two or three times the usual number of patrol vehicles (sent through at random times) to show a visible presence.
3. *Control*—Assigned their usual number of police patrol vehicles (one each beat), which cruised the area in their normal manner.

Contrary to expectations, the results of the Kansas City project suggest that variations in the level and visibility of police patrols made little difference in any of these areas tested. More directly stated, no significant differences were found in the rates of crime among reactive, proactive, and control beats. Nor, for that matter, were the community members' levels of fear reduced among any of these experimental sectors.

James Q. Wilson (1977) cautions that observers of the Kansas City project should not be misled by the findings. Wilson (1977:99) explains:

> The [Kansas City] experiment does not show that the police made no dif-ference and it does not show that adding more police is useless in control-ling crime.
>
> All it shows is that changes in the amount of random preventive patrol in marked cars does not, by itself, seem to affect, over one year's time in Kansas City, how much crime occurs or how safe citizens feel.

Along similar lines of reasoning, many methodologists have sought to explain the Kansas City project's findings as the result of problems in methodology. For example, since the community was never informed about the patrol changes, they could not immediately react to them. This includes lawbreakers who may well have not noticed that there were more or fewer patrol cars in various areas. As a result they never bothered to change their usual patterns of criminal behavior. In other words, had public notices been issued in, say the proactive sectors, and the public knew there would be increased patrol activity, different results may have occurred. As Wilson indirectly observed, and without public notice, the changes in patrol over one year's time may simply not have been enough.

Other observers have warned that the study should not be understood to mean that police have no effect on crime. Rather, the study should be under-stood as indicating that routine patrol has only a minimal effect on crime (Cord-ner and Trojanowicz 1992:6–7).

It is important to recognize that findings from a single study should never be taken as absolutely accurate. Certainly, the findings of a single study of one kind of preventive patrol strategy should not be construed as meaning all preventive patrol strategies may be unsuccessful.

Some proactive programs have adopted highly selective approaches to the apprehension of street criminals (Martin and Sherman 1986). One example of a proactive policing program that targets street criminals is the Metropolitan Police Department of Washington, D.C.'s "Repeat Offender Project" (ROP pronounced *rope*). The project began in 1982 with a special task force of 88 officers (later reduced to 60). The program was geared toward creating a selective identification and apprehension strategy. The basic strategy was to locate and apprehend individuals believed to be highly active criminals (Martin and Sherman 1986). The project planners slated two groups of individuals for apprehension: those people already wanted by the police who had one or more arrest warrants already issued, and those people believed to be criminally active, but who were not already wanted (no warrants had been issued). The first group was called "warrant targets," and the second "ROP-initiated targets."

The ROP experiment was found to increase the likelihood of arrests among targeted repeat offenders. By many measures, ROP appears to have succeeded in its manifest goal of selecting, arresting, and contributing to the incarceration of active repeat criminals. Nonetheless, evaluators of the ROP experiment are cautious of too strongly recommending such a strategy (Martin and Sherman 1986). They warn about the potential dangers inherent in a program that singles out not only fugitives, but others as well for surveillance and close monitoring.

Policies concerning law enforcement and crime prevention practices have resulted in an expanded concept (see Box 4.2) of community relations. In addition to maintaining open lines of communication and a good public image for police officers (a traditional public relations concept), recent community relations efforts include community-oriented policing, and problem-oriented policing strategies.

BOX 4.2 BLOCK WATCH IN ACTION: THE PHILADELPHIA EXAMPLE

An emergency call sends police officers rushing to the scene of an assault, where they find a young man who has been savagely beaten by a gang of thugs. They rush him to the hospital, talk to witnesses, and set off to catch the criminal who did it.

The criminal justice system knows its job: find the suspect, charge them, prosecute them, punish them if convicted. A corps of highly trained professionals—police officers, attorneys, judges, probation officers, correction officials, stand ready to do its part.

The victim and his family need help, and they need more than medical attention and a sympathetic interview. Police and prosecutors have come to recognize this need in recent years, but often their agencies are not equipped to do much about it.

When a crime like this occurred in Philadelphia recently, the victim's family received a telephone call from someone in the neighborhood offering to help. The caller was a member of the

continued

BOX 4.2 continued

block watch (sometimes called town watch, block watch, or neighborhood watch) in which local residents band together to keep an eye on their neighborhood and to alert police whenever they see something suspicious. In most communities, block-watch members play no role after a crime has been committed, but in Philadelphia many members have trained to provide crucial assistance to victims.

The call from the block-watch neighbor was simple: "How are you getting along? Is there anything I can do to help?" When the neighbor found that the victim's mother was distraught, she comforted her and helped her get information about her son.

Eventually, the young victim began to express a commonly held fear—that his attackers would assault him again if he pressed charges. The block-watch neighbor reassured him. When it came time to go to court, the neighbor escorted the victim and sat through the proceedings.

Such neighbor-to-neighbor involvement is common in northwest Philadelphia. It is the result of a pioneering partnership among police, a victim assistance program, and neighborhood block-watch organizations. Together, they help victims with short-term, immediate needs and with the long-term goal of making the neighborhood safer.

SOME BASIC ELEMENTS OF THE PHILADELPHIA BLOCK WATCH

- Reassuring the victim. Let victims know that neighbors are concerned and ready to help. This may involve nothing more than saying, "How are you getting along?" "I just wanted to say we're around the corner if you need some help." "Call me if you get scared."
- Stay with victims for an hour or two after a crime. Many people are afraid to be alone after a traumatic event. Having someone there is particularly helpful with elderly men and women, who sometime become virtual recluses after being victimized.

- Listening. Let victims express their fears, retell what happened, and reveal their worries about the future. Often neighbors are better listeners than friends and family who may be impatient with the victim's anxieties or contribute to the victim's feeling at fault for letting the crime occur. Neighbors may even be more effective than trained counselors because some victims trust only people they know and are intimidated by "professionals."
- Providing practical assistance. When a neighbor came home one night to find that burglars had ransacked her house after pushing in the skylight, a couple of agile block-watch members temporarily boarded up the roof to prevent anyone from returning. When another family had all their money, major appliances, and food stolen, the block watch lent them money from its treasury and collected food from the neighborhood. Block-watch members sometime baby-sit when victims make trips to the doctor or court.

  Accompanying victims to court or to local service. A mugging victim who ignored two court summonses to appear at a line-up agreed to go only when a block watch captain arranged for three neighbors to accompany her. One block watch captain pleaded to get permission from a badly bleeding—but uninsured—victim to call an ambulance but ended up driving the injured man to the hospital to spare him the $100 ambulance fee.
- Helping victims obtain other help. This might include filing with the crime victim's compensation program or requesting financial assistance from a community safety program, or seeking local professional counseling.
- Helping victims make informed decisions. One block-watch captain strongly encouraged a mugging victim who was reluctant to report the crime to telephone the police. The volunteer had learned in training that reporting helps victims regain a feeling of control over their lives. He also explained to the victim that insurance compensation often depends on reporting the crime to the police within 48 to 72 hours.

- Explaining the criminal justice system. Let victims know what to expect when police arrive and what will happen in court.
- Providing liaison with police and prosecutor. When victims are afraid to leave their homes, a block watch can persuade the police to increase local street patrol or persuade the

prosecutor to ask the court's warrant unit to make an extra effort to locate a defendant who may have jumped bail.

From Peter Finn, "Block Watches Help Crime Victims in Philadelphia." *National Institute of Justice Reports.* Washington, D.C.: NIJ Printing (November-December 1986):2, 5.

COMMUNITY-ORIENTED POLICING EFFORTS

Chiefly as the result of several major riots during the 1960s—notably the Watts riots during the summer of 1965 and the Miami Riots in 1968—police agencies began to reevaluate their links and lines of communication with the communities they served. Urban riots, while certainly not a new phenomenon, were new for the police personnel of the 1960s. Black and Hispanic communities grew more and more concerned over the way police officers interacted and used excessive force when dealing with minority residents.

During the 1970s, Dade County, Florida, became a focal point for many racial disturbances and several riots. Between 1970 and 1979, Dade County experienced 14 outbursts of racial violence (Alpert and Dunham 1988). These major incidents, along with a great many minor clashes between minority groups and police officers, culminated in 1980 with what came to be called the McDuffie riots. The McDuffie riots resulted in an enormous amount of violence and damage, ending after 3 days with 18 people dead, $80 million in property damage, and more than 1,100 people arrested.

In the 1990s, police again were witness to racially triggered unrest and riots such as the 1991 Los Angeles riots following the acquittal of officers involved in the Rodney King incident (see Box 4.3).

For nearly four decades, police have been concerned about diffusing tensions and dissension among minority community residents and restoring the legitimacy and image of police in the eyes of the public. The police cannot operate effectively if they do not have the respect and legitimacy bestowed upon them by their community. The police have been faced with a serious challenge. They must try to prevent or quell riots, while at the same time minimize property damage, injury and loss of lives, and reduce their already damaged and negative image.

In many ways, during recent years, police agencies have experienced a resurgence of efforts to foster improved police community relations. This resurgence is sometimes represented more as a department philosophy than actual tactics. It is a proactive approach to policing intended to reduce crime and fear of crime, maintain order, while also responding to the specific needs of the community (Trojanowicz and Carter 1988; Eck and Spelman 1987).

BOX 4.3   THE RODNEY KING INCIDENT

In 1991, after being stopped for suspicion of driving under the influence by the California Highway Patrol, an African American later identified as Rodney King was severely beaten. The beating, which included punches, kicks to the head, the use of an electric shocking device, and 52 "power baton strokes" from several officers of different police agencies was captured on home video. King suffered nine skull fractures and a shattered eye socket, among his other injuries. The officers involved in the beating were charged with assault, but were acquitted after their first trial in Los Angeles, California. Their acquittal ignited a riot across the Los Angeles community that raged like wildfire and cost 50 people their lives (Siegel 1998). Two of the officers were later convicted on civil rights violations in a federal court. On April 19, 1994, a Los Angeles court awarded Rodney King $3.8 million in damages stemming from his arrest and beating. Several years later, King was arrested for driving under the influence while visiting relatives in New Castle, Pennsylvania.

Some of the early attempts by the police to improve their image and legitimacy in the eyes of the public involved alterations in the police organization's bureaucratic structure. For instance, community relations units were created, and civilian review boards. Yet, both of these early efforts were fairly limited in their scope and effectiveness. Community relations units had virtually no effect on how street officers behaved when interacting with residents. Similarly, street officers strenuously resisted the idea of outsiders or civilians sitting in judgment in police matters.

During the past several decades a number of communities have implemented a community policing philosophy and various programs guided by the philosophy. Several of these programs have been examined by researchers and are discussed in the following sections.

TEAM POLICING

Many American police agencies have striven to improve their patrol effectiveness, while simultaneously improving police-community interactions. Once such approach frequently associated with the community-oriented policing philosophy is team policing. In its most elemental form, team policing brings together groups of officers and a supervisor over specified community area (Martin and Sherman 1986; Belknap et al. 1987). The team typically develops its own strategies for patrol and deployment, its working hours, and its methods and procedures (within the confines of agency policy). The central purpose of most team policing schemes is to increase the police-community partnership in repressing crime and to involve community residents in policing efforts. A second purpose, related incidentally to the first, is the reduction of fear of crime in a given community. For example, the Lansing, Michigan, South Precinct opened its doors on May 22, 1996. The precinct is located in a remodeled high school building and is responsible for 60 percent of the patrol area, and handle 51 percent of the calls for service for the city. The detectives in the precinct are paired off and operate as investigative teams. The patrol officers are assigned to two teams each under the supervision of a sergeant. The sergeant's responsibility is to manage the team's activities including team meetings, problem-solving initiatives, educational meetings with neighborhood groups, and opening up lines of communication between the citizens and officers in the patrol area.

STOREFRONT POLICING

Storefront policing substations were an innovation that placed officers in the communities that appeared to need them most. Imitating an earlier Japanese storefront policing experiment, Detroit was among the original cities to create mini-stations during the mid-1970s (Holland 1985). In a short time, a number of cities were experimenting with variations on the Detroit mini-station format.

In some instances, in addition to staffing these storefronts with uniformed officers, it was common for off-duty officers to stop by, assist in locating stolen bicycles and lost dogs, help residents with various social service and utility problems, and visit with local residents. Typically storefront stations were located in high-crime areas or areas populated by large proportions of welfare recipients and elderly people—who are prime crime targets. The operative assumption was that community residents would be more willing to walk into a police station located in an unpretentious and convenient setting such as their own neighborhood (Eck and Spelman 1987). These storefront police stations were well received by communities and did serve to improve communications between local residents and the police. There was even some evidence that the presence of these storefront stations served to reduce the fear of crime (Brown and Wycoff 1987). Even today, many jurisdictions continue to offer storefront police substations in high-risk and potentially troubled communities.

An example of a modern day storefront approach is the Community-Oriented Policing Substations (COPS) used by the West Spokane, Washington, police department. The first COPS opened its doors in 1992, and was fully operated by volunteers from the area. Since 1992, more than a dozen other COPS have been opened. The Spokane Police Department, in association with a number of human service organizations, have trained 2,000 volunteers to staff COPS. These volunteers are instructed on the proper methods of taking a police report, deal with minor neighborhood nuisances, disseminate resource information, and coordinate communications between area residents, public agencies, and the police.

Figure 4.11
Storefront police mini-stations are frequently staffed with uniformed officers.

CITIZEN ACADEMIES

The 1990s have brought with them another community involvement innovation, namely, **citizen academies**. The basic intent of citizen academies is to create a stronger partnership between citizens and the local police department. Academies range in length from 6 to about 12 week programs designed to provide citizen recruits with firsthand information about how police departments operate. The underlying objective is to acquaint local residents with law enforcement's role in serving and protecting the community and generally to improve the community members' quality of life. In addition, the academies expose community residents to the tasks police officers face in the daily performance of their police duties.

Usually, sessions at these civilian academies are taught by officers and department personnel in their own areas of expertise. Sessions cover a range of topics including demonstrations by various specialty and tactical units (K-9, forensics, etc.), information about domestic violence and child abuse, use of force, special community education and drug resistance programs, youth gangs, police patrol operations, and planning and budgeting. Many citizen academies additionally allow citizen recruits to take part in a ride-along program in police cars with regular patrol officers.

REDUCING THE FEAR OF CRIME

Past research has led to the conclusion that fear of crime may lead to neighborhood demoralization, which in turn may lead to higher crime rates (Brown and Wycoff 1987). Fear reduction programs, consequently, fall under the purview of proactive policing strategies. Naturally, not all programs designed to fight fear in communities fall under the auspices of the local police agency. Nor for that matter, are all studies on reductions of fear of crime necessarily accurate, owing to variations in their styles of measurement (Ferraro and LaGrange 1987). Nonetheless, when there is fear in a particular community, and as we have already seen police have moved steadily toward community-oriented policing, fear reduction programs do frequently fall into the hands of the police and offer some degree of reassurance. During the 1970s, many municipal agencies sought to improve community relations by developing Officer Friendly programs. In **Officer Friendly programs**, officers attended elementary school assemblies, provided demonstrations in local shopping centers and, in general, tried to get youth to feel safe and comfortable interacting with police officers.

The increased interest in fear reduction and the benefits it seems to have for improving social order within the communities have once again forced both police and the public to rethink their images of the police officer. Throughout the past three decades, society has witnessed a vast array of proposals and strategies intended to draw the police and the communities they serve closer together. Increased responsibilities for police-community relations units, team policing, mini-stations, a return to foot patrols, and Officer Friendly programs are only a few of the innovations and experiments carried out during the last several decades (Eck and Spelman 1987; Rosenbaum 1987). These trends may be understood as a pattern towards creating, or perhaps more accurately, reestablishing, a closer working relationship between the police and their community (the public). These efforts have led to the evolution of neighborhood watch groups, along with the other community-oriented policing programs mentioned above. Most neighborhood watch organizations instruct both local residents and merchants to watch more closely the activities around them and the neighborhood and to contact police whenever they observe suspicious circumstances or persons.

THE "BIG THREE" COMMUNITY CRIME PREVENTION STRATEGIES

While the police obviously cannot be everywhere at the same time, their omnipresence can be felt in communities where the law enforcement consciousness of residents has been raised. Usually, what this means is that local residents have realized that the police simply cannot effectively operate in the absence of a working partnership with the people they serve. Dennis Rosenbaum (1987:104) identifies what he and Feins (1983) call "the big three" community crime prevention strategies and suggests that policing has entered "the heyday of community crime prevention." According to Rosenbaum (1987) these "big three" crime prevention strategies include **block watches** (neighborhood watch organizations), **operation I.D.** (personal property engraving for identification purposes), and **home security surveys** (to assess the safety of community residents' homes).

Block Watch

Block watch has enjoyed a widespread and enduring use by communities and the police. Steven Lab (1988:37) has described the neighborhood block watch as follows:

> The basic goal of neighborhood watch is increasing community awareness and problem solving. This can be accomplished through a variety of methods. Foremost among these is the bringing together of neighbors and residents of an area. Often, the resulting groups and activities are referred to as a neighborhood watch. Mutual problems and goals among participating individuals lead to increased feelings of communal needs and, possibly, joint action.

Neighborhood watch programs have received considerable public support in opinion polls, and national policy has encouraged block-watch types of organizations with the "Community Anticrime Program" and the "Urban Crime Prevention Program" (see Debow and Emmons 1981, Gallup 1981, Feins 1983, Roehl and Cook 1984, Cunningham and Taylor 1985, Garofalo and McLeod 1989).

The exact extent to which communities make use of block-watch programs in the United States is not known. However, many police agencies, of all sizes, are involved in such programs. Similarly, the duration of block watches may vary from one area to the next. In one community in western Pennsylvania, the local police established a block-watch program after a wave of more than 60 burglaries swept across a middle-class neighborhood section. The residents were very anxious to get involved and work together for their common interest—

until the burglaries in the area stopped. At that point, attendance at block-watch meetings dropped, and the program waned.

Neighborhood watch programs, like other volunteer organizations, are difficult to organize, maintain and to keep members motivated. They tend to arise in middle- and upper-class neighborhoods, where residents have property loss concerns. Like the western Pennsylvania example, most neighborhood watch programs are prompted by some sensational crime, or wave of criminal behavior. In many cases, block-watch programs come and go at different times in a community's history, reflecting changes in crime awareness levels among neighborhood residents. Nevertheless, they do provide a useful outlet for police-community relations activities and are at least partially effective at increasing neighborhood cohesiveness—at least for short periods. In terms of long-term effectiveness, most block programs fail to remain operative long enough to offer much long-term law enforcement benefit. Nevertheless, their repeated resurrection in neighborhoods over time does serve to reintegrate police with neighborhoods as community residents change over time.

Operation I.D. Programs

Operation I.D. programs, are sometimes credited with having been started in Monterey Park, California, in the early 1960s (LaGrange 1993). Like block-watch programs, Operation I.D. programs have received considerable local and national support. Frequently, such property identification programs are undertaken and coordinated jointly with the local neighborhood watch organizations and the police. Basically, these programs involve marking personal possessions with an identification mark or number series (frequently one's driver's license or social security number). In the event that this property is stolen and later recovered, it can be more easily identified and returned.

In many jurisdictions, local law enforcement agencies will provide an "electric pencil," which can be borrowed and used to engrave identification marks on property such as televisions, stereos, personal computers, typewriters, bicycles, and so forth. It is also recommended in most operation I.D. programs, that residents photograph their possession, particularly small objects such as jewelry, in order to increase the likelihood of its identification if recovered after being stolen (Purpura 1984).

Home Security Surveys

Home security surveys borrow heavily from the tradition of business risk-management (see Purpura, 1984). In some instances, local law enforcement agencies will provide a security checklist for a resident to use to survey his or her home or business. In other jurisdictions, often as part of the department's neighborhood watch program, an officer will actually come to the resident's home or place of business and survey the premises. Checklists typically contain questions about the types of door (solid or hollow), windows, locks, sliding doors, alarms, lighting, and landscaping. In addition to identifying points of potential risk, officers frequently will sit down with the resident and discuss ways to safely correct these security weak points.

POLICE AND THE TRAFFIC FUNCTION

As you go racing down the highway at 80 miles per hour and glance in your rearview mirror just in time to see the police car behind you switch on its lights and siren, a moment of terror comes over you. Okay, so you were speeding—a little. But the real question or rationalization that runs through your head is, "What's this cop doing chasing down poor honest speeders when there are serious criminals out there?" Of course, when you have just been cut off by some other daredevil motorist doing 80 and you are forced to slam on your brakes, the words that flash through your mind are different. Now it runs something like, "So, where are the police when you need them?" Certainly, in the last instance you would gleefully laugh as you whirled by watching the officer ticket that reckless driver. The difference, of course, is that in the first case it is you and in the second case it is someone else.

The streets and roadways of America are inextricably linked both to automobiles and the crimes connected with cars. In addition to the literal traffic laws that govern the highways, expressways, and local streets, every conceivable category of crime regularly involves cars. Cars and roadways are used to reach and escape from targets of crime, to transport ill-gotten goods and criminals, to smuggle guns, drugs, illegal aliens, and to move rape, murder, and ransom victims. It has become commonplace for officers to encounter serious felons while making routine traffic stops. Once stopped, even for a minor violation, it may be learned during a routine check that the motorist is wanted by police for some serious crime.

In addition, during a traffic stop, drugs or other illegal contraband frequently may be observed on the seats or the floor of the vehicle. For instance, during one week in June 1987, the Massachusetts State Police arrested nine individuals on drug charges resulting from three separate traffic stops. These nine arrests added to the 130 drug-related arrests that had occurred during traffic stops made by Massachusetts State Police between January 1987 and June 1987 (Tan 1987).

The traffic function in policing includes two basic duties: traffic control and accident investigation. As in other aspects of policing, who is involved in each activity is an organizational decision based upon personnel numbers and cost-effectiveness (see Box 4.4). In smaller departments the patrol division is responsible for all police operations, including traffic. In such cases both traffic and patrol duties belong to patrol officers. In larger departments specialized traffic units have evolved to handle traffic control and accident investigations. The logic behind these specialized units is twofold. First, accident investigation and reconstruction is a time-consuming operation and one that requires specialized

BOX 4.4   LEFT-SIDED POLICE STOPS

Usually, when one sees a police officer stop a motorist on the roadways, one expects to see the officer approach the motorist on the driver's side. This is sometimes referred to as a left-side approach. However, in 1994, the California Highway Patrol began to approach the motorist from the passenger seat side. This right-side approach is believed to be a safer procedure. First, standing on the right side protects the officer from oncoming fast moving traffic. Additionally, standing on the right side of the motorist's vehicle, the officer has a better visual vantage of the motorist. For example, in order for the motorist to draw a weapon and shoot at the officer, he or she will need to turn their body towards the right side of the vehicle, allowing a fraction of time for the officer to respond. Many officers have been shot and killed by felons stopped for a traffic citation. Often, officers are shot point-blank through the window of the driver's side as they approach the vehicle. By 1997 several other state patrols had joined the California Highway patrol's lead in making right-side stops.

training and skills. It simply is not practical to train all officers to be specialists in accident investigation and reconstruction.

Second is the plain fact that many officers do not enjoy working traffic details. Some officers do not believe that writing citations is "real police work," although the definition for what constitutes "real police work" seems rather amorphous. Others just do not like the idea that they will be ruining someone's day by issuing a traffic citation (Hale 1994).

Many police managers believe that traffic control should be the responsibility of all members of the patrol force. Even where departments have specialized traffic units, patrol officers should not entirely ignore traffic law enforcement because there is such a specialized unit. An effective patrol officer should know their patrol area well. This includes knowing which corners seem to be accident prone owing to trees on their corners and poor visibility, or straightaways where people have a tendency to speed.

Many police managers argue that there is a positive relationship between an aggressive traffic enforcement policy and crime prevention. The basic logic behind this assumption is as follows: When traffic enforcement is an integral part of the patrol function, officers are in a better position to detect and apprehend criminals. Most crimes involve the use of an automobile or other motorized vehicle in order to escape from the scene of a crime. Thus, unless a suspect is apprehended at the crime scene, it is likely, he or she will be intercepted during a pursuit on the roadways.

TRAFFIC CONTROL

The traffic control function of patrol officers, of course, is likely the most obvious and familiar role for the public to relate to. At one time or another, each of us has seen an officer directing traffic on some busy street corner or when a signal light has broken down. To be sure, some of us have received traffic citations for having passed through a stop sign or traveled faster than a posted speed limit or for driving a vehicle that has not been correctly maintained (with broken lights, a defective muffler, improper registration, etc.). We may have resented receiving these citations. In a more rational moment it may be possible to realize what the actual purpose of these traffic laws are: safety. The most important element involved in all traffic law enforcement is the prevention of traffic accidents and serious injuries to drivers and pedestrians.

Because traffic control is such a necessary, but complex task, and also because of the enormous numbers of automobiles on the roads, it would be impossible to stop every violator of a traffic or vehicle safety law. As a result, traffic divisions in police departments, as with other aspects of police work, practice selective enforcement. **Selective enforcement** of traffic laws typically means targeting the more serious offenders. For instance, two cars may pass an officer watching for speeders. One may be clocked on radar going 67 miles an hour in a 55 zone. The other, however, may be traveling at 70 miles an hour. It is likely, in this scenario, that the officer will pursue the motorist speeding at 70. Selective enforcement may also mean focusing on particular traffic violations at specific locations, or at certain times (stops to check for proper car registration, sobriety, possession of a driver's license, etc.).

ACCIDENT INVESTIGATION

Traffic safety programs and safe roadways are extremely important aspects of the police traffic function. **Accident investigation** involves the collection and assessment of facts surrounding automobile collisions. Accident investigations are conducted chiefly for three basic reasons: (1) to preserve human life by collecting information that can be used to prevent similar accidents in the future, (2) to assist insurance companies in determining fault or liability, and (3) to determine if there is criminal culpability on the part of any involved motorist.

In practice, many accident investigations amount to little more than collecting the statements of parties involved, and from possible witnesses. Although skid marks, the amount of physical damage to a vehicle, and other elements of physical evidence may be recorded by the officer, little investigation or actual use of these elements is undertaken unless a serious injury or death has occurred.

SUMMARY

This chapter has examined patrol work. As presented, patrol can be understood as a complex function within police organizations. Patrol encompasses not only law-enforcing activities, but also a variety of social service and public relations

Figure 4.12   *The police traffic function includes accident investigations.*

tasks. The patrol division is in many ways the core around which all other police functions revolve.

Because police agencies are among the very few official representatives of local government that operate on a 24-hour basis, they are often called upon to perform tasks that one would not typically associate with law enforcement. As a partial response to this call for service, as well as in an effort to improve and increase the patrol's presence on the street, experiments in scheduling have been undertaken.

Changes in styles of criminal activity and advances in technology have resulted both in an alteration in styles of policing from reactive to proactive, and also in modes of patrolling. Foot patrol has given way to a variety of more effective modes of motorized and even airborne patrolling activities, although a revitalization of a form of foot patrol has also recently emerged.

Similarly, innovative strategies and experiments in community policing have increased the feeling of confidence in police agencies while at the same time decreased the fear of crime in many communities.

REFERENCES

Adams, Thomas F. *Police Field Operations*. 3d ed. Englewood, N.J.: Prentice Hall Career and Technology, 1994.

Alpert, Geoffrey P., and Roger G. Dunham. *Policing Multi-Ethnic Neighborhoods*. New York: Greenwood, 1988.

Alpert, Geoffrey P., and Roger G. Dunham. *Policing Urban America*. 2d ed. Prospect Heights, Ill.: Waveland Press, Inc., 1992.

Barker, Thomas, Ronald D. Hunter, and Jeffrey P. Rush. *Police Systems and Practices.* Englewood Cliffs, N.J.: Prentice Hall Career & Technology, 1994.

Belknap, Joanne, Merry Morash, and Robert Trojanowicz. "Implementing a Community Policing Model for Work with Juveniles." *Criminal Justice and Behavior,* 14(1987):211–45.

Bittner, Egon. *The Function of Police in Modern Society.* Cambridge, Mass.: Olegeschlager, Gunn, and Haine, 1980.

Brown, Lee P., and Mary Ann Wycoff. "Policing Houston: Reducing Fear and Improving Service." *Crime and Delinquency,* 33(1987):71–89.

Cordner, Gary. "Community Policing: Elements and Effects." *Police Forum,* 5 (3)1995:1–7.

Cordner, Gary, and Robert Trojanowicz. "Patrol." In *What Works in Policing? Operations and Administration Examined.* Gary Cordner and D. Hale (eds.) Cincinnati, Oh.: Anderson Publishing Co., 1992.

Cunningham, W. C., and T. H. Taylor. "Private Security and Police in America." *Report for the National Institute of Justice.* McLean, Va.: Hallcrest, 1985.

DeBow, F., and D. Emmons. "The Community Hypothesis." In *Reaction to Crime.* D. Lewis (ed.) Beverly Hills, Calif.: Sage, 1981.

Eck, John, and William Spelman. *Problem Solving.* Washington, D.C.: Police Executive Research Forum, 1987.

Feins, J. D. *Partnerships for Neighborhood Crime Prevention.* Washington, D.C.: Department of Justice, National Institute of Justice, 1983.

Ferraro, Kenneth F., and Randy LaGrange. "The Measurement of Fear of Crime." *Sociological Inquiry,* 57(1987):10–101.

Gaines, Larry K., Victor E. Kappeler, and Joseph B. Vaughn. *Policing in America.* Cincinnati, Oh.: Anderson Publishing Co., 1997.

Gallup, George H. *The Gallup Report #200.* Princeton, N.J.: Gallup Poll, 1981.

Garofalo, J., and M. McLeod. "The Structure and Operations of Neighborhood Watch Programs in the United States." *Crime and Delinquency,* 35(3)1989:326–344.

Hale, Charles D. *Police Patrol: Operations and Management.* 2d ed. Englewood Cliffs, N.J.: Prentice Hall Career and Technology, 1994.

Holland, Lawrence H. "Police and the Community: The Detroit Mini-Station Experience." *FBI Law Enforcement Bulletin,* 54 (February 1985):1–6.

International Association of Chiefs of Police. *The Patrol Operation.* Rockville, Md.: IACP, Bureau of Operations and Research, 1977.

Kaplan, David E. "Bomb-Sniffing Tests Provoke a Dogfighter." *U.S News and World Report,* 24 November, 1997, 42.

Kelling George, Tony Pate, Duane Dieckman, and Charles E. Brown. *The Kansas City Preventive Patrol Experiment: A Summary Report.* Washington D.C.: Police Foundation, 1974.

Kelling George, Tony Pate, Duane Dieckman, and Charles E. Brown. "Kansas City Patrol Experiment." In *Policing Society.* W. Clinton Terry III. (ed.) New York: Wiley, 1985.

Lab, Steven P. *Prevention: Approaches, Practices and Evaluations.* Cincinnati, Oh.: Anderson Publishing Co., 1988.

LaGrange, Randy L. *Policing American Society.* Chicago: Nelson-Hall Publishing, 1993.

Lundman, Richard J. "Police Patrol Work: A Comparative Perspective." In *Police Behavior: A Sociological Perspective.* Richard J. Lundman (ed.) New York: Oxford, 1980.

Martin, Susan E., and Lawrence W. Sherman. "Selective Apprehension: A Police Strategy for Repeat Offenders." *Criminology,* 24(1986):155–74.

McLean, H. "A Zap in the Dead of Night." *Law and Order,* 36(10)1988:26–31.

Moore, Daniel T., and J. Glen Morrow. "Evaluation of the Four/Ten Schedule in Three Illinois Department of State Police Districts." *Journal of Police Science and Administration,* 15(1987):105–109.

Moore, Mark H., Robert C. Trojanowicz, and George L. Kelling. "Crime and Policing." *Perspectives on Policing* series. Washington D.C.: National Institute of Justice, Department of Justice, 1988.

More, Harry W., and W. Fred Wegener. *Effective Police Supervision* (2d ed). Cincinnati, Oh.: Anderson Publishing Co., 1997.

Potter, Joan. "Aviation Units: Are They Worth the Money?" *Police Magazine,* 2(1979):22.

Purpura, Philip P. *Security and Loss Prevention.* Boston: Butterworth–Heinemann, 1984.

Reiss, Albert J. *The Police and the Public.* New Haven, Conn.: Yale, 1971.

Roehl, J. A., and R. F. Cook. *Evaluation of Urban Crime Prevention Programs.* Washington, D.C.: Department of Justice, National Institute of Justice, 1984.

Rosenbaum, Dennis P. "The Theory and Research Behind Neighborhood Watch: Is it a Sound Fear and Crime Reducing Strategy?" *Crime and Delinquency,* 33 (1987):103–34.

Sharp, Arthur G. "Computers Are a Cop's Best Friend." *Law and Order,* November, 1991:41–45.

Siegel, Larry J. *Criminology.* 6th ed. Belmont, Calif.: West/Wadsworth Publishing Company, 1998.

Skolnick, Jerome H., and David H. Bailey. *The Blue Line: Police Innovation in Six American Communities.* New York: Free Press, 1986.

Tan, Kim L. "Police Cracking Down on I-95 Drug Traffic." *The Boston Herald,* 11 June, 1987, 6.

Trojanowicz, Robert, and David L. Carter. *The Philosophy and Role of Community Policing.* East Lansing, Mich.: National Center for Community Policing, 1988.

Uniform Crime Reports for the United States, 1994. Washington, D.C.: GPO, Table 78, pp. 296–356.

Wilson, James Q. *Varieties of Police Behavior: The Management of Law and Order in Eight Communities.* Cambridge, Mass.: Harvard University Press, 1968.

Wilson, James Q. *Thinking About Crime.* New York: Vantage, 1977.

Wilson, James Q., and Barbara Boland. *The Effect of Police on Crime.* Washington, D.C.: U.S. Department of Justice, 1979.

Wilson, James Q., and George Kelling. "Broken Windows: The Police and Neighborhood Safety." *Atlantic Monthly,* March 1982:29–38.

QUESTIONS FOR REVIEW

Objective #1:

- What is the basic field operation for all local level police agencies?

Objective #2:

- What is meant by law enforcement calls?
- What type of call is the request assistance to free a child from a locked bathroom?

Objective #3:

- How would you define order maintenance?

Objective #4:

- What are the 11 elements basic to traditional patrol operation?
- What additional elements might one add to those used in traditional patrol operations, in modern police agencies?

Objective #5:

- What are the basic responsibilities of a patrol officer arriving at the scene of a crime?
- Why should the initial responding officer carefully assess the crime scene?
- Who is responsible for conducting follow-up investigations?

Objective #6:

- What are the four primary activities associated with the deployment of patrol forces?

Objective #7:

- What is the difference between a four-ten scheduling structure and a four-two structure?
- On what issues might an agency determine whether to use two or three 12-hour shifts?

Objective #8:

- What is meant by a beat?
- How might one define a precinct?

Objective #9:

- Why are motorcycles not always practical for pursuit?
- When are K-9 officers viewed as expendable?
- Why are helicopters used to pursue suspects fleeing in automobiles?

Objective #10:

- When police establish alcohol sobriety checkpoints, is this an example of proactive or reactive policing?

- When officers arrive at the scene of a burglary following a silent alarm, is this an example of proactive or reactive policing?

Objective #11:

- What are some of the reasons that police began developing community relations programs?
- What motivates the initiation of many block-watch programs?

Objective #12:

- What are the primary reasons for speed limits?
- For what purposes are traffic accident investigations undertaken?

5 Investigations, Juveniles, and Special Units

CHAPTER OBJECTIVES

After reading this chapter you should be able to:

1. Describe what is meant by the investigative unit or division.
2. Offer an explanation for why detectives had such a slow development in municipal policing.
3. Discuss the primary objectives associated with the investigation process.
4. Differentiate between crimes against persons units, crimes against property units, and general assignment units.
5. Discuss the utility and limitations of task forces.
6. Explain how police investigate a crime.
7. Consider the nature of routine cases, common cases, and special attention cases.
8. Describe various aspects of undercover police work.
9. Indicate the positive aspects of the internal affairs division.
10. Consider the type of pressure that leads many juveniles to become involved in drug use.
11. Discuss the program focuses of DARE.
12. Outline the principal purpose of SWAT teams.

DIVISIONS OF LABOR IN THE POLICE ORGANIZATION

Law enforcement agencies vary in complexity and in their number of personnel. In larger departments, the division of labor exceeds mere allocation of tasks by the same officers during different portions of the day (the small department's

KEY TERMS		
	task forces	vice laws
	forensics	undercover
crimes-against-persons units	routine cases	light cover
crimes-against-property units	common cases	deep cover
general assignment units	special attention cases	internal affairs division
uttering	clearing cases	project DARE
kiting	conviction	SWAT teams

"Andy Taylor" kind of arrangement). In larger departments the operational tasks are divided into different divisions or units that specialize in a given function or set of activities. Thus, the "operations bureau" may contain separate patrol, traffic, investigations, narcotics and vice, juvenile, and special tactical or emergency units. Figure 5.1 shows this general division of departmental units in

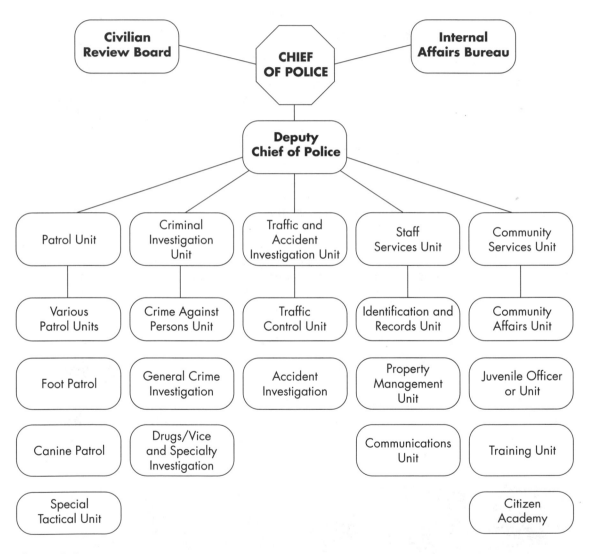

Figure 5.1
Basic Organizational Chart of an Average Police Department.

a hypothetical *average* police department. Naturally, larger departments will have a greater number of division and a more complex structure. In Chapter 4, patrol and traffic were considered. In this chapter, the focus will be on investigations, narcotics and vice, and the juvenile details.

THE INVESTIGATIONS DIVISION

The investigations division is a specialized unit primarily involved with identifying and apprehending violators of fairly serious crimes. Less serious criminal offenses tend to remain under the purview of the uniformed patrol officer. Although a kind of split appears to occur between patrol and investigative units, this tends to be more artificial than real. The investigative units will likely concentrate on crimes such as murder, rape, major robberies, stalking, and aggravated assaults. But the patrol unit often shares in the responsibility for apprehending the perpetrators of these serious crimes, as well as the responsibility for handling lesser crimes. In fact, a great many cases that originate in the patrol unit are resolved by patrol officers and never reach the desks of investigators.

Although there is a considerable amount of shared responsibility, there is a certain amount of resentment between officers in patrol and investigative units. Much of this friction is perceptual, and derived from the "special privileges" and autonomy associated with detectives. The public and the media have romanticized detective work. It has literally been elevated to the level of a glamorous and adventurous career. From detective Andy Sipowicz to Axel Foley, from Joe Friday to Kojak, the role of the detective has been presented as an adventurous and even glamorous job. Intensifying this situation is the tendency of both the public and the media to assume that investigators are solely responsible for breaks or apprehensions in big crime cases. Frequently, patrol officers perceive their efforts as the real police work, for which investigators take undeserved credit. One may certainly question why investigators seem to enjoy this position of privilege—if indeed they do. Let us consider the role and function of the police detective.

THE POLICE DETECTIVE

Detective, as a noun, makes its first appearance in lay parlance in the 1840s in order to identify the police organizational position of an investigator (Klockars 1985; Kuykendall 1986). The central function of early detective work in police organizations was apprehension. The early history of the detective, both in England and colonial America, was filled with controversy. Kuykendall

(1986:175) details seven general perceptions of early (chiefly private) detectives:

1. [They] investigated only either difficult and serious or easily solved cases.
2. [They] worked primarily for profit and usually only for middle and upper classes.
3. [They] spied on citizens to acquire information about their actual and possible political and criminal activity.
4. [They] acted as agent provocateurs or thiefmakers to incite crime and entrap citizens.
5. [They] used secrecy, deceit, treachery, coercion, and brutality to acquire information.
6. [They] participated with criminals to both create and cover up illegal behavior.
7. [They] used and manipulated informers.

In England these perceptions of early detectives were perhaps more pronounced than in early American versions. Yet, the slow development of investigative agencies, such as the Federal Bureau of Investigation, and the covert activities of some early private detective agencies (such as those of the Pinkerton Agency during union strikes at coal mines) certainly affected American attitudes about detectives. The slow move toward formal and organized detective bureaus in American police agencies, in fact, may reflect public mistrust and fear of detectives. The romanticism of contemporary detectives, in turn, may represent an attempt to compensate for these feelings of distrust and apprehension. Today, merely mentioning the word *detective* and some mysterious trench-coated sleuth springs to mind.

For many, the investigative function centers around solving crimes reported to or discovered by the police (Gaines et al. 1997; Osterburg and Ward 1997). Berg and Horgan (1998:6), however, identify eight primary objectives commonly associated with the investigative process:

1. Deal with emergencies.
2. Determine if a crime has been committed and, if so, what crime.
3. Establish crime scene priorities.
4. Identify suspects.
5. Apprehend the suspects.
6. Gather and preserve evidence.
7. Recover stolen property.
8. Assist in prosecution and conviction of the defendant or defendants.

Investigators must sift through all available information and determine which pieces can be linked together to accomplish all of the above. Investigative units frequently are separated from the regular patrol chain of command. In large measure, they possess an autonomous parallel chain of command that works hand-in-hand with other divisions of the police department (e.g., patrol, narcotics, etc.). The image of the detective enjoying higher prestige than other categories of police officers may rest on the fact that they frequently receive higher pay, more regular work hours, greater control in what they do, and less supervision. It is not unusual, for example, for a detective sergeant to receive a higher salary than a patrol sergeant and for this detective sergeant to work a regular non-rotating shift.

In many jurisdictions, detectives within a given unit are organized around a particular type of crime: homicide, robbery, forgery, and so forth. In some other jurisdictions, detectives are assigned to cases according to their geographic area of occurrence. Along similar lines, Thomas Reppetto (1985) describes the overall organization of American police detective work as having historically fallen into two basic orientations, territorial generalists and headquarter specialists. The former were typically attached to a local precinct and worked directly or indirectly with local patrol officers. These detectives investigated a wide assortment of large and small cases. In the case of headquarter specialists, investigators were organized into squads (much like today's) specializing in particular categories of crime.

Most large metropolitan police departments organize their detective units around three central details. These include a unit specializing in various crimes against people, a unit designed to investigate crimes against property, and a unit of detectives to handle general investigative assignments. Detectives assigned to **crimes-against-persons units** investigate cases in which people have been physically harmed, abused, violated, or threatened. Examples of such crimes include murder, aggravated assault, rape, and armed robbery.

Officers in **crimes-against-property units** pursue criminals who have in some manner stolen or severely damaged material goods and objects. Thus, property-unit detectives may find themselves searching for car thieves and shoplifters one day, and burglars or pickpockets the next. Or, property detectives might be assigned to locate youths believed to be vandalizing and destroying car windshields or systematically stealing items from parked cars.

In partial contrast to crimes-against-persons and crimes-against-property units, **general assignment units** are less specific in the categories of crime it handles. To some extent, this third unit receives cases that fall between the cracks of the other two units. General assignment officers are likely to deal with flim-flam and confidence games, frauds, keeping an eye on Gypsies as they migrate through a given city or jurisdiction, forgery (signing someone else's name, typically to a check), **uttering** (intentionally issuing bad or worthless checks), and **kiting** (intentionally writing checks for more than a balance will cover, expecting to add to the balance before the check needs to clear).

In some police departments detective divisions are further subdivided into specialty units or task forces. **Task forces**, by definition, are usually established as temporary squads of detectives to accomplish a specific, limited task (see Box 5.1).

In 1986, for example, the Tallahassee, Florida, police department put together a small task force of both detective and patrol officers. The central purpose of this task force was to identify and apprehend people involved in sales and distribution of crack cocaine. Similar task forces were also established in

BOX 5.1 DETECTIVE SPECIALIZATIONS

Crimes Against Persons
- Homicide
- Rape
- Aggravated assault
- Stalking
- Narcotics
- Prostitution and vice

Crimes Against Property
- Car theft
- Shoplifting
- Pick-pocketing
- Vandalism
- Burglary

General Assignment
- Frauds
- Confidence games
- Gypsy-associated crimes
- Forgery
- Uttering
- Kiting

Special Task Forces
- Major robberies
- Serial rapes
- Serial murders
- Stings (special apprehension efforts)
- Narcotics sweeps

many larger cities like New York and Boston, where the use of crack was seen as potentially growing to epidemic proportions.

Similarly, special anti-crime squads or task forces assigned to expose organized crime and racketeering have a long history in investigative work. During the 1920s. the Los Angeles police department had its "Crime Crusher" squads during the 1930s there were various FBI "Get Dillinger" and "Public Enemy Number One" squads (Reppetto 1985).

The use and existence of such highly specialized detective units is quite literally akin to the proverbial double-edged sword. On the one hand, these kinds of task forces tend to pull together the best-skilled and frequently most energetic investigators, and by nature usually possess strong support and often financial backing from their administrations. As a consequence, these special task force units customarily achieve dazzling results.

On the other hand, since these units do put together the best officers and spend increased amounts of department funds on time and equipment, they may be a drain on these resources in other units. More mundane crimes—the bulk of the case loads—are likely to be under-investigated or unresolved.

Another potential problem one might associate with these special task force arrangements is overemphasis by police managers, supervisors, and administrators of solving what might be called high-fear crimes. Illustrations of these high-fear crimes include the serial murders in New York, Los Angeles, central Ohio, and Atlanta. The murder sprees have been attributed respectively in the media to the "Son of Sam," the "Hillside Strangler," the ".22-caliber killer," and the "Atlanta Child Killer." In 1997, in the face of a wave of unresolved bombings at Planned Parenthood clinics in Atlanta, and the 1996 Atlanta Olympic bombing, the Atlanta Police department established a task force. All of these cases created instant fear fever among members of each community. This fear was all the more damaging to people in these communities because the killers and bomber remained at large for long periods of time. Although detectives who worked on these cases certainly made every effort to capture the culprits, many Americans could not understand why it was so difficult. Using their television images of such notable detectives as Kojak, Columbo, Cagney and Lacey, and Simone and Sipowicz, Americans found it difficult to accept that in the real world, crimes are not always resolved in a neat, 60-minute format.

It may well be that a proportion of the mystique that surrounds detective operations is the impression that a detective has certain hard-to-gain skills and intellectual prowess; that investigating a serious crime requires enormous scientific knowledge; and that detective work is more important and much more exciting than uniformed street patrol. It may come as a surprise to many people, but detective investigations, as with a considerable amount of all police work, involve routine, rather tedious chores. Often, detectives find themselves knee-deep in paperwork (see Box 5.2), form processing, and various clerical tasks that are much less exciting than activities many patrol officers undertake daily.

Although some true detection can be associated with detective work, it is usually proportionately less than television and the movies would have the

---

BOX 5.2 "WHO LOVES YA BABY?" THE KOJAK SYNDROME

Detective stories and books bulge Americans' library shelves and television is filled with detective programs and movies. Although periodically a program about uniformed police officers, such as *Hill Street Blues* and *High Incident,* attracts the attention of American viewers, such programs are not nearly as numerous or successful as detective shows. The extent to which the police detective has been popularized in books, television, and in the movies has a profound effect upon the way real-life police detectives operate. Some of the sophisticated forensic equipment used by television detectives may only be used by a few large city agencies. But there is a tendency for real detectives to attempt to use television detectives' investigative techniques, rather than rational strategic plans to solve crimes (Goldstein 1977). Sometimes, life does imitate art. The fictional television character of Kojak, for example, not only further promoted the image of detective as supersleuth, but actually affected police organizations and management styles. In June 1981,

Sam Souryal wrote an article titled, "The Kojak Syndrome: Meeting the Problem of Police Dissatisfaction through Job Enrichment." In this article, Souryal identified the "Kojak Syndrome" as increasing dissatisfaction among police officers with their agency's policies, working conditions, misguided supervision, political interference, and a long list of other grievances. Lt. Theo Kojak, although a fictional character, idealized the police detective for many officers as well as the public. Kojak simply would not allow red tape to interfere with his investigations. Often against the advice of his supervisors, Kojak cut through red tape and pushed his investigation to the limit regardless of whose toes he had to step on. This "Kojak Syndrome"—although certainly present among detectives for a long time—has only begun to be addressed administratively during the past decade or so. The result is that a number of changes and adaptations in police policy have emerged in order to improve police managerial styles (Souryal 1986).

public think. It is similarly debatable whether a detective necessarily requires significantly greater skill or knowledge than patrol officers possess. Certainly, it is undeniable that a considerable amount of detective work amounts to little more then a lucky communication with someone in the community, and checking out leads on somewhat of a hit-or-miss basis. It is only in fictional accounts of detective investigations that bank robbers, drug dealers, and bunco artists are regularly apprehended and successfully prosecuted.

For example, on a dark night in March of 1997, Ennis Cosby, the son of actor Bill Cosby, was brutally shot to death as he changed the tire on his car along an East Hollywood, California, road. Police and detectives pulled out all stops to find the murderer of Ennis Cosby. Yet, in spite of an eyewitness, and a composite sketch shown in the newspapers and the nightly news for a week, it took a telephone tip to locate a suspect nearly a month after the shooting.

In the real world of cops and robbers, and with the exception, perhaps, of murder, most crimes go unsolved. As shown in Table 5.1, between 1982 and 1992 less than half (about 44 percent) of all violent crime investigations result in an arrest. By comparison, less serious crimes such as various property crimes average arrests in only about 17% to 18% of the cases during this same period (Sourcebook 1994).

Table 5.1
Percent of offenses cleared by arrest, by type of offenses, 1982–1992.

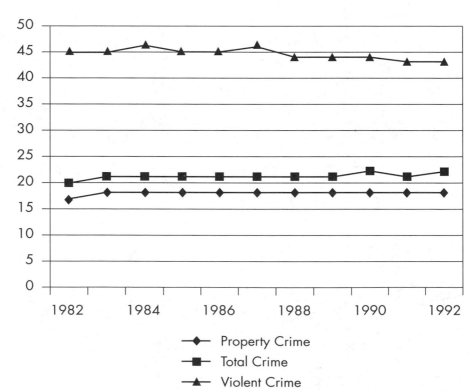

One logical explanation for this phenomena rests upon our society's attitude about life and property and the relative social value placed upon human life compared to property. Although the public may be angered by thefts and robberies, they are outraged by the taking of another person's life. As a result, police agencies frequently expend more effort and personnel power to investigate a killing than they do typical cases of burglary or robbery. The public seldom balks when huge amounts of personnel and money are spent on special efforts to apprehend serial murderers like David Berkowitz (the Son of Sam killer in New York during the 1970s). If, however, like amounts of money were spent on robberies and similar property crimes, the public would strenuously object.

INVESTIGATION

Detectives principally are involved with law enforcement activities after a crime has been committed and identified, either by police or a community resident's complaint. Typically, by the time detectives receive the case, it has already received preliminary investigation by the uniformed officers who responded to the initial call. The uniformed officer's detailed notes may provide important leads and clues the detective can use to solve the case.

Certainly, it is possible for detectives to enter a case at different points, depending upon such factors as the seriousness of the offense, the time at which the crime occurs, their physical proximity at the time the crime is identified, or the personal interest a given detective—or the community—may have for a particular case. Although some large departments do provide 24-hour investigative coverage by assigning detectives to each shift, many mid-size and smaller departments do not. In these smaller agencies, detectives may be formally scheduled for day shift (8 A.M. to 5 P.M.), Monday through Friday, and share in the on-call responsibilities during other shifts and during the weekend. If a serious crime occurs, investigators may get called in, even if they are not officially on call.

Many crimes that occur, such as residential burglaries or commercial break-ins, simply can wait until morning or until Monday when the detectives come in to the office. Until then, uniformed officers responding to the call are responsible for the case. Again, owing to television portrayals, many victims of such crimes as a residential burglary are disappointed to learn that a forensic team is not rushing to the scene. Although the science of criminal investigations or **forensics** is quite advanced technologically, it also can be very expensive. In the real world, not every police department has its own crime lab. Further, it would be very expensive to bring even a single forensic technician to the scene of every residential burglary. It is often pointless to send forensic technicians to the scene until after a detective has had an opportunity to assess the situation. In many cases, there would be no benefit.

Over the past decade, a growing number of police agencies nationally have arranged for their uniformed officers to carry small forensic field kits in their patrol cars. When summoned to a burglary call, they will routinely dust for prints if there are obvious points of entry or exit (a jimmied window or door, broken glass, etc.). For the most part, this activity is undertaken as a public relations endeavor rather than a real law enforcement one. While any prints lifted at the scene are sent along to the detectives, it is infrequent that these prints are actually used to locate or identify a suspect. In some cases, particularly when either the patrol officer or the detective recognizes some similarities between a current case and previous ones, these prints might be used to determine if the same criminal has committed both crimes. In some cases, where the department has access to an automated fingerprint indexing system or AFIS (AFIS will be discussed in detail later in this text), the fingerprints may be computer checked against the existing database and a suspect identified. Fingerprinting and its use in identifying suspects will be more fully discussed in Chapter 9.

Perhaps the easiest way to demonstrate the way detectives investigate a criminal case is to follow one through the system. Allowing for certain variations of agency policy or local ordinance, there is a general pattern, as can be seen in Figure 5.2.

First, a crime must occur and be brought to the attention of the police. For the purpose of our example, let us consider a home burglary. After the homeowner calls in the report, a patrol officer in the vicinity is notified and sent to the scene. Once there, the officer will take careful notes about the burglary and fill out an incident report as part of the preliminary investigation. This initial report will be sent to the investigative unit, where one of the detectives will be assigned to conduct a follow-up investigation. To begin, investigators typically read through their assigned cases and sort them into what amounts to three different priorities: routine cases, common offenses, and special attention cases.

In **routine cases**, the circumstances of the offense indicate the next obvious step to be taken. These cases are straightforward, although perhaps requiring long hours of leg work and even longer hours of interviewing witnesses, victims, and suspects.

The second category includes those cases that are straightforward, but less promising. These **common cases** will be checked against an officer's personal file as well as the department's. But, because of their rather common characteristics, the investigator does not view them as likely to be readily solved at this time. A symbolic investigation will be undertaken and the victim contacted to see if any additional information might be added to the report. Following this, the investigator will file the case as unsolved (open).

Finally, cases may be viewed as serious, regardless of how few leads and clues seem readily available. These **special attention cases** will require the investigator to examine the existing evidence as well as the crime scene in order to locate any leads or clues missed by the responding officer. Investigators will additionally canvass the neighborhood, actively seeking information and/or witnesses to the crime. In serious cases, investigators may additionally call in a

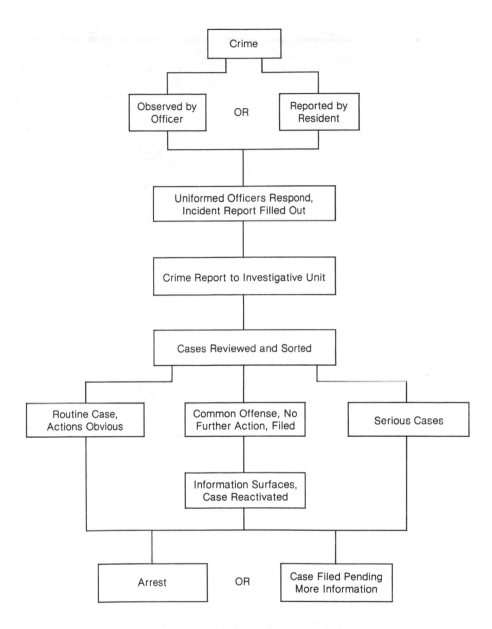

Figure 5.2
Typical crime investigation sequence.

forensic team and the use of other kinds of laboratory techniques that may be available (at local or state crime laboratories, or even the FBI's laboratory facilities). For example, on March 27, 1997, local sheriff's deputies from the San Diego, California, sheriff's department, responding to a telephone tip, discovered 39 dead bodies in a large private home in Santa Fe, near San Diego. After an investigation and autopsies, the Sheriff's department learned that this was a mass suicide by a cult of people who believed in extraterrestrial life. They had

Figure 5.3
Thirty-nine bodies were found at the Heaven's Gate compound in Santa Fe, California, the apparent victims of a mass suicide.

been convinced by their leader (David Whitehead, AKA David Ono) that a spaceship was following the Hale-Bopp comet. By committing suicide, these people were told, they would simply throw off their human containers, so that they could be elevated to a higher life form and meet with the spaceship marked by the comet. While this case did not really offer much criminal mystery, it nonetheless required some special attention in its investigation.

Returning to our burglary example, it is likely that the case will be viewed as either routine or common. As a routine case, the investigator might recognize something reminiscent of a similar recent burglary. In this situation, the other case file will be sought and comparisons may lead to sufficient information for an arrest. Or, nothing may come from the comparison. In this event, and following a perfunctory investigation and perhaps adding some notes from the follow-up investigation, the case is filed.

Unlike television, where virtually every case is satisfactorily resolved by at least an arrest, in the real world it just does not always end happily ever after. There are several elements about resolving or clearing cases that bear consideration.

CLEARING CASES

The concept of **clearing cases** refers to how the case is resolved. In some cases, this means an arrest is made. In other cases, this may refer to a case cleared by an adjudication of guilty. In some situations, cases may even be cleared through clerical procedures. The type of crime under investigation will certainly affect whether a case will be cleared by an arrest, a prosecution, or simply filed away (to be cleared clerically at a later time). Homicides, although not the most common crime that police must deal with, do tend to have the highest rate of cases cleared by arrest. The national rate for homicides cleared by arrest averages 75% to 85% annually (Sourcebook 1995). Conversely, and as illustrated in

Figure 5.4
Vice and narcotic squads reflect and enforce the morals as well as the laws of a community.

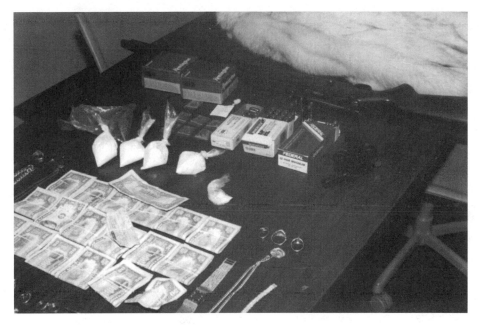

Table 5.1, the annual clearance rate (from arrest) for most property crimes is appreciably lower, usually between 17% and 20%. Similarly, clearance rate by arrest for violent personal crimes, such as rape and assault, also tend remain below 50% annually.

To a large measure, this disparate clearance by arrest reflects how police tend to invest a greater amount of time and resources in serious crimes. Implicit in this rate of clearance is the social attitude of a greater priority being placed on human life—both the injuring and taking of it—than on monetary or property losses from thefts.

Finally, it is important to note that clearance is not synonymous with **conviction**; that is, arrest is not an assurance that the individual will be found guilty in a court of law. Whether or not each offender arrested is later convicted is a decision of the courts, not the police. As a result, a great many more cases may be cleared by arrest than will actually result in conviction.

As suggested at the beginning of this chapter, investigative divisions are frequently composed of several specialized units. Among the more common specialty units are the vice or morals squad and the narcotics unit (frequently a single combined squad). In the next section, this unit is described in detail.

VICE AND NARCOTICS SQUADS

Vice laws may be summarized as those statutes that reflect the morals of a community's residents. Because of their social significance, vice laws, perhaps to a greater extent than most other laws, come under frequent community and law enforcement debate and negotiation. Although somewhat less controversial than questioning whether prostitution should be illegal, laws against illicit drug use are also reflective of changing social values.

In a broad sense, vice laws encompass an array of "victimless crimes" associated with prostitution, gambling, and drug use. Vice and narcotics officers often set themselves up as customers in order to apprehend people actively involved in these law violations. For example, in response to residents' complaints, undercover detectives might begin frequenting some public men's rooms in order to be solicited by a male prostitute, who will subsequently be arrested.

In some instances, policewomen pose as prostitutes and await propositions to perform sexual acts for money. In all of these situations, the investigators must be careful not to initiate the solicitation and thereby entrap someone. Similarly, officers must not actually engage in any sexual contact with the individual they are arresting. Occasionally, in an effort to get charges dropped, a perpetrator may accuse the arresting officer of having engaged in sex just prior to the arrest. Such accusations, along with substantiated cases of corruption on the part of some officers, have led to criticism of covert police operations that might violate personal rights of average citizens.

UNDERCOVER POLICE WORK

As a result of continued necessity for clandestine investigations, vice and narcotics officers must take elaborate precautions to avoid discovery by the law violators. To this end, and to some degree because of the serious risk of becoming corrupted by the very elements they are attempting to police, vice and narcotics officers frequently report directly to the chief of the department. By shortening the links in the chain of command, vice and narcotics officers are afforded both increased insulation against accidental or unintentional departmental leaks about operations and increased autonomy in the field.

Much of law enforcement heavily relies upon the authority vested in the role of the officer. Traditionally, this has come to be represented by the uniform, badge, squad car, and other outward symbols of police authority (Wilson 1978; Miller 1987). But for obvious reasons, these outward symbols of police authority can also limit an officer's ability to collect information and evidence covertly.

The term **undercover** can be used as a kind of generic label to identify decoy work, sting operations, and police intelligence-gathering efforts (Marx 1980). Regardless of the exact nature of the assignment, undercover officers are only effective if their activities remain secret.

According to George Miller (1987), there are two types of undercover work, light cover and deep cover. Jay Williams and L. Lynn Guess (1981) have similarly distinguished between "partial" and "deep" cover with approximately the same meaning as Miller. Officers assigned to **light cover** typically work a regular tour of duty. These officers may assume different names and identities and wear plainclothes during their work shift. But, at the end of their shift, these disguises come off, and they go to their homes and families.

In contrast, **deep cover** is elaborate. Officers assigned to a deep cover operation must entirely submerge themselves in their disguised identities. To a large measure, these officers must temporarily become the individuals they pretend to be. Officers must remain in character 24 hours a day. In fact, as Michel Girodo (1984) observes, deep cover operations are often open-ended in duration and last several months or even years.

Because by definition deep cover requires a more complete immersion in some criminal group or organization, one might expect that the officer must be highly experienced, skilled, and trained in police work. Ironically, more often than not, undercover officers are selected immediately after graduation from the police academy.

In many jurisdictions, persons with no police training—or affiliation—at all are hired as undercover officers. The logic here, of course, is that to be effective, undercover officers must not be known to the group they plan to infiltrate. George Miller (1987:31) quotes one of his subjects as stating:

> I had no academy training. The Personnel Officer offered me the undercover assignment after I submitted my application. I took the civil service exam alone . . . and received mailed notification a week later that I had passed. I met the Chief and [my supervisor] in a hotel room to get sworn in.

Frequently, police administrators select undercover officers on the basis of some particular need in a specific case. These may refer to the requirements of a certain ethnic type, language requirement, age, gender, or special skill or knowledge. Obviously, having a black officer attempt to gain information about the activities of several Ku Klux Klansmen would be preposterous. By the same token, asking a white officer to infiltrate a Haitian cocaine-smuggling ring would have disastrous results.

In some cases, the investigation requires very youthful appearance, such as when then the investigation takes police to high school students or on high school campuses. Sometimes, youthful appearance is used in prostitution investigations, since the working girls are less likely to suspect a boyish-looking man of being a police officer (see Figure 5.5).

The nature of both vice and narcotics investigations is highly sensitive, and the chief or supervisor must be kept appraised of all facets of an investigator's activities nearly all of the time. Yet, it is difficult to supervise or communicate with deep cover officers, since direct contacts with the office would jeopardize the cover. Consequently, the deeper one's cover, the more limited and infrequent are supervisor-contacts (Williams and Guess 1981; Miller 1987).

As Gary Marx (1985) indicates, the enormous effect of isolation from other, more legitimate contacts while in deep cover can have serious and unintended consequences. "Playing the crook," as Marx describes it (1985:109), may amplify an officer's already-existing feeling of cynicism about the effectiveness

Figure 5.5
Sometimes youthful-looking police are used undercover on high school or college campuses.

of law enforcement and the role of a police officer. The officer may begin to find it just as easy to employ illegal tactics as legal ones, even to accomplish departmental goals. In time, an officer under deep cover may become the very felon the officer set out to apprehend.

One illustration of the dangers of deep cover operations is that of a northern California police officer who spent 18 months investigating the Hell's Angels. Although he was ultimately responsible for a number of arrests for serious felonies and received high praise from his supervisors, the officer paid a heavy price. His carousing with the Angels while undercover led to both alcohol and drug dependency. These, in turn, resulted in the break-up of his family, loss of his position through forced resignation, and sentencing to prison after a series of bank robberies (Linderman 1981).

Similarly, some officers who work under deep cover for prolonged periods of time, develop genuine feelings of friendship with the felons they need to investigate and ultimately arrest. When it comes time to make the arrests, some of these officers develop emotional problems over their violation of a sense of friendship and locality with these individuals (Barker, Hunter, and Rush 1994).

Ironically, in the face of what may be the most dangerous segment of policing, undercover work, officers frequently describe their task as a game (Hicks 1973; Miller 1987). It is described as a matching of wits of the officer and the felons, a contest of skill and ingenuity. But, it is a contest the officer cannot really afford to lose. For the officer, a loss might mean death.

Adding to the general dangers of undercover work is the fact that officers sometimes find it impossible to carry a gun while undercover. Miller (1987) points out that many undercover officers have never received any training in the use of firearms. This being the case, what is a problem for some may be a benefit for others. The increasingly youthful age of those involved in drug sales and distribution, along with other violent criminal activity have resulted in undercover officers investigating children. "Narc," as undercover investigators are sometimes called, find it necessary to infiltrate adolescent groups on high school and college campuses. In many instances, theses officers are not permitted to carry weapons. Unfortunately, nobody has shared these rules with the youthful felons who continue to carry and use weapons.

INTERNAL AFFAIRS: POLICING THE POLICE

It has been suggested that for a democratic society to operate effectively, the public must be protected from arbitrary practice of public officials (Redford 1969; Bent and Rossum 1976). The police, as a governmental agency with both legal and symbolic authority, must ensure that their policies and practices offer sufficient control over law violators, while not jeopardizing the liberty of law-abiding citizens.

To be sure, some amount of police misconduct and corruption can be avoided by careful screening of recruits, followed by effective standardized training and proficient supervision. Unfortunately, despite police entrance examinations, psychological screenings, and local and state level standards of training, police malpractice continues to occur.

Most large and many mid-sized police departments have formal mechanisms for investigating allegations of police malpractice. These departmental investigations generally are handled by a specialized unit of detectives commonly referred to as the **internal affairs division** (IAD). Although it is safe to say that most internal affairs units make earnest attempts to ferret out corrupt and disreputable officers, it would be naive to think this can be accomplished completely.

The efforts of the IAD are sometimes hampered by the media. For example, television and newspapers may hear about allegations of police wrongdoing and, in their zeal to report the facts, inadvertently turn allegations into fact regardless of the actual outcome of the investigation. Further inhibiting the responsibility of internal affairs detectives is the cloak of secrecy that is immediately drawn over a department when accusations of improper conduct arise. Curiously, as leery of outsiders or non-police affiliated people as police officers are, they are more suspicious of internal affairs detectives. No on in the police organization is more feared, and despised, than the "head hunters" or internal affairs officers. The President's Commission on Law Enforcement (*Task Force Report* 1967:194) made special note of this attitude when it wrote: "Policemen all too often, because of misplaced locality, overlook serious misconduct by other officers." Although it is now 30 years later, this attitude continues to persist.

The hostility leveled at internal affairs officers results, in part, because these detectives have sometimes used questionable practices during their investigations.

But, in part, other officers are suspicious because they either do not understand the purpose or disagree with the need for such an investigative unit (Territo and Smith 1985; Barker 1994). What, then, is the goal and purpose of internal affairs units?

Realistically, no police department will ever be immune to some officer's misconduct at some time or another. It is, however, the civic as well as legal responsibility of each department to make concerted efforts to assure that police integrity and behavior is exemplary. If police officers are to maintain public trust and continue representing, both in a real and symbolic sense, American ideals such as liberty and freedom, they must remain detached from corruption, misconduct, and malpractice. The manner in which a department deals with community residents' complaints about unacceptable police conduct strongly reflects on that agency's capacity to maintain the public's trust. An open system, where residents neither fear reprisal nor anticipate cover-ups, is essential for reliable law enforcement operations (Carter 1986).

JUVENILE DIVISION

During the past several years, police have found it necessary to become involved with juveniles with increasing frequency. Research has shown that serious and violent crimes are being committed by juveniles at an alarming rate. Delbert Elliot and David Huizinga (1983, 1987), for example, conducted a national panel study and reported that many youths commit illegal acts multiple times daily. According to the *Sourcebook of Criminal Justice Statistics* (1993:428), there were 1,943,138 arrests of people under the age of 18. In addition to their involvement in violent crimes and property crimes, juveniles are rapidly committing increasing numbers of alcohol, narcotics and drug-related offenses. Occasionally, undercover officers discover a case they are working involves a juvenile. In most instances, the department's juvenile unit is notified and sometimes actually drawn into the investigation.

The enormity of juvenile crime in the United States has necessitated increasingly stringent actions on the part of the police. The juvenile unit, or juvenile detail as it is sometimes called, is an attempt to curb delinquency. As a general rule, the juvenile detail is a specialized unit within the detective division. The responsibilities of juvenile officers typically include handling any case that relates to children or adolescents. Consequently, juvenile officers may work with youths who have committed crimes or who have themselves been victims of crime.

A youthful offender's status as a juvenile is established by each state's statute. Among several relevant factors used in statutes is a youth's age. Many states include as juveniles all people under the age of 18. Other states may set the upper limit at 17, and still others at 16. In a few states, the age of juvenile jurisdiction is limited to those 13 years old or younger. Even when a youth falls under the age provision for juvenile status, however, he or she may be handled as an adult under certain circumstances. For instance, if the nature of the crime is sufficiently violent and premeditated, the courts may handle the youth as they would an adult after transferring jurisdiction through petition. The violence by juveniles became so severe during the late 1980s and early 1990s that several states began using a reverse petition system for extremely violent juveniles. For example, in the early 1990s, Pennsylvania began automatically to place juveniles accused of violent crimes into adult criminal court regardless of age. It then became incumbent upon a youth under the age of 18 to petition into family court where he or she would be handled as a juvenile case.

JUVENILE GANGS

Gang activity is another problem related to juveniles that is confronting the police. Gangs have been found to be actively involved in the illegal drug industry, racketeering, and murder. Studies have shown that juvenile violence rates are highest in urban areas where teenage gangs thrive (Block 1990). Gang killings may result from warfare between rival groups over neighborhood territory or control of the local drug trade; drive by shootings where enemies are killed and innocent bystanders are sometimes caught in the crossfire. These killings account for thousands of deaths each year (Ewing 1990). For example, a study on street gangs in Chicago conducted by Carolyn and Richard Block (1993) indicated that between 1987 and 1990, street gangs in Chicago were responsible for more than 9,000 acts of violence including 288 homicides.

Traditionally, the police response to gangs was to seek ways of preventing intergang warfare. In some departments, this meant special gang units separate from or attached to the juvenile divisions developing. The activities of these special units was to collect intelligence information on various gangs and to intervene when possible intergang violence was imminent. This strategy was largely unsuccessful, and homicide by gang members continued to increase annually. In Los Angeles alone, for example, the Bloods and Crips (two notorious gangs) have been responsible for as many as one homicide each day (Spergel 1990).

A more recent strategy to controlling gang violence involves police treating gangs as organized criminal groups. This means using various techniques usually used on more traditional organized crime organizations. These techniques include the use of informants, promises of immunity and relocation of witnesses, electronic surveillance and long-term deep cover operations. Additionally, efforts have been undertaken to create special statutes to make prosecution easier (Moore and Kleiman 1989).

Unfortunately, most anti-gang enforcement activities have been less than successful (Klein and Maxson 1994). For the most part, gangs are not as highly organized as police once thought. In fact, they are fairly loosely organized groups with rapidly changing leadership. When police concentrate attention on gangs, it frequently causes these gangs to become more organized and cohesive—exactly the opposite of what the police would like.

Some police authorities advocate increased efforts in the area of police community relations. These efforts, it is suggested, should emphasize encouragement of civic and community leaders and local organizations to work against gangs. Local police agencies can assist by encouraging community residents to place stricter supervision over their children, increasing structured recreational and athletic activities for youths after school and on weekends, and providing educational motivation and support.

JUVENILES AND DRUGS

As already indicated, among the problems facing police in America today, is the problem of juvenile involvement with illegal drugs. Research demonstrates that most American youth experiment with drugs—either licit or illicit ones. Prevention programs, therefore, frequently operate from the standpoint that experimentation represents youthful ignorance about the drug's dangerous effects. However, research suggests that drug experimentation, and potentially regular use are actually the result of a number of complex social relationships with peers. Regardless of what one chooses to call these relationships, they can be easily understood as *peer pressures*. The social benefits from "being cool," or "being in," or "being one of the in crowd," certainly outweigh any negative health or delinquency consequences that may be associated with drug experimentation or regular use.

Recognizing that drug prevention programs really amount to resisting not just the drugs, but certain types of social or peer pressure, in 1983 the Los Angeles Police Department in cooperation with the Los Angeles Unified School District developed **Project DARE** (Drug Abuse Resistance Education). Believing that drug intervention programs that focus on junior and senior high aged youths came too late, DARE targeted elementary school aged children. Police officers involved in DARE must be specially trained and certified. They teach a school-based program designed to emphasize four focus areas:

1. To provide accurate information about tobacco, alcohol and other drugs.
2. To teach students decision-making skills.
3. Provide students with ideas and strategies to resist peer pressure.
4. Give students ideas for alternatives to drug use.

Today, DARE elementary curriculum is taught to over 5.5 million children each year. Over 16,000 police officers have been certified to teach DARE throughout the United States. Nationally, DARE has expenditures of approximately $700 million annually (Cauchon 1994). In addition, in many jurisdictions, DARE curriculum continues to be administered in junior high school classes as well as elementary ones (see Figure 5.6).

In the face of soaring rates of delinquency and juvenile misbehavior, the police have become an important resource for battling juvenile criminal involvement. Today, it is usual for police officers to have a considerable amount

Figure 5.6
DARE officers provide anti-drug information and alternative behaviors to elementary and junior high school aged juveniles.

of contact with a large number of young people in the community. The importance, of the juvenile police officer should not be underestimated.

SPECIAL WEAPONS AND TACTICS (SWAT) TEAMS

One final type of specialty unit that has become increasingly popular among many municipal police agencies is the Special Weapons and Tactics (SWAT) team (see Figure 5.7). These squads of specially trained officers are regarded both by citizens and police personnel as elite teams of highly trained and skilled law enforcement agents (Alpert and Dunham 1988).

Typically, **SWAT teams** are called to the scenes of ongoing, dangerous situations after more conventional strategies have failed, or when serious and imminent threats to peoples' lives exist (a sniper on a rooftop, a hostage held in a store by robbers, a husband wheeling a shotgun while keeping his family locked in their apartment, etc.). In some jurisdictions, these units simply are called *tactical units*.

In some jurisdictions other euphemisms or friendlier-sounding names are given to these units. For example, in San Jose, California, their tactical unit is known as MERGE (Mobile Emergency Response Group and Equipment). But, regardless of what one calls these units, they are designed to respond to critical incidents.

Members of these tactical teams have received firearms and strategic planning training, as well as training in climbing and rappelling, handling highjackings and other hostage situations, and riot control tactics. During the 1960s and

Figure 5.7
Special tactical teams are used by many departments during hostage situations or critical incidents.

1970s, SWAT teams emerged to assist regular patrol officers faced with increasingly angry crowds during the turbulent anti–Vietnam War era and racial unrest in many large cities.

By the 1980s, SWAT units had grown increasingly useful for, among other things, gaining access to "crack houses." Crack houses are usually well fortified residences where crack cocaine is sold. These homes frequently have steel reinforced doors and windows with only small gun slits for defensive purposes. In an effort to combat these fortress-like houses, several tactical teams nationally have converted the gun turret of a surplus military tank into a battering ram.

SUMMARY

Chapter 4 offered the general impression that uniformed officers were the thin blue line that separated order from disorder in society. This chapter sought to move a step further and offer an examination of the contributions made by a number of specialized police units. Chapter 5 began with a discussion of the investigative division and police detectives. Included in this discussion of detectives and their work was an attempt to debunk some of the fictional accounts of detection from books, films, and television. But, it was also the purpose of this chapter to demonstrate the impact that fictional accounts of detective work may hold for real detectives as suggested by the "Kojak Syndrome."

This chapter additionally illustrated a typical crime investigation sequence. In this instance, the intention was to indicate some of the ways investigators handle criminal cases.

The vice and narcotics squads and undercover work in general were discussed in light of their dangers and risks for corrupting officers. Along similar lines, internal affairs units were considered with regard to their purpose as watchdogs of the public trust as invested in police officers.

The juvenile detail was examined in the chapter in order to relate it to investigative work, drug investigations, and gang activity. It was suggested that crimes committed by juveniles are among the most costly and numerous in America today. Finally, this chapter examined tactical units, and the important role they play to protect both citizens in the community, and police officers.

REFERENCES

Alpert, Geoffrey P., and Roger G. Dunham. *Policing Urban America*. Prospect Heights, Ill.: Waveland, 1988.

Barker, Thomas, Ronald D. Hunter, and Jeffery P. Rush. *Police Systems and Practices*. Englewood Cliffs, N.J.: Prentice Hall Career and Technology, 1994.

Bent, Alan E., and Ralph A. Rossum. *Police, Criminal Justice, and the Community*. New York: Harper and Row, 1976.

Berg, Bruce L., and John Horgan. *Criminal Investigation*. 3d ed. Westonville, Oh.: Glencoe/McGraw Hill, 1998.

Block, Carolyn Rebecca. "Chicago Homicide from the Sixties to the Nineties: Have Patterns of Lethal Violence Changed?" Paper presented at the Annual Meeting of the American Society of Criminology, Baltimore, Md., November 1990.

Block, Carolyn Rebecca, and Richard Block. *Street Gang Crime in Chicago*. Washington, D.C.: National Institute of Justice, 1993.

Carter, David L. "Police Abuse of Authority." In *Police Deviance*. Thomas Barker and David L. Carter (eds.) Cincinnati, Oh.: Pilgrimage, 1986.

Cauchon, D. "Study Critical of D.A.R.E. Rejected." *U.S.A. Today,* October 4, 1994:2A.

Elliot, Delbert and David Huizinga. "Social Class and Delinquent Behavior in a National Youth Panel: 1976–1980." *Criminology,* 21(1983):149–177.

Ewing, Charles Patrick. *When Children Kill*. Lexington, Mass.: Lexington Books, 1990.

Gaines, Larry K., Victor E. Kappeler, and Joseph B. Vaughn. *Policing in America*. Cincinnati, Oh.: Anderson Publishing Co., 1997.

Girodo, Michael. "Entry and Re-entry Strain in Undercover Agents." In *Role Transitions*. Vernon L. Allen and Evert va de Vliert (eds.) New York: Plenum, 1984.

Goldstein, Herman. *Policing a Free Society*. Cambridge, Mass.: Ballinger, 1977.

Hicks, Randolph D. *Undercover Operations and Persuasion*. Springfield, Ill.: Thomas, 1973.

Huizinga, David, and Delbert Elliot. "Juvenile Offenders: Prevalence, Offender Incidence, and Arrests Rates by Race." *Crime and Delinquency,* 33(1987):206–223.

Klein, Malcolm, and Cheryl Maxson. "Gangs and Crack Cocaine Trafficking." In *Drugs and Crime: Evaluating Public Policy Initiatives*. D. Mackenzie and C. Uchida (eds.) Thousand Oaks, Calif.: Sage, 1994:42–60.

Klockars, Carl B. *The Idea of Police*. Beverly Hills, Calif.: Sage, 1985.

Kuykendall, Jack. "The Municipal Police Detective: An Historical Analysis." *Criminology,* 24(1986):175–201.

Linderman, Lawrence. "Undercover Angel." *Playboy,* July 1981:134–136, 142, 220–235, 244.

Marx, Gary T. "The New Undercover Police Work." *Urban Life,* 8(1980):399–446.

Marx, Gary T. "Who Really Gets Stung? Some Issues Raised by the New Police Undercover Work." In *Moral Issues in Police Work.* Fredrick A. Ellison and Michael Feldberg (eds.) Newark, N.J.: Rowmon and Allanheld, 1985.

Miller, George I. "Observations on Police Undercover Work." *Criminology,* 25, 1987:27–46.

Moore, Mark, and M. Kleiman. "The Police and Drugs." *Perspectives on Policing.* Washington, D.C.: NIJ and the Program in Criminal Justice Policy and Management, Harvard University, 1989.

Osterburg, James H., and Richard Ward. *Criminal Investigation: A Method for Reconstructing the Past.* 2d ed. Cincinnati, Oh.: Anderson Publishing Co., 1997.

President's Commission on Law Enforcement. *Task Force Report: The Police.* Washington, D.C.: GPO, 1967.

Redford, Emmette S. *Democracy in the Administrative State.* New York: Oxford, 1969.

Reppetto, Thomas A. "The Detective Task: State of the Art, Science, Craft?" In *The Ambivalent Force.* Abraham S. Blumberg and Elaine Niederhoffer (eds.) New York: Holt Rineholt and Winston, 1985.

Souryal, Sam. "The Kojak Syndrome: Meeting the Problem of Police Dissatisfaction Through Job Enrichment." *Police Chief,* June 1981:60–64.

Spergel, I. "Youth Gangs: Continuity and Change." In *Crime and Justice: A Review of Research.* M. Tonry and N. Morris (eds.) Chicago, Ill.: University of Chicago Press, 1990.

Territo, Leonard, and Robert L. Smith. "The Internal Affairs Unit: The Policeman's Friend or Foe?" In *Critical Issues in Law Enforcement.* Harry W. More, Jr. (ed.) Cincinnati, Oh.: Anderson Publishing Co., 1985.

U.S. Department of Justice, Bureau of Statistics. *Sourcebook of Criminal Justice Statistics.* Washington, D.C.: GPO, 1993.

U.S. Department of Justice, Bureau of Statistics. *Sourcebook of Criminal Justice Statistics.* Washington, D.C.: GPO, 1994.

U.S. Department of Justice, Bureau of Statistics. *Sourcebook of Criminal Justice Statistics.* Washington, D.C.: GPO, 1995.

Williams, Jay R., and L. Lynn Guess. "The Informant: A Narcotics Enforcement Dilemma." *Journal of Psychoactive Drugs,* 13(1981):23–245.

Wilson, James Q. *The Investigators.* New York: Basic, 1978.

QUESTIONS FOR REVIEW

Objective #1:

- Why do many police agencies have separate patrol and investigative units?

Objective #2:

- What type of investigations did early English detectives undertake?
- Why is there a cloak of romantic mystery surrounding American detectives?

Objective #3:

- List the four primary objectives associated with the investigative process.

Objective #4:

- Which type of detective division investigates homicides?
- When a bank is robbed, which detective division is likely to be called in?

Objective #5:

- Why can police task forces succeed in investigations, where the usual investigative techniques may fail?
- What may be described as a limitation of task forces?

Objective #6:

- What do detectives do when they initially receive a criminal case?

Objective #7:

- How might a detective classify a purse snatching? How come?
- How might a detective classify a residential burglary? How come?

Objective #8:

- What is meant by light cover operations?
- What is meant by deep cover?

Objective #9:

- How do the activities of the internal affairs division preserve police integrity?

Objective #10:

- Why do many juveniles ignore health risks, and experiment with drugs?

Objective #11:

- How many program focuses for DARE are discussed in this chapter?
- List the program focuses for DARE listed in this chapter.

Objective #12:

- What is the central purpose of SWAT teams in police departments today?

6 Criminal Investigation

CHAPTER OBJECTIVES

After reading this chapter you should be able to:

1. Explain the investigative process.
2. List the four primary objectives of officers involved in criminal investigations.
3. Differentiate inductive from deductive reasoning.
4. Describe the general nature of a preliminary investigations.
5. Outline various activities associated with conducting a preliminary investigation.
6. Define *modus operandi*.
7. Describe what is meant by a police complaint.
8. Consider the informational role of witnesses to crimes.
9. Express why good written and oral skills are important to police officers involved in criminal investigations.
10. Indicate the six questions used as a writing guideline in this chapter.

SCIENTIFIC DETECTION

The process of **criminal investigation** is a scientific and systematic series of activities designed to use various pieces of information and evidence to explain the events surrounding a crime, identify a suspect, and link that suspect to the crime. In this process, police and detectives use fingerprints and other evidence found at the scene of the crime, computers and other sophisticated technological and chemical advances, and logical reasoning to solve the crime.

In this brief chapter, it would be impossible to adequately or completely draw out the process of criminal investigation. In fact, entire texts have been written on the subject of criminal investigation (see Berg and Horgan 1998;

KEY TERMS	deductive reasoning	complaint
	preliminary investigation	complainant
criminal investigation	corpus delicti	cop speak
inductive reasoning	modus operandi	

Swanson, Chamelin, and Territo 1996; Bennett and Hess 1994; Osterburg and Ward 1992). Instead, this chapter will outline several of the major areas where patrol officers are likely to be involved in the process.

As indicated in Chapter 2, many police departments are large enough to have a separate detective bureau or division. In such agencies, criminal investigations are handled by these units. In smaller agencies, where patrol officers rotate into investigative positions or where there are no formal investigators, the patrol unit handles the investigations. In either case, criminal investigation is a systematic reasoning and thinking process. The primary objectives of an officer involved in a criminal investigation are to:

1. Establish that a crime has been committed.
2. Locate and identify information leading to the apprehension of a suspect.
3. Recover stolen property and evidence linking the suspect with the crime.
4. Assist the state in prosecuting a defendant once charged with the crime.

Investigators must sift through all available information and evidence, and make use of various laboratory techniques to determine which can be linked together to accomplish all of the above objectives. Let us consider an example of these objectives.

On June 12, 1994, Nicole Brown Simpson and her friend Ronald Goldman were found brutally murdered outside of Nicole's home in fashionable Brentwood, Los Angeles, California. Both had died from vicious wounds received from a knife or other sharp cutting instrument. The police arrived and sought to determine if a crime had been committed (objective #1). This first objective was a fairly simple task, given the numerous cuts and stabs, and types of wounds each victim had received. Next, the arriving officers began to secure the area and to seek information and evidence that would assist in identifying the killer (objective #2).

Although not immediately taken in to custody, Nicole Simpson's estranged husband Orenthal James Simpson—better known to sports fans as O. J.—became the prime suspect. The police investigative team deduced O. J. Simpson was their suspect using various pieces of evidence discovered at both the crime scene and his own home about two miles from Nicole's (objective #3). During the trial, evidence collected at the crime scene, field reports, and officer testimony were used in the prosecution of O. J. Simpson (objective #4).

Investigators must carefully examine the crime scene. As information and evidence are located, an investigator can begin to make reasoned connections between these and perhaps a suspect. These reasoned connections can be either inductive or deductive in nature.

INDUCTIVE REASONING

Inductive reasoning moves from particular and apparently separate observations, or pieces of information or evidence, and draws a general conclusion or inference. For example, suppose a victim is found lying dead on a bed, with a bottle of sleeping pills, and another of vodka on the bed table. The investigator could, using inductive reasoning, infer that the victim died as a result of suicide. However, this is what the investigator thinks may have happened to the victim not necessarily what did occur. When an autopsy and an investigation are undertaken, additional information and evidence may be illuminating. The autopsy may indicate that there were insufficient amounts of alcohol and sleeping pills in the body to kill the victim. It may also indicate that the victim died from suffocation. An investigation of the bathroom trash container may uncover a plastic bag with traces of the victim's saliva on the inside. Thus, the circumstances and evidence may indicate the victim was murdered, and the killer tried to make it look like a suicide.

DEDUCTIVE REASONING

Deductive reasoning is the process of reaching a conclusion and testing it against available particular facts. In other words, one moves from a general observation to a particular conclusion. For instance, suppose the investigator in our scenario, in addition to the general appearance of suicide drawn from the presence of the pills and vodka bottles, notices ligature-type bruising around the victim's neck. In this case, he or she may deduce that the victim has not committed suicide by himself. This particular conclusion might be drawn, since there is no sign of either a cord or ligature, or the plastic bag that will be discovered later during the investigation. Hence, someone had to move the missing item after the victim's death. Whether this was a case of assisted suicide, or murder, will still remain to be resolved.

It is important to note that whether investigators use inductive or deductive reasoning, any conclusions drawn are based on careful reasoning and systematic collection of information and evidence.

THE PRELIMINARY INVESTIGATION

The activities that take place at the scene of a crime immediately following its report to or discovery by police officers are all part of the **preliminary investigation**. In most cases, many of these activities are initially undertaken by members of the uniformed patrol unit of the police agency responding to the call for assistance (Berg and Horgan 1998).

Sometimes, when a patrol car is dispatched, the call requires immediate action in order to save a life or apprehend an offender. These may be calls for robberies in progress assaults, riots, domestic disturbances, or prowlers. Other types of crimes such as prostitution, gambling, auto thefts, bad checks, or various forms of fraud, may not require immediate response, and will be handled as time allows.

The patrol officers who answer a particular call typically are responsible for certain important aspects of the eventual investigation. For example, the officer who first arrives at the scene of a crime must immediately determine what has happened and whether anyone is injured. The officer must assess whether a criminal act has been committed and, if so, the type of crime. Should the initial facts prove unfounded or of a non-criminal nature, the matter can be closed with the first report. If, on the other hand, the officer's findings indicate that a criminal law violation has been committed, then proof of the *corpus delicti* part of the particular offense must be established. ***Corpus delicti*** is Latin for "body of the crime," and represents the basic elements of an offense specifically set forth in the criminal statutes. In other words, it is the facts constituting or proving the body of the crime, or the elements, which taken together, demonstrate the commission of a crime.

PROCEDURES IN A PRELIMINARY INVESTIGATION

Whenever a crime has been committed, the criminal has disturbed the surroundings in one way or another. It is the investigating officer's task to find the manner in which the crime scene has been altered. From clues found at the crime scene, the officer seeks to identify and apprehend the criminal. Disturbances to the crime scene can be caused by curious onlookers, "helpful citizens," the victim, persons attempting to conceal the crime, members of the media, and others.

Certain procedural steps must be taken by the officer at the scene to create a strong foundation from which to work. The nature and circumstances of the case will determine the order of investigative steps, but the following rules have general application to most types of criminal investigations:

1. *Be alert and waste no time in beginning the investigation.* It is important that the responding officer be ready to act or react to unexpected situations that might jeopardize his or her life.

2. *Assess the scene for emergency situations.* The officer should determine whether there are injured victims, witnesses, or suspects at the scene. It is important for officers to always be mindful that saving a human life comes before protecting private property. The officer should also determine if additional personnel, medical professionals, or specialty units (e.g., SWAT teams) may be required.

3. *Determine whether or not a crime has been committed and, if so, what type of crime it is.* Make a rapid visual inspection of the scene and the situation. The original information received by the dispatcher may have been incomplete, inaccurate, or distorted. What was called in as a domestic disturbance by neighbors may turn out to be an accidental injury while cutting up a salad in the kitchen. What was dispatched as a gang fight may actually be a minor argument between teens playing basketball. Conversely, a call about shoplifters in a small

grocery store may actually be an organized attempt to scare the proprietor into paying protection money.

4. *Instruct people involved in the situation at the crime scene, not to touch or disturb anything.* In crimes that will require a forensic investigation, it is important that nothing at the scene of the crime is altered, moved, or handled. Such molestation of items could damage or destroy potential sources of evidence.

5. *Separate, calm, and take statements from witnesses and victims.* The responding officer or a designee will need to take statements from each of the witnesses and victims. It is important to have each witness and victim offer his or her recollection of the events, without their comparing stories and details. Obtain a description, if possible, of any suspect(s).

6. *Isolate and preserve the crime scene.* Rope or tape off the area, post guards, and barricade the location if necessary. Exclude unauthorized people from the scene. Limit authorized personnel to those actually necessary to carry out required duties. Make certain the critical area remains under constant protection until processing is complete.

7. *Commence accurate chronological notes of the crime scene investigation.* Record the date, time of arrival, visibility, weather, lighting, identity of associate(s), their time(s) of arrival and activities at the scene, and any other conditions that may have bearing on the crime or its investigation.

8. *As soon as possible, contact dispatch to broadcast an initial description of the suspect(s).* The description of the suspect(s) should be obtained during the interviews with witnesses and victims. It should be as complete as time will allow.

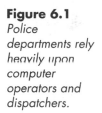

Figure 6.1
Police departments rely heavily upon computer operators and dispatchers.

But, it is important to recognize that time is of the essence. The sooner an initial broadcast is made, the greater the likelihood of an apprehension. There will be time later to transmit a secondary, more complete description of the suspect(s).

9. *Arrange for photographs, sketches, and in some departments, videotapes of the crime scene as is.* Naturally, this assumes that the crime was a fairly serious felony. In most major felony cases the use of cameras and sketches are a must. Courts are interested in knowing the condition of the scene at the time of the arrival of police, as well as the location of various relevant pieces of evidence.

10. *Plan the area to be searched in order to preclude the possibility of any section being overlooked.* Crime scene searches should be undertaken using a systematic procedure to insure that no physical evidence is missed. This may mean walking across the area with a single straight line of searchers. It may mean spiraling in from an outside corner, or dividing the area into smaller zones or quadrants.

11. *Place one person in charge of the search.* During the crime scene search, a single officer should be responsible for the coordination of all search efforts. Generally the ranking detective on the scene is in charge. Assignments should be given out by this officer; he or she will also be responsible for assuring that an irrefutable chain of custody of all evidence taken is maintained.

12. *Place an identification mark on all physical evidence found at the crime scene.* The officers involved in searching the scene should place their initials or some other identification mark on any item found. If items are too small or might be damaged, they should be placed into a sealed container, and an identification mark placed on that container.

13. *Create a detailed inventory of all things taken from the crime scene.* It is important that this inventory be detailed and comprehensive. Include the amount or quantity, make, size, model, type, serial number, color, and any other identifiable characteristics.

14. *Compile a complete, accurate report of the investigation.* The report should contain a description of all activities undertaken during the investigation. List all facts that can be substantiated through personal knowledge, physical evidence, or statements made by victim and witnesses.

In many departments, where a separate detective division operates around the clock, investigators may arrive soon after the uniformed patrol officers have secured the area. In these cases, it will be the detectives who will direct most of the activities undertaken at the crime scene. In smaller departments, the tasks described above are likely to be undertaken by patrol officers.

MODUS OPERANDI

Modus operandi is a Latin term for mode or method, of operation. In police work it describes the activities used by criminals in the preparation and commission of a crime. The earliest published material dealing with modus operandi appeared in 1913 by Major Sir Llewelyn W. Atcherley, then Chief Constable of the West Riding Constabulary, Yorkshire, England (*Modus Operandi and Crime Reporting Manual* 1964). August Vollmer, former Chief of Police in Berkeley, California, is credited with developing a modus operandi index during the early 1900s. Although various refinements have been made to this system, it has remained largely intact and is an effective tool for police investigations.

It was once believed that every criminal followed a particular M.O. and would rarely, if ever, change the type of crime they committed or their methods of committing it. Today it is generally believed that while many criminals seldom change their M.O.'s others intentionally do so. Such information aids in investigations. For example, in the 1970s it was a relatively simple matter for New York police officers to recognize the work of David Berkowitz, the "Son of Sam," also called the ".44-caliber killer." All of Berkowitz's victims were young females, with the single exception of a long-haired male whom police believe Berkowitz mistook for a woman. All were shot with the same type of weapon, at close range, and at night. Yet, it was not solely on the onus of his M.O. that Berkowitz was eventually captured. It actually resulted from an unpaid parking ticket he received on the night of one of his murders.

Modus operandi can also assist in more subtle ways. For instance, let's say a small pocket mall suffers a wave of burglaries, each being committed during the early morning hours of 2:00 A.M. to 4:00 A.M., and all involving entry through a ceiling or skylight. It could be inferred that the same individual(s) committed all of these burglaries. If safes are burglarized in each crime, and no other items are stolen or damaged, the likelihood that the same party or parties are committing all of these burglaries increases. Now let's say the burglaries suddenly stopped in this community, and similar methods of entry, commission time, and targets of theft occurred in a nearby pocket mall of stores. One could now infer that the burglar or burglars have moved on. The likelihood of these burglaries, in both communities, being unrelated is quite small.

Although the inferences drawn from M.O. are not certainties, they can greatly assist investigators in their pursuit of criminals. In reality, some criminals do commit several different types of crimes and may even intentionally change the type of crime they commit or their methods. Consequently, while a suspect's modus operandi may lead an investigator to him or her, it is important never to eliminate a suspect solely because his or her M.O. may have changed (Berg and Horgan 1998).

SOURCES OF INFORMATION ABOUT CRIMES

Police learn about crimes from a number of sources. In some cases, victims will contact police departments directly and bring a complaint against someone. In other situations, witnesses, friends of the victim, neighbors, or bystanders may contact the police and report a crime. But, these other people may not always be able to file a complaint. In the following section, complaints and complainants will be discussed.

COMPLAINTS AND COMPLAINANTS

At its basic level a **complaint** is a request for police action and/or assistance. Complaints may be filed by a victim of crime or by some others doing so on behalf of a victim of crime. For example, the parents of a juvenile who has been the victim of an assault may file a complaint with the police. The neighbor of a child, who believes this child is being neglected or abused, should notify the police, but may not be permitted to file a complaint. In this situation, it may be the police or a social service agent who actually will file a complaint.

In recent years, many jurisdictions have provided officers a means of filing a complaint in certain domestic violence situations. In such cases, the officer becomes the complainant. The **complainant**, then, is the individual seeking some action by the police. Complainants are especially important during the initial stages of a police investigation. Complainants will provide the basic information surrounding the crime. They may be able to describe a suspect and the various details, events, and circumstances leading up to and during commission of the crime.

Complainants come from all walks of life. They are generally persons who have a personal interest in the case and are invariably ready and willing to furnish all of the information required. Data provided by complainants to an officer may seem trivial at times. But officers must remember that when a complainant tells the police something, he or she is likely to perceive this information as very important. How an officer handles the filing of a complaint and the interviewing of the complainant may affect the public image of his or her agency, and indirectly, of the police in general.

Every complainant should be taken seriously until they demonstrate that their complaint has no basis in fact or reality. Thus, even mentally deficient and alcohol- or drug-impaired complainants may furnish valuable and necessary information. However, when it is determined that the complainant's statement holds no basis in fact, the interview should be terminated and appropriate referrals or action taken regarding the complainant.

For example, if an agitated, drug-addicted street person has just witnessed the stabbing of another street person, he may be the only source of information about this crime. In this case, the police will be interested in holding the complainant and talking with him after he has sobered up.

On the other hand, it may be an individual who claims that the silver foil helmet he is wearing protects him from the Alphacenturian visitors masquerading as store clerks in the supermarket. In this case, the police may consider referring the man to a psychiatric facility for an intake examination and evaluation. Whenever troubled or psychotic complainants become repeaters, their names should be placed in some kind of a file. In some departments this may mean an electronic file in the agency's computer system. In other agencies, this may mean a paper file created on three-by-five-inch cards and maintained in an index near the complaint desk or counter, or information desk. This will provide a reference for officers in the future to check the file when they suspect a complainant is mentally troubled.

INFORMATION FROM WITNESSES

Solutions to many cases are obtained simply by talking with people and obtaining information about what these people may have seen or heard. Knowledge about a victim's background, habits, associates, and enemies is also helpful. Descriptions of cars, objects, and suspects provide other pertinent data. During the preparation for an interview, the officer/interviewer should consider the kinds of questions a defense attorney might ask each witness at the trial. Questions by the defense are likely to challenge the credibility of the prosecution's witnesses. These may be directed at such factors as their physical or mental condition, emotional state, and their experience, education, and knowledge levels. Witnesses do not have to be advised of their constitutional rights; however, no threats or promises of any kind should be made to them to obtain statements.

Witnesses are often hastily questioned at the scene of a crime immediately after the reported violation. At these times, witnesses are questioned in order to obtain fast information that might immediately lead to the apprehension of the perpetrator. This includes information about the suspect that may be broadcast to other officers or agencies. Following these preliminary activities at the crime scene, the investigating officer will want to conduct more extensive interviews with witnesses and victims. (Interviewing is discussed in Chapter 7.)

REPORTS AND REPORT WRITING

Effective communication is an essential to police work and criminal investigation is no exception. If officers are to communicate effectively they need both solid oral and written skills. Their oratory skills should include clear annunciation, ordered and uncomplicated presentation and suppressed use of **cop speak** or police jargon (Berg and Horgan 1998).

Poor oral or written communication skills may limit an officer's ability to acquire necessary information to solve a crime. Furthermore, these weaknesses may interfere in the officer's ability to present testimony in court. Writing skills such as note-taking and report-writing are simply critical tools in the investigation of crimes. Among the more accurate images shown in many television and movie versions of police work is the large amounts of paperwork associated with police activities. Underplayed in these fictional accounts are the problems that can be caused by poorly written reports.

Police reports must contain accurate, concise, clear, and complete information. These reports serve as records of the investigative efforts, and the criminal incident. Police reports are official records of the activities of a government agency and are used in a variety of ways. Every investigation should be complimented by an accurate report. Good report-writing is so important that a number of police agencies in the United States have employed technical writers to instruct their officers on writing techniques.

Police reports provide information to fellow officers working on a case, to supervisors, and administrators who may need to determine resource allocations for a case, and to the prosecuting attorney who may try the case. Reports also may be used in court to outline a case to the jury, refresh an officer's memory about a case investigation, or clarify points offered in testimony. Investigative reports play key roles throughout the criminal justice process. Reports begin as notes taken during the preliminary investigation, continue to record events during the follow-up investigation, and emerge again during the trial and perhaps even during an appeal. Since reports can sometimes create the foundation for a prosecution, it is very important that investigators be mindful about how reports are produced.

In the recent double murder trial of O. J. Simpson, the defense initially sought to impugn the police investigation by showing that investigators had botched their reports. The defense team claimed that the investigators had failed to maintain an accurate chronology of events, that specific forms were not always filled out completely; and that in contradiction of department policy, plain sheets of note paper had been substituted for certain forms (Berg and Horgan 1998).

For many people these items may seem like very minor flaws: it is just such minor flaws, however, that can damage an entire prosecution. Reports communicate the thoughts of the officer who wrote them, description of events and actions, and frequently even motives. If there are errors in police reports, these may be interrupted by defense counsels, jurors, and the media as errors in facts or mistakes in procedures.

GUIDELINES FOR WRITING REPORTS

There are no magic wands that can be waved, or incantations uttered that will immediately make all patrol officers proficient writers. There are, however, a number of structural elements that should be included an any well-written police report. These elements are similar to those structured questions often taught in journalism and research methods classes. These elements involve an attempt to answer six basic questions: who, what, when, where, how, and why (Berg and Horgan 1998). Answering these questions ensures that, at minimum, these important pieces of information are included in all investigative reports.

THE ELEMENTS OF WHO, WHAT, WHERE, WHEN, HOW, AND WHY

Who?

Who were the people involved? When considering this issue, the officer should determine who were the principal people involved in the case? That is, who were the complainant, the victim and the witness(es)? Who are the suspects? The question of "who" also includes recording the names of the investigators involved and, for felonies, noting which officer(s) was first to arrive on and secured the crime scene?

What?

What has occurred? In effect, what was the crime? As well, what were the events that surrounded the criminal event? For purposes of the police report, as much detail as possible should be included concerning what has occurred. If there are victims, detail the circumstances of their injury or victimization. If property has been stolen, a detailed account and description of what objects are missing should be included. The report should reflect information such as the actions of suspects, what evidence has been located, what special knowledge, skill or expertise may have been necessary to commit the crime, what was reported that is not substantiated by the facts or physical evidence, and certainly, what further actions may be warranted by the police.

Where?

Where did the incident occur? When handling the question "where" it is important for the officer to obtain correct information about addresses including names of streets, type of building, house, apartment, store, etc. Identifying where in a given location a crime, or portion of a criminal event took place is likewise important.

When?

When did the incident occur? This inquiry considers such elements as when during the day the crime occurred, the day of the week, the month? Additionally, officers should consider when the crime was discovered? In short, officers should be concerned with any information regarding the times associated with the various aspects of the crime and the investigation.

How?

How was the event accomplished? Regarding this question, the officer should include all information that shows or suggests how the criminal event took place. This may include the modus operandi, as well as information about how the suspect(s) may have arrived on or fled the scene. If available, the report also should contain information regarding how the suspect may have obtained information necessary to commit the crime (e.g., lock combinations, alarm system details, floor plans, etc.).

Why?

Why has this crime occurred? Actually, this question speaks to the possible motives of the criminal. Motives usually are nothing more than deductions based upon experience, evidence, and available facts. Nonetheless, officers should not overlook the question of "why," or avoid considering apparent motives for the crime. The officer may consider such things as the following: Why did so much time elapse before the crime was reported? Why is a witness so anxious to point out a guilty party? Why was the victim so frightened to speak with the police? Why has this suspect committed the crime against this particular party, store, organization, and so forth? In some cases, such as robbery or burglary, the answer to some of the "why" questions may be apparent. It may be assumed that the crime was committed to obtain possessions, most likely for liquidation into cash. The actual use of that money, once obtained, as a motivating factor is secondary. In other words it doesn't mater if the indirect reason for the crime was to obtain money for wealth or for drugs.

However, it is always worthwhile to consider why a suspect chose one particular victim over another or one premises over some other premises. In certain kinds of crimes, such as traffic accidents there are seldom motives. On the other hand, in homicides the motives may take considerable investigation to uncover, and may not be immediately available to the initially arriving officer during his or her preliminary report. In any event, answers to the general question "why" are still important to pursue in investigative police reports.

Keeping these six elementary questions (who, what, when, where, how, and why) in mind when writing police reports provides a kind of skeleton on which the reporting officer can hang the facts of the case. Naturally, the order in which these questions are presented and answered will vary according to the facts of a case and the reporting officer's own writing style. In fact, in some cases, it may not be necessary to obtain answers to all six questions. It should be further understood that these questions should not be literally transcribed in one's report. Nowhere in the report does one actually need to write down "Where did the incident occur?" followed by the answer to that question. The questions are a guide, especially for inexperienced report writers to use in order to ensure that all necessary points of an investigative report are covered.

Frequently, a brief first paragraph that contains a synopsis of the entire report in the who, what, when, where, how, and why order serves as the completed report for 80 percent of misdemeanor crimes reported. For longer, more complicated reports, the elements of the crime should be organized and presented in a logical fashion. This sort of logical organizational style reduces the possibility of omitting or forgetting any essential elements of the report. It proves an especially effective strategy when creating a lengthy narrative report. A clearly written and organized introductory paragraph may save a report that is otherwise not well organized or well written.

In report writing, as in all other phases of police work, good judgment, a good working knowledge of procedures and department policy, and some practice are all required. As in all writing, the author should consider his or her *audience*. For police reports, the audience is likely to include other officers, supervisors, administrators, and prosecuting attorneys. Whenever possible, inexperienced report writers should obtain advice about improving their writing skills from more experienced writers.

SUMMARY

This chapter describes criminal investigation as a scientific and systematic consideration of information and evidence. The purpose of these activities is directed toward uncovering and explaining the events surrounding a crime, and to identify and link a suspect to the crime. The chapter details four primary objectives of officers involved in criminal investigation.

As well, Chapter 6 discusses inductive and deductive reasoning, and activities associated with the preliminary investigation. The chapter further indicates the importance of the initial responding officer being ready for the unexpected and for emergency situations at the scene of a crime.

In addition, this chapter explains what is meant by modus operandi and how this information may assist police to identify suspects and solve certain crimes. The chapter also considers various sources of information used by police to investigate crime. This discussion examines complaints and complainants and information provided by witnesses.

Finally, Chapter 6 explores the importance of police reports, and some guidelines for writing them.

REFERENCES

Bennett, Wayne W., and Karen M. Hess. *Criminal Investigation*. 4th ed. St. Paul, Minn.: West Publishing Co., 1994.

Berg, Bruce L., and John Horgan. *Criminal Investigation*. Westerville, Oh.: Glencoe Publishing Company, 1998.

Osterburg, James W., and Richard H. Ward. *Criminal Investigation*. Cincinnati, Oh.: Anderson Publishing Co., 1992.

State of California, Department of Justice, Division of Criminal Law and Enforcement, Bureau of Criminal Identification and Investigation. *Modus Operandi and Crime Reporting Manual*. Sacramento, 1964.

Swanson, Charles R., Neil C. Chamelin, and Leonard Territo. *Criminal Investigation*. 6th ed. New York: The McGraw-Hill Companies, Inc., 1996.

QUESTIONS FOR REVIEW

Objective #1:

- What is meant by criminal investigation?

Objective #2:

- What are the four primary objectives of an officer involved in a criminal investigation?

Objective #3:

- What is the basic definition for inductive reasoning?
- When an officer decides a homicide is drug-related, because drugs are found at the scene, is this a deduction or an induction?

Objective #4:

- At what point in an investigation does the preliminary investigation take place?
- Typically who is involved in a preliminary investigation?

Objective #5:

- What is the first task commonly associated with a preliminary investigation?
- Why are witnesses and victims separated before being questioned?

Objective #6:

- What is meant by modus operandi?

Objective #7:

- How might one define a police complaint?
- When can a police officer file a domestic violence complaint (become the complainant)?
- Why should complaints and information provided even by drug addicts be considered by the police?

Objective #8:

- What sort of information might a witness provide to a criminal investigation?

Objective #9:

- How might a poorly written police report effect a prosecution?
- Who generally reads police reports?

Objective #10:

- When writing police reports to whom does the question of "who" refer?
- What is the importance of including information on motives ("why") about a crime's commission?

7 Interviews and Interrogations

CHAPTER OBJECTIVES

After reading this chapter you should be able to:

1. Differentiate between police interviews and police interrogations.
2. Explain the importance of preparation before conducting an interview.
3. Detail the effects of rapport during interviews.
4. List different types of witnesses commonly interviewed by police.
5. Define the concept of custody.
6. Specify what the *Miranda* warnings are.
7. Describe how to arrange an interrogation.
8. Suggest different interrogation approaches.
9. Distinguish between confessions and admissions.
10. Consider how police may use the polygraph to encourage confessions.

GATHERING INFORMATION

During any police investigation, one of the most important elements will be obtaining information. Logic dictates that information derives largely from people. As a police officer, then, one is expected to be an effective communicator, and able to interview people. In law enforcement, there are chiefly two methods for obtaining information: interviewing and interrogation. **Interviews**, may be defined as conversations with a purpose, namely, to gather information (Berg 1998a, 1998b). Typically, this information is obtained from witnesses and victims of a crime. Interrogations, on the other hand, may be defined as another method for obtaining but from slightly different sources than interviews. **Interrogations**, gather information from suspects of crimes, their families, and their associates.

KEY TERMS	rapport	admission
	custody	polygraph
interviews	Miranda *warnings*	
interrogations	confession	

Figure 7.1
The primary way police gather information is by speaking with people.

Additionally, one might differentiate interviews from interrogations by the general demeanor of the officers conducting each type of information gathering method. In the case of interviews, an officer's attitude and demeanor should be open, friendly, and conversational. There is a tacit assumption that during interviews the officer is working with a willing respondent. During interrogations, however, there is a shift to a more adversarial attitude and demeanor and the assumption that one is working with someone who is not willingly volunteering information. Interrogations, by nature, tend to be more formal, antagonistic, challenging, and competitive than interviewing (Berg 1998b).

Legally, one can make an additional distinction. One does not usually interrogate someone who is not in custody (a *custodial interrogation*). Once someone is taken into custody, information police obtain from them cannot be used in court unless they have been advised of their Constitutional rights. Information gathered during the course of a police interview, and recorded in an officer's field notes is admissible in court.

Police officers ask many questions of a wide variety of different types of people. Often, patrol officers, must interview victims of crimes, informants, interested bystanders, witnesses, adults, children, the aged, men, women, professionals, blue- and pink-collar workers, the curious, the disinterested, the reluctant, and sometimes even a few suspects. The purpose of this chapter will be to familiarize the reader with various guidelines for interviewing, and several different types of possible subjects of interviews.

GENERAL GUIDELINES FOR INTERVIEWS

Human beings are a strange breed of gossiping, curious, and talkative folks. Once started, most people will talk about their successes, their failures, their plans, their dreams, and ironically, a near compulsion to talk about crimes or wrongs they may have committed. Psychological experts suggest that criminals, like anyone else, possess an intense desire to share experiences with others. This feeling causes many criminals to confess their crimes. Theodor Reik (1959) suggested that when an individual commits a crime he or she is haunted by the guilt feelings caused by violating personal ethical standards, and the terrible truth begs to be told through confession. Reik termed this a compulsion to confess. Reik's theory fits many police cases where officers have encountered people who virtually demand to be heard and then confess openly and completely to heinous and unspeakable crimes. After confessing, these criminals seem to be relieved, and ready to accept whatever punishment they receive.

The key to good interviewing is to deal with every interview as a separate situation, one potentially requiring a slightly different tack on the part of the interviewer. Not every witness can be interviewed in the same way. Nor for that matter does every suspect have a compulsion to confess. As a good interviewer or interrogator, one must develop a keen sense of judgment about how to handle certain interviews, to recognize that something you are doing is not working, and when to shift to various different strategies.

INTERVIEW PREPARATIONS

Officers need to make certain preparations prior to beginning any interview. Even when interviewing someone at a crime scene there are certain preparations that are possible. For example, victims and witnesses should be immediately separated to avoid their talking about the event and potentially contaminating each other's stories. Next, the officer should know who is being interviewed, and introduce him or herself to this person. The officer should also try to know how the person is involved in the case (e.g., victim, witness, suspect), where the events took place, and any other available information about the crime. The more information an officer has about the case and the people involved, the better the officer will be able to maintain control over the interview.

Officers conducting interviews should begin by establishing a rapport with the respondent. **Rapport** is a kind of relationship that develops between the officer and the individual being interviewed. In this relationship, the respondent feels that the officer has a kind of empathy for him or her, or identifies with his or her situation (Berg 1998b). Providing some simple human courtesies can go a long way towards establishing and maintaining rapport during an interview. When an interview occurs immediately following a crime, allow a few minutes to pass before beginning. This will provide the respondent some time to compose him or herself. It is also important to be mindful about the location of the interview. Large crowds, other family members, the media, certain weather conditions, noises, or any anxiety-producing situations may interfere with the officer's ability to establish rapport. People being interviewed should always be treated with respect, and be addressed by their proper name or title (Mr., Dr., Mrs., Ms., Sir, etc.). Unless permission is offered or obtained do not address someone being interviewed by their first name.

When conducting interviews, it is necessary to listen carefully to what is being said. In Western culture, it is common to interrupt speakers in order to interject one's own view or comment. During interviews it is very important not to interrupt the respondent by saying things like, "Oh, yeah, I know what you mean" or "Uh huh, that's just what I thought" or similar comments and well-intended interruptions. Such interruptions have a tendency to close down the respondent. While they may have been about to tell you all sorts of information, once you interrupt, this information may be lost. It is also critical that officers learn the difference between pauses for breath, for effect, for the respondent to recompose him or herself, and the completion of a statement. Good listening skills during interviews and interrogations will yield much more information than sloppy listening skills. The FBI even includes a segment on listening skills as part of their interview and interrogation training for new agents.

INTERVIEWING WITNESSES AND VICTIMS

Police solve crimes simply by talking with different people and obtaining information about what these people may have seen or heard. Little things such as something a suspect may have said, or the way he or she said it, descriptions of cars, objects, and the suspect all may provide pertinent data. When preparing to interview a witness or a victim an officer should consider the kinds of questions he or she will ask. The officer should also consider the types of questions a defense attorney might ask the witness or victim at trial. Defense attorneys are likely to ask questions that challenge the credibility of the prosecution's witnesses or the character and veracity of the victim. These may include addressing their physical condition or mental facilities; their emotional state, knowledge or experience, living conditions, occupation, and so forth. Unlike suspects, witnesses and victims do not have to be advised of their constitutional rights; however, officers should never make threats or promises of any sort to witnesses in order to obtain his or her cooperation.

Except in those situations where direct action is necessary following the commission of a crime and where time is of the essence, the investigating officer can be successful interviewing witnesses and victims by considering ten basic rules. These rules are shown in Box 7.1.

BOX 7.1 TEN BASIC RULES TO INTERVIEWING WITNESSES

1. *Plan ahead.* Make appointments at the convenience of the witness. When interviewing business and professional people, offer to conduct the interview at their workplace rather than in their homes or at the police station.
2. *Arrange for privacy.* Witnesses are more comfortable, relaxed, and willing to talk with the police when they know their conversations will not be overheard or interrupted. Whenever possible arrange a quiet and private location for the interview.
3. *Ideerly.* Before beginning any interview, be sure to politely introduce yourself to the witness. Remember, it is easier to speak with a person with a name than to an anonymous police officer.
4. *Assemble case facts in advance.* When preparing for an interview, an officer should gather all available information and facts about the case.
5. *Have direction.* Interviewing officers should know what they are after before beginning a line of questions. In other words, the officer should know the objective of the interview.
6. *Be timely.* Interviews should be conducted as soon as possible after the crime, while the information is still fresh in the witness' mind.
7. *Avoid interruptions.* Encourage the witness to do most of the talking. Do not paraphrase or reshape statements made by the witness. Avoid interrupting the witness or interjecting extraneous commentary.
8. *Be a good listener.* Use good listening skills and allow the witness to completely tell what happened before you begin another line of questions.
9. *Adjust your level of interviewing.* Officers conducting interviews should adjust their level of language, pace, and demeanor according to how the witness being interviewed reacts or indicates a need for changes.
10. *Demeanor and rapport.* Always remain polite, friendly, and courteous. These attributes are more likely to obtain rapport, details about events, and the truth, than a discourteous, unfriendly, offensive, or disinterested behaviors.

TYPES OF WITNESSES

Some witnesses will be forthcoming with responses, during interviews, while others may be evasive or hesitant to answer questions. In the following sections, different types of witnesses that police commonly encounter are discussed.[1]

Willing Witnesses

This type of witness is cooperative and often volunteers information about the event. Willing witnesses may even seek out the police in order to offer their information about a crime.

Eyewitnesses

Eyewitnesses are among the most important types of witnesses for police to locate. An eyewitness literally means "someone who has observed a crime or some portion of a crime." It is important when interviewing eyewitnesses that they be allowed to tell their story completely. After they have completed their version of events, the interviewing officer should ask various clarifying questions.

Unwilling or Reluctant Witnesses

There are a number of reasons some witnesses may be unwilling or reluctant to answer questions posed by the police. Resentment of police, stubbornness, fear, apathy, fugitive status themselves, or even a relationship with a suspect may influence people to be unwilling or reluctant witnesses.

Silent or Disinterested Witnesses

These individuals choose to offer no information or assistance to police. There are a number of reasons why people may take this position. For example, some people simply do not want to become involved in a police matter. Others may fear any contact with the police or the courts. There are even some people who simply delight in seeing the police fail.

Unreliable Witnesses

Witnesses of this sort may be mentally deficient, publicity seekers, children with vivid imaginations, people with personal axes to grind, or pathological liars. It is sometimes helpful, when interviewing this type of witness, to remind him or her that lying to the police has serious repercussions.

Frightened Witnesses

Such witnesses often fear that suspects or their associates will retaliate against them should they cooperate with police. Frightened witnesses genuinely believe that if they assist the authorities, people will lay in wait to harm them. It is necessary to reassure these types of witnesses that retaliation is extremely rare.

Biased Witnesses

These witnesses willingly, often anxiously, furnish information to the police. These statements, however, may be prejudiced toward the suspect or victim in some manner. A personal or romantic relationship between a witness and the suspect may tend to bias the witness' statement. In some cases, hostility towards a neighbor, an ex-friend, or even a relative who is now a suspect may be very strong.

Hostile Witnesses

These are people who do not intend to furnish any useful information to the police. They tend to be antagonistic and resentful that the police are even asking them questions. It is important for a police interviewer to try to determine the cause of the hostility if he or she expects to gain any useful information from these types of witnesses. Sometimes, appealing to civic responsibility, personal pride, religion, decency, family, or justice may be helpful.

Timid Witnesses

Sometimes, timidity results from a witness feeling self-conscious or shy when speaking with police officers. In other cases, timidness may arise from a lack of confidence or from poorly developed language skills. Police interviewers should be understanding and patient with timid witnesses.

Deceitful Witnesses

When police interviewers encounter what they believe may be a deceitful witness, it is important to check out this assumption. Allow them to tell their story without interruption. When they have finished, ask them to repeat various parts of their statement to see how consistent it remains. After they have made a number of apparently false and inconsistent statements, confront them with the falsehoods and inconsistencies, and remind them abut the serious consequences of offering perjured testimony, and lying to the police.

INTERROGATING SUSPECTS

Conducting interrogations is somewhat more difficult than interviewing a witness or a victim. The first difficulty is that suspects are not always immediately apprehended and available for questioning. Even after a suspect is located by the police, he or she may not be willing to make any statement, let alone an admission of guilt. Many people mistakenly believe that the main purpose of an interrogation to obtain a confession from the suspect. In reality, the main purpose of an interrogation is to gain from a suspect, or from people associated with the suspect, information about a criminal event.

As a matter or practice, an officer advises a suspect of his or her rights whenever the individual has been taken into custody. **Custody** may be defined as any detainment of an individual by a police officer where that individual feels he or she is not free to leave. One standard rule of thumb used by many street officers is to "Mirandize" whenever the conversation with a person moves from an interview to an interrogation—even if the individual has not yet officially been placed into custody.

Figure 7.2
Conducting interrogations is somewhat more difficult than interviewing a witness or a victim.

A suspect who has been taken into custody must be warned, at the time of their arrest, of their protection under the Fifth and Sixth Amendments. These include one's right to be safe from self-incrimination and the right to have the assistance of counsel in one's defense. Before the police begin an interrogation, they often again advise individual of his or her constitutional rights. These rights were established in the case of *Miranda v. Arizona* (1966).

Ernesto Miranda, a 25-year-old, mentally-impaired man, was arrested in Phoenix, Arizona. He was charged with kidnapping and rape. Miranda was arrested in his home and taken to a police station where he was identified by the victim. Following an intensive 2-hour interrogation, Miranda signed a written confession and was later convicted and sentenced to 20 to 30 years in prison. This conviction was affirmed in his appeal to the Arizona Supreme Court. Miranda continued his appeal, eventually having it heard by the U.S. Supreme Court. The appeal's argument rested heavily on the fact that Miranda had never been warned that any statement he made could be later used against him, and that he had been unaware of his right to have legal counsel present during interrogation.

The *Miranda* case was one of four similar cases heard simultaneously by the Supreme Court. Each case dealt with the legality of confessions obtained by the police from suspects held *incommunicado* and without benefit of full warnings about their constitutional rights. The other cases included *Vignera v. New York* (1966); *Westover v. United States* (1966); and *California v. Stewart* (1966).

The major constitutional issue decided by the court in all four cases was the admissibility of statements obtained from suspects questioned in custody (or otherwise denied freedom). Under the provisions of the Fifth Amendment, "no person . . . shall be compelled in any criminal case to be a witness against himself." Taken literally, this means that a defendant cannot be required to testify in court. It also means that a suspect cannot be physically or psychologically compelled to confess nor be made to confess under fear or duress. In the opinion of the high court, Miranda had given in to psychological pressures from the "third-degree method" employed by the police during his interrogation. Miranda's conviction was overturned and the court established specific procedural guidelines for the police to follow before attempting to interrogate suspects. These procedures are more commonly referred to as *Miranda* warnings.

Anyone who has seen television police shows during the past 30 years is familiar with the basics of the **Miranda warnings**. Although variations on the warnings exist in different jurisdictions, all share basic characteristics. Before being questioned while in custody you are entitled to be advised of certain rights:

1. You have the absolute right to remain silent. You do not have to make any statement or answer any questions. Anything you say will be taken down and can later be used against you in a court of law.
2. You have the right to speak with an attorney, to be represented by an attorney, and to have an attorney present during questioning.
3. If you cannot afford an attorney, but desire one during questioning, one will be provided by the court at no charge.
4. If you want to answer questions now, without an attorney present, you will still retain the right to stop answering questions at any time.

The *Miranda* decision has been hailed by many legal scholars as the most significant legal case of the twentieth century. For others, the *Miranda* case has been seen as a serious impediment to carrying out the task of maintaining justice in America.

Shortly after the *Miranda* decision in 1966, several studies sought to examine its impact on police officers' behavior. Among the most systematic studies were those conducted by Michael Ward and associates (1967) in New Haven, Connecticut; Pittsburgh, Pennsylvania; and Washington D.C.

Each study found that while *Miranda* warnings were routinely given to suspects in custody, there was little effect on the law enforcement process. Ward et al. (1967) suggest that *Miranda* warnings reduced the ability of police to obtain confessions during interrogation in relatively few cases. Often confessions occurred later during interrogation, once plea negotiations had begun. Thus, Ward et al. indicate that confessions during interrogation were largely unhampered by *Miranda*.

INTERROGATION PREPARATION

When preparing to conduct an interrogation, the officer should review all available information currently held regarding the case. This should include the criminal incident report, notes on the victim, witnesses, and any information already known about the suspect. Interrogations should never be conducted as impromptu events. Preparation before interrogation may seem time-consuming and somewhat unnecessary. Actually it should take only a few minutes and can result in excellent results. Even when only a little information is available, a good interrogator will go through this data before beginning.

ARRANGING INTERROGATIONS

Sometimes it is necessary to conduct an interrogation in the field. However, in most cases, it should be possible to put off an interrogation until the suspect can be taken to a location, such as the police station, where the interrogating officer has better control of the setting.

Usually, there are at least two officers present during the questioning of a suspect. When the suspect is female, at least one of these officers should also be female. Regardless of how many officers may be present during the interrogation, only one officer at a time should asked questions. After the original interrogator has exhausted a line of questions, other officers in the room, in turn, may ask questions regarding specific points. In some situations, a second or even a third officer may interject a pertinent question at appropriate times. This will work, as long as there is no apparent conflict in the control of the interrogation, and it does not persist to a confusing extent. One advantage to have more than a single officer present during an interrogation is that it safeguards against unfounded allegations of misconduct, unethical tactics, false charges, or other complaints that a suspect might make. In some larger departments, the entire interrogation is videotaped to provide a visual record that can easily safeguard against false allegations.

INTERROGATION APPROACHES

There are a wide variety of interrogation approaches. To some extent, the circumstances of a case and the particular characteristics of a suspect will direct the interrogating officer to a particular approach. There are, however, several broad, generally accepted approaches commonly used during interrogations. These include:

1. The logical approach
2. The emotional approach
3. Indirect or direct lines of inquiry
4. Deflating or inflating ego
5. Understating or overstating facts

THE LOGICAL APPROACH

The logical approach is based upon rational reasoning. One begins with the assumption that the suspect being interrogated is relatively reasonable and rational. If there is considerable evidence available, an officer using this approach will discuss these issues in fact with the suspect with the notion that once confronted with the overwhelming evidence, the suspect will likely discuss his or her involvement in the crime. When little evidence is at hand, this approach does not make false claims to the suspect. Such false claims are likely to be read as weakness—which they are—by a logical suspect. Instead, when little evidence is available, the logical approach dictates that the interrogating officer meticulously go over the suspect's statement, possible alibi, and explanations to assure consistency. When inaccurate or implausible statements or alibis are offered, the suspect should be challenged to indicate the flaws in his or her defense.

THE EMOTIONAL APPROACH

When using the emotional approach the interrogating officer is actually appealing to a suspect's underlying sense of decency, morality, spiritual belief or values, family orientations, pride, sense of fair play, or other similar reasons for coming clean and telling the truth.

The approach is sometimes more effective with first-time offenders who have committed a negligent criminal act or a law violation because of anger, passion, or other emotional motivation. Interrogating officers should be calm, patient, and offer understanding about how the suspect might have felt, or why the suspect might have committed the particular crime.

INDIRECT AND DIRECT LINE APPROACHES

The indirect line of inquiry is an attempt to draw out the truth without specifically addressing the literal facts or circumstances of the case. For example, rather than asking a suspect, "Did you hold up the bank on Maple Street today?" One might ask, "So, have you ever been walking on Maple Street?" This question might be followed with, "Have you ever been in the bank on the corner of Maple and Oak street?" Finally, the questioning officer might ask, "By the way, do you have any information about the bank robbery that took place at the bank on Maple and Oak earlier today?" It's a little like sneaking-up on the truth, rather than coming out immediately and asking. It is also a non-accusatory style of questioning. Indirect lines of inquiry are sometimes useful when the suspect seems shy or nervous about talking, but nonetheless desires to talk with the police.

Direct lines of inquiry work best with experienced criminals when considerable evidence or information about the crime already exists. In such cases, an officer can lay it our before the suspect and directly ask, "So, how about telling me how you got involved with this robbery?"

DEFLATING OR INFLATING EGO APPROACHES

Sometimes if an interrogating officer challenges a suspect's abilities, knowledge, skill, or intellectual capacity he or she will become sufficiently agitated to admit involvement in a crime. For instance, an officer might discuss the facts of a case where a suspect has broken into a home and bypassed the burglar alarm. While discussing the crime with the suspect, the officer might say, "Gee, I don't know why we are talking with you, its clear you're not smart enough to bypass an alarm system." Or, the officer might discuss a fairly skillful crime with a suspect, but describe its execution as amateurish, or carelessly undertaken.

Inflating a suspect's ego may also work to encourage him or her to admit involvement. For example, the officer might praise a suspect on the enormous skill it must have taken to accomplish some criminal activity; or the tremendous knowledge one must need to carry out some aspect of the crime. The purpose, then, of deflating or inflating a suspect's ego is to push and individual defending his criminal prowess, or into taking credit for some alleged criminal mastery.

UNDERSTATING OR OVERSTATING FACTS APPROACHES

In some situations, it is better to understate the nature or penalties of a crime. For example, if a suspect stands accused of a heinous and brutal rape and murder, he may be charged with a capital crime. In this case, with the death penalty potentially hanging over his head, the questioning officer might not want to use words such as murder and rape. Instead, when questioning the suspect, the officer might use euphemisms such as, "the incident," "the event," the "accident," or whatever understatement sounds less threatening and ominous to the suspect.

On the other hand, in some cases, the questioning officer might overstate the severity of a crime's penalty in order to arouse a response from the suspect. For example, in a case where the penalty might range from 3 to 7 years, the officer might fixate on the seven years when talking with the suspect. When two or more individuals are suspected as working together in a crime, the investigator might overstate information to one of them, in order to turn him or her against the other. For example, in a jewelry store burglary, where $100,000.00 in gems are stolen, the officer might ask one of the suspects what became of the $250,000.00 in stolen jewels. This might simply get a rise from the suspect who might correct the officer—thereby indirectly indicating knowledge about the facts in the case. Or, it may cause the suspect to think that his or her partner had been holding out on them, angering the suspect into a slip of the tongue.

CONFESSIONS AND ADMISSIONS

Television versions of police work frequently speak of confessions and admissions of guilt. But, what exactly do these terms mean? A **confession** can be defined as a voluntary statement in which a person admits to participating in or commission of some criminal act or law violation.

An admission is not synonymous with a confession. An **admission** is a statement by an individual that contains information or facts about a given crime, but falls short of a full statement of involvement. By themselves, admissions of involvement in a criminal activity may not necessarily incriminate a suspect. One might, for example, offer an admission statement about being with another suspect, just before the other suspect committed a rape, but this does not represent any actual involvement in the criminal act itself. In an admission, then, the individual is not confessing to a crime, only admitting knowledge of a certain fact pertaining to that crime.

THE POLYGRAPH

The **polygraph** is a mechanical device that permits the operator to assess deception associated with stress as manifested in physiological data. The word *polygraph* actually means *many writings*, and typically involves the simultaneous recording of respiration, blood pressure and heart rate, and even the skin's electrical resistance. Because the polygraph uses physiological data, it is unnecessary for a subject hooked to the machine to actually verbally respond to a question. The polygraph will measure and reflect the somatic and emotional effects from being asked the question. Simply being asked questions will cause endocrine system and the nervous system to gear up the body in order to protect it from impending stress or danger. This involves changes in blood volume, effecting changes in blood pressure and pulse rate, along with an increased respiration. In addition, there is also a change in skin resistance. Each of these changes is recorded by the polygraph (Hollien 1990).

Perhaps the most important aspect of a polygraph examination is the examiner and his or her ability to accurately make assessments and judgments about the charts created by the polygraph and the physical mannerisms of the subject. An examiner needs to check the various ink lines created by the machine that represent the various physiological rates as questions are asked of the subject. Two types of questions traditionally are asked during a polygraph examination. The first type of questions is called *control* questions. These will be used as a standard of truthfulness, against which the examiner can compare patterns created when the subject is asked questions about the crime or *investigative questions*. By comparing the patterns produced by both sorts of questions, the examiner judges whether deception is taking place (Bull 1988). Differences in the patterns are believed to be caused by stress and various somatic and emotional protective responses of the nervous system (Abrams 1991).

In one study of law enforcement agencies in the United States it was found that 93 percent of the responding agencies did use polygraphs in their investigations. Of these agencies, nearly three-quarters used sworn personnel as their polygraph examiners (1991). The question does arise, however, regarding how accurate polygraphs actually are—regardless of how frequently agencies use them in investigations.

Even among avid polygraph supporters, opinion differs regarding how reliable the polygraph is. Most agree that the machine can detect physiological changes in the subject at least 75 percent of the time, and perhaps as often as 85 percent or 90 percent of the time. However, most admit variation does occur. The variation is chiefly dependent on several distinct variables including the machine itself, the subject, and the operator or examiner. Because of these factors, while continuing to be very useful in police investigations, polygraph results are not yet accepted in courts as absolute evidence. However, at least 30 courts in the United States allow polygraph results into evidence if both parties agree, and 13 states do so even if opposing counsel objects (Rafky and Sussman 1985).

More often than not, polygraphs fail to detect lies, rather than to verify truths. As a result, they continue to prove beneficial for cross-checking and validating statements. One important reason to use the polygraph, then, is to eliminate suspects. Many police departments and prosecutors use the polygraph to see if a suspect is telling the truth and hence removed from the primary list of suspects. In fact, many criminals believe that polygraphs are *truth machines.* Consequently, polygraphs sometimes have a significant psychological effect on a suspect. Telling a suspect that you would like to verify his or her statement with a polygraph test sometimes leads to a confession. While the actual test is not admissible in court, the confession is.

It is important to note that witnesses, suspects, and victims cannot be compelled to undertake a polygraph test. Like admissions and confessions, subjects are protected against self-incrimination by the Fifth Amendment. Subjects can, however, voluntarily submit to a polygraph.

SUMMARY

Chapter 7 describes various strategies and approaches associated with police interviews and interrogations. The chapter begins by differentiating between interviews and interrogations. Next, the chapter discusses issues related to interview rapport. Following this section, the chapter details various types of witnesses, and strategies for officers to use when interviewing each. Next, the chapter examines the nature of custody, and how this relates to application of the *Miranda* warnings.

REFERENCES

Abrams, S. "The Directed Lie Control Question." *Polygraph,* 20(1)1991:26–32.

Berg, Bruce L. *Qualitative Research Methods for the Social Sciences.* 3rd ed. Boston: Allyn and Bacon, Inc., 1998a.

Berg, Bruce L., and John Horgan. *Criminal Investigation.* 3d ed. Westerville, Oh.: Glencoe/McGraw Hill, 1998b.

Bull, Ray H. "What is the Lie-Detection Test?" In *The Polygraph: Tests, Lies, Truth and Science,* Geoffrey Davies (ed.) Beverly Hills, Calif.: Sage Publications, 1988:1–10.

Hollien, Harry. *The Acoustics of Crime, the New Science of Forensic Phonetics.* New York: Plenum Press, 1990.

McCloud, Douglas G. "A Survey of Polygraph Utilization." *Law and Order,* September 1991: 123–124.

Rafky, D. M., and R.C. Sussman. "Polygraphic Reliability and Validity: Individual Components and Stress of Issues in Criminal Tests." *Journal of Police Science and Administration,* 13(4)1985:280–296.

Reik, Theodor. *The Compulsion to Confess: On the Analysis of Crime and Punishment.* New York: Farrar, Straus and Giroux, 1959.

Ward, Michael, Richard Ayres, David W. Hess, Mark Schantz, and Charles H. White-bread II. "Interrogations in New Haven: The Impact of Miranda." *Yale Law Journal,* 76(1967):1530–1538.

CASES CITED

California v. Stewart, 384 U.S. 436 (1966).
Miranda v. Arizona, 384 U.S. 436, 86 S.Ct. 1602, 16 L.Ed. 2d 694 (1966).
Vignera v. New York, 384 U.S. 436 (1966).
Westover v. United States, 384 U.S. 436 (1966).

NOTE

[1] Much of this section derives from Bruce L. Berg and John Horgan, *Criminal Investigation.* 3d ed. Westerville, Oh.: Glencoe/McGraw Hill, 1998:133–135.

REVIEW QUESTIONS

Objective #1:
- How might one define a police interview?
- What is a police interrogation?

Objective #2
- Why should an officer prepare before beginning an interview with a witness or victim?

Objective #3:
- How does good rapport between the interviewer and the respondent improve the quality of the resulting interview?

Objective #4:
- What makes a reluctant witness reluctant?
- What is meant by a biased witness?

Objective #5:

- What is meant by police custody?

Objective #6

- What is meant by protection from self-incrimination?
- When are the *Miranda* warnings usually given by the police?

Objective #7

- Why should distractions be kept to a minimum during an interrogation?
- How often should interruption be allowed during the course of an interrogation?

Objective #8

- What is meant by the logical approach in interrogations?
- What is the underlying objective in using a deflating ego approach during an interview?

Objective #9

- Would it be considered a confession, if an individual admitted to owning a .38-caliber pistol, when a .38-caliber pistol was used in a murder?
- How might you define an admission?

Objective #10:

- How do some police agencies use the polygraph to encourage confessions?

8 Constitutional Regulations and the Police: Life, Liberty, and the Pursuit of Criminals

CHAPTER OBJECTIVES

After reading this chapter you should be able to:

1. Describe the role of the American peace officer.
2. Distinguish between arrests with warrants and warrantless arrests.
3. Define probable cause.
4. Explain the exclusionary rule.
5. Discuss the good-faith exception to the exclusionary rule.
6. Consider the nature of inevitable discovery.
7. State the history of vehicle searches.
8. Detail the rules associated with stop and frisks.
9. Describe three techniques commonly used in field searches of suspects.
10. Explain voluntary searches.
11. Discuss open field doctrine.
12. Define inadvertent intrusions.

THE AMERICAN PEACE OFFICER AND CONSTITUTIONAL PROTECTIONS

In the preceding chapter, proper rules for interviewing and interrogation were discussed. This included a brief discussion on *Miranda* as a constitutional safeguard against self-incrimination. *Miranda*, however, is not the only protection afforded to citizens against the improper actions by police (or other agents of the government). This chapter will re-examine *Miranda*, in some detail, as well as a number of other constitutional limitations on police officers intended to ensure liberty and personal privacy for citizens.

KEY TERMS		
	immediate control	*frisk*
	incident to the arrest	*voluntary consent*
warrant of arrest	*exclusionary rule*	*open field doctrine*
probable cause	*good-faith exception*	*curtilage*
reasonable suspicion	*inevitable discovery*	*inadvertent intrusions*

Earlier chapters have alluded to the concept of law enforcement officers as peace officers. "Peace officer" is a generic term that includes people employed by some branch of the government and sworn to uphold the laws of the United States and state, county, or city that employs them. Peace officers are typically divided according to their level of governmental employer. Federal officers are employed by the federal government, whereas state officers are employed by a given state. The sheriff and his or her deputies are employed by the county or parish, and the municipal police are employed by the cities of incorporated counties (Stuckey 1986).

Customarily, one thinks of the principal task of peace officers as including maintenance of public order, deterring criminal activity, and apprehending those who violate the law. But the modern American peace officer has an expanded role in society. Peace officers must actively work with communities not only to deter crime, but also to relax fear of crime among community residents (see Chapter 4). Peace officers serve as extensions of public welfare and public health agencies by diverting juveniles, alcoholics, some homeless people, and drug addicts from deeper penetration of the judicial system. In many police agencies, peace officers have moved into areas of criminal pattern research and planning. Peace officers assure that emergency conditions such as floods, hurricanes, riots, or other natural disasters do not result in civil disorder, looting, or other socially dysfunctional activity.

In many ways the American peace officer is the most visible component of the criminal justice system. He or she is charged with the responsibility of preserving the liberty of Americans, often at considerable personal risk both physically and emotionally. It is interesting to note that much of what we think of today as justice originated in the writings of Plato. This is somewhat ironic because in Plato's original formulation, he located guardians (enforcers of the state's laws) near the top of his ideal society's social structure.

In fact, Plato maintained that rulers could only be successful after they served as guardians. As guardians, potential rulers were understood to gain wisdom, valor, courage, and temperance—the four cardinal virtues of Plato's ideal society. The irony, of course, is that police officers today find themselves at the lower end of the social structure of society, but aspire to preserve justice through only slight variations on the original four cardinal virtues.

It is important to recognize that temperance or moderation that affect control over police actions and behaviors is embodied in both the U.S. Constitution and Supreme Court decisions. Yet, controversy has long accompanied various Supreme Court decisions that affect police practice. On the one hand, there are outcries that certain decisions have handcuffed the police and provided an officially sanctioned way for felons to be set loose on society. On the other hand, many maintain that Supreme Court reviews of legal cases assure that liberty is maintained for citizens and integrity upheld for the law enforcement community.

It would be both naive and incorrect to insist that criminals have never been released on some technical error made by either the judicial system or the police. But it is similarly inaccurate to elevate mistakes made in particular situations to the level of institutionalized permission to commit crime. Furthermore, it is critical to keep in mind the fact that whenever constitutional rights are maintained, all in society benefit. In the United States, the encroachment on the rights of individuals by the police or other governmental agencies historically has not been tolerated.

Unfortunately, high-profile cases—such as the assault on Rodney King by police officers after stopping him for an alleged speeding violation—gain widespread and continuing media coverage. Stories such as King's suggest abuse of police authority and police brutality that is not representative of the vast majority of officers in the nation (see Box 8.1). For example, one recent research study conducted in Washington state reported that only 4 percent of all brutality charges against the police were substantiated. Most of the charges, it turned out, had to do with verbal comments and alleged insults (Dugan and Breda 1991). More recently, in a special report prepared at the request of the Los Angeles County Board of Supervisors, it was reported that misconduct cases in the Los Angeles Sheriff's Department were down by 30 percent in 1994, 25 percent in 1995, and 23 percent in 1996, indicating a steady downward trend (Seventh Semiannual Report 1997).

BOX 8.1   RODNEY KING STORY

It was a cool, clear evening in late spring of 1991. Rodney King a 25-year-old African-American man was driving his car. Suddenly, a police officer began to pursue. According to police reports, rather than pulling over, King sped up, and attempted to elude the police. Officers claimed to have clocked King at 115 miles per hour—although the 1988 Hyundai's manufacturer later reported that the vehicle is not capable of speed beyond 100 miles per hour.

Eventually, King's car was stopped, and King was pulled from the vehicle. Officers reported that King acted in a wild and non-compliant manner, suggesting he may have been on some sort of drugs. In their effort to subdue King, he was twice shocked by electronic stun guns. The stunning had little effect, further increasing officer's suspicions that he may have been high on drugs. Officers continued to attempt to arrest King, who they maintained persisted in resisting and refusing to comply with officer's orders. In all, King was struck 52 times with nightsticks; kicked in the face, stomach, and back; and was left with 11 separate skull fractures, missing teeth, a crushed neck bone, and a broken ankle. A witness told reporters that she heard King begging officers to stop beating him, but they continued their assault (Time 1991).

The entire episode was captured on an amateur video, taped from a nearby balcony. The 2 minutes of videotape was repeatedly shown over national news programs, creating a national furor over police brutality. The notoriety led the Justice Department to call for a review of law enforcement violence across the country. Four Los Angeles police officers were indicted for beating Rodney King. In 1992, all four were found not guilty after a jury trial. The verdict touched off a riot in Los Angeles that raged for days, and resulted in deaths, injuries, and millions of dollars in property damages. In a later federal case for civil liberties violations, the accused officers were found guilty of having violated Rodney King's civil rights.

Figure 8.1
The courts assure that the police do not infringe on the constitutional rights of citizens.

The Constitution of the United States is designed to protect the rights and interests of the American people—especially under the provisions set forth in the Bill of Rights. Five amendments principally deal with civil liberties relevant to police and policing. These include the First, Fourth, Fifth, Sixth, and Four-

---

BOX 8.2   SELECTED AMENDMENTS TO THE U.S. CONSTITUTION

AMENDMENT 1
*[The Freedoms of Religion, Speech, and Press; Right to Assembly]

Congress shall make no law respecting an establishment of religion, or prohibiting the free exercise thereof; or abridging the freedom of speech, or of the press; or the right of the people peaceably to assemble, and to petition the government for redress of grievance.

AMENDMENT 4
*[Limiting the Right of Search]

The right of the people to be secure in their persons, houses, papers, and effects, against unreasonable searches and seizures, shall not be violated, and no Warrants shall be issued but

upon probable cause, supported by Oath or affirmation, and particularly describing the place to be searched, and the person or things to be seized.

AMENDMENT 5
*[Guarantee of a Trial by Jury; Protection from Double Jeopardy and Self Incrimination; Private Property to be Respected]

No person shall be held to answer for a capital, or otherwise infamous crime, unless on a presentment or indictment of a Grand Jury, except in cases arising in the land or naval forces, or in the Militia, when in actual service in time of war or public danger; nor shall any person be subject for the same offense to be twice put in jeopardy

Figure 8.2
Officers must prepare affidavits requesting arrest and search warrants.

teenth Amendments. The full content of each is shown in Box 8.2. From these amendments and the various Supreme Court decisions that modify and affect their application, guidelines for the performance of law enforcement officers and the law are established.

of life or limb; nor shall be compelled in any criminal case to be a witness against himself, nor be deprived of life, liberty, or property, without due process of law; nor shall private property be taken for public use, without just compensation.

AMENDMENT 6
*[Rights of the Accused]

In all criminal prosecutions, the accused shall enjoy the right to a speedy and public trial, by an impartial jury of the State and district wherein the crime shall have been committed, which districts shall have been previously ascertained by law, and to be informed of the nature and cause of the accusations; to be confronted with the witnesses against him; to have compulsory process for obtaining witnesses in his favor, and to have the Assistance of Counsel for his defence.

AMENDMENT 14
*[Federal and State Citizenship Defined]

Section 1. All persons born or naturalized in the United States, and subject to the jurisdiction thereof, are citizens of the United States and of the State wherein they reside. No State shall make or enforce any law which shall abridge the privileges or immunities of citizens of the United States; nor shall any State deprive any person of life, liberty, or property, without due process of law; nor deny to any person within its jurisdiction the equal protection of the laws.

*Explanations of amendments; subhead in brackets not included in the Constitution.

ARRESTS BY POLICE

The specific laws for arrest by police officers may vary slightly from one state to another. However, there are broad guidelines that allow us to discuss arrest procedures in general. First, officers must make lawful detentions if courts are to regard these arrests and any accumulated evidence as legitimate. Second, police officers have the ability to make two different types of valid arrests: with and without an arrest warrant.

A **warrant of arrest** is a document ordering a police officer to arrest the person named and to deliver that person to the court of magistrate issuing the document. The warrant of arrest is deemed executed once the named person is taken into custody.

On some occasions, the actual identity of an offending party may not be known by the police. Although investigations may have secured relevant evidence and information to identify a suspect, his or her real identity may be unknown. Under such circumstances, and provided the information and evidence is sufficiently compelling, some courts will permit a complaint to be filed under the name of John or Jane Doe or, for record-keeping purposes, any pseudonym selected by the police agency.

In most jurisdictions a warrant remains valid until successfully executed or withdrawn by the issuing court. In some states the warrant may be executed only in the county of the court issuing the warrant. In most states, however, the warrant may be executed through out the issuing court's state.

Arrest with a Warrant

When an arrest with a warrant occurs, it means that a complaint has been duly filed and placed before a magistrate or judge. If after reading the complaint the magistrate or judge finds probable cause, and arrest warrant will be issued. In most situations an arrest warrant is lawful even when the arresting officer does not have the warrant in possession at the time of the arrest. However, upon request, warrants must be shown to the arrested person as soon as possible. A sample arrest warrant is shown in Box 8.3.

Arrest without a Warrant

In contrast, arrest without a warrant may occur under certain conditions. For example, a lawful arrest can be made without a warrant whenever an officer has probable cause to believe that a person has committed a felony. In such an instance involving a felony, it is immaterial whether the officer was actually present during the commission or attempted commission of the crime. Police officers may also make arrests without warrants when a crime (either a felony or a misdemeanor) has actually been committed or attempted in the officer's presence. Historically, the authority to make such warrantless arrests derives

BOX 8.3   EXAMPLE OF AN ARREST WARRANT

The People of the State [Any State] vs.

[Arrestee's Name] Defendant(s)

CASE NUMBER
0000000

ARREST WARRANT

In the County of _____ [Any County] _____
The people of the State of _____ [Any State] _____ to any police officer of this State:

A complaint on oath has this day been laid before me that the crime of [designation of crime] was committed and accuses [the arrestee's name] thereof. You are therefore ordered to arrest the accused forthwith and bring him before a judge of this court.

ENDORSEMENT FOR NIGHT SERVICE

For good cause shown to this court, I direct that this warrent be served at any hour of the day or night.

Dated at_____ (place) this _____ day of _____, 19_____

[Signature of judge or magistrate]

from the English common law tradition. In the case of common law, peace officers were permitted to make an arrest if they had probable cause to believe a felony had been committed. In most jurisdictions today, peace officers are authorized to make warrantless arrests on the basis of court decisions and/or state statutes. How certain court decisions arose and affect today's policing practices will be discussed next. Among the court decisions, perhaps the most heralded, yet controversial, is the right not to incriminate oneself provided by *Miranda*. The specific case of *Miranda* was previously discussed in Chapter 7. During the past several decades, however, the *Miranda* decision has been the subject of considerable public and legal attention. Originally, many of the critics of the *Miranda* decision felt that it placed a stranglehold on the ability of police to gain information. However, the trend of restricting information gained prior to apprising suspects fully of their *Miranda* rights began to shift in 1980 with the case of *Rhode Island v. Innis*.

The *Innis* case bears an eerie similarity to another case (*Nix v. Williams* 1984) which occurred in 1984 involving Robert Anthony Williams and the kidnapping and murder of Pamela Powers (the facts of this case are detailed later). In the *Innis* case, a Providence, Rhode Island, cab driver was found slain. He had been killed by a shotgun blast to the back of his head. Police investigations soon resulted in the arrest of Thomas Innis. While in custody, Innis was read his *Miranda* warnings four times. Eventually, Innis asked to speak to an attorney. Police immediately discontinued their interrogation. But, as officers were driving Innis to an appointment with counsel, they passed a school for handicapped children. One of the officers in the cruiser remarked, "God forbid one of them (referring to the children) find a weapon with shells and they might hurt themselves." Innis was noticeably moved by the comment, and immediately instructed the officers to turn the car around, and led them to where he had hidden his weapon.

When the U.S. Supreme Court reviewed the *Innis* case, it ruled 6–3 that no violation of the suspect's rights had transpired. Innis, at the time of his disclosure, was not in the process of interrogation within the meaning of *Miranda*.

Not long after Innis (1980), several other cases emerged that seemed to loosen the constraints imposed by the *Miranda* doctrine. In *California v. Prysock* (1981), for example, Randall Prysock, a youthful killer, was read his *Miranda* rights, and he informed police Sergeant Byrd that he did not want to talk to him. Later that day, in the presence of Prysock's parents, Sergeant Byrd carefully went through each of Prysock's rights under *Miranda* and elaborated on each in order to assure the juvenile understood the meaning of his rights. When asked, "Now, having all these legal rights in mind, do you wish to talk to me at this time?" young Prysock responded, "Yes."

The exchange was tape-recorded, but was briefly interrupted at this point by Prysock's mother. She asked if her son would be permitted an attorney at a later time, even if he made a statement now. Sergeant Byrd assured her he could and that he was entitled to have one present now, if he desired, as well.

Prysock's statement, made after the lengthy explanation of his rights, was used against him during his murder trial. When the Supreme Court reviewed the case, it held that the *Miranda* warnings were valid even when not given word for word, as decreed by Chief Justice Earl Warren in *Miranda v. Arizona* (1966).

In 1984, another exception to the rigid rules of *Miranda* arose. In *New York v. Quarles* (1984), the Court voted 5–4 to create an exception when "overriding consideration of public safety" are at stake. The *Quarles* case involved a rape suspect, armed with a .38-caliber revolver, running into a crowded supermarket as he fled the scene of an assault. A patrol officer named Kraft, notified by the victim of the attack, pursued the suspect into the market. When Officer Kraft cornered the suspect, he noticed the man's shoulder holster was empty. Without reading him his rights, the officer shouted, "Where's the gun?" The suspect pointed toward where the gun lay. The recovered weapon was subsequently used as evidence in the man's trial. The Court's decision was to allow the gun's admission as evidence and to uphold the convictions of Quarles. The Court stated:

> We conclude that the need for answers to questions in a situation posing threat to the public safety outweighs the need for the prophylactic rule protecting the Fifth Amendment's privilege against self-incrimination.

A number of other cases followed during the decade, each slightly loosening the rigidity many police associated with *Miranda*. For example, in *Colorado v. Connelly* (1986) the Court held that if a suspect waives his or her rights and voluntarily makes statements while irrational—as in believing he or she is "following the advice of God"—these statements are admissible. Furthermore, the Court ruled that when a suspect waives *Miranda* rights—believing the interrogation is to focus on some minor criminal involvement, but the questions shift to a more serious crime—any confession is valid, provided that there has been no misrepresentation or deception used by the police (*Colorado v. Spring* 1987). In the case of *Connecticut v. Barrett* (1987) the Court ruled that when a suspect invokes his or her rights and refuses to make written statements, but later voluntarily offers oral statements to police, the statements are admissible. The Court held that defendants have the right to choose between speech and silence. Finally, reinforcing the Court's *Prysock* ruling in *Duckworth v. Egan* (1989), the Court held that a suspect need not be given his or her *Miranda* warnings in exactly the wording outlined in *Miranda v. Arizona*. The important element in any rendering of *Miranda* warnings is that the information reasonably conveys the suspect's rights.

PROBABLE CAUSE: SEARCHES, SEIZURES, AND ARRESTS

It will become apparent that the issue of reasonable or probable cause is relevant to both searches and lawful arrests. Thus, the question of what constitutes probable cause for searches and arrests warrants requires some consideration. Courts have generally held that **probable cause**, also characterized as **reasonable suspicion**, is evident if a person of average intelligence and foresight (ordinary prudence) would be led to believe that a crime has been committed. In other words, probable cause may exist even when there may be some doubt. But, for the arrest to be lawful, more than mere suspicion of a crime being committed is necessary (Stuckey 1986; Ferdico 1996). The next question that naturally arises is, "How is probable cause established?" Occasionally, officers making routine traffic stops will sometimes notice contraband in plain sight. In most instances, this observation will provide sufficient probable cause for a summary arrest.

Similarly, the tradition of warrantless searches concurrent with an arrest are usually permissible. In other words, if a lawful arrest of a fleeing bank robbery suspect is made at a bus terminal and the suspect is carrying a suitcase, a search of the suitcase would be proper. But, as one might suspect, there are certain restrictions. First, the arresting officer(s) must make the search of the offender's person immediately upon arrest; and second, the search of the area beyond the offender's person is limited to the area within his or her immediate control. **Immediate control** typically has been given to mean approximately within one arm's reach. The reasoning behind this limitation is to restrict the search to a location where the felon might reasonably have concealed a weapon or contraband immediately prior to arrest.

The restriction placed on the scope of a search that is **incident to the arrest** (occurs immediately after the arrest) can be traced to the Supreme Court case of *Chimel v. California* (1969). Before this case, police officers had been permitted to search all areas in the immediate vicinity of the arrested party. Following the *Chimel* case, officers were not permitted to search an entire house without a duly authorized search warrant (see Box 8.4). In short, the scope of the search is limited to approximately the length of the physical extension of an arm's length from the suspect.

An exception to *Chimel* is "protective sweeps." In *Maryland v. Buie* (1990), the Court held that when a warrantless arrest takes place in a suspect's home, officers may search "all parts of the premises" if they have reason to believe that another potentially dangerous person may be hiding in the areas to be searched (Bohm and Haley 1997). It may additionally be lawful to conduct a more extensive search incident to an arrest when it is possible that someone else on the premises might otherwise destroy evidence.

The next question to ask is "what about searches without warrants that may occur when not incident to an arrest?" Does the average individual have the right to expect the privacy of home, for example, to be maintained under the Fourth Amendment? Can one refuse entry to duly sworn officers who want to come in an look around, but who do not have a warrant in their possession? These concerns were addressed in the case of *Mapp v. Ohio* (1961) and have established a doctrine commonly referred to as the "exclusionary rule".

THE EXCLUSIONARY RULE

Perhaps the major way limitations upon searches and seizures have come about has been the exclusionary rule. The exclusionary rule is founded in the Fourth Amendment of the Constitution. It is intended to assure that individuals are protected from illegal searches and seizures. In practical terms, the **exclusionary rule** means that police must follow certain lawful guidelines when searching for and seizing material as evidence.

Under this rule, evidence illegally obtained is excluded from the judicial process. Typically, this results when a motion to suppress the illegally seized evidence is granted by the court. In making such determinations, the courts consider the facts surrounding the identification, location, or collection of evidence and whether the seizing of this evidence was lawful. Related to this are concerns about probable cause in cases of frisks (discussed later) and searches. The exclusionary rule long has been viewed as controversial since it is applied to a case *post factum* (after the fact). In other words, when the motion to suppress is requested, the justice system has already identified the suspect and located evidence that incriminates this suspect. When a judge grants a suppression motion, the illegally obtained materials may not be used against the defendant. Thus, without sufficient evidence, an apparently guilty murderer-rapist may walk out of a courtroom free, simply because the very evidence that indicates his guilt—sometimes conclusively—cannot be used against him. In fact, it can be suggested that the public outrage from such an instance has given rise to a danger-

BOX 8.4   A COPY OF A SEARCH WARRANT

Search Warrant

TYPE - OR PRESS FIRMLY WITH BALL POINT PEN

REORDER FROM **Garlits** INDUSTRIES, INC.   30 N. PENNSYLVANIA AVE., MORRISVILLE, PA 19067-1110 (215) 736-2660

Commonwealth of Pennsylvania

COUNTY OF _____

SS: **APPLICATION FOR**
SEARCH WARRANT
AND AFFIDAVIT

WARRANT CONTROL No.

J 09993

DATE OF APPLICATION

INVENTORY No.

(Name of Affiant)   (Police Department or address of private Affiant)   (Phone No.)

being duly sworn (or affirmed) before me according to law, deposes and says that there is probable cause to believe that certain property is evidence of or the fruit of a crime or is contraband or is unlawfully possessed or is otherwise subject to seizure, and is located at particular premises or in the possession of particular person as described below.

IDENTIFY ITEMS TO BE SEARCHED FOR AND SEIZED (be as specific as possible):

SPECIFIC DESCRIPTION OF PREMISES AND/OR PERSONS TO BE SEARCHED (Street and No., Apt. No., Vehicle, Safe Deposit Box, etc.):

NAME OF OWNER, OCCUPANT OR POSSESSOR OF SAID PREMISES TO BE SEARCHED (If proper name is unknown, give alias and/or description):

VIOLATION OF (Describe conduct or specify statute):

DATE OF VIOLATION

PROBABLE CAUSE BELIEF IS BASED ON THE FOLLOWING FACTS AND CIRCUMSTANCES (See special instructions below):

ATTACH ADDITIONAL PAPER (5) COPIES IF NECESSARY   ☐ CHECK HERE IF ADDITIONAL PAPER IS USED.

PLEASE READ AND FOLLOW THESE INSTRUCTIONS CAREFULLY

1. If information was obtained from another person, e.g., an informant, a private citizen, or a fellow law officer, state specifically what information was received, and how and when such information was obtained. State also the factual basis for believing such other person to be reliable.
2. If surveillance was made, state what information was obtained by such surveillance, by whom it was obtained, and state date, time and place of such surveillance.
3. State other pertinent facts within personal knowledge of affiant.
4. If "nighttime" search is requested (i.e., 10 P.M. to 6 A.M.) state additional reasonable cause for seeking permission to search in nighttime.
5. State reasons for believing that the items are located at the premises and/or on the person specified above.
6. State reasons for believing that the items are subject to seizure.
7. State any additional information considered pertinent to justify this application.

Signature of Affiant   Address of Private Affiant   Badge No.   District/Unit

Sworn to and subscribed before me this _____ day of _____ 19___ . Office
Address

_____ (SEAL) Mag. Dist. No. _____

Signature of Issuing Authority

AOPC 410-80

ORIGINAL APPLICATION

BOX 8.4 *CONTINUED*

TO LAW ENFORCEMENT OFFICER: WHEREAS, facts have been sworn to or affirmed before me by written affidavit(s) attached hereto from which I have found probable cause, I do authorize you to search the premises or person (described on the reverse side), and to seize, secure, inventory, and make return according to the Pennsylvania Rules of Criminal Procedure, the items described on the reverse side.

* ☐ This Warrant should be served as soon as practicable but in no event later

than _____ ☐ A.M. ☐ P.M. _____ , 19 _____

and shall be served only during daytime hours of 6 A.M. to 10 P.M.

Issued under my hand this _____ day of _____ ,

19 ____ , at _____.M. o'clock. *(Issue time must be stated)*

(SEAL)

_____

(Signature of Issuing Authority)

Mag. Dist. No. _____ Office Address _____

Date Commission Expires _____

** ☐ This Warrant should be served as soon as practicable but in no event later

than _____ ☐ A.M. ☐ P.M. _____ , 19 _____

and may be served anytime during day or night.

Issued under my hand this _____ day of _____ ,

19 ____ , at _____.M. o'clock. *(Issue time must be stated)*

(SEAL)

_____

(Signature of Issuing Authority)

_____ Phone No. _____

Title of Issuing Authority _____

**The issuing authority should specify a date not later than two (2) days after issuance. PA. R. Crim. P. 2005(d).*
***If issuing authority finds reasonable cause for issuing a nighttime warrant on the basis of additional reasonable cause set forth in the accompanying affidavits and wishes to issue a nighttime search warrant, only this section shall be completed. PA. R. Crim. 2006(b).*

Printed by Garlits Industries, Inc.

ously increasing vigilante mentality. Many people who take the law into their own hands, do so with the rationalization that they fear the justice system is incapable of effectively punishing the criminals (Ferdico 1996).

The exclusionary rule, however, does serve an important role in the judicial process. The role concerns placing necessary restraints upon the authority of the police to intrude in the personal lives of private citizens. Furthermore, if the police violate the laws of the land in order to obtain evidence against criminals, they have themselves become lawbreakers. The Supreme Court has suggested that when this occurs, it is *de facto* (in effect) the government that becomes the outlaw, and that such activities breed contempt for law (*Olmstead v. U.S.* 1928). In effect, such contempt for the law on the part of police breeds the vigilante attitude evident in much of today's society. After all, one can rationalize, if the police are above the law, why not the average citizen? The obvious and ultimate extreme of this attitude is anarchy.

The application of the exclusionary rule has been one of the most controversial aspects of controls placed on the behavior of police officers. Its opponents argue that the exclusionary rule provides guilty people with a technical loophole through which they gain ill-deserved freedom. From this perspective, the safety of society is jeopardized and the basic principles of the justice system are undermined. In contrast, proponents point to the exclusionary rule as among the most important protective cornerstones of freedom. They maintain that it protects American citizens from becoming subjects in a police state where officers are willing to use any means to investigate a crime. Without the provisions of the exclusionary rule, homes could be broken into, phones arbitrarily tapped, individuals strip-searched, and cars stopped and impounded—all in the name of law enforcement. In many ways, the exclusionary rule stands as an important demarcation between democracy and totalitarian governments. In spite of the necessity to maintain the rights of residents, the exclusionary rule is frequently attacked. In fact, during the 1980s a number of exceptions to the exclusionary rule emerged in the decisions of the Supreme Court. The **good-faith exception** to the exclusionary rule, for example, suggests that illegally obtained evidence should not be excluded if it can be shown that the evidence was obtained in good faith. What this actually means is that the officers, in the performance of their duties, believe that they are acting in accordance with the law when they obtained the evidence. Although both the American Bar Association and the American Civil Liberties Union opposed the widespread adoption of this doctrine, many states nonetheless endorsed its use.

In 1984, two cases marked the beginnings of the good-faith exception to the exclusionary rule. The first case was *U.S. v. Leon* (1984), and the second *Massachusetts v. Sheppard* (1984). The *U.S. v. Leon* case involved the Burbank, California, Police Department and an investigation of a drug trafficker. After investigators received a confidential tip, the suspect, Leon, was placed under surveillance. Investigators applied for a search warrant based upon information gathered during the surveillance. The warrant request went through all appropriate channels and was issued by a state judge. A search of Leon's three separate places of residence resulted in the discovery of a large amount of drugs and other evidence. A ruling in a federal district court, however, suppressed all of the evidence gathered in this case. The federal district court ruled that the original affidavit used to request the search warrant failed to adequately establish probable cause.

The government petitioned the U.S. Supreme Court to consider whether the evidence gathered by officers in this case was gathered in good faith, and as such, the validity of the warrant should be executed in court. The Court ruled that when law enforcement officers have acted in objective good faith or their transgressions have been very minor, evidence may be admissible.

In the same year, the Supreme Court reviewed the case of *Massachusetts v. Sheppard* (1984), and further reinforced the concept of "good faith." The *Sheppard* case began on May 5, 1979, when the Boston police discovered a woman's body behind the YMCA in the Roxbury section of Boston. Her hands and feet had been bound with wire, and she had been set on fire in an attempt to conceal or destroy evidence of her murder. This was the ninth in a series of unsolved murders of young women; she was identified as Sandra Boulware.

Detective Emmett McNamara told reporters that the police had spoken with Boulware's boyfriend, Osborne (Jimmy) Sheppard. Sheppard was released shortly after questioning, after providing the police with an alibi for his activities during the day and evening of the slaying. However, upon further investigation, the police determined that Sheppard had lied. Having become convinced that Sheppard was the prime suspect, the police wanted to search his home for possible evidence of the murder. Fearing that Sheppard might destroy evidence if he were given sufficient time, the police planned to obtain a search warrant immediately. The police also were working under the pressure of an increasingly frightened Roxbury population who wanted the individuals responsible for the string of murders arrested quickly.

Unfortunately, the investigating officer could not find the correct form for applying for a search warrant for a premises. What he did find was a form for requesting a search warrant for drugs. The officer scratched out the phrase "Controlled Substances" on the form to adapt it. On a separate sheet of paper the officer specified the location of the residence to be searched and the places within the residence (the basement and second floor). The officer also indicated that the evidence being sought included wire and blood samples. Next, the officer took his amended application for a search warrant to the magistrate. The magistrate read the form and the attached sheet. Although he saw the place where the officer had scratched out the words: "Controlled Substances," he missed another instance of this phrase—that had not been removed. The warrant was issued, the premises searched, and evidence was found. The evidence included blood samples that matched the blood of the slain woman, and wire matching the piece that was used to bind her hands and feet.

Sheppard was arrested and charged with the murder of his girlfriend. In court, he was initially convicted on the weight of the evidence collected in his home. After his conviction and sentence to life in prison, his attorney motioned for a new trial. The attorney's grounds were that the search warrant was not proper and thus its execution invalid. Invoking the exclusionary rule, Sheppard's attorney sought to have all evidence obtained during the search suppressed.

The attorney maintained that in addition to failing to correctly indicate the charges, the warrant was on an improper form and was incorrectly stapled. The Supreme Judicial Court of Massachusetts agreed with the defense counsel and ordered a new trial.

The case was appealed to the U.S. Supreme Court. On the last day of its 1983–84 session, the Supreme Court reversed the Massachusetts Supreme Court decision and reinstated Sheppard's conviction in a 6–3 decision.

By virtue of this decision and of *U.S. v. Leon* (1984), if the police can convince the court that evidence was seized in good-faith reliance on the existence of valid judicial authority, the evidence will be admissible in court proceedings. This is true even if the authority for the seizure is subsequently found to be invalid. In other words, the objective intentions and procedures of the officer(s) and magistrate involved are measured, rather than the technical correctness of the document (the search warrant).

Critics of the assault on the exclusionary rule suggest that these cases foretell a new era of weakening the rule in general (Misner 1986). There seems little question that the nation's courts are moving in the direction of granting police and other agencies greater leeway in their law enforcement practices. This is apparently true even if it means restricting the rights of criminal suspects and jeopardizing the rights of private citizens in general.

For instance, in 1984, the Supreme Court adopted the "inevitable discovery exception" to the exclusionary rule. In effect, **inevitable discovery** refers to the idea that police will eventually uncover evidence—with or without the aid of the suspect.

The Court ruled in the case of *Nix v. Williams* that evidence the police may have obtained illegally, but that would eventually have arisen through legal means, may be admitted as valid evidence in court (Ferdico 1996).

Briefly, the case involved Robert Anthony Williams and the murder of 10-year-old Pamela Powers. On Christmas Eve 1968 in Des Moines, Iowa, Powers was abducted and killed. From witnesses, the police managed to identify and arrest Williams in Davenport, 160 miles away. He was read his *Miranda* rights and escorted back to Des Moines by two officers. These officers had agreed not to question or interrogate Williams during the trip back, and they did not.

Almost offhandedly, one of the officers remarked during the drive home abut the sadness that the little girl's body would not lie buried somewhere under the snow and that she deserved a burial especially at Christmas time. Williams was touched with remorse at the officer's words and voluntarily led them to where the child's body could be found. By a vote of 5–4, the Supreme Court ruled that the officers' behavior had violated Williams's rights under the Fifth Amendment.

After two appeals of the case, the Supreme Court reversed itself in June 1984. The Court concluded that search parties would have eventually have found the little girl's body, even if Williams had said nothing. The Court had, in effect, incorporated the doctrine of inevitable discovery into the more common understanding of exclusion and *Miranda*.

The expansion in the ability of police officers to work beyond the limits of the exclusionary rule has had little negative effect on the justice system. The rule itself, however, remains critically important. The exclusionary rule offers a vital, symbolic expression of the basic protections guaranteed to all American citizens. In fact, its existence may be the explanation for why most police officers do not even think about violating rights of privacy afforded to private citizens.

VEHICLE SEARCHES

The question of scope during a lawful search following an arrest is again the focus of concern when considering automobiles. Discussion of the practices of searching vehicles is usually begun with consideration of *Carroll v. California* (1925). In this case, the Supreme Court established a clear distinction for searches of people, vehicles, and premises. Essentially, the Court held that a warrantless search of a vehicle was legitimate, provided the police had probable cause to believe the vehicle contained evidence or contraband. As with lawful searches in general, warrantless searches of automobiles have been a problematic procedural area for the police. For instance, while the *Carroll* case provided a doctrine for permitting police to search a vehicle, it did not specify the extent to which this search was permissible. If a vehicle was stopped, did the police have the right to inspect the truck? What if a package was found in the trunk? Could the police lawfully open if for inspection? Could the police lift the rear bench-seat to search below it? Could they enter a locked glove box compartment? Was it permissible to search passengers in the car?

Even with more recent cases, one finds procedural problems and confusion over the permissible scope of a search. For instance, in *Chambers v. Maroney* (1970), the Court ruled that warrantless searches of vehicles are lawful, since cars are movable and, once alerted, occupants of a vehicle could certainly destroy or conceal evidence. Yet, little attention is paid to the scope of the search in this ruling. Further clouding the waters were later cases, such as *Robbins v. California* (1981) and *U.S. v. Ross* (1982).

In the first case, a police officer observed a car weaving and driving erratically on a California highway. Upon stopping the vehicle, the officer smelled marijuana smoke as the car's door opened. A search of the vehicle located two wrapped packages. These packages were opened by the officer, inspected, and found to contain marijuana. The California Supreme Court, however, held that the opening of these sealed packages for inspection without a warrant exceeded the legitimate scope of the vehicle search.

In the second case, *U.S. v. Ross* (1982), scope of a vehicular search was finally addressed. The U.S. Supreme Court reversed the decision of a District of Columbia court concerning the warrantless search of a narcotics dealer's car trunk and later location of drugs therein.

In this case the police received a telephone tip (tips are discussed later in this chapter) from a reliable informant about a man known as Bandit selling narcotics from the trunk of his car (Katz 1983). The informant further indicated that he had just seen Bandit complete a drug deal, and that he had been told by Bandit that more drugs remained in the car's trunk. The informant described Bandit, his car's location, and the vehicle itself. When the police arrived, they found the car, but no one matching Bandit's description. A computer check of the vehicle's license plate revealed that it was registered to a man named Albert Ross. Ross matched the physical description of Bandit given to the police by their informant.

The officers drove off to avoid alerting the suspect. When they returned, they observed the vehicle being driven from its parking spot. The officers ordered the driver to pull over and saw a man matching the description of Bandit. The officers searched Ross and observed a bullet on the front seat of the automobile. While searching the interior compartment of the car, they found a gun in the glove compartment. Ross was handcuffed and arrested. The officers next took Ross's car keys and opened the truck. They found two containers. One was a closed but unsealed brown paper bag, and the other a zipped red leather pouch. In the paper bag, the officers found glassine envelopes containing a white powder, later identified as heroin. The leather pouch was left undisturbed. The paper bag was replaced in the trunk and the vehicle transported to the police headquarters (Katz 1983; Zalman and Siegel 1991).

At trial, Ross's motions to suppress the heroin discovery were denied, and he was convicted of possession of heroin with intent to distribute. The Court of

Appeals for the District of Columbia heard the *Ross* case twice, but did not reverse the findings of the lower court.

When the case reached the U.S. Supreme Court, the Court ruled that police officers who have legitimately stopped an automobile, and who have probable cause to believe that contraband is concealed somewhere within it, ". . . may conduct a search of the vehicle that is as thorough as a magistrate could authorize in a warrant particularly describing the place to be searched. "The automobile exception established by *Ross* now stands as a general exception to the search warrant requirement for vehicles. It has been suggested that the widening of automobile exceptions to the Fourth Amendment limitations on privacy intrusions have been in the name of law enforcement expedience. But the Supreme Court defends against such claims by stating that the Fourth Amendment guarantee against unreasonable searches and seizures mandates "that searches conducted outside the judicial process, without prior approval by judges or magistrate, are per se unreasonable . . . " (Katz 1983).

In the case of *California v. Carney* (1985) the Supreme Court added another reason for treating the searches of automobiles differently from searches of a person's home. By expanding the general reasoning of *Ross* (1982) the Supreme Court concluded that there is a lesser expectation of privacy in an automobile or other licensed vehicle. In *California v. Carney,* the Court also had an opportunity to comment on the definition for what constitutes an "automobile." Carney lived in a mobile motor home. Police suspected that he was trading drugs for sexual favors, and placed his motor home under surveillance. During one afternoon, while Carney was stopped in a parking lot in downtown San Diego, a youth was observed entering the motor home. The youth stayed for nearly an hour and a quarter. Upon exiting the motor home, police stopped and questioned the youth. The police learned that the youth had been given drugs in exchange for allowing Carney sexual contact. The youth and the police returned to the motor home, knocked, and after Carney came to the door, entered the motor home—without a warrant—and seized drugs concealed therein.

Carney argued that because the vehicle was also his home, it was protected under the same Fourth Amendment protections as any immobile home. He maintained that the police could not, therefore, search his home without a search warrant. The Supreme Court, however, disagreed, stating that the motor home was a van. As a mobile vehicle, a motor home is subject to similar licensing and regulations required of any other automobile or motorized vehicle. Therefore, the reasoning went, expectation of privacy in a van is equivalent to what one expects in an automobile and not a private residence.

It is important to note the manner in which both the *Ross* and the *Carney* rulings address the scope of a vehicular search. First, they do not provide that when an officer has probable cause to search an automobile, he or she may do so without a warrant in every part of the vehicle where contraband could be concealed. This includes containers and packages wherein the contraband or evidence could conceivably be hidden. One cannot irresponsibly search places in the vehicle where the suspected contraband simply could not be. This has given rise to the rule of thumb that officers may not search glove compartments if they are looking for an elephant. In other words, it would be impossible to conceal an elephant in the small confines of a glove compartment. Consequently, the officer has no authority—without a search warrant—to examine those areas of the vehicle where the contraband or evidence could not conceivably by concealed.

This maxim of not seeking elephants in glove compartments came into question in the case of *New York v. Class* (1986). In this situation, a New York City police officer entered the vehicle he and his partner had stopped for a traffic violation. The full details of the case are described in Box 8.5. In brief, one of the officers, while looking for the vehicle's identification number (VIN), found a gun, and the driver of the car was arrested. The case eventually reached the Supreme Court, where the officer's actions were ruled necessarily intrusive and justifiable under the circumstances (see Box 8.5).

Putting aside for a moment the actual case of *Class*, the actions of the Supreme Court suggest several important implications for law enforcement. First, the ruling expands usual understandings of the Fourth Amendment exception for automobiles. In effect, the Court may have opened a door through which police officers can be granted carte blanche to search automobiles that have lawfully stopped (Maclin 1987:19ff). For example, could a police officer open a glove compartment in order to look for a vehicle registration certificate or proof of insurance? How about when a lawfully conducted roadblock has been set up? Can the officers involved willfully open the car door or the car's hood in order to check that identification numbers on engine heads match VINs on dashboards? If, in the course of these activities, the officer happens to observe contraband, is its seizure legal? Naturally, no single Supreme Court decision answers all questions that arise. But, it remains important to think about some of the implications that may yet surface from this particular ruling. As Kilpatrick (1986) indicates, it is important to recognize that Supreme Court decisions are not intended to make police or public policy. Indeed, it should be readily apparent that while Supreme Court decisions may provide loose guidelines for officers performing warrantless searches, there are really no explicit rules.

Most police departments do provide their officers with ad hoc or department limits on conducting searches. Offices should be knowledgeable about these departmental policies. Nonetheless, it is conceivable that an overzealous police officer may exceed the scope of a lawful search, particularly with regard to an automobile. The two central reasons for this, of course, are the mobility of the cars and the potential risk to the officer.

STOP AND FRISK

The vagueness associated with rules for searching vehicles also directs us to a more general concern and exception to the laws requiring warrants, namely,

BOX 8.5 *NEW YORK V. CLASS:* SEARCHING FOR ELEPHANTS IN GLOVE COMPARTMENTS

The question of whether police officers making routine traffic stops can justifiably search the glove compartment of the vehicle (without a warrant) touches upon important Fourth Amendment rights to privacy. Whether the officer's need to intrude outweighs the private citizen's expectation of privacy is usually the key issue in this controversy. The case of *New York v. Class* (1986) provides an opportunity to examine this issue in detail.

In the *Class* case, two New York City police officers, Lawrence Meyer and William McNamee, observed a 1972 Dodge with a broken windshield exceeding the speed limit by ten miles an hour. Meyer and McNamee, driving in an unmarked police car, turned on their lights and siren and ordered the car, driven by Class, to stop. After stopping, Class got out of his car and approached Officer Meyer. He offered the officer the vehicle's registration certificate and proof of insurance. Meyer then learned that Class had no driver's license.

At the same time, Officer McNamee (who had neither seen the automobile documents nor learned of Class' unlicensed status) went to the vehicle to inspect the car's vehicle identification number (VIN). He first opened the driver-side door, since this is where the VIN plate is often placed on older vehicles. When he found no VIN, and while still outside the vehicle, he looked at the left-hand corner of the front windshield. In many vehicles made after 1969, the VIN plate is located on the dashboard and visible from outside of the car. Still unable to locate the VIN because papers on the dashboard obscured the view, McNamee entered the vehicle to move the papers he believed could be covering the VIN plate.

Once inside the vehicle, however, Officer McNamee observed the handle of a .22-caliber pistol protruding from beneath the seat. The officer seized the weapon, and Class was arrested for possession of the gun. He was issued summonses for driving without a license and for driving with a broken windshield. A search of

Class additionally found he was in possession of .22-caliber ammunition.

At trial, Class moved to suppress the finding of the gun, but was denied the motion. Justice William Holland of the Bronx Supreme Court ruled that the search for the VIN had been reasonable and that McNamee's intrusion into the vehicle was justified, notwithstanding any lack of probable cause to believe the car had been stolen because the defendant's conduct (exiting the car and approaching the officer, and being unlicensed) made the officer's actions quite reasonable. Class was convicted of the weapons charge and was sentenced to a period of probation not to exceed 5 years.

On appeal, a four-justice majority of the appellate division affirmed the conviction without opinion. The New York Court of Appeals, however, concluded that the police intrusion was without adequate objective justification and reversed the decision (*New York v. Class*, 1984). Writing for the court, Judge Kaye noted that one does not have a legitimate expectation of privacy in locations observable by a passerby. But there are locations, inside the car, including the area beneath the seat that cannot be viewed from the outside, which an individual legitimately expects will remain private.

The case reached the U.S. Supreme Court, where the Court reinstated the guilty verdict 7–2. In its ruling, the Court indicated that because of its physical characteristics, transportation function, and pervasive regulation, the automobile has been traditionally viewed as possessing a lesser degree of privacy than a private home. The Court also acknowledged that a "car's interior as a whole" is subject to the same degree of Fourth Amendment protection. But, in the situation presented in *Class*, if he had stayed in his car and acceded to a request to remove the paper obstructing the VIN plate, Officer McNamee

continued

BOX 8.5   *CONTINUED*

"would not have needed to intrude into the passenger compartment."

The Court further explained the dilemma confronting Officer McNamee. On the one hand, if he allowed the defendant Class to return to the car to remove the obstructing papers, Class could have reached the pistol under the seat (or any other potentially hidden weapon) and caused injury to the officers. On the other hand, and as the officers did act, McNamee could continue to detain Class outside the vehicle and move the papers himself without fear of potential risk.

From this, Justice O'Connor noted that warrantless searches were permissible in certain law enforcement contexts, in spite of their substantial intrusiveness. Under the doctrine derived from *Terry v. Ohio* (1968), the constitutionality of a warrantless search is to be judged by balancing the need to search against the intrusion the search entails. Three important factors existed to justify McNamee's search. First, the safety of the officers was served by the intrusion. Second, the intrusion was kept to a minimum, and third, the search stemmed from at least some probable cause created by suspicious behavior on the part of the individual affected by the search, namely, Class. When weighed against the governmental interests, Class' own reasonable expectation of privacy was simply not as compelling. This is particularly true since there is no reasonable expectation of privacy concerning the VIN plate and since Class had committed two traffic violations prompting the initial stop.

frisking a suspect. At this juncture it would be useful to consider how stopping and frisking someone may also intrude upon the privacy of private citizens.

A **frisk** or pat-down is a cursory search of an individual's person. In general, it accompanies a field interview and is not considered an exploratory search. Typically, the only items for which an officer can search during a frisk are weapons. However, if the frisk uncovers other contraband incidental to the search for weapons, the discovery of these items of contraband is sufficient to justify a more thorough search.

Most frisking is conducted quite causally and involves patting down the outer garments of a suspect with the palms of one's hands. One should begin at the head and work the hands along the outside of the clothing wherever a weapon might be found. One should never place hands inside of the suspect's clothing, unless the outside patting has revealed something that feels like a concealed weapon.

Usually, when an officer stops someone for questioning (conducting a field interview), it is because something about the individual has provoked suspicions or the individual may be believed to be in possession of certain bits of information relevant to a crime, or because the officer has observed or been notified of a violation of law. Certainly, then, what is unknown about the individual being stopped may mean that a frisk for safety reasons is advisable. The appearance of the individual being frisked should not override the need to conduct the frisk. Many officers have been injured by underestimating the ability of a small person to pull a weapon suddenly and use it.

The delicate balance between the rights and liberties of private citizens and the government's need to abridge these Constitutional guarantees is tested daily in the course of police work. Among the most often cited doctrines connected with appropriately maintaining this balance is the case of *Terry v. Ohio* (1968).

In this case a Cleveland detective, Martin McFadden, observed John Terry and another man, Richard Chilton, standing on a street corner. McFadden watched as they walked back and forth along a strip of the block and paused each time to look inside the same store's window. Following each promenade past the store window, the men stood on the corner and chatted. McFadden grew suspicious and suspected that they were casing the store for a burglary. Suddenly, a third man, Katz, appeared but left almost immediately. Detective McFadden followed Terry and Chilton as they walked several blocks and again met up with Katz.

McFadden approached the three men, identified himself as a police officer, and asked their names. The men mumbled something fairly inaudible, which led the officer to spin Terry around and pat him down. Keeping his frisk to the outer garments, McFadden detected a gun in the pocket of Terry's overcoat, but was unable to remove it. He ordered all three men to face a wall with their hands raised over their heads, and removed the gun. McFadden next proceeded to frisk each man, which resulted in the seizing of another revolver from the pocket of Chilton. No weapon was found on Katz.

Terry and Chilton were each charged with carrying concealed weapons, but the defense moved for a suppression of the evidence of the weapons. While the trial court did not accept the prosecution's claim that the guns had been seized incident to a lawful arrest, it did permit the gun as evidence. The court justified

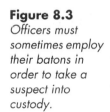

Figure 8.3
Officers must sometimes employ their batons in order to take a suspect into custody.

the inclusion of these guns as evidence by indicating that while the officer did have probable cause to be suspicious of these men given their behavior, he did not have probable cause to make an arrest. However, given his suspicions, McFadden was justified in frisking these men for his own protection, since he had probable cause to believe they might be armed.

In effect, the *Terry* case established a distinction between an investigative stop for questioning and an arrest. The case also distinguished between a frisk of outer clothes (for the protection of the officer) and an intensive search for evidence. The defendants Terry and Chilton were found guilty. The case was appealed and was subsequently heard by the Supreme Court, which upheld the convictions.

FIELD SEARCH TECHNIQUES

Field searches are typically conducted when an officer has reasonable cause to believe that an individual who has been stopped may be armed and a threat to his or her safety or prior to any arrest (Adams 1994).

1. The individual should be placed in an off-balanced position. This may be accomplished in one of three ways:
   - **Kneeling Position**. Have the subject kneel on both knees and cross his feet one over the other behind him or her. Have the subject interlace their fingers and hands behind their head. Slight pressure on the leg and a hand on the subjects hands provides considerable control during the hand search.
   - **Standing Position**. Have the subject stand with feet spread widely (about two times their shoulder width). Have the subject place his or her interlaced fingers behind their heads. Have the subject lean back slightly and arch his or her back as you search.
   - **Prone Position**. Have the subject lie face down on the ground with arms outstretched and legs spread widely. This submissive position makes it difficult for the subject to make furtive or aggressive moves against the searching officer.
2. Always handcuff the suspect prior to beginning the search. This will add to your ability to maintain control over the subject.
3. Whenever possible, have a second officer maintain a cover position during the search.
4. Always search using only one hand. Reserve the other for defense, or to secure and control the subject during the search.
5. Conduct a systematic search. Begin at the head and slowly working your way down the body to the feet. Be carefully to remove and check hat or head coverings, long hair, and wigs. These are locations where blades, razors, or other implements may be hidden. Be mindful to check all possible places of concealment (e.g., the inside collar of shirts, under arms by armpit areas, belts and belt buckles, waistbands and cuffs of pants, etc.).

6. Speak clearly and in plain language to the subject. Be brief in your commands, and do not attempt to make explanations.
7. Never turn you back on a suspect—even when cuffed.
8. Never begin the search until you are certain the subject is under your control.

VOLUNTARY CONSENT SEARCHES

Warrantless searches may also be lawfully undertaken if the individual in immediate control of an area gives voluntary consent. In effect, **voluntary consent** means one consents to permit the police to search one's premise, automobile, or person: one has waived one's Constitutional rights under the Fourth Amendment. Again, because the restrictions on police behavior are established to assure the safety and privacy of the average innocent citizen, there are limitations.

The question of consent, of course, remains of concern. For example, imagine being a marijuana farmer several miles from the nearest town or city when a knock comes at your door. You open the door and are confronted by 10 or 12 law enforcement agents brandishing badges and pointing their guns at you. Now assume the officers have sufficient probable cause to arrest you: They know you own the land, and they have observed 60 acres of marijuana growing between your corn stalks. For the officers to lawfully search your home a quarter of a mile from the fields still requires a warrant—or your consent. A large unfriendly officer asks, "May we come in and look around?" The likelihood is you will yield to the guns pointed at you, rather than saying something like, "Well, actually the place is a mess, and I'd rather you didn't." Thus, the question of exactly how voluntary this consent may have been can be raised.

In most cases, courts are reluctant to accept the uncorroborated word of an officer who maintains that a voluntary waiver has been obtained. As a result, individuals who do waive their rights may be asked to verbally consent in the presence of several officers as witnesses or to first sign statements indicating they have consented to the searches without warrants. Similarly, courts may view voluntary consent to search as legitimate provided that the individual has been informed of the prerogative to refuse consent. But, even with these restrictions, and as illustrated in the preceding example, voluntary consent could be obtained through duress and later may be challenged in court.

For example, in *Florida v. Bostick* (1985), voluntary consents were challenged. In their effort to curb the drug trade, the Broward County, Florida, sheriff's department had developed a practice where they would board a bus, and with the consent of passengers, search their luggage. During one such instance, they discovered cocaine in the luggage of Terrance Bostick, who was arrested and subsequently convicted on charges of drug trafficking. The Florida Supreme Court later ruled that the search was unconstitutional. The court felt that a reasonable passenger, in the same situation as Bostick, would not have felt free to leave the bus to avoid questioning by the police.

In 1991, the U.S. Supreme Court reversed the Florida Supreme Court (in *Florida v. Bostick* 1985). The High Court felt that the Florida Supreme Court had erred in interpreting Bostick's feelings that he was not free to leave the bus. In other words, Bostick was a passenger on a bus that was scheduled to leave, and as such, he would not have felt free to leave the bus even if the police had not boarded it. Bostick's movements were confined, but only because of his free decision to travel by bus to begin with. Thus, Bostick was confined not so much by the police actions as by his own decision that he might miss the bus were he to exit it to avoid police questioning. The Court concluded that police warrantless searches are permissible so long as officers do three things:

1. Ask individual passengers for permission before searching their possessions.
2. Do not in any way coerce passengers to consent to a search.
3. Do not suggest that cooperation and consent to be searched is mandatory.

In effect, passengers still must be willing to voluntarily consent to be have their property searched for this variation of warrantless search to be legal.

THE OPEN FIELD DOCTRINE

Related to the searches of private property are the open field and abandoned property doctrines. Both provide exceptions to the requirement of a search warrant. For the most part, the singular controversy has been at what point the yard ends and the open field begins. In other words, where domiciles are protected from unreasonable searches assured by the Fourth Amendment end and unprotected open fields begin (Albanese 1988; Gardner and Anders 1995; Ferdico 1996).

The open field doctrine was established in the case of *Hester v. United States* (1924). **Open field doctrine** concerns the collection of evidence in an open area or field. The *Hester* case involved an investigation by ATF officers who suspected that Hester was manufacturing alcohol illegally in his home. When Hester realized that the officers were approaching his home, he and a confederate fled across a field adjacent to the house—both carrying bottles. The two men were pursued by federal officers, one of whom fired his weapon. Hester and his associate dropped the bottles they were carrying, which were later found to contain illegally produced liquor. The officers, who did not have any search warrants, arrested Hester and his companion. They were later convicted.

On appeal, the conviction of the two men was overturned on the grounds that the officers had made an illegal search and seizure. Eventually, the case reached the U.S. Supreme Court, which reversed the appeal decision and reinstated the conviction. In its decision the High Court stated:

> The defendant's own acts, and those of his associates, disclosed the jug, the jar, and the bottle—and there was no seizure in the sense of the law when the officers examined the contents of each after it had been abandoned . . . the special protection accorded by the Fourth Amendment to the people in their "persons, houses, papers, and effects," is not extended to the open

field. The distinction between the latter and the house is as old as the common law.

Since *Hester*, the decision for what constitutes a house or domicile and where the property legally viewed as a portion of this domicile ends has been fairly well established. Stated simply, all of the area and buildings in that area ordinarily used by the people dwelling there are considered part of the domicile's **curtilage**. The protection of the Fourth Amendment assured to a person in his home, therefore, extends to this curtilage as well.

The 1984 case of *Oliver v. United States* illustrates both the concept of yard, and curtilage, and the general understanding it limits. In the *Oliver* case, two narcotics agents with the Kentucky State Police went to Oliver's farm to investigate allegations that marijuana was being grown. When they arrived, the officers drove past Oliver's house to a locked gate with a "no trespassing" sign on it. A small footpath visible to the officers led around one side of the gate. The officers walked around the gate and down a road for several hundred yards. The two officers passed a barn and a parked camper truck. At about this point, someone stepped out from behind the camper and shouted, "No hunting is allowed, come back here." The officers identified themselves as Kentucky State Police and moved toward the camper. When they arrived no one was there. The officers renewed their investigation of the property and soon located a field of marijuana about a mile from Oliver's house. Oliver was subsequently arrested for manufacturing a controlled dangerous substance.

Later, during trial, it was brought out that the officers had searched the property without a search warrant, and Oliver was not convicted. The Court of Appeals reversed the decision, and the U.S. Supreme Court accepted a petition to hear the case and upheld the conviction. The Court ruled:

> The rule of *Hester v. United States*, that we reaffirm today, may be understood as providing that an individual may not legitimately demand privacy for activities conducted out of doors in fields except in the area immediately surrounding the home.

The Court, therefore, found the two officers' search of the property lawful—even in the absence of a warrant. As the Court expressed it, "It is not generally true that fences or no trespassing signs effectively bar the public from viewing open fields in rural areas" (*Oliver v. United States* 1984).

More recently, the High Court has further extended the limits of plain view by including the concept of inadvertent intrusions. The notion of **inadvertent intrusions** may be understood as an officer observing evidence or contraband—even within a domicile—provided that officer is legally present in that domicile. In other words, police officers do not have to shield their eyes while in a house under a properly executed warrant. If they casually observe contraband not listed in the warrant, and not previously expected, they may legally seize this material as evidence (*Horton v. California* 1990).

The purpose of the plain view doctrine is to accommodate the reasonable needs of police officers with privacy in situations where it would be ridiculous to extend Fourth Amendment rights. The basis of these limitations is to allow a reasonable amount of flexibility to the police in observing suspicious items and seizing them (Zalman and Siegel 1991).

SUMMARY

This chapter began with a brief reexamination of the social and law enforcement role of the peace officer. Included in this exploration was a consideration of the nature of arrest, constitutional concerns regarding citizen rights, probable cause, exclusions of evidence for violations of law or citizen's rights, and various aspects of searches and seizures.

Throughout the chapter's discussion of the various restrictions and limitations on the authority of police officers, an attempt was made to express the necessity for preserving constitutionally guaranteed rights, including those of the accused. Plato's concept of temperance seems to best capture the essence of what the Constitution and Supreme Court decisions do for the American style of policing.

The purpose of this version of temperance is not to provide avenues of escape for guilty parties. Rather, the intended purpose for preserving constitutionally guaranteed rights is to protect those who may be wrongfully accused of a criminal offense.

REFERENCES

Adams, Thomas F. *Police Operations*. 3d ed. Englewood Cliffs, N.J.: Prentice-Hall Career and Technology, 1994.

Albanese, Jay S. *The Police Officer's Dilemma: Balancing Peace, Order and Individual Rights*. Buffalo, N.Y.: Great Ideas Publishing, 1988.

Bohm, Robert M., and Keith N. Haley. *Criminal Justice*. New York: Glencoe/McGraw Hill, 1997.

Dugan, John, and Daniel Breda. "Complaints About Police Officers: A Comparison Among Types and Agencies." *Journal of Criminal Justice*, 19(1991):165–71.

Ferdico, John N. *Criminal Procedures for the Criminal Justice Professional*. Minneapolis/St. Paul: West Publishing Co., 1996.

Katz, Lewis R. "*United States v. Ross*: Evolving Standards for Warrantless Searches." *The Journal of Criminal Law and Criminology*, 74(1983):172–196.

Kilpatrick, James J. "*Miranda v. Arizona*: Twenty Years Have Not Improved It." *Criminal Justice Ethics*, 5(1986):2,59–60.

Maclin, Tracey. "*New York v. Class*: A Little-Noticed Case with Disturbing Implications." *The Journal of Criminal Law and Criminology*, 78(1987):1–86.

Misner, Robert. "Limiting Leon: A Mistake of Law Analogy." *Journal of Criminal Law and Criminology*, 77(1986):507–545.

"Seventh Semiannual Report of Special Counsel Merrick Bobb and Staff." Prepared at the direction of the Los Angeles County Board of Supervisors, in response to the *Kolts Report*, Los Angeles, California, 1997.

Stuckey, Gilbert B. *Procedures in the Justice System*. 3d ed. Columbus, Oh.: Merrill, 1986.

"Police Brutality!" *Time*, 25 March, 1991:18.

Zalman, Marvin, and Larry J. Seigel. *Criminal Procedures: Constitution and Society*. Minneapolis/St. Paul: West Publishing Co., 1991.

CASES CITED

California v. Carney, 471 U.S. 386, 105 S.Ct. 2066, 85 L.Ed.2d 406 (1985).

California v. Prysock, 453 U.S. 355,101 S. Ct 2806, 69 L.Ed 2d. 696 (1981).

Carroll v. U.S., 267 U.S. 132 (1925).

Chambers v. Maroney, 399 U.S. 42,51 (1970).

Chimel v. California, 395 U.S. 584, 97 S.Ct. 2861, 23 L.Ed. 2d 685 (1969).

Colorado v. Connelly, 479 U.S. 157 (1986).

Colorado v. Spring, 479 U.S. 564 (1987).

Connecticut v. Barett, 479 U.S. 523 (1987).

Duckworth v. Eagan, 109 S.Ct. 2875 (1989).

Florida v. Bostick, No. 89-1717 (1985).

Hester v. United States, 44 S.Ct. 445 (1924).

Horton v. California, 110 S.Ct. 2301, 47 CrL 2135 (1990).

Mapp v. Ohio, 395 U.S. 643,644 (1961).

Maryland v. Buie, U.S. 110 S.Ct, 1093, 108 L.Ed.2d 276 (1990).

Massachusetts v. Sheppard, 104 S.Ct. 3424 (1984).

Miranda v. Arizona, 384 U.S. 436,86 S.Ct. 1602,16 L.E.d.2d 694 (1966).

New York v. Class, 106 S.Ct. 960 (1986).

New York v. Quarles, 467 U.S. 649 (1984).

Nix v. Williams, 104 S.Ct. 250 (1984).

Oliver v. United States, 104 S.Ct. 1735 (1984).

Olmstead v. United States, 277 U.S. 438, 485 (1928), Justice Brandeis, dissenting.

Rhode Island v. Innis, 446 U.S. 291 (1980).

Robbins v. California, 453 U.S. 420 (1981).

Terry v. Ohio, 392 U.S. 1 (1968).

U.S. v. Leon, 468 U.S. 104 S. Ct. 3405 (1984).

U.S. v. Ross, 456 U.S. 798, 102 S.Ct. 2157, 72 L.Ed.2d 572 (1982).

QUESTIONS FOR REVIEW

Objective #1:

- What is the role of the peace officer in America?

Objective #2:

- When may an officer make an arrest without benefit of an arrest warrant?
- Under what circumstances should an officer have an arrest warrant before making an arrest?

Objective #3:

- What is meant by probable cause?

Objective #4:

- What is the purpose of the exclusionary rule?
- Who is the exclusionary rule intended to protect?

Objective #5:

- What is meant by the good-faith exception to the exclusionary rule?

Objective #6:

- How might one define inevitable discovery?

Objective #7:

- Why has the scope of a vehicular search been extended?
- When can an officer enter the driver's compartment of vehicle?

Objective #8:

- What parts of the body are searched during a stop and frisk?

Objective #9:

- Describe the standing search.
- How is a seated search accomplished?

Objective #10:

- What is meant by a voluntary search?
- What is required in a voluntary search of passengers on a bus?

Objective #11:

- Does open field doctrine apply to evidence found in the curtilage of a 2domicile?

Objective #12:

- What is meant by an inadvertent intrusion during a search?

9 Criminalistics and the Police

CHAPTER OBJECTIVES

After reading this chapter you should be able to:

1. Describe the nature of criminalistics.
2. Talk about the origins of American forensic laboratories.
3. Differentiate between direct and indirect evidence.
4. Explain why crime scenes must be well documented before objects are moved.
5. Detail how fingerprints are created.
6. Define different types of fingerprints.
7. Describe various methods for developing invisible fingerprints.
8. Discuss automated fingerprint identification system technology.
9. Describe blood-typing's role in police investigations.
10. Examine DNA technology in police work.
11. Contrast various biological specimens sometimes found in evidence.
12. Consider how guns, bullets, and barrels may each serve a purpose as evidence in a criminal case.

FORENSIC SCIENCE AND SCIENTIFIC INVESTIGATION

Criminalistics, or what may be more broadly referred to as forensic science, can be defined as the scientific investigation of crime. Stated simply, forensic

---

KEY TERMS

criminalistics
evidence
direct evidence
indirect evidence
fingerprints
bulb
ten-print card
latent prints
visible prints

invisible prints
plastic prints
manual searches
Automated Fingerprint
   Identification Systems (AFIS)
bloodstains
blood samples
reagents
blood-typing
antigens
Rh factors

deoxyribonucleic acid (DNA)
double helix
Restricted Fragment Length
   Polymorphism (RFLP)
Polymerase Chain Reaction
   (PCR)
Amplified-Fragment Length
   Polymorphism (AMPFLP)
ondontology
ballistics
rifling

science involves the use of various natural sciences (chemistry, physics, biology), photography, and computers to solve crimes, and to identify and locate suspects. Patrol officers typically do not conduct forensic examinations at crime scenes. Patrol officers do often secure and protect a crime scene. When forensic examinations are required, a team of specialists will be called to the scene. Nonetheless, police officers can be profoundly affected by the work of forensic science.

In some crimes, forensic science plays a major role in establishing that a particular implement was used in the commission of the crime. In other cases, various items such as blood traces or semen stains identified by the forensic team may lead the police to a particular suspect. In many other cases, forensic science may never even enter the picture. Unlike many television shows would have the public think, not every lawyer has a forensic scientist on the payroll. For that matter, most lawyers are not amateur criminalists. Similarly, not every police agency has the resources to provide a forensic team for every crime, or to operate a crime laboratory.

Unfortunately, television shows have created a number of misconceptions and misunderstandings about what police forensic labs can accomplish. While some of the technologies depicted on television can certainly be used by forensic laboratories in some large metropolitan cities, most of the sophisticated techniques and equipment are beyond the budgetary reach of the average town or municipal police agency. Although these technologies may exist, the cost of certain services mean they are used for only major crimes and not the more routine and mundane ones.

This chapter will discuss the general area of forensic science and its role in police work. The chapter will begin with a brief description of the origins of forensic labs in the United States. Next the chapter will consider the nature of evidence and how it is collected. Following this, the chapter will examine some of the major evidence-gathering strategies used during crime-scene investigations.

THE ORIGIN OF AMERICAN FORENSIC LABORATORIES

Some historians point to a crime laboratory established in Los Angeles in 1923 as the first to be set up in America. Others, suggest that the most well-known early forensic laboratory was established by the Chicago police in 1929. It was during that same year that Chicago witnessed one of the most vile and bloody gangland, execution-style murders recorded, commonly referred to as the St. Valentine's Day Massacre. Seven Chicago hoodlums and their associates were lined up against a brick wall and sprayed for several minutes with rounds fired from machine guns, shotguns, and .45-caliber automatic pistols (Wilson 1975).

Several witnesses reported that they had seen men carrying weapons escape from the scene in what appeared to be police cruisers and that they were wearing some sort of uniforms. The community leaders of Chicago were appalled. In their attempt to restore faith in local law enforcement, civic leaders established a special coroner's jury to investigate the circumstances of the crime and allegations of the witnesses.

Among those appointed to this special coroner's jury was Bert A. Massey, a local businessman and financier. With Massey's financial backing, Col. Calvin Goddard, an independent forensic consultant, was brought into the case. Goddard maintained a small laboratory in New York City and by 1929, when he was summoned to Chicago, had already established himself as an expert in firearms (Wilson 1975). In cooperation with the special coroner's jury, Goddard recounted an extremely complete description of the slaying of those seven individuals on St. Valentine's Day, based on his examination of the physical evidence collected at the scene. His evaluation was published in the first issue of the *American Journal of Police Science* (Goddard 1930) [This journal was later published as a section in the prestigious *Journal of Criminal Law and Criminology*, which subsequently split into two separate journals].

The law enforcement community and Massey were so impressed with the accomplishments of Goddard that they urged him to move permanently to Chicago. As inducement, Massey offered to assist financially in establishing a modern crime laboratory. Goddard agreed and, with the $125,000 donated by Massey, established his forensic laboratory at the Northwestern University Law School.

During their nearly 70 years of existence, American crime labs have been controlled by various individual state and local police agencies. These labs resist

Figure 9.1
A crime lab.

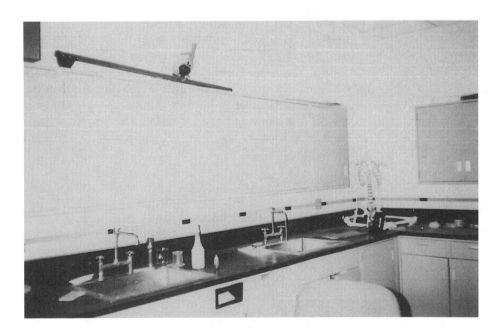

Figure 9.2
Fuming boxes are used to develop certain types of fingerprints.

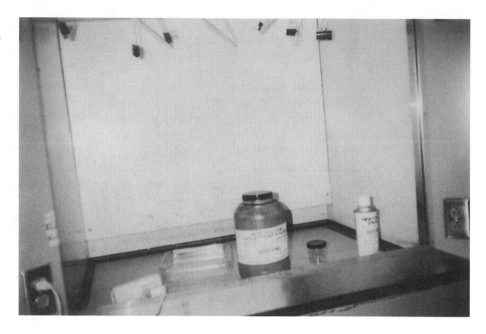

guidance and control from the federal government. In time, these labs became extremely individualistic, reflecting the interests and priorities of local police officials and often the limited scientific qualifications of the personnel who staffed them. The criteria used by each lab to hire personnel, examine evidence, and validate findings were unique to each laboratory. At least in part this explains the lack of consistency among crime labs across the nation in terms of capabilities, quality controls, and expertise of personnel. In the 1990s, many crime laboratories resemble large clusters of laboratories under a single roof. Each laboratory specializes in its own area or branch of science, such as pathology, toxicology, odontology, DNA, explosives, or ballistics. Each laboratory operates with its own specialized equipment, ranging from scanning electron microscopes to emission spectrographs, from atomic absorption spectrometers to equipment for thin-layer chromatography and electrophoresis.

EVIDENCE

A police investigation must be concerned with both people and things (Berg and Horgan 1998). As Chapter 7 indicated, considerable information can be obtained by interviewing and interrogating people. In addition, the use of various types of physical evidence can provide important information for a police investigation. **Evidence** is defined as any physical item that helps in establishing the facts in a related criminal case. Evidence is found at the scene of the crime or on the victim, or in or near the suspect's home or hiding environment.

Figure 9.3
Evidence is stored until needed in court.

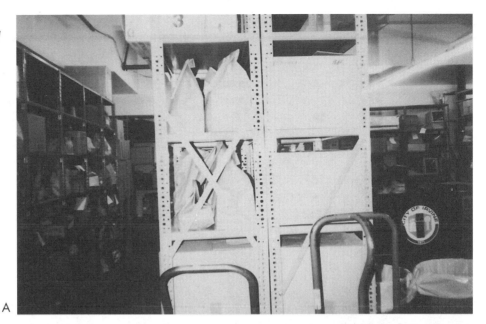

A

B

Evidence is the material that the prosecuting attorney will use to demonstrate the state's argument when presenting the case against a defendant. Evidence, for the most part, arises as one of two major types, direct and indirect evidence.

Direct Evidence

Typically, **direct evidence** is viewed as *proof in itself* of the guilt or innocence of the defendant. In terms of implementation, this means some type of eyewitness testimony concerning the crime at hand. For example, assume that two men, Mr. Katz and Mr. Diaz, are in a bar arguing. Katz draws a gun from his belt and fires it at Diaz in the presence of the bartender. Katz drops his gun and flees the bar. Any official statement given by this bartender concerning what he saw will be direct evidence against Katz.

But what if the bartender had gone to the storeroom while the two men were arguing, heard a shot, and returned to find Diaz on the ground bleeding and Katz gone? The bartender certainly could offer direct evidence concerning the argument he witnessed prior to going into the back room. He could even place Katz in the bar just before the shooting. But the bartender could not provide direct evidence that Katz shot Diaz.

Obviously, neither police nor prosecutors can rely upon eyewitness testimony only. Fortunately, various kinds of indirect pieces of evidence can also be used to establish a case against a suspect and a defendant. For example, in our illustration of the barroom shooting, it may be possible to identify Katz's fingerprints on the gun. Such a piece of physical evidence, in addition to the events leading up to the shooting seen and heard by the bartender, may be sufficient to convince a jury that Katz is guilty of shooting Diaz.

Indirect Evidence

Stated simply, **indirect evidence** includes physical evidence or circumstantial pieces of information. In other words, it is evidence that in itself cannot demonstrate the guilt or innocence of a defendant. Nonetheless, physical evidence does provide the pieces of the puzzle that, once put together, form a picture complete enough to show a defendant's guilt or innocence. The old adage that "you can't get a conviction with a case built entirely on circumstantial evidence" is patently untrue. In fact, a good many felons sitting in prison can attest to the invalidity of that saying.

In many crimes, unlike the illustration of Katz and Diaz, all that the police have is a victim and a crime scene. If it is a major crime, such as a homicide or robbery of a large sum of money, a forensic team will be called in to examine the crime scene. The identification of various pieces of physical evidence, in fact, is viewed by many police officers as more reliable than eyewitnesses who can always lie, make mistakes, or have a change of mind. But physical objects, imprints, and traces of various biological substances cannot, by themselves, lie.

Naturally, the reason that physical objects cannot lie is they cannot speak. In order to hear what physical evidence has to say about a crime, police agencies and the courts must rely upon experts. These forensic experts or criminalists, as they are sometimes called, are charged with the responsibility of explaining what various pieces of physical evidence mean. Forensic experts, in an ideal sense, are people with specialized training and experience in a number of different scientific and academic areas. Using their various expertise, these experts decipher otherwise silent pieces of evidence for police officers and courtroom judges and juries.

COLLECTING PHYSICAL EVIDENCE

The success or failure of a police investigation often depends on the thoroughness of the crime scene investigation and the ability of the police to secure, preserve, and collect physical evidence. Physical evidence may initially offer a certain amount of information merely because of its position or location at the crime scene.

Movies and television often show some patrol officer stumbling into a crime scene and discovering a dead body on the ground with a gun laying next to it. Inevitably, the officer picks up the gun—usually by placing a pen or pencil in the barrel—and places it in a pocket. In reality, that just isn't how things happen. The first order of business for a patrol officer discovering a homicide scene will be to notify his or her supervisor, and to secure the area. Even when the forensic team arrives, no one is going to insert a pen or pencil into the barrel of the gun, for this action might damage potential evidence (e.g., gunpowder or lead residue). Furthermore, nothing in the crime scene will be touched, moved or in other ways molested until it is documented.

Documentation of crime scenes usually refers to drawn sketches and still photographs showing the crime scene exactly as it is found in order to preserve in time the proximity and juxtaposition of all potential material objects at the scene.

DOCUMENTING THE CRIME SCENE

Among the most important tasks to be undertaken at the scene of a serious crime is to assure that an accurate, precise, and objective record is made of the scene's appearance and of objects found there. Both drawn sketches and photographs should be taken before any object of potential evidence is touched or moved.

Photographs provide a comprehensive visual record of the crime scene and will assist throughout the investigation and subsequent prosecution. Likewise, drawn sketches allow the investigating officer to depict the physical location of various objects or pieces of evidence in proximity at the crime scene. These too will become valuable during the investigation and prosecution sequences of the case.

During recent years, many police agencies have additionally begun to videotape the crime scene and investigative proceedings at the scene. Videotapes provide an additional visual record of events during the investigative process but should not substitute for either sketches or still photographs.

LOCATING AND IDENTIFYING EVIDENCE

After the crime scene has been secured and documented, a coarse and general examination of the scene may be undertaken. During this stage of the crime scene investigation, forensic technicians, sometimes with the assistance of patrol officer or investigators, seek items that are clearly apparent to the naked eye. These may include indications of pry-bar marks or other tool marks by windows and door jams that have been forced open, paint chipped by prying, broken glass panes, damaged locks, small objects strewn about the room, blood spatters, articles of clothes, weapons, etc.

During this stage of the crime scene investigation, officers and technicians will seek items and implements that may have been involved in some aspect of the crime. For example, in the event of a homicide by strangling, the logical instrument is some sort of cord or ligature. In a shooting incident, the search might be for the gun or spewed shell casings; in a stabbing, a knife or sharp instrument, and so forth.

In the world of television make-believe it often appears that after a crime occurs, a forensic team rushes in and in a matter of minutes (usually following several commercials) the team finds conclusive and clear-cut evidence that identifies a suspect, beyond reasonable doubt. In the real world of police and bad guys, however, things move much slower and are frequently far less dramatic and conclusive.

FINGERPRINT EVIDENCE

Usually as part of the initial coarse examination of the crime scene, fingerprint evidence is sought. Fingerprints and palm prints are often described as among the most valuable sorts of physical evidence one can find at a crime scene. Occasionally prints produced by bare feet also provide clues to the identity of a suspects.

Loosely speaking, **fingerprints** refers to any impression of the friction ridges on a person's hands and fingers (Berg and Horgan 1998). Fingerprints are composed of lines, whorls, arches and ridges unique to every individual. All portions of the body that are subjected to fairly continuous and vigorous use, are subject to development of these friction ridges (Kirk 1974). These body surfaces include the fingers, palms of the hand, toes, and the soles and heels of the feet.

Fingerprints are created by the lines and ridges on the rounded first joint or **bulb** of each finger and thumb. These ridges are distinct and unique in every individual. Even when one intentionally attempts to damage or remove these friction ridges, in order to alter or obliterate the conformation of these ridges, they have a tendency to repair themselves to their original configuration.

Records of fingerprints derive from a fairly wide assortment of origins. For example, each time a person applies for a position with any governmental agency, the person is fingerprinted and sometimes photographed. In many states, applications for gun, liquor, driver's, nursing, and medical licenses require the applicant to provide a thumbprint or set of fingerprints.

Figure 9.4
Fingerprints are composed of lines, whorls, arches, and ridges unique to every individual.

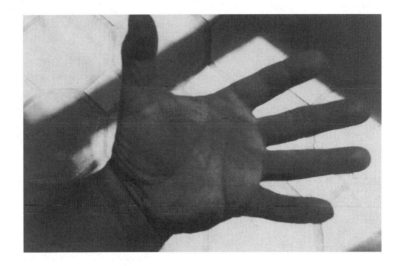

Figure 9.5
Fingerprints are taken at the station and compared with those on file.

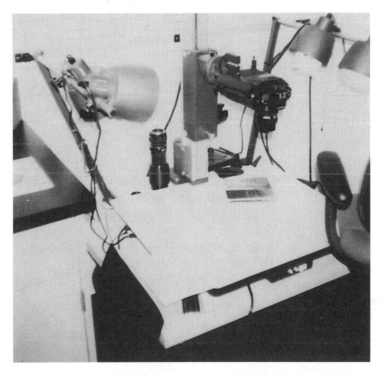

In the late 1970s, the Educational Testing Services, the people who are responsible nationally for administering the Law School Aptitude Test (LSAT), among other entrance examinations, began taking the thumbprints of all applicants prior to each LSAT.

In the early 1980s, in partial response to a massive rise in the value of silver, coin dealers, jewelers, and old-silver buyers began to require thumbprints of anyone selling more than $100 worth of silver or gold. The purpose here was to maintain a record of the seller in the event it was later discovered that the precious metal sold had been stolen.

In the late 1990s, a number of states began calling for the thumbprinting of anyone who purchased ammunition. The idea was to maintain a record of ammunitions purchases, even though there are many illegal guns in circulation. Also in the 1990s, a number of the nation's banks began to require thumbprints of customers cashing large denominated checks.

Of course, one of the obvious places where police agencies obtain records of an individual's fingerprints is during the booking of a suspect for some offense. At that time, copies of all ten fingerprints of the suspect are imprinted on a file card called a **ten-print card** (see Box 9.1). Some agencies have additionally begun to take prints of a suspect's palm. These prints have, until recent years, been stored in various index files and, when used, required a hand search and an extremely time-consuming, thorough comparison when a latent print was found at a crime scene. As will be discussed later, the advances in computer technology have also moved in the direction of fingerprint identification.

In addition to maintaining a set of ten-print cards in each local police department, police agencies regularly provide copies of their ten-print cards to central clearinghouses and storage houses. Among the leading fingerprint clearinghouses, as one might expect, is the Federal Bureau of Investigation (FBI). The FBI has served as a fingerprint clearinghouse since 1930. Typically, when an agency submits a ten-print card to the FBI, it will receive in return a cumulative listing of all of the times that the clearinghouse indicates the individual has been arrested and fingerprinted.

The FBI has been developing an integrated computer system scheduled for beginning operation by the year 2000. This system will combine an automated fingerprint indexing system with other identification and statistical information. Once operational, agencies will be able to contact the system, and in addition to running fingerprints, they will be able to search the National Crime Information Center (NCIC) databases as well. They will also be able to access an Interstate Identification Index and several other record banks (Berg and Horgan 1998; AFIS User Review 1998).

TYPES OF FINGERPRINTS

There are a number of different types of fingerprints frequently found at a crime scene. These include latent prints, visible prints, invisible prints, and plastic prints.

BOX 9.1 TEN-PRINT CARD

Ten Print Card

LEAVE BLANK

TYPE OR PRINT ALL INFORMATION IN BLACK

FBI LEAVE BLANK

LAST NAME NAM   FIRST NAME   MIDDLE NAME

STATE USAGE

ALIASES

CONTRIBUTOR
OR
I

FL0120000
SO
LAKE CITY FLA

SIGNATURE OF PERSON FINGERPRINTED

DATE OF BIRTH DOB
Month   Day   Year

THIS DATA MAY BE COMPUTERIZED IN LOCAL, STATE AND NATIONAL FILES

DATE ARRESTED OR RECEIVED DOA

SEX | RACE | HGT. | WGT. | EYES | HAIR

PLACE OF BIRTH POB

DATE SIGNATURE OF OFFICIAL TAKING FINGERPRINTS

YOUR NO. OCA

LEAVE BLANK

CHARGE

FBI NO. FBI

CLASS.

SID NO. SID

REF.

FINAL DISPOSITION

SOCIAL SECURITY NO. SOC

NCIC CLASS - FPC

CAUTION

1. R. THUMB	2. R. INDEX	3. R. MIDDLE	4. R. RING	5. R. LITTLE

6. L. THUMB	7. L. INDEX	8. L. MIDDLE	9. L. RING	10. L. LITTLE

LEFT FOUR FINGERS TAKEN SIMULTANEOUSLY   L. THUMB   R. THUMB   RIGHT FOUR FINGERS TAKEN SIMULTANEOUSLY

Reel	Check Name*	ANA* Yes ☐ No ☐	Add D.O.B.* Yes ☐ No ☐	1	2	3	4	5
	Aliases for Input*		CHQU	6	7	8	9	10
			Old F/P Class					
Frame	Old Height	Old Weight	Old Hair	Blocking Out	Blocking Out Reference		Classed By:
	Mod. P.O.B.* Yes ☐ No ☐	Add SSN* Yes ☐ No ☐	In NCIC Yes ☐ No ☐				Idented By:
	FDLE No.	Reel and Frame		Blocked Out By:	Mod. Reel and Frame* Yes ☐ No ☐		Verified By:

Latent Prints

Impressions transferred to a surface by perspiration or oil and other substances from the rides of fingers, toes, palms, and feet are referred to as **latent prints**. Latent prints are sometimes created by substances such as blood, paint, mud, grease or others, carried on the hands or feet. The term latent print is commonly used generically to almost any sort of print found at a crime scene.

Visible Prints

Visible prints are a classification of fingerprints given to latent prints created by soiled or stained fingers or palms. **Visible prints** are easily observable with the naked eye, and include impressions left in deposits of dust or other similar substances on solid, nonporous surfaces.

Invisible Prints

Invisible prints may be found on either porous or nonporous surfaces. **Invisible prints** are not immediately observable to the naked eye. These latent prints require treatment by various powders, chemicals, gases, and lights to make them visible.

Plastic Prints

These are a variation of visible prints created in soft substances. **Plastic prints** are commonly formed in substances such as butter, wax, putty, grease, and even paint; any substance that forms a kind of mold of the fingerprint when touched creates a plastic print.

LIFTING AND PRESERVING FINGERPRINTS

Because fingerprints have a long-standing and established tradition as a reliable means of identification, they are eagerly sought at major crime scenes. To preserve prints for later identification, several techniques are available, including developing or making visible, invisible latent prints.

PHOTOGRAPHING FINGERPRINTS

Before making any attempt to lift a fingerprint, it should be photographed. When photographing faint prints there is a possibility that normal room light may be inadequate. Forensic scientists, therefore, have sought ways to enhance

Figure 9.6
Fingerprints may be developed in a variety of ways.

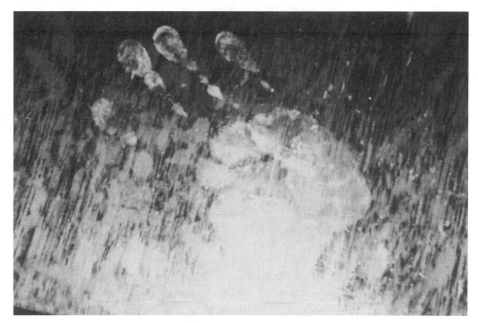

the quality of a photographed print. Among the several techniques used to enhance fingerprint photographs are laser lights and combined use of laser lights and enzyme treatments (Menzel et al. 1984).

DEVELOPMENT TECHNIQUES

Before an invisible print can be photographed or lifted, it must be visible. There are a number of ways to make these prints visible. The most common technique is to use various powders.

Powders

Traditionally, fingerprint powders are white or black; today, powders may also come in an assortment of colors including fluorescents. Usually, the background color on which the latent print has been left determines the color of powder to use in order to produce a good contrast. To develop the print, the powder is applied with a small brush or a feather, spreading the powder gently across the area where the invisible print is believed to exist.

Some powders are not only colored, but magnetic as well. Magnetic powders are useful when dusting on ferrous, or iron-containing surfaces. Magnetic brushes and powders are particularly useful when they can be used for dusting overhead, slanting, or vertical surfaces.

Lifting Prints

The phrase "lifting prints" is quite a literal description of this process. Fingerprints are lifted with a length of clear cellophane tape. The procedure involves placing one end of the tape just beyond the print to be lifted. The tape is straightened, and gently pressed over the print and just a little beyond. After the tape has been placed, it may be left there to protect the print and the entire object sent to the lab for examination. Of the object is immobile or too large to move, the tape is carefully lifted from the object's surface and transferred to a card. The powder, dusted over the print to make it visible, will adhere to the adhesive of the tape creating a perfect image of the print once the tape is pressed onto a card.

Rubber fingerprint lifters may also be used when recovering fingerprints. These devices are particularly useful for removing prints from surfaces that are curved or difficult to photograph. Rubber lifters usually are composed of a thin, flexible material coated with an adhesive on one side. The procedure for lifting is similar to that already described. However, in this case, a protective transparent cover is removed form the rubber lifter, exposing the adhesive side. After paling the lifter over the print, and lifting it from the surface of some object, the protective covering is replaced over the print and the adhesive.

Fingerprints should always be photographed prior to any attempt to lift or transfer them from their original location. It is likewise important to photograph plastic prints since they may be damaged by attempts to dust or lift them.

Fuming

In some cases, invisible prints can be made visible by fuming them with various chemicals such as cyanoacrylate vapors that polymerize or bond with an invisible print, producing a visible chemical reaction in the form of a residue deposit on the print. Iodine has also been used to fume prints and create a visible tracing of the fingerprint outline. Other chemicals commonly used to develop prints include silver nitrate, and Ninhydrin and commercial mixtures such as Chem Print.

FINGERPRINT FILES AND SEARCHES

At one time all fingerprint identification searches were undertaken by hand. These **manual searches**, depended largely on what was called the Henry System of fingerprint identification. The search involved a fingerprint classifier determining the primary fingerprint classification in order to assure that the correct suspect was being considered. This was especially important when multiple suspects were known by the same or very similar names. If a match was found, the criminal jacket for that suspect was located and sent to the investigating officers.

The location of fingerprints using this manual method were laborious and time-consuming efforts. Even with several fingerprint classifiers working diligently, it could take many hours or days to match a single latent print located at a crime scene with one already on file in the classification files.

AUTOMATED FINGERPRINT IDENTIFICATION SYSTEMS (AFIS)

During the past twenty years, computer technology has rocketed forward in every possible way. Computers have significantly altered and improved many aspects of police work, including in the area of forensics and fingerprint classification and identification. Among the leading advances in this area is the **Automated Fingerprint Identification System (AFIS)**. This computer technology rose to national recognition in 1985, when the Los Angeles police department identified and arrested Richard Ramirez as the notorious "Night Stalker." The Los Angeles police were assisted in their investigation by a computer built by the Nippon Electric Co. of Japan. AFIS sorted through 380,000 electronically stored ten-print cards and hit on a best fit with Richard Ramirez. Ramirez was arrested 2 days after his card was identified and charged with killing 17 people. Experts have estimated that it would have taken a single fingerprint technician 67 years to make the same ten-print identification from manual files (Elmer-De Witt 1985).

In 1986, the Massachusetts State Police purchased a slightly more advanced version of AFIS than the one used in the Los Angeles investigation. The Massachusetts AFIS had the capacity to sort through 250,000 ten-print cards in just under 3 minutes and reported up to ten best hits.

An unanticipated benefit of AFIS has been to eliminate multiple jackets in a given jurisdiction. In other words, the same individual arrested in different local jurisdictions may have used different names. By running the ten-print card through the system, aliases are identified and collapsed into a single file.

AFIS uses a mathematically created image of a fingerprint and identification of up to 250 characteristics for each print (Buracker and Stover 1984). In addition to scanning, classifying, storing, and retrieving these fingerprint images, the system can reproduce them on a plotter or terminal screen for visual comparisons. Standard ten-print cards can be scanned electronically, digitized, and made readable by the computer system to create the databank of fingerprint records.

LIVE DIGITAL FINGERPRINTING

A related innovation in fingerprinting is the live digital fingerprint-scanning process. This scanning process permits one to scan a suspect's finger with an electro-optical system and to convert the resulting fingerprint image to a digital form. This digital information is displayed on a computer terminal and can be printed out onto a standard ten-print card, transmitted from its originating site to some other location, or sorted for later use (Bennett 1987).

During the past ten years, AFIS computers have expanded and are used today in virtually every state in the nation. These systems have made an extraordinary impact on the ability of agencies to identify suspects from latent prints. Unfortunately, in the absence of an inexpensive way for small law enforcement agencies to access these various AFIS databases, much of their potential utility is lost. The sharing of fingerprint data among police agencies must certainly be the next step. The development of large clearinghouse fingerprint database networks, such as the one proposed by the FBI to begin by the year 2000, will be a major stride forward.

SHOE AND TIRE IMPRESSIONS

In the same manner that a finger or hand may leave an impression in dust, mud, or other pliable materials, so too may a shoe or automobile tire. Usually, one thinks of these impressions as occurring in the outdoors. Often, these shoe and tire tread impressions are as distinct as fingerprints. Like tools, these items frequently have identifiable flaws or nicks that show up in the impressions left in mud, dirt, and even in snow (Ojena 1984; Bennett and Hess 1994). These impressions are usually first photographed and are then cast in plaster or latex, depending on the medium in which the impression has occurred. Casting procedures are detailed in Box 9.2.

Fingerprints, shoe, and tire impressions have their greatest value to police when they are found in locations to which limited or authorized persons have access (Adams 1985, 1994). In public places and places of business, for example a grocery store, prints found on a countertop or vending machine or any other accessible object in the premises are reduced in value in a criminal investiga-

---

BOX 9.2 PROCEDURES FOR CASTING IMPRESSIONS

Some departments prefer to use dental casting, or various latex materials, when making castings. Others continue to primarily use plaster. The steps for casting a plaster impression set forth below:

Step 1: Create a retaining frame or dam completely around the impression approximately 2 inches from the impression's edges. This may be created using plastaline clay, wood, or metal.

Step 2: Very carefully coat the impression with several layers of shellac, hairspray, or similar lac-

quer material. Allow each layer to dry before applying the next. This will produce a sealer effect against which the plaster will be poured. Apply a light coat of linseed oil, or sprinkle talcum powder to the final layer of sealer.

Step 3: Mix a sufficient amount of plaster to fill the casting frame about half full.

Step 4: Pour the plaster into the casting frame, being certain to cover the entire impression. Fill the frame until it is about half full.

Figure 9.7
Tires leave identifying markings in soil and other soft materials.

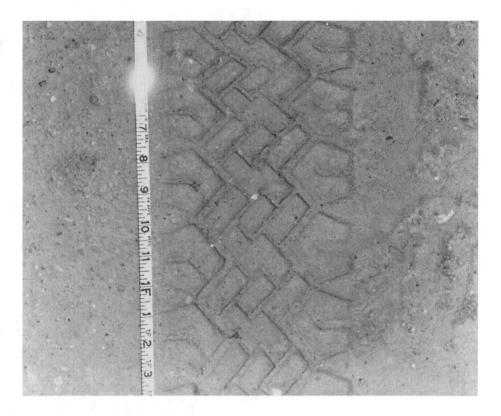

tion. Certainly, a good defense attorney can allege that the defendant may have touched some object when in the premises for some lawful purpose during normal business hours. Conversely, fingerprints of an intruder found in someone's private dwelling, where the suspected intruder had no authorization or legitimate access, become very incriminating pieces of evidence.

Step 5: Place several strips of nylon gauze (commonly used when taping drywall) across the surface of the casting. This will provide additional strength to the final casting. Finish filling the casting frame with plaster.

Step 6: As the cast begins to set, but before it is done drying, etch an identification mark, the date, and the case number into the back of the impression.

Step 7: After the cast has dried and hardened it can be removed from the casting frame. Do not attempt to remove half hardened casts; this could result in damage to the impression casting.

Step 8: After removing the casting from the frame, carefully wrap it, label the outer wrapping of the package, and transport it to the crime laboratory.

Figure 9.8
Photos and castings of shoe prints can aid in identifying suspects.

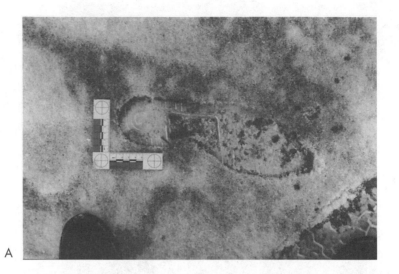

A

B

OTHER KINDS OF PHYSICAL EVIDENCE

Almost anything found at a crime scene may be used as evidence, provided that it is germane to the investigation. Even something as innocent as glass particles may offer an important clue in a criminal investigation and later become useful as evidence.

BLOOD AS EVIDENCE

Blood is perhaps the most obvious—and among the most common—form of evidence found at the scene of a violent crime. Blood may be found in very small trace amounts, puddles, pools, spatters, or droplets. Blood can be extremely useful as evidence whether it is found wet or dry, soaked into fabrics or furniture, or spattered on the walls, ceiling, or floor. Dried specimens of blood are referred to as **bloodstains**. **Blood samples**, on the other hand, usually refer to small amounts of blood collected from pools or directly from suspects or victims.

Extreme caution is necessary when handling blood at crime scenes. While it remains an excellent form of evidence, it also can be a serious health hazard for officers. This is true whether the blood specimens being handled are wet or dry. Working with hepatitis- or HIV-contaminated blood samples increases one's risk

Figure 9.9
Blood found at a crime scene can aid in the investigation.

of contracting these diseases. Most police agencies have strict policies about wearing protective gloves and masks when handling blood evidence or dealing with bleeding victims and witnesses. It is important to maintain these precautions diligently.

Blood is usually fairly easily identified at a crime scene since it is a highly visible fluid which is hard to remove from many fabrics and carpeting. Even when felons do try to remove this incriminating crimson fluid from carpeting, weapons, or other objects, trace elements of the blood sometimes remain. Forensic technology has advanced to a point where even minute traces of blood may be detected by using certain **reagents**, or substances used to enhance and detect or test for the presence of blood. The reagent luminol, for example, can detect very minute traces of blood—even if the area has been cleaned with detergents or bleach. One limitation of this product is that it must be used in total darkness.

BLOOD TYPING

Blood typing involves classifying certain aspects of the blood into different categories. Classification of red blood cells is accomplished by identifying the presence of specific substances on the cell's surface or membrane. These substances are called **antigens**. Among the large number of antigens found on the red blood cell's membrane, scientists recognize those designated A, B, and O as the most important. An individual with the genes for either A and O or B and O will develop only the A or B antigen. Accordingly, the possible blood types are A, B, O, and AB.

Another antigen of great medical and classification importance is the Rhesus or **Rh factor** so-called because it was first studied in rhesus monkeys. Rh factors determine whether an individual's blood type is positive or negative. In addition to these more commonly known antigen systems, there are others that help to identify genetic and antigen structure. Using these structural patterns, it can be determined whether a particular blood sample was likely to have come from a specific individual. As a result, knowing someone's blood type and Rh factor, can assist police in eliminating a suspect as well as incriminating one.

For example, let's say a sample of blood found at the scene of a murder is A–. A test of the victim's blood proves to be B+. This means that the victim is not the source of the blood, and any suspect in this murder will have to have A- blood. In addition to blood typing, other elements of biological specimens may prove helpful during criminal investigations.

BIOLOGICAL SPECIMENS AND DNA TYPING

Have you ever looked into the face of a newborn baby, and exclaimed, "Gee, she looks just like her mother. She has her eyes and mouth shape!" Or have you ever noticed that children may look like their grandparents or that everyone in the family has blond hair? These family characteristics seem to repeat themselves over and over throughout the family's ancestry.

The physical appearances of human beings, and often their likelihood of contracting certain kinds of diseases, are actually related to the biochemical blueprint that also makes people different and unique. Determination, prediction, and to a certain extent even alteration of how people may look, can be considered scientifically through the study of genetics.

Deoxyribonucleic acid (DNA), is a naturally occurring substance believed to be the principal component of cellular chromosomes. It is the biochemical factor that unlocks the varieties of similarities and differences that arise through reproduction and heredity. As an aid to law enforcement and criminal investigation, DNA typing and profiling is in its infancy. The typing and profiling of DNA actually was a by-product of the genetic research into gene splicing and cloning that arose in molecular biology during the 1970s. It was not used in a forensic situation until 1985. Today, DNA profiling or fingerprinting are seen as an enormous advance by both prosecution and defense attorneys alike. Among prosecutors, there is the possibility of presenting positive identifying evidence associated with a particular crime or crime scene. The linkage between a suspect and a crime scene has very strong suggestive value and can be very convincing to a jury. In other words, if a specimen of blood, semen, or hair found on the clothing of a victim has been convincingly shown to be from a particular suspect, this goes a long way towards persuading a jury of the suspect's guilt.

Conversely, for defense attorneys, DNA findings can effectively sway a jury and convince them that their client could not possibly have been the guilty party. Even fragments of bone, saliva, or urine may be used in current DNA profiling tests. Although slow to be introduced as evidence in the courts at first, by 1989, 25 states had begun to allow DNA test results to be admitted as evidence. In 1988, DNA was successfully used as evidence in a Florida rape case (*Andrews v Florida* 1988). This case is briefly described in Box 9.3.

BOX 9.3   THE CASE OF TOMMY LEE ANDREWS

In 1987, an Orlando jury convicted Tommy Lee Andrews of sexual battery and related offenses, partially on the basis of a DNA analysis made on his blood and semen. The specimens had been taken form the rape victim. During the trial, Dr. Michael Baird, an expert on DNA analysis, testified that there was a clear match. Dr. Baird also indicated that the chances that the matching DNA bands would be duplicated in some other person's cells was less than 1 in 839 million (*Criminal Justice Newsletter* 1988).

DNA PROFILING OR FINGERPRINTING

Pictorially, the DNA molecule looks a little like a twisted ladder, or a spiral stair-case, and is called a **double helix**. The steps of the ladder contain four chemical subunits or nitrogenous bases: guanine [G], adenine [A], thymine [T], and cytosine [C]. Each step is composed of a predictable pair of these bases. A is always paired with T, and G always with C. The combinations A-T and G-C are called base pairs. When a sugar (deoxyribose) is linked to a phosphate group and to one of the four nitrogenous bases (G,A,T,C,), the resulting molecule is called a nucleotide.

The possible number of arrangements for nucleotides is virtually infinite, and the human genetic code is believed to contain three billion combinations. However, only a small portion of these base pairs are actually responsible for unique traits in humans that can be useful for forensic investigations.

DNA is folded into microscopic bundles called chromosomes and exist in all cells that contain a nuclei. Thus, while DNA is present in the blood, it is not present in red blood cells themselves, since they do not have a nuclei. Other cells present in blood, however, do contain nuclei and DNA.

Scientific advances in molecular biology have permitted scientists to unravel the DNA code and to examine pieces of DNA. This in turn permits forensic scientists to look for similarities and differences between pieces of DNA obtained from different individuals. For example, a small fragment of DNA code may be represented as shown in Figure 9.10.

All human cells contain 46 chromosomes comprising 23 donated from each parent, creating a unique DNA structure built from a randomly alternating series of base pairs.

For forensic purposes, there are two procedures typically used to examine DNA: Restricted Fragment Length Polymorphism, and Polymerase Chain Reaction. **Restricted Fragment Length Polymorphism (RFLP)**, usually requires a larger quantity of sample than PCR, and it may take several weeks to actually complete the analysis. It is a laborious technique that employs various radioactive labeled reagents, requiring considerable specialization and special laboratory practices. **Polymerase Chain Reaction (PCR)**, on the other hand, is much easier to use, works on very small samples, and offers results in much briefer time periods. The differences arise in the laboratory results. RFLP population results can be individualized to a segment in the population as small as one in several billion. PCR results, however, may isolate an individual only in the order of one person in several thousand.

In 1993, the FBI began conducting validation tests on an innovation called Amplified-Fragment Length Polymorphism. **Amplified-Fragment Length**

Figure 9.10
The DNA molecule looks like a twisted ladder, and is called a double helix.

Polymorphism (AMP-FLPS), combines PCR's ability to make many copies of DNA evidence with the resolving power that comes from examining fragment length polymorphisms, the principal strength of RFLP. Using AMP-FLPS, forensic scientists will be able to perform DNA tests in a matter of days, rather than weeks. As a result, there will be even greater confidence in the conclusions about the evidence than from current tests (*FBI Law Enforcement Bulletin* 1992).

Vernon Gabreth sums up the view of many law enforcement officers regarding DNA profiling when he writes, "It's like the criminal leaving his name and address and social security number at the scene" (Gabreth 1990). Since DNA can maintain its integrity for prolonged periods even in dried specimens, its use can be helpful both in current and reopened past cases.

OTHER BIOLOGICAL SPECIMENS AS EVIDENCE

There are two additional biological elements that may be found at the crime scene and provide useful clues to the identity of a suspect. These include semen and hair.

Semen, like blood, may assist in identifying a suspect through Rh testing and typing. Additionally, both blood and semen may be used to undertake DNA test comparisons between samples taken from the victim or the crime scene, and specimens obtained form a suspect.

Hair can be a valuable, though sometimes overlooked, piece of evidence, and means for personal identification. Human hair grows from follicles in the skin at a rate of approximately 1/2 inch a month, although this may vary. Hair can be found in a wide variety of places on the body. Unlike body fluids such as blood and semen, the human hair generally retains its structural features for a very long period of time. Because of its nature, hair is an ideal source of information about the individual from which it came. For example, hair can be used to identify both the sex and the race of a person (Moenssen, Inbau, and Starrs 1986).

While hair cannot absolutely identify a particular individual, as for example a fingerprint might, scientific examination of hair can fairly convincingly rule out having come from a particular individual. Often, eliminating one of several suspects can be as important as identifying a particular one. Hair can also be valuable in police investigations because it tends to store a number of substances ingested by the body, including certain chemicals and drugs. In fact, a 2-inch length of hair taken from a suspect could reveal under scientific testing information about various drug substances this suspect may have used or ingested during the past 4 months.

NON-BIOLOGICAL SPECIMENS AS EVIDENCE

In addition to various biological specimens such as blood, semen, and hair, a number of non-biological specimens often can be helpful in police investigations.

Frequently these are collected and examined as small or even microscopic pieces of trace evidence. These include fibers, glass fragments, and paint chips.

Skip Palenik (1988) suggests that there are five basic techniques typically used by forensic technicians when collecting microtraces: handpicking, adhesive tape, vacuuming, and scraping (Palenik 1988:164). Each of these techniques is described in Box 9.4.

BOX 9.4 MICROTRACE COLLECTION TECHNIQUES

Handpicking. Handpicking literally means the removal of particles from some medium by means of a gloved hand or some inorganic implement (tweezers forceps, probes, magnets, and so forth). Handpicking is usually the first technique employed to locate and collect microtraces. It is useful for collecting particles that are numerous, large enough, or sufficiently color distinctive to contrast with their background. The shattered glass particles are an example of particles suitable for handpicking.

The major advantages to handpicking are its ability systematically to detect, recover, and isolate particles from contaminants in a single step. Identification of the location where the handpicked particles were found is relatively easy.

Adhesive Tape. Similar to the use of cellophane tape to lift fingerprints, cellophane adhesive tape is used to collect traces of minute particles from areas where handpicking may be ineffective. Once the particles adhere to the tape's mastic, they may be protected by folding a clean piece of tape over the particles. Another protective technique, originally advocated by Max Frei-Sulzer during the 1940s, places the strip of tape with the collected particles sticky side down on a microscope slide or plastic sheet (Frei-Sulzer 1951; Palenik 1988).

During examination of these particles, the slide can be placed directly under a microscope, or particular samples of the microtraces may be carefully removed. In removing samples, sections of the tape can be cut out, lifted, and used without damaging or contaminiating the remaiing particles.

Adhesive tape is particularly useful for removing fiber fragments that might otherwise go unnoticed or undetected were simple handpicking used alone. Unfortunately, because adhesive tape depends upon its mastic to lift various minute particles, this technique is ineffective on wet, oily, or excessively dusty surfaces.

Vacuuming. The vacuuming technique of microtrace collection is regarded as a highly efficient, although non-discriminating strategy. Vacuuming can remove microscopic fragments of fiber or other substances from carpeting, fabric, and other woven materials. However, vacuuming collects *all* particles in the area being covered and makes it necessary later to distinguish potentially useful microtraces from run-of-the-mill lint and dirt traces.

Forensic vacuums use very tiny filter cassettes to improve the technician's ability to identify specific locations where particles were found. Unlike the family Hoover, which may take weeks of household vacuuming before its filter bag is filled, these tiny filter cassettes take only a few seconds. Once they have been used, they are removed, bagged, and labeled to identify the location from which the dust has been obtained, just as with any larger pieces of evidence.

Washing. Washing, as a technique for collection of microtraces, is typically used to dislodge or loosen particles adhering to some medium. Some stains or deposits of mud or other soil harden significantly when dry. In order to remove pieces for examination and analysis, one might need to pick strenuously, potentially damaging materials that may be trapped below the surface of the stain. In such an instance, washing the stain to loosen and remove particles can be most useful.

ODONTOLOGY AS A FORENSIC INVESTIGATIVE TECHNIQUE

Related to the more microscopic examination of physical evidence is an increasingly useful technique known as **odontology** or bite-mark identification. For example, cavalier burglars sometimes make themselves sandwiches and leave half-eaten remains on kitchen tables. Also, teeth are commonly used as weapons (both offensively and defensively) during assaults and sexual attacks.

Among the incriminating evidence used against Ted Bundy in his trial for killing two Florida State University students were comparison bite marks left in the breasts of the women by their killer and a casting made from a bite Bundy had taken from an apple while incarcerated.

By examining the impression of the bite mark in some object or the flesh of a victim and comparing it to the suspect's bite structure, an identification may be possible. Unlike fingerprints, however, bite-mark identification is not viewed as exacting. Even in the case of Ted Bundy, experts called in to identify the comparison bite marks could only claim that the markings could have been made by the same person (Swanson et al. 1996).

Some stains, such as those caused by blood or seminal fluid, can be classified by Rhesus (Rh) factors and protein type, as well as being subjected to various other laboratory analysis tests. These traces can therefore be extremely useful in identifying suspects. These substances, however, tend to dry rapidly and create stains. Although moist stains, such as damp stains of blood or semen, may be collected on a blotter and allowed to dry. Dry stains, however, on floors, fabric, and garments present slightly different problems. Frequently, one can successfully scrape some of the dry blood from a hard, smooth surface, such as a floor. Alternatively, however, a mild saline and water solution could be used to moisten the stain sufficient to blot it.

Scraping. Scraping can be a useful strategy in loosening stains, such as blood or semen, where little danger of damaging participates is apparent. Also, scraping can be a useful technique to dislodge microtraces from clothing. The usual procedure is to scrape the garment gently with a metal spatula. The garment should be held over some large, clean material (plastic garbage bags, or large sheets of paper, for example) to capture particles that fall.

Among the five microtrace collection techniques discussed, scraping is the least efficient. There are several reasons for this. First, running the spatula down the garment in an attempt to knock particles off the fabric is not efficient and many particles will remain lodged in the garment's fibers. Second, and more serious, is the potential for nearly uncontrollable contamination from minute airborne particles. Traces of pollen, lint, dust, ash, and the like spin about us all the time. Anyone who wears eyeglasses can attest to that.

The damage these incredibly small particles can do is well understood by clean-room facilities workers where microchips and printed circuit boards are produced. Even a single particulate can destroy or irreversibly damage a microchip.

The scraping of a garment, then, not only loosens potential pieces of evidence, but large amounts of fibers and particles that are simply present in the air. Additionally, contaminants are likely to fall onto the capture sheet from the air itself.

GUNS, BULLETS, AND BARRELS

Among the more accurate television images of forensic science promulgated in the United States is that the most common type of physical evidence concerns guns, bullets, and rifle-barrels. Perhaps because of the enormous number of violent crimes each year involving shootings, the United States is teeming with firearms experts.

Less accurately portrayed in the media is the ease with which one can make a convincing identification of a bullet or cartridge fired from a particular gun. Although this is typically an important question in a shooting, it is not always answered as simply in the real world as in some police drama on television.

Frequently, the bullets recovered in a shooting fragmented or became significantly misshapen from their impact against bone, a wall, a tree, or other solid objects. Also, the weapon that fired the bullet may have become damaged by rust, clogged with mud, worn, or intentionally damaged after use, making identification of a signature or identifiable marking or striations on either the discharged bullet or cartridge impossible.

In spite of the difficulty associated with it, the examination and identification of fired bullets, or what is more properly called **ballistics**, is an important area in forensic science. First, bullets and cartridge cases typically are materials left behind at a crime scene. Second, in many cases markings on bullets and/or cartridges created by a particular weapon are sufficiently unique that they are like fingerprints, hence the concept of the weapon's signature.

Firearms evidence may include weapons such as revolvers, pistols, rifles, and shotguns, or loaded cartridges, misfired cartridges, casings, bullets, powder residues, shot pellets, and even wads from muzzle-loading black powder weapons and some older shotguns. Many of these objects may offer additional clues to the identity of the shooter, because it may reveal a fingerprint or have materials such as blood, hairs, or fibers attached.

The essential question usually asked in a shooting investigation is whether a particular weapon fired the bullet found. In order to answer this question, once a suspect and weapon are located, test firings are undertaken. Typically, this will involve firing the suspected weapon into a special tank filled with water. The water creates resistance to slow and eventually stop the bullet, but without causing serious damage or fragmentation to it. Also, water will not impart extraneous striations and markings on the soft lead of unshielded bullets. Jacketed ammunition (usually copper shielding) requires fewer precautions against potential damaging when test-fired.

After test firing and collecting the spent bullet, a comparison can be made of markings on the test slug and the one(s) obtained at the crime scene. Under magnification, both intentional tooling and rifling grooves left from the weapon's barrel and idiosyncratic irregularities in a barrel should become apparent.

Barrels of Weapons

As suggested above, a critical element in the identification of a bullet and the determination that it came from a particular weapon is the markings left on a bullet by the weapon's barrel. Gun barrels typically leave significant markings on bullets that pass through them. Virtually all modern handguns and rifles—with the exception of shotguns—possess internal barrel grooves known as **rifling**. A barrel's rifling results from one or another of several manufacturing methods, which leave grooves cut into the lining of the barrel. These grooves offer the bullet stability of flight, by causing the bullet to move with a rotary motion (a spin) as it is propelled through the barrel. This activity, however, creates striations and markings on the bullet.

Variations consistently occur in the process of rifling a gun's barrel. These irregularities may be affected by flaws in the tools used to cut the rifling, different depths of cut, and even different methods of creating the rifling.

SUMMARY

This chapter has examined generally the role of police and forensic science during the collection of evidence. The chapter began with a brief description of early crime laboratories. Next, the chapter considered the nature of evidence. In this regard, evidence was divided into two major categories, direct and indirect evidence. Direct evidence was described as proof in itself of the guilt or innocence of a suspect. Contrasting this, indirect evidence was depicted as circumstantial or fragmented pieces of information that cumulatively suggested the possible guilt or innocence of an individual.

A large portion of this chapter examined various types of physical evidence. These included various biological specimens such as blood, semen, hair, and DNA profiling. This segment of the chapter included a general description of coarse examination of crime scene for large objects such as weapons, furnishings, objects, etc. As well, this included the search for latent fingerprints and similar imprints. The chapter later shifted focus to consider microtraces of evidence such as fibers, glass, and paint fragments that may be located at crime scenes, on suspects, or on incriminating objects. Finally, the chapter concluded with a discussion on firearms, and various elements associated with firearms identification.

REFERENCES

Adams, Thomas F. *Police Field Operations*. Englewood Cliffs, N.J.: Prentice Hall, 1985.
Adams, Thomas F. *Police Field Operations*. 3d ed. Englewood Cliffs, N.J.: Prentice Hall, 1994.

Bennett, Robert A. "Refining the Art of Fingerprinting. "*New York Times,* 11 November, 1987:D10.

Bennett, Wayne W., and Karen M. Hess. *Criminal Investigation.* 3d ed. Minneapolis/ St. Paul: West Publishing Co., 1994.

Berg, Bruce L., and John J. Horgan. *Criminal Investigation.* 3d ed. Westonville, Oh.: Glencoe/McGraw-Hill, 1998.

Buracker, Carroll and William Stover. "Automated Fingerprint Identification-Regional Application of Technology. "*FBI Law Enforcement Bulletin,* 53(1984):1–5.

"DNA Fingerprinting Upheld in First Appellate Level Challenge. "*Criminal Justice Newsletter,* 1 December, 1988:3–4.

Elmer-De Witt, Phillip. "Taking a Byte Out of Crime." *Time,* 14 October, 1985:96.

"DNA Technology Update." *FBI Law Enforcement Bulletin,* April 1992:5.

Gaberth, Vernon, J. "Application of DNA Technology in Criminal Investigations." *Law & Order,* March 1990:70–73.

Goddard, Clavin. "The Valentine Day Massacre: A Study in Ammunition-Tracing." *American Journal of Police Science,* 1(1930):60–78.

Kirk, Paul. *Criminal Investigation.* 2d ed. New York: Wiley, 1974.

Menzel, E. R., J. Everse, K. E. Everse, T. W. Sinor, and J. A. Burt. "Room Light and Laser Development of Latent Fingerprints with Enzymes." *Journal of Forensic Science,* 29(1984):99–109.

Moenssen, A. A., F. E. Inbau, and J. E. Starrs. *Scientific Evidence in Criminal Cases.* 3d ed. New York: Foundation Press, 1986.

Ojena, S. M. "A New Improved Technique for Casting Impressions in Snow." *Journal of Forensic Sciences,* 29(1984):322–325.

Palenik, Skip. "Microscopy and Microchemistry of Physical Evidence." In *Forensic Science Handbook Volume 2.* Richard Saferstein (ed.) Englewood, Cliffs, N.J.: Prentice Hall, 1988.

Swanson, Charles R., Neil C. Chamelin, and Leonard Territo. *Criminal Investigation.* 6th ed. New York: The McGraw-Hill Companies, Inc., 1996.

Wilson, Charles. "Crime Detection Laboratories in the United States." In *Forensic Science: Scientific Investigation in Criminal Justice.* Joseph L. Peterson (ed.) New York: AMS Press, 1975.

CASE CITED

Andrews v. Florida, No.87-2166 (1988).

NOTE

[1] Information regarding biological fluids has been taken from Maria Josefi (ed.) *Handbook of Forensic Science.* Washington D.C.: Department of Justice, Federal Bureau of Investigation, 1995. Additional information was obtained from David Bigbee, *The Examination of Serological Evidence.* Quantico, Va., Federal Bureau of Investigation Research and Training Center, 1989.

QUESTIONS FOR REVIEW

Objective #1:
- How might one define criminalistics?
- What types of disciplines are often associated with forensic sciences?

Objective #2:
- What does the St. Valentine's Day Massacre have to do with early American forensic laboratories?

Objective #3:
- What is meant by direct evidence?
- When evidence is said to be "proof in itself of a person's guilt," is this direct or indirect evidence?

Objective #4:
- Why must a crime scene be photographed and sketched before items of evidence are collected and removed from the scene?

Objective #5:
- What are "friction ridges?"
- What part of the finger is the bulb?
- How can someone permanently alter their fingerprints?

Objective #6:
- What is meant by an invisible print?
- How are plastic prints formed?

Objective #7:
- Traditionally, what color are fingerprint powders?
- Why are some fingerprint powders fluorescent-colored?
- How might iodine be used to develop an invisible print?

Objective #8:
- How does AFIS technology speed fingerprint searches?

Objective #9:
- What are the four major typing groups for blood?
- How might blood type and Rh factors assist in eliminating a suspect?

Objective #10:
- What are the two primary types of DNA tests used in forensic police work today?
- What is DNA?

Objective #11:

- How might semen assist a criminal investigation?
- What sort of information can hair found at a crime scene tell the crime laboratory?

Objective #12:

- How are striations on the sides of bullets formed?
- Why might it be difficult to identify a particular bullet found at a crime scene as having been fired from a specific gun?
- How is rifling created?

10 Computers and the Police

CHAPTER OBJECTIVES

After reading this chapter, you should be able to:

1. Discuss the advantages to law enforcement offered by computers and suggest some problems computers may cause police.
2. Talk about the historical development of computers in policing.
3. Consider the role of computers in police communications.
4. Describe various types of databases and information management systems.
5. Examine the value of computer programs to the area of forensics.
6. Differentiate between cyberpunks and cyber-criminals.
7. Specify five major categories of computer crime.
8. Consider how police investigate computer crimes.
9. List procedures used for securing a computer taken as evidence.

THE COMPUTER AS A DOUBLE-EDGED SWORD

On the surface, it would appear that the advances in computer technology would be an enormous benefit to a variety of law enforcement processes. However, computer technology actually is a kind of *sword* that cuts in two directions. On one edge of the blade are the many benefits to law enforcement such as data management, ease in report writing, communications, criminal identification, document and photographic enhancement, and training, to name but a few.

On the other edge of the blade, however, are the advantages offered to individuals who engage in criminal behavior. The threats from computer-equipped criminals has grown more serious during the past decade because computer costs have dropped radically, while computers' powers have increased geometrically. The computer industry estimates that by the turn of the century, one out of every five homes in America will possess a personal computer.

KEY TERMS		
	ports	bootable disk
	hackers	boot-up
information systems	cyberpunks	parking the hard drive
stand-alone program	cyber-criminals	diddled data
interface	antivirus programs	voice mailbox

In spite of their potential capacity as an aid to police work, the computer has not yet come of age. There are several reasons for this. For example, although costs have dropped radically, many small departments in towns, boroughs or even small cities simply do not have the budgetary resources for an advanced computer system. Furthermore, although educational requirements are changing and increasing nationally, many agencies simply do not have sufficient numbers of computer-literate officers to make it practical. Moreover, many officers are resistant to expand their understandings of computers. In addition, there are some lingering questions about the use of computers, computer information networks, and rights to privacy.

It seems safe to argue, however, that as the educational requirements among entry-level officers increases, resistance towards computerization will diminish. Certainly, at the federal and state levels, computerized information and data storage systems are being revamped and upgraded. Many states have poured millions of dollars into an automated fingerprint indexing system (AFIS). At the federal level, the FBI AFIS databanks contain more than 18 million print records of offenders born in or after 1929. It has been estimated that this bank is used for searches in excess of 30,000 times daily for both criminal justice and non-criminal justice purposes. The system processes more than 246,000 searches each month (Wilson and Woodward 1987; Berg 1995; Berg and Horgan 1999).

The FBI also has been working on an integrated computer system scheduled to be completely up and running by the year 2000. This integrated computer system will combine AFIS capacity with other sorts of identification and

Figure 10.1
Computers are apparent throughout many police departments.

Figure 10.2
Officers use computers for many factes of their work.

statistical records information. Once on line, agencies will be able to contact the system, and in addition to running latent prints, be in contact with National Crime Information Center (NCIC) data. As well, they will be able to access an Interstate Identification Index, and several other informational record banks (Van Duyn 1993).

COMPUTER APPLICATIONS IN POLICING

Although computer use and development is quickly growing across the country, it is still in its infancy as a tool in law enforcement and criminal investigation. In 1964, only a single city, St. Louis, could boast having a police computer system. By 1968, 10 states and 50 cities had established state-level computer based informational systems for law enforcement use (Birchler 1989). Today, virtually every city of more than 50,0000 people has some sort of law enforcement-related computer support, communications, and/or investigation system.

COMPUTERS AND COMMUNICATIONS

Mobile Data Terminals (MDTS), 911 enhanced systems, portable computers and even fax systems have been finding their way into police cruisers during the past decade. These devices allow officers to enter or retrieve information directly into the department's computer, see information such as names, addresses, and even street directions to a location, on screen, and write store reports or interviews, and even enter computerized traffic ticket data (Monopoli 1996). The St. Louis County Police Department have been using a Computer-Assisted Report Entry (CARE) system for several years (Gaines et al. 1997). Dennis George (1990) suggests that this system reduces the time required of police officers to write reports and increases their accuracy.

The computerization of these and other records increases an agency's accuracy, decreases labor costs, and eliminates redundant paperwork. An added administrative benefit is that these various computerized communications devices provide a means for supervisors to monitor officers while they are in the field. With the proper configurations and interface capacities, officers in the field can even access national, regional, or state databases such as AFIS.

The National Law Enforcement Telecommunications System (NLETS), for example, is a computer link telecommunications network. It has the potential for connecting all law enforcement agencies in the country with a database containing driver license, motor vehicle registration, and criminal history records. Using this system, a federal investigator in Spokane, Washington, could obtain a suspect's criminal history from a police agency in New Jersey.

The National Center for Analysis of Violent Crime (NCAVC) currently uses several advanced computer systems to assist their investigations of violent crimes. One system is the Violent Criminal Apprehension Program (VICAP), which is operated through the FBI. This information management system provides a means for investigators to compare elements of a criminal's *modus operandi* with those of other crimes contained in the database. This program allows

Figure 10.3
Mobile data terminals (MDTS) can be found in many police cruisers across the country.

Figure 10.4
Mobile data terminals (MDTs) increase officer efficiency in the field.

investigators to project criminal patterns and project a serial criminal's geographic movements from one jurisdiction to another (Gaines et al. 1997).

LARGE DATABASES

In 1965, the FBI took up the challenge brought by advances that were emerging in computer technology. By 1967, the FBI had created a central repository and clearing center for the nation, containing computerized information about missing and wanted persons and for stolen property. This system was called the National Crime Information Center (NCIC). Today, NCIC holds more than 6,000,000 active records and processes more than 250,000 inquires daily.

Information system is an industry term for computer systems that manage and manipulate information. They have grown in use by police agencies across the country. While these do not manage as large a database as several of the federal systems do, they have had a tremendous impact on police departments. The follow section will describe several of the areas that such *information systems* have assisted.

COMPUTERS AND SUSPECT IDENTIFICATION

In addition to storage places for potentially huge databases, computers also are useful for aiding in the identification of suspects. A growing number of police agencies in the United States have begun using a computerized imaging system to replace their *rogues gallery* of mug books. In these systems, photographs are stored in a computer and easily retrieved for a victim or witness to view. For the past several years, New York City has successfully used an automated mug-shot file called the Computer-Assisted Terminal Criminal Hunt (CATCH).

A witness or victim provides the investigator with any identifying information he or she has. These may include a capped tooth, a scar, beard, eyeglasses, or whatever. It may further include particulars about how the crime was committed. These pieces of information are entered into CATCH as parameters. As a result, only pictures of known suspects that have such features—fall into the parameters—will be selected by the computer for viewing. Obviously, this saves countless hours of unproductively having a witness or victim scan through hundreds of mug shots in traditional mug books.

A number of software companies have also developed programs that assist in creating a composite picture of a suspect. These programs contain a library of photographed facial features (e.g., noses, eyes, lips, ears, etc.). These features can be brought together on a computer screen to create a composite face. The witness or victim scans thought the facial features, selecting those that most closely match their memory of the suspect. Facial hair, glasses, scars, and skin tone can all be added or adjusted. Once the witness or victim is satisfied with the composite, an attached camera produces a photographic copy for distribution (Schmitt 1992).

PROGRAMS FOR CRIMINAL INVESTIGATION

The kind of software programs used by police agencies can be dichotomized. First, there are programs that are designed in-house by an officer with sufficient computer expertise to write and customize a program. Second, there are commercially vended programs that offer various levels of support to an agency. Most agencies tend to favor a commercial vendor for a records management system that may additionally carry a program designed to assist criminal investigation. In fact, among the literally hundreds of vendors who produce software to law enforcement agencies, only a handful offer *stand-alone* criminal investigation programs (Pilant 1993). A stand-alone program is one that does not require assistance from a larger more encompassing of multifaceted program. As illustration of this might be a program designed for recording criminal incident reports that operated largely like a word processing program with special forms. While one might be able to create and store files containing criminal incident forms, one might not be able to compare these with previous incident forms from ten years ago on a stand-alone program or system.

Most criminal investigation programs are modules that are either part of a records-management system, are able to draw from one and integrate information, or are sold as adjunct programs to a main management package; this is because criminal investigation generally makes use of information derived from a number of sources that become aspects of the police agency's records. For instance, incident reports, field interviews, criminal histories, witness, victim, and suspect statements, and evidence descriptions all can be entered into a record management program. Then, using a relational database associated with this main system, criminal investigators can retrieve and manipulate information in a number of ways. A stand-alone system would either require the duplicate entering of various pieces of information, or it may be limited to certain functions (see Box 10.1). Furthermore, stand-alone systems may not be able to interface or communicate and share data with various department database and management systems, further limiting their usefulness (Pilant 1993).

An example of this more encompassing sort of technology is Ameritech's Records Information Management System (RIMS). This package includes two separate systems in one integrated program: a record management module and a computer-assisted dispatch module. Like many records management programs, RIMS ties together information entered into the files. However, RIMS completes this operation automatically. In addition, RIMS contains an automatic solvability function, criminal profiling segment, a crime analysis component, and a case management capacity. What is particularly useful, is that all of these components are able to interface with a separate Automated Control of Evidence (ACE) module. ACE features a segment what allows the user to simultaneously

BOX 10.1 STAND-ALONE COMPUTER SYSTEMS AND COMMUNITY POLICING

Community-oriented policing has become an increasingly important element in many police agencies across the country. In Alexandria, Virginia, it is part of the daily routine of the department. Officers are assigned to each of the city's civic associations and are expected to keep citizens apprised of the rises and falls in crime for every community in the city.

These community liaison officers, until recently, found that these tasks were enormously time-consuming. Regularly keeping up with local crime rates was further complicated by the complexity of the department's computerized information system. The resolution was to develop a separate personal computer database that could interface and download information from the departments larger information system (Campbell 1994).

Department administrators called this new system "Quick Query". The primary purpose of this system was to improve the ability of liaison officers to quickly locate and then share information with community associations. In addition, this information could be accessed and used by

patrol officers, investigators, supervisors, and administrators.

An important factor included in the design of QQ was maintaining control over timeframes covered by the queries, types of incidents culled from the system, and the geographic limits of the searches (Campbell 1994). As well there were concerns that it be **user-friendly**. In other words, that it be easy enough for even the most computer-shy officer to use. To accomplish this, the program was designed to be fully menu-driven. In fact, after typing in one's personal code number, it is possible to perform all of QQ's functions using only six keys (four cursor keys, the escape and the enter keys).

By using QQ, the liaison officers in the Alexandria, Virginia, police department can more quickly and efficiently address the crime problems in their respective communities. Combining this computer resource with the ideal of community policing allows the department to provide enhanced services at a minimal cost to its citizens.

cross-reference the database in several different ways. It also provides a *tool program* that permits a user to identify relationships between cases, property, and people (Pilant 1993). Police agencies can even purchase optional components that will allow the user to interface with NCIC, work with a crime lab function, or network with other precincts or districts and permits entry of data from these other sites.

Many agencies, however, find that certain types of stand-alone systems do offer distinct advantages over comprehensive records management systems. First, they tend to be far less expensive than comprehensive integrated record management systems. Second, they can be designed to meet a department's specific criminal investigation styles, polices, or practices. The Homicide Investigation and Tracking System (HITS), for example, originally was developed for use by the officers in the State of Washington. HITS stores, collates, and analyzes characteristics of all murders and sexual offenses. The information is available statewide to assist in solving these cases (Pilant 1994). In addition, operations specialists for HITS advertise in various law enforcement and criminal justice trades sources, offering to provide information and assistance to agencies interested in developing their own version of HITS.

Another example of a stand-alone system is Oxnard, California, Police Department's Gang Offender Comprehensive Action Program (GOCAP). This program is networked between the police department, probation department, and the courts to identify and track gang members (Pilant 1994). The basic database consists of information taken from field interview cards on known gang members. This information consists of everything the agencies know about the gang member, such as gang affiliation, any aliases or nicknames, and even descriptions of tattoos and samples of an individual's graffiti. In effect, this allows every member of the police department to have accurate, up-to-date information on gang members at the touch of a few buttons.

COMPUTER PROGRAMS AND FORENSICS

Criminal investigation has made good use of computer technology in the area of fingerprint analysis and identification. However, there have also been large strides made in the use of computers in the area of forensics. The Metro Dade County Police Department, in Florida, for instance was among the first agencies to combine and computerize their property and evidence management records with their crime lab operations (Pilant 1992).

Metro Dade's crime lab services about 30 cities in Florida, and processes more than 1,000 cases each month. Before computerizing their system, paperwork backlogs and serious time delays plagued the lab and allowed too much room for error. In 1992, the department began using the Laboratory Information Management System (LIMS). This is a powerful and sophisticated program that automatically assigns case numbers and bar codes, tracks evidence, and even creates case files containing the court case number, the name of the attorney(s) handling the case, an evidence list, primary officer investigating, and the judge assigned to the case. LIMS has the capacity to generate a daily report on chemical tests, and statistics that allow officers to determine whether there has been an increase or decrease in case loads, if there have been shifts in the drug profile of an area, or even if there has been a change in the prevalence of one type of drug or another (Pilant 1992).

In another area of forensic investigation, new computer-assisted *forensic imaging* technology has arrived. In 1987, the FBI's Special Projects Section received a request from the Newark, New Jersey, field office. Agents asked if it were possible to take a photograph of long-time fugitive, John List, and produce an age-enhanced version. List had eluded authorities since murdering his family in 1970 (O'Donnell 1994).

The Special Projects Section was intrigued by the idea, and using newly acquired computer systems, the visual information specialists produced an age-enhanced image of John List. This photograph was then sent to the field officers. The agents publicized the photo in various national publications, and List was recognized by one of his neighbors. List was living under the assumed name of Robert P. Clark. The woman who recognized Clark as List dared Clark's wife to confront her husband. The wife did not.

In 1989, the television show *America's Most Wanted*, featured a plaster bust prepared by a forensic artist based on the age-enhanced photographs. Although by this time Clark had moved, the neighbor who originally recognized him was now convinced that Clark was really List. The FBI was contacted, and although Clark denied being List when confronted, fingerprint records from the gun permit application he filed a month before killing his family proved otherwise (O'Donnell 1994).

In addition to enhancing the age of an adult suspect, the computer programs, like the one used in the List case, are also capable of creating an age-enhanced image of a child's photograph. This permits investigators to see what a 10-year-old child might look like 12 years later when she is 22 years old.

The introduction of three-dimensional digital imaging offers yet additional forensic potential. For example, by manipulating a digitally created three-dimensional skull image, forensic artists are able to rotate facial images on screen and produce more detailed facial expressions and features.

The use of computers to assist forensic artists clearly has brought vast amounts of improved assistance to the field of investigations. Further advances in the computerization of forensic images promise to provide criminal investigation with even greater benefits in the future.

CRIMES INVOLVING COMPUTERS

As suggested in the beginning of this chapter, in addition to the benefits to criminal investigation, computers pose a liability as well. In particular, over the past several decades, computers have rapidly gained prominence in the area of crime.

When computers first began emerging in the 1940s, most were complex, large (sometimes filling an entire room) and difficult if not impossible for the average person to operate. In these early days, it was common for computer engineers to use complex languages such as Fortran to communicate with the device and create programs. Even as computers began to enter business settings, it is likely that few of the corporate managers had the skills necessary to use these cumbersome and complex machines. This lack of computer skills placed these corporate managers at the mercy of professional programmers, and venders of early packaged computer programs. If a problem arose with the computer program, or if the computer crashed, it became necessary to call in the vendor or a specialized computer consultant. It is not difficult to imagine that there were many unscrupulous people who saw an opportunity to swindle unknowing companies, and seized it. Minor problems might require days of repair work and huge bills, rather than a few minutes and a couple of dollars.

Today, with the advances in menu- and icon-driven, user-friendly programs, and even voice-command mode in some personal computers, the opportunities for computer-related crimes has leaped to extraordinary proportions. It is not uncommon, today, to find children in lower elementary grades receiving computer instructions. Many children, as young as 2 or 3 years of age, already have begun mastering computer skills as they play with an assortment of games and computer-based books. While many of our parents may have been nearly completely computer illiterate, our children—even as children—are not.

Several writers have noted that with the explosion in the amount of computer equipment available to the public, and the increasing numbers of people knowing how to use it, there is little wonder that computer-related crimes are increasing (Albanese 1988; Manning and White 1990; Sites 1991; and Berg and Horgan 1999). Table 10.1 lists some of the more common computer crime-related terms and their meanings.

Table 10.1 *Common Terms Related to Computer Crimes*

Antivirus Program	A program designed to detect a *computer virus* that has attached itself to a program on a disk or hard disk. Most antivirus programs contain a sub-program intended to cure the program by removing the virus.
Backdoor	A glitch in a computer system that permits someone entry, even without a proper code or password. Sometimes this can be accomplished by gaining entry to a non-secured segment of a program, and opening a window between the non-secure and secure segments.
Browsing	Involves the unauthorized examining of someone else's data after an unlawful entry into another's computer files.
Computer Virus	A program designed to attach itself to some other program, and to attack and destroy the program. Sometimes, viruses are designed to ride one program into a system, but to attack and destroy data or memory in the computer's main drive. Some viruses are simply obnoxious, rather than really destructive. In this case, they may cause a computer to automatically shut down, or to show disks as blank even when data is present.

Data Diddling	A procedure sometimes used by insiders. Involves placing false information into a computer, as in the placing of a false name on a payroll, or paying out to a fraudulent bill.
Digital Signature	A means of including an electronic authorization in electronically produced documents. May involve strategic placement of names, dates, times created, and so forth.
Encryption	Creation of electronic cipher into which material is encoded and decoded. Material can not, however be decoded without the correct key to the cipher.
Fraud	As it relates to computer crimes, fraud represents any use of trickery, deception or falsification, involving computers, to obtain money, services, or property.
Hacking	The illegal entry into a computer system, usually through trial and error, or systematically using a random digit program, a modem, and an automatic caller.
Impersonation	In computer-related crimes, this involves the unauthorized use of someone's identity, code, or password. It is sometimes associated with calling card or voice-mail frauds as well.
Masquerading	Similar to *impersonating* where an unauthorized user uses someone else's identity code or password.
Picks	These are programs designed to break through, or bypass security locks and safeguards intended to prevent unauthorized duplication of software programs.
Program Piracy	The unauthorized copying of commercial programs.
Salami Slice	The establishing of an unauthorized account in a company or bank's computerized records. At some regular interval, a small amount, perhaps even fractions of a cent, are systematically placed in the unauthorized account. Sometimes these transfers go unnoticed for long periods of time, because the amounts are covered by rounding figures. These pennies and fractions of pennies eventually can amount to hundreds of thousands of dollars.
Smart Cards	Electronic identification cards, sometimes cued to a digitized fingerprint or retinal identification screening device. Designed to assure the user of a computer is authorized to be so using.
Super-Zapping	The use of repair, diagnosis, or maintenance programs to sidestep antitheft programs on a corporate computer systems. Although some manipulation of the program may be necessary, once inside, the *super-zapper* soon is able to control the system's operations.
Time Bomb	A virus scheduled to "explode," or begin its work, on a specific date, time, or holiday. If undetected for long, it may destroy all files in a computer's memory (see *Trojan horse*).
Trap Door	A similar phenomenon to a *back door*. Usually, however, trap doors are intentionally left in by a computer programmer, so that he or she can gain entry, no matter what antitheft or security measures may be added on later.
Trashing	The taking of information from discarded printout, computer disks, or tapes. This can sometimes uncover important information and may occur in governmental or industrial espionage cases.
Trojan Horse	A hidden program which may lay dormant until a particular program is called up, or a particular time or date occurs in the computer clock and calendar. Then, the Trojan horse program *awakens*. Sometimes Trojan horses contain computer virus programs. Other times they run specific program tasks or data manipulations (see *time bombs*).

For many types of computer crimes, all one needs is a personal computer (PC) equipped with a modem, the right software, and the desire to commit a crime. Regardless of security programs and passwords designed to limit access to a remote telephonic **ports** or computer access hook-ups, large corporate or governmental computer systems may still be vulnerable to invasion.

Computers operated by the U.S. Department of Defense, various defense contractors, utility companies, universities, hospitals, research institutes, banks, and an assortment of *Fortune 500* companies all have been invaded by **hackers**. Hackers are people proficient in the use of computers and computer technology. Sometimes these are teenagers simply interested in being able to get in, change a grade or their telephone bill, in order to demonstrate that they actually did it! Sometimes, however, these invasions have a more sinister purpose. They may be accomplished as part of some espionage plan against the government or private industry, or simply as a criminal means of obtaining services or money. Hacker Kevin Mitnick, for example, stole 20,000 credit card numbers—and used them to obtain an and estimated million dollars—until his capture in February 11, 1995. Mitnick's capture by the FBI was assisted by Tsutomu Shimomura, a researcher at the San Diego Supercomputer Center. Shimomura got involved because Mitnick allegedly broke into his home computer last Christmas and stole thousands of data files (*USA Today* 1995).

As another example, a number of years ago, a computer operator for Wells Fargo, one of the leading bonded money movers in the United States, electronically transferred several million dollars into his own Swiss bank account. The transfer occurred on a Friday afternoon, and was not discovered until Monday. The thief had nearly three full days to escape to Switzerland. He has never been apprehended.

The threat of hackers is so significant that the federal government employs a group of "professional hackers" to regularly test the security effectiveness of defense and other sensitive government computers. These people regularly attempt to "break in" to federal computers simply to assure that it is not possible—or more correctly—very difficult—to get in.

CYBERPUNKS AND CYBER-CRIMINALS

During the early 1980s a group of science-fiction authors began writing in a particular style that seemed to set them apart from others of the time. It was both this style and several common concepts woven throughout their stories that separated them from other science fiction writers. This genre of writing quickly began to be labeled by a number of names, including "radical hard science fiction," "outlaw technologists," "the eighties wave," "the neuromantics," and even "the mirror-shades group." The label that soon overwhelmed all others was "cyberpunks."

From this seemingly innocent literary origin, the label of cyberpunk has grown into an actual counterculture with its own magazines, music, artifacts, and beliefs. Cyberpunks today hold a quasi-philosophical view of the world that examines and criticizes modern technological advances as typifying the fall of humanity. Cyberpunks predict a kind of technological apocalypse that will result in huge decaying cities, humans and machines merging into one, and human-free thought becoming mediated through computers. Subscribers to this cyberpunk way of thinking are very concerned about contemporary states of technology because they both fear, and desire to understand this apocalyptic future.

Cyberpunks serve an interesting purpose. They underscore small details that many people overlook in modern cyber-culture. This includes making computer networks more cautious about security and the potential dangers of hackers infiltrating their systems. Cyberpunks are well versed in the use of computers and the many uses of computers—both lawful and otherwise. But the term "cyberpunks" has frequently been mistakenly seen a synonymous with "cyber-criminals."

Cyberpunks, in their purest sense, are technological outlaws, radical computer hackers driven by a moral concern about technology's role in future society and culture. In some cases, their interventions—although illegal—are not dissimilar to radical environmentalists who have come to be called environmental terrorists because of their sometimes violent or overzealous attempts to protect the environment.

Cyber-criminals, on the other hand, some of who may well have started out as cyberpunks, regularly break the law for criminal purposes. There is no altruism in their acts, only profit motive, or a desire to disrupt computer systems in some terroristic manner, and often with some terroristic purpose.

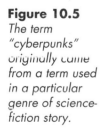

Figure 10.5
The term "cyberpunks" originally came from a term used in a particular genre of science-fiction story.

Until recently, the criminal justice system has not addressed the criminal misuse of computers. In 1979, the U.S. Department of Justice defined computer crime as "any illegal act for which knowledge of computer technology is essential for its perpetration, investigation, or prosecution" (Parker 1983:23). More recently, an National Institute of Justice report indicated that there are five distinct categories of computer crime: internal computer crimes, telecommunications crimes, computer manipulation crimes, support of criminal enterprises, and hardware or software thefts (Conley and McEwen 1990:3).

INTERNAL COMPUTER CRIMES

This category of crime includes any alteration to an existing computer program that causes that program to operate in a manner other than its original design. This could include changes in the program that causes losses or deletion of data, prevents access by legitimate users, destroys segments of the computer's memory sectors, cause the computer to crash or shut down without warning, and so forth. Typically the causes of these sorts of problems generically are called viruses. Viruses can be envisioned as attaching themselves to some other program when that program is placed into a "contaminated computer." Frequently, viruses are transferred from one computer to another when one shares programs on disks, with friends or colleagues. However, viruses also can enter a computer when one signs onto a contaminated computer bulletin board while surfing the Internet. In many cases, if the infected computer is discovered soon after a virus has attached itself, the computer can be "cured" by running any of a number of commercial antivirus programs. **Antivirus programs** combat specific viruses. While antivirus programs often contain an index of as many as 100 viruses they can combat, these programs must be updated regularly. New viruses are constantly finding their way onto the Internet and into unwitting users' computers. Unfortunately, when a virus lies undiscovered in a computer for too long, it can ruin the data on a computer's hard disk (Berg and Horgan 1998).

Telecommunications Crimes

Telecommunications crimes involve the illegal access to or use of computer systems over telephone lines. This may involve someone using a random-digit program in order to determine a valid access code into a computer system, or misuse of toll-free numbers, calling card numbers, illegal access to automatic teller machines (ATMs) and voice mail systems (see Box 10.2). In addition, telecommunications crimes include the misuse of computer bulletin boards or creation of underground bulletin boards in order to carry out various criminal activities. These may include sale or solicitation of child pornography, drugs, stolen property, or even murder for hire. During recent years, terrorists have even begun to use bulletin boards in order to send and receive messages, and to provide members with information about law enforcement activities (Berg and Horgan 1998).

BOX 10.2   CRIME AND TECHNOLOGY: FRAUD AND VOICE MAIL

As technology advances, so too do the various ways criminals adapt to these innovations. An example of this can be seen in increases recently in the illegal use of stolen calling card numbers, and the theft of calls from commercial voice mail services.

Most of us are familiar with voice mail. Typically, it involves a recorded message telling the caller a list or menu of numbers to press on a touch tone phone to reach some intended calling destination. In some cases, one may need the extension number of someone in particular in order to bypass or exit the phone mail system. If the intended party is not available, the voice mail recording instructs the caller on how to leave a voice message in a **voice mailbox**. These systems allow the owner of the voice mailbox to call in and using a tone or password code, retrieve his or her voice messages.

Criminals, however, have discovered ways to commit voice-mail fraud, usually against businesses equipped with a toll-free (1-800) number (Thrasher 1994). The processes involves a caller leaving a personal, nonbusiness-related message for another individual in a business' voice mailbox, using a toll-free number. Then, when the other individual retrieves the message, he or she can return the personal call, again using the company's toll-free number. The loss will be reflected in the long distance telephone bills the company will receive at the end of the billing cycle. Often, these bills can run into staggering amounts, especially when the fraud involves long-distance overseas numbers (Thrasher 1994).

Other variations on this fraud may involve obtaining and using a voice-mail code number. Frequently, voice-mail systems include a remote code that allows a member of the company to make a long distance call through the system, in a manner similar to a calling card. If this code is learned by an unscrupulous person, it may be misused or even sold. Corporations have sustained losses from such frauds exceeding $1,000 in just the first few hours following the report of a stolen corporate calling card or code number. In once case, the loss to the corporation exceeded $220,000 after only 13 hours of fraudulent use (Thrasher 1994).

Many state statutes define fraud as the *obtaining of money, property, or services by trick, deception, or false pretense*. Therefore, the unauthorized use of toll-free numbers, calling codes and calling cards can be prosecuted. Since voice-mail fraud may cross several jurisdictions, or even involve international calls, state and local prosecutors sometimes must work with a Federal prosecutor in order to process a case.

The unauthorized use of ATM or credit cards with personal identification numbers (PINs) has become a increasing problem for police agencies. While various safeguards have been taken to reduce the likelihood of unauthorized use of bank account and credit lines through ATMs, it continues to be a serious criminal problem. This is especially true with the advance of the bank-issued debit card (see Box 10.3).

Many banks and credit card companies warn customers from keeping their PINs with their ATM access or credit cards. Yet, many customers persist in writing their PINs directly on the cards—so they will not forget it. In some cases, the customer will write it on a slip of paper, their car registration, or social security card. Unfortunately, if they carry these documents with their ATM or credit cards they have provided open access to their credit and bank accounts should their wallet or purse be lost or stolen.

Figure 10.6
Banks and credit card companies warn customers against keeping their PIN on their person with their ATM access or credit cards.

Figure 10.7
Automated Teller Machines (ATMs) pose a potential risk to users, and a challenge to would-be computer criminals.

A

B

BOX 10.3 THIEVES CASH IN ON ATM

It was a crisp November afternoon in Portland, Oregon, but for the thieves who stole Karen Smith's bank card must have thought Christmas had come early! The thieves calmly cruised from automated teller machine to another in broad daylight, spending hours at a time withdrawing money.

In a 54 hours, the thieves managed to make 724 withdrawals totaling $346,770. Authorities have called this one of the five largest automated teller fraud cases in U.S. history. According to Detective Jim Muzyn, who investigated the case, the thieves repeatedly ran the card through the machine just as fast as their fingers could press the buttons. They were apparently courteous thieves, however, and periodically stopped long enough to allow a *real* bank customer to use the machine.

Usually there are computer safe guards such as a $200.00 per day limit on withdrawal intended to prevent exactly this sort of crime. However,

owing to a serendipitous problem with the bank's software, and changes that were being made, no such limits were in force for the thieves.

When the computer showed that the account was empty, the thieves simply used empty deposit envelopes to make fake deposits. Then, they withdrew the bogus funds from the already empty account. The crime spree began on Friday, November 18, when the thieves broke into Smith's van while she attended a high school football game in Gresham, a Portland suburb. They found Smith's purse in the van containing her bankcard, and her social security card with her personal identification number written on it. The card was used for the first time just moments after the break in, and the rest is history.

The thieves literall emptied several of the 48 ATMs they hit during their spree. But several of the machines were equipped with hidden cameras, and the thieves were identified and arrested (Bob Baum 1994).

A growing number of banks now issue an ATM card that also serves as a debit credit card. This means the user can make regular charges against the balance of money currently held in the user's bank account. Thus, when stolen, this card can be used like a credit card—where no personal identification number is required and an individual's bank account effectively can be emptied. As a result of these debit cards, even if one has intentionally concealed his or her PIN, the money in the account remains vulnerable.

COMPUTER MANIPULATION CRIMES

These types of crimes involve changing data or creating records in a system for the specific purpose of advancing some other crime. For example, one might create false entries in a company's electronic bookkeeping ledger, and place corporate funds into these dummy accounts.

In the early 1960s and 1970s, a number of banks were subjected to computer manipulation crimes. In those days, banks routinely left blank deposit slips out on tables for the convenience of their depositors. The slip had a series of computer scannable numbers at its bottom that told the computer what bank branch it was, and that these were not personalized account deposit slips.

Criminals, however, discovered that they could print duplicate slips containing their own personal account numbers on the slip. Then, whenever a customer used one of these slips, replaced by the criminal, the customer's money was deposited into the thief's account. Most banks have now abandoned the use of blank slips left out on counters (Berg and Horgan 1998).

SUPPORT OF CRIMINAL ENTERPRISES

Computer programs are not only an aid to legitimate businesses, but to illegal ones as well. For instance, computer-based account ledgers can be used by criminals to keep track of their drug business, or profits and expenses when running an organized auto theft ring. E-mail (electronically written and transmitted messages) can be sent between members of criminal conspiracies to keep one another informed. Electronic bulletin boards can be created, or used to solicit or advertise pornographic materials, weapons, drugs, or even criminal services. Computers even may be used by criminals to maintain information or to simulate a planned crime.

HARDWARE AND SOFTWARE THEFTS

The theft of computers, monitors, and other hardware devices seems rather uncomplicated. Theft of software, however, has a number of more subtle shades of ambiguity. Software piracy is a serious problem because of its relative ease to accomplish. It involves the unauthorized duplication and distribution of software programs. The Business Software Alliance, a Washington, D.C., based trade group, estimates that software piracy may cost the industry $15.2 billion in lost sales each year (Slind-Flor 1995). In fact, the group claims such misappropriations of technology cost $482.00 each second, $28,900.00 per minute, and $1.7 million each hour (Slind-Flor 1995).

While some software companies have developed safeguards or *locks* on their programs intended to prevent unauthorized duplication, these efforts are not always successful. It is a simple task to obtain *pick programs* designed to bypass the very security measures intended to prevent duplication. Adding to the problems related to this type of crime is the attitude of many consumers of commercial programs. Many do not recognize the problems caused by making a duplicate program for a friend. Others do not believe it is a crime, if no fee is charged for the duplicate program. Still others rationalize that at the cost of programs, *they are entitled to make copies.*

The lack of clear and unambiguous definition for what constitutes computer crime is a problem for law enforcement agencies. Further complicating matters is the fact that several different categories of computer crime may overlap, creating a potential problem in determining charges. Furthermore, while some new laws are emerging, many of the laws used to prosecute computer criminals simply were not created for these sorts of prosecutions. Software piracy, for example, has been prosecuted under state "trade secret acts," but these tend to come in a variety of different forms. In some cases of data theft, the action has been prosecuted under a 1919 federal statute enacted to deal with interstate transport of stolen automobiles (Slind-Flor 1995). In other words, prosecution of software and data code pirates has not been an easy task. Finally, computer illiteracy and fear of computers on the part of police tends to hinder some investigations and prosecutions.

To resolve some of these problems, police departments must begin hiring or cultivating officers with computer skills and technical competence. As time progresses, large police departments may need to assign officers to special computer units whose job it will be to handle crimes related to computers and computer technology.

On February 1, 1996, Congress overwhelmingly passed the Telecommunications Act of 1996. This was the first comprehensive rewrite of the Communications Act of 1934, and dramatically effects telecommunications equipment and services, cable television, radio and television broadcast regulations, and the Internet and online computer services.

In a subpart of the Act titled "Communications Decency Act of 1996," criminal penalties are noted for the "knowing" transmission over the Internet of material considered "indecent to minors." These provisions also make it a crime to make any computer network transmission without the intent to "annoy" or "harass" the recipient.

It should be clear that computers and computer criminals are increasing in their prevalence in our society. It should be just as clear that police agencies must become more computer-competent if they are to combat these cyber-criminals.

INVESTIGATION OF COMPUTER CRIME

When the police receive a report about a computer crime, typically they follow their general report policy. Appropriate forms will be filled out, and the information given to the department detectives. The investigator who is assigned to the case will conduct the primary investigation. This, like any preliminary investigation, will likely begin with the investigator questioning the complainant.

Next, the investigator will interview other potentially related parties. These may be other employees at the business where the computer crime occurred, past employees, service contractors, and anyone else who might provide relevant information.

For the most part, investigation of computer crimes run fairly parallel to other types of investigations, especially those involving what may be categorized as white-collar crimes. Sometimes an employee or executive of a company accidentally stumbles over indications that some sort of data manipulation or similar computer crime has taken place. In other situations, a routine or surprise audit or repair order may have brought the crime to the attention of the authorities. This discovery of a computer crime is not unlike the way many embezzlement schemes are uncovered. Borrowing from such standard embezzlement cases, investigators should determine which employees might have had access to or reasons to be involved with entrees or computer operations related to the eventual computer crime.

In other more traditional street crimes, evidence is often found in the tangible form of weapons, fabric fragments, hair, blood, glass, semen, and so forth. But in computer crimes, evidence may be in the form of electronic records or sophisticated data codes. A mistake during the collection or securing of this evidence could easily destroy or lose this evidence forever. It is critical, therefore, that investigators move cautiously and slowly when dealing with the collection or preservation of computer crime evidence. If an investigating officer is not conversant in computer lingo, or comfortable and knowledgeable about computer hardware, he or she should seek the assistance of a computer specialist.

Following the initial investigation and report, officers should develop a plan for the continued investigation of the crime. Although the investigation may deviate from this plan along the way, it will assist officers to have some guidelines for their follow-up investigation. The plan should include, at minimum, the following elements:

- The names and telephone numbers of special computer consultants, if any are to be used in the investigation.
- The nature of the crime (e.g., data manipulation, data piracy, false transfer of funds, etc.).
- The names and addresses of any known people suspected of being part of the crime.
- The type of hardware or software involved.
- The names and addresses of any witnesses who might have information about the crime.
- The personnel needs for the investigation.
- An approximation of how long the investigation should take.

When considering the nature of the crime, it should also be determined if this is a local, state, or federal law violation. If possible, the officer might consider what statutes have been violated. The appropriate prosecuting attorney should be contacted and if necessary, his or her aid solicited.

SECURING A COMPUTER AS EVIDENCE

Seizing a computer as evidence must be undertaken very carefully. Many computer criminals are capable of booby-trapping their computers. Touching a certain key on the keyboard, or even switching the computer on or off could easily set the trap in motion and destroy evidence. As Stites (1991:164) and Noblett's

(1992:10–15) suggest, whenever an officer finds a computer involved in a crime and it is to be seized, there are certain basic guidelines he or she should follow. These guidelines include:

1. Photographing the entire area of the computer, including how cables and connections are hooked-up.
2. Never touch the keyboard, and if the computer is not turned on, leave it that way! If the computer is already on, photograph the screen.
3. Restrict the handling of all computer evidence to a single officer.
4. If the computer has any disks in its drives, carefully remove these and treat them as one would treat any piece of evidence (carefully tag and record it).
5. Disconnect the plug from the wall in order to return it off. Do not use the computer's on and off switch.
6. Place a clean (reliably free of viruses) **bootable disk** (a disk with the DOS operating system on it) into the disk drive. If the computer has more than one drive, place a bootable disk into each drive. Next, replug the computer into the wall receptacle. Normally, computers **boot-up** or start-up in drive A, however, this can be easily altered, and start-up could occur in the other drive.

   Once the computer has been started, the hard drive (usually C or D drive) should be parked to prepare the computer for transport. **Parking the hard drive** means placing the head in a neutral position on the drive so that data will not be damaged by the jogging of the machine during transport. Many machines come equipped with their own parking programs which use the commands *park, ship,* or similar terms. Do not attempt to use the machine's own parking command. Officers or departments should invest in an inexpensive parking utility program that should be on the bootable disk.

7. Once the hard drive is parked, place a blank diskette in each of the drives bays, and seal each with evidence tape.
8. Again, remove the plug from the wall, and only after the machine is off, remove all of the connecting cables from the rear of the machine. Be careful to label which cable was attached to which connection point—this is very important. If the machine has been altered, replacing cables to incorrect connections may destroy files on the hard disk when the machine is next powered up.
9. Be sure to take into custody anything having to do with the computer that may be in the area. This may include disks, peripheral equipment such as a mouse, an external CD-ROM drive, printouts, manuals, printer ribbons discarded in the wastebasket, and so forth.
10. Be careful to keep any seized disks away from magnetic fields.
11. Make a through inspection of the immediate area around the screen and keyboard before moving the computer. Look carefully for labels, tags, or notes containing numbered series or terms that may actually be passwords or cryptographic keywords. Just as some law-abiding citizens write their

PINs on the back of bank cards, some criminals leave their computer passwords near the computer.

12. Once the aforementioned items have been accomplished, the computer is secured for transportation.

When investigating a computer crime in a large organization, it is sometimes necessary to develop an undercover operation (Berg and Horgan 1999). It should go without saying, but it is very important that the officers used in this operation possess strong computer skills and understanding of computer technology if the operation is to be successful. Sending in undercover officers who do not understand computers will likely alert offenders about police presence. Furthermore, having the necessary computer skills will permit these officers to know evidence when they find it.

The conducting of interviews and interrogations in a computer cases are essentially the same as in any other investigation. Similarly, the requirement of preserving suspects' rights during searches or seizures of evidence remain consistent with rights of suspects in other crimes.

Among the major problems associated with investigating computer crimes in general, is the need to determine if the crime was committed by someone in the organization; someone outside the organization; or someone outside the organization with the assistance of someone inside of it. As well, it is important to determine what exactly the crime is, and what statutes may have been violated. It is additionally important that investigators do not overlook, or accidentally destroy potential pieces of evidence. Finally, and given the ambiguities with classifying computer crimes, the problems associated with prosecuting some types of computer crimes, and the negative public relations and press that may occur, it may be necessary for an organizational victim to determine if it would better serve justice to handle the crime administratively, rather than though the criminal justice system.

Another problem facing the investigation of computer crimes is the reluctance of some victims to prosecute a computer felon. Many large corporations, financial organizations, and even governmental agencies do not report, or fail to pursue prosecution of offenders. Their fear often rests on undesired negative publicity. Large corporations may not want it known that a hacker was able to by pass its computer security strategies and gain entry. A financial organization such as a bank may be even more reluctant to have its depositors learn that someone may have broken through and **diddled data** or altered information in depositor accounts.

Finally, there is the problem of applying criminal sanctions when hackers go through foreign countries to commit their crimes. Because the Internet allows a computer user to communicate anywhere in the world, hackers can actually relay their calls through foreign countries. The danger here, of course, is that many small countries on the Internet do not have laws specifically making hacking activities illegal. Since the hacker has gone through this country, it is not always possible to enforce criminal sanctions.

SUMMARY

The computer age has arrived in many police agencies across the United States. In some departments this may involve the modest introduction of a personal computer for writing and storing reports. For many larger departments, it represents large information systems, or computer networking systems. The area of criminal investigations has similarly moved in the direction of increased computerization.

A number of specialized computer modules and stand-alone system have emerged to assist criminal investigation. Among these are various forensic programs that can assist identifying suspects buy creating composite pictures, or enhancing or aging existing photographs. Even the forensic laboratory has gained from recent advances in specialized computer programs. Some computer programs even allow officers to simultaneously consider various elements of a criminal investigation contained separately in a larger report management system.

Unlike the early days of computers, today's computer crimes are relatively easy for the average person to commit, and infinitely more difficult to detect. Computer crimes may involve internal computer crimes, telecommunications crimes, computer manipulation crimes, support of criminal enterprises, and hardware or software thefts.

The investigation of modern-day computer crimes sometimes requires specialized computer skills or expertise. Criminal investigators should seek various resources to assure that computer culprits do not succeed in their criminal endeavors.

REFERENCES

Albanese, Jay S. "Tomorrow's Thieves." *The Futurist.* September/October 1988:26.

Baum, Bob. "Thieves Cash in with Stolen Card." *The Indiana Gazette*, 11 February. 1995:22.

Berg, Bruce L. "The Computer In Criminal Investigation." Paper presented at the annual meeting of the Academy of Criminal Justice Sciences, Boston, Mass., March 1995.

Berg, Bruce L., and John Horgan. *Criminal Investigation.* 3d ed. Westonville, Oh.: Glencoe/McGraw-Hill, 1998.

Birchler, Mark. "Computers in a Small Police Agency." *Law Enforcement Bulletin,* January 1989:7–9.

Campbell, J. J. "Computer Support for Community Oriented Policing." *The FBI Law Enforcement Bulletin*, 62(2)1994:16–18.

Conley, C. H., and J. T. McEwen. "Computer Crime." *NIJ Reports,* January/February, 218(1990):2–7.

Gaines, Larry K., Victor E. Kappeler, and Joseph B. Vaughn. *Policing in America.* 2d ed. Cincinnati, Oh.: Anderson Publishing Co., 1997.

George, Dennis. "Computer-Assisted Report Entry: Toward a Paperless Police Department." *Police Chief,* March 1990:46–47.

Manning, Walt W., and Gary H. White. "Data Diddling, Salami Slicing, Trojan Horses. Can Your Agency Handle Computer Crimes?" *Police Chief,* April 1990:46–49.

Monopoli, Daniel M. "Mobile Data Terminals: Past, Present, and Future." In *Computerization in the Management of the Criminal Justice System.* Richard Scherpenzeel (ed.) Helsinki/The Hague: HEUNI, 1996.

Noblett, Michael G. "Computer Analysis and Response Team (CART): The Microcomputer as Evidence." *Crime Laboratory Digest,* 19(1)1992:10–15.

O'Donnell, Gene. "Forensic Imaging Comes of Age." *The FBI Law Enforcement Bulletin,* 63(1994):5–10.

Parker, D. B. *Fighting Computer Crime.* New York: Scribner, 1983.

Pilant, Lois. "Equipping A Forensics Lab." *Police Chief,* 59(1992):37-47.

Pilant, Lois. "Computerizing Criminal Investigations," *Police Chief,* 60(1993):29–40.

Pilant, Lois. "Information Management." *Police Chief,* 61(1994):31–47.

Schmitt, Judith Blair. "Computerized ID Systems." *Police Chief,* 59(1992):33–45.

Sites, Clyde M. "PCs: Personal Computers, or Partners in Crime?" *Law and Order,* September 1991:161–165.

Slind-Flor, Victoria. "Cyber-Criminals Thrive as Laws Lag: Prosecutors Struggle to Pursue Software Theft with Statutes from the Model T Era." *National Law Journal,* 6 November, 1995:A1.

Thrasher, Ronald R. "Voice Mail Fraud." *The FBI Law Enforcement Bulletin,* 63(7)1994:1–4.

"Hacker Not Very Difficult to Catch." *USA Today,* 20 February, 1995:3B.

Van Duyn, Lowell C. "The FBI's 21st Century Integrated Computer System—AFIS." *Law Enforcement Technology,* April 1993:40–41.

Wilson, Thomas F., and Paul L. Woodward. *Automated Fingerprint Identification Systems: Technology and Policy Issues.* Washington, D.C.: U.S. Department of Justice, Bureau of Justice Statistics, April 1987.

QUESTIONS FOR REVIEW

Objective #1:

- What are some of the ways computers assist police departments in their day-to-day activities?

Objective #2:

- How large were computers when they first entered the commercial market?
- Why were computer vendors and specialists necessary when computers were first began to enter the corporate arena?
- By 1968, how many states had established state-level computer-based information systems for law enforcement?

Objective #3:

- What sort of computer advances have been added to many modern police cruisers?
- What is the purpose of the National Law Enforcement Telecommunications System (NLETS)?

Objective #4:

- What is meant by the term "information system?"
- What is meant by a "stand-alone program?"
- What is the purpose of Oxnard, California, Police Department's Gang Offender Comprehensive Action Program (GOCAP)?

Objective #5:

- What is the purpose of forensic imaging?

Objective #6:

- How would you define "cyberpunk?"
- What definition might one offer for a "cyber-criminal?"

Objective #7:

- What type of crime is the theft of a telephone calling card number?
- If a person made copies of a legitimately purchased computer program and gave these to friends, how might this crime be classified?

Objective #8:

- How does a computer crime investigation usually begin?
- What sort of guidelines should police follow when conducting a computer crime investigation?

Objective #9:

- Why should you never turn off a suspect computer?
- What is meant by a "bootable disk?"

11 Police Discretion

CHAPTER OBJECTIVES

After reading this chapter you should be able to:

1. Describe what is meant by police discretion.
2. Discuss decision-making as it regards distribution of traffic citations.
3. Consider discretion in officer-involved shootings.
4. Explain what factors might determine whether or not an officer will make an arrest.
5. Talk about the myth of full enforcement.
6. Differentiate between reasonable and excessive force.
7. Express what role liabilities play in the police decision-making process.
8. List the four progressive stages of permissible force.
9. Define deadly force.
10. Discuss the fleeing felon rule.
11. Consider the importance of firearms training.
12. Examine whether one can predict which officers are likely to use excessive force.

DISCRETION AND DECISION-MAKING

Of the wide assortment of concerns that confront police officers daily, discretion is surely among the most complex. Police officer discretion may or may not at least appear to deteriorate into discrimination, violence, unfair access to protection, or other abuses of official authority. Research remains inconclusive about the extent to which extralegal variables such as race, gender, ethnicity, age, and demeanor affect officer discretion (Icove 1990; Cox 1996; Royberg and Kuyken-

KEY TERMS		
	reasonable force	deadly force
	excessive force	shooting reviews
police discretion	intentional torts	fleeing felon rule
myth of full enforcement	negligent torts	shoot-don't-shoot
discrimination by police officers	managing force used by police	

dall 1997). Yet, there is little question that these factors do influence an officer's thinking. It would be difficult to argue that personal judgments are not inoculated by one's life experiences, personal hang-ups, and prejudices. Often, however, it is very difficult to accurately draw a line between discretion and discrimination.

Discretion in law enforcement, and for that matter throughout the entire criminal justice system, is not a new phenomenon. Still, serious examination of officer decision-making, with an eye on curbing the wide latitude that police discretion allows, did not arise until the late 1960s and early 1970s. As part of a larger social movement directed toward reducing arbitrariness and discretion practiced by many American social institutions, a movement to infuse rules in the police decision-making process arose (Hanewicz 1985).

Some police sources suggest that various judicial attempts to minimize or regulate discretionary decision-making by police may have actually hand-cuffed police. In these instances the inferences is that police require a greater, not lesser, degree of discretionary powers. It would be difficult to dispute Howard Cohen's (1986:27) claim that "the use of discretion is not an option for police officers; it is a necessary, unavoidable part of the job."

With few exceptions, all police activities require some degree of discretion and decision-making. These decisions may involve simply selecting what the officer sees as the best course of action in a mundane situation. Or, these decisions may require the officer to decide whether to shoot and perhaps kill a suspected criminal.

This chapter examines the problems with discretion in policing. Included are considerations of the range of choices and their social implications. The chapter will review various strategies designed to reduce or regulate police exercise of authority. Along with this discussion will be a consideration of the police officer as policy maker. The chapter will additionally consider the use of force, including deadly force.

DISCRETIONARY SITUATIONS

Police discretion, according to Sykes, Fox, and Clark (1985:172), ". . . exists whenever an officer is free to choose from two or more task-relevant, alternative interpretations of the events reported, inferred, or observed in a police-civilian encounter."

When police interact with private citizens, it is usually for one or another of the following reasons: Some sort of educational purpose (as in school or neighborhood watch lectures); some sort of informational purpose (as in offering directions); some sort of law enforcement purpose (issuing a traffic citation or making an arrest); or some sort of service activity (as in assisting an elderly couple get their heat back on a cold winter evening). Any police decision based on controversial issues or factors could create significant real and public relations problems for a police department.

During the recent past, social scientists have become increasingly interested in the discretionary nature of decision-making by police officers. Douglas Smith (1987) points out that throughout the past several decades, studies repeatedly indicate that law alone is an ineffective predictor of police behavior where decision about arrest are concerned (see Banton 1964; Black 1970; Lundman 1974; Smith and Vishner 1981; Berk and Loseke 1981; Icove 1990). In one early study of American policing, Michael Banton (1964) remarked that the most striking thing about police officers was their frequent choice *not* to make an arrest. This observation by Banton has resulted in others pursuing examinations of the rather routine aspects of police work, which in turn has increased scholarly knowledge about the complexities of the police role and decision process.

Various past studies provide the basis for a useful typology of situations in which police discretion typically arises. These situations include traffic citations, juvenile arrests, police shooting incidents, and daily police policies.

Traffic Citations

Among the most obvious situations in which police discretion arises, and perhaps the least distasteful for most people, is during the issuance of a traffic ticket. In one study, John Gardiner (1969) found that Dallas police officers wrote as many as 20 times the number of traffic tickets as police in Boston—although the cities had approximately the same population size (Walker 1983). Similarly, Richard Lundman found discrepancies in the issuance of traffic citations and the making of traffic stops. In his investigation Lundman (1980) found that only 47 percent of 293 violators were issued citations.

Figure 11.1
Citizens sometimes interact with police to obtain information or directions; but sometimes they come in contact with police only if they receive a traffic citation.

Referring to production pressures and ticket quotas, Jerome H. Skolnick (1966, 1986) describes how police may lie in ambush near tricky intersections in order to assure capture of their quotas of traffic violators. But, once they had met their quotas, they would not necessarily continue this practice.

The largest problem with discretion during traffic citations is the possibility of sensitive variables, such as race and gender, affecting the officer's decision. In other words, many African Americans and Latinos believe they are regularly stopped when driving through ostensibly white neighborhoods, simply because of their race. One method that police officers can use to assure that they are not charged with allegations of racism or sexism is to always indicate their *probable cause* for stopping the vehicle. If the subject was speeding, this should be stated clearly during the stop. If the subject has passed a stop sign, this should be explained. In other words, officers should never stop a vehicle without cause. In fact, officers should question their reasons for stopping a vehicle if a law has not been broken and no other probable cause exists.

Unfortunately, what is less easily monitored is the decision whether to actually issue a citation or a warning once the vehicle is stopped. Some departments actually have policy regarding this situation. However, such policies are rather difficult to enforce. As a result, officers with some prejudice against certain groups of people can issue more citations against these people, simply by never allowing them warnings.

Juvenile Arrests

Studies repeatedly demonstrate that police use a wide degree of discretion in dealing with juveniles. There is considerable indication that a juvenile's race and social class influence a officer's decision about arrest. Evidence tends to suggest that minority and poor youths are represented disproportionately in arrest statistics. For instance, in 1994 white youths accounted for 66.2 percent of all arrested persons under the age of 18; they accounted for 59.7 percent of arrest for total index crimes (by persons under 18 years of age) (UCR 1995). By comparison, African-American youths under the age of 18 accounted for 31.9 percent of all arrests, and 38.3 percent of all index crimes (UCR 1995). Other racial groups accounted for about 2 percent of all arrests, and 2 percent of total index crimes (UCR 1995). White youths obviously accounted for the largest percentage of juvenile crimes. However, African-American youths seem to represent a disproportionate number of arrests since they comprise only about 13 percent of the U.S population (Hollman 1993; Bohm and Haley 1996).

Many studies have indicated that the seriousness of a crime affects the decision-making processes. Most police juvenile encounters involving a felony result in an arrest. On the other hand, most police juvenile encounters tend to involve minor offenses and delinquent behaviors. When offenses are minor, it is likely that a number of extralegal variables influence the police decision-making process (see as examples Black and Reiss 1970; Lundman, Sykes, and Clark 1978; Berg 1986).

Gender also appears to affect the decision-making process of arrests in police officer-juvenile encounters—particularly in minor offenses. However, the studies in this area tend to have mixed findings. In spite of an increasing number of females committing crime, male juveniles continue to be taken into custody more frequently. For example, the Port Authority Police of New York and New Jersey reported 2,515 contacts with youth for the calendar year 1985. Only 97 youths were taken into custody; 34 females and 63 males (Port Authority 1986). Systematic research on the impact of gender on decision-making is limited. However, at one time there did appear to be some police bias in favor of girls who commit serious offenses, and against them when the offense was trivial or is not a crime traditionally associated with females (Cavan and Ferdinand 1981). Some research, however, suggests that any gender bias that may have existed in the past has significantly diminished or disappeared (Sampson 1985).

Such conflicting research would tend overall to support the notion that gender does influence police-juvenile encounters at least sometimes.

Police Shootings

Police shootings engender heated debates and will be discussed in greater detail later. For now, it should be sufficient to point out that there is considerable research that suggests race and situational circumstances can influence an officer's decision to shoot. Jay Albanese (1988:125), for example, reports that a survey of five major studies on police shootings reveals discrimination. The studies, which include 11 different cities, suggest that African Americans tend to be shot by police two to four times more often than whites. For instance, in a Philadelphia study by Robin (1963) where 22 percent of the population was African-American, 88 percent of the shooting victims also were African-American. In a study of shootings in Chicago by Harding and Fahey (1973) where the African American population was 33 percent, the African American shooting victims accounted for 75 percent. In Milton et al. (1977), seven cities were investigated with an average African-American population of 39 percent. The average percentage of African-American shooting victims was 79 percent. In New York City (Fyfe 1978) where the African-American population was 20 percent, the percentage of black shooting victims was 60 percent. In Los Angeles, Meyer's (1980) found an African-American population of 18 percent and a African-American shooting victim percentage of 50 percent.

In a review of the literature on police shootings, James Fyfe (1988:189) reported that "regardless of the care employed in restricting officers' shooting, every study that has examined this issue found that blacks are represented disproportionately among those at the wrong end of the police guns." Most population studies suggest a national African-American population of approximately 13 percent. In his effort to outline some of this research Fyfe (1988) cites a study by Takagi (1974). Takagi (1974:29) found that among 2,441 males

Figure 11.2
Police shootings are reviewed carefully to assure the gun play conforms to law and departmental policy.

A

B

reported by the National Center for Health Statistics to have been killed by American police officers from 1960–1968, 1,188 (48 percent) were African American. In another study, Harring et al. (1977) reported that death rates for African-Americans at the hands of police officers nationwide were as much as ten times those of whites.

In partial contradiction to allegations of discrimination in police shootings, Arnold Binder and Peter Scharf (1982) suggest that comparisons of African-

American victims with the proportions of African Americans arrested for violent crimes might be a more reliable indicator of discrimination in police shootings (Albanese 1988:126). In fact, Binder and Scharf (1982:19) found that when "one compares victimization rates with arrest rates, one comes up with remarkably close numbers." In further support of this notion, several ancillary findings in other studies suggest that African Americans appear to possess guns when involved in police shootings more often than do whites (Fyfe 1978; Meyer 1980).

Binder and Scharf also point out that it may be a mistake to equate African-American shooting victims with African Americans in the general city population, as most studies tend to do. Binder and Scharf assert that police seldom shoot certain kinds of people—college professors, doctors, merchants, and so forth—whether they are white or African American. Hence, it is not race per se that may make one more prone to being shot; it is exposure to certain types of situations that increase one's likelihood of being shot. If one is involved in law violating, one is more likely to be exposed to situations in which a shooting is possible than if one does not break the law.

These findings and observations account for some of the disparities that exist in the proportion of African Americans (as compared with whites) injured of killed in police shootings. As Fyfe (1988:191) comments, "Researchers have found close association between racial distributions of police shooting subjects and measures of the risk of being shot at, such as arrests for murder, robbery, aggravated assault, weapons offenses, and burglary . . . arrests for FBI Crime Index offenses . . . and arrests for violent Crime Index offenses." It remains questionable, however, how accurate arrest proportions are as an indicator of discrimination in police shootings. Certainly, arrests may be tainted by discriminatory decision-making practices that result in greater numbers of African-Americans than whites being arrested.

Nonetheless, some studies that examine whether both arrest and deadly force statistics result from discriminatory police practices suggest they do not (see Fyfe 1981; Blumberg 1981). Mark Blumberg found that regardless of race, approximately seven in ten of those individuals shot by Atlanta police and half of those shot by Kansas City police from 1971 to 1978 had attacked officers with weapons. Blumberg also found that regardless of the intensity of officer response shooting victims (assessed on the basis of the number of officers who shot and the number of shots fired) or the results of shooting (measured by the ratio of non-fatal to fatal wounds) varied by subjects' race.

One interpretation of the various contradictions observable in these studies on police shootings is a kind of measurement imprecision: the failure of many researchers to consider the setting in which the police shooting occurred. Indeed, some settings, like some neighborhoods, are seen by police officers as more safe than others. Realistically, an officer operating in an area perceived as dangerous may be more likely to misinterpret a furtive movement than in a neighborhood perceived as safe. If this interpretation is correct, then at least some of the explanation for why police shooting rates reflect disproportionate numbers of African Americans may rest on the location of these shootings, rather than the race of the individuals shot.

In fact, according to Harry W. More (1992) most police use-of-force situations occur at night in public locations, and in high-crime areas of big cities. These incidents typically involve on-duty, uniformed officers firing their weapons at suspects. Since armed robbers pose a significant threat to the lives of both the police and citizens, "the police are more likely to shoot suspects wanted for armed robbery than for any other crime" (More 1992:48).

Policies for Routine Police Functions

The area of policies for routine functions refers to prioritizing investigation, arrest, and use-of-force policies as routine control and order maintenance issues. One of the principal problems associated with even mundane police activities is the general absence of statutory or legislative guidelines (Walker 1983; Goldstein 1985). Even when they do exist, the language may be vague or conduct criminalized (defined as illegal) broadly to avoid loopholes. As a result, police must make decisions abut various alternative forms of action that fall within their purview, but may not be outlined specifically in department policy.

In his attempt to study law enforcement policies, Kenneth Culp Davis (1975) surveyed 21 district police stations in Chicago and asked if a person would be arrested for drinking in a public park. Officers at 3 of the district stations answered they would arrest the person, 4 answered they would probably make an arrest, and 11 said they would not arrest the person or would probably not do so.

In some instances, even when standard guidelines are adopted, controversy persists. Consider, for example, the issuance of a *Miranda* warning. Violations of the *Miranda* may result from when the warning is given, the order of the elements included in the warning, or even the age and maturity of the suspect receiving the warning.

To a large extent, even when official policies do exist, officers must rely upon their training, resourcefulness, and often their imagination to get through a tour of duty. Unfortunately, this leads to inconsistencies in policy application as officers operate in situations with a variety of circumstances.

TO ARREST OR NOT TO ARREST?

As suggested above, the police must make many decisions daily. Among these decisions, of course, is whether to make an arrest. This problem actually is fairly complex. For example, even when statutes provide that an arrest *may* be made, and with the exception of certain felonies, it is typically at the discretion of the officer. There also are decisions on which charges should be made.

For example, consider an officer called by a complainant at 2 A.M. because a neighbor has been playing loud music and seems to be drunk. Upon arriving at the scene, the officer observes the neighbor urinating in his front yard. As the officer approaches the neighbor, he raises his fist in the air, shouts some obscenity, and then rushes back in to the house, slamming the door.

Should the officer make a summary arrest for disorderly conduct? In most jurisdictions, disorderly conduct is an arrestable statutory crime. If an arrest is made, is the charge of disorderly conduct sufficient or should additional charges of resisting be included, since the man ran into his house? What about public lewdness, or public indecency, owing to the act of urinating on the lawn? Or, perhaps, the officer should simply find out what's happening and counsel the man to lower the music and to stop urinating on his lawn.

It is rather common for officers not to make arrests—even as in the example above, where there are certainly sufficient reasons to do so. In some situations, the demeanor of the offenders may sway an officer one way or another. In other situations, the way in which the officer was summoned may play a role. In other words, an officer might respond in one way if dispatched by a superior and in quite a different manner if summoned by a private citizen running up to the cruiser. In other situations, the seriousness or nature of the crime may affect the decision of whether to arrest. Another factor that can affect an officer's decision about arrest concerns previous encounters. If the officer has repeatedly been called about an individual or the individual is known to be a local troublemaker, this too may affect the decision. Some research suggests that hostile suspects are more likely to be arrested, but not so much because their demeanor connotes disrespect for police authority. Rather, hostile suspects tend to be arrested because they are more likely to commit crimes in the presence of the police (Klinger 1994).

A less frequently discussed issue involves an officer's decision to make an arrest, or to search, knowing full well that there is insufficient probable cause or no appropriate warrants. Nonetheless, there are circumstances, gray areas as they are sometimes referred to, in which an officer will chance a motion to suppress evidence in order to find a cache of drugs or weapons. What leads the officer to this decision is a desire to rid the streets of what the officer expects to find—even if it means losing the case, not filing a case, or not even filing a formal report. In some instances the officer may feel justified to violate the law in order to preserve the peace and protect the community.

For instance, an officer is called to a family dispute and during the course of calming things down notices a shotgun hanging on the wall. Upon closer inspection, the officer finds that it is loaded and unlocked. Should the officer, after calming the parties down, leave the gun in the house? Even assuming that its owner has the correct papers or necessary license, the officer might choose to remove the weapon and instruct the owner to retrieve it from the station in the morning. Technically, the officer has no legal power to remove the private property from the house. The decision to do so, however, may follow from the level of hostility the officer encounters upon arrival. Many people might be shocked at the idea that a police officer would intentionally break the law to maintain the peace. Ironically, many of these same people would be appalled if the officer left the gun and one of the parties killed the other.

The necessity for police officers to exercise discretion without benefit of viable guidelines places tremendous pressure on them. The exercise of discretion is not the problem; it is the abuse of discretion that is. The abuse of discretion might be reduced by the adoption of rigid guidelines. But guidelines can never be sufficiently inclusive to stipulate all the elements and facts that might arise in various situations. In fact, the more complicated the guidelines, the less flexible they are likely to be under different circumstances. The types of activities that police officers face daily are enormously varied and complex. The police must respond to each new situation with confidence, authority, and discretion.

On the other hand, completely uncontrolled discretion can lead to officers enforcing the law according to their personal standards and values. Such sidewalk justice creates a completely untenable situation of highly selective lawfulness. As mentioned throughout Chapter 8, among the basic tenets of American law enforcement is the notion of full access to lawful protection for all people. In addition to access to law enforcement protection, Americans are constitutionally guaranteed that when two people violate the same law, they will receive equal treatment under the law. Yet, as already suggested, police do not always respond to similar sets of circumstances in identical ways.

The situation of limited enforcement, or more accurately selective enforcement of laws is difficult for many officers to acknowledge. The admission that some people who break the law go free, while others are made to pay the full price levied by the justice system, tends to fly in the face of the equal legal protection concept. Nonetheless, the rhetoric of full enforcement of all the laws, or the myth of full enforcement, as Wayne LaFave (1965) and Samuel Walker (1983) describe it, persists. What is meant by full enforcement of the law? In effect, the **myth of full enforcement** means that all laws are uniformly applied and enforced in every applicable situation.

One reason for the perpetuation of this myth involves the legal truth that police officers are not authorized to ignore or not enforce the law. In fact, in most states, the failure of an officer to enforce the law is at least a dereliction of duty and may be a criminal offense.

Another reason for the myth's persistence is the failure of the public to comprehend that real police work is not like television. The bad guy is simply not always captured in a neat 30- or 60-minute format in the real world. In the face of this kind of public sentiment, police administrators and police organizations vigorously guard against intrusions by civilians. In other words, unlike the public's perception, law enforcement is not the singular function of the police nor accomplished by bumbling detectives who can only solve crimes with the assistance of civilian novelists or private investigators. But, until these frames of reference are corrected, police executives will continue to be reluctant to openly discuss departmental policies or procedures.

Samuel Walker (1983) points to a third factor connected with the persistence of a myth of full enforcement; namely, the image of police authority. The police rely heavily upon their ability to imply or express the threat of an arrest in order to maintain control over many situations. To admit openly that certain laws are not usually enforced or may be frequently ignored could undermine their image of authority and might create problems in maintaining order. For instance, across the state highways of the United States, a fairly consistent unspoken enforcement policy is an approximate 10-mile-per-hour leeway above the posted limit of 55 and about 5-miles-per-hour leeway above the 65 miles an hour limit. Naturally, one travels at speeds in excess of the posted limit at one's own peril, as it is a statutory violation. But, violation of this particular statute is not one especially likely to result in a citation (Langworthy and Travis 1994:294–295).

FACTORS AFFECTING THE MYTH OF FULL ENFORCEMENT

For many experts on policing, the resistance among police agencies to debunking the myth of full enforcement is seen as a serious impediment to professional growth in policing (Davis 1975; Goldstein 1985; Walker 1983). Increasingly, police officers have been called upon to offer greater conformity in their application of criminal law during an arrest (More 1985). Also, police agencies during the 1980s developed numerous departmental policies for routine police activities. These included how and when to call in a K-9 team; how to secure a crime scene; use of force policies; firearms policies; courtroom demeanor policies; *Miranda* warning policies; stop-and-frisk policies; social service referral policies; and juvenile rights policies. Each of these policies moves in the direction of an accountability system, but one that does not rigidly remove certain elements of discretion.

In most instances, police officers retain the right to determine whether to arrest, whether to stop and question suspicious people, and a host of other discretions. In many agencies police discretion is affected by factors related to the criminal justice system as a whole. These may include limitations on financial or personnel resources, time lags in court processing, seriousness of the offense and likelihood of conviction, and related concerns.

Owing to serious limits on time, money and officers, law enforcement agencies simply cannot effectively enforce all law violations all of the time. As a result, most agencies develop informal priority systems. In effect, the agency's administrators and supervisors are making discretionary decisions about which offenses and law violations will warrant enforcement and which will not.

Another factor related to the imposition of discretionary decision-making among police involves situational factors. Douglas Smith (1987) examined discretion among police officers responding to situations in which there was violence. Smith found a number of extralegal variables did influence police decision-making. Smith stated that social factors, such as race and gender of the parties involved and their demeanor, significantly influence whether police choose to handle the problems by medication or arrest.

Police officers frequently describe an acquired ability to assess an individual and determined if he or she is a suspicious person. In some instances, this may mean the individual fits the officer's image or stereotype of a drug user, pimp, hustler, or simply a person of low moral character. The obvious problem with this, of course, is that it may go far beyond acceptable discretion, to arbitrariness. An example of this arose in the case of Edward Lawson (see Box 11.1).

A third factor that plays heavily in discretionary decision-making by police is the individual characteristics of officers. Police, like all members of society, have been socialized into accepting or rejecting various values, attitudes, and beliefs. Some officers may feel more strongly about one issue than others, but all police officers have fairly strong opinions on some issues that may seriously affect their decision-making. Albert Reiss (1971:134) argues that officers act on

BOX 11.1   SUSPICIOUS PEOPLE OR SUSPICIOUS POLICE? THE CASE OF EDWARD LAWSON

It has been argued that among the more serious problems with police discretion is that it encourages police to abuse their legitimate authority. "Terry stops" (referring to *Terry v. Ohio*, 1968), in which an officer stops and frisks a person who has demonstrated suspicious actions or behaviors have been fairly well regulated with departmental policies and through court cases. However, simple stops of suspicious persons to question them or obtain identification have until recently been less restrained. Often, an individual who in some manner "stands out" is subjected to a stop and questioning by police. But, such unwarranted stops appear to exceed the limits of police authority and discretion. This conclusion is supported by the U.S. Supreme Court decision in the case of *Kolender et. al v. Lawson* 1983.

The Circumstances and Facts of the Case:
Edward Lawson was a resident of California who, for over 30 years, enjoyed walking. Lawson walked everywhere and often did so at late hours of the night. Although perhaps eccentric, this desire to walk and to do so at odd hours is perfectly legal. But, the thirty-six-year-old Lawson has an appearance that made many police offic-

ers suspicious of his behavior. Lawson was a tall, muscular black man, with long braids known as dreadlocks. In Jamaica, Lawson's appearance would be fairly commonplace. In fact, in San Francisco, where he later moved, his appearance is indistinguishable from others who dress in extraordinary styles of clothing or wear their hair in styles that more conservative types might call strange. But, in San Diego, where Lawson resided during the 1970s, his appearance, coupled with his walking at odd hours, made him a prime target for frequent suspicious-person stops (Press and Sandza 1982).

Between March 1975 and January 1977, Lawson was stopped and questioned by police officers approximately fifteen times. When stopped, police referred to a California statute that prohibited loitering or wandering "upon the streets or from place to place without apparent reason or business, and who refuses to identify himself and to account for his presence when requested by any peace officer to do so, if the surrounding circumstances are such as to indicate to a reasonable man that the public safety demands such identification" (California Penal Code, Section 647e). Violation of this statute was a misdemeanor.

the basis of their personal "moral belief." In some instances, this means the officer views the "suspect as guilty, and an arrest is therefore just." On other occasions, officers may believe that an individual is innocent—regardless of evidence to the contrary—and the arrest is unjustified.

It would be naive to think that some police officers do not allow racial, sexual, social class, demeanor, or other extralegal elements to affect their decisions of whether or not to arrest individuals. Among the more controversial questions regarding discretion is whether racial bias may disproportionately influence arrest decisions. A survey of studies on this topic suggests that most are unable to conclude that racially biased decisions predominate. Rather, research repeatedly reports that police officers are more likely to consider the nature and seriousness of the offense and the demeanor of the suspect than they are to consider race (Terry 1967; Reiss 1971; Black 1980; Cox 1996; Bohm and Haley 1997).

Discrimination by police officers typically refers to undue decision-making influences from age, gender, race, or ethnicity. In the real world of policing, many officers must actively resist stereotyping certain categories of people. Because of experience in the field, education, and training, or simple prejudice, police officers are more likely to stop and question a young African-American man than, for example, a middle-aged white man who seems to be acting suspiciously.

In all, Lawson was arrested five times, convicted once, and served several weeks in jail. In every instance of a stop or arrest, the officers involved were white. The Lawson case demonstrated a need to take a serious look at the issue of identification and whether police have a constitutional right to arrest people for strolling the streets and because they refuse to identify themselves.

Lawson did appeal his conviction to the U.S. Supreme Court, which reversed it on the grounds that the status under which Lawson had been convicted was simply too vague. The problem with the statute, then, was not that police had initially stopped a suspicious person. Rather, the Court found: "Although the initial detention is justified, the state fails to establish standards by which the officer my determine whether the suspect has complied with the subsequent identification requirements." The High Court's concern was that this statute provided police officers with discretion for "virtually unrestrained power to arrest and charge a person with a violation' and, consequently, "furnishes a convenient tool for harsh and discriminatory enforcement by local prosecuting officials against particular groups deemed to merit their displeasure" (*Kolender et al. v. Lawson*, 1983).

Edward Lawson, a fairly tall, muscular black man, had been repeatedly stopped by California police officers for no more reason than he looked "suspicious." His appearance, although perhaps out of the norm for the areas he walked (upper-class-white neighborhoods) would not seem to justify either his 15 stops or 5 arrests. Nor would it justify his being handled roughly by the police each time he was stopped and detained. Assessments of Lawson, chiefly because he was out of place in the view of the officers, erroneously identified him as a person who needed to be stopped. The case of Edward Lawson rather clearly illustrates the tension between police claims of a need for discretionary stops and the rights of private citizens.

The literal point at which good policing ends and discrimination begins is difficult or impossible to identify in every case. In other cases, it is not quite as difficult. For example, during one of Edward Lawson's stops, he was pulled from a coffee shop by an officer who was seeking a one-legged white man (Press and Sandza 1982).

USE OF FORCE

Police in America are given the authority to use reasonable force in a variety of situations. Lawmakers and the courts do not expect police officers to operate in life-threatening situations without defending themselves, but neither do they permit officers to use unnecessary or unreasonable bullying tactics or force. **Reasonable force** can be defined as the amount of force required to bring a situation under control, or to effect a lawful arrest. **Excessive force** can be defined as the use of force that exceeds what is necessary under a given circumstance to bring a situation under control or to effect an arrest.

EXCESSIVE FORCE

Clemens Bartollas and Loras Jaeger (1988:176) outlines three categories of excessive force, or police brutality:

1. Situations in which emotions of both the police and the participants are high, such as riots or mass demonstrations. Tempers flare on both sides, and the police often are difficult to control. Direct orders by supervisors are often disregarded at these times, and police discipline collapses.
2. Situations in which a police group or organization systematically and in regular patterns inflicts excessive force, or brutality on citizens. This is most common in areas where there is racial hostility between the police and citizens.
3. Situations in which the police, during their day-to-day activities, use force beyond that which is necessary to control the situation, or make an arrest.

Most police officers admit that at some time in their career they lost control of a situation and used excessive force or more force than was necessary, either to control a situation or make an arrest. David L. Carter (1985:322–323) has similarly developed a tripartite definition for excessive force. Carter's typology offers a broadly encompassing reference to physical abuse (excessive force), verbal (psychological) abuse, and legal abuse (violations of civil rights).

Physical Abuse—Excessive Force

This category of abuse is described as involving the use of more (physical) force than is required of an officer to fulfill his or her duty in a given situation.

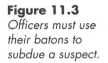
Figure 11.3
Officers must use their batons to subdue a suspect.

Verbal-Psychological Abuse

Verbal-psychological abuse arises when an officer verbally assaults, ridicules, or in other ways demeans or harasses an individual.

Legal Abuse—Violations of Civil Rights

The legal abuse or violation of civil rights may arise in conjunction with other categories of excessive force, or alone. It amounts to any violation of the private citizen's constitutional rights.

DECISION-MAKING AND POLICE LIABILITY

Civil litigation against police officers also has had a major effect on law enforcement decision-making policies. Lawsuits can result from an assortment of reasons (Adams 1994). These may include dereliction of duty, misrepresentation of duty, unlawful detention, or failure to follow appropriate departmental policies. Certainly, lawsuits against police can be seen as appropriate and necessary means of censuring errant officers and remedying with monetary awards for damages. But lawsuits against police officers can additionally be viewed as a nuisance and an ineffective means for a person to vent frustrations toward society for which he or she has no other, more appropriate outlet. Whether or not police administrators like the situation, the possibility of a lawsuit has provided an additional control over police discretion and decision-making.

Legal actions taken against police officers sometimes arise because of the type of service officers provide to the public, and their status as agents of the government (Kappeler 1993). Whenever an officer fails to perform his or her official duties, performs them in a negligent or inappropriate manner, or abuses authority, the possibility of civil liability exists. However, civil litigation against police officers is not always the result of their failure to perform their duties, or performing them negligently. A surprising number of liability cases have arisen because of allegations of officer misconduct and abuses of authority, ranging from false arrest to excessive use of force.

Police officers can be held liable in both state and federal courts. However, civil suits in federal courts seem to have become more common during recent years (Roberg and Kuykendall 1993). The length of time for getting to court, at the federal level, is frequently shorter than in state court. Furthermore, it is easier for the plaintiff—the individual bringing a lawsuit—to obtain documents form police departments. Additionally, if the plaintiff is successful, the defendant can be made to pay the cost of the plaintiff's legal counsel (del Carmen 1991).

Under state law, a *tort* is a civil wrong where the action of one person is in violation of a legal duty required by law, and which causes injury to another person or damages his or her property. There are two types of legal actions used in civil liability suits against police officers. These include, *intentional* and *negligent torts*. **Intentional torts** involve situations where an officer causes some type of physical or mental harm to another person. The most common situations that might provoke an intentional tort lawsuit involve cases of excessive force, false arrest, false imprisonment, assault, wrongful deaths, intentional infliction of emotional or mental distress, misuse of legal procedures, invasion of privacy, illegal use of electronic surveillance devices, and defamation of character.

Negligent torts involve some kind of breach of lawful duty to act appropriately or responsibly. The major difference between intentional and negligent torts is that, in the former, the officer's mental state is important. On the other hand, in the case of the latter, it is not. For example, the negligent operation of a police cruiser, or the failure to take appropriate action such as respond to a call for service are examples of situations that could result in negligent torts.

Officers can use several defenses in civil liability suits involving intentional torts, including good faith and probable-cause. In the *good-faith* defense, the officer tries to demonstrate that he or she was not aware that the damaging action was illegal. In a *probable-cause* defense, the officer attempts to demonstrate that the action(s) taken were lawful.

In negligent tort cases, there are several defenses used by police officers. Some of these include a defense based on discretionary acts, sudden emergency, contributory negligence, and assumption of risk. The discretionary-acts defense is generally based on those acts that are not required of police officers, or if the action was required, the officer had discretion about the time, nature, and extent of his or her activities. The sudden emergency defense is based on the argument that in some situations an officer has to act from instinct rather than having the time to exercise reasonable judgment. When a plaintiff in a civil suit can be shown to have contributed to his or her injuries or damages, the officer is not held liable. Finally, a police officer cannot be held liable if a citizen does something dangerous after having been warned not to do so by the police; in effect, the individual assumes the risk themselves.

In addition, some potential risks of lawsuits are so predictable that they have forced some police agencies into effecting strict policies. For example, in California, the Los Angeles County, Sheriff's department has a formal policy about pursuing stolen cars. Once a vehicle suspected of being stolen has been confirmed as stolen, the officers may not pursue for more than about one mile with lights and sirens. In other words, if the car thief bolts, and tries to lead the deputies on a high-speed chase, the officers can not pursue. The logic behind this policy has largely to with the civil liability associated with property damage and personal injures that often occur during high-speed pursuits. Officers may contact other agencies and request assistance, allowing them to continue the chase, but may not themselves continue. Failure to break off the pursuit could result in a formal reprimand, and as much as a week's suspension.

NON-DEADLY FORCE

Speaking generally, most people do not strenuously object to police officers arresting people who are suspected of committing crimes. Even people being arrested often resist only slightly and then frequently only with verbal resistance, demanding to know why they are being arrested, or insisting that the officer has made a mistake. In some instances, of course, people being arrested do resist with force. Throughout the late 1970s and 1980s, police agencies and training academies began to generate various policies and procedures regarding use of force during an arrest.

In addition to circumstances arising during an arrest, most guidelines specify that the use of force may be lawfully employed when conducting searches and seizures, to prevent escapes of people in custody, in self-defense and the defense of others (i.e., to protect one self or others from bodily injury or death), to prevent the commission of an offense, and to prevent suicide or self-inflicting injury.

The amount of force used by an officer is usually described in agency procedures as limited to that which is no greater than necessary and reasonable in a given situation. This is sometimes delineated in guidelines as variable depending upon certain aspects of the situation, such as the nature of the offense, the behavior and response of the subject against whom force is to be used, the presence and actions of third parties, physical odds against the officer (substantial differences in size or weight), and the feasibility or availability of alternative actions. It is generally understood that an officer acting alone may be required to resort to a much greater degree of force than might be necessary if another officer were present.

MANAGING THE USE OF FORCE

One goal of every police department should be to use force of any type only as a last resort—and only after all other alternatives have been considered or exhausted. Both the public and police agencies must realize that in some situations, force not only is necessary but required if serious injury or death to police officers or other people is to be avoided (Roberg and Kuykendall 1997). Thus, police agencies must learn to manage force. The concept of **managing force used by police** literally means creating some system of rules, guidelines, and accountability regarding the use of force by officers.

When officers become too concerned about avoiding the use of force, they may avoid risky situations, begin getting injured more frequently on the job, or fail to prevent private citizens from being injured or killed.

For example, when officers who have used necessary force to effect difficult arrests begin being cited or repeatedly questioned for such behavior, they may begin to avoid making the arrests at all. This, in turn, may leave dangerous and violent offenders in the community.

Policy guidelines for use of force must be compatible with state and federal laws and provide clear conduct rules in various situations. The important element, of course, is not to punish officers who do explicitly follow their department guidelines when using force—even if negative public relations outcomes occur.

PROGRESSIVE STAGES OF PERMISSIBLE FORCE

Often, policy guidelines for non-deadly force describe a five-stage scale of escalating intensity. Figure 11.4 illustrates the five general stages usually detailed.

- *Stage one*. The first stage is customarily the *verbal command stage*, and involves officers identifying themselves (when not in uniform) and informing suspects that they are under arrest. This stage may include verbal orders related to a frisk and handcuffing, but cannot move beyond use of words unless a subject is physically uncooperative and offers resistance or attempts to escape custody.
- *Stage two*. The second stage arises in the event that the suspect offers simple physical resistance and may be termed *physical strength* or *skill stage*. Police officers are trained in defensive restraint and take-down procedures. Although physical force is required during this second stage, it is restricted to the officer's training and skill with bare hands.
- *Stage three*. The third, or *service baton stage* represents the need for an officer to employ a fairly high level of physical force. The suspect may be fairly

Figure 11.4
Escalating Levels of Permissible Force by Police Officers

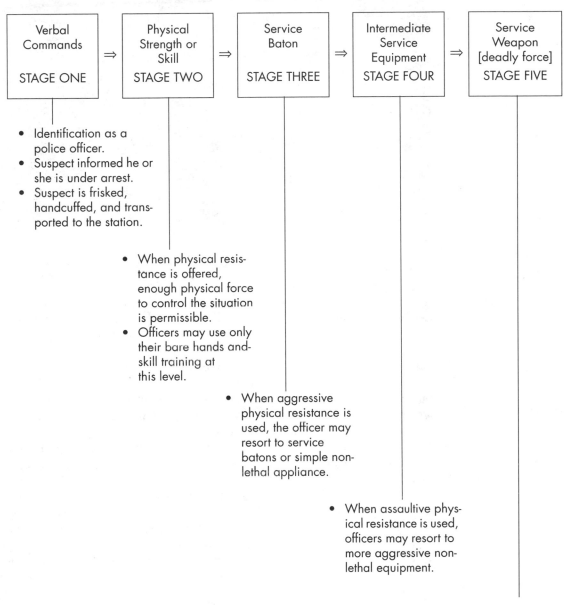

Verbal Commands		Physical Strength or Skill		Service Baton		Intermediate Service Equipment		Service Weapon [deadly force]
STAGE ONE	⇒	STAGE TWO	⇒	STAGE THREE	⇒	STAGE FOUR	⇒	STAGE FIVE

- Identification as a police officer.
- Suspect informed he or she is under arrest.
- Suspect is frisked, handcuffed, and transported to the station.

- When physical resistance is offered, enough physical force to control the situation is permissible.
- Officers may use only their bare hands and-skill training at this level.

- When aggressive physical resistance is used, the officer may resort to service batons or simple non-lethal appliance.

- When assaultive physical resistance is used, officers may resort to more aggressive non-lethal equipment.

- If the suspect uses a gun or other dangerous weapon, the officer may use deadly force.

Figure 11.5
Police use an assortment of non-lethal devices, including various types of batons.

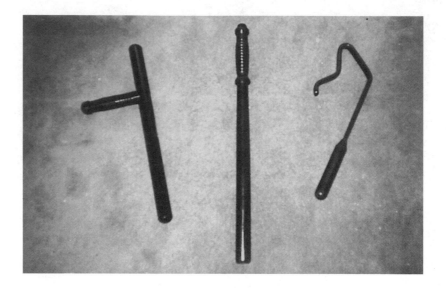

aggressive in his or her resistance (e.g., assaultive, kicking, biting). If the suspect further escalates the level of resistance by using a weapon other than a gun, the officer may use a service baton, or other non-lethal device depending on specific laws in various jurisdictions). These may include a stun gun, pepper spray, or other devices. Again, police officers are trained in the use of their service batons and other devices.

- *Stage four.* The fourth stage is an *intermediate weapons stage.* In this stage, officers make use of an assortment of non-lethal weapons including rubber bullets, bean bag rounds, nets, foam sprays, and electronic devices. These actions are frequently used when apprehending a difficult and resisting DUI suspect, or to end an automobile chase.
- *Stage five.* The fifth and final stage occurs in the event that the suspect being placed under arrest resorts to resistance with a gun, or demonstrates serious intention to resist with *deadly force.* At this juncture, the officer may draw a gun loaded with live rounds and fire. Situations related to this fourth stage may vary by policy in different jurisdictions. For example, in some jurisdictions, a suspect standing less than twenty feet from the officer and who is away wielding a knife is considered sufficient for the officer elevate to level 4. In other jurisdictions, unless the suspect makes a lunging or menacing move toward the officer (or some other person) the situation may not be sufficient.

Police officers obviously will be required at times to resort to physical force to enable them to carry out fully their official duties. The use of force by police officers, however, is an issue of great concern to society, individual officers, and police administrators. Cries of "police brutality" are hurled at police whether they are accurate or not.

Unquestionably, the lawful use of force must be controlled and confined so that an officer is neither subjected to unnecessary civil and criminal liability or inhibited from complete performance of duties. Toward this end, police agencies have created fairly explicit procedures for officers to follow when confronted with situations that require the use of force. In addition to the general sequence of ascending force, officers are expected to decrease their force as a situation warrants. A situation that may require the officer to use a service baton one minute may require only verbal commands a few minutes later. In fact, as Geoffrey Alpert (1985) and Samuel Chapman (1986) have both indicated, often an officer's best weapon is his or her mouth and the spoken word.

DEADLY FORCE

Policing is a unique occupation, except perhaps for the military, since it is the only one that authorizes its personnel to use deadly force as part of the performance of their duties. Briefly, **deadly force** may be defined as ". . . such force readily capable of or likely to cause death or serious bodily harm" (Alpert and Fridell 1992:12).

The foremost element in the decision to use deadly force is whether the officer has sufficient cause to believe that the suspect poses a real, probable, and imminent threat of serious physical harm either to the officer or others. Similarly, it is not constitutionally unreasonable to use all necessary measures, including deadly force, to prevent escape of dangerous suspects. In other words, if a subject has threatened with officer with a weapon, or there exists probable cause to believe that the subject has committed a crime involving the inflicting

Figure 11.6
Police officers are permitted to meet deadly force with deadly force.

of physical harm or has placed someone in fear of physical harm through threats, deadly force is permissible to prevent an escape. In the absence of these factors, however, police officers may not use deadly force to effect arrests or prevent escapes.

As mentioned with regard to the use of force generally, one important factor that offers a kind of controlling or tempering effect on the use by police of deadly force is litigation against police officers. Less regularly considered, however, are the administrative and personal ramifications that accompany an officer-involved shooting.

Whenever an officer discharges a weapon in a deadly force situation, in most jurisdictions the event is administratively reviewed. This is sometimes referred to as a *shooting review*. During **shooting reviews**, the events of the officer involved shooting are considered, and a determination is made about whether the shooting was the appropriate line of action to have taken. As part of this shooting review, the officer may be subject to criminal and civil jeopardy, should the review find the shooting was unnecessary or inappropriate. Individually, the officer may be held in violation of state laws, as well as federal ones for civil rights violations. The department for which the officer works also may be subject to civil liabilities.

In addition to these various criminal and civil problems, police officers involved in shooting situations may carry away a serious emotional scare. An assortment of stressful situations may impair the health of police officers. The psychological effects of being involved in a shooting situation, whether the suspect is injured or killed, is quite dramatic. In the even of death, however, the officer must reconcile the taking of another human being's life. Too, the officer must deal with the reality that his or her own life had been in serious peril—an enormously discomforting thought.

To be sure, the use of deadly force by police officers is extremely controversial and complicated. There are three primary focuses for consideration of police officers' use of deadly force. These include the fleeing felon rule, firearms training, and predictability about those who are likely to resort to the use of deadly force.

The authority for police officers to use deadly force derives from English common law. Under this legal tradition, an arresting officer was permitted to use deadly force to prevent the escape of a fleeing felon. Officers were not, however, permitted to use deadly force to prevent escapes from fleeing misdemeanants. The justification for such permissible lethal force was that most felonies during the late fourteenth and fifteenth centuries were punishable by death (see Chapter 2).

FLEEING FELONS

As English common law was the central basis for both the early and modern American legal system, it is not surprising to find that the fleeing felon rule found its way into the early laws in America. Under the provisions of the **flee-**

Figure 11.7
Officers are no longer permitted to use deadly force when pursuing a fleeing felon who poses no immediate threat to the community.

ing felon rule, officers could shoot felons as they fled from the scene of a crime, or escaped from custody. The number of crimes classified as felonies has risen significantly since fifteenth-century England. Interestingly, as the felony crimes increased in number on the American legal books, the imposition of the death penalty for felony crimes decreased. By the late nineteenth century, the historical justification for the fleeing felony rule had all but disappeared (Albanese 1988; Blumberg 1993).

Most state laws continue to permit police officers to use any force—including deadly force—necessary and reasonable to arrest an individual suspected of a felony. The latitude once provided by the fleeing felon rule, however, has been drawn into serious question during the past decade. Scrutiny of policies surrounding shooting fleeing felons has risen as the result of two primary factors. First, the enormous amount of criticism and bad publicity departments receive every time an officer fires a weapon at a felony suspect claiming, "I thought I saw a weapon!" only to recover none. Second is the case of *Tennessee v. Garner* (1985), and the ramifications to the fleeing felon rule across the country as the result of the Supreme Court's ruling.

At the time of the *Garner* case, 19 states had fleeing felon statutes and 4 others had no statutes, but apparently followed the "fleeing felon rule"; and 22 other states used some variation of the violent fleeing felon rule. All of these states reconsidered their laws on fleeing felons following the *Tennessee v. Garner* (1985) ruling (Kaune and Tischler 1989).

An important underlying question regarding the use of deadly force in instances of fleeing felons is whether this action is constitutionally permissible. At one time, when cases involving police use of deadly force reached courts, it was an unacceptable defense that the fleeing felon rule violated the rights of the suspected felon. But in 1985, after the U.S Supreme Court heard and ruled in the case of *Tennessee v. Garner,* state laws and agency policies on use of deadly force were drastically changed (see Box 11.2). The Court ruled that the shooting of an individual who posed no immediate threat to the safety of others was a violation of the Fourth Amendment ban against unreasonable seizure.

BOX 11.2   FLEEING FELONS: THE CASE OF *TENNESSEE V. GARNER* (1985)

It began on October 3, 1974 at about 10:45 p.m. Two Memphis police, Elton Hymons and Leslie Wright, received a radio call to investigate a prowler. When the officers arrived, the found a woman standing on her porch who told them that she had heard someone breaking into the house next door. As Wright radioed the dispatcher to indicate their disposition, Hymon moved to the rear of the house where the prowler(s) had been heard. Suddenly, a door slammed, and Hymon saw someone run across the back yard and toward a 6-foot chain-linked fence. Hymon shied his flashlight in the direction of the runner and observed what he believed to be a 17- or 18-year-old youth. Scanning with his light he could see no sign of a weapon in the hands of the youth who appeared to 5'6" or 5'7".

In fact, the youth was Edward Garner, a 15-year-old, 5'4" eight grader who weighed approximately 100 pounds. As Garner crouched at the bottom of the fence, Hymon identified himself as a police officer and ordered him to halt. Garner ignored the order and began to climb the fence. Believing that Garner was the prowler and that he would clear the fence and evade capture, Hymon fired his server revolver. The shot stuck Garner in the back of the head, and he was taken by ambulance to a local hospital. Garner died from his wounds while still on the operating table.

At trial, Hymon justified his use of deadly force by indicating that he had convinced that Garner would evade pursuit and, under Tennessee law, he was permitted to use his weapon in such circumstances. The statute reads: "[If] after notice of the intention to arrest the defendant, he either flees or forcibly resists, the officer may use all the necessary means to effect the arrest" (Tennessee Code, Section 40-7-108, 1982). The U.S. Supreme Court (*Tennessee v. Garner,* 1985) ruled:

> The use of deadly force to prevent the escape of all felony suspects, whatever the circumstances, is constitutionally unreasonable. It is not better that all felony suspects die than that they escape? Where the suspect poses no immediate threat to the officer and no threat to others, the harm resulting from failing to apprehend him does not justify the use of deadly force to do so. It is no doubt unfortunate when a suspect who is in sight escapes, but the fact that the police arrive a little late or are a little slower afoot does not always justify killing the suspect. A police officer may not seize an unarmed, nondangerous suspect by shooting him dead.

As a result of the *Garner* case, many departments voluntarily altered their general shooting policies. States that had fleeing felon laws were forced to strike them. Yet, the High Court did not unanimously agree on its findings. The vote was 6–3. It is likely that this lack of unanimity is reflective of a wider social attitude of the public's regarding the shooting of fleeing felons by police officers.

The position taken by the High Court in *Garner* has been strongly criticized by some law enforcement officials who feel that it leaves the police officer in the precarious position of deciding whether the suspect is dangerous. Like any other decision related to police work, decisions about the use of deadly force are inescapable. But, unlike the decision to write a citation or not to arrest some juvenile shoplifter, use of deadly force is an irreversible decision.

FIREARMS TRAINING

In most jurisdictions, departmental policies on use of force are separate from guidelines on use of deadly force. Many police departments have long adopted a defense-of-life shooting policy or some guideline geared to empower an officer for self-protection or the protection of others from imminent threat of serious bodily harm or death. But, as suggested in the four-stage model of ascending force, the use of an officer's service weapon (deadly force) is permissible only in circumstances in which it cannot be avoided.

As part of this policy orientation, police academy training in firearms has moved in the direction of restrained use of weapons. Although not all circumstances can be outlined in a classroom, many academies have gone to the increased use of role-playing and scenario discussions in order to get officers practiced in selecting alternatives to deadly force. Unfortunately, the game-like circumstances of these activities cannot duplicate the rapid breathing and pounding heart from an adrenal surge as an officer is actually confronted with the decision to use, or not to use deadly force on the street. As Alpert and Fridell (1992:95) suggest: As important as having proficiency in the use of firearms is having the skill to make the appropriate decision to shoot or not to shoot in a practical situation, and having the skill to minimize the possibility of a shooting.

In the past, academy training in firearms was geared toward preparing recruits to qualify with their weapons. What this literally meant was the ability safely to load and discharge a prescribed number of rounds and strike a graded target with sufficient accuracy to reach a required score within a limited time frame.

While most police academy programs spend as much as 40 or 48 hours on the shooting range in firearms training, the majority of this time is spent practicing or attempting to qualify. This type of training acquaints the recruit with firearms safety, proper procedures for cleaning weapons, correct and appropriate non-hostile firing postures, and at least a minimum degree of accuracy when shooting.

Although some academies limit the bulk of their firearms training to stationary targets, others employ pop-ups or movable ones. The training in these cases is usually centered around the concept of shoot-don't-shoot. The notion behind this **shoot-don't-shoot** activity is to provide recruits with practice at making very fast decision about whether deadly force should be used. Typically, characters on pop-ups and targets depict good guys and bad guys. When a target appears, the officer must rapidly assess whether to fire. The shoot-don't-shoot style of training has grown in popularity. As technology improved, the cardboard and wooden pop-up targets were replaced by interactive computer/television laser systems and interactive video disc systems like the Firearms Training System (FATS). Although far more sophisticated, the basic technology of these computerized laser systems is similar to children's toys such as those produced by Nintendo and Sega.

In the case of FATS, a standard Smith and Wesson Model 66 .357 Magnum revolver has been adapted with a laser-emitting device and is supplied with a simulator. The basic 40 scenarios in the system's package have been developed by the Federal Law Enforcement Training Center.

The interactive television programs allow an officer to watch a complex set of circumstances before deciding whether or not to shoot, rather than responding to a two-dimensional drawing as it pops up. In many ways, these interactive programs do not offer a simple shoot-don't-shoot situation. Instead, the officer views a scene in which a series of decisions must be made, simulating at least partially the kinds of decisions officers must make on the street (see Scharf and Binder 1983; Geller 1985).

The interactive program also shoots back, complete with a loud gun blast and appropriate responses from onlookers. Because they are computer linked, interactive programs also can assess whether a shooter has fired a weapon too soon or too late. In complete systems such as FATS, the computer can both display on the screen and provide a complete print-out of the officer's reaction time, the officer's accuracy by number of hits and misses, and even whether the officer fired before or after the suspect. These last factors may actually set this style of firearms training above others.

Although obviously not duplicative of real life, the realization by a recruit that he or she had fired upon a good guy or hesitated too long before firing, allowing the bad guy to kill a hostage, can be quite sobering. Considerable benefit can be derived if classroom discussions follow these practice shoots, and recruits learn when they should shoot and when they should avoid shooting entirely.

The interactive television and video disk systems have also grown in popularity because of their flexibility and relative cost-effectiveness. Because they are fairly compact and can be adapted to any regular television, these systems can be used in the classroom itself. These devices also provide recruits with practice in firing at moving targets. During the recent past, many police departments have lost civil lawsuits for wrongful deaths when the courts learned the officers had not undergone training in moving targets.

In addition to classroom instruction, role-playing, and interactive television systems, many academies conduct simulated training exercises. In some instances, this may involve the use of an actual residence, a warehouse or school building during off-hours, In other situations, police training facilities have built streets complete with storefronts, two-story buildings, alleys, and other common buildings. Combined with more traditional target-shooting, these more interactive decision-based strategies may represent what William Geller (1985) has referred to as the new frontier in police shooting.

PREDICTING MISUSE OF DEADLY FORCE

If social scientists were able to devise some means to predict accurately the profile of a trigger-happy or excessively violent police officer, this discussion would be unnecessary. Sadly, just as it has yet to be determined with any accuracy which felons will be recidivists, no study exists that convincingly offers a profile or composite of officers who are most likely to misuse their weapons or to be brutal (Geller 1985; Blumberg 1985).

There are, however, several worthwhile relationships suggested in the literature. For example, Van Wormer (1981) suggests that female police officers are less likely to use their guns than male officers. In fact, as Robert Homant and Daniel Kennedy (1985) point out, female officers are better than male officers at verbally reducing volatile and potentially dangerous domestic fight situations. Second, younger officers, perhaps owing to less street experience, are more likely than older, more experienced officers to resort to their service weapon. Third, and as suggested by James Fyfe (1980; 1981) and William Geller (1985), the rate of violence in a community and the rate of assaults upon police officers appears to be related to occurrences of police shootings.

But, even these suggested relationships must be viewed through cautious eyes. Female officers have only relatively recently been permitted full patrol duties. As a consequence, their recorded presence and activities in high-crime, high-risk situations is dwarfed by comparison with those experienced by male officers. It may be some time before any meaningful longitudinal patterns can be accurately addressed. Regardless the second relationship that police experience may have less to do with the situation than military experience prior to becoming a police officer. Until the mid-1970s most police officers possessed prior military training. This included previous self-defense and firearms. It is conceivable, then, that the additional tactical training that some older officers received in the military contribute to their being less likely to resort to deadly force. At least for the present, the most credible relationship appears to come from the suggestion that shootings are more likely to occur in certain geographic areas in which crime rates and assaults on police officers are highest.

SUMMARY

This chapter examined the basic issue of police discretion, including its limitations and the need for its control. In addition, this chapter explored the tension between the need for selective enforcement of certain laws, while simultaneously assuring full constitutional protection to all people. The chapter further suggested that police work is a complicated matrix of situations that often present an officer with a unique set of circumstances. As a result, police officers cannot rigidly enforce the law.

But there is a serious need to assure that police officers do not exceed their discretionary limits. Uncontrolled discretion may lead to reckless and arbitrary whim or to the implementation of discriminatory or excessively brutal practices. In an effort to control the exercise of discretion by police officers, many agencies have created formal guidelines and procedural policies. These guidelines are often lengthy and extensive, but permit sufficient latitude and/or options so that the police officer may flexibly apply them in varied situations.

As the chapter indicates, the use of force—particularly deadly force—operates in the face of a number of competing factors. These factors include the rights of the police to protect themselves, their duty to protect the lives of third parties, and the legislated responsibility to suppress community violence, reduce crime, and provide security and access to law enforcement for all through use of reasonable and necessary force. All of these obligations must be balanced against the assurance of constitutional guaranteed rights of the suspect. These rights include individual liberty, equal protection under the law, and most importantly, the constitutional right of everyone to be presumed innocent until proven otherwise in a court of law.

The chapter also considered various controlling and tempering elements, such as guidelines and departmental procedures. In addition to the department policies, another source of control of police discretion discussed was civil litigation. The mere mention of civil litigation against police officers is proving a significant motivating factor for officers to adhere carefully to their departmental guidelines. Beyond these legal and constitutional factors, the chapter considered the social factors and effects using deadly force may have for police officers themselves.

Finally, this chapter detailed the use of both non-deadly and deadly force. Regarding the former, the chapter explored a model of ascending force and its implications for police officers. With respect to deadly force, the chapter first discussed the constitutionality of the fleeing felon rules. Finally, the chapter considered the nature of firearms training and the ability of agencies to predict brutal or trigger-happy officers.

REFERENCES

Adams, Thomas F. *Police Field Operations*. 3d ed. Englewood Cliffs, N.J.: Prentice Hall, 1994.

Albanese, Jay S. *The Police Officer's Dilemma: Balancing Peace, Order and Individual Rights*. Buffalo, N.Y.: Great Ideas, 1988.

Alpert, Geoffrey P. *The American System of Criminal Justice*. Beverly Hills, Calif: Sage, 1985.

Alpert, Geoffrey P., and Lorie A. Fridell. *Police Vehicles and Firearms: Instruments of Deadly Force*. Prospect Heights, Ill.: Waveland Press, 1992.

Banton, Michael. *The Policeman in the Community*. New York: Basic Books, 1964.

Bartollas, Clemens, and Loras A. Jaeger. *American Criminal Justice*. New York: Macmillan, 1988.

Berg, Bruce L. "Arbitrary Arbitration: Diverting Juveniles into the Justice System." *Juvenile and Family Court Journal*, 37(1986):31–42.

Berk, Sarah F., and D. Loseke. "Handling Family Violence: Situational Determinants of Police Arrest in Domestic Disturbances." *Law and Society Review*, 15(1981):313–344.

Binder, Arnold, and Peter Scharf. "Deadly Force in Law Enforcement," *Crime and Delinquency*, 28(1982):1–23.

Black, Donald J. "The Production of Crime Rates." *American Sociological Review,* 35(1970):733–48.

Black, Donald J. *The Manner and Custom of the Police.* New York: Academic, 1980.

Black, Donald J., and Albert J. Reiss, Jr. "Police Control of Juveniles." *American Sociological Review,* 35(1970):63–77.

Blumberg, Mark. "Race and Police Shooting: An Analysis in Two Cities." In *Contemporary Issues in Law Enforcement.* James Fyfe (ed.) Beverly Hills, Calif.: Sage, 1981.

Blumberg, Mark. "Research on Police Use of Deadly Force." In *The Ambivalent Force.* Abraham Blumberg and Elaine Niederhoffer (eds.) 3d ed. New York: Holt, Rinehart and Winston, 1985:334–339.

Blumberg, Mark. "Controlling Police Use of Deadly Force: Assessing Two Decades of Progress." In *Critical Issues in Policing.* 2d ed. Roger Dunham and Geoffrey Alpert (eds.) Prospect Heights, Ill.: Waveland Press, 1993.

Bohm, Robert M., and Keith N. Haley. *Introduction to Criminal Justice.* New York: Glencoe, McGraw-Hill, 1997.

Carter, David L. "Police Brutality: A Model for Definition, Perspective and Control." In *The Ambivalent Force.* 3d ed. Abraham Blumberg and Elaine Niederhoffer (eds.) New York: Holt, Rinehart and Winston, 1985:321–330.

Cavan, Ruth and T. Ferdinand. *Juvenile Delinquency.* New York: Harper and Row, 1981.

Chapman, Samuel G. *Cops, Killers and Staying Alive.* Springfield, Ill.: Charles C. Thomas, 1986.

Cohen, Howard. "Exploring Police Authority." *Criminal Justice Ethics,* 5(1986):23–30.

Cox, Steven M. *Police: Practices, Perspectives, Problems.* Boston: Allyn and Bacon, Inc., 1996.

Davis, Kenneth Culp. *Police Discretion.* Minneapolis/St. Paul, Minn.: West Publishing Co., 1975.

del Carmen, Rolando. *Civil Liabilities in American Policing.* Englewood Cliffs, N.J.: Brandy, 1991.

Fyfe, James J. "Shots Fired: An Examination of New York City Police Firearms Discharges." Unpublished Dissertation, State University of New York at Albany. Albany, N.Y., 1978.

Fyfe, James J. "Geographic Correlates of Police Shootings: A Microanalysis." *Journal of Research in Crime and Delinquency,* 17(1980):101–113.

Fyfe, James J. "Observations on Police Deadly Force." *Crime and Delinquency,* 18(1981):376–89.

Fyfe, James J. "Police Use of Deadly Force: Research and Reform." *Justice Quarterly,* 5(1988):165–206.

Gardiner, John A. *Traffic and the Police: Variations in Law Enforcement Policy.* Cambridge, Mass.: Harvard University Press, 1969.

Geller, William. "Officer Restraint in the Use of Deadly Force: The Next Frontier in Policing Shooting Research." *Journal of Police Science and Administration,* 13(1985):153–157.

Goldstein, Herman. "Police Policy Formulation: A Proposal for Improving Police Performance." In *Critical Issues in Law Enforcement.* Harry W. More Jr. (ed.) Cincinnati, Oh.: Anderson Publishing Co., 1985.

Hanewicz, Wayne B. "Discretion and Order." In *Moral Issues in Police Work.* Fredrick A. Elliston and Michael Feldberg (eds.) Totowa, N.J.: Rowman and Allanheld, 1985.

Harding, Richard W., and Richard P. Fahey. "Killing by Chicago Police, 1969–70: An Empirical Study." *Southern California Law Review,* March 1973:284–315.

Harring, S., T. Platt, R. Speiglman, and P. Takagi. "The Management of Police Killings." *Crime and Social Justice,* 8(1977):34–43.

Homant, Robert J., and Daniel B. Kennedy. "Police Perceptions of Spouse Abuse: A Comparison of Male and Female Officers." *Journal of Criminal Justice,* 13(1985):29–47.

Hollman, Fredrick W. *Current Population Reports: U.S. Population Estimates by Age, Sex, Race, and Hispanic Origin: 1980 to 1991,* Series P25-1095. Census Bureau. Washington, D.C.: GPO, 1993.

Icove, D.J.. "Research Review: Police Use of Discretion." *FBI Law Enforcement Bulletin,* 59(10)1990:21.

Kappeler, Victor E. *Critical Issues in Police Civil Liability.* Prospect Heights, Ill.: Waveland, 1993.

Kaune, Michael M., and Chloe A. Tischler. "Liabilities in Police Use of Deadly Force." *American Journal of Police,* 8(1989):89–106.

Klinger, David A. "Demeanor or Crime? Why 'Hostile' Citizens are More Likely to be Arrested." *Criminology,* 32(1994):475–493.

Lafave, Wayne R. *Arrest: The Decision to Take a Suspect into Custody.* Boston: Little Brown, 1965.

Langworthy, R. H., and L. F. Travis. *Policing in America: A Balance of Forces.* New York: Macmillan, 1994.

Lundman, Richard J. "Routine Police Arrest Practices." *Social Problems,* 22(1974):127–41.

Lundman, Richard J., Richard Sykes, and J. P. Clark. "Police Control of Juveniles: A Replication." *Journal of Research in Crime and Delinquency,* 15(1978):74–91.

Lundman, Richard J. *Police Behavior: A Sociological Perspective.* New York: Oxford, 1980.

Meyer, Marshal W. "Police Shootings of Minorities: The Case of Los Angeles." *Annals of the American Academy of Political and Social Science,* November 1980:98–110.

Milton, Catherine H., J. W. Hallack, J. Larder, and G. L. Albrecht. *Police Use of Deadly Force.* Washington, D.C.: Police Foundation, 1977.

More, Harry W. Jr. (ed.) *Critical Issues in Law Enforcement.* Cincinnati, Oh.: Anderson Publishing Co., 1985.

More, Harry W. Jr. *Special Topics in Policing.* Cincinnati, Oh.: Anderson Publishing Co., 1992.

Port Authority of New York and New Jersey. *Annual Report.* New York: Youth Services Unit, 1986.

Press, Aric, and Richard Sandza. "The California Walkman." *Newsweek,* 19 July, 1982:58.

Reiss, Albert J. *The Police and the Public.* New Haven, Conn.: Yale, 1971.

Roberg, R. Roy, and Jack Kuykendall. *Police and Society.* Belmont, Calif.: Wadsworth, 1993.

Roberg, R. Roy, and Jack Kuykendall. *Police Management.* 2d ed. Los Angeles, Calif.: Roxbury Publishing Company, 1997.

Robin, Gerald D. "Justifiable Homicide by Police Officers." *Journal of Criminal Law, Criminology and Police Science*, June 1963:225–31.

Sampson, Robert J. "Sex Differences in Self-Reported Delinquency and Official Records: A Multiple-Group Structural Modeling Approach." *Journal of Quantitative Criminology*, 1(1985):345–367.

Scharf, Peter, and Arnold Binder. *The Badge and the Bullet: Police Use of Deadly Force*. New York: Praeger, 1983.

Skolnick, Jerome H. *Justice Without Trial*. New York: Wiley, 1966.

Skolnick, Jerome H. "Deception by Police." In *Police Deviance*. Thomas Barker and David L. Carter (eds.) Cincinnati, Oh.: Pilgrimage, 1986.

Smith, Douglas A. "Police Response to Interpersonal Violence: Defining the Parameters of Legal Control." *Social Forces*, 65(1987):767–82.

Smith, Douglas A., and Christi Vishner. "Street-Level Justice: Situational Determinants of Police Arrest Decisions." *Social Problems*, 29(1981):167–177.

Sykes, R., J. Fox, and J. Clark. "A Socio-Legal Theory of Police Discretion." In *The Ambivalent Force*. Abraham S. Blumberg, and Elaine Niederhoffer (eds.) New York: Holt Rinehart and Winston, 1985:171–183.

Takagi, P. "A Garrison State in a 'Democratic' Society." *Crime and Social Justice*, 15(1974):34–43.

Terry, Robert. "Discrimination in the Police Handling of Juvenile Offenders by Social Control Agencies." *Journal of Crime and Delinquency*, 14(1967):218.

Uniform Crime Reports for the United States 1994. U.S. Department of Justice, Federal Bureau of Investigation. Washington, D.C.: GPO, 1995.

Wormer, Katherine. "Are Males Suited to Police Patrol Work?" *Police Studies*, 3(1981):41–44.

Walker, Samuel. "Employment of Black and Hispanic Police Officers: Trends in Fifty Largest Cities." *Review of Applied Urban Research*, 11(1983):33–40.

CASES CITED

Kolender et al. v. Lawson, 461 U.S. 352,360,361 (1983).
Tennessee v. Garner, 105 S.Ct., 1694 (1985).

QUESTIONS FOR REVIEW

Objective #1:

- What is meant by police discretion?

Objective #2:

- How might the demeanor of the suspect effect whether an officer writes a ticket for a speeder?
- Why might a white police officer write more tickets against African-American drivers than white ones?

Objective #3:

- Do more African Americans than whites become involved in police-civilian shootings? How come?

Objective #4:

- How might being hostile affect whether an officer arrests you?
- How might being female affect whether or not an officer arrests you?

Objective #5:

- What is meant by the myth of full enforcement?

Objective #6:

- How might you define reasonable force?
- What is the usual definition for excessive force?

Objective #7:

- Why might it be dangerous for an officer to worry too much about liabilities in shooting situations?

Objective #8:

- What level of force would use of a baton fall under?
- Would it be excessive force if an officer drew his or her service weapon when a suspect lunged toward him or her wielding a broken bottle?

Objective #9:

- How might you define deadly force?

Objective #10:

- How did the case of *Tennessee v. Garner* (1985) effect the fleeing felon rule?
- From where did the fleeing felon rule originally derive?

Objective #11:

- Why do police officers need to know more about firearms than safety precautions?
- Why should officers receive practice and training in shooting moving targets?

Objective #12:

- What are the problems associated with trying to predict violent or brutal police officers?

Part III

Police Culture

12 Women and Minorities in Law Enforcement

CHAPTER OBJECTIVES

After reading this chapter you should be able to:

1. Describe the history of women in policing.
2. Explain why women officers originally were relegated to the role of matrons—even after being hired as police officers.
3. Compare female officers' performance with male officers.
4. Consider some of the obstacles that originally blocked the way to promotions for women in policing.
5. Define defeminization of women in policing.
6. Briefly define what is meant by a police personality.
7. Discuss institutionalized discrimination.
8. Communicate what is meant by cultural diversity.
9. Detail what is meant by double marginality.
10. Discuss the role of cultural diversity training.

WOMEN AND LAW ENFORCEMENT

As many alert readers may have noticed, throughout this text, police officers have not been referred to as male, or using gender specific terms such as "policeman." This has been no accident. The situation of women in policing in the United States is similar to that of various cultural minorities working in our nation's law enforcement agencies. Historically, cultural minorities have found their access and promotions blocked by both institutionalized forms of discrimination (such as height restrictions) and personal prejudices held by administrators. Similarly, women in law enforcement, historically, have been limited in their ability to ascend the ranks into command positions because of

KEY TERMS

stereotypic masculine qualities

defeminization
police personality
institutionalized discrimination

cultural diversity
double marginality

gender barrier. These gender barriers include fairly widespread beliefs about women being less capable of performing police work as well as men, and general misgivings about men and women working together in dangerous jobs. These gender biases have certainly improved during the past several decades, however, many male officers continue today to have difficulty working with women officers (Hale 1992).

FROM MATRON TO POLICE OFFICER

Many historians suggest that women first entered the business of law enforcement around 1845 when the New York Police Department hired two police matrons (Milton 1972; Berg and Budnick 1986; Berg 1992). Yet it is not until 1893, 48 years later, that Chicago's metropolitan police department appointed Marie Owens a police officer (Higgins 1951). In 1905 Lola Baldwin was hired as a police officer in Portland, Oregon. Officer Baldwin's principal duties were to handle a growing number of young prostitutes who were soliciting local lumberjacks, miners, and vacationers in the area (LaGrange 1993). In 1910, Los Angeles hired the first woman police officer with full arrest powers, Alice Stebbins Wells. Her hiring received considerable fanfare and publicity—most of it negative. Throughout America at that time, the public's strong displeasure with police officers had been based upon the belief that no "self-respecting women would want to work with debauched women and criminals" (Feinman 1986:84).

When women began to enter police work in the nineteenth century, it was chiefly in response to increased concern by society over social problems involving women and children, especially young girls. Many of these problems were beyond the interest of male police officers or other distributors of public services. Fundamental changes in social living, rapid urbanization, immigration, and increases in technological requirements in the workplace all contribute to vast increases in unemployment. The nineteenth century witnessed a steady increase in the number of women arrested and incarcerated for drunkenness, prostitution, disorderly conduct, theft, and vagrancy. As the incidence of crime by females and child-related crimes increased, police departments felt the need to have matrons present in the station to handle these cases. Thus, the presence of women in police work chiefly arose from a social-work basis and not one of law enforcement or crime investigation.

Partially as a residual from this ingrained social-worker orientation of police matrons, women officers continued to operate in police agencies in this general capacity until the late 1960s. Their police work was typically limited to assisting in cases involving women, children, and teenage girls (Talney 1969; Hamilton 1971; Feinman 1986). Although the hiring of Alice Stebbins Wells set off a nation wide series of hirings of women throughout the 1920s, female officers were not permitted to involve themselves in what male officers would call "real police work." Real police work, to them, involved patrol work, investigating all sorts of crime, and apprehending suspects.

As with other male-dominated occupations, World War I brought women into the labor market, including operational areas of law enforcement. By the close of World War I, women were employed in some police capacity in more than 220 cities. Frequently, women operated in a separate women's bureau such as New York's famous women's precinct, established in spring of 1921 (Hamilton 1971). Clarice Feinman (1986) outlines the specialized duties of early women police officers in New York's and other cities' women's bureaus. These duties including handling cases involving juvenile delinquency, female victims of sex crimes, women criminal suspects, abandoned infants, missing persons, vice squads, matron duty, and clerical work. Although there were additionally a few women assigned to units involved in active police work such as detective bureaus, these were very few. Even when a woman police officer did find herself working in the role of a more traditional law enforcement officer, she was paid an appreciably lower salary than men in her unit and typically was restricted to the rank of patrol officer throughout her career.

By the end of World War I, various social reform movements, spearheaded by an assortment of women's organizations, had concluded that a significant need existed for women in policing. Throughout the war years, female officers had filled an important gap in law enforcement dealing with children and women. Policewomen of this era had argued that they should maintain the social service orientation they had been limited to. In a manner of speaking, female officers projected a fairly consistent false consciousness that supported their role as nurturing social workers and not fully involved patrol officers. In Mary Hamilton's own words (1971:183), "The policewoman has been likened to the mother. Hers is the strong arm of the law as it is expressed in a woman's guiding hand."

This maternal social-service role of women officers extended beyond merely working with juveniles. The attitude and belief that arose was that women officers were somehow better-suited than men when it came to dealing with women offenders and victims, runaway girls, and children of assorted ages. Unlike her male counterpart, whose policing tools were his gun and baton, female officers used tools of counseling and report writing, and assumed a maternal role. "As mothers of the nest generation," Mary Hamilton (1971 [1924]) once said, female offenders must be viewed as a threat to society. Hamilton also stated:

> a policewoman who corrects a vicious environment is saving boys and girls
> from lives of crime and this is exactly what a policewoman does do. There
> are anti-social dangers, backwardness, truancy, incorrigibility, and asocia-
> bility, which if not detected during early childhood become definite causes
> of crime. To correct these before they become fixed is the duty of the public
> schools today. If our children are to be saved for the good of society every-
> one must join together—the parents, the teachers, and all community

workers. To this group belong the policewoman. [Mary Hamilton 1971:153]

To a large measure, comparing the work of policewomen to social workers and other community workers increased the acceptance of women officers. In this role, women were not a threat to male officers. Even in today's law enforcement community, female officers frequently face a similar catch-22. As Berg and Budnick (1986:317) reported:

> On the one hand, women may choose to assume traditional feminine roles while working in law enforcement (i.e., caretaking, nurturing, and matronly roles). Certainly, these traditional female roles pose no threat to male officers. . . . On the other hand, female officers who do emulate male officers are frequently seen as a career threat by these male officers (these female officers are on patrol and may be considered for command positions just as the male officers are).

During the early days of women in policing, the assertion was that women's abilities were different from male officers. This allowed them to fill a unique position in policing rather than a duplicative one and further led to tolerance of policewomen. Although some female officers did desire to be real peace officers and enter the realm of patrol and investigation, they performed their tasks in fashions consistent with their presumed natural abilities (Feinman 1986). In most instances, women officers were deployed as decoys in vice raids and continued to investigate rape, abortion and prostitution cases. It was not until the 1960s that any real significant changes began to emerge in the roles and functions of American policewomen.

Throughout the 1960s various federal equal employment laws assisted women and other minorities in their attempts to gain parity with white men in the labor force (Townsey 1982; Berg and Budnick 1986, 1987). For example, both the Equal Pay Act of 1963 and Title VII of the Civil Rights Act of 1964 banned the gender-based discrimination previously practiced by labor unions and various non-government employers. Similarly in the 1970s, additional federal actions and legislation laid the foundation for increased equality for women and other minority police officers. For instance, in 1971, the U.S. Supreme Court in *Reed v. Reed* declared that any state law discriminating on the basis of sex violates the equal protection clause of the Fourteenth Amendment (Milton 1972; Feinman 1986). This decision was buttressed in 1973 in the case of *Frontiero v. Richardson*. In this case, the Supreme Court ruled that sex, like race, is a characteristic that must be justified if used as a classification of people for legislative purposes (Milton 1972; Feinman 1986).

It was not until the 1964 Civil Rights Act was amended under Title VII of the 1972 Civil Rights Act that women in policing began to achieve a social and functional status even remotely similar to that of their male colleagues. This amendment, commonly referred to simply as Title VII, prohibited employment discrimination on the basis of race, creed, color, sex, or national origin (Charles 1982; Gaines et al. 1997). In addition to increasing the regulatory powers of the

Equal Employment Opportunity Commission, Title VII's passage meant that women could negotiate identical terms and compensations for work similar to that performed by men.

In what may have been informally a situation related to Title VII, Pennsylvania in 1972 became the first state constabulary to offer both male and female state troopers identical work responsibilities—including road patrol. A number of other states fell in line behind Pennsylvania, and by 1984 all but South Dakota and Wyoming had women functioning as peace officers in their state police forces (UCR 1985). In the wake of these civil rights achievements, other legislation followed. The Revenue Sharing Act of 1972, the 1978 Pregnancy Discrimination Act, and the 1979 Justice System Improvement Act had significant impact on the advancement and growth of women and other minority groups in the labor market. These acts made it more difficult to continue to institutionally discriminate against women and other minorities.

HOW DO FEMALE OFFICERS COMPARE TO MALE OFFICERS?

There have long been a research interest regarding the question of whether women make effective police officers. There is additionally a considerable amount of interest directed toward the question of how great an impact, if any, policewomen are making on police organizational structures and policies (Homant 1983; Homant and Kennedy 1985).

In a review of nine major evaluations of women in policing, Merry Morash and Jack Green (1986) indicted that women were found to be less capable than their male counterparts only in a single study. However, Morash and Green raised serious objections to all of these studies because each suffered from a host of methodological problems. For example, they all failed to examine differences within the same gender groups and to take into account that indexes used to assess male and female officers represent many areas of variation. Variance and distribution scores were often ignored so that when female and male officers' scores differed widely, it was impossible to determine whether this represented a majority of females differing significantly from males or that a few extreme scores had skewed the results.

Morash and Green additionally indicated that these studies each defined positive attributes for the police in terms of **stereotypic masculine qualities**. The stereotypic masculine qualities included attributes such as assertiveness, aggression, authoritativeness, courage, and so forth. These studies also often measured qualities that had little or nothing to do with actual police work. Finally, there was confusion among these studies as to whether arrests were always the most desirable outcome in police-citizen encounters (see Whitaker and Phillips 1983), in other words, whether arrests accurately measured police effectiveness. Morash and Green concluded that collectively the nine evaluations of policewomen suggested that while gender differences do not immediately disqualify women from policing, they do have implications for police employment. Put simply, one could interpret the findings as suggesting that only a limited number and certain type of woman should be in policing.

Robert Homant and Daniel Kennedy (1985:30) indicated that, "any research that attempts to compare policewomen with policemen threatens to raise more problems than it answers." For example, because of the disparate numbers of women in policing, it is rather difficult to obtain large, representative samples of them. Even were one to attempt a matched sample, there are countless variables that might be employed to match the two groups of men and women, none of which would necessarily represent accurately either male or female officers. At least as problematic as sampling difficulties is the question of how one goes about interpreting differences between policemen and policewomen (Homant and Kennedy 1985). Does one attribute identified differences to a cultural socialization process, such as the one that promoted the false consciousness manifested in the 1920s; are differences the result of gender-based differences; are they an artifact of police training of the style of research; might differences between male and female officers result from life experiences that create certain attitudes, values, or motivations, and did these occur prior or subsequent to joining the force; finally, how does one explain similarities? Then again, how does one explain the highly likely overlap that may result from all the factors as explanations for differences?

Early research on women police officers tended to be directed to the question of whether women were suited for police work because of their emotional temperament and nurturing mother image. Later research, particularly that undertaken in the face of the various pieces of legislation of the late 1960s and 1970s, began to consider the rigors of physical endurance and agility required of policemen and women who wanted to be police. In spite of adversities, research repeatedly indicated that women performed their policing tasks, even physically demanding ones, as well as men (Block and Anderson 1974; Sherman 1975). One traditional belief has been that women officers are less effective than male officers in making felony arrests. In an examination of 2,293 officers in Texas and Oklahoma, James David (1984) convincingly established that the arrest rates for male and female officers were almost identical. In another study, Grennan (1988) examined violent police confrontations and found that female officers used their firearms less frequently than male officers, had fewer instances of injuring citizens, and were no more likely than males to be hurt themselves.

Research began to suggest that the biggest differences between male and female officers was how they approached their work (Hale and Wyland 1993; Gilligan 1982; Worden 1993). For example, Gilligan (1982) notes that male officers tend to adhere to a "morality of justice," whereas women officers subscribe to a "morality of care." This translates into men enacting justice through rigorous enforcement of rules and laws. Women, on the other hand, continue to nurture, and protect through attempts at solving problems without necessarily depending on official sanctions and force. As a result, female officers are able to accomplish the same ends as male officers, but less aggressively. Unfortunately, this lack of aggression is misread by many male officers as a sign of weakness or indicating inadequacies in the female officer's performance. Ironically, with modern day police policy emphasis on community relations and community policing, the more gentle and diplomatic approaches of female officers are receiving wider acceptance (Gaines et al. 1997).

Regardless of their actual performance records, female officers continue to face considerable resistance to their presence in policing. Today, policewomen only represent about 8.8 percent of the nation's sworn officers (Reaves 1996).

PROMOTION OF POLICEWOMEN: MOVING UP THROUGH THE RANKS

Although a number of policewomen achieved the rank of detective during the 1930s and 1940s, few were ever able to move higher than the rank of patrol officer. In part, the discrimination was justified along the lines of educational qualifications. Since policewomen did women's work they were not trained in a comparable manner to male officers and consequently, could not pursue the same promotional schedules. In 1952, several New York City policewomen applied to take the competitive examination for promotion to the rank of sergeant, but were refused because New York City's civil service agency had no job description for women above the rank of officer (Feinman 1986). In 1961 another New York City policewoman applied to take the sergeant's examination and was denied. But this time, Officer Felicia Shpritzer took the case to court. Two years and three court battles later, Officer Shpritzer was permitted to take the examination, which she passed (Feinman 1986).

Another early leader in the promotion effort was Gertrude Schimmel. Officer Schimmel had met and worked with Felicia Shpritzer during their early years in New York law enforcement. Schimmel had also taken and passed the sergeant's examination in 1964. In 1971, Schimmel made law enforcement history by being the first women to obtain the rank of deputy inspector, the highest uniformed position in the New York Police Department (Milton 1972).

Although there have been increasing numbers of women officers successfully gaining rank in the nation's police forces, they have also been described as less qualified and less efficient than male officers. Women officers may receive lower performance evaluations from their male evaluators for several reasons, chief among them, perhaps, the fear by male officers of increased competition for a small number of promotions (Wexler and Quinn 1985). Harriman (1985) asserts that while effective women managers have been found to differ little from effective male managers in their attitudes, motivations, and behaviors, their careers, nevertheless, progress more slowly than those of males.

Susan Martin (1989) reported that in a review of studies on leadership, no differences in behavior between sexes were found after controlling for situational and various demographic variables. Martin also notes, however, that several studies tend to link effective leadership traits with stereotypical, masculine traits and consequently regard women as less effective leaders (see Harriman 1985).

While there have been apparent increases in the numbers of women entering policing careers, most police agencies continue to underrepresent female officers. Some of the resistance women officers must confront takes the form of sexual harassment; other forms include reluctance of male officers to partner with them, or patronizing behavior by male officers. Martin (1990) and Morash and Harr (1995) suggest some not-too-veiled forms of harassment include displays of explicit pornographic pictures in the locker rooms, and inappropriate or off-color comments and jokes about female officers and their sexuality.

Possibly as a response to obstacles and criticism levied against them, many women officers appear to feel a need to abandon femininity to compete with male officers and advance in the police ranks (Berg and Budnick 1986). This has been described as the defeminization of policewomen and has been the subject of considerable debate and research (Heffener 1976; Martin 1979, 1980; Gross 1981; Berg and Budnick 1986, 1987).

DEFEMINIZATION OF POLICEWOMEN

Put simply, **defeminization** may be defined as the acceptance and emulation by women of traditional male gender-role behaviors, attitudes, and traits. These attributes may be understood to include being active, authoritative, assertive, autonomous, and daring. In other words, defeminized policewomen are described as having taken on what sociology textbooks call traditionally masculine characteristics (see Schaefer and Lamm 1989). Heffner (1976) and to some extent Van Wormer (1981) indicate that masculine characteristics are perceived as beneficial for patrol officers, regardless of their possessor's gender.

Some research has suggested that defeminization is the consequence of tokenism and results from policewomen attempting to gain acceptance of their male peers by outdoing them (Martin 1979). Unfortunately, this attempt by some policewomen to become supercops frequently works against them. Instead of being embraced by their fellow officers, they are perceived as serious threats to the careers of male officers. After all, these women are a double threat: they demonstrate their abilities are better than many of the male officers, and they meet affirmative action requirements maintained in most departments. Possibly as a response to the perception that policewomen pose a career threat, it is not uncommon for male officers to demean or ridicule defeminized female officers (Gross 1983; Morash and Harr 1995).

Some research has suggested that many male officers believe that they must be "chivalrous" and protect policewomen when they are partnered with them. Quoting one of their subjects, Bryant and his associates (1985) state:

> The thing is, a lot of men are still very protective toward women. I've been crewed with policemen before, when we had an incident car, and if it is a

rough situation they'll say, "Stay there" because they really do protect you—they protect you like their wives!

The kind of situations Bryant et al. (1985) describe place policewomen in a serious double bind. On the one hand, if the officer remains in the car, she fails to provide backup for her partner and may both increase his danger and set herself up for a charge of dereliction of duty or even cowardice. On the other hand, if she gets out of the cruiser to do her job as a police officer—which even the greenest male rookie would be expected to do—her male partner may become injured due to his preoccupation with protecting her.

Several studies during the 1980s concluded that policewomen may feel compelled to sacrifice at least some of their femininity if they desire to be accepted by male officers, as well as seriously considered for advancement beyond the rank of sergeant (Kennedy and Homant 1981; Gross 1983; Berg and Budnick 1986). In one study, Sally Gross (1983) assessed data collected in a study of 288 trainees attending the Southeast Florida Institute of Criminal Justice during 1982–1983. In her preliminary findings, Gross found that more successful female academy recruits displayed a number of masculine mannerisms:

> Women who show masculine behavior rather than feminine ones will get along better with academy classmates. This is consistent with previously reported findings that women's acceptance is a function of peer relations and fitting in, which in this environment means exhibiting masculine traits . . . [By the end of eight weeks of training] . . . the more feminine they [recruits] were, the worse they felt about themselves.

Confounding her preliminary findings, in later more thorough examinations, Gross (1986) began to observe that other females (those exhibiting at once both masculine and feminine characteristics) tended to gain the greatest success during their time in the academy.

Many people in society may look at these masculine characteristics as detracting from policewomen's *expected* feminine role as women. As a consequence, many policewomen themselves may be faced with certain role strains. Their confidence and self-image as wives, mothers, sisters, and friends—as well as police officers—may invoke serious emotional conflicts and stress for some policewomen. In some cases, the only solution may be leaving the police force. For other the resolution may come from defeminizing at least during the working hours. In many cases, some compromise, either in terms of restricted advancement or the type of assignments, may allow a policewoman to cut a niche in her department.

The possible career pathways of police women are graphically displayed in Box 12.1. As suggested in the diagram, some women may join the police already predisposed to conducting themselves in a masculine manner, in short, already defeminized. Other women may enter the field of law enforcement with no predisposition. Finally, a third category of women may enter the academy as androgynous.

BOX 12.1   A MODEL OF THE POLICEWOMEN'S CAREER PATH CHOICES

[TYPES OF FEMALE POLICE RECRUITS ENTERING THE ACADEMY]

Masculine Women   Androgynous Women   Feminine Androgynous

[WHILE ATTENDING THE POLICE ACADEMY]

Potential for:
    Simple change of mind about career decision.
    Role strain.
    Role conflict.
    Occupational stress.

Options:
    Quit the academy.
    Defeminize (adopt masculine characteristics)
    Maintenance of original gender characteristics
    (Masculine, androgynous, or feminine).

- -
[AFTER ATTENDING THE ACADEMY]
- -

Rookies now confronted with increased probability of:
    Role conflicts.
    Role strain.
    Stress . . . . [Rookies Unable to Adapt]
                EXIT POLICING

[Successfully Adapted Rookies]
CONTINUE A POLICE CAREER

MASCULINE AND ANDROGYNOUS ROOKIES	ROOKIES MAINTAINING THEIR FEMININITY
[FIELD POSITIONS] Fair Potential for Command (Self-Assessment of Job Satisfaction)	[NON-FIELD POSITIONS] Low Potential for Command (Self-Assessment of Job Satisfaction)
[TOO LOW] EXIT POLICING	[High Satisfaction] ORIENT TOWARD CAREER STATUS	[TOO LOW] EXIT POLICING	[Adequate Job Satisfaction] ORIENT TOWARD CAREER STATUS

Adapted from Berg and Budnick, "Defeminization of Women in Law Enforcement: A New Twist in the Traditional Police Personality," *Police Science and Administration* 14(1986):318.

Perhaps the singular most important function of the police academy beyond basic training in a state's code is the development of uniform behavior within a department to establish objective, rather than subjective decision-making skills in the field (Harris 1973; Bittner 1980; Berg 1990).

Standardized behavior has several compelling advantages. First, it reduces the likelihood of public antagonism from disparate behavior. Second, it offers a consistent, externalized protocol for officer behaviors; formal (written) rules and procedures, report forms, and so forth. Third, standardized behaviors offer a means for administrators to plan and coordinate systematically the activities of those under their command.

THE POLICE PERSONALITY AND POLICEWOMEN

Regardless of various conflicting social roles and pressures, women continue to make advances toward equality in the ranks of policing. One major obstacle that policewomen still need to overcome, and one that is not generally associated with other occupations, is the "police personality." It remains controversial whether one enters policing already in possession of a police personality or if one adapts to the police culture by fostering this stereotypic persona.

The **police personality** is thought generally to be a combination of characteristics and behaviors that have come to be commonly used to stereotype police officers. Often these characteristics are given to include a desire to be in control of situations, assertiveness, cynicism, an authoritarian attitude, a wish to be aloof from civilians, an increased solidarity with other officers, and a tendency to be physically aggressive.

In part, this type of personality may have grown out of profiles of police recruits of the past. Until the mid-1970s, police officers entering the nation's police academies were predominantly white males, ranged in age from 21–25, and had both military and combat experience. Perhaps as a consequence of this kind of recruit, it is understandable that the average citizen's image of police officers was once of an authoritative, paramilitary, perhaps violent, take-charge-kind-of-guy. Add to this the various violent police civilian encounters during the anti-war protests and sit-ins of the 1960s (e.g., the 1968 Democratic Convention in Chicago) and the idea of a police personality becomes rather vivid.

Although the concept of a police personality is very easy to identify, its actual existence is not as easily demonstrated empirically. As Daniel Kennedy and Robert Homant (1981:347) indicate, ". . . Numerous studies reach essentially the opposite conclusion and tend to suggest that policing contains the same range of personality types likely to be found in any occupation." The police personality will be more extensively considered in Chapter 13, along with issues of police culture and subculture in general.

Several researchers have argued that the token representation of women on police forces is insufficient to hasten changes in attitude among the majority group of white male officers. Certainly, in spite of many advances in progressive departments, women in policing have not risen in numbers beyond token representation in American police agencies nationally (see Martin 1989:323–324; Reaves 1996). One explanation for this token status may be that access to police positions has been systematically denied to women. This systematic denial or institutionalized discrimination, is detailed in the next section.

INSTITUTIONALIZED DISCRIMINATION IN POLICING

Each of us has at some time or another felt discrimination. Perhaps it was a teacher or camp counselor who chose some other kid because he or she liked that child better. An aunt who preferred your brother and lavished him with gifts while ignoring you. The captain of the sandlot baseball team who chose you to fill the last spot on the team, or maybe some employer who chose another candidate because that person was not (or was) a particular religion, race, age, or gender. This kind of individual discrimination, although unkind, operates chiefly on a one-to-one basis. But there is additionally a more systematic and encompassing type of discrimination: institutionalized discrimination.

Institutionalized discrimination is defined here as denial of opportunities and equal rights to individuals and groups that results from the habitual operations of an organization or institution in society. In other words, discrimination that arises from the structure and/or policies of an organization, agency or institution.

Figure 12.1

At one time Asians and Latinos had difficulty becoming police officers because of institutionalized discrimination in the form of height requirements.

For example, in 1966, the streets of Chicago's Puerto Rican neighborhoods were repeatedly filled with rioters. As with other minority communities during the volatile 1960s, Chicago's Puerto Rican residents voiced complaints of police brutality, harassment, and unprovoked assaults. When the dust had settled and the media and federal investigations began to emerge, it was discovered that the Chicago Police Department did not have even a single Puerto Rican officer on the force. Inquires found that the department had been adhering to a height requirement that exceeded the average height of most Puerto Ricans.

The use by police agencies of height or physical agility requirements—ones that meet the physical stature and abilities of white males but not women and certain minorities—to restrict entrance by women or minorities has been called institutionalized racism (Locke 1980). In essence, institutionalized racism may be understood to exist in policing when agency procedures create or perpetuate situations of advantage for the dominant group (white males) to the exclusion or restriction of minority groups (Chesler 1976; Locke 1980; Townsey 1982). In spite of many advances made in the direction of removing various forms of institutionalized discrimination, the lowering of the height bar came slowly in many departments. In 1997, the Los Angeles police department became one of the first departments to completely remove any height restrictions for entrance.

CULTURAL DIVERSITY IN AMERICAN POLICING

The term **cultural diversity** is the current vernacular used to describe a group or agency with mixed racial, ethnic, and gender composition. During the past four decades, American police departments have been moving in the general direction of a more culturally diverse composition. Since the 1970s, most police agencies have made efforts to recruit and hire women and members of various cultural minorities. Of course, not all departments have undertaken these efforts willingly. Some agencies have only moved forward to increase the number of minority officers in their agencies in the face of numerous blue-ribbon national commissions advocating such changes and following sometimes lengthy legal battles that resisted these changes. In some cities, Hispanic and black officers were not hired until sufficient political pressure was levied by local black communities. Jack Kuykendall and David Burns (1980) state that in some departments, the hiring of black officers came only after church and civic groups created enough political pressure.

The increased hiring of Hispanic officers, which occurred during the 1980s, is of fairly recent origin (Carter 1985). So, too, is the rise in hirings among Asian officers. This surge in seeking Asian recruits emerged during the late 1980s after police departments recognized the growth of Indo-chinese neighborhoods in many of America's larger cities. Because Asian officers have only recently entered American police work, little empirical research has examined the impact of their hirings. Some commentaries, however, suggest that many Vietnamese people look down on the job of police officer and may discourage their children from joining the force (Early 1989). The explanation here may rest on the residual fears of many older Vietnamese immigrants who remember that in Vietnam, the police were the ones pulling people out of their homes at night and shooting them. Today, when recruiting officers try to sell policing as a possible career for young Vietnamese men and women, their families look upon such work with trepidation.

Black and Hispanic officers, however have been surveyed to a greater extent than Asian officers. For example, Samuel Walker conducted two studies (in 1983 and 1988) that examined black and Hispanic officer representation in police departments of 50 of the largest American cities. He found that about half of the departments reported significant gains in minority recruitment. The other half, however, indicated either no appreciable gain, or a decline in the number of minority officers (Walker 1989).

Black police officers, ironically, have been working in municipal police forces since 1872, when Chicago hired its and the nation's first black officer. By 1894, there were approximately 23 black officers serving in Chicago (Walker 1980:61). Sullivan (1989) found that in 1970, only 3.9 percent of the nation's police force was black, although blacks represented 11.1 percent of the nation's population. By 1994, 11.3 percent of the officers in police departments across the country were African American and 6.2 percent Hispanic (Reaves 1996).

In spite of a rather long historical affiliation with police work, black officers continue to be underrepresented on police forces of even several of the country's largest city police departments (Kuykendall and Burns 1985; Reaves and Smith 1996).

Figure 12.2
An increased hiring of Hispanic officers occurred during the 1980s.

A CLOSER LOOK AT THE BLACK POLICE OFFICER

In the late 1950s and 1960s, some agencies recognized specific reasons for bringing black and other minority officers into the ranks. These departments believed that in order to represent community interests more effectively, the force needed to be better represented by community members. Frequently, however, this translated into hiring black officers to patrol black neighborhoods, where they were permitted to arrest only black suspects (Sullivan 1989).

In his book *Black Police, White Society*, Stephen Leinen (1984:166) states:

> Over time, white police have come to share a set of occupational values and beliefs about minority groups that set them [referring to the police as an aggregate] apart from significant segments of the black community. The recruitment of greater numbers of blacks into the lower ranks in the early 1970s was part of a large effort designed to narrow this distance.

Leinen suggests that police agencies assumed that the new black recruits, by virtue of their natural cultural links to the community, would re-establish both the police role and image in those neighborhoods.

These assumptions, although viewed as progressive for their time, failed to consider how black community residents viewed black police officers. Since white officers were viewed as the enemy, as much for their symbolic position in the system as for their being white, it was the police who were the real enemy, not only the white police officers, but black ones as well. Many of these black officers resented the department's efforts to restrict their assignments to what were high-crime, dangerous slum precincts (Alex 1969; Leinen 1984).

An odd sort of institutionalized discrimination arose. Chiefly because they were black and presumed to have a greater affinity for black community problems, inexperienced rookie officers found themselves working in far more hazardous areas than most of their more seasoned white colleagues.

Even as black officers were increasing their representation in some police departments, their role in police work remained restricted. Typically, black officers were denied high profile positions or liaison roles between the department and other elements of the justice system or public. Activities such as honor guards in parades, public relations positions, head of special task forces, and other specialized assignments were seldom offered to black officers.

Similar to the discrimination evident in evaluations of female officers, black officers too were institutionally discriminated against during performance evaluations. In turn, these low-scoring evaluations were used to determine raises, promotions, and specialized assignments. Stephen Leinen reported that by the mid-1960s only 22 law enforcement agencies had black officers ranking above patrol officer. Even when black officers were granted raises or promotions in rank, these promotions seldom placed them in command positions. Even black lieutenants were expected to walk beats (Alex 1969). Again, questions concerning their effectiveness on the job often inaccurately addressed their minority status, rather than the more objective problems of this type of an assignment for any inexperienced officer. One might even question whether black officers might not have been placed on certain hazardous duty patrols because they were viewed as expendable by white commanders.

Nicholas Alex (1969) has indicated that during the early push for black officers, these men suffered from what he termed **double marginality**. By double marginality, Alex meant that officers were unable to please their white colleagues, while at the same time, they were despised in their own black community because they were police officers—regardless of their skin color.

In his examination of conditions, Alex (1969) found that the manner in which black police officers interacted with other blacks ranged from those suggesting that black suspects should be treated differently and better than white ones, to black officers responding much more harshly than necessary to black suspects (Alex 1969).

CULTURAL DIVERSITY TRAINING

Many police academies across the nation now regularly include, as part of their curriculum, a session on cultural diversity. The idea here is to improve recruit officers' understanding about the various cultural groups they will be in contact with once they hit the streets. The hope is that by better understanding various nuances of peoples' cultures, better cooperation and interactions will result. Unfortunately, this process does not always operate as intended. In fact, for many officers, just hearing the term "cultural diversity training" causes them to cringe.

The cringing arises not so much from the initial training received by many recent recruits, but rather, among veteran officers being sent to in-service "cultural diversity training sessions," or "cultural sensitivity training. The explanation here is that many departments require cultural diversity training for officers who have had some sort of altercation with one cultural group or another. Thus, when an officer is notified that he or she is to undergo several days of diversity sensitivity training, it is viewed as a punishment, not a learning experience.

Certainly, progress has been made regarding entry by minority officers to police work. But it is equally certain that police departments remain largely composed of white males, and that this is particularly true of upper-level command positions (see *Who Is Guarding the Guardians* 1981; Leinen 1984; Polk 1995).

SUMMARY

As this chapter outlined, women and minority officers have been working in police agencies for more than 150 years. However, it is only during the past 30 years or so that women and minority members have been permitted to function as full police officers. This chapter has examined a number of historical problems both women and other minorities have been forced to contend with in their efforts to gain acceptance by police organizations and the communities they serve.

This chapter began with an examination of women in policing and traces their historical roots as nurturing matrons to present-day issues about becoming defeminized. In addition, this chapter discusses a number of changes in civil rights laws throughout the 1960s and 1970s, which provided access to police positions for many previously excluded groups of minorities. As part of this consideration, this chapter discusses the nature of institutional discrimination and its effects on women and minority officers.

Finally, this chapter briefly considers the nature of cultural diversity in general. As the chapter implies, the police are guardians of society's value and legal system. But, when police departments and their minority communities are at odds with one another, serious strain and discontentment results. The expansion of cultural diversity training in police academies is one good step towards securing a stronger working relationship between police departments and the communities they serve.

Although impressive steps have been made for both women and minority police officers, it will still take a considerable amount of time and serious effort before equality is to be realized. For example, women and minority police officers are being actively recruited. Yet, even with increases in numbers among the lower ranks, there remains a disparity in the number of women and minority officers who hold command and high-ranking administrative positions. In short, while definitely improved, the problems that women and minority police officers have endured in the past are not over today.

REFERENCES

Alex, Nicholas. *Black in Blue: A Study of the Negro Policeman.* New York: Appelton-Century-Croft, 1969.

Berg, Bruce L. "Who Should Teach Police: A Typology And Assessment of Police Academy Instructors." *American Journal of Police,* 9(2)1990:79–100.

Berg, Bruce L. *Law Enforcement and Introduction to Police in Society.* Boston: Allyn and Bacon, Inc., 1992.

Berg, Bruce L., and Kimberly Joyce Budnick. "Defeminization of Women in Law Enforcement: A New Twist in the Traditional Police Personality." *Journal of Police Science and Administration,* 14(1986):314–19.

Berg, Bruce L., and Kimberly Joyce Budnick. "Defeminization of Women in Law Enforcement: Examining the Role of Women in Policing." In *Police and Law Enforcement,* 5. Daniel B. Kennedy and Robert Homant (eds.) New York: AMS, 1987.

Bittner, Egon. *The Function of Police in Modern Society.* Cambridge, Mass.: Oelege-schlager, Gunn, and Hain, 1980.

Block, Peter, and Deborah Anderson. *Policewomen on Patrol: Final Report.* Washington, D.C.: Police Foundation, 1974.

Bryant, L. D. Dunkerley, and G. Kelland. "One of the Boys?" *Policing*, 1(1985):236–44.

Carter, David L. "Hispanic Perception of Police Performance: An Empirical Assessment." *Journal of Criminal Justice*, 13(1985):487–500.

Charles, Michael T. "Women in Policing: The Physical Aspects." *Journal of Police Science and Administration*, 10(1982):194–205.

Chesler, M. "Contemporary Sociological Theories of Racism." In *Towards the Elimination of Racism*. P. Katz (ed.) New York: Pergamon, 1976.

David, James. "Perspectives of Policewomen in Texas and Oklahoma." *Journal of Police Science and Administration*, 12(1984):395–403.

Early, D. E. "Police Departments are White Male—and Changing." *San Jose Mercury News*, 28 April, 1989:f1–f2.

Feinman, Clarice. *Women in the Criminal Justice System*. New York: Praeger, 1986.

Gaines, Larry K., Victor E. Kappeler, and Joseph B. Vaughn. *Policing in America*. Cincinnati, Oh.: Anderson Publishing Co., 1997.

Gilligan, C. *In a Different Voice: Psychological Theory and Women's Development*. Cambridge, Mass.: Harvard University Press, 1982.

Gross, Sally. "Socialization into Law Enforcement: The Female Police Recruit." Final Report for the Southeast Florida Institute of Criminal Justice. Miami, Fl., 1981.

Gross, Sally. "Women Becoming Cops: Development Issues and Solutions." Report for the Southeast Florida Institute of Criminal Justice. Miami, Fl., 1983.

Gross, Sally. Comments offered during discussion at the Annual Meeting of the Academy of Criminal Justice Sciences. Orlando, Fl., (March 1986).

Grennan, S. "Findings on the Role of Officer Gender in Violent Encounters with Citizens." *Journal of Police Science and Administration*, 15(1)1988:78–85.

Hale, D. "Women in Policing." In *What Works in Policing: Operations and Administration Examined*. Gary Cordner and D. Hale (eds.) Cincinnati, Oh.: Anderson Publishing Co., 1992.

Hale, D., and S. M. Wyland. "Dragons and Dinosaurs: The Plight of Patrol Women." *Police Forum*, 3(2)1993:1–6.

Hamilton, Mary E. *The Policewomen: Her Service and Ideas*. New York: Arno Press and *The New York Times*, [1924] 1971.

Harriman, A. *Women/Men/Management*. New York: Praeger, 1985.

Harris, Richard N. *The Police Academy: An Inside View*. New York: Wiley, 1973.

Heffner, P. "The Impact of Policewomen on Patrol: Contributions of Sex-Role Stereotypes to Behavior in an Astereotypic Setting." Unpublished doctoral dissertation. Department of Psychology, Wayne State University, Detroit, 1976.

Heffnernan, William, and Timothy Stroup. *Ethnics: Hard Choices in Law Enforcement*. New York: John Jay, 1985.

Higgins, Lois L. "Historical Background of Policewomen's Service." *Journal of Criminal Law and Criminology*, 41(1951):822–35.

Homant, Robert J., and Daniel B. Kennedy. "Police Perceptions of Spouse Abuse: A Comparison of Male and Female Offenders." *Journal of Criminal Justice*, 13(1985):29–47.

Kennedy, Daniel B., and Robert J. Homant. "Nontraditional Role Assumption and the Personality of Policewomen." *Journal of Police Science and Administration*, 9(1981):346–55.

Kuykendall, Jack L., and David E. Burns. "The Black Police Officer: An Historical Perspective." In *The Ambivalent Force*. Abraham S. Blumberg and Elaine Niederhoffer (eds.) New York: Holt, Reinhart and Winston, 1985. Originally published in *Journal of Contemporary Criminal Justice*, 1(1980):4–12.

LaGrange, Randy L. *Policing American Society*. Chicago, Illinois: Nelson-Hall, Inc., 1993.

Leinen, Stephen. *Black Police, White Society*. New York: New York University, 1984.

Locke, H. "Racial Altitude and Institutional Racism: Display Issues." *Social Development Issues*, 4(1980):7–20.

Martin, Susan E. "*Police*woman and Police*woman*: Occupational Role Dilemmas and Choices of Female Officers." *Journal of Police Science and Administration*, 7(1979):314–23.

Martin, Susan, E. *Breaking and Entering: Policewomen on Patrol*. Berkeley, Calif.: University of California Press, 1980.

Martin, Susan E. "Female Officers on the Move?: A Status Report on Women in Policing." In *Critical Issues in Policing: Contemporary Readings*. Roger G. Dunham and Geoffrey P. Alpert (eds.) Prospect Heights, Ill.: Waveland, 1989.

Martin, Susan E. *Women on the Move? A Report on the Status of Women in Policing*. Washington, D.C.: Police Foundation, 1990.

Milton, Catherine. *Women in Policing*. Washington, D.C.: The Police Foundation, 1972.

Morash, Merry, and Jack Green. "Evaluating Women on Patrol: A Critique of Contemporary Wisdom." *Evaluation Review*, 10(1986):230–55.

Morash, Merry, and R. Haar. "Gender, Workplace Problems and Stress in Policewomen." *Justice Quarterly*, 12(1)1995:113–140.

Polk, O. E. "The Effects of Ethnicity on Career Paths of Advanced/Specialized Law Enforcement Officers." *American Journal of Police*, 18(1)1995:1–21

Reaves, B. A. *Local Police Departments, 1993*. Washington, D.C.: U.S. Department of Justice, 1996.

Reaves, B. A., and P. Z. Smith. *Law Enforcement Management and Administrative Statistics*. Washington, D.C.: Bureau of Justice Statistics, 1993:37–48.

Schaefer, Richard T., and Robert P. Lamm. *Sociology*. 3d ed. New York: McGraw-Hill, 1989.

Sherman, Lawrence J. "Evaluation of Police Patrol in a Suburban Police Department." *Journal of Police Science and Administration*, 3(1975):434–38.

Sullivan, Peggy S. "Minority Officers: Current Issues." In *Critical Issues in Policing: Contemporary Readings*. Roger G. Dunham and Geoffrey P. Alpert (eds.) Prospect Heights, Ill: Waveland Press, 1989.

Talney, R. "Women in Law Enforcement: An Expanded Role." *Police*, 14(1969):49–51.

Townsey, Dianne Roi. "Black Women in American Policing: An Advancement Display." *Journal of Criminal Justice*, 10(1982):455–68.

Uniform Crime Reports for the United States. U.S. Department of Justice, Federal Bureau of Investigation. Washington, D.C.: GPO, 1985.

Van Wormer, Katherine. "Are Males Suited to Police Patrol Work?" *Police Studies*, 3(1981):41–44.

Walker, Samuel. *Popular Justice*. New York: Oxford, 1980.

Walker, Samuel. *The Police in America: An Introduction*. New York: McGraw-Hill, 1983.

Walker, Samuel. "Racial Minority and Female Employment in Policing: The Implication of 'Glacial' Change." *Crime and Delinquency*, 31(1985):555–572.

Walker, Samuel. *Employment of Black and Hispanic Police Officers, 1983–1988: A Follow-up Study*. Omaha, Neb.: Center for Applied Urban Research, University of Nebraska at Omaha, February 1989.

Wexler, Judice Gaffin, and Viki Quinn. "Considerations in the Training and Development of Women Sergeants." *Journal of Police Science and Administration*, 13(1985):98–105.

Whitaker, Gordon P., and Charles David Philips (eds.) *Evaluating Performance of Criminal Justice Agencies*. Beverly Hills, Calif.: Sage, 1983.

"Who is Guarding the Guardians? A Report on Police Practice for the U.S. Commission on Civil Rights." Washington, D.C.: GPO, 1981.

Worden, A. P. "The Attitudes of Women and Men in Policing: Testing Conventional and Contemporary Wisdom." *Criminology*, 3(2)1993:203–237.

QUESTIONS FOR REVIEW

Objective #1:

- In what year did women first enter policing?
- In what city was the first woman hired as a police officer?
- In what state was the first female officer allowed to conduct full patrol activities?

Objective #2:

- Why were women believed to be more nurturing than men?
- What were the primary duties of early police women?

Objective #3:

- In what ways do women officers outperform men?

Objective #4:

- Why were so few female officers promoted above the rank of sergeant prior to 1972?

Objective #5:

- What is meant by defeminization of women in law enforcement?
- Why might defeminized female officers fair better than very feminine female officers?

Objective #6:

- What is meant by a police personality?

Objective #7:

- Why would a minimum height requirement of 5' 10" be an example of institutionalized discrimination?

Objective #8:

- How might you define the phrase "cultural diversity?"
- Why is cultural diversity important to policing?

Objective #9:

- Why were early black officers said to experience double marginality?

Objective #10:

- Why do many officers regard cultural diversity training as a punishment?

13 Police Subculture

CHAPTER OBJECTIVES

After reading this chapter you should be able to:

1. Describe two myths about police behavior.
2. Explain the concept of a police subculture.
3. Define what is meant by culture.
4. Detail the process of socialization.
5. Discuss why minimum training standards are necessary.
6. Differentiate between desocialization and resocialization at the police academy.
7. Consider the role of field training for police officers.
8. Talk about police cynicism and authoritarian behavior.
9. Consider how one acquires a police personality.
10. Describe the concept of police *esprit de corps*.
11. Discuss the occupational role of police officer.
12. Express what is meant by styles of policing.

TWO MYTHS ABOUT POLICE BEHAVIOR

Until recently, sociologists, criminologists, and others who study the police were blinded with a type of myopia when it came to police officers. This myopia involved taking for granted that they knew what the police as a social institution really is and who becomes police officers. This myopic view prevented many researchers from raising questions about the institution and who actually enters police work. In turn, this led to two prevalent myths about police behavior. For some, police were idealized as altruistic personalities who ministered

KEY TERMS	stress-reaction training	anomie
	total institutions	police esprit de corps
subculture	desocialization	reference group
culture	resocialization	anticipatory socialization
copspeak	cynicism	formal socialization
socialization	authoritarians	style of policing

the law exactly and without discretion, bias, or prejudice. For others, the myth was that police officers were authoritarian personalities who administered the law however they wanted to, swaggering through life enforcing laws against whomever they chose whenever they saw fit. This meant that police officers enforced laws against private citizens according to their racial, social, and even sexual prejudices.

Unlike either of these extremes, police are neither free to enforce laws in an arbitrary or whimsical fashion, nor are they expected to rigidly enforce all laws at all times. Police officers are influenced by a wide variety of social forces, as are other members of society and social institutions. A variety of mechanisms for social control moderate the actions of police officers. Some of these control mechanisms are informal and identical to those that each of us learn during our lifetimes through the process of socialization. Other control mechanisms are formal and rely upon written laws, codes, and policies.

This chapter explores the police not only as a social institution, but also as a social group operating in our society. Theoretical explanations for why police may behave in certain ways, possess certain kinds of personalities, or perform their duties in specific ways are explored. The central purpose of this chapter is not to identify exactly what the police as a social institution is, but rather to consider who specific officers might be.

THE NEED FOR GROUP SUPPORT

All social groups seek some form of individual and group security. Two major emphases of this sense of security is physical security (protection from physical harm), and material security (protection of one's property). But social groups also require a less tangible type of security, namely, emotional security. To assure emotional support, empathic understanding, like values and beliefs, and shared ways of seeing and doing things, the police have evolved what is commonly referred to as a police subculture. Many textbooks define a **subculture** as a culture within a culture, or a small subset of some large cultural group.

The formal concept of a police subculture was originally advanced in a work by William A. Westley titled *Violence and the Police* (1970). This book resulted from Westley's study 20 years earlier of the police in Gary, Indiana. In a manner similar to Studs Terkel's 1974 examination of the "Royal Blue" construction workers and their social norms and occupational pride, Westley examined police from the perspective of an occupational subculture. As Westley (1970:11) expresses it, his goal was to "isolate and identify the major social norms governing police conduct and to describe the way in which they influence police action in specific situations."

In his research, Westley identified police as grouping together into what he described as a distinct subculture. Westley, and later other researchers, stressed the importance of a distinct police subculture in shaping the views, attitudes, and behaviors of police officers.

Westley, in fact, indicates the attitudes the police subculture supports or encourages are perpetuated in policing. Conversely, those elements the police subculture does not endorse are short-lived. For example, if the police subculture accepts or condones gift-taking by police officers, new recruits will learn to approve of this behavior and see it as normal. Westley's argument further suggests that police view the public as the enemy. This Westley explains, results from the police officers never meeting private citizens on particularly good terms. Most meetings are with citizens who would prefer no contact with the police. Westley describes these sorts of meetings as representing "an unpleasant job, a threat, the bad ones, unpleasant and whining, self-concerned, uncooperative, and unjust" (1970:49). What results is a kind of us-versus-them attitude among many police officers.

Because of the perceived public hostility, Westley argued that police officers began to rely heavily—or exclusively—upon other officers for their support. Hence, a kind of self-imposed social isolation envelops police. It is this symbolically circumscribed social support and friendship network that Westley calls the police subculture.

In one recent review of modern policing, Malcolm Sparrow and his associates (1990:51) identified six core beliefs described as underscoring the police subculture. These include:

1. We are the only real crime fighters. The public wants the police officer to fight crime; other agencies, both public and private, only play at fighting crime.
2. No one else understands the real nature of police work. Lawyers, academics, politicians, and the public in general have little concept of what it means to be a police officer.
3. Loyalty to colleagues counts above everything else. Police officers have to stick together because everyone is out to get the police and make their jobs more difficult.
4. It is impossible to win the war against crime without bending the rules. Courts have awarded criminal defendants too many civil rights.
5. Members of the public basically are unsupporting and unreasonably demanding. People are quick to criticize police unless they need the police themselves.
6. Patrol work is the pits. Detective work is glamorous and exciting.

Taken together, these six beliefs summarize the general cloak that shrouds the police; what Westley described as the *blue curtain* that separates the police from private citizens. Michael Brown (1981) has similarly talked about a police subculture. Brown, however, specifies three core values that, he maintains, ground officers to the police subculture: honor, loyalty, and individualism. *Honor* is the officers' claim to prize work well done and services rendered to the community. Since part of an officer's expectation is to provide service, police officers do not expect to be honored by either their departments or the public. This makes it all the more important that the officers honor one another. *Loyalty* is required in the police subculture. It is expected to be instantaneous and unflinching and, according to Brown, loyalty is the most important characteristic a rookie officer can display to veteran officers. Among the illustrations Brown offers is the bond that develops between partners.

Loyalty and honor are directed toward others. In contrast to this, Brown suggests that the more self-centered value of *individualism* also grounds officers to their police culture. Individualism is characterized by officers receiving reward from involvement in police work, the thrill of a chase, or making a good arrest.

Elizabeth Reuss-Ianni (1984) characterized the police culture as divided between two systems or codes, formal and informal. Reuss-Ianni maintains that the formal code is represented by the law, rules, regulations, policies, and procedures of the agency. The informal code, however, fills in the cracks and becomes the actual way officers go about their work. This informal code is passed from experienced officers to less experienced officers through various social activities and training situations.

To better understand all of these various interpretations of police subculture, it may be useful to consider a more general definition of what is meant by the concepts of *culture* and *subculture*.

CULTURE

Virtually all introductory sociology textbooks have a chapter on culture. Each will offer a slightly different definition for what this term represents. But, at some level, all of these variations amount to the same thing. Specifically, **culture** refers to a society's total way of doing things. It includes all human-made objects, knowledge, beliefs and values, customs, laws, technologies, and virtually all other products of human endeavor. Additionally, all definitions of culture convey the notion of generational inheritance. In short, one generation teaches the next generation the group's cultural elements. Sharing a similar culture is what allows us to define various different societies. Typically, one thinks of a society as a group of people residing within an identifiable territory and sharing a common culture (Stark 1998).

SUBCULTURE

Within the confines of the overall, or dominant, culture of a society, one finds various smaller subgroupings. Members of these subgroupings, while sharing in many of the dominant culture's values, norms, and other social ideas and patterns, differ distinctly in some manner. Each of us belongs to various subgroups that powerfully influence our beliefs and behaviors: social clubs, friendship cliques and groups, families, school classes, churches and synagogues, and so forth. But these social organizations fail by themselves to adequately represent the nature of a subculture.

Subcultures frequently develop an *argot* or specialized language that both distinguishes them from the dominant culture's as well as establishes fairly clear lines between ingroup members or subgroup members and outgroup members or nonsubgroup members. These groupings are sometimes identified by sociologists as simply a distinction between insiders and outsiders (see Becker 1963). **Copspeak** offers an example of a distinctive argot used by insiders, the police. When the police are searching for a child rapist, they may speak about hunting a *skinner* or a *short-eyes*. New York City's transit police use the term *lushworker* to describe people who rob drunks and sleeping passengers on the subway trains (Theroux 1982:74). But more important than a distinct argot is the *weltanschauung* or ideological worldview that permeates the subculture. Stated differently, members tend to share deeply certain ways of looking at people and situations, ways of behaving, and values (Gaines, Kappeler, and Vaughn 1997).

The real and exaggerated sense of danger inherent in police work is part of this worldview and part of what may be termed the police folkway. Unquestionably, some of what police officers do is very dangerous and risky behavior. However, much of the day-to-day activities of patrol officers is fairly routine and not particularly dangerous. Nonetheless, police officers often view citizens as potential sources of violence, as assailants and enemies. This symbolic assailant concept is often passed from older training officers to younger less experienced ones in the course of casual conversations as well as during specific training exercises. Eventually, this perception is ingrained as part of the young officer's general way of looking at citizens. It has become part of his or her worldview.

Often police officers are not even aware of the significant influence membership in this subculture holds over them. Yet it is common for police officers to seek the companionship of other officers rather than civilians, to avoid social activities that might draw them into civilian social circles, to avoid mention of their occupation unless directly asked, and to generally foster an attitude of *them* (civilians) and *us* (police officers).

Entrance into the police subculture does not automatically occur when one puts on a police uniform. Entrance is gained slowly through a learning process that allows the individual to gain both knowledge and internalize values appropriate to the group. In short, entrance into police culture requires one to adopt a police *weltanschauung* or worldview. Sociologists call this learning process **socialization.**

Socialization into police culture is a process by which recruits acquire the various values, attitudes, and acceptable behaviors in policing. It is similar to other forms of "occupational socialization" (see Klofas, Stojkovic, and Kalinich 1990; Berg 1990a; Roberg and Kuykendall 1997). In addition to the increased social support among peers that arises from membership in the police culture, behaviors in the police organization remains remarkably stable. This is true in spite of personnel or policy changes.

Figure 13.1
Children role-play cops and robbers as part of their socialization into society.

Stuart Scheingold (1984) suggests that three features of police work tend to encourage initiation in the police culture. First, in the past the traditional police officer came from the working class or the lower middle class. Hence, they shared similar backgrounds, values, and ways of looking at the world. Even in today's police departments and in the face of higher educational requirements, police recruits primarily come to the job sharing basic middle-class views and values. Second, Scheingold indicates that police share a particularly stressful working experience. This, in turn, tends to create solidarity between officers. Third, Scheingold (1984:98) states that "the police live and work together within a largely closed social system that tends to cut them off from the outside and their ideas." Young recruits realize, often in the academy, that their social networks change the moment they become police officers. This literally may mean replacing many—or all—of one's old friends with new police friends.

By this juncture, it should be clear that the nature of a police subculture and the perception of them-versus-us creates a dilemma for the police. On the one hand, police must emotionally detach or distance themselves at least partially from their neighbors and other civilians in order to operate effectively. Certainly, it would be difficult to enforce laws against people who were close friends with any consistency. It is similar to the generally held taboo against surgeons operating on their own family members. Such situations create extreme anxiety and reduce effectiveness.

On the other hand, when the police distance themselves from civilians and their non-police neighbors, they are perceived as secretive, divisive, and tainted in some manner. The notion that policing is in some manner a tainted occupation is a view held by many private citizens. This perception assumes that police are, in general, just slightly better than the criminals they arrest. When a police officer is indicted in a crime, many civilians hold this instance up as a prime example of police law-breaking. Some commentators suggest that the police often perceive a more extreme antagonism on the part of the public than what really exists (Alpert and Dunham 1988). Yet, the contempt for the police because they are thought to be just a little dirty or because they had the discretion not to write that ticket but did, is a fairly common attitude among civilians. A new recruit learns quickly that, even if the public does not appreciate the work undertaken by the police, other police officers do.

The remainder of this chapter will examine various aspects of the police subculture, including entrance during police training, its effects on cynicism and authoritarianism, and the police personality. Stated generally, the remainder of this chapter examines various nuances of the *culture of policing*.

THE POLICE ACADEMY

Sir Robert Peel aptly suggested in the nineteenth century that the selection of good candidates for police training is the first step in assuring a high-quality police force. The next step, of course, becomes the training itself. It seems unreasonable to expect a high caliber of law enforcement protection from a poorly trained or untrained police force, irrespective of the motivation or dedication of the officers (Holden 1986). Yet, in 1965, the International Association of Chiefs of Police (IACP) learned that the vast majority (85 percent) of police agencies in the United States did not offer any formal training to new officers. According to Jack Kuykendall and Peter Usinger (1975), in many jurisdictions new officers were issued guns, badges, and rule books, but no formal training.

Today, this phenomenon has virtually reversed. What has not radically changed, however, is the variety of formal training programs that exist across the country. In some jurisdictions, the police academy is a double structure. Recruits must first attend a standard training program. In Florida, for example, this minimum period is 320 hours of classroom instruction. After completing this initial training, the recruit is certified to serve as a police officer in the state of Florida. The second component of academy training involves any training specialized required by the recruit's hiring agency. For example, in the state's capital of Tallahassee, the police department requires an additional 40 hours of classroom training, the sheriff's department an additional 20 hours.

The minimum training to gain certification for policing ranges from a low of about 120 hours in Missouri to a high of 954 hours in Hawaii. Table 13.1 shows how, what, and the number of hours police recruits are trained is substantially different from state to state. Differences also exist within states among various agencies.

Table 13.1

Minimum Training Hours Required for Entry-Level Policing

STATE	TOTAL NUMBER OF HOURS REQUIRED	HUMAN RELATIONS	FORCE & WEAPONRY	COMMUNI-CATIONS	LEGAL TRAINING	PATROL & CRIMINAL INVESTI-GATION	CRIMINAL JUSTICE SYSTEMS	ADMINIS-TRATION
Hawaii	954	17	153	65	133	444	29	113
Rhode	661	42	65	0	48	480	0	26
Vermont	553	4	80	30	74	330	3	32
Maine	504	27	62	17	73	277	21	27
West Virginia	495	14	98	20	120	195	36	12
Pennsylvania	480	76	88	10	94	196	16	0
Maryland	471	0	0	0	73	366	0	32
Massachusetts	460	35	132	28	90	167	8	0
Utah	450	19	73	27	49	247	15	20
Connecticut	443	23	48	8	64	284	11	5
Indiana	440	21	73	4	83	192	32	35
Michigan	440	9	105	8	48	244	0	26
Washington	440	34	152	24	85	145	0	0
New Hampshire	426	20	75	8	60	205	8	50
New Mexico	421	30	69.5	18	56	238.5	9	0
Arizona	400	24	110	16	78	135	12	25
California	400	15	80	15	60	185	10	35
Iowa	400	33	75	12	44	175	13	48
Kentucky	400	6.5	84.5	3.5	75.5	182.5	6	41.5
South Carolina	382	18	77	12	72	178	2	23
Texas	381	14	48	18	68	233	0	0
North Carolina	369	28	64	20	72	170	0	15
Delaware	362	12	64	17	87	174	6	2
Montana	346	22	77.5	14	19.5	183.5	15	14.5
Nebraska	341	36	58	10	62	158	2	15
Colorado	334	19	55	22	79	141	18	0
Florida	320	24	39	18	54	158	9	18
Kansas	320	34	42	20	45	170	1	8
Mississippi	320	8	70	20	50	153	7	12
Wyoming	320	10	71	14	53	119	33	20
North Dakota	313	10	23	20	84	139	16	21
Idaho	310	0	47	9	51	169	16	18
New Jersey	310	26	40	13	49	116	17	49
Arkansas	304	14	60	6	19	190	0	15
New York	285	9	38	7	44	169	10	8
Alabama	280	14	49	8	48	138	3	20
Ohio	280	16	42	10	76	111	20	5
Oregon	280	14	64	12	62	104	8	16
Alaska	276	1	20	7	74	139	13	22
Georgia	240	18	45	5	47	110	2	13
Louisiana	240	16	57	8	36	78	5	40
Tennessee	240	2	50	7	31	136	8	6
Wisconsin	240	18	30	9	16	121	10	36
Nevada	200	8	28	11	46	96	2	9
South Dakota	200	17	32	8	22	109	6	6
Missouri	120	3	23	10	28	55	1	0

Note: Data obtained through a mail survey of law enforcement training directors. Oklahoma, Illinois, Virginia, and Minnesota were omitted from the study due to incomplete data on curriculum content.
Source: U.S. Department of Justice, *Sourcebook of Criminal Justice Statistics, 1986*. Washington, D.C.: U.S. Government Printing Office, 1986:16

While variations in the duration and content of police basic training do differ, efforts have been undertaken to standardize this level of police instruction. In most states, for example, training commissions, such as the commission on Peace Officer Standards and Training (POST) in California, have been established to develop minimum entrance level training requirements for police work. These commissions additionally assist in the development of police training programs for law enforcement agencies (Hale 1994).

INSIDE THE ACADEMY

In spite of differences in the content and duration of police academies across the country, all share in the process of shaping new recruits' views on policing and civilian life, crime and order, and their principle goals and functions as police officers.

The police academy is perhaps the first formal occupational socialization process a recruit comes in contact with within the law enforcement organization. Some police training programs are intentionally designed to break down the recruit, in order to build him or her up as a police officer. This technique is sometimes referred to as **stress-reaction training** in police academies. Sociologically, this concept derives from two related stages of an indoctrination process intended to socialize group members into various total institutions. **Total institutions** are defined as settings or organizations in which members are isolated in real or symbolic terms from the rest of society. Members of total institutions are subject to the control and authority of the administrative staff. Examples of total institutions typically include prisons, mental institutions, religious cults, the military and paramilitary agencies such as the police.

Two stages are associated with this indoctrination process: desocialization and resocialization (Goffman 1961). During **desocialization,** the organization or training program attempts to strip away the self image and outsider perspective of the recruit. These perspectives, values, and beliefs, of course, are the result of previous years of socialization in the large society while a private citizen. **Resocialization,** then becomes the replacement of these old ways of thinking and believing with values, outlooks, and self-images supportive of the organization. Hence, the process of occupational socialization (Klofas et al. 1990).

In the police academy, desocialization can be most clearly observed during the first few days. Recruits are frequently reminded of their outsider status through numerous degradation rituals. These may include being required to have military haircuts (crew-cuts or very short-cropped hair), maintaining high-gloss shines on their shoes or boots, wearing uniforms clearly distinguishable from those of real police officers, having orders and frequently derogatory names barked at them by instructors, or following near-ritualized routines (Berg 1990a).

For example, in some police academies, it is common for recruits to halt, come to attention, and state, "Sir, by your leave, sir!" whenever they walk by an

Figure 13.2
Recruits dress alike at the academy as part of the desocialization and resocialization process.

A

B

academy instructor (Berg 1990b). Failure to recite these lines immediately might earn the errant recruit a punishment of 25 push-ups. In other academies, the interaction between recruits and instructors resembles a very formal college class.

John Broderick (1987) suggests that there are essentially three types of police academy orientations. First, there is the "plebe system," modeled after basic military training. In such academies, recruits are placed under considerable stress, and tend to learn policing skills by rote. Emphasis is placed on obedience, loyalty, and looking sharp. Second is the "technical training model." This approach is similar to advanced military training, in that it teaches useful operational skills, the use of equipment, and solving problems. The third approach, according to Broderick, is the "college system." Under the college system, communications, problem solving, and professionalism are emphasized. Each of these academy orientations tries to produce good police officers, and has both certain advantages and disadvantages. All undertake varying activities designed to desocialize recruits during the first portion of the academy training.

As time in the academy progresses, these desocialization rituals tend to lessen and dissipate. In their place, various resocialization rituals appear. For example, awards are given to recruits who master various police skills. A top-gun award, for instance, may be given to the recruit who achieves the highest score during firearms training. Or, an academic award may be given to the recruit who achieves the highest overall grade point average from classroom instruction. However, throughout the academy experience there is the subtle understanding among recruits that they will still have to prove themselves out on the streets, perhaps during field training.

FIELD TRAINING

The idea for field training is sometimes credited with having been originated in 1972 by the San Jose, California Police Department (Gaines et al. 1997). Stated simply, a field training program attempts to create a smooth transition for recruits out of the academy and into the real world of police work on the streets. In a national survey of 588 police departments of all sizes, McCampbell (1987) found that 64 percent of those responding had some sort of formal field training program. An advantage to this on-the-job, or near apprentice training program is that it provides a formal mechanism to closely monitor and evaluate the recruit, as well as a means for extending standardized training procedures.

For a field training program to be successful, it is critical that well-qualified, experienced officers be selected as field training officers (FTO). The impact of these FTOs should not be underestimated. If a recruit is told by his or her FTO that everything learned in the academy is bunk, that recruit may well believe the FTO. If on the other hand, the FTO provides guidance and explanation for information and material learned at the academy, the overall training process for the recruit is improved (Roberg and Kuykendall 1997).

Recruits typically receive field training during their initial probationary period with the department. Usually, this probationary period is fairly structured in an effort both to allow the recruit to experience a variety of police situations, as well as to allow the recruit to demonstrate what he or she has learned at the academy. Frequent evaluations will be made of the recruits' performance. Often, these evaluations are made by different FTOs each supervising the recruit in different areas of police work.

THE ACADEMY CLASSROOM EXPERIENCE

Before reaching the field training level, recruits spend many weeks in the academy classroom. In these classes, recruits are instructed in penal code statutes necessary for their work, certain constitutional restrictions and privileges, motor vehicle laws, standardized procedures and protocols, the use of firearms, emergency first aid–first responder, communications skills (oral and written), and the use of an assortment of police equipment—radios, batons, cuffs, gas masks. The necessity for standardized training should not be underemphasized. It is enormously important that the police use objective procedures, forms, and records. The use of established procedures assures more systematic standards for behavior, creates a measure of consistency in officers' responsibilities, and allows administrators to plan and coordinate agency activities more systematically.

In many academy training programs, the recruits move out of the classroom and into the field toward the end of their program. As they do, the romanticized and idealized role of the police officer that many possessed when they entered the academy gives way to a more realistic one.

Typically, all occupations in America indoctrinate new members into their way of thinking and doing things. These occupationally specific ways of thinking are usually based upon the various activities with which participants are routinely involved. Doctors, for example, tend to look for organic or medical cures to various problems they confront and may attempt to restore harmony in situations of conflict. Lawyers may seek remedies to problems or question participants in a situation in search of the truth. Automobile mechanics may consider a problem by examining how it got started, how various things fit together, how one participant stalls the situation or another participant's comments flare into an argument. In other words, these occupational views carry over into each member's every day life and activities.

Importantly, this notion of ways of thinking and behaving extends far beyond the mere semantics presented here. For police, perhaps even more than for some other occupations, such a *weltanschauung* eventually permeates the officer's belief and value orientations. Walking beats with experienced FTOs exposes recruits to this other type of socialization process. They begin to see the world they have signed on to protect and work in, and they begin to hear and learn about the police worldview from their training officer. In many cases, this field training period conveys a good and positive image of police work. In other cases, however, this period conveys a cynical image of the world and the justice system.

CYNICISM AND AUTHORITARIANISM

In his classic book, *Behind the Shield: The Police in Urban Society* (1969), Arthur Niederhoffer, himself a former police officer, argued that cynicism and authoritarianism were inevitable aspects of the police personality. The police are, after all, confronted daily with the worst sorts of violence and inhumanity. For example, police must deal with individuals such as Jesse Timmendequa, who in his own confession admitted to having first fondled, and then strangled 7-year-old Megan Kanka in 1994 (Bai 1997); officers must handle pregnant teenage girls who go to their proms, secretly deliver babies, and then discard these new-borns in the trash (Harden 1997); the police must even work with cult members' remains after they commit mass suicide (Thomas 1997) and so forth. As a consequence, it seems understandable that their view of the world might be slightly distorted. As a matter of definition, **cynicism** may be understood as a negative or distrustful attitude about things. Cynical people are often thought to view the actions of others as motivated by self-interest. **Authoritarians** can be seen as persons who adhere to a general philosophy of blind submission to authority.

In his research, Niederhoffer claimed that it was possible to distinguish between two focuses of cynicism among police officers: general cynicism directed toward the public and a specific cynicism targeted at the police system itself. Regarding the first form of cynicism, Niederhoffer felt that it was experienced by all ranks and types of officers. But the second, more specific form of cynicism, according to Niederhoffer, although fairly common among patrol officers, was not felt by what he termed the professional police officers. These were individuals who optimistically looked ahead to a transformed police system that they could eventually administer.

Niederhoffer attributed the origins of police cynicism to anomic situations the officers encountered in their work. **Anomie** is a concept coined by the sociologist Emile Durkheim (1951 [1897]). Durkheim introduced the term to describe a loss of direction felt in situations in which an individual's behavior becomes ineffective. The definition of anomie is sometimes given simply as normlessness. In other words, anomie is not knowing the rules governing a certain situation and consequently not being able to behave effectively.

Relating this notion to the police, Niederhoffer maintained that the acquisition of a cynical attitude by police officers occurred as a result of failures and frustrations form the job. For some, this led to job dissatisfaction and alienation—isolation and increased feelings of separateness from the community. For others, these cynical feelings were believed to motivate renewed commitment to the job.

It has been suggested that police officers are socialized into a culture of policing. In some cases, this socialization process begins when they enter the police academy. Niederhoffer, for example, maintained that while most police officers were authoritarians, it was the police system that had transformed them. He was quite adamant that officers do not enter policing with this particular trait.

In other cases, it is suggested that some form of police socialization occurs much earlier and may, in fact, be attributed as the motivating factor for the individual's decision to join the police force. There has been extensive research directed at the question of whether people enter the police possessing certain characteristics or personality types (Alpert and Dunham 1980). If this latter argument is accurate, then applicants for police work may share certain traits long before they enter policing as a career.

Carpenter and Raza (1987) found that police applicants differed from other occupational groups in several specific ways. First, police applicants, as a group, were more psychologically healthy, "less depressed and anxious, and more assertive in making and maintaining social contacts." Second, Carpenter and Raza found that police officer applicants were a more homogeneous group of people and that this greater homogeneity may be the result of their sharing certain personality characteristics which led them to decide on a career in policing. Finally, the researchers found that police officers tended to be similar to military personnel in their conformity to authority and chains of command.

Research, such as that of Carpenter and Raza's has led to a questioning of the methodological accuracy of Niederhoffer findings and conclusions regarding authoritarianism and cynicism. Regoli (1976), for example, argued that Niederhoffer had tapped into what were really five different types of cynicism, not a single type with two focuses. According to Regoli, these were cynicism directed toward the public, police dedication to duty, police solidarity, organizational functions, and training and education. Thus, Regoli suggests that cynicism must be viewed as multidimensional. As such, cynicism may be interpreted as more than simply a single attitude.

Wilt and Bannon (1976) also identified several problems with the earlier Niederhoffer study. In their work on Detroit police recruits, Wilt and Bannon found a substantially lower rate of cynicism than Niederhoffer (1969) had in his sample of police officers in New York City. They felt that several of Niederhoffer's questions reflected realism (how the world actually is) rather than cynicism (how the officer believes the world ought to be). Wilt and Bannon concluded that the rise in cynicism they found among recruits during the first few weeks of training may have been a result of the cynicism projected by the more experienced and jaded officers instructing at the academy.

Later studies concluded that cynicism among police officers may be related to work alienation and job dissatisfaction, and that these factors are themselves related to an officer's level of education, duration of service, social class, ethnicity, gender, and the size of the department (Regoli, Poole, and Hewitt 1979; Lester 1980; Berg, Gertz, and True 1984; O'Connell, Holzman, and Armandi 1986; Carpenter and Raza 1987).

Niederhoffer's notion that occupational tasks contribute to the transformation of police officers' attitudes, whether one-dimensionally or multidimensionally, do appear, as Wilt and Bannon suggest, to be amplified or begun at the police academy. Yet, it remains questionable whether various attitudes such as authoritarianism or cynicism result from the kinds of people electing to become police officers (predispositions to these attitudes) or from the socialization process of becoming a police officer (Burbeck and Furnham 1985; Broderick 1987).

ACQUIRING A POLICE PERSONALITY

Throughout the 1970s two main explanations for how police acquire a police personality competed for acceptance among researchers: the predisposition and the socialization models. The predisposition model maintains that certain personality traits of individuals who become police officers are significantly different from those people who choose other careers. The idea conveyed by this model is that people with certain specific personality traits (such as a need to control situations, cynical views of the world, etc.) seek law enforcement careers, where such traits are encouraged (Rokeach et al. 1971).

The other, and slightly more persuasive model argues that the attitudinal and value differences identified between police and civilians results from a transformation or resocialization of the individual into a police orientation. Usually, this theoretical perspective considers both the structural elements of police work and the process by which recruits are identified and selected for the job of police officer.

The general question of how (or when) one acquires a police personality remains filled with controversy. To be sure, arguments can be aired both for and against the predisposition model. However, currently available research does not tend to support the idea that people entering policing possess personality characteristics that are disproportionately different from people entering other careers.

FORMULATING THE POLICE WORKING PERSONALITY CONCEPT

The idea of a police personality first began to gain public awareness in the late 1960s. The 1960s were a turbulent period for the police and the country. Anti-war protests were a regular occurrence, as were racially motivated neighborhood fights and riots. In the face of a series of political assassinations and attempted assassinations, and general civil unrest across the country, police officers frequently found themselves assailed as brutal, mindless stormtroopers. With these social situations as a backdrop, it is easy to understand criticism of the police as secretive, violent, cynical, and authoritarian. The concept of a police personality associated with these negative characteristics, then, fast gained popularity as a stereotype. The perpetuation and reinforcement of this stereotype among private citizens was frequently accentuated by media representations and factual accounts of violent police and citizen encounters.

Jerome Skolnick (1966) is sometimes credited with developing the concept of a "working personality" in his book *Justice Without Trial*. Skolnick's book examines police attitudes and discretion and suggests that police develop a working personality as a consequence of their work environment. Police working personalities, then, are not the result of pre-existing traits. It was Skolnick's contention that two principle elements in policing—danger and authority—lead to the development of a police personality. According to Skolnick (1966:42), "Danger typically yields self-defense conduct." Officers quickly learn to be continually concerned for their own safety.

Skolnick believes that the potential dangers from police work (both real and perceived) lead officers to grow uneasy with civilians, making these officers more suspicious of people in general. Being hyper-suspicious, these officers tended to isolate themselves from private citizens. Instead, police officers were described as seeking the social support of other officers. Skolnick (1966:42–70) indicated that in order to deal with danger, the officers develop a "perceptual shorthand to identify certain kinds of people" who pose a greater threat to safety then others. This perceptual shorthand amounts to a mental listing of various visual clues and signals, with special emphasis on a person's physical appearance.

Regarding the use of authority by police, Skolnick looks to their authority to restrain residents and, thereby, effectively deny them liberty. Since many individuals, when denied their liberty (placed under arrest), resist or challenge the officer's prerogative, the officer's perception of danger is reinforced. Skolnick also implies that the police learn to use their authority as a defensive mechanism. Indeed, arrest or the threat of arrest, physical force or the threat of physical force, and even the potential for deadly force provide an officer with a powerful means for effective control over people and situations.

Studies by David Bayley and Harold Mendelson (1969) and Joel Lefkowitz (1975) began to dispute the supposed police personality stereotype held by the general public. In a study of the Denver Police, Bayley and Mendelson (1969:15) found that "on all personality scales the data show that policemen are absolutely average people." According to Bayley and Mendelson, police recruits may even be more idealistic when they first enter the academy than members of the general population.

Reviewing the research conducted up to that point, Joel Lefkowitz (1975) commented that most of the literature suggested mere opinions that police officers were more authoritarian than other occupational categories and not empirical evidence. He concluded that while police personalities do differ in systematic ways from private citizens' these differences were effectively neutral. In other words, while the police may be more conservative in their attitudes and behaviors, they are not necessarily pathological in their authoritative approach.

In a study by Elizabeth Burbeck and Adrian Furnham (1985), the researchers reviewed the literature on attitudes of the police and pointed toward a kind of police world view distinguishable from the general population's. For example, police officers were found to place considerable emphasis on concrete or terminal values, such as the family, mature love, and specific work accomplishments. Conversely, officers tended to have lesser concern over nontangible, abstract values such as equality.

Whether the police personality is acquired before entering the academy, as a result of the academy training, or once the officer enters the field remains unclear. Similarly, there are questions about whether classroom instruction at the academy and field experience as officers are equally useful. To be sure, a fair amount of an officer's training is accomplished in the classroom. But, an enormous amount of how an officer will use (or not use) book knowledge can only be accomplished through structured experience gained in the streets, while on the job (Rubenstein 1973; Van Maanen 1974; Brown 1981; Bennett 1984). As already suggested, the harsh realities of the kinds of people and problems officers must contend with may create anomic situations for these officers. In response, these officers may invoke various defensive mechanisms. The defensive mechanisms, then, may de-emphasize what some have called the softer, more abstract affective values and require increased emphasis on harder, more concrete ones (Burbeck and Furnham 1985; Alpert and Dunham 1988).

Similarly, these defensive mechanisms may move officers into positions of social isolation from their neighbors and, in some cases, even from family members. What results is an extraordinary type of group unity among police officers collectively. This mutual support and solidarity among police provides the social cement that binds together the police subculture. The confidence, shared feelings of threat and isolation, and support offered to one another enable officers to endure the hostility, conflict, contempt, and disapproval confronted daily. Some researchers have argued that loyalty is among the most important elements associated with the police subculture.

Michael Brown (1981), for example, writes in *Working the Street*:

> As one patrolman expressed the matter, "I'm for the guys in blue! Anybody criticizes a fellow copper, that's like criticizing somebody in my family; we have to stick together." The police culture demands of a patrol unstinting loyalty to his fellow officers, and he receives, in return, protection and honor: a place to assuage real and imagined wrongs inflicted by a (presumably) hostile public; safety from aggressive administrators and supervisors; and the emotional support required to perform a difficult task. The most important question asked by a patrolman about a rookie is whether or not he displays the loyalty demanded by the police subculture.

In addition to offering emotional support, increasing self-esteem, and self-confidence, and solidarity among officers has roots in officer survival needs. Bittner (1980) has detailed these survival concerns in his elaboration on the *esprit de corps* associated with the institution of policing.

ESPRIT DE CORPS

Egon Bittner's book, *The Future of Police in Modern Society*, outlines the notion and nature of police *esprit de corps*. Briefly, Bittner defines **police *esprit de corps*** as a version of the traditional military "code of honor and secrecy." According to Bittner (1980:63):

The *esprit de corps* has some basis in the realities of police work and is, in its own way, purposeful. Policing is a dangerous occupation and the availability of unquestioned support and loyalty is not something officers could readily do without. In the heat of action it is not possible to arrange, from case to case, for the supply of support, nor can the supply of such support be made dependent on whether the cooperating agents agree about abstract principles. The governing consideration must be that "so long as 'one of us' is in peril, right or wrong, he deserves help."

To a large measure, however, and as several commentators on policing have observed, this "fraternal spirit" is a double-edged sword. While it is indeed a comfort in the lives of officers, its may also produce serious ethical problems. For example, what on the surface may appear a uniform buddy system may actually have an infinite variety of collusive arrangements.

At some level officers may be bound together entirely as a single group. At another level, however, there may be smaller bunchings of solidarity that pit one group of officers against another. The corruption and secrecy uncovered by the Knapp Commission, which will be discussed in Chapter 15, encompassed an entire city's police organization. Officers lied for one another to conceal graft, vice, and racketeering, both from the public and superior officers. Many of the superiors were themselves involved in rampant corruption. Another example of a corruption of the *esprit de corps* can be witnessed by the "Exam-Scam" of the Boston Police (1978–1987). In this instance, police officials and a number of officers were alleged to know about police promotion exams being stolen for as long as 6 years before any action was officially taken (Doherty 1987). These officers and officials may well have remained mum because of the spirit of "one for all and all for one"—at all costs.

Although the police may not be, as many perceive, one big happy family, officers are required to work with and depend upon one another (Bittner 1980). As a result, even in situations where one officer may be disapproving of another's actions, it may be difficult to do anything about it actively. The 1973 film *Serpico* illustrates the problems faced when honest officers turn in dishonest ones. Although a slightly fictionalized account, the film chronicles how Frank Serpico, a real New York City police officer, blew the whistle on a number of extremely dishonest officers at the height of the Knapp Commission hearings. More important for our current discussion, the film shows how, after doing so, other officers were unwilling to be his partner. In fact, the opening scene of the film, which is then presented in flashbacks, shows Frank Serpico and other vice officers attempting to enter an apartment where drugs are being sold. At a critical moment, when Serpico has wedged himself between the partially opened door to the apartment and the door jamb, his fellow officers fail to assist him. He is trapped, and shot in the face at point-blank range. Although Serpico did survive the shooting, he suffered partial paralysis and, shortly after his recovery, quietly resigned from the police department.

It should be obvious that police work requires absolute trust in one's co-workers. The veil of silence that sometimes envelops a segment of a police department, then, may reflect this need for mutual dependency. While this cloak of secrecy may not originate as a malevolent situation, certainly it may easily become one. But, it must be remembered that when such a situation arises, it likely is a fairly small number of police officers who have undermined the trustworthiness of the police institution. This area of police corruption will be more comprehensively considered in Chapter 15. For now, it is important to note that despite the opposite appearance, the culture of policing is not intended to indoctrinate people into breaking the law or covering up law violations of other officers.

THE OCCUPATIONAL ROLE OF THE POLICE OFFICER

This book has previously discussed the idea that when one hears the phrase "police work," one conjures images of police cars with lights flashing and sirens wailing as they race to the scene of a crime. Some people may envision an officer crouched in a defensive combat position with gun trained on some highly dangerous criminal. Still others may imagine the sport coats and shirt and ties of detectives Sipowicz and Simone. To be certain, when the average person thinks about police officers, who they are, and what they do, this vision is clouded by media representations of the police as supercops.

As part of this imagery, civilians tend to think about the police as one-dimensional creatures whose days and nights are filled with a never-ending stream of excitement, danger, and intrigue. There is a tendency, therefore, to think of police as preoccupied exclusively with crime and crime fighting. But police start out their lives as private citizens. They are subject to the same social problems, prejudices, costs of living, conflicts with parents and friends, and general life decisions as others in society.

Unfortunately, the line separating the real life of police officers from their media-created counterparts has grown increasingly blurred. Many of the stereotypes that the public holds for police are based on the belief that most of an officer's work time is spent dealing with criminals and enforcing laws. These stereotypes seldom depict accurately the actual nature of the occupational role of the police officer. The term *role* has been used by social scientists in a variety of ways, depending in great measure upon the focus of their research (Zurcher 1983). It typically refers to various behavior patterns and attitudes expected of individuals who occupy specific social categories. In a general sense, these social categories include formal status positions in the social structure of society, as well as informal, more temporary statuses. In the case of the former, one might think of mothers, fathers, teachers, and police officers as examples. In the case of the latter, one might consider being a member of the audience at a rock concert, a patron of a record store, or a player on a sandlot softball team.

In addition to these more regular status categories, there are labels used to categorize people in society that reflect either cultural or subcultural values. For example, Van Maanen (1974; 1985:147) suggests that many police officers view their occupational world as comprising three categories of people: suspicious persons, people the police have reason to believe may have committed a crime, assholes, people who fail to accept or understand the police officer's definition of a situation; and know-nothings, people who fit neither of the other two categories but who are not police and, therefore, do not know what the police are really about.

In examining these various role categories, some social scientists concentrate upon roles as static elements of an already established social structure of society. From this vantage, roles are considered with regard to how they influence the behavior of people. Others depict roles in a more fluid and flexible manner. In these cases, roles are seen as arising in social settings and are viewed with regard to how individuals influence, alter, or maintain certain behavioral expectations (Zurcher 1983; Holstein and Gubrium 1995).

Throughout this section, police roles have been alluded to and will be further discussed as behavioral expectations for an officer (Heiss 1981:95). The *should* concept derives from several sources, including expectations generally held for recognized formal or fixed role categories, with less formal and emergent roles, and with the officer's self-concept. Role labels and behavioral expectations are learned through the process of socialization.

It is safe to suggest that some people grow up feeling favorably toward the police, while others feel antagonistic. These attitudes may reflect the kinds of orientation each person has received during early home life. Many people have heard small children who, when asked what they want to do when they grow up, respond, "I want to be a police officer." Other children, however, never mention policing as a possible career choice. Whether the first kind of child really does become a police officer may be significant.

The literature is replete with research demonstrating that the occupational socialization process begins before an individual becomes a regular member of the occupation. Brim and Wheeler (1966), Merton and Rossi (1968), and even Klofas et al. (1990) argue that applicants for a given occupational role begin to anticipate the demands and expectations of their future occupation. Typically, the urge to choose a given occupation as a career is related to one's reference group(s).

A **reference group**, in some cases, may be a real and existing group. It may include one's family members, friends, or social associates who are members of or who may be knowledgeable about some occupation. In some other cases this may represent an imagined or idealized reference group—provided by television, newspaper accounts, the movies, or one's own imagination. In any case, this period in the career decision process, unconsciously as it may be, has been labeled by Richard Bennett (1984) as anticipatory socialization.

According to Bennett (1984) **anticipatory socialization** is the first in a three-stage process of becoming a police officer. The second stage, called **formal socialization**, refers to the recruit's exposure to more experienced police officers in the academy and while a probationary officer. The third stage of continuing socialization involves reinforcement of beliefs and values while working in the field. As a trainee, Bennett (1984) hypothesizes, the police officer grows increasingly similar to more experienced officers in terms of cognitive ways of seeing things. In other words, novice police officers begin to acquire what this chapter has repeatedly referred to as a police *weltanschauung* or worldview. This third stage of the socialization process into policing involves learning appropriate ways of thinking and acting in order to function successfully in the everyday work world of police officers. The actual rate of speed that this socialization process requires, according to Bennett, varies according to certain socioeconomic status, race, and educational level. A less controversial situation concerning the culture of police than predisposed or socialized personalities, is the concept of styles of policing.

POLICE OFFICER STYLES

Earlier discussions in this chapter regarding the culture of policing, police personalities, and roles laid the foundation for understanding various styles of policing. Stated differently, in order to comprehend why and how styles of policing differ among officers and to some extent among police agencies, it was first necessary to indicate some of the possible origins of the strains on the police officer's value system and perceptions.

For definitional purposes, **style of policing** refers to a kind of working attitude. This working attitude, like its collateral concept, the working personality, is used by officers to manage and interpret various aspects of their law enforcement lives. For instance, some police officers may view their jobs simply as a petty bureaucratic positions in civil service. As such, the officer may see his or her principal role as a paper pusher with a gun. Others officers may see themselves as sentinels whose mission it is to protect society from the ravages of vile criminals. The diversity in policing styles is based upon a number of influences, ranging from personality variables to police institutional goals and regulations. Michael Brown (1981:223) defines the concept of styles of policing as follows:

> A patrolman's operational style is based on his response to . . . the difficulties and dilemmas he encounters in attempting to control crime . . . [and] the ways in which he accommodates himself to the pressures and demands of the police bureaucracy.

Like others, Brown further suggests that the officer's style of policing is related to how aggressively and how selectively the officer chooses to operate in the streets. Aggressiveness includes the idea of proactively attempting to initiate crime control measures and criminal apprehension. It also includes the notion of how forcefully the officer will respond to challenges to authority. Selectivity refers chiefly to the officer's use of discretion. Discretion, in turn, refers both to the decision to initiate and pursue crime detection prevention activities and the intensity of these pursuits.

Carl Klockars (1985) suggests that such aggressiveness and selectivity has led some officers to a social dilemma he describes as the "Dirty Harry Problem." Klockars explains that the Dirty Harry problem derives its name from the popular 1971 Warner Brothers film character, Police Inspector Harry (Dirty Harry)

Callahan. Briefly, the Dirty Harry problem involves the question of "when and to what extent does the morally good end warrant or justify an ethically, politically, or legally dangerous means to its achievement?" (Klockars 1985:429). In other words, is the forceful or marginally legal use of police authority characteristic of the Harry Callahan character ever really justifiable? Klockars (1985:437) concludes that it is never justifiable to employ a "dirty" style of policing even "to achieve some unquestionably good and morally compelling end."

TYPOLOGIES OF POLICING STYLES

As police officers develop their particular styles of policing, each must weigh the consequences of his or her decisions. On one side of this moral scale are the social injustices that confront officers every day. Along with these are realities about civil liabilities, the judicial system, the bail system, and constitutional restrictions on lawful searches and seizures that often appear to work in the favor of wrongdoers.

Against these pessimistic concerns the officer must weigh moral responsibility, maintenance of the law of the land in order to preserve liberty, and a conscious attempt not to violate department policy. As the officer weighs these various elements, the officer is confronted with the enormous temptation to use a Dirty Harry approach. To do so, of course, removes the thin blue line that symbolically stands between social order and disorder (Skolnick and Bayley 1986).

William G. Doerner (1985), a university professor who became a police officer, describes how rookies search for a style of policing. Doerner (1985:396) writes:

> I maintain that the work group molds the officer's personality. I call it street survival. Rookies find themselves under tremendous pressure and tend to gravitate from one end of the pendulum to the other in their search to find a comfortable style of policing. Every rookie knows his or her reputation needs to be established before being fully accepted as a fellow officer. Hence, rookies tend to be impetuous, aggressive, and very rough around the edges. They need to learn when and how to bullshit on the street, how to read the interactional cues and body language that dictate appropriate courses of action and impending danger.

Against the preceding ideas and concepts, it should be easier to understand how styles of policing are formed. It should also soon become clear, if it is not already, that an officer's style of policing affects both the officer's immediate community and the society at large.

A number of studies have tried to identify, and classify various police styles in formal role categories. These classification schemes, sometimes called typologies, attempt to generate categories that represent particular approaches or models in policing. The purpose of such classification schemes has been to provide political leaders, the public, and police administrators with information on the perceptions and priorities of police officers. This information, in turn, has been used to rearrange departmental policies in order to encourage certain styles and discourage others. This has proven particularly beneficial in reducing police-community relations conflicts.

At one time, the literature on policing styles chiefly identified four primary categories or models of policing styles: crime fighter, social agent, law enforcer, and watchman. Each of these are considered below.

The Crime Fighter

Officers who fall into this category see their role primarily as serious battlers of crime. In terms of priorities this type of officer sees crimes against people as the most serious and property crimes much less so. Mundane misdemeanors are viewed as trivial and better suited for social service agencies than the police. From this perspective, police personnel time and financial allocations should be directed predominately toward interception of serious criminals.

Crime fighters are almost exclusively interested in dealing with actual crime, rather than paperwork or social service calls. Although they are often first on the scene of a serious assault, murder, or burglary, they may ignore radio calls in their areas concerning traffic accidents or other minor incidents. In many ways, these crime fighters fit the public's image of the supercops of fiction. They are no-nonsense, old-style crime fighters, who frequently use more force than may be required to maintain order in a street situation (Brown 1981; Doerner 1985).

The Social Agent

As a virtual opposite of the crime fighter stands the social agent type of officer. A major function of police officers involves answering a variety of social service calls. Supporters of the social agent style of policing argue that police officers should recognize this reality. Accordingly, supporters recommend spending more time and effort on activities that simply need to be done and less effort on imagining that the singular role of policing is crime fighting.

The social agent may even point out that historically, policing included health, sanitation, and fire protection. Hence, social agents conceive the notion of community security in a broad, generalized context that includes crime prevention and criminal apprehension as mere elements among others.

The Law Enforcer

In a manner similar to the crime fighter, law enforcers have a tendency to emphasize investigation, interception of crimes, and apprehension of criminals. In contrast to the crime fighter, however, law enforcers do not make a distinction between serious and trivial crimes. Like other types of police officers, law enforcers see being involved in police work, such as investigating serious or major crimes, as desirable and rewarding. But, law enforcers also see the necessity of enforcing all statutes and ordinances—no matter how minor. The law is the law! Law enforcers are reminiscent of the fictional Officer Joe Friday character made famous by the popular 1960s television series *Dragnet*. They work by the book, letter of the law, and "Just the facts, ma'am," as Officer Friday was so often heard to say. Or, in a more contemporary vein, similar to the 1980s and 1990s futuristic comic book character Judge Dredd (played by Sylvester Stallone in the 1995 movie version). Dredd's argument usually was that the law was always right, simply because it was the law.

The Watchman

While both the crime fighter and the law enforcer stress enforcement of the law, watchman-style policing emphasizes order maintenance. If this means enforcing the law, so be it. On the other hand, if maintaining public order means ignoring minor infractions or brushing off requests for social service assistance, then watchmen will do this as well. The priority among watchmen is preservation of the social and political order of society. James Q. Wilson (1968) is frequently credited with coining this description. According to Wilson (1968:141):

> The police are watchman-like not simply in emphasizing order over law enforcement but also in judging the seriousness of infractions less by what the law says about them than by their immediate and personal consequences. . . . In all cases, circumstances of person and condition are taken seriously into account.

William Muir (1977) has also classified four types of police officers. These include professional, enforcers, reciprocators, and avoiders. This typology was created when Muir examined the "perspectives" by which police officers viewed their jobs, as well as the "morality of coercion," that is, whether the use of force was acceptable for the police officer (Roberg and Kuykendall 1997).

Professionals

Professional police officers are those who have an integrated sense of coercion and have sympathy for people's problems. Professional officers carefully consider an array of possible solutions and mediate the "rule of law" and citizen needs when determining which solutions to select. Furthermore, professional police officers understand that their job requires them to assume a number of different social roles including that of enforcer, social worker, and counselor.

Enforcers

Enforcers tend to be cynical and are coercion-oriented. These officers tend to hold to a "tough-guy" sort of self-image. From this perspective, enforcers may go a little overboard with law enforcement activities and see themselves as standard bearers of the law: protecting law-abiding citizens from the ravages of criminals. They are seldom empathetic and see the law in terms of strict "black and white" issues.

Reciprocators

These officers are sympathetic toward citizens and have difficulty applying coercive force. Reciprocators desire to help people and may hesitate to use force against citizens. Typically, a reciprocator would prefer to give a citizen the benefit of the doubt rather than make the arrest. These officers may shun law enforcement activities and focus more on civic activities and servicing citizens.

Avoiders

Avoiders are officers who actively avoid use of coercion and have little sympathy for people. For the most part, these individuals are actually unsuitable for police work.

MODERN POLICING STYLES

During the more recent past, however, John Broderick (1987) offered a modern typology of policing styles that may be more suitable for modern police practice. Broderick's typology incorporates both types of officers and styles of policing. Unlike earlier typological classification systems, Brodrick's does not reify his proposed categories. Instead, Broderick cautions that his is an analytic schema in which some characteristics found in one category may be found in others as well. Broderick further asserts that not all police officers may be neatly cast into one or another of his proposed categories, giving the impression that his may not be an exhaustive set of categories.

Broderick's typology, however, draws together characteristics commonly associated with police personalities and suggests how these variables tend to overlap with styles of policing. In doing so, "he [the police officer] provides a useful and convenient way of examining a very complex area of human behavior" (Broderick, 1987:4). Broderick's classification system includes enforcers, idealists, realists, and optimists. Each is detailed below.

Enforcers

Enforcers are similar to the crime fighter and emphasize clearing the streets of criminals. Although they place a high value on maintaining social order within the community, they place a low value on individual rights, due process, and empathic understanding of civilians.

Idealists

In contrast to enforcers, idealists sincerely believe in the law. They view procedure, department policy, statutory law, and due process as potential solutions to criminal activity in society. Idealists look at constitutional rights afforded all citizens, even criminals, as necessary to preserve social order. Idealists also see education as important and may seek college degrees—sometimes in fields other than law enforcement. Hence, officers fitting this category may report lower levels of commitment to policing than those in other categories.

Realists

Unlike enforcers and idealists, realists place little emphasis on either preservation of individual rights or maintenance of the social order. Officers falling into this category tend to be cynical and dissatisfied with the failure of the criminal justice system. Often, these officers become alienated from their colleagues, administrators, and the community they police. They may withdraw into themselves and avoid making any difficult decisions.

Optimists

Broderick's final category, the optimist, perceives his or her role as a police officer as really making a difference. These officers see their mission as one that assists people, and it brings them intrinsic reward. In may ways, optimists are reminiscent of the social agents described earlier. Although fighting crime is seen as a necessary part of the job, the primary function of policing is seen as providing service to the public.

Other researchers have identified characteristics and models similar to those suggested by Broderick (see for example, Hatting, Engel, and Russo 1983; Walsh 1986; Peak 1993; Roberg and Kuykendall 1997). A central theme through all attempts to typologize policing is that police officers are not a homogeneous group. Although police officers share many characteristics, interests, and ideas, each officer responds to the demands of the job in a distinct manner. How officers begin to react in police situations eventually settles into what Doerner (1985) called "a comfortable style of policing."

SUMMARY

In the preceding discussion of the culture of policing, it has been suggested that research has uncovered certain variables commonly associated with police officers. These variables, or more accurately traits, have been long believed to represent certain stereotypic expectations about how a police officer is likely to think and act. These stereotypic role expectations have given rise to the concept of a police personality.

The research and understanding about police personalities, however, remains somewhat inconclusive. Of particular controversy is the question of whether police recruits are somehow selected because they display predispositions favorable to acquiring a police personality or acquire a police personality through socialization after joining the force, irrespective of predisposition.

The existence of a police subculture has been suggested to represent the collective result of a group's need to create a socially supportive and secure network. This subculture provides officers with assistance in coping with alienation, stress, and difficulties emerging from performance of their role as law enforcers. In other words, the police subculture provides coping and defensive mechanisms for officers.

The existence of and socialization into the culture of policing is not unlike other occupational subcultures. A portion of the socialization process is designed to instruct neophyte officers about specialized ways of speaking (argot) that insiders use. Another portion of the process acknowledges certain ways of doing things. finally, and perhaps the most important aspect of this indoctrination into the occupational subculture of policing, is a transferring of their particular way of seeing the world, a police *weltanschuungen*.

The preceding chapter has also examined the extension of a general police personality concept and considered the officers' working personalities and policing styles. In this regard, it has been suggested that a number of typologies have been generated by research. Although each varies slightly with its categorical labeling, all tend to share a basic premise. This premise concerns the diversity among police officers in terms of how they operate in their daily policing activities. In short, in spite of many common characteristics and interests, police react differently from one another even in similar situations.

REFERENCES

Alpert, Geoffrey, and Roger G. Dunham. *Policing Urban America.* Prospect Heights, Ill.: Waveland Press, 1988.

Bai, Matt. "A Report From the Front in the War on Predators." *Newsweek,* 19 May, 1997:67.

Bayley, David H., and Harold Mendelson. *Minorities and the Police.* New York: Free Press, 1969.

Becker, Howard S. *The Outsiders: Studies in the Sociology of Deviance.* New York: Free Press, 1963.

Bennett, Richard R. "Becoming Blue: A Longitudinal Study of Police Recruit Occupational Socialization." *Journal of Police Science and Administration,* 12(1984):47–58.

Bennett, Richard R., and Theodore Greenstein. "The Police Personality." *Journal of Police Science and Administration,* 3(1975):439–45.

Berg, Bruce L., Marc Gertz, and Edmund True. "Police Riots and Alienation." *Police Science and Administration,* 12(1984):186–90.

Berg, Bruce L. "First Day At The Police Academy: Stress Reaction Training As a Screening Out Technique." *Journal of Contemporary Criminal Justice,* 6(2)1990:89–105.

Berg, Bruce L. "Who Should Teach Police: A Typology And Assessment of Police Academy Instructors." *American Journal of Police,* 9(2)1990:79–100.

Bittner, Egon. *The Function of Police in Modern Society.* Cambridge, Mass.: Oelege-schlager, Gunn and Haire, 1980.

Brim, Orville G., and Stanton Wheeler. *Socialization After Childhood.* New York: John Wiley, 1966.

Broderick, John. *Police in a Time of Change.* 2d ed. Prospect Heights, Ill.: Waveland Press, 1987.

Brown, Michael K. *Working the Streets: Police Discretion and the Dilemmas of Reform.* New York: Russell Sage Foundation, 1981.

Burbeck, Elizabeth, and Adrian Furnham. "People Officer Selection: A Critical Review of the Literature." *Journal of Police Science and Administration,* 13(1985):58–69.

Carpenter, Bruce N., and S. M. Raza. "Personality Characteristics of Police Applicants: Comparisons Across Subgroups and with other Populations." *Journal of Police Science and Administration,* 15(1)1987:10–17.

Doerner, William G. "I'm Not the Man I Used to Be: Reflections on the Transition from Professor to Cop." In *The Ambivalent Force* 3d ed. Abraham S. Blumberg and Elaine Niederhoffer (eds.) New York: Holt Rinehart and Winston, 1985:394–99.

Doherty, William F. "Class Action Suit Accuses Bellotti of Failure to Halt Police Exam Thefts." *The Boston Globe,* 8 December, 1987:1,30.

Durkheim, Emile. *Suicide.* Translated by John A. Spaulding and George Simpson. New York: The Free Press, [1897] 1951.

Gaines, Larry K., Victor E. Kappeler, and Joseph B. Vaughn. *Policing in America.* 2d ed. Cincinnati, Oh.: Anderson Publishing Co., 1997.

Goffman, Erving. *Asylums: Essays on the Social Situation of Mental Patients and Other Inmates.* Garden City, N.Y.: Anchor, 1961.

Hale, Charles D. *Police Operations and Management.* 2d ed. Englewood Cliffs, N.J., 1994.

Harden, Blaine. "Teen in Prom Baby Case Is Charged with Murder." *Los Angeles Times,* 25 June, 1997:A14.

Hatting, Steven H., Alan Engel, and Phillip Russo. "Shades of Blue: Toward and Alternative Typology of Police." *Journal of Police Science and Administration,* 3(1983):319–326.

Heiss, Jerold. "Social Roles." In *Social Psychology: Sociological Perspectives.* M. Rosenberg and R. H. Turner (eds.) New York: Basic, 1981.

Holden, Richard. *Modern Police Management.* Englewood Cliffs, N.J.: Prentice Hall, 1986.

Holstein, J. A, and J. F. Gubrium. *The Active Interview.* Thousand Oaks, Calif.: Sage, 1995.

Klockars, Carl B. *The Idea of Police.* Beverly Hills, Calif.: Sage, 1985.

Klofas, John, Stan Stojkovic, and David Kalinich. *Criminal Justice Organizations, Administration and Management.* Pacific Grove, Calif.: Brooks/Cole, 1990.

Kuykendall, Jack, and Peter Usinger. *Community Police Administration*. Chicago: Nelson-Hall, 1975.

Lefkowitz, Joel. "Psychological Attributes of Policemen: A Review of Research and Opinions. *Journal of Social Issues,* 31(1975):3–26.

Lester, David. "Are Police Officers Cynical?" *Criminal Justice Review,* 2(1980):51–56.

McCampbell. M. S. *Field Training for Police Officers: The State of the Art.* Washington, D.C.: GPO, 1987.

Merton, Robert K., and Alice Kitt Rossi. "Contributions to the Theory of Reference Groups Behavior." In *Readings in Reference Group Theory and Research.* Herbert H. Hyman and Eleanor Singer (ed.) New York: Free Press, 1968:26–68.

Muir, William K. *Police: Streetcorner Politicians.* Chicago, Ill.: University of Chicago Press, 1977.

Niederhoffer, Arthur. *Behind the Shield: The Police in Urban Society.* Garden City, N.Y.: Anchor, 1969.

O'Connell, Brian J., Herbert Holzman, and Barry R. Armandi. "Police Cynicism and Models of Adaptation." *Journal of Police Science and Administration,* 14(1986):307–313.

Peak, Kenneth J. *Policing America.* Englewood Cliffs, N.J.: Regents/Prentice Hall, 1993.

Regoli, Robert M. "An Empirical Assessment of Niederhoffer's Police Cynicism Scale." *Journal of Criminal Justice,* 4(1976):231–241.

Regoli, Robert M., Eric M. Poole, and John D. Hewitt. "Exploring the Empirical Relationship Between Police Cynicism and Work Alienation." *Journal of Police Science and Administration,* 7(1979):336–339.

Reuss-Ianni, Elizabeth. *Two Cultures of Policing.* New Brunswick, N.J.: Transaction, 1984.

Roberg, Roy R., and Jack Kuykendall. *Police Management.* 2d ed. Los Angeles, Calif.: Roxbury Publishing Company, 1997.

Rokeach, Milton. *The Nature of Human Values.* New York: Free Press, 1973.

Rokeach, Milton, Martin G. Miller, and John A. Snyder. "The Value Gap Between the Police and the Policed." *Journal of Social Issues,* 27(1971):155–171.

Rubenstein, Johnathan. *City Police.* New York: Farrar, Straus and Giroux, 1973.

Scheingold, Stuart A. *The Politics of Law and Order: Street Crime and Public Policy.* New York: Longman, 1984.

Skolnick, Jerome H. *Justice Without Trial.* New York: Wiley, 1966.

Skolnick, Jerome H., and David H Bayley. *The New Blue Line: Police Innovation in Six American Communities.* New York: Free Press, 1986.

Sparrow, Malcolm, Mark Moore, and David Kennedy. *Beyond 911, A New Era for Policing.* New York: Basic Books, 1990.

Stark, Rodney. *Sociology.* 7th ed. Belmont, Calif.: Wadsworth Publishing Company, 1998.

Terkel, Studs. *Working.* New York: Random House, 1974.

Theroux, Paul. "Subway Odyssey." *New York Times Magazine,* 31 January, 1982:20–23, 71, 74–76.

Thomas, Evan. "Web of Death." *Newsweek,* 7 April, 1997:26–35.

Van Maanen, John. "Working the Streets: A Developmental View of Police Behavior." In *Reality and Reform: The Criminal Justice System.* H. Jacobs (ed.) Beverly Hills, Calif.: Sage, 1974.

Van Maanen, John. "The Asshole." In *The Ambivalent Force*. Abraham S. Blumberg and Elaine Niederhoffer (eds.) New York: Holt, Rinehart and Winston, 1985:146–58.

Walsh, William F. "Patrol Officer Arrest Rates: A Study of the Social Organization of Police Work." *Justice Quarterly*, 3(1986):271–90.

Westley, William A. *Violence and the Police*. Cambridge, Mass.: MIT Press, 1970.

Wilson, James Q. *Varieties of Police Behavior: The Management of Law and Order in Eight Communities*. Cambridge, Mass.: Harvard, 1968.

Wilt, Marie G., and James D. Bannon. "Cynicism or Realism: A Critique of Niederhoffer's Research into Police Attitudes." *Journal of Police Science and Administration*, 4(1976):38-45.

Zurcher, Louis A. *Social Roles*. Beverly Hills, Calif.: Sage, 1983.

QUESTIONS FOR REVIEW

Objective #1:

- What two myths are commonly held about police behavior?

Objective #2:

- What types of things does the police subculture provide officers?
- Why do most police officers have other police officers as friends?

Objective #3:

- How do most textbooks define culture?

Objective #4:

- What is the purpose of socialization?
- When does socialization begin?

Objective #5:

- What is meant by minimum training standards?
- Why do the number of hours of minimum training differ in various jurisdictions?

Objective #6:

- What is the purpose of desocialization?

Objective #7:

- What type of information is generally learned during field training?
- Why can a probationary officer receive better supervision in a field training structure than on his or her own?

Objective #8:

- What is meant by police cynicism?
- How might one define authoritarian personality?

Objective #9:

- According to the chapter, when does one acquire a police personality?

Objective #10:

- What is meant by a police *esprit de corps?*

Objective #11:

- How are occupational roles learned?

Objective #12:

- What is the major purpose of considering various styles of policing?
- How does the Idealist and the Realist categories of policing styles differ?

14 Police Ethics

CHAPTER OBJECTIVES

After reading this chapter you should be able to:

1. Delineate between moral, immoral, amoral, and illegal behavior.
2. Describe ethical police regulations and standards.
3. Explain what is meant by the police-community social contract.
4. List five ethical standards associated with the police-community social contract.
5. Discuss the differences between authority and power.
6. Consider the nature of persuasion and force.
7. Detail the nature of organizational ethics.
8. Explore the dilemmas of ethics among police supervisors and administrators.

ETHICAL STANDARDS

Police ethics, as in all professional ethics, must be anchored to a larger and broader moral perspective. A moral perspective is a point of view that highlights the moral and ethical dimensions of behaviors and situations. This moral perspective helps us better understand human behaviors, so that we can make value-laden judgments about what is good or bad, and what is right or wrong (Cohen and Feldberg 1991).

Policing, from this moral perspective, can have some clear rights and wrongs. For instance, when an officer refuses to take a bribe, in exchange for losing evidence, he or she not only following department policy and the laws of malfeasance, but he or she is doing the right thing. Except for the situations of an undercover operation investigating corrupt behavior, there can be no moral justification for taking such a bribe.

KEY TERMS	illegal behavior	authority
	ethics	power
moral behavior	regulations	persuasion
immoral behavior	standards	force
amoral behavior	social contract	organizational culture

On the other hand, policing also provides possibilities for some less clear situations of right and wrong. For example, an officer received a note on the seat of his patrol car, attached to the note is $50,000. The note reads:

Do not arrive at the warehouse district at your usual time tonight. Arrive fifteen minutes later.

The officer has several options. First, the officer can report the incident to his or her superior, who could arrange a stake-out at the warehouse district. Second, the officer can say nothing, keep the money, and show up to the warehouse district fifteen minutes later. Or, third, the officer could keep the money, say nothing, and show up at the warehouse district on time, and even potentially make an arrest. In the first case, the officer's actions are clearly right. In the second case, it would seem the actions are wrong. But in the third case, the waters get a little darker. The officer has not betrayed his or her oath, nor seemingly accepted a bribe—since there was no omission of duty or commission of any sort of favor. The problem here seems to be, rather than the officer committing an overt action that we can clearly label wrong, the moral failing comes from sort of a non-action—a kind of double-cross against a criminal—and hence against a bad person. Still, the concept of a "double-cross" seems to be sneaking and immoral.

Police must also deal with other, even more subtle forms of moral behavior. For example, an officer arrives at the scene of a shooting. The victim, who is known to the officer as a local drug addict and dealer lies bleeding, but alive, on the ground. While the officer is checking the victim, and awaiting the paramedics to arrive, the man suddenly stops breathing. The officer now must decide whether or not to administer mouth-to-mouth resuscitation. As he considers his next action, a number of concerns flash through the officer's mind: the man is dirty and smelly, and may have AIDS, the man is generally repulsive to the officer, there is little good offered to society by this man, etc. After a brief moment, the officer decides not to administer mouth-to-mouth, and simply to wait for the paramedics. The man is dead when they arrive eight minutes later. From our moral perspective, has the officer actually done anything wrong? Has any law been broken in this instance, or has the officer behaved in an amoral manner? Is there, perhaps, a distinction we choose to make between moral, amoral, and illegal behaviors.

The distinctions can be described in the following ways: **moral behavior** is judged as good conduct (**immoral behavior**, then, becomes bad conduct). **Amoral behavior**, is conduct deemed outside of that to which moral distinction or judgments apply. **Illegal behavior**, from this moral perspective, is behavior that violates law and can be judged as either moral or immoral. **Ethics,** then refers to the study and analysis of what constitutes moral, immoral, and amoral behaviors (Souryal 1992; Pollock 1994).

During an average person's usual day-to-day activities, judgments do not require a very refined moral perspective. Deciding what cereal to have for breakfast, or whether to wear the red or blue skirt simply are not moral decisions. Each of us operates with a basic notion of common decency that is widely shared throughout our society. We have learned it from our parents, scout leaders, teachers, clergy, and various other role models. We pick it up from experiences, observations, and specific instruction. This is not to say we are necessarily even aware that we are learning a moral system, or that this is some carefully articulated moral theory. Rather, it is what we refer to as "common decency," and it is at the heart of our ability to assess right from wrong, and good conduct from bad. For example, most people in society believe that it is wrong to kill another person simply because you get angry with them; it is wrong to molest small children; and it is even wrong to cheat at Monopoly. Conversely, it is usually believed to be right to keep your word when making promises, paying your debt when borrowing money, helping the less fortunate, and so forth.

Common decency can take most of us a very long way in life as we deal with others during the course of everyday living. However, when it comes to thinking about how police officers make moral judgments, we quickly realize that one cannot easily understand all actions and behaviors simply in terms of moral decency (Cohen and Feldberg 1991).

It is also apparent that what is right and wrong may not always be the same as what is moral or immoral: the concepts are not always synonymous. Many people use the law as their main source for judging moral behavior (Pollock 1994). From such a perspective, if something is not illegal, it must be all right. Political figures, for example, make campaign promises which they never mean to keep; they received benefits including those that provide personal financial gains from deals they make while in office, and when exposed as having violated their public trust, their defense is, "I never broke the law." This rationalization if generally unacceptable to most people in society. Strict adherence to the law still leaves considerable room for immoral or amoral and unethical behavior.

In addition to adherence to laws, various groups in our society, such as the police, have regulations that govern their activities. **Regulations** typically represent rules and policies that come from the administrative body responsible for the operation of that group or organization. Regulations may include sanctions for those who violate these rules and policies. The adherence to these regulations creates a set of guidelines or **standards** for the organization's membership. Regulations and standards establish parameters for ideal behavior that organizational or occupational members can seek to achieve. Failure to comply with some regulations or standards may not be equated with immoral behavior as easily as criminal lawbreaking (Pollock 1994). Frequently, police officers who violate some departmental regulation receive a sanction. This might come in the form of a suspension, a letter of reprimand, or even dismissal from the force. Yet, the officer may not be branded unethical or criminal.

As implied, some behaviors by police officers may be considered violations of law, while others simply violations of regulations or policy. The relationship between violations of law and of regulations can be visualized as shown in Figure 14.1. Some areas of behavior will be governed exclusively by ethical precepts, some by laws, and others by an overlap of both law and ethical prescriptions.

Figure 14.1
Ethical standards and the overlap of legal standards.

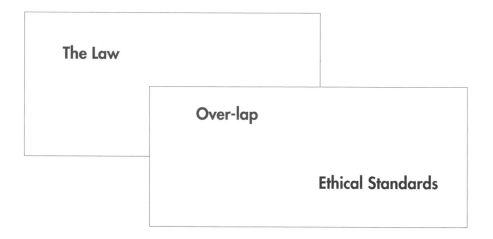

The Law

Over-lap

Ethical Standards

POLICE AND ETHICAL STANDARDS

In spite of situations such as the videotaped media blitz of the beating of Rodney King, allegations of evidence tampering in the O. J. Simpson case, and an assortment of other media propelled cries of unethical police behavior, police officers actually compare well with other professionals in citizen surveys rating honesty and ethical standards (Gallup 1990; La Grange 1993). Twenty-five occupations were listed in the survey ranging from physicians and other traditional professions to car salesmen and labor union leaders. Police, who were neither the highest social status or highest paid occupation listed, ranked seventh in ethical standards and honesty. Unfortunately, scandal tends to sell more newspapers (see Box 14.1).

BOX 14.1   MARK FUHRMAN AND TRUTH

Throughout the O. J. Simpson murder trial, Detective Mark Fuhrman was questioned about tainting evidence. However, the big turn came when he was caught in a lie about having uttered a racist slur several years earlier. Under oath, Fuhrman insisted that he had not used the term "nigger" at any time during the past 10 years. Yet, the defense counsel produced four witnesses and a tape recording contradicting Fuhrman's statement. Fuhrman repeatedly maintained that he had forgotten about the tapes, and that they were made at a time when he was trying to develop a screenplay (Abrahamson 1996). The tape contained the use of the "n-word" 41 times and included statements by Fuhrman bragging about his illegal and unethical behavior.

In October of 1996, almost exactly one year after the jury had acquitted O. J. Simpson in the slaying of his ex-wife Nichole Brown Simpson and Ronald Goldman, Fuhrman's perjury case was resolved with his entry of a plea of "no contest" (Fleeman 1996). In return for his plea, Fuhrman was sentenced to 3 years of probation.

Perhaps the saddest part in the Fuhrman case is that other officers of the Los Angeles Police Department—as well as in other departments across the nation—must live down the shame of Fuhrman's unethical conduct in the courtroom, and the field.

It is important to note that public opinion of police officers can change very rapidly. This is especially true when the media repeatedly shows some unpopular or unethical activity undertaken by the police. For example, in a March 1991 Gallup poll, citizens were asked, "In some places in the nation, there have been charges of police brutality. Do you think there is any police brutality in your area, or not?" The survey was undertaken just two weeks after the video of the beating of Rodney King was repeatedly shown on television (Gallup 1991). The results showed that more than one of every three people felt that police brutality existed in their area. It is likely that if these same citizens were asked to rank police on honesty and ethical standards in this poll, many would have ranked officers much lower than seventh in a group of twenty-five.

THE SOCIAL CONTRACT OF POLICING

Police officers operate in their communities only so long as the community members allow them to do so. If all of the community members jointly agreed to disregard the police in their community, it would be virtually impossible for the police officers to effectively operate. Thus, a kind of social contract exists between the police and the community. In this police-community **social contract**, the police agree to protect the lives, liberty, and property of community members; in exchange, community members agree to vest officers with a certain authority to operate in the community (Cohen and Feldberg 1991). This means that police are given the legitimate authority to enforce the laws and maintain the peace, and if necessary, to legally take another person's life. Yet, there are certain provisions, standards, and regulations by which these tasks are expected to be accomplished.

Keeping in mind this notion of a social contract, there are five basic ethical standards from which one can legitimately make moral assessments about police behavior. These five standards include the following:

1. *Fair access to law enforcement.* Police must offer equal opportunities and access to their protection for all members of the community.
2. *Support of the public trust.* Police must operate within the law, and never betray the faith (public trust) that the community members have in their positions as police officers.
3. *Maintenance of the peace, safety, and security.* Officers must undertake their duties under the framework of maintaining the peace, safety, and security of the community.
4. *Justice system teamwork.* Police activities must be undertaken as a team effort. The police are just one component of the justice system. In addition, officers

must work with other law enforcement agencies—prosecutors, probation officers, judges, and so forth.

5. *Unbiased and objective police work*. Police work often requires the officer to set his or her personal values and feeling aside, if he or she is to operate effectively. By holding one's own feelings and values in check, police officers can conduct themselves in a more objective and unbiased manner.

FAIR ACCESS TO LAW ENFORCEMENT

The general nature of fair access to law enforcement was discussed in detail in Chapter 12. To briefly reiterate, all citizens have an equal right to call upon police officers for certain obligatory tasks. These include things such as personal safety or protection and recovery of personal property. On the other hand, there are certain tasks that go above and beyond the usual. These may include certain activities that not all police agencies offer in every community. For example, in many areas, citizens may telephone the police and arrange a motorcade for a funeral or a wedding; some departments will provide escort service to merchants carrying bank deposits during certain holidays; some departments provide guest speakers to local community groups, and so forth. Not all agencies offer these services. However, following the provision of fair access to law enforcement, in those that do offer these services, they must be available to any citizen who requests them.

SUPPORT OF THE PUBLIC TRUST

Support of the public trust refers to police work as a public trust. It implies quite directly the nature of the social contract with the community. Police are expected and permitted to use their authority for the public's welfare. There should be no attempt by police to improve their personal position in the community at the expense of the community's safety, welfare, or trust. This public trust provides officers with the ability to perform their job as police officers. This includes their prerogative to stop and question suspicious or dangerous-looking people in the area to intervene in domestic disputes; investigate allegations of child molestation, abuse, or neglect and to apprehend suspects in criminal matters. If citizens themselves exercised these authorities, the community would quickly turn into one run by vigilantes and mobs.

MAINTENANCE OF THE PEACE, SAFETY, AND SECURITY

This third ethical standard requires police officers to operate in the community in a lawful manner. It requires officers to develop and exercise good judgment, and to maintain the Constitution of the United States. It is particularly relevant when one considers the nature of the police as protectors of the public trust. While officers are authorized to stop and question suspicious and dangerous looking people, and even to frisk or search some parties when they are stopped and questioned, there are rules and laws about how these activities must be accomplished. Certain felonies will require an officer to make an arrest. However, in order to smoothly maintain the peace, it may be necessary under some circumstances not to make an arrest for certain minor misdemeanors. For example, while gambling is illegal in many communities, it would not serve any positive purpose to go around searching for and breaking up petty nickel and dime poker games. Nor, for that matter, would such a probe result in effective peacekeeping maintenance.

Officers must be able to balance between the safety and security of the community, and actions and activities that may actually undermine keeping the peace in that community. Laws are a tool for enhancing the safety and security of a community. Enforcing these laws is a technique by which police officers manage to maintain social order. In fact, when law enforcement threatens the peace of the community, it ceases to function as intended.

JUSTICE SYSTEM TEAMWORK

The police are just a single element in the larger system of criminal justice. When the various groups work together, they operate as a team; a team whose joint efforts are greater than any of the single organization's might otherwise be. The police, in fact, are only a small portion of the larger governmental branch of enforcement. When these different agencies work together, they are also more likely to operate effectively. For example, when a serial killer strikes, a local police agency may begin the investigation. However, it is likely that the offender will not be caught without the assistance of other law enforcement agencies and the FBI.

For police departments to operate as efficient organizations, every officer must cooperate as a teammate. When officers are individually focused, rather than group or team focused, the peace, safety and security of a community may be jeopardized. Since police work is based on a team effort model, any behaviors by officers to undermine this goal may be viewed as detracting from the moral standard of the department. From this standard's perspective, abuse of one's authority, "hotdogging" or grandstanding, or even covering up other officer's wrongdoings are all abuses of the teamwork spirit.

UNBIASED AND OBJECTIVE POLICE WORK

As this text has discussed previously, police officers are frequently called upon to function as society's referees. Merchants sometimes call the police when a customer has become too irate, a neighbor may call the police when the people next door are having what sounds like a knock-down, bang-up fight, bartenders may call the police when patrons become too drunk or abusive, and motorists must sometimes be pulled apart by police after some sort of traffic accident. Thus, it is extremely important that the public see police officers as unbiased and objective (see Box 14.2). Furthermore, it is important that police are not perceived as taking advantage of their position of authority.

AUTHORITY VERSUS POWER

Carl Klockars (1984) has described police control as comprising the following elements: authority, power, persuasion, and force. **Authority** the legitimate right to move others to your influence. Power, however, is a little different. **Power** is sometimes mistakenly used as a synonym for authority but power may not always represent the absolutely legitimate ability to move others to your influence. In fact, power implies that there may be resistance to overcome,

---

BOX 14.2   CITIZEN GROUPS OVERSEE POLICE MISCONDUCT

Across the United States, the number of police departments involved with citizen reviews rose 74 percent between 1990 and 1994 (Lewis 1997). About 80 cities now have some sort of review process in place, with much of the growth among smaller and midsize cities.

It would seem that accountability of the police has won acceptance, not only in the minds of citizens, but among police agencies as well. Moreover, these review boards provide a mechanism to assure police remain objective during the performance of their duties. The various televised police scandals that seem to arise in waves every few months have focused national attention on the tensions that exist between police and, frequently, people of color. Rather than taking these assaults lying down, many police agencies and their communities have begun developing citizen review boards to help restore confidence in the justice system.

Advocates of these review boards suggest that they are needed because police departments have demonstrated in the past that they are not very good at policing themselves. Historically, police are charged with misconduct in only about

10 percent of police investigations spurred by citizen complaints. Citizen review boards, then, become a means for handling citizen complaints about police that involve people who are not themselves sworn officers. Thus, the objectivity of the officers need not be questioned.

Through the eyes of the average citizen, the more dispassionate and detached an officer is at the scene, the more objective and credible he or she fills the role of police officer. The more emotional or personally involved, the less trustworthy the officer will seem to handle the situation fairly. In other words, this standard requires the officer to set aside his or her personal and emotional feeling about people and situations and to demonstrate objectivity. However, to be really effective as a police officer, he or she must still convey to the citizen that he or she is genuinely concerned about the situation and the person's problems. It is a very difficult tightrope for the officer to walk. On the one hand, he or she can remain fairly detached and hence objective. On the other hand, if there is too much detachment, the officer may become or appear jaded and cynical.

Figure 14.2
*Police have the
authority to stop
speeders and
issue traffic
citations.*

and that this resistance can be coerced or crushed. An example may better illustrate these two terms. If an officer pulls your vehicle over to the side of the road for driving 8 miles above the posted speed limit, it is within his or her authority to do so. On the other hand, let's say an officer has just completed a short high-speed chase of a drunk driver. During that chase, the drunk has sideswiped several cars, and perhaps even forced another driver off the road. The officer orders the drunk out of his vehicle, but the drunk refuses and tosses several beer cans at the officer. At this point, with adrenaline pumping, the officer draws his weapon (now loaded with rubber bullets) and orders the drunk from the car. The drunk complies at this point, not because of police authority, but because of the coercion resulting from the drawn gun.

Persuasion also may be used in response to resistance, but persuasion does not seek to crush the resistance or engage in immoral behavior. Instead, persuasion, attempts to motivate someone to move in the general direction or according to the directions of another individual. In effect, persuasion means convincing someone to do what you desire them to through signs, symbols, and argument that convince the other party he or she should comply. Finally, force may be required to get people to do what one wants them to do. **Force** usually means physically making an individual comply with one's wishes. This differentiates it from the three previous types of control over others. Whereas force implies physical contact to move others, the other terms convey the idea of controlling the situation through mental domination.

ORGANIZATIONAL ETHICS FOR POLICE

All organizations have an organizational culture. **Organizational culture** includes the formal values, guiding beliefs, understandings, and ways of thinking shared by members of the organization (Daft 1995). Many organizations have a value system that has been articulated in some formal sense such as a written code of ethics. For police, a code of ethics suggests the kind of behavior expected of every officer. Davis (1991) explains that there are three different kinds of codes: the first code directs attention towards a kind of ideal professional; the second, offers principles or guidelines that relate to the organization's value system. The third type of code provides mandatory rules of conduct for members and serves as a structure for discipline.

Since the late 1980s, police officers have followed a code of ethics promulgated by the International Association of Chiefs of Police (*Police Chief* 1990; 1992). This code of ethics (see Box 14.3) is similar to the first type, that is, it creates a mental image of a nearly perfect police officer which the average officer can aspire to. The problem with this code of ethics, however, is its relevance to the average officer (Swift, Houston, and Anderson 1993). The basic argument against the code is that it expects such perfect conduct that it becomes irrelevant

BOX 14.3 LAW ENFORCEMENT CODE OF ETHICS

As a law enforcement officer, my fundamental duty is to serve the community; to safeguard lives and property; to protect the innocent against deception, the weak against oppression or intimidation, and the peaceful against violence or disorder; and to respect the constitutional rights of all people to liberty, equality, and justice.

I will keep my private life unsullied as an example to all. I will maintain courageous calm in the face of danger, scorn or ridicule; develop self-restraint; and be constantly mindful of the welfare of others. Honest in thought and deed both in my personal and official life, I will be exemplary in obeying the laws of the land and the regulations of my department. Whatever I see or hear of a confidential nature or that is confined to me in my official capacity will be kept ever secret unless revelation is necessary in the performance of my duty.

I will never act officiously or permit personal feelings, prejudices, animosities, or friendships to influence my decisions. With no compromise for crime and with relentless prosecution of criminals,

I will enforce the law courteously and appropriately without fear of favor, malice, or ill will, never employing unnecessary force or violence and never accepting gratuities.

I recognize the badge of my office as a symbol of public faith, and I accept it as a public trust to be held so long as I am true to the ethics of police service. I will never engage in acts of corruption or bribery, nor will I condone such acts by other police officers. I will cooperate with all legally authorized agencies and their representatives in the pursuit of justice.

I know that I alone am responsible for my own standard or professional performance and will take every reasonable opportunity to enhance and improve my level of knowledge and competence.

I will constantly strive to achieve these objectives and ideals, dedicating myself before God and my chosen profession . . . law enforcement. I will constantly strive to achieve these objectives and ideals, dedicating myself before God to my chosen profession.

to the real lives of officers. This wide gap between the expected and the real behaviors of officers is detrimental to the basic validity and credibility of the code. In fact, it would be largely impossible for officers to actually and completely embrace the behaviors outlined in the code.

Proponents of the code argue that it is valuable specifically because it provides an ideal for all officers to strive for. It is a goal to have officers strive for these high ideals—even if they never actually realize them completely. Certainly, no one would endorse a code that required mediocrity. It would also serve no purpose to have a code that instructed officers to be unbiased and objective unless he or she had really strong emotional feelings about one party over another; to be courageous unless there were serious dangers; or to be honest in thought and deed whenever it were convenient. The code was intended to outline the highest of standards, a high-jump bar placed at 25 feet so that by trying to achieve these goals, officers could always be improving themselves—yet recognizing that no officer will ever be perfect.

Unfortunately, the police code of ethics offers little control over police conduct. In more traditional professions,[1] violations of a code of ethics bring sanctions and other forms of pressure. Since the police code of ethics is not actually an obtainable pattern of conduct, it does not.

At one time, ethics were taught in most police academies as a very small segment of the overall curriculum. During the mid-1990s this began to change. Chiefly as a result of such publicized cases as the beating of Rodney King, the allegations of misconduct of Detective Mark Fuhrman during the investigation of Nicole Brown Simpson's murder, and the handling by federal officers of arrests at Ruby Ridge, Idaho, and Waco, Texas, ethics became a much bigger part of law enforcement training. Many of the larger academies in cities such as New York, Texas, Los Angeles, and Washington, D.C., began offering ethics training that ran several weeks in length. Furthermore, many departments began to require in-service modules on ethics to reinforce the original academy training. Police work is somewhat unpredictable and encounters a wide range of situations; it is difficult to develop consistent rules of ethics for all possible occurrences. The basic idea behind the additional emphasis on ethics during training was to improve the ability of officers to internalize appropriate policing norms and values. Once internalized, these values and norms should provide proper guidelines for police conduct in a variety of situations.

In addition to improving procedures, guidelines, and internalized values among officers, departments can maximize ethical behavior by assuring that supervisors' and administrators' conduct serves as an example to line officers (Pollock 1994). Supervisors and administrators may have certain ethical concerns that are unique to their positions. Budget and allocations problems, decisions about the use of drug testing, affirmative action hirings, claims of sexual harassment, citizen complaints, and promotional selections all present ethical problems for supervisors and administrators. For example, many police executives have moved up through the ranks. Often, they move faster and higher than officers they have served with on the line. Suddenly, friends and ex-partners are now subordinates. Yet these people may also still be friends. In some cases, these officers may expect special treatment based on their friendships. These expectations create an interesting ethical dilemma for the superior. Police supervisors and administrators also must contend with ethical problems related to questions of seniority or education in assigning certain tasks or allocating resources such as new equipment. They must make command decisions when they learn about an officer's drinking problems or drug use, accusations of officer misconduct or sexual harassment, and an assortment of other problems. In short, it can be fairly difficult for supervisors and police executives both to behave ethically, and to demonstrate ethical conduct. Sam Souryal (1992:186) described ethical leaders as those with "a mental state that is characterized by vision, enlightened reasoning, and moral responsibility." In many ways, this too may be a difficult "code" to live up to.

SUMMARY

This chapter began with a general discussion about the concept of police ethics. It offered definitions for several important terms including moral, immoral, and amoral behavior. Next, the chapter attempted to show both the distinction and overlap between legal behavior and ethical conduct. The chapter also discussed how police behavior may be regulated through implementation of policies, rules, and procedures. The chapter examined standards of conduct and considered the police implications of a police code of ethics. Next the chapter explored the police social contract. This included elaboration on five heuristic standards of ethical conduct that apply to police officers. In addition, the nature of police authority and police power were discussed. Finally, the dilemmas of organizational ethics were briefly considered and the nature of ethics among supervisors and police executives described.

REFERENCES

Abrahamson, Alan. "Mark Fuhrman Apologizes." *The Seattle Times*, 8 October, 1996:1.

Cohen, Howard S., and Michael Feldberg. *Power and Restraint: The Moral Dimension of Police Work*. New York: Praeger, 1991.

Daft, Richard L. *Organization Theory and Design*. 5th ed. Minneapolis/St. Paul: West Publishing Co., 1995.

Davis, Michael. "Do Cops Really Need a Code of Ethics?" *Criminal Justice Ethics*, 10(2)1991:14–28.

Fleeman, Michael. "Mark Fuhrman Pleads No Contest to Perjury, Gets Three Years Probation." *Associated Press International*, 3 October, 1996.

Gallup, George, Jr. *The Gallup Poll*. Princeton, N.J.: The Gallup Poll, February 1990:23.

Gallup, George, Jr. *The Gallup Poll*. Princeton, N.J.: The Gallup Poll, March 1991:20.

Klockars, Carl. "Blue Lies and Police Placebos." *American Behavioral Scientist*, 27(4)1984:529–44.

La Grange, Randy L. *Policing American Society*. Chicago, Ill.: Nelson-Hall Inc., 1993.

"Law Enforcement Code of Ethics." *Police Chief*. International Association of Chiefs of Police. January 1992:16.

Lewis, Mark. "Police Misconduct Triggers Growth of Citizen Oversight." Article #25. The American News Service. Brattleboro, Vt., 1997.

"1989 Police Code of Ethics." *Police Chief*. International Association of Chiefs of Police. January 1990:18.

Pollock, Joycelyn M. *Ethics in Crime and Justice*. 2d ed. Belmont, Calif.: Wadsworth, 1994.

Souryal, Sam. *Ethics in Criminal Justice: In Search of the Truth*. Cincinnati, Oh.: Anderson Publishing Co., 1992.

Swift, Andrew, James Houston, and Robin Anderson. "Cops, Hacks, and the Greater Good." Paper presented at the Academy of Criminal Justice Sciences, Kansas City, Mo., March 1993.

NOTE

[1] The question of whether police are members of a true profession will be considered in Chapter 17 of this text.

QUESTIONS FOR REVIEW

Objective #1:

- How might you define moral behavior?
- How might the term amoral conduct be defined?

Objective #2:

- What purpose is served by police agency regulations and standards?

Objective #3:

- What is meant by the police-community social contract?

Objective #4:

- State the five ethical standards associated with the police-community social contract.

Objective #5:

- Define authority.
- Define power.

Objective #6:

- How does persuasion differ from force?

Objective #7:

- What purpose is served by organizational ethics?

Objective #8:

- Why are police supervisors and administrators confronted with different ethical dilemmas than are line officers?

15 Police Deviance and Corruption

CHAPTER OBJECTIVES

After reading this chapter you should be able to:

1. Define officer integrity.
2. Describe police deviance and police corruption.
3. Discuss the nature of police gratuities.
4. Differentiate between a bribe and extortion.
5. Consider the meaning of non-feasance, misfeasance, and malfeasance.
6. Justify enforcement priorities in police departments.
7. Delineate between rotten-apple and rotten-pocket theories of police corruption.
8. Consider how various external factors contribute to police corruption.
9. Explain occupational opportunity's role in police corruption.
10. Discuss ways of controlling police corruption.

THE LINE BETWEEN DEVIANCE AND CORRUPTION

Chapter 13 discussed the proper and ethical behavior of police officers. Chapter 14 considers an important related issue, namely, police misbehavior. An important question related to this issue is whether all police misbehavior should be placed at the same point on an imaginary continuum of deviance. The fact that some police officers misbehave, as will be discussed in this chapter, should not cloud the fact that *most police officers are honest and possess a high level of moral integrity.*

Integrity is concerned with officer violations of organizational guidelines and regulations, in effect, violations of department policies and procedures (Roberg and Kuykendall 1997). The activities and behaviors may involve lying,

KEY TERMS

integrity
police gratuities
meat eaters

grass eaters
bribe
extortion
non-feasance
misfeasance

malfeasance
enforcement priorities
police corruption
citizen police academies

accepting certain gratuities, and various forms of corruption (e.g., accepting money to permit gambling, drug sales or distribution, shakedowns, etc.), other criminal behaviors committed either on or off duty (including theft, use of illegal drugs, abuse of alcohol, spousal abuse, or other forms of family violence). In addition, there are other forms of behavior that may create questions of integrity among police officers. For example, working a second job or *moonlighting* may be permitted by some departments, but raise certain questions. For example, is the officer paid in cash or by check. If the salary is in cash, one might question whether it is being claimed by the officer on his or her taxes. Does the officer conduct any private activities during duty time, or make use of department equipment during private time? And, importantly, are decisions the officer makes while moonlighting different from those he or she might have made if on duty? Many, if not most police departments, face these sorts of integrity problems at some time or another.

Many Americans have almost grown used to reading about various police scandals and crimes reported in the news media. During the 1980s in Miami, scarcely a week went by without some report of police indiscretion. In this period almost 10 percent of the city's police were either jailed, fired, or disciplined in connection with a scheme in which officers robbed and sometimes killed cocaine smugglers on the Miami River, then resold the drugs (Lacayo 1993). Throughout 1983, the headlines reported on Luis Alvarez, an officer accused for and later acquitted of shooting Nevell Johnson. Johnson, an unarmed black man, was shot at a video arcade as Alvarez attempted to take him into custody (Stuart 1983). Newspapers also reported on Dade County, Florida, police officers involved in cocaine smuggling, theft, and murder (see Peterson 1986; *United Press International* 1987; *Associated Press* 1987).

In 1991, another huge media story of police misconduct broke. In this case, newspapers and television newscasts were filled with images of Rodney King being beaten by Los Angeles police officers. Here too, the later acquittal of officers during their first trial, touched off a powder keg of violence and rioting across Los Angeles. In 1997, two officers were accused in Los Angeles of taking a woman stopped for a traffic citation to a hotel and raping her. Similar types of sexual misconduct have been reported in other states.

On a larger scale of police misbehavior, newspapers in the 1980s reported on a 4-year FBI investigation into police corruption in Philadelphia capped by the arrest in 1986 of Eugene Sullivan for alleged RICO (racketeering laws) violations. Sullivan, considered by many Philadelphians the next candidate for police commissioner, was the 29th officer convicted during this FBI probe (see *The Washington Post* 1986).

In Los Angeles, following the Rodney King incident, Mayor Tom Bradley created a commission to investigate the excessive force allegations against police officers in Los Angeles. This commission soon merged with one created by then Chief of Police Daryl Gates. This commission became known simply as the "Christopher Commission." This commission conducted a massive investigation into police use of force and heard from more than 50 expert witnesses, 150 rep-

Figure 15.1
Officers are trained in the use of non-lethal force, and expected to use their skills appropriately.

resentatives of community organizations, private individuals, and more than 500 current and retired police officers (Peak 1993).

The Christopher Commission found that there were a significant number of Los Angeles Police Department officers who were actively involved in using excessive force against the public—despite the fact they violated department guidelines and the California Penal Code. As in most departments across the country, police policy in Los Angeles called for officers to use the minimum amount of force necessary to control a situation and a suspect.

Beyond these very public investigations and media accounts of police misconduct, each of us has likely heard of some type of police indiscretion. It may have been a story from a friend that claimed that a police officer had stopped an attractive motorist in order to obtain her telephone number. Or it may have involved a police officer accepting money in exchange for not issuing a speeding ticket. It may even have been the allegation that a police officer suggested that extraneous in exchange for sexual favors he or she would not write a citation. Perhaps it was the observation that a police officer left a restaurant without paying the check, or seeing a handcuffed suspect smacked or hit by an officer as he placed this suspect into a police cruiser. Certainly, these situations happen, and perhaps more often than many police administrators would care to acknowledge. The question is, are these all examples of corruption? Can there be gradations in corruption, that is, certain amounts that can be tolerated? Or is corruption absolute and clear-cut in every instance? Answers to these questions should be come apparent as this chapter examines systematic and occupational factors that make deviance and corruption sometimes seem endemic to police work. This chapter will also consider ways of controlling the problem of police ethical and legal violations.

WHAT IS POLICE CORRUPTION?

Police corruption should not be tolerated. Yet, what police corruption actually means seems a little vague. For some, police corruption occurs when an officer acts in a manner that places his or her personal gain ahead of duty, resulting in the violation of department procedures, criminal law, or both (Lynch 1989; Cox 1996).

In police work, like many other occupations and professions, it is difficult to make hard-and-fast statements about accepting or distinguishing between friendly gifts, gratuities for service, bribes for favors, and general corruption or misuse of one's official position.

For example, with the drop in numbers of students applying to law schools, many schools have taken to subtly soliciting student referrals. Special informational conferences are held where pre-law school advisers are brought to some law schools from all across the country with all expenses paid. These pre-law advisers are wined and dined. They are put up at the best hotels, and given tours of the school's facilities. Naturally, the intention here is to impress these advisors, but certainly not to bribe them—right?

The apparel industry is notorious for its wooing of out-of-town buyers. These buyers are frequently treated to expensive meals and hotels and, in some instances, even provided with prostitutes. Many buyers accept these gratuities and do not view them as bribes because they claim not to be swayed by them. The buyers' argument is that unless they can make a profit from a line of clothes, they aren't going to buy it regardless of the gifts and good times provided by the seller. These dividends are merely seen as the "perks" of the job, not bribes.

When you leave a mailman a card with $5 stuffed into it at Christmas time, this is not a bribe or gratuity, just a Christmas present. It's just like the bottle of top-shelf liquor one might buy for his or her boss.

It is likely that most police officers at some time have been offered some sort of gratuity. Similarly, it is very likely that many have taken one. Gratuities to police officers typically are quite small. Perhaps the delicatessen prepares sandwiches at half-price for uniformed police officers or the local grocery tosses the beat cop a couple of steaks on his or her birthday or a turkey on Thanksgiving. Maybe the dry cleaner gives a reduced rate for cleaning police uniforms, the gas station may repair private cars owned by officers for cost, and the local doughnut shop may offer police officers free coffee—and, of course, a doughnut.

While these gratuities are rather petty in value, most police agencies are likely to discourage, or forbid, their officers from accepting them. Some departments may even regard the acceptance of even petty items as a serious breech of their ethical policy and procedures and sanction the offending officer. In some ways one might even suggest that the acceptance of even petty gratuities runs counter to the Law Enforcement Code of Ethics discussed in Chapter 14. For many people, police officials and private citizens alike, accepting even that fabled free cup of coffee is viewed as potentially lessening the fair access to law enforcement protection to which all people are entitled.

Stated differently, the retailer presenting the gift is buying additional police protection. The usual cliché is to suggest that while the officer sits sipping free coffee in the restaurant, the restaurant owner, at least indirectly, is receiving increased police protection. Without debating this point, there may be other less arguable illustrations of preferential treatment by police and increased access to protection. Consider, for example, a row of stores damaged by a storm and being looted. Whether consciously or unconsciously, it is likely that a store owned by someone who has offered even petty gratuities will receive slightly better attention than one owned by a person who has offered the officer nothing.

Some police administrators, however, see nothing wrong with officers getting items "for cost." In other words, reduced-rate items and services are seen as distinguishable from freebies. In these instances, the discounts, and even an occasional cup of coffee, are viewed as a courtesy to the officer by an appreciative person. The implication here, of course, is that police deviance or corruption has not occurred unless it involves cash or the outright gift of products (a free television, a pair of shoes, or a washing machine).

The perhaps not-so-obvious problem with this is how the public views such transactions. Policing is sometimes regarded as a slightly tainted occupation. This involves a somewhat pervasive attitude among private citizens that the police are all dishonest, it's simply a matter of degree. Consequently, when officers are seen receiving reduced rates for products or services—especially just

Figure 15.2
When officers eat in restaurants, they must be careful to avoid the impression of improper behavior or repeipt of gratuities.

for doing their duty—many people are affronted. The operative assumption is that when an officer is willing to accept a half-priced dinner, he or she is also likely to take a bribe. Perhaps this officer is also likely to steal drugs from the property room to sell on the street, as occurred in New York in the late 1960s (see Box 15.1). Although it may seem a big jump from a discounted meal to becoming a drug dealer, it is a small step in the minds of many people. Patrick Murphy, former commissioner of the New York city police, once said that for police officers, "except for your paycheck, there's no such thing as a clean buck" (Elliston and Feldberg 1985:267).

There has been a great deal of interest in police corruption. In addition to journalistic accounts and successful movies, such as Paramount Pictures' 1973 film *Serpico*, and Warner Bros. (1982) movie *Prince of the City*, several corrupt officers have described their activities in fairly well-read stories and books (Schecter and Phillips 1973; Barrett 1973; Clemente and Stevens 1987). Throughout the 1970s, the public witnessed a number of large scale investigations into criminal behavior by police officers and police organizations in New York, Philadelphia, Chicago, and Indianapolis ("The Knapp Commission Report" 1973; Pennsylvania Crime Commission 1974; Beigel 1974). During the 1980s, the media again drew attention to police improprieties as it identified police corruption from drug smuggling and protection to murder (Golden 1987; Phillips 1987). During the 1990s, the media again focused attention on police misconduct, this time with particular emphasis on brutality and sexual harassment (Christopher Commission 1991; Peak 1993).

It is indisputable that corruption exists in some police departments. From their moment of formation during the nineteenth century, police departments

BOX 15.1   THE FRENCH CONNECTION: WHAT'S A LITTLE HEROIN AMONG FRIENDS?

In 1962, two New York City police detectives, Eddie Egan and Sonny Grosso, stumbled onto a multimillion dollar, international drug-smuggling operation. The smugglers operated out of Marseilles, France, importing raw opium from Turkey and exporting heroin into the United States through various New York City ports. The case became known as the French Connection. After a lengthy investigation that was subsequently made into several feature movies, the drug ring was crushed. Nearly 100 pounds of uncut heroin, valued at more than $30 million, was confiscated during the investigation, and placed for *safekeeping* in the New York City Police Department's property room. Unfortu-

nately, sometime between 1962 and 1972, 80 pounds of heroin from the French Connection case, and approximately another 88 pounds of heroin and 31 pounds of cocaine from other cases was discovered to be missing. Apparently, these drugs were stolen right out from under the police's watchful eyes, taken from the property room. The thieves cleverly replaced the drugs with powdered sugar. In spite of an extensive investigation, the thieves involved in this crime have never identified or brought to justice. One thing that seems certain: to have pulled off this crime, someone from the police department had to have been involved (Inciardi 1990).

in various cities have been riddled with scandals and corruption: abuses of power, sales of promotions, elaborate systematic schemes of protection and racketeering. Still, the vast majority of police officers in America should not be classified as corrupt; the few who are outright crooked, however, bring disgrace to the entire occupation.

Police corruption may be viewed as a number of different activities. Some observers find acceptance of gratuities and corruption as synonymous, while others see these as distinguishable. Howard Cohen and Michael Feldberg (1983:31) attempt to clarify this ambiguity and define **police gratuities**:

> Any goods or services which are given to law enforcement officers because they are law enforcement officers, which are not part of their regular remuneration.

For some observers, the ambiguity inherent in defining police gratuities owes to two complicating factors. These factors include the intent of the person offering the gratuity and the effect of the gratuity on the behavior of the officer. In other words, if a gift, service, or discount is given freely with no intent to prejudice or gain greater access to police services, and the offering results in no actual behavioral changes in the officer's performance of his or her official duties, then these gratuities would seem harmless. From this vantage, such gratuities would not appear to represent police corruption.

Extending this notion of gratuities, one begins to see that corruption in some manner involves misuse of one's official authority. This broad canopy of corruption includes both misuse that may result in personal gains to an errant officer, as well as unnecessarily using force, making unreasonable searches, sexual harassment, or moral turpitude (immoral activities).

To better understand the various forms police corruption may take, a number of social scientists have developed categorical schemes. For example, in 1972, the Knapp Commission investigated what may be the most widely publicized investigation of police corruption of this country's history (see Box 15.2).

In its report, the commission categorized dishonest officers into two principal categories: "Meat eaters" and "grass eaters." **Meat eaters** were described as those officers who aggressively misuse their police powers for personal gain. **Grass eaters**, on the other hand, simply accepted the payoffs that the happenstance of their police work threw their way. The Knapp Commission concluded that while meat eaters received huge sums of money as payoffs and filled the newspaper headlines, they represented the tip of the iceberg. The much larger body of the iceberg, which remained under water, was the grass eaters. As the Knapp Commission report suggested, the great number of grass eaters tended to create an image of corruption as respectable—or at least acceptable behavior.

Other categorical schemes of police corruption have been suggested. Michael Johnson (1982:75) says that police corruption may be divided into four major categories: internal corruption, selective enforcement/non-enforcement, active criminality, and bribery and extortion.

According to Johnson (1982), *Internal corruption* occurs among police officers and involves bending or breaking department rules and regulations as well as criminal law violations. An example of this sort of corruption might be the theft and sale of police promotional exams in the Boston Police Department (see Stewart 1987).

BOX 15.2   A BRIEF HISTORY OF THE KNAPP COMMISSION'S ACTIVITIES

It was on August 3, 1972, then Mayor John V. Lindsey of New York was given a 34-page preliminary report drafted by Whitman Knapp. Knapp chaired the "Commission to Investigate Alleged Police Corruption" in New York City. The report had taken a full 2 years to compile and offered a summary from a detailed examination of police corruption run rampant throughout the New York City Police Department. This report would eventually result in numerous firings and indictments of police officers throughout all five boroughs of New York City.

The probe into police misconduct had begun on April 23, 1970, when Lindsay appointed a five-member committee that came to be known as the "Rankin Committee." This panel consisted of J. Lee Rankin, the city corporation counsel; Police Commissioner Howard R. Leary; Investigation Commissioner Robert K. Ruskin; New York County District Attorney Frank S. Hogan; and Bronx District Attorney Burton B. Roberts. These men were given the responsibility of examining the general procedures used by New York City for investigating cases of police corruption (Burnham 1970; Dempsey 1972).

The Rankin Committee was charged with three principal responsibilities: (1) consideration of the procedures employed by the police department to investigate allegations of police corruption; (2) to offer recommendations for improvements in these general procedures; and (3) to investigate the specific charges of corruption and other allegations of police misconduct that grew out of the announcement of the committee's formation.

By May 11, 1970, the Rankin Committee had received 375 complaints of police misconduct. Among these were 316 that specifically spoke to alleged police corruption. The committee report indicated the following breakdown for these complaints:

Eleven percent of the complaints alleged a payment of money or other item of value to a policeman who could be identified with a fair degree of certainty; in thirty percent of similar complaints the officers could not be identified; in 7 percent of the complaints an identified officer was charged with failure to take necessary police action; in 48 percent of the total number of complaints an unidentified officer was charged with failure to take action. [Rankin Committee Report 1970]

The Rankin Committee's final report to Lindsey asked that an independent investigative body be appointed to replace it and that this body be charged with the responsibility of a full investigation into police corruption in the city. Within one week's time, Lindsay appointed a "Committee to Investigate Allegations of Police Corruption," also known as the Knapp Commission. The members of the Knapp Commission included Whitman Knapp, a New York attorney who had previously served as head of the indictment and Frauds Bureau of the New York County District Attorney's Office; Cyrus W. Vance, secretary of defense during President Lyndon Johnson's administration; Joseph Monserrat, president of the Board of Education; Franklin Thomas, a former deputy police commissioner for legal matters; and Arnold Bauman, a former assistant U.S. attorney for the Southern District of New York (Dempsey 1972). Arnold Bauman later resigned and was replaced by John E. Sprizzo, a former assistant U.S. Attorney and professor of law at Fordham University.

Selective enforcement or non-enforcement involves misuse of police authority and discretion. This behavior amounts to a failure to enforce laws in a fair or appropriate manner. For example, if an officer chose to let a speeder go with a verbal warning, it would be a legitimate use of discretion. But, if the officer allowed the speeder to drive off because a $50 bill was clipped to the driver's license—money the officer took—it would represent corruption.

Once established, the Knapp Commission drew its authority to make an investigation from the executive order of the mayor. This order provided both subpoena powers for the commission (to assure that witnesses would come in to speak with the commission) and funds for an operating budget.

FINDINGS OF THE KNAPP COMMISSION

The Knapp Commission (1973:1) reported:

> We found corruption to be widespread. It took various forms depending upon the activity involved, appearing at its most sophisticated among plainclothesmen assigned to enforcing gambling laws. In the five plainclothes divisions where our investigations were concentrated we found a strikingly standardized pattern of corruption. Plainclothesmen, participating in what is know in police parlance as a "pad," collected regular bi weekly or monthly payments amounting to as much as $3,500 from each of the gambling establishments in the area under their jurisdiction, and divided the take in equal shares. The monthly share per man (called the "nut") ranged from $300 and $400 in midtown Manhattan to $1,500 in Harlem. When supervisors were involved they received a share and a half. A newly assigned plainclothesman was not entitled to his share for about two months, while he was checked out for reliability, but the earnings lost by the delay were made up to him in the form of 2 months' severance pay when he left the division.

The Knapp Commission also reported corruption among the remaining divisions, which they had not investigated in depth. The commission report also suggested that several other forms of corruption existed. These included a slightly less organized payment system among narcotics officers called "scores," where officers sometimes received huge amounts of cash; shakedowns of individuals by the general investigative detectives; payments by officers to other officers in order to secure better assignments or to speed paperwork; and uniformed officers, particularly those assigned to patrol cars, found to be participating in gambling pads—although much smaller ones than the plainclothesmen's.

The commission included the police officers' sense that the public had become preoccupied only with "police corruption" and had lost sight of the fact that corruption existed in other agencies as well. The officers viewed this as unfair and believed that it tended to intensify their general feelings of alienation and hostility toward their jobs not just in New York City, but everywhere. Interestingly, this attitude is similar to how members of delinquent subcultures are traditionally described as justifying (or rationalizing) their law violations (Cohen 1983; Sykes and Matza 1957; Matza 1964).

The Knapp Commission has also been given credit for having denounced the "rotten-apple theory" of police corruption. In this theory, individual officers are viewed as corrupt—as rotten apples that must be removed from "an otherwise clean barrel." Thus, identification of individual corrupt officers, according to the theory, does nothing to remedy a more complex or extensive problem. The commission examined and rejected this theoretical explanation. They concluded that a much greater good would be accomplished by thoroughly examining the barrel, as well as the apples it contains.

Active criminality, as implied, represents actual participation in illegal behavior. For instance, *The Cops Are Robbers* by Gerald Clemente and Kevin Stevens (1987) details how Clemente and other police officers routinely burglarized retail stores they had been expected to protect. In fact, police burglary rings have long troubled both large and small cities across the nation (Simpson 1977; Stoddard 1983).

Bribery and extortion are goal-directed activities designed to obtain financial gains for police officers through misuse or abuse of their authority. Although similar in nature, one may distinguish between bribery and extortion according to who initiates the transaction. A **bribe** typically is initiated by a private citizen. In **extortion**, the bribe is usually initiated by the officer.

Jay Albanese (1988) defines three basic forms of police corruption: Nonfeasance, misfeasance, and malfeasance. Each of these is detailed as follows:

Non-Feasance

Non-feasance may be understood as an omission duty or an officer's failure to perform his or her lawful duty. For example, when an officer stops a motorist who was exceeding the speed limit but chooses not to issue the citation because the driver shows remorse, this behavior is technically non-feasance.

Misfeasance

A **misfeasance** may be classified as the failure of an officer to perform his or her lawful duty in an appropriate manner. For instance, a misfeasance is committed if an officer on patrol peeps through windows hoping to see people undressing or undressed, under the guise of patrolling the neighborhood.

Malfeasance

An officer has committed a **malfeasance** if he or she commits an act that simply could not be performed as part of his or her lawful duties. For example, an officer answers a burglary call at a retail store. Arriving after the burglar has fled, the officer nonetheless enters the store and goes shopping. That is, the officer takes items from the store and allows the retailer to think the burglar stole these items.

It is fairly clear to see that all cases of malfeasance can be classified as corruption. Yet, many instances of non-feasance and misfeasance may not represent clear-cut examples of corruption. Some non-feasance and misfeasance may represent deviance—stretches in the social limits of tolerance. But this, in itself, may not represent corruption. In many police departments, a choice is made to establish enforcement priorities. In essence, these **enforcement priorities** set patterns of police activities in which petty offenses are either ignored entirely or given only superficial attention. In such instances, it is the organizational policy, rather than an individual officer or group of officers, that is responsible for the non-feasance or misfeasance.

AN UNINTENTIONAL EFFECT OF ENFORCEMENT PRIORITIES

The idea behind enforcement priorities is not intentional non-feasance. Rather, it is to ensure that the more serious crimes, and crimes for which suspects are most likely to be apprehended if action is taken immediately, receive the greatest priority by investigators. Thus, in an ideal sense violent crimes, homicides, and major robberies should receive greater attention than incidents of shoplifting or car theft.

There is also the possibility that some misfeasance is unintentionally created through simple officer error or from a lack of understanding about a particular law. For example, if an officer believes that a suspect who *has not* been advised of his constitutional rights has been *Mirandized*, and in casual conversation learns about additional crimes or evidence of other crimes, this information may become useless. The officer did not intentionally, or willfully violate the suspect's rights or potentially destroy elements of the state's case. Rather, the officer simply goofed.

What remains, at this junction, is the suggestion of a working definition of police corruption. It must be sufficiently broad to capture the vast diversity of inherently corrupt activities, but adequately narrow to avoid inclusion of minor acts of deviance, and unintended non-feasance. Jay Albanese (1988:113) offers a useful definition for **police corruption**:

> Illegal acts or omissions by a law enforcement officer in the line of duty who, by virtue of his official position, receives or intends to receive, only gain for [him or herself] or others.

It is important to note two central focuses evident in this definition—that the illegal behavior or omissions must occur while on duty and that these activities are undertaken with the intention to receive a reward. In other words, part of the definition is that these activities are profit motivated—whether this profit is cash, merchandise, or political favor. Taken together, these components of Albanese's definition suggest that police corruption is inherently the misuse of police authority for personal advantage or gain.

Albanese's definition is generally workable. However, it does possess at least two serious limitations. By stressing the idea that the illegal behavior must occur while on duty, a wide variety of behaviors are eliminated. Consider, for instance, an officer who, while on duty, gains information about when a wealthy local resident will be away on vacation. While off-duty, the officer could use this information and burglarize the home of this wealthy local resident. While still within the general spirit of Albanese's definition, it certainly does not really comply with then specifics of an illegal behavior committed while on duty.

A second limitation rests on the fact that Albanese's definition directs attention to the individual and away from the department or institution of policing. Later in this chapter this will be shown to be somewhat imprecise.

Several researchers have offered additional insights to and explanations for police corruption. For the most part, these may be divided into one or the other of three kinds: explanations that focus on individual officers, explanations that center on departmental or organizational problems, and explanations that identify contributory problems from outside the department.

CORRUPTION OF INDIVIDUAL OFFICERS

Individual explanations of police corruption see the locus of initial illegal behavior as originating among particular police officers. Supporters of this perspective argue that if a few rotten apples were eliminated from police agencies, corruption would vanish. When one thinks about this sort of officer, one may well imagine someone of low moral character who is unable to resist the temptation of fast-but-dirty money or illegal deals and negotiations. Another image related to this type of officer is an officer who misuses authority for personal gain, rationalizing that since the job pays poorly and he or she works so hard, the officer deserves certain perks. In contrast to the officer of low moral character, this second type more aggressively seeks opportunities to receive financial gains or favors in return for omissions of duty (e.g., not making an arrest, not issuing a citation, not reporting a safety or health violation, etc.).

The explanation of a few rotten apples spoiling the barrel was fairly popular during the 1960s (Peterson 1960; Goldstein 1977). Today, however, few law enforcement researchers fully embrace this explanation of police corruption. As Samuel Walker (1983:180) says:

> By focusing on the individual it explains corruption in terms of the moral failure of a few officers. According to this view, corruption spreads because the rotten apple spoils the rest of the barrel . . .
>
> Despite its popularity, the rotten apple theory is rejected by most experts. First, it fails to explain the pervasiveness and persistence of police corruption—otherwise one would have to assume that there are an enormous number of "bad" people recruited into police work. On the contrary, studies of police recruitment indicate that persons attracted to policing are relatively idealistic . . .
>
> Second, the rotten-apple theory fails to explain the difference between departments and differences within a particular department over time . . .

Walker also suggests that if one accepts the rotten-apple theory, one must additionally accept the notion that at least some police departments have attracted a disproportionately high number of rotten apples—and have done so for a very long time (see Box 15.3).

BOX 15.3 SOME "BLUE-COAT CRIMES"

Ellwyn Stoddard (1983) suggests that there are a number of "blue-coat crimes," or crimes committed by individual officers. These types of individually based unethical and criminal behaviors may include the following:

1. *Mooching*: receiving free items such as coffee, meals, groceries and so forth.
2. *Chiseling*: seeking free admission to entertainment or expecting price discounts for purchases.
3. *Favoritism*: using window decals or courtesy badges or cards to gain immunity from traffic citations (sometimes even extending this courtesy to spouses, friends, and family members).
4. *Discrimination*: acting upon one's prejudicial feelings about a minority group member; being physically abusive or unfair in dealings.
5. *Extortion*: demands for contributions to police benevolent groups, purchase of tickets to police functions, payments to avoid traffic citations, etc.
6. *Bribery*: receipt of cash, or items of value for past or future assistance in avoiding prosecution. The acceptance of payoffs or protection money would also fall under this category.
7. *Night shopping*: appropriating expensive items from retail stores and attributing the loss to some criminal activity such as a burglary. Usually accomplished while investigat-ing an unlocked or open door, or an actual burglary.
8. *Shakedowns*: a type of extortion where officers accept money from citizens in lieu of enforcing the law.
9. *Perjury*: provision of an alibi or in some other manner covering up for a fellow officer. May also include lying about the behaviors of a defendant in order to assure a conviction.
10. *Premeditated theft*: the actual planning and execution of a crime which cannot be explained as a "spur of the moment" impulse. Theft differs from shakedowns only in regards to the intentional planning of the premeditated theft.
11. *Case fixing*: as a form of corruption, case fixing has occurred at all levels of the criminal justice process and may involve not only police officers but bailiffs, jurors, prosecutors and judges. The most common form of case fixing involves bribing an officer for not being arrested; it may involve paying an officer to perjure him or herself on the witness stand.
12. *Drug abuse*: the abuse of drugs by a police officer may motivate the officer to commit a variety of illegal or corrupt behaviors in order to support his or her drug addiction, or to cover-up the fact of this addiction.

(Adapted from Stoddard 1983:340-341).

Writing shortly after the Knapp Commission (1973) had concluded its investigation, former New York City Police Commissioner Patrick Murphy (1973:72) stated:

> The "rotten-apple" theory won't work any longer. Corrupt police officers are not natural born criminals, nor wicked men, constitutionally different from their honest colleagues. The task of corruption control is to examine the barrel, not just the apples—the organization, not just the individuals in it, because corrupt police are made not born.

Two things should be evident about individual explanations of police corruption. First, they insufficiently account for changes in idealistic recruits who become corrupt shortly after becoming police officers. Secondly, individual explanations do not specify why certain departments have historically and consistently had greater amounts of corruption than other departments.

Patrick Murphy's comment suggests a second and slightly more popular type of explanation: corruption viewed as originating in the structure of the police organization, or organizational culture (Daft 1995).

CORRUPTION OF DEPARTMENTS

Departmental explanations of police corruption look at the small groups of officers who typically band together within police departments. These police cliques may serve positive ends. But, in some instances, these cliques may foster sentiments antagonistic to their jobs, the community they serve, or even the justice system. This mutual support of one another's negative and antagonistic feelings may lead to corruption. Lawrence Sherman (1974) described this situation as a *rotten pocket*. Sherman further suggests that rotten-pocket departments may be subdivided into those with pervasive, unorganized corruption. In the first case, a majority of police in a given department are corrupt, but have little contact and make few cooperative efforts in their illegal personal gains. Gerald Clemente (Clemente and Stevens 1987) describes this sort of department in *The Cops Are Robbers* (see Box 15.4).

In the second case, the department may be seen as filled almost entirely with officers actively involved in systematic and organized corruption. Departments with organized corruption are places where bribes, payoffs, and shakedowns are routinized to the extent that they become mundane aspects of daily police activity. Robert Daley's 1978 book *The Prince of the City*, illustrates this sort of organized corruption. The book details the story of Frank Leuci, a New York City detective, whose testimony against officers involved in crime made him an outsider in his department.

Richard Lundman (1980:140–141) outlines five principal elements that distinguish individual police deviance from organized corruption:

First, for police behavior to be seen as departmentally or organizationally corrupt, "it must operate in a manner contrary to norms or rules maintained by legal institutions outside of the police department."

BOX 15.4   HOW COPS GO BAD: GERALD CLEMENTE'S TARNISHED BADGE

One may certainly question how cops, who entered the field of law enforcement with altruism and good intentions, became involved in the largest bank robbery in American history. In his book *The Cops Are Robbers* (Clemente and Stevens 1987), one-time police Captain Gerald Clemente describes his evolution from law enforcer to lawbreaker. His criminal career culminated in the 1980 Memorial Day weekend bank robbery of the Depositors Trust in Medford, Massachusetts. The estimated haul in this robbery was approximately $25 million dollars in cash and jewels.

Second, to distinguish between individual deviance and organized police corruption, the "deviant act must be supported by internal operating norms which conflict with the police organization's formal goals and rules. . . ."

Third, in order to maintain the subterranean norms of illegal behavior, a socialization process "supportive of police misconduct" must exist to indoctrinate recruits.

Fourth, a general condition of mutual and "peer support of the misbehavior of colleagues" must be present throughout the department.

Finally, for police misconduct to be organizationally corrupt, "it must be supported by the dominant administrative coalition of the police organization." The idea of a deviant police subculture and negative results from its related, secret *esprit de corps* are certainly implied in Lundman's elements.

It is likely that some conditions that arise within departments will make organized corruption more or less conducive. In other words, there may be an interrelationship of certain groups of officers as rotten pockets and certain organizational structures or agency administrators and policies that lead to organized corruption. The third possible explanation of police corruption mentioned previously is the effect of external factors.

EXTERNAL FACTORS THAT EXPLAIN CORRUPTION

The external factors explanation of police corruption draws heavily from sociological theory. From this perspective, police corruption is seen as the latent effect of society's attempt to execute certain unenforceable or socially controversial laws (Barker 1986). These may include behaviors that are violations of statutes or ordinances, but that all parties have engaged in voluntarily, such as gambling, prostitution, and drug use—the so-called victimless crimes. These crimes are difficult to enforce, both because there are few complaints and because pervasive attitudes permissive of these activities tend to exist throughout society.

While external-factor explanations contribute to some species of police corruption—such as bribes and payoffs—these are rather limited in their applicability. For example, this theory fails to explain why an officer might be willing to fix a traffic ticket for a local politician or why an officer who desires a new color television might turn to burglary to obtain it.

THE OCCUPATIONAL OPPORTUNITY EXPLANATION

A more promising explanation of police corruption arises when one considers law enforcement from an occupational perspective. Police misbehavior and corruption, then, become forms of occupational deviance. All occupations present their members with various opportunities to use, or more accurately misuse, their position or authority for personal gain. Stockbrokers may use insider information to make themselves wealthy. Members of the supermarket night stock crew may make themselves expensive steak dinners while working. Department-store salespersons may place sale tags on full-priced merchandise for friends, relatives, or themselves. University professors may trade undeserved grades for cash or sexual favors from students. Automobile factory workers may take tools home in their lunch pails. Occupational opportunity and human greed frequently combine to produce deviant situations.

With regard to police officers, most are placed in circumstances that present them with opportunities for misconduct at some time or another. Even in the smallest of exurbs (beyond the suburbs), patrol officers may base an arrest decision on some extralegal criteria, accept money for letting a speeder go unticketed, or use physical force to effect an attitude adjustment with a smart-mouthed teenage suspect.

Given the enormous amount of work-related deviance/corruption apparent in various occupations and professions, why is there special concern about police deviance? One explanation, of course, is that the occupational setting of police officers, and the accompanying opportunity structure, offers a far greater range of choices and corrupting circumstances. Also, compared with other occupations, the public has far less compassion for transgressions committed by police officers (Coleman 1985). After all, no other occupation has been officially granted the authority to preserve liberty, even to the extent of taking another person's life.

Additionally, policing provides access to numerous occasions to engage in occupationally deviant activities that do not provide a material or financial gain. For example, police officers are required to testify in court as part of their law enforcement duties. In spite of having taken an oath to tell the truth, some officers may bend this truth or lie in order to improve the likelihood of a conviction (Ericson 1981; Barker 1986).

Some acts of perjury, such as lying under oath, suggest commonly understood types of corruption, such as having taken a bribe. Some acts of perjury, however, do not. Occasionally, an act of police perjury simply reflects an over-zealous officer's attempt to get a conviction at any cost. It well may be that the defendant is a known felon, who whether guilty or not of the current crime, is seen by the officer as guilty of some crime. In this case, the end of obtaining the conviction—even to the extent of perjury—may outweigh the means of obtaining it in the mind of the officer. But no matter how noble the intentions, this sort of perjury remains a misuse of one's authority. It is police deviance in the truest tradition of Dirty Harry—yet it is characteristically different from police corruption.

Jerome Skolnick (1986:125) offers the following explanation for why police officers may lie or perjure themselves:

> The policeman lies because lying becomes a routine way of managing legal impediments—whether to protect fellow officers or to compensate for what he [or she] views as limitations the courts have placed on his [or her] skepticism of a system that suppresses truth in the interest of the criminal. Moreover, the law permits the policeman to lie at the investigative stage,

when he [or she] is not entirely convinced that the suspect is a criminal, but forbids lying about procedures at the testimonial stage, when the policeman is certain of the guilt of the accused.

There is another problem related to the opportunity for police officers to perform misconduct. This other inducement is the huge economic base many organized criminal operations possess today (see Berg and Horgan 1998, "Organized Crime"). For many criminals a large cash payoff to the police is simply a business expense. With the increased importation of cocaine in tons rather than in pounds, millions of dollars are at risk when police seize a shipment. A $10,000 payoff to a police officer, then, is chicken-feed. As a result, police officers sometimes find themselves offered bribes that amount to as much or more than they earn in an entire year. For example, if a high-level drug smuggler is arrested, it might be cheaper to spend $50,000 or $100,000 to arrange for an officer to lose evidence than to go to prison for many years.

The high degree of discretion characteristic of policing and the independent and largely unsupervised patrols of officers further increase the possibilities for corruption. In addition, discretionary decisions, such as whether to make an arrest, are essentially invisible to the greater public. In short, most police activities go unseen by the average private citizen. Unless one is witness or victim to a crime, one seldom gets to see real police work. When a person does happen to see police in action, such as officers leaving the scene of a burglary, it is virtually impossible to know whether legitimate police activities or misconduct have occurred. This ambiguity additionally increases the conduciveness for police deviance and corruption.

The various factors inherent in policing as an occupation provide an opportunity that can facilitate police misconduct and potentially police corruption. It is extremely important to emphasize that the vast majority of law enforcement officers, like the majority of other occupational group members, do not take advantage of their positions and authority. The majority of police officers remain law-abiding bearers of the trust society has bestowed upon them.

In fact, when alleged wrongdoing is identified, police officers frequently rush to the defense of the organization, even at the expense of the accused officer(s). Although civilians under law are innocent until proven guilty, the police are more often treated (particularly by other officers) as guilty until proven innocent. This general trend has resulted in a somewhat unusual attitude within police organizations. Since the officers in a given department rally to condemn the suspected party in the group, the agency itself is presented as exempt from any responsibility for the misconduct (Goldstein 1986). An illustration of this occurred in Boston on February 2, 1988. Boston Police Commissioner Francis M. Roache fired a rookie police officer 6 days after the officer had brandished a gun and pointed it at the head of a cab driver during a dispute. The entire incident was inadvertently captured on videotape by a nearby shopping mall's surveillance camera. During the press conference Commissioner Roache called specifically to announce this firing he said, "There is no way this type of activity will be tolerated in this department" (Ribadeneira 1988:16).

In a subsequent newspaper article (Stewart 1988), it was reported that Boston Police Department officials had twice tried to nix the offending officer's police appointment. Their reason was her arrest in 1980 on two counts of assault and battery with a dangerous weapon—her foot. The charge was a felony and a conviction would have automatically disqualified her from appointment as a police officer in Massachusetts. However, the charges were reduced to two counts of assault and battery, misdemeanors. The appointment went through because the department did not have sufficient cause to reject the recruit.

The question, of course, becomes, "Is the organization really exempt from responsibility simply because it has fired this officer and filed charges against her for yet another assault and battery?" Although largely a rhetorical question it does certainly offer a direction for police agencies to move in. Specifically, supervisors and administrators need to become responsible for their personnel. These commanders also need to be sure that departmental policy and procedure have been clearly articulated and understood by subordinate officers. The attitude of some administrators who, after the fact, claim, "I knew that so-and-so was a time bomb, waiting to go off" is insufficient. No action on the part of an administrator is action! The consequences of the bomb, should it go off, are indeed the legal and civil responsibility of both the offending officer and the agency—including the department's administrative leaders.

CONTROLLING POLICE CORRUPTION

The question that should arise about now is, "If the occupation of policing virtually facilitates corruption, how is it to be controlled?" Management accountability is perhaps the most important, effective, and perhaps most difficult, proactive tool for preventing, detecting, and intervening in police corruption (Bracey 1989; Cox 1996).

Trojanowicz (1992:2) states that supervisors can have an important influence on corrupt activities, but he also states:

> Supervisors must go the extra distance to ensure that the officers under their command treat people with respect and that they have not crossed the line . . . The good news is that departments which have embraced Community Policing have taken an important step in fostering a climate where the average citizens may well feel encouraged to share any such concerns or suspicions."

In the United States, interests in controlling or monitoring police conduct first began to gain impetus in the 1950s. As part of a national judicial trend that addressed the question of due process, the U.S. Supreme Court grew more critical of cases involving poor police practices. Throughout the 1960s, and with the ruling set forth in such cases as *Mapp v. Ohio* (1961), *Miranda v. Arizona* (1966), and *Terry v. Ohio* (1968) the tone for the judicial review of police conduct was set.

Also during the 1960s, the police found themselves facing urban rioting and massive political protests. Protesters and disgruntled citizens, many of whom had been injured at the hands of police who were attempting to control public disturbances, added their voices to a growing demand for more effective mechanisms to express complaints about police conduct (Goldstein 1986). What evolved was a fairly widespread movement calling for the establishment of civilian review boards.

The civilian review board process involved the creation of a group of civilian advisers to review allegations of police misconduct. Although this style of police monitoring is fairly popular with many police executives today, it met with considerable resistance among both officers and administrators in the 1960s (Epstein 1982; Walker 1983). With the development of community policing strategies during the 1980s, civilian review boards have become fairly commonplace in many police departments. As a similar extension to this community outreach approach to policing, many departments across the nation have developed **citizen police academies**. These citizen police academies are structured courses that allow private citizens an opportunity to learn, firsthand, how police departments operate. It also provides a mechanism whereby the average citizen will become more comfortable discussing—with police supervisors—problems they can now recognize or may witness when officers do not appropriately perform their police duties.

Another approach to controlling police misconduct is through increased training and education. As suggested in Chapter 12, much of a police officer's formal occupational socialization occurs at the police academy and during the first few months on the street. Thomas Barker (1983) suggested that many police recruits enter the academy already believing that some amount of corruption is present in every police department. These recruits, then, need to be carefully instructed not only in the laws they are expected to uphold, but the laws and ethical canons they themselves are expected to follow.

Many academies traditionally offered brief courses in police ethics. A growing number of these academies, however, have begun to increase the emphasis placed on this training, and the length of time devoted to the subject. While the press is still filled with many stories of police misconduct, only time will tell whether this new emphasis on proper police behavior will have a meaningful effect on police conduct. While police organizations have come a long way from the corruption-riddled agencies of the 1960s, in many ways they have taken only a few very short steps forward.

SUMMARY

This chapter began with the premise that not all gratuities taken by police officers necessarily constitute corruption. In developing this argument the chapter asserts that one consideration involves whether the gift or service interferes with fair access to law enforcement protection and services all people are entitled to. Another serious problem associated with gratuities is how the public perceives them. Speaking generally, there tends to be an attitude among people that accepting even that free cup of coffee may symbolically represent potential, if not actual, police corruption. The chapter also draws attention to the notions of intent and effect with regard to gratuities and police officer behavior. When a gift or service is given without the intent to gain greater access to police protection or gain preferential treatment in any manner, and when this gift does not result in a change in the officer's behavior, there seems little objective harm.

In an effort to distinguish various sorts of police deviance (e.g., rule bending) from police corruption (law violations), the chapter examines a number of categorical schemes. Included among these were explanations that were directed toward individually corrupt officers (sometimes referred to as rotten apples). Explanations directed toward the department and cliques of corrupt officers were identified in text as rotten-pocket arguments. Finally, explanations that considered various factors external of the police department and individual officers were discussed. These external explanations included certain difficult-to-enforce crimes and social attitudes.

The chapter concluded with an examination of police corruption as a variety of occupational deviance. Included in this discussion were several recommendations for controlling police corruption.

REFERENCES

Albanese, Jay S. *The Police Officer's Dilemma: Balancing Peace, Order, and Individual Rights*. Buffalo, N.Y.: Great Ideas, 1988.

Associated Press. "Corruption Figure Disappears in Miami; Second Hospitalized." *Washington Post* November 19, 1987:22.

Barker, Thomas. "Peer Group Support for Police Occupational Deviance." In *Police Deviance*. Thomas Barker and David L. Carter (eds.) Cincinnati, Oh.: Pilgrimage, 1986.

Barrett, J. K. "Inside the Mob's Smut Racket." *Readers Digest* November 1973:128–33.

Beigel, Herbert. "The Investigation and Prosecution of Police Corruption." *The Journal of Criminal Law and Criminology*, 65(1974):135–156.

Berg, Bruce L., and John J. Horgan. *Criminal Investigation*. Westonville, Oh.: Glencoe Publishing Co., 1998.

Bracey, Dorothy H. "Proactive Measures Against Police Corruption: Yesterday's Solutions Today's Problems." *Police Studies*, 12(24)1989:175–179.

Burnham, David. "Graft Paid to Police Said to Run into Millions," *The New York Time*, 25 April, 1970:1, 18.

Christopher Commission. Independent Commission on the Los Angeles Police Department. Los Angeles, Calif., 1991.

Clemente, Gerald, and Kevin Stevens. *The Cops Are Robbers*. Boston: Quinlan Press, 1987.

Cohen, Howard, and Michael Feldberg. *Ethics for Law Enforcement Officers*. Boston: National Association of State Directors of Law Enforcement Training, 1983.

Coleman, James. *The Criminal Elite*. New York: St, Martin's, 1985.

Cox, Steven M. *Police: Practices, Perspectives, Problems*. Boston: Allyn and Bacon, Inc., 1996.

Daft, Richard L. *Organizational Theory and Design*. 5th ed. Minneapolis/St Paul: West Publishing Co., 1995.

Daley, Robert. *Prince of the City: The True Story of a Cop Who Knew Too Much*. Boston: Houghton-Mifflin, 1978.

Daley, Robert. *Prince of the City*. Videotape produced by Burt Harris. New York: Warner Home Video. Screenplay, Jay Presson Allen and Sidney Lumet, 1982.

Dempsey, Lawrence. "The Knapp Commission and You." *The Police Chief* November, 1972:20–29.

Epstein, David G. "The Complaint: Advisory Reflections to the Law Enforcement Agency Head." *The Police Chief* May 1982:58–61.

Elliston, Fredrick A., and Michael Feldberg. "Gratuities, Corruption, and the Democratic Ethos of Policing." In *Moral Issues in Police Work*. Fredrick A. Elliston and Michael Feldberg (eds.) Newark, N.J.: Rowman and Allanheld, 1985.

Ericson, Richard V. "Rules for Police Deviance." In *Organizational Police Deviance*. Clifford D. Shearing (ed.) Toronto: Butterworth, 1981.

"Former Officer in Philadelphia Receives 13-Year Sentence." *Washington Post* March 4, 1986:A20.

Golden, Daniel. "Can Police Corruption be Stopped?" *The Boston Globe* November 15, 1987:A25.

Goldstein, Herman. *Policing a Free Society*. Cambridge, Mass.: Lippincott, 1977.

Goldstein, Herman. "Controlling Police Deviance." In *Police Deviance*. Thomas Barker and David L. Carter (eds.) Cincinnati, Oh.: Pilgrimage, 1986.

Inciardi, James A. *Criminal Justice*. 3d ed. New York: Harcourt Brace Jovanovich Publishers, 1990.

Johnson, Michael. *Political Corruption and Public Policy in America*. Monterey, Calif.: Brooks/Cole, 1982.

Klockars, Carl B. *The Idea of Police*. Beverly Hills, Calif.: Sage, 1985.

Knapp Commission Report. *The Knapp Commission Report on Police Corruption*. New York: Braziller, 1973.

Lacayo R. "Cops and Robbers." *Time* October 11, 1993:43–44.

Lundman, Richard J. "Police Patrol Work: A Comparative Perspective." In *Police Behavior: A Sociological Perspective*. Richard Lundman (ed.) New York: Oxford, 1980.

Lynch, G. W. "Police Corruption from the United States Perspective." *Police Studies*, 12(4)1989:165–170.

Matza, David. *Delinquency and Drift*. New York: Wiley, 1964.

Murphy, Patrick. "Police Corruption." *The Police Chief* December 1973:36–72.

Peak, Kenneth J. *Policing America*. Englewood Cliffs, N.J.: Regents/Prentice Hall, 1993.

Pennsylvania Crime Commission. "Report on Police Corruption and the Quality of Law Enforcement in Philadelphia." St. Davids, Pa.: Pennsylvania Crime Commission, 1974.

Peterson, Bill. "Miami Virtue, or Vice?" *The Washington Post* January 12, 1986:6, A11.

Peterson, Virgil. "The Chicago Police Scandals." *Atlantic* October 1960:58–64.

Phillips, Frank. "Bribery Allegations Reported in Lowell." *The Boston Globe* October 16, 1987:1, 24.

Rankin Committee Report. "Report on Police Complaints Made to Rankin Committee April 24, 1970–May 11, 1970." May 13, 1970.

Ribadeneira, Diego. "Officer Seen on Tape is Fired." *The Boston Globe* February 2, 1988:14.

Schecter, L., and W. Phillips. *On the Pad*. New York: Putnam, 1973.

Sherman, Lawrence. *Police Corruption*. Garden City, N.Y.: Doubleday/Anchor Books, 1974.

Simpson, Anthony. *The Literature of Police Corruption*, 1. New York: John Jay, 1977.

Skolnick, Jerome H. "Deception by Police." In *Police Deviance*. Thomas Barker and David L. Carter (eds.) Cincinnati, Oh.: Pilgrimage, 1986.

Stewart, Richard. "Boston's Voided Police Tests: Perception a Costly reality." *The Boston Globe* November 23, 1987:1.

Stewart, Richard. "Police Request to Bypass Fired officer was Denied by State." *The Boston Globe* February 6, 1988:1.

Stoddard, Ellwyn R. "Blue Coat Crime." In Carl B. Klockars, *Thinking About Police*. New York: McGraw-Hill Book Company, 1983:338-349.

Stuart, Reginald. "Officer Indicted in Miami Shooting." *The New York Times* February 18, 1983:A18.

Sykes, Gersham, and David Matza. "Techniques of Neutralization: A Theory of Delinquency." *American Sociological Review*, 22(1957):644–70.

Trojanowicz, Robert. "Preventing Individual and Systematic Corruption." *Footprints*, 4(1)1992:1–3.

United Press International. "Suspension of 30 More Officers Predicted in Miami Police Scandal." *The Washington Post* November 23, 1987A5.

Walker, Samuel. *The Police in America: An Introduction*. New York: McGraw Hill, 1983.

QUESTIONS FOR REVIEW

Objective #1:

- What is meant by officer integrity?

Objective #2:

- At what point does police behavior become police corruption?

Objective #3:

- Why are even small gratuities frowned upon in many police departments?
- How might receiving even a free cup of coffee be a problem for police officers?

Objective #4:

- If a police officer tell a motorist he will not write a ticket if the motorist pays him $50, is this a bribe or extortion? How come?

Objective #5:

- How might you define non-feasance?
- What would you label a situation where an officer correctly complete the information required on a traffic citation?

Objective #6:

- If a rape is reported to the police at the same time as a burglary of a house, which should be investigated first? How come?

Objective #7:

- What is meant by a police department with a rotten-pocket?

Objective #8:

- What are considered external factors in police corruption?

Objective #9:

- What is meant by the role of opportunity in police corruption?

Objective #10:

- How might police agencies manage police corruption?

Part IV

The Forecast for Policing

16 Hazards of Policing: Danger, Stress, and AIDS

CHAPTER OBJECTIVES

After reading this chapter you should be able to:

1. Discuss the real and perceived dangers of police work.
2. Explain what is meant by the phrase "personal weapons."
3. Consider stress in police work.
4. List various types of stressors commonly associated with police work.
5. Differentiate between stress and eustress.
6. Talk about why some officers may self-medicate with alcohol or other drugs.
7. Explain why police stress counseling programs originally derived from alcohol counseling programs.
8. Define role-conflicts in police work.
9. Suggest how stress may be related to police officer suicides.
10. Consider why AIDS may be seen as a new police stressor.

DANGERS IN THE POLICE ENVIRONMENT

Among the many elements that exist in the police officer's occupational environment, danger has long been identified in research as among the most important determinants of police attitudes and behaviors (see Niederhoffer 1969; Goldstein 1977; Bennett and Greenstein 1975; Bennett 1984; Albanese 1988; Peak 1993; Cox 1996). As suggested in Chapter 12, long before a recruit ever seriously considers a career in law enforcement, he or she is being subtly conditioned about danger by various factors in society. The media—television shows, motion pictures, novels, stories, magazines, newspapers and so forth—each paint a romanticized, adventure-filled picture of police work. For many potential recruits, *dangerous* quickly becomes synonymous with *adventurous*.

KEY TERMS	task-related stressors	chronic stress
	individual stressors	AIDS
personal weapons	eustress	Human Immunodeficiency Virus
external stressors	role conflict	(HIV)
internal stressors	acute or situational stress	AIDS-Related Complex (ARC)

When youthful recruits do eventually enter the police academy, they are subject to the police socialization process. Speaking generally, recruits enter the academy believing they are already fully informed about danger. Based upon their pre-policing socialization process, they associate police work with danger and adventure.

Recruits are issued their guns, nightsticks, and handcuffs, and are trained in the academy to use these instruments—both offensively and defensively. These too may initially be viewed as very clear symbols of the danger of police work. Occupationally speaking, however, these are simply tools of the trade. They are not, in fact, significantly different from the medical instruments (hypodermics, stethoscopes, tongue depressors, etc.) used regularly by medical students as they become doctors.

It is undeniable that police work encompasses a number of tasks and functions that effect a set of potential risks to safety not present in other occupations. In fact, there appears to be an unusual amount of stress and related health problems associated with police work. This stress is also commonly seen as related to other social problems that plague police officers, such as spousal abuse, divorce, alcoholism, drug abuse, and even suicide. As a matter of fact, many police officers are injured, and some are killed in the line of duty.

Both the law enforcement community and the general public take the killing of a police officer very seriously. For instance, even before many states had begun reinstating the death penalty for the crime of homicide during the early 1980s, most already carried a capital sentence on their statutes for the killing of a police officer.

Traditionally, newspapers and television newscasts spend several days discussing the circumstances surrounding the killing of a police officer. Large numbers of police and police officials often attend the funerals of a fallen comrade—even when they may not have personally known the slain officer. More remarkable, perhaps, officers attend the funeral, even when the fallen comrade was a canine! In January 1988, a Dallas, Texas, police officer was killed by a deranged homeless person. The street person wrestled the officer's gun away from him and then shot the officer three times. More than 1,000 fellow police officers and city officials attended a memorial service in the officer's honor.

In February 1988, a Boston, Massachusetts, officer was killed as he attempted to break down the door to a drug dealer's apartment. Shots were fired through the door as Detective Sherman C. Griffiths struck it with a sledgehammer. He was critically wounded in the head and died 11 hours later (Lewis 1988). More than 700 officers and police officials attended his funeral.

One week after the Boston shooting, another officer was gunned down, this time in New York City. At 3:30 A.M. on February 26, 1988 Officer Edward Byrne was shot three times in the head—execution style—as he sat in his patrol car. Officer Byrne had been assigned to a fixed patrol outside the home of a state's witness in a large-scale crack case. The witness had received death threats, and his home had been fire-bombed two weeks before Byrne's shooting (Fried 1988).

On March 9, 1993, officer Howard E. Dallas of the Garden Grove, California stopped a man for a traffic violation, and was shot to death when he went to speak with the driver. His bleeding body was found with his service weapon still holstered (Boucher 1997). After a 4-year investigation, police in California finally located a suspect in Officer Dallas' shooting (Boucher 1997).

The occurrence of police killings certainly draws considerable public attention and is a genuine problem. But the publicity tends to mask a problem at least as serious: stress from officers' perception of danger. What is interesting about this perception of danger, and its concomitant stress, is the fact that while the risk of danger is very high in police work as an occupation, the reality of danger is relatively low. It may be that there is a lower level of actual danger in police work because of the precautions taken as a result of the perception of danger's threat. In other words, compared to the number of officers actually working in the field, the number of officers who are seriously injured or killed is relatively small. As Table 16.1 illustrates, in 1994 a total of 76 officers were killed during incident-related actions nationally. When one stops to consider that in 1994 there were more than 600,000 full-time sworn officers nationally, the number of officers killed begins to pale. In full, fewer than about one out of every 8,000 law enforcement officers were actually killed in the line of duty during 1994.

In fact, the killing of a police officer is a relatively rare occurrence (compared to the number of officers in the field). As Table 16.2 illustrates, during the period of 1985–1994, a total of 708 officers were killed in the line of duty. This approximates an average of 71 officers killed each year, a figure slightly lower than the actual number of deaths during half of these years. Yet, in other occupations, such as construction, mining, agriculture, fishing and forestry, public utilities, wholesale and retail, and even manufacturing more than 10,000 thousand people die each year in occupationally related incidents (Cox 1996).

Another element related to the dangers associated with police work is injury in the line of duty. As Table 16.3 suggests, during the 10-year period of 1985–1994 an average of 65,853 police officers were injured nationally. Another glance at Table 16.3 and some quick calculations reveal that the vast majority of those injuries were from the combined categories of personal weapons and other dangerous weapons. Typically, **personal weapons** include feet, elbows, fists, and teeth (biting wounds). Similarly, other dangerous weapons represent items such as lamps, keys, and pens used as weapons against an officer. While injuries can an are sustained, most do not result in long-term disabilities. In one study by David H. Bayley and James Garofalo (1989:6), the researchers report that "the unambiguous fact is that patrol officers rarely face violence in encounters with the public." Bayley and Garofalo (1989) found that officers faced physical danger only occasionally and then the violence frequently was not directed against them.

This discussion is not intended to diminish the very real potential dangers in police work. For example, on February 28, 1997, when the quiet afternoon was shattered by the sound of automatic gunfire as two masked bank robbers

Table 16.1

Law Enforcement Officers Killed During 1994 (by circumstances at scene and type of assignment)

Circumstances at Scene	Total	2-Officer Vehicle	1-Officer Vehicle Solo/Assist	Foot Patrol Solo/Assist	Detective Special Assign Solo/Assist	Off-Duty
Total	76	6	19 / 24	1 / 0	3 / 11	12
Disturbance calls	8	0	3 / 4	0/0	0/0	1
Bar fights, man with a gun, etc.	4	0	1 / 2	0 / 0	0 / 0	1
Domestic disturbances	4	0	2 / 2	0 / 0	0 / 0	0
Arrest situations	31	2	5 / 10	0 / 0	2 / 4	8
Burglaries in progress	3	0	1 / 0	0 / 1	0 / 0	0
Robberies in progress or pursuing robbers	16	0	2 / 5	0 / 0	0 / 1	8
Drug-related matters	3	1	1 / 0	0 / 0	1 / 0	0
Attempted other arrests	9	1	1 / 4	0 / 0	0 / 3	0
Civil disorders, mass disturbances, riots, etc.	0	0	0 / 0	0 / 0	0 / 0	0
Handling transporting custody of prisoners	1	0	1 / 0	0 / 0	0 / 0	0
Investigating suspicious persons	15	3	4 / 4	1 / 0	1 / 0	2
Ambush situations	6	1	1 / 0	0 / 0	0 / 4	0
Mentally deranged	4	0	1 / 1	0 / 0	0 / 2	0
Traffic pursuit and stops	11	0	4 / 5	0 / 0	0 / 1	1

Source: *Sourcebook of Criminal Justice Statistics, 1995.* Table 3.162, p. 379, US Department of Justice Statistics, Washington, D.C.: U.S. Government Printing Office, 1996.

took on nearly 200 Los Angeles police officers, the risk of injury or death was very great (Shuster and Smith 1997). In the end, the two robbers were killed, ten officers injured, and three civilians had been hit by gunfire (Shuster and Smith 1997). Incidents such as this foiled bank robbery bring to mind Bayley and Garofalo's (1989) warning that precautions are necessary since a single act of violence may have catastrophic results for an officer and the public.

Nonetheless, the discussion offered here is intended to keep consideration of potential risks to police officers in perspective. Furthermore, the tables presented in this chapter merely focus on the "physical assaults on officers." To

Table 16.2

Law Enforcement Officers Killed 1985–1994 (by circumstances at scene and type of assignment)

Circumstances at Scene	Total	2-Officer Vehicle	1-Officer Vehicle Solo/Assist	Foot Patrol Solo/Assist	Detective Special Assign Solo/Assist	Off-Duty
Total	708	83	233 / 119	5 / 6	46 / 110	106
Disturbance calls	119	24	41 / 37	0 / 0	1 / 6	10
Bar fights, man with a gun, etc.	54	11	12 / 17	0 / 0	1 / 6	7
Domestic disturbances	65	13	29 / 20	0 / 0	0 / 3	3
Arrest situations	269	25	45 / 46	2 / 3	15 / 73	60
Burglaries in progress	27	5	12 / 3	0 / 0	1 / 3	3
Robberies in progress or pursuing robbers	93	7	14 / 12	1 / 1	3 / 7	48
Drug-related matters	53	5	4 / 4	0 / 0	8 / 32	0
Attempted other arrests	96	8	15 / 27	1 / 2	3 / 31	9
Civil disorders, mass disturbances, riots, etc.	0	0	0 / 0	0 / 0	0 / 0	0
Handling transporting custody of prisoners	35	5	10 / 1	0 / 1	10 / 8	0
Investigating suspicious persons	114	12	50 / 18	2 / 2	7 / 11	12
Ambush situations	61	5	18 / 2	1 / 0	10 / 8	17
Mentally deranged	13	3	4 / 3	0 / 0	0 / 3	0
Traffic pursuit and stops	97	9	65 / 12	0 / 0	3 / 1	7

Source: *Sourcebook of Criminal Justice Statistics, 1995.* Table 3.161, p. 378, US Department of Justice Statistics, Washington, D.C.: U.S. Government Printing Office, 1996.

date, little empirical research has calculated the emotional impact on police officers from being placed regularly in situations where one could be killed or injured. In other words, placed in what James Fyfe (1989) terms "potentially violent situations or PVs." Little emphasis has been directed toward the emotional toll paid by officers when colleagues in their department or city have been permanently disfigured, disabled, or killed.

In spite of there being little information available concerning the emotional or psychological effects from potential dangers, instructors in police academies today regularly discuss the unpredictability of danger in policing. They train

Table 16.3

Assault on Law Enforcement Officers and Percent Receiving Personal Injury, 1985–1994 (by type of weapon)

Year	Total Victims	Firearms	Personal Weapons	Knife or Cutting Instrument	Other Dangerous Weapon
1985	61,724	2,793	51.953	1,715	5,263
1986	64,258	2,852	54,072	1,614	5,721
1987	63,842	2,789	53,807	1,561	5,685
1988	58,752	2,759	49,053	1,367	5,573
1989	62,172	3,154	51,861	1,379	5,778
1990	72,794	3,662	59,101	1,641	7,390
1991	62,852	3,532	50,813	1,493	7,014
1992	81,252	4,455	66,098	2,095	8,604
1993	66,975	4,002	53,848	1,574	7,551
1994	64,912	3,168	53,021	1,513	7,210

Percent Receiving Personal Injury

Year	Total Victims	Firearms	Personal Weapons	Knife or Cutting Instrument	Other Dangerous Weapon
1985	33.7 %	20.8 %	33.9 %	27.4 %	41.1 %
1986	33.7 %	22.3 %	33.9 %	29.9 %	38.3 %
1987	33.3 %	21.7 %	33.5 %	30.7 %	38.4 %
1988	35.8 %	27.3 %	35.6 %	32.3 %	42.1 %
1989	35.2 %	30.2 %	35.0 %	30.5 %	40.8 %
1990	36.3 %	29.4 %	36.1 %	29.4 %	42.5 %
1991	37.6 %	30.8 %	37.5 %	30.6 %	43.5 %
1992	36.5 %	25.5 %	36.9 %	30.4 %	40.9 %
1993	35.9 %	27.4 %	36.4 %	31.0 %	36.3 %
1994	35.7 %	26.3 %	36.3 %	29.4 %	36.7 %

officers to be suspicious of most if not all citizens they encounter; and instruct them on policies to call for backup in potentially dangerous situations (Barker et al. 1994).

In many ways, and as the remainder of this chapter will indicate, it is not the reality of a gunman shooting an officer during the course of a robbery or a traffic stop that is the most serious threat to the life or health of this officer. Rather, it is the stress created from knowing that such a situation could occur (Cullen et al. 1983).

Figure 16.1
Toy guns and replicas may create dangerous situations for police officers.

A

B

POLICE WORK AND STRESS

The problem of stress as related to police work has received considerable attention throughout the past 20 or more years. As Samuel Walker (1983:277) suggests, much of the early writing on the subject was alarmist and frequently exaggerated. Estimates of suicides, divorces, and alcohol and drug dependency among police officers were often disproportionate to reality. As one might expect, the strongest supporters of such alarmist mythology are often police officers themselves. Ironically, the fear or concern created by such a police folk belief is itself likely to increase police officer stress more rapidly than actual death and injury situations occur.

A somewhat more even-handed approach to stress and police work begins with the recognition that stressful situations occur among all occupations. As a result, the cardiovascular diseases, hypertension, ulcers, depression, stress-induced diabetes, alcohol-drug abuse, and assorted other somatic afflictions are not unique to law enforcement officers.

Elements usually thought to contribute to occupational stress or stressors include the loss of a sense of efficacy; reduced participation in decision-making processes; disillusionment with organizational goals; inequities in hiring, firing, and promotional structures; and task overloads. In addition to these general stressors, police work has several job-specific stressors. Ironically, the most devastating stressor is actually a paradoxical combination of long, tedious periods of inactivity, coupled with brief, unpredictable periods of severe and lethal danger.

Although trouble and volatile situations may arise only four or five times during an 8-hour shift, if that frequently, police are trained to be ever aware of potential threats to safety (see Whitaker 1982; Bayley 1986; Bayley and Garofalo 1989; Barker et al. 1994). The innocent-looking drunk sleeping in the alley could just as easily be a look-out for a burglar already inside a building. The three youths casually standing under a street lamp smoking cigarettes may actually be waiting for a woman to pass so they can grab her handbag. Police are repeatedly taught that nothing is necessarily as it seems. This sort of near paranoid concern with even mundane things certainly can create emotional stress.

Too, patrol activities can lead to various health problems, such as poor eating and sleeping patterns, and leg or back problems. Related to these various stressors, of course, are assorted family conflicts, arguments with spouses, spousal assaults, divorce, heavy drinking and/or alcoholism, and a potential host of medical afflictions (Schwartz and Schwartz 1975; Goolkasian, Geddes, and DeJong 1989).

Discussions of police stress usually identify sets of stressors in similar ways. For example, quoting William Kroes (1976), Leonard Territo and Harold J. Vetter (1981) have grouped stressors into four categories: organizational practices; criminal justice system practices and characteristics; public practices and characteristics; and police work itself.

Clinton Terry III (1985:400) has similarly identified four types of police stressors (see also Blackmore 1978, 1985; Stratton 1978; Wallace 1978; Ayres 1990; Hale 1994). The four categories include external stressors, internal stressors, task-related stressors, and individual stressors.

External Stressors

External stressors, according to the literature, include frustrations from the American judicial system. These include seeing many arrests end up in dismissal in the courts, or seeing lenient treatment of felons who are convicted. External stressors may also involve a sense of a lack of support from the public. This may include disdain for local media coverage of police or crime-related incidents, resentment of civilian committees and governmental bodies that may be empowered to intervene in or affect performance of police officer functions.

Internal Stressors

Internal stressors represent a wide array of institutional problems. These may include flaws in training, non-functional procedures, insufficient or inadequate equipment, short pay and long hours, lack of identity, and a generally vague and unsatisfying system of rewards and recognition for good police work. Other internal stressors may be related to various forms of political favoritism or nepotism at the hands of supervisors, which limit or delay advancement. Internal stressors also may result from a kind of self-fulfilling prophecy in which officers define police work as stressful and identify instances that justify this definition.

Task-Related Stressors

Task-related stressors can be identified as those elements that stem from the performance of police duties. These may include shift rotations, role conflict, boredom, repeated exposure to violent or brutal crimes, a fragmented sense of the job and its responsibilities, and the long-term fear for personal safety.

Individual Stressors

In contrast to the other three stressors, **individual stressors** are chiefly idiosyncratic, that is, they originate within the individual officer. These stressors may include feelings of self-doubt, marital problems, difficulties arising from being a member of a minority group, difficulties arising from an inability to get along with other people, and various physical and mental health problems.

One important point that should be made is that none of these stressors must be real in order to have an effect on the officer. For example, if an officer believes that a supervisor is racist, this situation will be stress-provoking even if it is entirely untrue. If an officer is confronted by a man who draws what the officer believes to be a real handgun, the fear that runs through the officer is very real. If the officer later learns that the gun in question is a toy, it will likely make little difference. The emotional trauma the incident aroused will have already had some effect on the officer.

This phenomenon is similar to the concept of a self-fulfilling prophecy and derives from a theory credited to W. I. Thomas (Thomas and Swaine 1928). According to Thomas, situations that are defined as real by people, become real in their consequences. In other words, if an officer believes that the felon's hand in his pocket holds a gun, the officer will respond to that situation. The objective reality that the felon's hand clutches a toy or a roll of pennies is of no importance. The officer's emotional and somatic effects from the felon's simulation of a gun will be identical to those the officer would experience if confronted with a real gun.

EUSTRESS AND ITS EFFECTS ON THE POLICE ORGANIZATION

Eustress is a term coined by Hans Selye (1975) meaning "good stress." Organizationally induced eustress is often seen as a positive management approach in policing (Leonard and More 1987; Roberg and Kuykendall 1997). The use of eustress assumes that an individual can and will take a positive view of certain life events. Thus, one's attitude can determine whether an experience is perceived as pleasant or unpleasant. By adopting a positive attitude, one can convert unpleasant stress into productive and pleasant stress. The result, then, becomes a more gratifying and satisfying work environment.

Some stress from police work can be identified as very harmful to officers (Farmer 1990). Some other stress can be viewed as both helpful and necessary for officers' healthy survival in police work. According to Selye, the total absence of stress can be lethal. In fact, Seyle (1975:83) suggests that appropriate amounts of stress should be viewed as the "spice of life."

Police managers may use stress, or perhaps what might be termed *anxiety*, to deal with employees' response to the organizational structure of the department. In these cases, managers attempt to create a work environment based upon an awareness of how officers view their department. But the overall attitudes and the morale of officers are taken into consideration. Department policies, in turn, are developed in an effort to maintain a high level of job satisfaction. In order to accomplish this, the organization accommodates individual officers with regard to their levels of stress endurance and ability to adapt to stressful situations that occur in police work.

The overall emphasis of this orientation is that the organization is to use stress that exists in the workplace in a positive way. The rationale is that occupational stress can and should contribute to individual health, productivity, and physical well-being.

STRESS AND THE OFFICER'S FAMILY

When an individual signs on as a law enforcement officer, he or she has accepted more than merely a job or career. As Leonard Territo and Harold Vetter (1981) suggest, policing is a way of life for both the police officer and his or her family. Francis T. Cullen and his associates (1985) have suggested that police stress falls along two discernible dimensions, one involving the family and the other involving the job.

Most occupations expect employees to work during some specified period of hours and then to stop working and go home to a private life. For example, a taxicab driver can switch off his or her *on duty* light, climb out of the cab, and go home as a private person. Once home, the cab driver can kick back and discuss the cute or annoying events of the day with his or her spouse, friends, or other relatives. A police officer cannot as easily turn off the job, or even discuss all of the days events with friends or loved ones.

First, police officers are never really off-duty. Rather, they are off the clock. A private person can ignore most crimes—even some felonies—they witness in progress or merely call the police and report the crime. Under similar circumstances, an off-duty officer could be charged with dereliction of duty if he or she made no attempt to intercede. When a neighbor hears a prowler at 3:00 A.M. who gets called—the officer neighbor next door and two minutes away, or the police department?

Second, police officers find it difficult to leave their feelings about the job at the precinct. As a result, they frequently bring their frustration, disappointments, fears, and dissatisfactions home into their living rooms and to their families. Conversely, and like any other kind of worker, police officers may bring anger, hostility, or family problems to their job. Many of us have been stopped by a police officer for a traffic infraction. During those moments of waiting for the officer to walk from the cruiser to our car's window, certainly many people are whispering to themselves, "I hope this cop didn't have a fight at home this morning before coming to work!"

It is only recently that police administrators have begun to recognize that discord in an officer's family life can contribute to serious disruptions in the officer's effectiveness. Also, it is only during the past several years that police agencies have acknowledged that police work stress is carried home to the family—sometimes in the form of spousal abuse. Many of the perceived threats to safety experienced by police officers are perceived by their spouses and children as well. In many cases these stressors adversely affect the health of family members as seriously as they affect officers themselves. With this in mind, some agencies, such as the Kansas City, Missouri, police department have established programs that involve spouses in an effort to reduce stress (Saper 1980).

STRESS, COPING, AND ALCOHOLISM

To be sure, police stress is much more than an abstract concept. Stress can lead to a host of somatic and psychological problems. For some, the use of alcohol—or other drugs—may serve as a form of self-medication for stress. Violanti, Marshall, and Howe (1985) imply that police officers may drink in order to unconsciously relieve symptoms of stress—as a kind of coping strategy.

In fact, early police stress programs were directed almost exclusively at officers with alcohol problems. Among the earliest programs was one founded by Monsignor Joseph Dunne, a chaplain with the New York City police department. Between 1958 and 1966, Dunne fought the red tape and cynical attitudes of the police bureaucracy in order to establish an alcoholism program for officers.

A large portion of Dunne's problems stemmed from the social attitude that problem drinking was and individual's own problem and reflected a character flaw. Institutionally, the department handled drinking on the job or intoxication while on duty as a disciplinary problem. Violators were subject to suspensions, being docked 30 days' salary, and put on a year's probation. Because of the severity of these penalties and the stigma of having an alcohol problem, many supervisors resisted reporting their personnel when minor drinking incidents arose (e.g., the smell of alcohol on an officer's breath). In 1966, under a new and more forward-thinking administration, Dunne successfully organized an alcohol-counseling program.

Throughout the late 1960s, a number of police agencies began to take serious action to reduce the effects of police problem drinking. In New York, Philadelphia, and Chicago police departments established in-house counseling programs to work with alcoholic officers. As psychologists began working with these officers, they soon realized that alcoholism was not the problem, but merely a symptom. The problem was police stress.

More extensive counseling programs began to emerge, first on the West Coast in Los Angeles, under the directorship of Doctors Martin Reiser and William Kroes (Blackmore 1978). But, by the mid-1970s, most large city police departments had developed some type of counseling services for their officers. In some cases this meant simply arranging with a local psychologist or social worker to provide crisis intervention when needed. In some other departments, counseling services involved full-blown programs of stress management.

In 1974, the Boston Police stress program emerged, first as an alcohol counseling service, but eventually as a full-scale peer-counseling program. During the next 10 years, many other agencies innovated a variety of styles and types of counseling programs. Some, like those in the Detroit Police Department, operate as part of the agency's medical section and either provide officers with counseling or offer referrals to local counselors. Unfortunately, in many instances officers continue to resist seeking psychological services on their own. As a result, supervisors are still placed in a position of having to identify and direct officers to these services.

When officers are suspected of having a drinking problem, some agencies, such as the Denver Police Department, use closed-circuit television systems to record the officers and encourage them to join an in-house program (Territo and Vetter 1981). From this in-house program, many of the officers with more serious drinking problems are persuaded to enter a clinical treatment program at a local hospital.

Loo (1984) has suggested that, traditionally, police agencies have sought psychological services in a reactionary manner. Counseling services were implemented only in crisis situations or to resolve immediate problems, such as an officer's drug problem, low morale, and community complaints against police officers. Frequently, outside psychologists brought into these situations met with resistance and suspicion from the officers. The peer-counseling programs, which Boston and many other agencies have used, have enjoyed a fair amount of success as intervention strategies (Graf 1985). Klyver (1983), reporting on the Los Angeles Police Department's peer-counseling program, emphasizes the point that many officers with stress-related problems are unlikely to seek professional help. Yet, these same officers, argues Klyver, find it acceptable and comforting to discuss personal problems with colleagues or peer counselors.

ROLE CONFLICT AND STRESS

Among the many contributory factors to stress among police officers are role conflicts (Peak 1993). A **role conflict**, as used here, is defined as the expression of a set of patterned behavioral expectations associated with a given social position or status (father, mother, teacher, police officer, and so forth, (Thio 1997). Ralph Linton (1937) distinguished between status and roles by saying that individuals *occupy* a status, but they *perform* a role. Roles are interactionary because they define social behavior between people. However, roles are also relational because they define expectations of behavior between certain statuses. For example, one ideally defines the role associated with the status of parent in terms of behaviors or responsibilities associated with child rearing. In turn, one ideally defines the roles associated with such statuses as sons and daughters in terms of relational behaviors directed toward a parent.

Thus, roles are paired, and expected patterns of behaviors occur between these pairs (teachers and students, employer and employee, buyer and client, police officer and suspect, etc.) Since most individuals occupy many statuses or what is called a *status set*, they express a variety of roles. In fact, individuals often perform many roles while occupying a single status (Dabney and Berg 1996). This occurs because individuals perform variations in role behavior depending upon their relationship with the other person's role. Robert K. Merton (1968), a noted American sociologist, has defined these multiple roles attached to a single status as a *role set*.

Although several roles may be linked to a single status, they may not always be in accord. When this occurs, an individual can feel pulled in several different directions at once. Role conflict, then, is defined as this clash between roles corresponding to a single status. Ritzer's and Walczak's (1986) explanation for role overload similarly describes conflicting role expectations and resulting strain. In this instance, an individual is confronted with a role set filled with conflicting role expectations and finds it impossible to satisfy all of them

For example, a police officer might be assigned to a midnight-to-eight shift throughout the month of December. Traditionally, this officer may have spent Christmas Eve with the family at the home of his or her parents. Additionally, the officer may be assigned to work with an unmarried, inexperienced rookie who asked to work Christmas Eve hoping to get some good street experience.

In this hypothetical case the officer experiences conflict in the attempt to be a parent, spouse, dutiful child, breadwinner, and field-training officer. Each of these is a status that demands focused time and energy. Under the circumstances, however, it will be impossible to simultaneously perform each role fully. Because the officer will not be able to fully perform all of these roles, a degree of role strain will result, hence, stress.

Stress that results from role conflicts may be reduced in several ways. For example, one might emphasize one facet of one's roles while withdrawing from those that cause conflict. In the hypothetical officer's case, this might mean withdrawing from certain family responsibilities or perhaps changing occupations.

Another way some individuals manage role conflicts is through what Merton (1968) refers to as *insulation strategies*. In this case, an officer might compartmentalize his or her life. Essentially, this involves limiting certain statuses and role behaviors to certain settings or during only specific times of the day.

For instance, many people are capable of changing their complete persona as quickly as switching on or off the lights. How they speak and act in their home may be very different from how they speak and behave in their work environment. If a family member enters the work setting for a visit, the persona may return to the at-home version.

This persona switching is similar to how most people switch from their everyday speaking voice to a *telephone voice* when the phone rings. Even people who are in the middle of an angry argument usually shift octaves slightly and produce a more melodious sounding voice when the argument is interrupted by a telephone call; this is particularly so when the individual does not immediately know who the caller is. Unfortunately, another way to eliminate the stress caused by role conflict is to obliterate it with alcohol, drugs, or ultimately through suicide.

POLICE STRESS AND SUICIDE

Arthur Niederhoffer (1969) described the unusually high incidence of suicide among police officers 30 years ago. Neiderhoffer (1969:101) states:

> After the necessary adjustments are calculated, the suicide rate for males in the general New York City population is about 15 per 100,000. The average police [suicide] rate of 22.7 is almost exactly 50 percent more than this.

Suicide, as related to police stress, is not a simple matter. Although less common among youthful officers, it does occur. Typically, the suicide of a young officer can be associated with some serious family crisis that is complicated by the everyday stress of police work.

Among older officers, suicide is more likely to be associated with alcoholism or drug abuse, severe physical illness, being connected to some illegal activity, or approaching retirement. While little empirical evidence has been amassed about the connection between retirement and suicide among police officers, some researchers have suggested such a relationship exists (see Territo and Vetter 1981). It is, for example, fairly widely known that people from many occupations frequently become depressed shortly after retirement. This depression may lead to a lack of interest in physical appearance and well-being, increased drinking, and ultimately to suicide.

Suicides by police officers are a serious problem facing the law enforcement community. In a study in Buffalo, New York, police officer suicides were found to be 53 percent higher than those of other city workers. Furthermore, it has been established that police officers are eight times more likely to commit suicide than to be killed in a homicide, and three times more likely to commit suicide than to die in job-related accidents (Roberg and Kuykendall 1997).

There are a number of possible reasons for the appearance that a disproportionately high number of police commit suicide. These include the following:

1. *Access to firearms.* Police are trained in the use of and have ready access to firearms. When crisis situations arise or stress overpowers a police officer, the access to a gun would make suicide easy.
2. *Psychological effects from exposure to brutality.* Police must deal with the victims of considerable violence and mayhem. This frequent exposure to brutality and murder may cause serious psychological distress for some officers. In some cases this psychological distress may become overwhelming.
3. *Erratic shift work.* The long hours of erratic shifts can alter the officer's normal sleep patterns, creating both a physical and emotional drain and stress. In addition, the changing hours of shift work may interfere in normal patterns of social and family interaction, further complicating various role conflicts that arise in the officer's life.
4. *Public image of officers.* The media and the public are often vocal in their criticism and accusations of police wrong-doings. This leads many good officers to feel badly about themselves and their occupation. The officer may become alienated from his or her community as well as the other members of the department. Ultimately, these feelings may develop into deep depression and even self-loathing.

AIDS: A NEW POLICE STRESSOR

The research on police work stress regularly divides two main types of stress endemic to policing: acute or situation stress, and chronic stress (see Ellison and Genz 1978; Violanti, Marshal and Howe 1985). The first type of stress, **acute or situational stress**, includes stressors of a short-term nature or those that are circumstance/situation based. These may include exposure to some traumatic or grotesque homicide scene, child victimization, or exposure to some sudden physically dangerous situation. The second type of stress, **chronic stress**, includes stressors of a long-term nature. These are typically police functions based, or the frustration that result from various role conflicts, police lifestyles, and agency processes.

The preceding discussion in this chapter has examined these two categories of stress in general terms. At this point, the discussion shifts to consideration of a specific and increasingly serious chronic stressor: police officer encounters with individuals with AIDS.

During the recent past, AIDS (Acquired Immune Deficiency Syndrome) has become both an increasingly serious public health concern and an emotionally charged stressor for people working in the justice and health fields. A fair amount of the stress associated with AIDS stems from fear and misinformation about contamination and transmission of the disease.

AIDS affects police officers in several important ways. First, many of the suspects and offenders police regularly encounter in their work are people who fit the profiles of high risk for AIDS (prostitutes, intravenous drug abusers). Consequently, street level law enforcement and corrections officers are concerned that they, too, may fall into an increased risk category for AIDS contamination. Second, in their effort to alert Americans to the seriousness of AIDS as a public health concern, the U.S. Surgeon General, various state departments of health, the Red Cross, and the mass media have inadvertently terrorized many police officers and health care workers. Recent research on AIDS transmission has shown that the risk of contamination from causal contacts such as saliva or biting is nearly impossible. But many law enforcement officers, convinced by the earlier scare campaigns, and reports in 1997 of a single case of alleged casual transmission, continue to perceive themselves as being in extreme risk for contamination.

Third, law enforcement officers could serve as a vital educational conduit through which accurate information about AIDS could flow to high-risk groups they encounter: intravenous drug abusers, prostitutes, and homosexuals. But first, the fear and misinformation under which many police officers currently labor must be cleared up (Hammett 1987a).

Finally, police are potentially affected by AIDS if an officer contracts the disease and continues working as a police officer. The fear of contamination already is very high among many police officers. The added pressure of perceived risks from working with someone with AIDS amplifies concern. To combat this potential problem, departmental policy and community relations problems must identify ways of educating officers and the community (Blumberg 1990).

Ironically, and as will be discussed in greater detail later, police officers and health care workers are as or perhaps more likely to contract hepatitis-B than they are AIDS. Hepatitis-B is a highly contagious infection transmitted by blood which results in liver damage, and frequently, in death. In fact, most of the law enforcement procedures concerning AIDS and handling people believed to be AIDS contaminated, are derived from protocols from the U.S. Department of Health and Human Service, and the U.S. Centers for Disease Control for hepatitis-B.

THE NEED FOR AIDS TRAINING FOR POLICE

One of the ways that police agencies can effectively respond to the problems of AIDS in their community, is with AIDS training for police personnel and staff. Among the important areas that training should address are the following:

- Timely information about AIDS and AIDS contagion.
- Frequently updated information should be regularly provided to personnel through in-service training sessions. Training modules during the academy are insufficient and fail to provide adequate updates and information changes.
- Printed information should be regularly provided to officers and staff. This material should be kept up-to-date.

- Presentations from knowledgeable people in the community should be encouraged. Having a presenter offer information in the form of a lecture, seminar, or even an informal discussion allows officers to formulate and ask questions. In turn, this may clear misinformation.
- All training related to AIDS should be focused on specific policing issues and situations. The purpose of these training elements should not be pieces of generic information about AIDS. Appropriate topics might include arrest and takedown procedures, searches, CPR and first-responder care, handling of evidence, clean-up at crime scenes, handling and disposal of contaminated materials, etc.
- While training programs at the academy should discourage complacency, it should likewise avoid alarmist tactics, folk information, or other forms of misinformation.

Given the present discussion, a natural question is "Exactly what is the nature of AIDS and what are the implications for police personnel?" Let us begin with the obvious first concern, defining AIDS.

AIDS DEFINED

AIDS is a disease characterized by an increased deficiency in the natural immune system of an individual, leaving the person highly susceptible to a wide range of opportunistic infections and other diseases (Hammett 1987a). People with AIDS become vulnerable to various health crises and illnesses that are normally not life-threatening to people with healthy immune systems.

AIDS is caused by a virus called **Human Immunodeficiency Virus (HIV)**. AIDS infects and destroys white blood cells, which are normally used by the body to fend off infections and illness. Infection with the virus HIV does not immediately lead to AIDS. Many people infected with the virus remain in perfectly good health for years without developing symptoms. It is not known whether all will actually develop AIDS. Others may grow more susceptible to infection and illness by varying degrees. These complications and illnesses are sometimes referred to as **AIDS-Related Complex (ARC)**. Although drug experiments and research are have recently shown some success at slowing the acceleration of the disease (Brittanica 1997), and the disease is preventable, once active it is almost always fatal (Koop 1987; Hammett 1987b).

TRANSMISSION OF AIDS

Although lethal if contracted, the AIDS virus is actually quite difficult to transmit outside of the body. The virus can be destroyed and disinfected by heat, many common household cleansers, bleaches, and by washing with soap and hot water.

In a manner remarkably similar to the transmission of hepatitis-B, the AIDS virus is primarily transmitted through exposure to contaminated blood, semen, and vaginal secretions. The indisputable means of transmission are through unprotected sexual intercourse and sharing of hypodermic needles among intravenous drug users. Until the early 1990s, women in the United States who were not IV drug abusers were not believe to be at much risk for HIV infection (in sharp contrast with several underdeveloped nations). However, today, it is clear that they are very much involved in the overall picture of AIDS, and potentially in transmission to their children (Medical Health Annuals 1989; Britannica 1997).

Finally, although in enormously decreased numbers since the mid-1980s, transmissions from contaminated blood used in transfusions during operations continue to appear.

The AIDS virus continues to be extremely unlikely to be transmitted through casual contacts such as sharing kitchen utensils, kissing, having saliva spat upon the skin—with cuts or abrasions—shaking hands, urine splashes, or other forms of non-sexual contacts (Hammett 1987b; Berg and Berg 1988; Lifson 1988; Blumberg 1990). There have been no documented cases of police officers, paramedics, correctional officers, or firefighters becoming infected during the course of their normal duties.

In fact, with the exception of a very small number of health care workers who attribute their contracting AIDS to having been accidentally pricked with contaminated needles or other exposures to blood, there are no reports of AIDS transmission from occupational activities (Ross and Krieger 1989). Even among these instances, there has been some controversy over whether some of these health care workers may not also have fit known high-risk groups (intravenous drug users, homosexuals, or sexually active with partners carrying the AIDS virus).

In spite of increasing numbers of identified cases of AIDS, the early breakdown of groups at highest risk to contract HIV has remained exceedingly stable. According to the U.S. Centers for Disease Control, as of March 1987, homosexual and bisexual males remained the largest category of people at risk and account for about 66 percent of all identified cases. Intravenous drug abusers compose the next largest risk category, accounting for 17 percent. Another 8 percent are represented by people who were both intravenous drug abusers and homosexual or bisexual males. Heterosexuals whose partners fell into one or another of the preceding categories comprised 4 percent of known cases. Hemophiliacs and transfusion recipients who contracted HIV represented 1 percent and 2 percent of the cases, respectively. The remaining 4 percent represented cases of incomplete information about risk due to death or refusal to identify with a particular category.

Most research continues to show that heterosexual transmissions of HIV infection is still considerably less common than among other higher risk groups in the United States and Europe (*Medical Health Annuals* 1989, 1990; Britannica 1997). Women, children, and heterosexual transmissions, however, do represent a substantial portion of the evolving global AIDS problem, especially in underdeveloped nations.

IMPLICATIONS FOR LAW ENFORCEMENT

AIDS has rapidly become a central concern in the law enforcement community. In one study of 35 police agencies, 33 reported that officers had voiced serious concerns about AIDS and their duties as officers (Hammett 1987b). This same study indicates that patrol officers from 94 percent of the departments surveyed reported anxiety about their potential exposure to AIDS.

Most police academies nationally now offer training designed to educate new police officers in AIDS safety. In some academy curricula, this may arise as part of the first-responder/first-aid training. In other academies, this may arise as a separate and specific course or series of lectures (Berg 1990). Many departments' in-service programs for officer survival have also augmented the training to include AIDS safety. A variety of AIDS-related concerns to law enforcement personnel and some appropriate educational elements are shown in Table 16.4.

Table 16.4   *AIDS-Related Law Enforcement Concerns*

Questions or Concerns	Answers
Are human bites likely to result in transmission of HIV?	Usually, the person doing the biting receives the victim's blood, and not the reverse. Since saliva is a poor medium for the HIV virus to be transmitted, it would seem most unlikely that a bite alone will result in infection. The wound should be made to bleed and then washed thoroughly.
Can spitting transmit the disease?	Viral transmission from saliva alone has received no support in the research literature. It is virtually an impossibility.
Do urine or feces of infected people contain the HIV virus?	Although HIV virus has been identified in the urine of infected people, the concentrations have been so small that transmission from this medium is usually judged impossible. There has been no documentation of HIV virus being found in feces.
Will cutting oneself with a contaminated needle necessarily lead to HIV infection?	Although even a single puncture could result in transmission, the majority of needle situations show risk of infection is very low. Receipt of repeated punctures or cuts from sharp contaminated objects, however, may lead to infection with the virus HIV.
Can one become infected during CPR or when performing other first-responder activities?	Although there are only minimal risks that one will become contaminated by performing CPR, masks and airways are strongly urged. During other first-responder activities, officers should be careful to avoid blood-to-blood contacts, and should keep open wounds covered. Rubber or latex gloves are strongly recommended
Are transmissions possible from causal contacts such as kissing, sharing food utensils, hand-shakes and the like?	There have been no documented cases of AIDS transmission as a result of solely casual contacts.
Is it possible to become contaminated by touching dried blood?	There have been no instances in which contamination has been traced to exposure to dried blood (such as during crime scene investigations). The process of drying appears to inactivate the HIV virus. Nonetheless, caution dictates wearing protective gloves and masks if the potential contact with even dried blood is great.

STRESS FROM PERCEPTIONS OF AIDS

There are essentially three areas where the threat of AIDS transmission operates as a stressor for police officers. These anxiety-producing situations include street apprehensions and searches, the lock-up, and during first-responder calls.

Street Apprehensions and Searches

Whenever an officer finds it necessary to make a formal arrest, there is the possibility of resistance or assaultive behavior on the part of the offender. As indicated in the preceding section, many of the injuries sustained by police officers each year occurring in connection with such apprehensions are from personal weapons—including teeth. The fact that it is extremely unlikely that for an officer to become contaminated from a simple bite wound from an AIDS-infected person is of little comfort to most police officers (Berg 1990).

In fact, it has been suggested by some researchers that for such a bite wound to have serious potential for contamination, the assailant would need to have a mouthful of contaminated blood and bite with sufficient ferocity to assure some of the contaminated blood gained entry into the officer's bloodstream. Although the HIV virus has been clinically isolated in saliva and tears, it is in such low concentrations as to render them ineffective as transmission media (Berg 1990; Blumberg 1990).

During searches, however, officers must be concerned about the possibility of being stuck by an unprotected and potentially contaminated hypodermic needle. Many officers will ask a suspect as they pat them down whether there is any need to worry about being stuck by a needle of any other sharp foreign object. Nonetheless, officers must use extreme care when frisking or otherwise searching a suspect.

Police Lock-ups

Another area of concern for many police officers involves police lock-ups and holding cell facilities. In addition to fears about bites and other assaults, officers tend to be anxious about an AIDS-infected person's threats or attempts to intimidate other prisoners. Also, there are concerns about contamination from being intentionally splashed with urine or spat upon by AIDS-infected prisoners. As with saliva, urine, while carrying very low concentrations of the HIV virus, is an unlikely transmission mechanism. No documented cases of AIDS have been linked to contaminated urine being splashed on someone.

First-Responder Calls

First-responder calls or the giving of immediate and temporary first aid to a victim, are fairly common for police officers. In some jurisdictions, local police agencies also house primary paramedic response teams or operate emergency ambulance services. Among the most stress-producing elements associated with fear of AIDS transmission involves cardiopulmonary resuscitation (CPR).

Even before the threat of AIDS contamination, performing CPR on people was somewhat problematic for many police officers. For example, it is not uncommon for people to vomit as they regain consciousness following CPR. In some situations, the vomit may contain blood as well as stomach contents. Because of this, a variety of *airways*, or mouth-masks with filters and one-way valves, are used. These one-way valves permit the officer to blow air in, but will not permit fluids from being expelled into the mouth of the officer—theoretically. Unfortunately, many officers remain dubious about the effectiveness of these masks even after repeated demonstrations.

Another element of anxiety related to first-responder activities concerns the treatment of bleeding and bandaging of wounds. Here, the anxiety involves concern over having contaminated blood come in contact with either one's skin or clothing. There are frequent instances when officers do come in contact with people injured in an automobile accident, hunting accident, or during the course of a crime. Because of frequency, the potential for coming into contact with contaminated blood might be fairly high.

Since people with AIDS should not be expected to wear a big scarlet "A" around their necks, it is impossible to know when an injured and bleeding victim carries the AIDS virus. Like many health care facilities, police departments have begun to adopt treatment protocols that assume that people are AIDS-infected. Often this includes the use of rubber or plastic gloves, protective masks, and airways when treating all people. It may mean sterilizing areas on the ground where blood has spilled with bleach.

HANDLING PEOPLE WITH AIDS: AGENCY PROCEDURES

In 1986, police agencies began to respond to the concerns and anxieties arising among police officers by issuing AIDS-related training bulletins and protocols (Minneapolis Police Department 1986; Skokie Police Department 1987; Baltimore County Police Department 1987). Typically, these notices were drawn from the agency's general communicable/infectious disease policies and guidelines and often borrowed heavily from procedures outlined for hepatitis-B.

Law enforcement officers, however, remain somewhat reluctant to provide hands-on service to known AIDS-infected people. At this time there is no evidence of any police officer falling victim to AIDS strictly from performance of police duties. Yet, the perception of risk about contracting AIDS is fast becoming among the most serious stressors facing police officers today.

Ironically, while law enforcement is perceived by many potential police officers as fraught with risk and danger, AIDS seems somehow more ominous then many other threats officers must face. The moment an individual becomes a police officer, he or she assumes a certain amount of this risk. Indeed, some officers are injured and killed in the line of duty. Individuals who enter law enforcement as an occupation have weighed these risks. The anxiety about AIDS that many officers feel today, then, must be weighed along with the other kinds of risks. Importantly, the fear of contamination does not free officers from their obligation to perform necessary police duties.

POLICE OFFICERS WITH AIDS

One question often left unasked in discussions on AIDS and the police is, "What should be done about police officers who contract the disease?" Mark Blumberg (1989) suggests that historically, police agencies have not hired openly homosexual people for police positions. Overt bans on homosexual applicants are both discriminatory and illegal in some states. In the past, institutionalized discrimination because an applicant was believed to be gay systematically prevented many homosexuals from entering policing. Even when departments did not openly or institutionally ban homosexuals, various elements in the recruitment and training of recruits may have been used as a means of screening out homosexual individuals (Blumberg 1989). Some agencies, however, actively seek homosexual recruits. San Francisco, for example, because of its large gay population, periodically recruits officers form the gay community (Shilts 1980:32–33). Active recruitment of gay officers, however, occurs in very few police departments. As a result, it is unlikely that many openly practicing homosexuals would seek employment as police officers or manage to secure positions if they did. Although based upon conjecture, it seems likely there are secret or closet homosexuals, just as there are in other occupations (Blumberg 1989). As a result, the potential for members of this high-risk AIDS group, practicing homosexuals entering policing, while not great, exists.

The other possible high-risk group that might enter policing is intravenous drug users. Refusal to hire drug abusers would not create any legal problems for police agencies. It has become a common practice in many police departments to refuse employment to applicants who have ever used heroin, cocaine, and even marijuana. These refusals may even occur when the drug use was experimental and happened many years before applying to the department. Although this later category of one-time, but discontinued, drug-user applicant has caused considerable policy debate among police administrators, no challenges of this position have yet occurred in the courts.

What one observes, then, is police departments generally are employing very few people who fall into the current high-risk for AIDS categories. In the face of this, it is understandable that police departments have not previously devoted a great deal of attention to the issue of police officers with AIDS. However, given that this disease has continuously grown in its spread pattern, and increases have occurred among women and heterosexual couples (where one spouse fell into a risk category) infected police officers are potentially inevitable.

Therefore, department policies concerning police officers infected with AIDS must begin to surface.

Essentially, there are two major issues police administrators and communities need to address regarding their response to officers with AIDS. First, what threat does the infected officer actually present to colleagues or the community (Blumberg 1989)? Second, how are community residents likely to respond to an infected officer, should they learn of his or her illness? Because of the futuristic nature of this problem, one is forced to speculate on possible resolutions to these concerns.

Since it has been established that AIDS is not spread through casual contacts that officers typically have with one another, police administrators must work to educate coworkers of the infected officer in order to reduce their fears. In this regard, police organizations are really no different from other work places where AIDS-infected personnel have been identified during the past several years. Through carefully planned training programs, many organizations have succeeded in reducing the fears of their employees.

Speculating on how the community might respond to the infected officer's presence is a bit more difficult. As previously mentioned, most daily work routines of police officers with coworkers will not extent beyond casual contacts with one another. This is not always the case with citizen-police situations. Police officers called to the scene of a traffic or industrial accident may have to assist people with serious gashes or open wounds. There is, therefore, a remote possibility that an infected officer could, under certain circumstances, contaminate the wounded person. Again, although possible, there as yet have been no recorded transmissions of the AIDS virus by contaminated persons administering first aid to someone. Nonetheless, educational programs sponsored by the police are likely to be the best method of allaying community residents' fears.

AIDS AND THE LAW

In addition to considering general procedures for working with or handling offenders who may be AIDS victims, law enforcement officers must be mindful of the law as it relates to AIDS. The bulk of law related to AIDS originally derives from those statutes that relate to discrimination in work places and assembly in public places, while some also concerns privacy and confidentiality (Luxenberg and Guild 1989).

Most jurisdictions have made it illegal to be fired from one's job strictly because of AIDS. Typically, statutes provide that so long as an individual is able to perform the tasks for which he or she had originally been hired, the person is entitled to continue working. It also is unlawful in most jurisdictions to refuse retail service to an individual on the basis of their being believed to be infected with the AIDS virus. Perhaps a more interesting trend evolving in the law, however, involves the criminalization of certain activities performed by people known to have AIDS. For example, there have been a number of cases where AIDS-infected prostitutes have been charged with attempted homicide or felony assault for having engaged in sexual acts without protection, and without warning their clients. Similarly, there have been cases where people, knowing they were AIDS-infected, sought to sell their blood to blood banks, and have been charged with attempted murder. People with AIDS who intentionally infect others have also been charged with assault (Associated Press 1987), and attempted murder. One of the more publicized cases involved James Vernall Moore, who was convicted of assault in 1987. The facts of the Moore case are as follows: Moore was a federal prisoner being held in Rochester, Minnesota. He had recently learned that he was positive for HIV. Although he was fully aware of the deadliness of his disease and how HIV could be transmitted, he bit two correctional officers during a scuffle (*U.S. v. Moore*, 1987). Moore was found guilty of assault and on appeal, Moore's conviction was upheld (Luxenberg, Guild, and Duber 1990).

On July 27, 1988, a military court found Private Adrian Morris Jr. guilty of two AIDS-related court-martial charges. Morris was convicted on charges of discrediting the Army and of sodomy with a former soldier. Morris had tested positive for the AIDS virus and subsequently failed to use condoms during sex. He was accused of threatening the health of his sexual partners by the military court (Doherty 1988). What impact the Morris case and the Moore case will have on future cases and to what extent the law will continues to criminalize such activities, will remain for the courts to determine. However, many states have enacted formal criminal statutes to deal with cases of reckless behavior by AIDS-infected people.

SUMMARY

This chapter began by introducing the notion of police work as a potentially hazardous occupation. The chapter points out that the actual dangers, while certainly real, may not be nearly as detrimental to the health of officers, as their perceptions of these dangers. In other words, the idea of certain dangers produces among officers a powerful emotional effect called stress. In turn, stress may contribute to police officers' developing a variety of somatic and psychological afflictions.

Stress was described as creating problems in both the everyday life of many police officers, as well as during the performance of their police duties. In order to combat these stress-related problems, many agencies have developed counseling programs. The chapter details how, in some agencies, these programs operate as integral parts of the medical unit. But, in some other agencies, the counseling programs are independent of organizational constraints and operate more as peer counseling programs.

Among the various coping strategies to which many officers have turned, alcoholism has long provided one means to adapt to stress. In fact, it was chiefly in an effort to treat officers with drinking problems that many early counseling programs began.

As if the traditional stressors of danger, boredom, shift work, and the like were not sufficient, a new and potentially lethal stressor has recently arisen—AIDS. This chapter discusses the current knowledge about AIDS and its transmission and describes several important implications AIDS cases hold for police personnel. These implications include perceived risks associated with street apprehensions, police lock-ups, and first-responder calls. The chapter concludes by suggesting the need to balance police officers' dysfunctional-alarmist panic about AIDS with comprehensive educational information about actual risks of contamination. These educational programs, as the chapter indicates, are necessary both in the communities and police agencies.

REFERENCES

Albanese, Jay. *The Police Officer's Dilemma: Balancing Peace, Order and Individual Rights.* Buffalo, N.Y.: Great Ideas, 1988.

Associated Press. "AIDS Patient Who Bit, Guilty of Lethal Assault." *Kansas City Times,* 25 June, 1987:A2.

Ayres, Richard M. *Preventing Law Enforcement Stress: The Organization's Role.* Alexandria, Va.: National Sheriff's Association, 1990:4–5.

Barker, Thomas, Ronald D. Hunter, and Jeffrey P. Rush. *Police Systems and Practices: An Introduction.* Englewood Cliffs, N.J.: Prentice-Hall, 1994.

Bayley, David H. "The Tactical Choices of Police Patrol Officers." *Journal of Criminal Justice,* 14(1986):329–348.

Bayley, David H., and James Garofalo. "The Management of Violence by Police Patrol Officers." *Criminology,* 27(1989):1–26.

Bennett, Richard R. "Becoming Blue: A Longitudinal Study of Police Recruit Occupational Socialization." *Police Science and Administration,* 12(1984):47–58.

Bennett, Richard R., and Theodore Greenstein. "The Police Personality: A Test of the Predispositional Model." *Journal of Police Science and Administration,* 3, 1975:439–445.

Berg, Bruce L. "Police Officer Stress and AIDS." Paper presented at the American Academy of Criminal Justice Sciences. Denver, Colo., March 1990.

Berg, Bruce L., and Jill Berg. "AIDS in Prison: The Social Construction of a Reality." *International Journal of Offender Therapy and Comparative Criminology,* 32, 1988:17–28.

Blackmore, John. "Are Police Allowed to Have Problems of Their Own?" *Police Magazine,* 1(1978):47–55.

Blackmore, John. "Police Stress." In *Policing Society.* W. Clinton Terry III. (ed.) New York: Wiley, 1985:393–399.

Blumberg, Mark. "The AIDS Epidemic and the Police." In *Critical Issues in Policing.* Roger G. Dunham and Geoffrey P. Alpert, (eds.) Prospect Heights, Ill.: Waveland, 1989.

Blumberg, Mark. *AIDS: The Impact on the Criminal Justice System.* Columbus, Oh.: Merrill Publishing Company, 1990.

Boucher, Geoff. "Long Road Leads to Suspect." *Los Angeles Times,* 31 July, 1997:1, A20.

Britannica Book of the Year 1997. Chicago, Ill.: Encyclopaedia Britannica, Inc., 1997.

"Communicable Disease Policy Guidelines and Procedures." *Department Training Manual of Procedures.* Towson, Md.: Baltimore County Police Department, 1987.

Cox, Steven M. *Police: Practices, Perspectives, Problems.* Boston: Allyn and Bacon, 1996.

Cullen, Francis T., Bruce G. Link, Lawrence F. Travis III, and Terrence Lemming. "Paradox in Policing: A Note on Perceptions of Danger." *Journal of Police Science and Administration,* 11(1983):457–462.

Cullen, Francis, T., Terrence Lemming, Bruce G. Link, and John Wozniak. "The Impact of Social Supports on Police Stress." *Criminology,* 23(1985):502–522.

Dabney, Dean A., and Bruce L. Berg. "The Active Interview: Considerations for Future Crime and Deviance Research." Presented at the American Society of Criminology, Chicago, Illinois, November 1996.

Doherty, Tim. "Soldier Convicted." *USA Today,* 28 July, 1988:3A.

Ellison, K. W., and J. S. Genz. "Police Officers as Burned-Out Samaritan." *FBI Law Enforcement Bulletin,* 47(1978):1–7.

Farmer, R. E. "Clinical and Managerial Implications of Stress Research on the Police." *Journal of Police Science and Administration,* 17(1990):205–218.

Fried, Joseph P. "Officer Guarding Drug Witness Is Slain." *The New York Times,* 27 February, 1988:1,34.

Fyfe, James. "Police/Citizen Violence Reduction Project." *FBI Bulletin,* May 1989:19–23.

Goldstein, Herman. *Policing a Free Society.* Cambridge, Mass.: Ballinger, 1977.

Goolkasian, Gail A., Ronald W. Geddes, and William DeJong. "Coping with Police Stress" In *Critical Issues in Policing: Contemporary Readings.* Robert G. Dunham and Geoffrey P. Alpert (eds.) Prospect, Heights, Ill.: Waveland Press, 1989.

Graf, Francis A. "The Relationship Between Social Support and Occupational Stress Among Police Officers." *Journal of Police Science and Administration,* 14, 1985:178–86.

Hale, Charles D. *Police Patrol: Operations and Management.* 2d ed. Englewood Cliffs, N.J.: Prentice Hall, Inc., 1994.

Hammett, Theodore M. *AIDS and the Law Enforcement Officer: Concerns and Policy Responses.* U.S. Department of Justice, National Institute of Justice, Washington, D.C.: GPO, 1987a.

Hammett, Theodore M. *AIDS and the Law Enforcement Officer.* U.S. Department of Justice, National Institute of Justice. Washington, D.C.: GPO, 1987b.

Klyver, N. "Peer Counseling for Police Personnel: A Dynamic Program in the Los Angeles Police Department." *Police Chief,* 50(1983):66–68.

Koop, C. Everett. *The Surgeon General's Report on Acquired Immune Deficiency Syndrome.* U.S. Department of Health and Human Services. Washington, D.C.: GPO, 1987.

Kroes, William H. *Society's Victim, The Policeman: An Analysis of Job Stress in Policing.* Springfield, Ill.: Thomas, 1976.

Kroes, William H., Bruce Margolis, and Joseph J. Hurrell Jr. "Job Stress in Policemen." *Journal of Police Science and Administration,* 2(1974):145–55.

Leonard, V. A., and Harry W. More. *Police Organization and Management.* Mineola, N.Y.: Foundation, 1987.

Lewis, Diane. "Police Arrest 2nd Suspect in Officer's Death." *The Boston Globe,* 20 February, 1988:1,22.

Lifson, Alan R. "Do Alternative Modes for Transmission of Human Immunodeficiency Virus Exist? A Review." *Journal of the American Medical Association,* 259(1988):1353–1356.

Linton, Ralph. *The Study of Man.* New York: Appleton-Century, 1937.

Loo, R. "Occupational Stress in the Enforcement Profession." *Canada's Mental Health* 1984:10–13. Cited by Francis A. Graf in "The Relationship Between Social Support and Occupational Stress Among Police Officers." *Journal of Police Science and Administration,* 14(1985):178–186.

Luxenberg, Joan, and Thomas E. Guild. "Health Privacy and AIDS." Paper Presented at the annual meeting of the American Society of Criminology, Reno, Nevada, November 1989.

Luxenberg, Joan, Thomas E. Guild, and Robin A. Duber. "Criminal Liabilities in the Transmission of AIDS." Paper presented at the annual meeting of the Academy of Criminal Justice Sciences, Denver, Colorado, March 1990.

Medical Health Annual. "AIDS." Chicago: Encyclopaedia Britannica, 1988.

———."AIDS: The Pattern is Changing." Chicago: Encyclopaedia Britannica, 1989:52–61.

———."AIDS." Chicago: Encyclopaedia Britannica, 1990.

Merton, Robert K. *Social Theory and Social Structure.* New York: The Free Press, 1968.

Minneapolis Police Department. "Infectious Diseases: What is AIDS?" *Training Journal Minneapolis Police Department,* No.9. Minneapolis: Minneapolis Police Department Training Unit, 1986.

Neiderhoffer, Arthur. *Behind the Shield: The Police in Urban Society.* New York: Doubleday, 1969.

Peak, Kenneth J. *Policing America.* Englewood Cliffs, N.J.: Prentice-Hall, Inc., 1993.

Reiser, Martin. *Practical Psychology for Police Officers.* Springfield, Ill.: Thomas, 1973.

Ritzer, George, and David Walczak. *Working: Conflict and Change.* 3d ed. Englewood Cliffs, N.J.: Prentice-Hall, 1986.

Roberg, Roy R., and Jack Kuykendall. *Police Management.* 2d ed. Los Angeles, Calif.: Roxbury Publishing Company, 1997.

Ross, Susan O., and John N. Krieger. "The Latest Studies on Occupational Exposure to HIV." *American Journal of Nursing,* November 1989:1424–1425.

Saper, Marshall. "Police Wives: The Hidden Pressure." *The Police Chief,* 47(1980):28–29.

Schwartz, Jeffrey A., and Cynthia B. Schwartz. "The Personal Problems of then Police Officer: A Plea for Action." In *Job Stress and the Police Officer: Identifying Stress Reduction and Techniques.* William H. Kroes, and Joseph J. Hurrell (eds.) Washington, D.C.: GPO, 1975:135–316.

Selye, Hans. *Stress Without Distress.* New York: Lippincott, 1975.

Shilts, Randy. "Police Come to Terms with the Gay Community." *Police Magazine,* January 1980:28–36.

Shuster, Beth, and Dough Smith. "Hours of Terror: Police Kill Two Suspects After Foiled Bank Heist." *Los Angeles Times,* 1 March, 1997:1, A29.

Skokie Police Department. "Acquired Immune Deficiency Syndrome." *Training Bulletin,* No.87-27. Skokie, Ill.: 1987.

Stratton, John B. "Police Stress, Part I: An Overview." *The Police Chief,* 45(1978):58–62.

Territo, Leonard, and Harold J. Vetter. "Stress and Police Personnel." *Journal of Police Science and Administration,* 9(1981):195–207.

Terry, W. Clinton III. *Policing Society*. New York: Wiley, 1985.

Thio, Alex. *Sociology: A Brief Introduction*. New York: Longman, 1997.

Thomas, William I., and Dorothy Swaine. *The Child in America*. New York: Knopf, 1928.

Violanti, John M., James R. Marshall, and Barbara Howe. "Stress, Coping, and Alcohol Use: The Police Connection." *Journal of Police Science and Administration*, 13(1985):106–10.

Walker Samuel. "Employment of Black and Hispanic Police Officers: Trends in Fifty Largest Cities." *Review of Applied Urban Research*, 11(1983).

Wallace, L. "Stress and Its Impact on the Law Enforcement Officer." *Campus Law Enforcement Journal*, 8(1978):36–40.

Whitaker, Gordon P. "What Is Patrol Work?" *Police Studies*, 4(1982):13–22.

CASE CITED

U.S. v. Moore, 669 F. Supp. 289 (D. Minn., 1987), 846 F. 2d. 1163 (8th Cir. 1988).

QUESTIONS FOR REVIEW

Objective #1:

- Where do police recruits get their basic image of police work as dangerous or adventurous?
- Of the over 600,000 sworn full-time officers in 1994, how many were killed in the line of duty?
- How can perceptions of danger be as serious in their consequences as actual dangerous situations?

Objective #2:

- How might one define "personal weapons?"

Objective #3:

- What are some of the basic causes of police stress?
- How does stress effect the health of a police officer?

Objective #4:

- What is meant by external stressors?
- What are individual stressors?

Objective #5:

- Why might a police administrator use eustress in his or her department?

Objective #6:

- How do some officers handle or adapt to their work-related stress?

Objective #7:

- Who was Monsignor Joseph Dunne?
- What is meant by a "peer-counseling" program?

Objective #8:

- What is meant by the term "role-conflict?"

Objective #9:

- What role does stress play in promoting police suicides?

Objective #10:

- Why are many police officers worried about contracting AIDS while on the job?
- How likely is it that an officer will contract AIDS from normal activities during a policing career?

17 Police Professionalism

CHAPTER OBJECTIVES

After reading this chapter you should be able to:

1. List traditional professions.
2. Define what is meant by the term professional.
3. Explain the concept of shadow-box professionalism.
4. Detail the evolution of police unions.
5. Explain what is meant by a police work slowdown, and a police department speedup.
6. Describe the purpose of the Law Enforcement Assistance Agency (LEAA).
7. Consider the purpose of police department accreditation.
8. Detail the origins of the concept of accreditation.
9. Suggest the benefits of police department accreditation.
10. Indicate the detriments from police department accreditation.

PROFESSIONAL POLICE OFFICERS OR POLICE PROFESSIONALS?

Throughout the twentieth century, policing as a social institution has undergone many organizational reforms. Often when one thinks of these changes, one simultaneously thinks of administrative efforts to make the police more professional. One might even suggest that many of the police reforms of the recent past occurred because of intentional efforts to achieve police professionalism.

The obvious question to ask next is, "Exactly what is police professionalism?" In fact, the nature of what police professionalism actually constitutes has

KEY TERMS

professional
new professionals
shadow-box professionalism

police work slowdown
police department speedups
Law Enforcement Assistance
   Agency (LEAA)

Law Enforcement Assistance
   Program (LEAP)
accreditation

been debated for decades. Many textbooks, including this one, will credit O. W. Wilson and August Vollmer as having spurred modern American policing in the direction of professionalism. But an answer to the question—what does police professionalism represent?—is not always offered. This chapter will examine what police researchers generally hold as a definition for police professionalism, as well as a number of related areas and factors. Among these related areas will be discussions of police unions, accreditation of police agencies, and the privatization of law enforcement services.

PROFESSION VERSUS THE PROFESSIONAL

To better understand the movement toward police professionalism, one must begin with a distinction between the concept of a professional in the traditional sense and a professional in the vernacular sense. When one hears the term "profession," several occupations are likely to come to mind: doctors, lawyers, professors, and even the clergy. These occupations have been long recognized as professions, and make up what one might call the traditional professions. Yet, in everyday language we often speak about a much wider variety of jobs as professional. One regularly hears basketball players and other athletes called professionals. Similarly, it is common to call a professional plumber to install your boiler, and a professional electrician to hang and hook up your ceiling fan. The term **professional**, then, has come to represent two distinct categories of occupation. First, and as the term is used most often in common parlance, professionals are people with specialized skills and training. Because these individuals possess specialized knowledge and skill, they receive salaries for their expertise. In short, professionals are the opposite of amateurs.

The second usage of the term "professional" directs attention to the more traditional connotation of the word. In this second case, the term refers to a specialized white-collar occupation that requires considerable formal education, membership or entrance standards, a body of theoretical knowledge, adherence to a system of socially regulated rules or a code of ethics, and the ability to self-regulate and sanction members (Goode 1960; Ritzer 1972; Swanson, Territo, and Taylor 1993; Barker, Hunter, and Rush 1994; Cox 1996).

Beyond the traditional professions, several other occupations have emerged as **new professionals**. These include such occupational categories as architects, social workers, teachers (elementary and secondary), nurses, bankers, stockbrokers, and accountants. These new professionals closely approximate the basic characteristics generally associated with the traditional professions. But, because high social status and prestige are commonly associated with the term profession, many occupations during the past several decades have sought to capture the title of professional. Police are a prime occupation that has diligently worked to this end. In spite of these efforts, and earnest attempts to move law enforcement in the direction of a profession, law enforcement has achieved little more that what might be called shadow-box professionalism.

SHADOW-BOX PROFESSIONALISM

The concept of **shadow-box professionalism** refers to the idea that some occupations attempt to professionalize by imitating attributes of more traditional professions. But rather than successfully replicating various necessary characteristics, shadows or near replications occur. In some respects, there may be a surface resemblance to a profession, but one that does not consistently hold up under the light of scrutiny. The light removes the casting of shadows. In the case of policing, attempts to effect professionalization have met with both resistance from within and without the institution of policing.

In the 1930s, the International Association of Chiefs of Police (IACP) established a committee for the professionalization of police. This committee put forth the notion that a profession should consist of five elements:

- An organized body of knowledge, constantly augmented and redefined, with special techniques based thereon.
- Facilities for formal training in this body of knowledge and procedure. Recognized qualifications for membership in, and identification with the profession.
- An organization that includes a substantial number of members qualified to practice the profession and to exercise an influence on the maintenance of professional standards.
- A code of ethics that, in general, defines the relationship of the members of the profession to the public and to other practitioners within the group and normally recognizes an obligation to render services on other than exclusively economic consideration. (Mannle and Hirschel 1988:300).

Although the theoretical end of this plan was quite noble and altruistic, the implementation was not. Typically, when the topic of police professionalism is discussed—even among police officers—financial compensation and working conditions are prime factors. The principal impetus to professionalize law enforcement has long been entangled with the attempt to increase the financial compensation for police work.

As a result, IACP's establishing of a code of ethics for police officers in 1957 tended to "window-dress" the general attempt to professionalize policing. Similarly, the establishment of uniform minimum standards for entrance did not actually begin to occur until sometime after 1964 and has not been fully accomplished yet. There also is little if any police theory that originates from the police professional exclusively. Rather, most police theory borrows from or identifies itself outright as originating from other fields and disciplines (psychology, sociology, and other cognate disciplines).

The question of whether policing is or should be considered a profession in the traditional sense, then, has been complicated by these and other factors. Among these other factors is the reality that policing involves both training and education and that these are not synonymous terms. In the case of training, police must acquire certain technical skills, such as how to direct traffic, how safely and accurately to use firearms, how safely and defensively to drive at high speeds, how to access information from a computer system, how to administer immediate first aid, and so forth.

In the second case, police officers must learn various cultural characteristics and theories about cultural value conflicts that may arise in the communities they police. How to use language and cogently write technical reports, how to think inductively, how to communicate effectively and supportively, how to access certain criminal patterns leading to theories of criminal motivation or cause, and so forth.

Along some dimensions, law enforcement might merit elevation to the status of a traditional profession. For example, were one to separate municipal police from certain federal agencies, such as the Federal Bureau of Investigation (FBI), one might make the argument for the FBI as a near-profession. Similarly, one might separate line officers from administrative officers and suggest that the administrators may resemble a professional group (see for example Witham 1985). However, in both of these illustrations, the weight of professionalism rests heavily on non-police qualification, rather than on police qualifications. The FBI agents are near-professionals by virtue of their simultaneous membership in more traditional professional groups, such as lawyers, or new professional groups, such as accountants—even though not all FBI agents actually are members of these other groups. Administrators are closer to a professional group by virtue of the new professional classifications of upper management administrators in general. In most respects, municipal law enforcement tends to be more trade-like than profession-like. As a consequence, many of the attributes of policing shadow rather than duplicate, the usual requisites for a traditional profession. Although some people continue to argue that policing is evolving into a profession, the point may be moot.

It is without question that police officers are considered by most people to be professionals as compared with amateurs. This public attitude carries with it the impression that police officers are highly trained and skilled at their jobs. The social status of law enforcement personnel is never likely to achieve the same social plane as that of physicians, lawyers, or clergy. In short, policing may never exceed the level of a shadow-box profession.

Ritzer and Walczak (1986) similarly describe policing and suggest at best it is a semi-profession. According to Ritzer and Walczak, professionalism is based more on a political (power) basis than it is on other issues. Police officers possess only a limited ability to control their clientele or to predict what situations they will find. This ability to plan systematically the activities of one's clientele is characteristic of more traditional professionals. For instance, when one arranges an appointment with a physician, one is usually given a date, time, and location for the meeting. The kinds of people police are capable of controlling typically possess little political efficacy. Some researchers describe these types of people as the underclass. Ritzer and Walczak conclude that police can most accurately be characterized as free semi-skilled workers.

Along related political lines of demarcation, Roberg and Kuykendall (1997) discuss police leadership along the lines of "professional vision." According to Roberg and Kuykendall (1997:242–243):

> A leader's vision can be professional or political, or both. A professional vision is one that identifies the responsibilities of individual police officers and the most appropriate strategies and methods to accomplish goals. A political vision is one in which the leader defines the most appropriate fit for police in a democratic society that is specific to a particular time period or community.

Again, this tends not to elevate policing much higher than to a level of highly efficient, but still only semi-skilled workers.

Yet, there seems to be a benefit from accepting policing as at least a shadow-box profession. Certainly, during the past 30 years, policing as an occupation has evolved into a better educated, more effective, and efficient work force. Characteristic of this evolutionary change is the growing emphasis in many police academies on decision-making, problem-solving skills, and ethical conduct. What has been reduced in emphasis is a focus on offensive and defensive physical tactics. A very serious emphasis has also been placed on formal education. Many jurisdictions now require entry-level patrol officers to possess a minimum of an associate's degree or two years of college as a basic requirement for hiring. In some jurisdictions, a baccalaureate is required. For example, since the mid-1980s, the Tallahassee, Florida, police department has required a baccalaureate degree of all its entry-level officers. In Massachusetts, several attempts have been made to pass legislation that would financially reward officers entering a department with college credits or degrees and

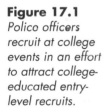

Figure 17.1
Police officers recruit at college events in an effort to attract college-educated entry-level recruits.

Figure 17.2
Students can ask questions about police careers at college career events.

increasing current officer's salaries as the college credits accumulate. In one national study conducted by the Police Executive Research Forum (PERF), it was reported what police executives would like to see colleges and universities doing for current and potential police officers. Contrary to what some people might expect, the majority of police executives do not want colleges and universities to teach police skills. Instead, they want these academic settings to provide graduates with a balanced understanding of police officers' roles and responsibilities, democratic values, tolerance, and integrity (Sapp, Carter, and Stephens 1989:1). The consensus was that a broad-based liberal arts curriculum should be part of every criminal justice program at U.S. colleges and universities.

Also, it was through the advances in professionalizing policing that nepotism and favoritism slowly yielded to civil service regulations for hiring and promoting officers. As the following section will detail, the ability of unions to take a foothold in policing also reflects an attempt to modernize and professionalize law enforcement.

POLICE UNIONS

Many authors have indicated the apparent relationship of police reform, police modernization, and attempts to professionalize policing (Neiderhoffer 1969; Folgeson 1985; Terry 1985; Skolnick and Bayley 1986; Walker 1992; Peak 1993; Cox 1996). Each of these activities has made deliberate efforts to advance police practice and performance. As Terry (1985:154) suggests, "The unionization of police forces has been difficult and traumatic." The basic arguments in favor of unions are labor, not professional ones. These have focused on improved working conditions, equipment, and better wages. As a result, as efforts to advance police unions progressed, they inadvertently impeded efforts to gain recognition as a traditional profession. In order to negotiate status, positions, and wage levels, traditional professions typically have relied upon their associations, not unions and collective bargaining units.

Police unions, and collective bargaining in police agencies, have received considerable attention throughout the past several decades. While the history of labor unions dates back to the late 1800s, active involvement in unions by police officers really did not occur until the 1960s and 1970s (Sapp 1985). Today, with the exception, perhaps, of teachers and firefighters, police are the most organized of public sector employees, with perhaps a much as 75 percent of all police officers holding membership in unions (Cole and Smith 1998:229).

Even excluding the issue of professions, there are several arguments that have been levied against police unions. First, it has been argued that police lose their right to strike when they accept positions as public service employees. The explanation here, of course, is that there is enormous potential for harm to the public from the sudden suspension of policing services. Since the threats of strike are the principal clout of a union, an immediate conflict emerges. A second argument concerns the ensuing problems that may arise between contractual negotiations between the union and administration, and the legal responsibilities of the police. For example, the union may prefer officers to work in safer environments, but setting such contractual limitations may simply be unenforceable, or prevent fair access to law enforcement protection. For instance, if the union determined that some high-crime neighborhood was too unsafe for the officers to patrol, the union might negotiate to exclude this area in its contract with the city. If such a contract were negotiated, people residing in these high-crime areas would not receive police protection.

A third problem of collective bargaining is that it creates a an adversarial relationship between union members (line officers) and management (police administrators). This adversarial attitude may carry over to the day-to-day police activities of these two workgroups, even after a collective bargaining agreement has been met. Furthermore, this relationship can undermine the authority of the administrators. If the union through collective bargaining determines the agency's policies, it, not the administrators are in charge.

While police strikes are for the most part illegal, **police work slowdowns** or speedups do occasionally occur. Under the guise of blue-flu, by-the-book slow-downs, or as has occurred in some small rural departments, department-wide resignations, walk-outs, and sick-outs among police do happen. Similarly, **police department speedups**, where officers write considerably more citations than they might otherwise, also occur. The intent in speedups is to aggravate the public sufficiently that they complain to the police chief or the town council. The hope is, that as a result, the chief and the town will listen more carefully to the desires—or demands—of the line officers.

Historically, police strikes have occurred since as early as 1889, when the police of Ithaca, New York (five officers), walked off their jobs because their pay had been reduced from $12 to $9 per week ("Police Labor Relations" 1973; More 1985). In 1918, 450 officers of the Cincinnati, Ohio, police department walked off their jobs to protest the firings of four officers. The four had been fired for attempting to organize the officers and hold a meeting in order to discuss a salary raise. Finally, perhaps the most famous police strike is the Boston Police Strike of 1919, regarded as the first fully organized labor strike by police officers.

As with earlier police labor actions, the Boston police were challenging extremely low salaries, poor work conditions, long work weeks, and unresponsive administrators. Officers first formed the Boston Social Club, which was chartered by the American Federation of Labor (AFL). In itself, this action was a direct violation of the city's police policy and 19 of the union leaders were summarily discharged. On September 19, 1919, in angry response to these firings, 1,117 officers from a full complement of 1,544 went out on strike. So outraged by their actions was Massachusetts Governor Calvin Coolidge that he fired and replaced all of the striking officers (Burpo 1971). It has been suggested that the response by police officers nationally to this mass firing for striking, may have been the dormancy of police unions for the next 40–50 years (Thibault, Lynch, and McBride 1990).

Indeed, the firing of these 1,117 officers was quite tragic, yet, a kind of silver lining to the dark cloud did surface. The Boston community had seen first-hand that the social and real property-damage costs from a police strike were extremely high. As a result, the officers who replaced the strikers were hired at a salary level $300 a year higher than their predecessors. Also, a benefit package was established that included a pension plan and city-supplied uniforms (Burpo 1971).

Before World War II, most police officers were fairly well off for poorly educated and largely unskilled laborers. Robert Folgeson (1985:169) quotes a Washington patrolman who told a congressional committee that police officers were not "fit for anything except police work for some kind of laboring work." The public attitude was that police officers received a sufficient salary, particularly since most supplemented their income with various payoffs. The officers' complaints of "long hours and short pay" were regarded by most people as no different from those of other laborers working in factories, on loading docks, or doing similar manual work (Fogelson 1985).

During and particularly following World War II, the general complacency of officers and the attitude of the public began to change. As the war came to an end, many veterans began to enter policing. With these men came their middle-class values, better educational levels, and greater demands for non-political promotions, improved salaries, and working conditions. Throughout the 1940s and early 1950s, police salaries and benefits barely kept up with inflation and were often much lower than factory workers'. In the mid-1950s, salaries began to improve and in many parts of the nation began to rise faster than the costs of living. But many officers across the country still found it necessary to moonlight in supplementary jobs as painters, salesmen, and in security positions (Folgeson 1985). Officers' dissatisfaction with their working conditions led many to leave policing for private industry or federal agencies. This dissatisfaction turned to outrage and alienation during the late 1950s and throughout the 1960s. It was during this period that the American Civil Liberties Union (ACLU) began to call for the creation of civilian review boards to hear what seemed to be a growing number of complaints against police officers. As well, the 1960s saw what seemed like a record number of U.S. Supreme Court decisions that protected the constitutional rights of accused criminals.

In addition, the 1960s were marked by riots and civil unrest that made the nation's social problems—including poverty, racism, and sexism—impossible to ignore. One of the central themes of the 1964 presidential campaigns was law and order. This issue continued as a main theme throughout most of the remaining years of the 1960s, and resulted in President Lyndon Johnson's creating the President's Commission on Law Enforcement and the Administration of Justice. The commission carefully examined the role of the police in American society, as well as the standards and requirements of police officers in cities across the nation, allegations of corruption and brutality, and the public's responses to law enforcement officers.

Police officers nationwide grew discontent and frustrated with their role and the public's attitude toward them. In response to the enormous anger and accompanying feelings of helplessness in the face of these social changes, police unions swept the nation's large city departments—with the exception of those in the South. The unionization of the 1960s created an enormous reform movement within policing agencies. As this reform movement grew in momentum, another federal agency, the Law Enforcement Assistance Agency (later to be changed to "Administration"), or LEAA as it is more commonly referred to, was created (see Box 17.1). The central purpose of the **Law Enforcement Assistance Agency** was to aid in the solution of problems uncovered during the examination undertaken by the President's Commission on Law Enforcement. As part of the agency's work it established the **Law Enforcement Assistance Program (LEAP)**, which provided grants of money for various police agency projects and programs. Also, LEAA worked for increased educational requirements among officers—and increased benefits for officers who achieved them. As a consequence, many of the nation's departments began to reward officers with increased salaries for returning to college and obtaining degrees.

But the existence of LEAA was controversial almost from its inception. Detractors saw it as symbolic of the Nixon administration's law-and-order platform, which itself was viewed as a means of arming police with the means to suppress legitimate grievances (Feeley and Sarat 1980). Supporters defended the expenditures and policies behind these as necessary for establishing order and the role of police in society. In 1980, after its federal funding had been removed, the LEAA began to fall out of existence.

BOX 17.1   THE RISE AND FALL OF LEAA

The growing need for police services during the turbulent 1960s and 1970s resulted in a large number of federally created investigations and commissions. In 1965 President Lyndon Johnson appointed the President's Commission on Law Enforcement and Administration of Justice. During that same year, Congress established the Office of Law Enforcement Assistance and Justice. Between 1967 and 1973 seven major national commissions were created to deal with the issues of crime control and the rising crime in America. Of considerable concern during this period was the civil unrest, riots, and violence in American streets. These activities had become commonly associated with anti-war and political demonstrations, and with what seemed to be a disproportionate number of political assassinations (see Finckenauer 1978).

Among the items identified as a problem by these investigations and commissions was the fragmented structure of law enforcement in America. Historically, policing has always been linked to local governments. As a result, police agencies, law enforcement practices, and procedures have traditionally reflected these fragmentations and regional nuances. However, crime is not subject to the same limitations. The fragmented structure and truncated nature of law enforcement efforts in America made systematic coordination on a larger than local scale quite difficult.

Chiefly in response to these conditions, Congress responded by establishing the Law Enforcement Assistance Administration (LEAA) in 1968. The agency was established under the auspices of the U.S. Department of Justice, under Title I of the Omnibus Crime Control and Safe Streets Act (Public Law 90–351, 90th Congress, June 19, 1968). LEAA was given a mandate to fund various research projects and programs to improve crime control and modernize the criminal justice system. Since law enforcement agencies were viewed as the primary crime deterrent tools in America, police agencies received a sizable piece of LEAA's multi-billion dollar pie. Between 1968 and 1977 LEAA disbursed over $6 billion to various crime control programs and research projects. The majority of these recipients (61 percent) were police agencies.

Unfortunately, little planning or careful consideration was given to many of the funded projects. A virtual funding frenzy occurred, and many departments obtained LEAA funds only to squander it on exotic or bizarre riot-control equipment (most of which arrived on the heels of the riot era).

Allegations began to surface concerning questionable projects and disproportionate levels of funds being allocated to police agencies. Critics quickly levied charges that while wild police projects were being funded, other segments of the criminal justice system were being ignored.

The bottom line in assessing the relationship between police unions and efforts to professionalize police agencies is whether they have improved the quality of policing. Some sources have concluded that unions have actually created significant problems in reforming corrupt departments (Bouza 1990; Murphy and Caplan 1993). As well, unions may well have been responsible for fragmenting the chain of command, contributing to racial tensions, requiring seniority over merit in promotional decisions, and resulting in lax or inefficient departments (Swanson, Territo, and Taylor 1993; Stone and Duluca 1994). On the other side of the ledger, however, police unions have improved officer morale by obtaining better salaries, educational incentives, fair procedures, and even better lines of communication (Swanson, Territo, and Taylor 1993; More and Wegener 1996).

By the late 1970s, a fairly strong movement to abolish LEAA had emerged. Plans were made for other federal agencies to take over some of LEAA's evaluation tasks, and LEAA was phased out of operation by 1982. Although LEAA did indeed fund some strange projects, it also provided an important and necessary federal–state–local link. Furthermore, LEAA did fund some very worthwhile criminal justice programs. For example, in Massachusetts funding permitted the experimental closing of juvenile institutions and their replacement with community-based facilities. Also, a number of prototype probation counseling, public defender, and police training programs were financed with LEAA seed money.

The abolishment of LEAA did not mark the elimination of all funding conduits for crime control and law enforcement improvement programs (such as LEAA's Law Enforcement Educational Program). Efforts to coordinate crime control on a larger scale were slowed, but not ignored. In 1980, Congress passed into law the Justice System Improvement Act. This act established the Office of Justice Assistance, Research, and Statistics (OJARS), which included the National Institute of Justice (NIJ), and the Bureau of Justice Statistics (BJS). The intention of the OJARS was to provide a funding source for criminal justice research and programming—but in a more limited way than had LEAA.

Particularly in the face of an increasing national drug problem in the United States, one can expect to see further growth in funding sources for criminal control. It even has been speculated that during the early 1990s, another attempt will be made to federally assist local law enforcement agencies, perhaps in the shape of a body one might call LLEA (Local Law Enforcement Agency).

POLICE AGENCY ACCREDITATION

One example of a project that began with an LEAA grant is the Commission on Accreditation for Law Enforcement Agencies, Inc., (CALEA). The LEAA initially funded what it believed to be an innovative idea conceived by IACP (Raub and Van Zandt 1986). This initial funding amounted to more than $5 million, which derived from the Department of Justice through LEAA (Cotter 1983). The fund was to be distributed over several years ending in 1983, when it was expected that CALEA would be able to support itself through self generated revenue as a non-profit organization (Diegelman 1983; Cotter 1983).

The original CALEA commission was composed of 21 members appointed by the executive board of IACP (the International Association of Chiefs of Police), NOBLE (the National Organization of Black Law Enforcement Executives), NSA (the National Sheriffs Association), and PERF (the Police Executive Research Forum). This original commission included 11 individuals with practical law enforcement experience, and 10 citizens representing a fairly wide gamut of educational, business, and political interests (Cotter 1983; Raub and Van Zandt 1986). Members of this commission were to serve 3-year terms.

The concept of accreditation has a long and rich history, although it is fairly new in the area of criminal justice and law enforcement. Accreditation developed in the United States when the New York State regents were established in 1787. The purpose of these regents was to monitor and certify that all colleges operating in New York State met certain basic standards. The New York State Legislature required that the regents make site-visits to each college and annually review the work of every college. From these visits and reviews, the regents were required to issue a written report to the legislature. From these early educational roots, accreditation spread to other settings, such as hospitals and mental institutions, in order to assure comparable training for student doctors without interfering with the quality of patient care. During the 1950s, accreditation spread to other disciplines and professions and, in 1974, accreditation entered the criminal justice arena when the Commission on Accreditation for Corrections (CAC) was founded. The question that arises, of course, is what is accreditation? Stated in basic terms, **accreditation** is the formal recognition that an agency or institution conforms to some specific body of regulations and standards. In the section that follows, the accreditation of law enforcement agencies is discussed.

Throughout the nation, police agencies have become voluntarily involved in seeking accreditation for their departments. James Cotter (1983:19), CALEA's first executive director, explains the accreditation of police agencies as follows:

> Accreditation is a process by which agencies bring themselves into compliance with a body of established standards; it is also a status awarded to agencies that meet or exceed all requirements of the standard.

The process of which Cotter speaks can be generally seen as constituting the initial attempts on the part of agencies to obtain accreditation. The status, on the other hand, involves being awarded the title of an accredited agency. Although few disagree about the improvements likely to occur during the process stage (improved equipment, entrance standards, training procedures, etc.), considerable controversy rages over the alleged benefits of obtaining the status of accredited. Also, now that more than 330 agencies have obtained accreditation, another consideration must be faced by CALEA: reaccreditation. Since agencies are permitted to retain their accreditation status for only five years, a kind of second level must be developed. In this second-level process, an agency must prepare itself to be visited again and maintain its minimum standard level.

SUGGESTED BENEFITS OF ACCREDITATION

Proponents of accreditation believe that the standardization of police agencies across the nation demonstrates commitment to excellence and furthers the cause of professionalizing policing. Among its manifest goals, accreditation seeks to establish a minimum standard of performance for all police agencies at a level that until recently only a few departments had reached. A number of benefits are suggested by the Commission on Accreditation (see Box 17.2). For example, the commission suggests that a more detailed knowledge of an agency's policies and procedures among line officers will lead to better service and fewer indefensible liability suits. Written and objective criteria for promotions and administrative actions should result in improved job satisfaction. Improvements in police-community relations are expected, owing to neighbor-

BOX 17.2   BENEFITS OF ACCREDITATION

The CALEA Commission claims ten principal benefits accrue to police agencies that complete the accreditation process. These benefits include:

1. Nationwide recognition of professional excellence;
2. Increased community understanding and support;
3. An elevation of employee confidence, and increased esprit de corps;
4. Improvement in confidence levels among state and local government officials;
5. "State-of-the-art" guidelines for evaluation and reform when necessary;
6. Clearly articulated and written proactive management systems, policies, and procedures;

7. Decreases or containment of insurance premiums;
8. Deterrence of liability litigation and increases in gaining out-of-court settlements;
9. Improved communications and coordination with neighboring agencies and other segments of the criminal justice community;
10. Increased access to information about modern law enforcement and training practices.

Adapted from Kenneth Medeiros, "Accreditation for Small Police Departments," *The Police Chief* 52(1985):40–41; and Kenneth Medeiros, "Accreditation as a Shield Against Liability and as a Protection for the Line Officer," presented during the Fifth Annual Conference on the Civil Liabilities of Law Enforcement Officials, Needham, Mass., 1988.

hood residents gaining confidence in the competence and professionalism of their local police officers. Other basic assumptions are that accredited police agencies will be more likely than unaccredited ones to provide both law enforcement and social services that exceed the minimum law enforcement mandates (Dearborn 1985; Smith 1987).

DETRACTIONS OF ACCREDITATION

Detractors of accreditation offer five major criticisms. First, they claim that standardizing all departments in the nation may be viewed as a first step in creating a national police force (Bartollas and Jaeger 1988:158). The fear of a national police force has long been a concern of the American people. Second, some critics view the broad and general minimum standards required by the commission as set too low. Often these standards appear elastic to a point of non-existence since an agency may petition not to comply with various mandates if these standard requirements go beyond local laws, policy, or budgetary constraints. As a result, an agency that gains accreditation may actually remain riddled with inadequate protocols, incompetent officers, and substandard equipment.

A third and similar criticism is a nearly chauvinistic attitude concerning who should determine an agency's standards. Many police executives resent the implication that their rules and policies are not as good as or better than those set by the commission (McAllister 1987). These executives suggest that in order to remain sufficiently flexible and generally applicable, many of the commission's standards require only the barest essentials for compliance. As a result, some police chiefs feel they would be taking steps backwards rather than forward by seeking accreditation.

A fourth criticism leveled against accreditation is that it may impede already progressive and modern departments from further progression. If local politicians see that the agency is able to achieve accreditation at the current level or training and performance, they may be reluctant to allocate funds to update equipment and technology, personnel needs, or advanced training.

Finally, and particularly in the northeastern regions of the nation where police unions have grown enormously influential, line officers view accreditation with skepticism. Their general view is that accreditation benefits administrators by providing a shield against department liabilities, media attacks, objective-appearing mechanisms for sanctioning patrol officers, and similar managerial benefits. But, little benefit is seen for the line officers themselves.

In fact, many line officers view the increased educational expectations, additional training, and advanced technology and equipment demands as quite threatening. In these instances, officers may turn to their unions to protect them from what they perceive as liabilities and risks to the security of their jobs. Interestingly, a minority of agencies located in northeastern states have sought and obtained accreditation. The majority of agencies that have successfully completed the accreditation process are located in southern and midwestern states. Unions were less successful in gaining strong footholds in the South than they were in the North.

A number of unanticipated consequences of the accreditation process have, however, occurred. For example a number of states have created coalitions to assist police agencies in the process of accreditation, thereby improving interagency cooperation (Cox 1996). A few agencies have even reported an insurance premium discount as a result of accreditation.

Perhaps the real question that remains is whether the status of accredited agency is actually a valuable as the process of its achievement. This history of police reform has witnessed resistance from within and without the justice system with virtually every change. Certainly, one element that may account for some of this resistance has been the concern and fear held by members over the perceived and anticipated effects of a given change. If a particular alteration is viewed as beneficial and requires little or no effort on the part of officers, one can expect little internal resistance. These sorts of reforms may include such things as salary increases, new patrol cruisers, reimbursements for voluntary educational course work, or pension packages.

On the other hand, if the anticipated change is perceived as threatening one's comfortable position in the organization, one's ability to gain rank and raises, and involves learning new procedures or acquiring certifications and/or additional amounts of education, resistance is likely to be quite high. For instance, many police officers acknowledge the usefulness of canine teams when conducting bomb and drug searches, the search for bodies, missing people, or tracking felons through rough terrain. Yet, serious resistance could be expected among many of these same favorably inclined officers were they told by an administrator that they were joining canine teams. Such a change would require their attending a specialized training program, learning how to be a dog handler, working and caring for their dogs, and assorted non-reimbursed financial expenses (e.g., medical care, food, toys, etc.).

In some ways, the prospect of going through an accreditation process may be perceived by line officers as similar to being told they are joining canine teams. Stated simply, this may be viewed as a lot of time, effort, and risk in order to obtain little tangible personal gain. In fact, for some officers, the prospect of their agency undergoing accreditation is seen as one in which potential for loss may be far greater than for gain.

For example, in order to obtain better work schedules, notice of promotion schedules, and even better positions on promotion lists, it is often who one knows. The existence of even subtle old-boy power networks is sometimes uncovered during the process of accreditation. Once identified, these old-boy structures can be eliminated through objective, written policies on promotion and salary increases. As a result the department power brokers may find themselves dethroned. Objectively, outsiders are likely to see this a very good thing. However, from an insider's perspective, especially one benefiting from this old-boy network, its destruction may not be well received.

What many detractors of police agency accreditation may miss is that once the accreditation status has been achieved, this is not truly an end in itself. This status is better viewed as a kind of holding position in a continuous process of reaccreditation. Viewed in this manner, the question of accreditation's worth as a status may be moot. The value of accreditation clearly rests upon the process of achieving it initially and maintaining it once obtained.

SUMMARY

This chapter began with an overview of professionalism and police reform during the twentieth century. Policing was examined in the light of traditional occupations, as contrasted with more vernacular understandings of the notion of professional. It was argued that while attempts have been made to professionalize policing, what has resulted amounts to little more than a reflection, or a shadow-box image of law enforcement as a profession.

The effects of and from police unions were detailed. In this regard, unions were suggested to represent the labor, rather than the traditional professional image many police agencies and administrators sought.

The contemporary issue of police agency accreditation was also considered. Following a brief historical account of the origins of police accreditation, the chapter considered several potential benefits from undergoing the accreditation process. It was indicated that even when agencies fail to complete their accreditation process, they might benefit. In these cases, benefits were described in terms of increases in officers' educational and training levels.

REFERENCES

Barker, Thomas, Ronald S. Hunter, and Jeffery P. Rush. *Police Systems and Practices.* Englewood Cliffs, N.J.: Prentice-Hall Career and Technology, 1994.

Bartollas, Clemens, and Loras Jaeger. *American Criminal Justice.* New York: Macmillan, 1988.

Burpo, John H. *The Police Labor Movement.* Springfield, Ill.: Thomas, 1971.

Bouza, A. V. *The Police Mystique.* New York: Plenum, 1990.

Cole, George F., and Christopher E. Smith. *The American System of Criminal Justice.* 8th ed. Belmont, Calif.: West/Wadsworth Publishing Co., 1998.

Colter, James V. "Accreditation Programs for Law Enforcement Agencies." *The Police Chief,* 50, March 1983:65–68.

Cox, Steven M. *Police: Practices, Perspectives, and Problems.* Boston: Allyn and Bacon, 1996.

Dearborn, David. "Police Department Aiming for National Accreditation." *The Glastonbury Citizen,* 2 May, 1985:6.

Diegelman, Robert F. "Accreditation for Law Enforcement." *The Police Chief,* 50, February 1983:18–19.

Feeley, Malcolm M., and Austin D. Sarat. *The Policy Dilemma: Federal Crime Policy and Enforcement 1968–1978.* Minneapolis: University of Minnesota Press, 1980.

Fogelson, Robert. "Unionism Comes to Policing." In *Policing Society.* W. Clinton Terry III (ed.) New York: Wiley, 1985.

Goode, William J. "Encroachment, Charlantism, and the Emergence of Profession: Psychology, Society, and Medicine." *American Sociological Review,* 25, December, 1960: 902–14.

Mannle, Henry W., and J. David Hirschel. *Fundamentals of Criminology.* 2d ed. Englewood Cliffs, N.J.: Prentice-Hall, 1988.

McAllister, Bill. "Spurred by Dramatic Rise in Law Suits, Police Agencies Warm to Accreditation." *The Washington Post,* 17 March, 1987:A7.

More, Harry W. Jr. (ed.) *Critical Issues in Law Enforcement.* Cincinnati, Oh.: Anderson Publishing Co., 1985.

More, Harry W., and W. Fred Wegener. *Effective Police Supervision.* 2d ed. Cincinnati, Oh.: Anderson Publishing Co., 1996.

Murphy, P. V., and D. G. Caplan. "Fostering Integrity." In *Critical Issues in Policing: Contemporary Issues.* Roger G. Dunham and Geoffrey Alpert (eds.) Prospect Heights, Ill.: Waveland Press, 1993.

Niederhoffer, Arthur. *Behind the Shield: The Police in Urban Society.* New York: Anchor, 1969.

Peak, Kenneth J. *Policing America.* Englewood Cliffs, N. J.: Regents/Prentice Hall, 1993.

"Police Labor Relations." IACP Public Safety Labor Reporter (1973). Cited in *Critical Issues in Law Enforcement.* Harry W. More Jr. (ed.) Cincinnati, Oh.: Anderson Publishing Co., 1985.

Raub, Richard A., and Jack Van Zandt. *First Accreditation of a State-Wide Law Enforcement Agency: Accreditation of the Illinois Department of State Police.* Illinois: Illinois Department of State Police, 1986.

Ritzer, George. *Man and His Work: Conflicts and Change.* New York: Appleton-Century-Crofts, 1972.

Ritzer, George, and David Walczak. *Working: Conflict and Change*. 3d ed. Englewood Cliffs, N.J.: Prentice-Hall, 1986.

Roberg, Roy R., and Jack Kuykendall. *Police Management*. 2d ed. Los Angeles, Calif.: Roxbury Publishing Company, 1997.

Sapp, A. D. "Police Unionism as a Developmental Process." In *The Ambivalent Force: Perspectives on Police*. 3d ed. Abraham S. Blumberg and Elaine Niederhoffer (eds.) New York: Holt, Rinehart & Winston, 1985.

Sapp, Allen D., David Carter, and Darrel Stephens. "Police Chiefs: CJ Curricula Inconsistent with Contemporary Police Needs." *ACJS Today*, 7(1989):1.

Skolnick, Jerome H., and David H. Bayley. *The New Blue Line: Police Innovation in Six American Cities*. New York: Free Press, 1986.

Smith, Robert. "Accreditation: Impact on Police Departments." *The Police Chief*, 54, March, 1987:37–38.

Stone, A. R., and S. M. Deluca. *Police Administration: An Introduction*. 2d ed. Englewood Cliffs, N.J.: Prentice-Hall, 1994.

Swanson, C.R., L. Territo, and R. W. Taylor. *Police Administration*. 3d ed. New York: Macmillan, 1993.

Terry, W. Clinton III. *Policing Society*. New York: Wiley, 1985.

Thibault, E. A., L. M. Lynch, and R. B. McBride. *Proactive Police Management*. 2d ed. Englewood Cliffs, N.J.: Prentice-Hall, 1990.

Walker, Samuel. *The Police in America: An Introduction*. 2d ed. New York: McGraw-Hill, 1992.

Witham, Donald C. *The American Law Enforcement Chief Executive: A Management Profile*. Washington, D.C.: Police Executive Research Forum, 1985.

QUESTIONS FOR REVIEW

Objective #1:

- Name three traditional professions.

Objective #2:

- What are the two possible definitions for professional?

Objective #3:

- What is meant by shadow-box professionalism?

Objective #4:

- What police action occurred in 1889, in Ithaca, New York?
- What occurred during the Boston Police Strike of 1919?

Objective #5:

- What is meant by blue-flu?
- How might a police department speedup manifest itself?

Objective #6:

- What was the central purpose of the LEAA?
- What was the purpose of the Law Enforcement Assistance Program, developed by LEAA?

Objective #7:

- How many members were appointed to the original Commission on Accreditation for Law Enforcement?
- What organizations were responsible for making these original appointments?

Objective #8:

- When, and where did the concept of accreditation develop?

Objective #9:

- What are some benefits afforded to police departments from obtaining the status of accredited?

Objective #10:

- What are some of the drawbacks to a police department becoming accredited?

18 The Future: Education, Training, and Privatization in Policing

CHAPTER OBJECTIVES

After reading this chapter you should be able to:

1. Discuss college education as an entry-level requirement for police officers.
2. Consider the differences between education and training.
3. Define what is meant by lazy-racism.
4. Describe some of the benefits of college-educated police officers.
5. Explain on-the-job-training in policing.
6. Indicate what is meant by credentialism.
7. Consider why a high school–level education may be insufficient for police officers.
8. Talk about the privatization of police services.

POLICING AS A CAREER

Policing, as this book as tried to demonstrate, is not a static phenomenon. Instead, policing is a very fluid and flexible activity that reflects both the needs and desires of the community and social structures of society. As each new layer is added to policing's social history, efforts to protect liberty increase.

In many ways, policing is likely to continue this pattern of bending and experimenting in its effort to better accommodate community demands for safety and freedom while attempting to avoid infringement of citizen's rights. Because of this desire to accommodate the people they protect, the roles and functions of police officers are deeply influenced by the community they serve. During the recent past, members of communities have begun to work with police officials to identify serious crime and crime-related problems and to consider various alternative resolutions (see Skolnick and Bayley 1986; Smith 1986; Sherman 1986; Bobinsky 1994).

KEY TERMS	lazy-racism on-the-job-training	credentialism

The purpose of this chapter is to review the way education and training in policing have been evolving, as well as their impact on the future of American policing.

Throughout this book numerous issues relating to policing have been identified and discussed. For the most part these have all related to a general mandate in policing to protect and serve the community. In addition, issues corresponding to crime investigation, stress, and risk have also been considered. The comprehensive nature of these items and the complexity of policing in general have required this book to offer only a scant look at each of these varied facets to policing. Nonetheless, this book has touched upon many of the major and timely aspects and elements commonly associated with police and policing.

It has also been the intention of this author to offer information about policing that was as realistic as possible. Often, students of policing foster highly idealistic, but equally unrealistic images of what and who the police are. As Chapter 11 expressed, this has created much consternation among new recruits and rookies as they begin their law enforcement careers.

In a study by M. Steven Meagher and Nancy Yentes (1986), police officers from two midwestern states were asked their reasons for becoming police officers. Meagher and Yentes (1986:320) found, as many previous researchers have, that the principal explanation centered upon a "desire to help people and the [financial and occupational] security associated with the job of policing" (see also Milton 1978; Ermer 1978; Charles 1982).

In a similar study, Harold P. Slater and Martin Reiser (1988) found that 49 percent of the officers asked why they chose police work as a career indicated service to the public. Forty-three percent indicated security and salary. Interestingly, the findings reported in both the Meagher and Yentes (1986) and the Slater and Reiser (1988) studies reflect nearly identical motivational reasons for both males and females. In other words, both men and women indicate they have selected a career devoted to service, while never expressing a desire to join the military or an authoritarian profession as a personal reason for joining the police force. The inference one can draw is that the old notion about certain personality types enter policing in disproportionate numbers should be put to rest. As with any other occupation, prospective members are concerned with financial considerations, job security, advancement, benefits, and even prestige. During the recent past, many police officers have looked at higher education as a potential shortcut to rapid advancement. Historically, however, the education movement in policing is a critical aspect in the modernization of the police as a social institution. It is important, therefore, to consider the role of higher education in law enforcement.

HIGHER EDUCATION AND POLICE OFFICERS

Among the more controversial elements associated with modern policing is the question of a need for college-prepared police officers. August Vollmer, the famous reform police chief of Berkeley, California, was among the earliest proponents of higher education for police officers. Vollmer urged adoption of a college education as a basic employment requirement as early as 1920. Yet little progress was made in this regard until the 1960s.

Historically, American law enforcement has not always viewed higher education for police officers as valuable. It is only after modern police reform models and attempts to achieve the status of professionals (see Chapter 17) emerged that education began to be viewed as a positive item. In the 1960s, with the influx of federal money through such programs as the Law Enforcement Education Program (LEEP), police departments and American colleges and universities began to direct their attention to higher education for police officers. Money was made available both for officers who desired to pursue college educations and for colleges and universities desiring to develop police oriented courses and programs. According to Richard A. Staufenberger (1980), only 184 institutions of higher education had established police-oriented programs prior to 1967. But, by 1974, over 1,030 institutions had developed law enforcement courses and programs.

Staufenberger (1977) also reports, as examples of the increase in college-educated police officers, that in 1968 only 11 officers in the Dallas Police Department and 6 percent of the officers in Florida had college degrees. But by 1975 the Dallas Police Department included 625 officers with completed bachelor's degrees, 21 officers with completed master's degrees, and over 450 officers actively pursuing college degrees. In Florida, by 1975, 23 percent of the state's officers had attended college, including 44 officers who had secured doctorates.

Several studies in the 1970s sang the praises of higher education for law enforcement officers. Bernard Locke and Alexander Smith (1976), for example, claimed that higher education reduced the tendency toward authoritarianism—a commonly employed personality description used in regard to police officers during the late 1960s and 1970s. In 1967, the President's Commission on Law Enforcement and Administration concluded that, "the complexity of the police task is as great as that of any other profession" (President's Commission 1967:124). The commission recommended that police departments begin to require a baccalaureate degree as an entry-level requirement. Few departments heeded the call in 1967. In 1973, The National Advisory Commission on Criminal Justice Standards and Goals urged that police agencies begin gradually to require some college education among new recruits. They recommended beginning with a requirement of 1 year of college during 1973, and increase to two year of college by 1975, 3 years in 1978, and a 4-year degree in 1982 (National Advisory Commission 1973:369). Again, few departments seemed anxious to respond to these suggestions.

There were many involved in policing, however, who suggested that college education could afford little for the average police officer (see Erickson and Neary 1975). The relatively boring and mundane activities usually associated with line-policing were suggested as prime reasons why higher education for police officers might be a waste of time (Sherman and Bennis 1977).

In 1983, James Fyfe reported on a study he conducted for the International City Management Association. Fyfe's survey asked educational questions of police department administrators. Fyfe (1983) reports that among the 1,087 responding agencies, only four indicated that they required a 4-year college degree as a condition of employment. Nearly 8 percent indicated they required a high school diploma or equivalency. In seemed increasingly clear that the various recommendations for college education as an employment requirement had not been meaningfully incorporated into policing ideology or police administration.

In 1989, the Police Executive Research Forum reviewed research, surveyed 502 departments, and visited seven departments to determine the then-current state of police officer education in the United States. They reported that the national average educational level had risen from 12.4 years of education in around 1967 to 13.6 years in 1989 (Carter, Sapp, and Stephens 1989).

According to George Cole and Christopher Smith (1998:213), "today most recruits have a college education, although officers in rural areas and small cities may have less education." While a much lower proportion of officers currently possess a baccalaureate degree, Cole and Smith (1998) suggest that about 60 percent of sworn officers have more than 2 years of college.

Several possible explanations have been offered for why police agencies failed to follow the various research and commission recommendations. Geoffrey Alpert and Roger Dunham (1988:186) suggest that at least one reason for not following the recommendation may have to do with concern over the potential effect such restrictions might have for minority applicants. For example, the Urban League has argued that any educational requirements for entry-level positions should be relevant to that job. In the case of police officers, the Urban League maintains that a high school diploma or its equivalent should be the maximum requirement for entry-level positions (Reynolds 1980).

As a consequence, the maintenance of the lowest common denominator, minimal educational requirements, may be a detriment rather than a benefit. Although a wider range of minorities may be eligible for admissions to the ranks of policing, the manifest appearance is a kind of lazy-racism. **Lazy-racism**, in this context, means a kind of institutionalized, and perhaps even unintended sort of race discrimination. In other words, the manifest appearance that there are no qualified minorities at higher educational levels—a subtle but racist attitude to foster, and one that is not true.

To be sure, other service-oriented occupations such as nursing have not lowered their educational standards in order to accommodate much large personnel needs than those occurring in policing. In fact, the trend in nursing for the past two decades is exactly the opposite. More and more, one finds hospitals, clinics, HMOs, and even doctors' offices eliminating diploma nurses (nurses who possess the status of a registered nurse, but who do not possess a baccalaureate degree). Many of these diploma nurses are being replaced by college-prepared nurses— even to the extent of importing them form foreign countries. Also, one can find an increasing number of bedside staff nurses who have master's degrees.

Figure 18.1
*The appearance
of minority officers
has become more
common in police
agencies across
the nation.*

Minimal educational requirements create a misconception about the complexity and sophistication of modern policing. If it were the intention of police agencies to acquire additional warm bodies, then fixing the maximum requirement at a high school diploma or equivalent might be adequate. Police work, however, simply cannot be equated with dock work, automobile repairing, operating telephone switch boards, laboratory technical work, or any other semi-skilled occupation for which a high school education might suffice at entry level.

Many people, especially those outside of law enforcement, fail to see the need for police officers to possess more than a very minimal education. However, as we enter the twenty-first century, police work has changed and requires rational and logical thinking, knowledge of other cultures, communications skills, writing and language skills, technical competence, and a variety of other social and technical skills that come from a college-level experience, and not a weekend of cramming for the General Educational Diploma (GED) test. High school and college experiences are vastly different. In most situations, one attends a high school located in the general vicinity of where one grew up. One attends along with many of the same peers one has grown up with in the community or with whom one attended middle and elementary schools. This homogeneous experience is quite stilted when compared with the kinds of broader cultural and geographic experiences one typically can expect at a 4-year college or university.

In truth, the requisite of a 4-year college degree may be slightly more than an entry-level police officer needs immediately upon joining a department—although this may well be debated. However, it would seem reasonable to

Figure 18.2
Police work cannot be equated with dock work or even automobile repair work.

expect future officers to be involved with college programs or possess an associate's degree as a minimal educational level.

While many academics and police executives agree that there are growing reasons for police officers to have a college education at entry-level, this argument has not been overwhelmingly accepted by all police officials. As these police officials are quick to point out, a college education does not necessarily translate into better police work. Often improvements in training standards can provide as effective (or more effective) paths to increased quality policing. Elizabeth Burbeck and Adrian Furnham (1985:62) have similarly written:

> Intelligence and education do not guarantee success in the police force, although they are of predictive use at the training school. Higher levels of education may paradoxically give rise to more dissatisfaction and higher wastage.

The question of police training requisites is itself problematic. For example, how many hours are necessary or sufficient during the academy to place officers safely in the field? What areas should be emphasized in the training program, and what proportion of hours should each area be given? At what levels should passing and failing be established? Should physical training be given equal, greater, or less time than more academic areas of study? Should rookie officers be permitted simply to begin police work after completing a classroom-training program, or should they be required to have a structured field training experience first? Unfortunately, a long and complicated debate is likely to arise, regardless of how one attempts to answer any of these questions. At least partially as a result of this circumstance, training is typically given a fairly low priority in nearly every police department across the country (Samaha 1997).

Many police chiefs would prefer to do **on-the-job-training** rather than send their recruits to an academy. In other words, these agencies would prefer to have less experienced officers trained while working with more experienced ones in the department. One reason for this is financial. While the recruit is attending the academy, the chief must pay an officer's salary without receiving the benefit of the officer's services.

Similarly, when it comes to in-service programs, police administrators are sometimes hesitant to pull officers from their usual duties in order to place them back into the classroom. Robert Meadows (1987) compared the perceptions of law enforcement training requirements as ranked by criminal justice educators (college and university professors) and police administrators. Meadows (1987:8) reported that both groups similarly ranked the value of several training areas: Both groups ranked patrol and investigation, force and weaponry, and communications as being the most important. The respondents also ranked human relations training last.

It is interesting to note that both educators and administrators have ranked human relations training as least important for recruits to learn. However, as Meadows (1987) explains, this may reflect uncertainty about how human relations training should be taught—and by whom (Berg 1990). This notion is not dissimilar to police educational questions raised by Lawrence Sherman's 1978 report, "The Quality of Police Education." Sherman's report delved into the disagreement over what kind of educational model is most effective for police officers. For example, a liberal arts background may be too general, a criminal justice one too focused, and law enforcement training too technical. The Sherman report made a number of recommendations intended to improve the field of policing education. For instance, it was critical of the criminal justice programs that required instructors to possess police field experience as a requisite for hiring. It was clear that this requirement limited the number of more academically trained instructors from securing positions in these programs. Too, the report recommended that criminal justice course material begin to emphasize theoretical and ethical considerations relevant to law enforcement, rather than merely the mechanical procedures of policing. Nonetheless, the debate and controversy over police educational needs persists, and various interest groups perceive the training requirements and functions of police officers differently (Berg 1994).

EXPERIENCE AS THE OFFICER'S BEST TEACHER

Another view of policing suggests that there is no substitute for street experience. Following this argument to its logical conclusion, neither material presented at the academy nor in the college classroom is as beneficial in dealing with confrontations in the real world. If this view of police learning is correct, then it follows that the best police officers should be the oldest, most seasoned field veterans. Also, the only people who could adequately make comments and judgments in a supervisory capacity are those still actively working the streets. In effect, the argument is analogous to the absurd claim that in order to study drug addicts, one must first be a drug addict. Few police officers would, therefore, argue as stated here, that only actively working police officers are competent to assess, supervise, or educate recruits.

David Bayley and Egon Bittner (1984) indicate that, "what police say about how policing is learned [experientially] is not incompatible with attempts to make instruction in the skill of policing more self-critical and systematic." Bayley and Bittner even recommend a kind of blending of theoretically based material with more practical experiential learning strategies. In this regard, frank discussion of actual case studies and the kinds of decisions that went into each would be instructive. Bayley and Bittner warn, however, that there is an important distinction to be made between having instructors excite recruits with war stories and offering authentic case examples for illustrative purposes. Related to this, then, it seems necessary that instructors themselves be well educated both in law enforcement issues and material and in educational procedures and techniques (Berg 1990).

THE VALUE OF COLLEGE-EDUCATED POLICE

The value of a police officer with a college education remains somewhat controversial. There is some research that suggests that college-prepared officers tend to perform their functions as police officers better than their non-college-prepared counterparts (see Sanderson 1977; Trojanowicz and Nicholson 1976; Bowker 1980; Worden 1990).

For instance, Robert Trojanowicz and Thomas Nicholson (1976:58) write that the college-prepared officer is:

> Willing to experiment and try new things as opposed to preferring the established and conventional way of doing things; assumes a leadership role and likes to direct and supervise the work of others; uses a step-by-step method for processing information and reaching decisions; likes to engage in work providing a lot of excitement and a great deal of variety as opposed to work providing a stable and secure future; and he values himself by his achievement of status symbols established by his culture.

But, other research indicates that there is little difference in performance between college- and high school–prepared officers (see Weirman 1978; Miller and Fry 1978). For example, R. P Witte (1969) compared two groups of police offices in the field. One group contained officers with college degrees, while the other was composed of high school graduates. Witte found that after 6 months, the crime rates in each group's area had remained relatively constant. Witte did report, however, that citizen complaints were fewer among the college-educated officers and that the response time in answering calls was faster than that of the high school–prepared officers.

Wayne Cascio (1977) and B. E. Sanderson (1977) found similar indirect evidence of a benefit from college preparation for police officers. In Cascio's research, the higher levels of education among Dade County, Florida, officers was associated with increased communication abilities, resulting in fewer on-the-job injuries during officer-citizen interactions, fewer sick days taken each year, and fewer allegations of unnecessary use of force. Sanderson (1977) found that educational levels among officers on the Los Angeles Police Department could be positively correlated with performance during an officer's academy training period and later with the likelihood of promotions.

Lee Bowker (1980) concluded in his review of the extant literature on higher education and policing that a college education had a number of benefits for police officers. These benefits included higher morale, a decreased amount of dogmatism and authoritarianism, more liberal social attitudes, and fewer disciplinary problems and citizen complaints (see also Finckenhauer 1975; Parker et al. 1976; Roberg 1978).

More recently, research conducted by Mark Dantzker (1992) showed that college-educated officers express greater job satisfaction when they first enter the profession; but, Dantzker also says the research showed that the positive effect is temporary and may wear away in about 5 years.

Regardless of the debate and controversy about college, officers interested in rapid advancement secure college degrees. It is perhaps ironic that because so many officers have sought college and graduate school educations, the mere possession of a college or graduate degree no longer assures rapid advancement.

For example, one study by Robert Fischer and his associates (1985) found that promotional chances are not enhanced by officers' possessing college degrees. Although most officers in the study who did obtain promotions possessed college degrees, it was not the degree that made, "a unique or essential contribution to the chances for promotion" (Fischer et al. 1985:335). Stated slightly differently, so many officers have now begun to accumulate college degrees that such credentials no longer set them apart form other applicants for promotion. Fischer's and his associates' finding about the plenitude of college-prepared officers may provide at least a partial explanation for the dissatisfaction to which Burbeck and Furnham (1985) and Dantzker (1992) refer. Since college-educated police officers are becoming more prevalent, their job dissatisfaction may be attributed to the effects of the mundane and routine patrol work typical in policing. In other words, college-prepared officers may have gained social tolerance and a greater depth of knowledge in college, but they have also likely accepted the idea that college preparation is the ticket to advancement. Yet, in policing, experience continues to be a necessary requisite for command positions—regardless of one's educational achievements.

What is particularly interesting about the Fischer et al. finding is that it suggests that there are a substantial number of college-prepared officers at all levels and ranks of law enforcement. Stated differently, policing is not administered disproportionately by overeducated ranking officers, nor is it commanded by undereducated, street-wise good-old boys. Instead, there is apparently a far more heterogeneous mix of educational backgrounds and professional police experiences.

FROM MAN-AT-ARMS TO POLICE SCHOLAR

It is necessary to emphasize that the historical transition from early watchmen to modern police officer has been a slow and deliberate plodding effort. Egon Bittner (1980) accurately points out that the early men-at-arms could not be modernized simply by the infusion of scientific courses of study or the acquisition of academic degrees. The kinds of scholarly, scientific bodies of knowledge existing during the early days of law enforcement were inappropriate for creating police scholars.

Also, many of the academics who instructed the scholarly courses in colleges and universities viewed police officers as unworthy of and not very interested in college education (Bittner 1980). These assumptions, if true, in combination with officers' perceptions that a college education would not significantly improve their positions in the police department, further slowed the educating of police officers.

It should be stressed that regardless of which side of the argument about degree requirements one stands, higher education in police work is certainly desirable. This is not to suggest that any course major in college is applicable to policing, although one might be tempted to make such a case, given the other life experiences and maturation college programs provide. This statement is intended to underscore the necessity in policing for officers to be educated in problem-solving and decision-making skills, along with knowledge of culture, psychology, technical writing, and computer technology. None of these areas can be adequately presented or mastered by students when presented in a programmed 2- or 4-hour module during the course of a 14-, 15-, or even 18-week academy class. As Bittner (1980:79) expresses it:

> The transformation of the conception of policing from the model of man-of-arms to the model of the trained professional whose training stands in some relationship to scientific scholarship, naturally involves the mobilization of specifically delineated programs of study and instruction.

Naturally, the development of such programs and courses of study are not being advocated to foster an image of policing as more scholastic. Rather, the implication is that police need to have greater guidance toward scholarly course work in areas that will enhance their knowledge and abilities as police officers. In turn, police officer recipients of graduate credentials who have been correctly schooled in scholarly methods and appropriate theories can eventually contribute to the scientific community in important and insightful ways.

A word of caution is also necessary concerning the potential in policing for some officers to become credentialists. **Credentialism** typically involves one or the other of two types. First, it may involve an agency arbitrarily establishing a high educational requirement for a position or rank, but one that may bear little or no relationship to the job. For example, the requirement of a master's degree in any academic discipline as a requisite for becoming a police captain. The argument might be made that the graduate school preparation, in general,

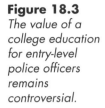
Figure 18.3
The value of a college education for entry-level police officers remains controversial.

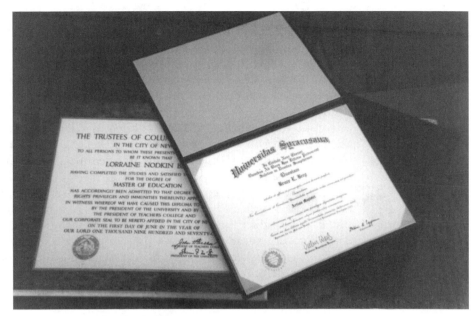

provides a potential administrative supervisor with various necessary pieces of knowledge. However, it would seem reasonable to expect that a master's in a police or social-scientific area would offer greater overall benefit than, perhaps, a degree in zoology, mathematics, or philosophy.

The second and closely related type of credentialism arises when an officer is in possession of a graduate degree—even in a related field—and as a consequence believes he or she should be exempt from various service time requirements (see Shernock 1992).

IS HIGH SCHOOL PREPARATION ENOUGH?

The standard of a high school diploma as a basic requirement for entry-level police positions, and other occupations, has prevailed for the past several decades. It can easily be argued that at one time this standard served a functional purpose, the identification of people possessing superior levels of formal education. But, today, where academic credential inflation has evolved to a virtual art form, the high school diploma no longer signifies—as it may have prior to World War II—above average mental ability or a significant level of educational accomplishment.

Harry More Jr. (1985:306) reports that in 1946, the U.S. Department of Health, Education, and Welfare claimed that less than one-half of the 17-year-old population had completed high school. By 1969, this figure had risen to more than 78 percent. By 1985, more than 93 percent of American youths between the ages of 14 and 17 years old were enrolled in high school programs and the majority of them were expected to obtain their diplomas (Molotsky 1984; Bogue 1985; Berg 1994).

Many people in society, however, claim that while the general population has attained high levels of education and academic credentials, these laurels are unnecessary for basic police functions and activities. In fact, during the early twentieth century, many commentators on policing suggested that policemen, as a class, were usually not well-educated or skilled mechanically or industrially. Police officers were regarded as possessing above-average in physical strength and appearance, but lacking sufficient persistence to acquire an education or learn a trade.

As Harry More noted in 1985, this attitude persists among many critics of contemporary police as well. The assumption is that issuing tickets, directing traffic, and conducting permit inspections simply does not require high levels of education. But these are not the only responsibilities of most contemporary police officers. In fact, in many modern agencies, these more mundane tasks have been delegated to civilian employees or private subcontractors. Thus, modern police officers are charged with more critical and pressing tasks, such as reducing fear and anxiety about crime among community members, resolving major crimes, preserving constitutional rights, neutralizing terroristic threats, investigating organized criminal activities, and assuring public safety in general. The necessity for police officers who are educated, articulate, tolerant of others, politically aware, and knowledgeable of the various social and cultural influences operating in the community they serve should be obvious.

EDUCATIONAL DIRECTIONS FOR THE FUTURE

The argument about the value of a college education for police officers rages on today, but with somewhat less intensity than it has previously. Some of the previous problems involved confusion among both academies and police officials concerning whether a college education for police officers should be vocational training programs. Indeed, many of the early junior college programs that arose during the LEEP years (the late 1960s and early 1970s) may have been more vocational than academic. Today, although some vocational programs persist, most of these early vocational programs have evolved into scholarly, academically oriented programs. Many of these one-time "police studies" programs have changed even their names to Departments of Criminal Justice, Criminology, or Justice Studies and are no longer designed exclusively for police officers or future police officers. Rather, serious students of all aspects of criminal justice have begun to fill the seats in many criminal justice programs.

The debate over where training ends and education begins, and whether more than merely high school preparation should be a national standard for entry-level police officers may not be settled soon. Yet, there is growing appreciation among ranking police officials for the value of a wide-range and in-depth knowledge in police and academic subjects. During the recent past, police researchers and police officials have begun to agree on many of their understandings of contemporary police issues. In keeping with this, one can expect a greater acknowledgment in all quarters of requirements in performance of police functions and their role in society.

Police work can no longer be viewed as an occupation of brawny but brainless people. It must begin to be seen as a skilled occupation of competitively educated, technically sophisticated, empathetic, and humane people. Too, reform and progress in policing must not be limited to the law enforcement community. Rather, as education and practice evolve in police circles, changes must consider the social contours, needs, and expectations of the community (Goldstein 1977; Radelet 1986; Berg 1990, 1994).

Until recently, police reform in America was guilty of "improving the police establishment without having given adequate attention to some serious underlying problems that grow out of the basic arrangements for policing in our society" (Goldstein 1977:8). During the recent past, the gap between police and scholars has grown smaller and consideration of decision-making processes among police, accountability, ethics, broad educational bases, and control have become more than merely strategies for improved police administration. These areas have incorporated substantive social scientific theories, public opinion, and police needs. But, perhaps more important, recent police reforms have addressed both police and societal problems as related to one another.

THE PRIVATIZATION OF POLICING

The history of policing has been traditionally intertwined with privately and publicly supported efforts. Many businesses employ security guards garbed in uniforms that resemble those of the local police, including, in many cases, weapons. The purpose of these private police officers, of course, is to secure their business employers against shoplifting and vandalism, and to provide personal safety for patrons and employees. Private security officers have become common sights in the private sectors of society, such as shopping malls, department stores, on many college campuses, in the lobbies of fancy buildings, and in a growing number of apartment complexes and residential gated communities. However, they have also grown in their appearance in such public sector locations as official security for federal court buildings and courtrooms, as additional security in county sheriff's jails, and in city run hospitals, parks, and recreational facilities.

In New York City, a number of private security forces augment city police by patrolling various sections of the city (Samaha 1997). For example, 29 uniformed security officers patrol a 50-block section of Manhattan. The unit is directed by a former borough commander, and the cost for the service is paid for by a self-imposed surtax on the local property owners (*Wall Street Journal* 1994). Similar private patrols protect Rockefeller Center, South Street Seaport, and Roosevelt Island (Samaha 1997).

Figure 18.4
Private security forces have begun to augment police patrols in a number of cities across the United States.

A

B

Today, about 4,000 private agencies employ nearly 1.5 million people in the security industry. It has been estimated that by the year 2000 businesses, individuals, and organizations will spend more than $100 billion annually on private security activities (Cole and Smith 1998). It can also be anticipated that during the coming decade, private security officers will find themselves more and more interwoven in the public sector of policing.

Many public officials and certainly police executives view the increasing use of untrained or semi-trained private security officers in public policing capacities as problematic (see for example Sherman 1990; Nasser 1993; O'Leary 1994). Other officials see the use of private police in the public sector as cost-effective and necessary in order to operate efficiently. The privatizing of law enforcement functions, then, may have some serious implications in the face of efforts to professionalize policing.

Several attempts have been made to examine the relationship between public and private policing. In one study sponsored by the National Institute of Justice and undertaken by WIlliam C. Cunningham and Todd H. Taylor (1983), several problems of both public and private police are considered. Among other things, Cunningham and Taylor note that both systems do share many similar goals. Both, for instance, seem to secure people and property from harm, identify and prevent criminal activity, and recover stolen property.

The study also indicates that most police officers continue to hold low opinion of the quality of contract security personnel, resulting in strain and discord when interacting with each other. Interestingly, by 1987, 35 states required guards and security patrol firms to be licensed, and more than 80 percent of all private firms were regulated by state or local agencies (Chaiken and Chaiken 1987). Unfortunately, in may jurisdictions, licensing represents filling out certain forms and registering with a local or state agency and not necessarily meeting any requirements or standards.

A GLIMPSE INTO THE FUTURE OF POLICING

It would be nice to have a crystal ball that one could look into and see the future as it actually will be. However, that remains in the realm of fantasy not reality. Nonetheless, one does not really need a crystal ball in order to consider the direction of policing in the future; all one needs to do is consider the basic trends from the past.

Therefore, it is reasonably safe to suggest that during the next several decades, policing will continue to advance in the areas of computers and sophisticated investigative technologies. It is also pretty likely that police academies and in-service programs will foster a heavier emphasis on ethics and integrity than may have been undertaken in the past. Furthermore, one can predict with considerable certainty that police line officers and administrators will be expected to become more accountable for their actions during coming years. Finally, police organizations will continue to move in the direction of professionalizing the occupation. As part of this continued effort, police officers will advance in their educational levels and expectations of educational requirements for entry-level officers.

It is also likely that the increasing violence, drug use, youth gangs, patriot groups, and techno-criminals (cyber-criminals) each will have significant impact on how police resources will be directed during the next several decades. These, along with legal developments, are likely to have significant effects on policing and police training in the future.

SUMMARY

This chapter began with a brief consideration of policing as a career as well as the relationship between policing and higher education. The focus in these examinations and throughout this chapter was on the various attitudes and arguments related to the issue of how much education should be required of entry-level police officers. The question of differences between "training" and "education" were additionally considered.

As outlined in this chapter, training was described as involving various skill acquisitions, whereas, education was depicted as a broader, more scientifically based accumulation of information and knowledge. As the chapter points out, the specific content of training, in itself, is somewhat problematic. In general terms training was described as the material and information offered in the police academy, in vocational college programs, and in the field. In contrast to this, education was described as more closely connected to scholarly college and university programs. The section concluded with the optimistic hope that current and future police reform will continue to move law enforcement in the direction of scholarly police advancements.

Finally, this chapter briefly reviewed another item of concern to police organizations, the privatization of policing and its potential impact. The chapter points out that private police and contracted police services in the public sector are not new. Yet, recent demands for various law enforcement services have required many police agencies to seek out greater amounts of private vendor service to augment their public police personnel. For some police officials, this has been viewed as a paradoxical and unsettling situation.

REFERENCES

Alpert, Geoffrey, and Roger Dunham. *Policing Urban America.* Prospect Heights, Ill.: Waveland, 1988.

Bayley, David H., and Egon Bittner. "Learning the Skills of Policing." *Law and Contemporary Problems,* 47(1984): 35–59.

Berg, Bruce L. "Who Should Teach Police: A Typology and Assessment of Police Academy Instructors." *American Journal of Police,* 9(1990):79–100.

———. "Education Versus Training." In *Critical Issues in Crime and Justice.* Albert R. Roberts (ed.) Thousand Oaks, Calif.: Sage, 1994:93–109.

Bittner, Egon. *The Function of Police in Modern Society.* Cambridge, Mass.: Oelegeschlager, Gunn and Haines, 1980.

Bobinsky, R. "Reflections on Community Oriented Policing." *FBI Law Enforcement Bulletin,* 63(3)1994:15–19.

Bogue, Donald J. *The Population of the United States: Historical Trends and Future Predictions.* New York: Free Press, 1985.

Bowker, Lee. "A Theory of Educational Needs of Law Enforcement Officers." *Journal of Contemporary Criminal Justice,* 1(1980):17–24.

Burbeck, Elizabeth, and Adrian Furnham. "Police Officer Selection: A Critical Review of the Literature." *Journal of Police Science and Administration,* 13(1985):58–69.

Carter, David L., Allen D. Sapp, and Darrel W. Stephens. *The State of Police Education: Policy Direction for the 21st Century.* Washington, D.C.: PERF, 1989.

Cascio, Wayne. "Formal Education and Police Officer Performance." *Journal of Police Science and Administration*, 5(1977):89.

Chaiken, Marcia, and Jan Chaiken. *Public Policing Privately Provided*. U.S. Department of Justice, National Institute of Justice. Washington, D.C.: GPO, 1987.

Charles, Michael T. "Women in Policing: The Physical Aspect." *Journal of Police Science and Administration*, 10(1982):194–205.

Cole, George F., and Christopher E. Smith. *The American System of Criminal Justice*. 8th ed. Belmont, Calif.: West/Wadsworth, 1998.

Cunningham, William C., and Todd H. Taylor. "Ten Years of Growth in Law Enforcement and Private Security Relationships." *The Police Chief*, 42, June 1983:30–31.

Dantzker, Mark L. "An Issue for Policing Educational Level and Job Satisfaction: A Research Note." *American Journal of Police*, 12(1992):101–16.

Erickson, James, and Matthew Neary. "Criminal Justice Education: Is it Criminal?" *Police Chief*, 42(1975):38.

Ermer, V. B. "Recruitment of Female Police Officers in New York." *Journal of Criminal Justice*, 6(1978):233–245.

Finckenhauer, James O. "Higher Education and Police Discretion." *Journal of Police Science and Administration*, 3(1975):450–57.

Fischer, Robert J., Kathryn M. Golden, and Bruce L. Heinnger. "Issues in Higher Education for Law Enforcement Officers: An Illinois Study." *Journal of Criminal Justice*, 13(1985):329–38.

Fyfe, James F. *Police Personnel Practices, Baseline Data Reports 15*. Washington, D.C.: International City Management Association, 1983.

Goldstein, Herman. *Policing a Free Society*. Cambridge, Mass.: Ballinger, 1977.

Locke, Bernard, and Alexander B. Smith. "Police Who Go to College." In *The Ambivalent Force*. 2d ed. Arthur Niederhoffer and Abraham S. Blumberg, (eds.) New York: Holt Rinehart and Winston, 1976.

Meadows, Robert J. "Beliefs of Law Enforcement Administrators and Criminal Justice Educators. Towards the Needed Skill Competencies in Entry-Level Police Training Curriculum." *Journal of Police Science and Administration*, 15(1987):1–9.

Meagher, M. Steven, and Nancy A. Yentes. "Choosing a Career in Policing: A Comparison of Male and Female Perceptions." *Journal of Police Science and Administration*, 14(1986):320–27.

Miller, J., and L. Fry. "Some Evidence on the Impact of Higher Education for Law Enforcement Personnel." *Police Chief*, August 1978:30–33.

Milton, Catherine H. "The Future of Women in Policing." In Alvin W. Cohn, (ed.) *The Future of Policing*. Beverly Hills, Calif.: Sage, 1978.

Molotsky, Irving. "31 States in College Test Scores." *The New York Times* December 19, 1984:B6.

More, Harry W. Jr. (ed.) *Critical Issues in Law Enforcement*. Cincinnati, Oh.: Anderson Publishing Co., 1985.

Nasser. H. E. "Private Security Has Become Police Backup." *USA Today*, 21 December, 1993:9A.

National Advisory Commission on Criminal Justice Standards and Goals. *Police*. Washington, D.C.: GPO, 1973.

National Commission on Law Observation and Enforcement (Wickersham Commission). Report on Police. Washington, D.C.: GPO, 1931.

O'Leary, D. "Reflections on Police Privatization." *FBI Law Enforcement Bulletin*, 63(9)1994:21–25.

Parker, L.C., M. Donnelly, D. Gerwtz, J. Marcus, and V. Kowalewski. "Higher Education: Its Impact on Police Attitudes." *Police Chief,* July 1976:33–35.

President's Commission on Law Enforcement and Administration of Justice. *Task Force Report: The Police.* Washington, D.C.: GPO, 1967.

Radelet, Louis A. *The Police and the Community.* 4th ed. New York: Macmillan, 1986.

Reiss, Albert J. Jr. *Policing a City's Central District—The Oakland Story.* U.S. Department of Justice. National Institute of Justice. Washington, D.C.: GPO, 1985.

Reynolds, Lee H. *Eliminators of Obstacles: Irrelevant Selection Criteria.* New York: Urban League, 1980.

Roberg, R. "An Analysis of the Relationship Among Higher Education Belief Systems and Job Performance of Patrol Officers." *Journal of Police Science and Administration,* 6(1978):344–66.

Samaha, Joel. *Criminal Justice.* 4th ed. Belmont, Calif.: West/Wadsworth, 1997.

Sanderson, B. E. "Police Officers: The Relationship of a College Education to Job Performance." *Police Chief,* 44(1977):62.

Sapp, Allen David, David Carter, and Darrel Stephens. "Police Chiefs: C.J. Curricula Inconsistent with Contemporary Police Needs." *ACJS Today,* 17(1989):1,5.

Sherman, Lawrence T. "Policing Communities: What Works?" In *Communities and Crime.* Albert Reiss and Michael Tonry (eds.) Chicago, Ill.: University of Chicago Press, 1986:343–86.

———. The Quality of Police Education. San Francisco, Calif.: Jossey-Bass, 1978.

———. "LEN Interview: Lawrence Sherman." *Law Enforcement News,* 31 March, 1994:9–12.

———. "Crackdowns: Initial and Residential Deterrence." In *Crime and Justice: A Review of Research.* M. Tonry and N Morris (eds.) Chicago, Ill.: University of Chicago Press, 1990.

Sherman, Lawrence T., and Warren Bennis. "Higher Education for Police Officers: The Central Issues." *Police Chief,* 4(1977):32.

Shernock, S. K. "The Effects of College Education on Professional Attitudes Among Police." *Journal of Criminal Justice Education,* 3(1)1992:71–92.

Skolnick, Jerome H. and David H. Bayley. *The New Blue Line: Police Innovation in Six American Communities.* New York: Free Press, 1986.

Slater, Harold P., and Martin Reiser. "A Comparative Study of Factors Influencing Police Recruitment." *Journal of Police Science and Administration,* 16(1988):168–175

Smith, Douglas. "The Neighborhood Context of Police Behavior." In *Communities and Crime.* Albert Reiss and Michael Tonry (eds.) Chicago, Ill.: University of Chicago Press, 1986.

Staufenberger, Richard A. "The Professionalization of Police: Efforts and Obstacles." *Public Administration Review,* November/December 1977:678–85.

———. *Progress in Policing: Essays on Change.* Cambridge, Mass.: Ballinger, 1980.

Trojanowicz, Robert, and Thomas Nicholson. "A Comparison of Behavioral Styles of College Graduate Police Officers vs. Non-College Going Police Officers." *Police Chief,* 43(1976):57.

"Security Guards Are Hired Increasingly to Fight Crime on the Streets." *Wall Street Journal,* 22 March, 1994:1.

Weirman, C. I. "The Educated Policeman." *Journal of Police Science and Administration,* 4(1978):450–57.

Witte, R. P. "The Dumb Cop." *Police Chief,* 36(1969):38.

Worden, Robert. "A Badge and a Baccalaureate: Policing Hypotheses, and Further Evidence." *Justice Quarterly,* 7(1990):565–92.

QUESTIONS FOR REVIEW

Objective #1:

- Why do many people feel police do not need a college-level education to get hired?
- Why is it necessary for police officers to have more education today than 20 years ago?

Objective #2:

- How might one delineate between education and training?

Objective #3:

- What is meant by the term lazy-racism?

Objective #4:

- How does on-the-job-training work?
- Why do some chiefs prefer on-the-job-training over in-service training programs held at the academy?

Objective #5:

- In what ways does a college education prepare police officers?
- Why might some college-educated officers become dissatisfied with work?

Objective #6:

- Why might a department create a position with an inflated requirement for a graduate degree?

Objective #7:

- Why might possessing a high school diploma no longer be sufficient for becoming a police officer?

Objective #8:

- Why might some agencies use private security officers to augment their own patrols?
- Why do many police administrators look skeptically at using private security officers in the capacity of police officers?

Index

A

Abandoned property doctrine, 192
Accident investigation, 106, 114
Accreditation, police agency, 421–425
Accused, rights of, 173. *See also* Miranda
    warnings
Acute or situational stress, 395
Adhesive tape to collect evidence, 220
Admissions, 165
AFIS. *See* Automated Fingerprint
    Identification System (AFIS)
African-Americans. *See* Race as factor
AIDS, 395–404
    definition, 397
    discrimination due to, 403–404
    implications for law enforcement, 399
    police officers with, 402–403
    police training for, 396–397, 399
    procedures for handling people with,
        401–402
    stress from perceptions of, 395–396,
        400–401
    transmission of, 397–398
AIDS-Related Complex (ARC), 397
Aircraft patrols, 88–89
Alcoholism of police officers, 391–392
Allocation of patrol, 75
Altruism of police, 309–310
Alvarez, Luis, 356
Ameritech Records Information
    Management System, 234–235
Amoral behavior, 342
Amplified-Fragment Length
    Polymorphism (AMP-FLPS),
    218–219
Andrews, Tommy Lee, 217
Anomie, 321
Anticipatory socialization, 328
Antigens (blood), 216
Antivirus computer programs, 236, 240
Arizona Rangers, 49–50
Arrests, 124, 174–177, 347

AIDS-related concerns, 400
    discretion in, 256–257, 259, 260–263,
        263
    gender as factor in, 264–266
    juvenile, 256–257
    probable cause and, 177
    race as factor in, 259, 264–266
    searches incident to, 177–178 (*See also*
        Searches)
    with warrant, 174, 175
    without warrant, 174–177
Asian police officers, 299–300
Assassinations, 35, 59
Assembly, right of, 172
Assize of arms, 24
Atlanta, Georgia, serial murders, 118
ATMs, unauthorized access to, 240–243
Authoritarianism of police, 310, 320–322
Authority
    misuse of, 363
    power *vs.*, 348–349
Automated Control of Evidence (ACE),
    233–234
Automated Fingerprint Identification
    System (AFIS), 122, 211–212,
    228–230
Automatic teller machines, unauthorized
    access to, 240–243
Avoiders (police style), 333

B

Backdoor (computers), 236
Ballistics, 222–223
Baltimore, Maryland
    history of policing, 31
    size of police department, 44
Barrels, gun, 222–223
Baton stage of force use, 270–272
Beat, the, 79–80
Berkowitz, David, 145
Biased witnesses, 158
Bicycle patrols, 87

Biological specimens. *See also* Blood as evidence
DNA typing, 216–219
hair, 219
semen, 219, 221
Block watches, 35, 95–97, 102–103
Blood as evidence, 215–219
antigens, 216
blood samples, 215
blood typing, 216
bloodstains, 215
DNA typing, 216–219
hepatitis or HIV contamination, 215–216
microtrace collection techniques, 220–221
reagents, 215–216216
Rh factor, 216, 221
Blood feuds, 17
"Blue curtain," 311
Blue-coat crimes, 367
Bootable disk, 247
Boot-up, 247
Boston, Massachusetts, Police Department
alcohol counseling program, 392
corruption, 326, 362, 371–372
history, 31, 32
police officer killed, 382
size, 44
strike, 418
Bow Street Runners, 26–27
Branch Davidians (Waco, Texas), 54–55, 351
Bribery, 364, 367, 369, 370
Broward County, Florida, Sheriff's Department
aircraft used by, 89
voluntary consent searches, 191–192
Browsing (computer files), 236
Bruce, Lenny, 8
Brutality
exposure of officers to, effect of, 395
police, 272, 299
Buffalo, New York, police suicides, 394–395
Bulb (fingerprint), 204
Bullets, 222–223
Bundy, Ted, 221
Bureau of Alcohol, Tobacco, and Firearms (ATF), 10, 60

Bureau of Investigation, 54
Bureau of Narcotics and Dangerous Drugs (BNDD), 56
Business Software Alliance, 244
Byrne, Edward, 382

C

California v. Carney, 185–186
California v. Prysock, 176–177
California v. Stewart, 160
Calls
law enforcement, 72
service, 71–72
Canine (K–9) teams, 90–92, 263
Cardiopulmonary resuscitation, 399, 401
Carlin, George, 8
Carroll v. California, 183
Case fixing, 367
Case law, 10
Chambers v. Maroney, 184
Chicago, Illinois
alcohol counseling program, police department, 392
blacks in police force, 300
history of policing, 31
juvenile gangs, 131
police discretion study, 260
police shootings, 257
Puerto Rican community, police discrimination against, 299
size of police department, 44
Valentine's Day Massacre, 198–199
women hired by police department, 288
Chief of police, 114
Chimel v. California, 178
Chiseling, 367
Christopher Commission, 356–357
Chronic stress, 395
Cincinnati, Ohio, history of policing, 31
Citizen police academies, 100–101, 373
Civil rights, violation by police of, 267
Civil Rights Act of 1972, 290–291
Civil unrest, 34–35, 97–98, 299, 356, 372–373, 419
Civilian review boards, 114, 348, 373, 419
Clearing cases, 124–125
Clemente, Gerald, 364, 368
Code of Hammurabi, 17–18
College education for police officers, 415, 430–441

Colorado v. Connelly, 176–177
Colorado v. Spring, 177
Commission on Accreditation for Law
    Enforcement Agencies (CALEA),
    421
Common cases, 122
Common law, 10
Communications, computers used for,
    229–231
Communications Decency Act of 1996,
    245
Community policing, 19, 73, 82, 93, 233.
    See also Community-oriented policing
    (COP)
Community relations, 34–36, 71. *See also*
    Civilian review boards
    citizen academies, 100–101
    citizen police academies, 100–101, 373
    crime prevention strategies, 35,
        102–104
    history of, 31–32
    reducing fear of crime, 101–102
Community services unit, 114
Community-oriented policing (COP), 36,
    97–98
    storefront policing, 35, 99–100
    team policing, 98–99
Community-Oriented Policing
    Substations (COPS), 99–100
Complainants, 146–147, 245
Complaints, 145, 146, 174
Computer crimes, 227, 235–249
    computer manipulation, 243–244
    cyberpunks and cyber-criminals,
        238–240
    definition of, 240
    evidence, securing computers as,
        246–248
    hackers, role of, 238, 248
    hardware and software thefts, 244–245
    internal, 240–243
    investigations, 245–248, 248
    support of criminal enterprises, 244
    terms related to, 236–237
Computer viruses, 236, 240
    antivirus program, 236
    antivirus programs, 240
    time bomb, 237
    Trojan horses, 237
Computer-Assisted Report Entry (CARE),
    230

Computer-Assisted Terminal Criminal
    Hunt (CATCH), 232
Computers, police use of, 227–235
    advantages and disadvantages of,
        227–231
    communications, use for, 229–231
    community policing, 233
    criminal investigation, programs for,
        232–234
    forensics and, 234–235
    large databases, 231
    stand-alone programs, 232–234
    suspect identification, 231–232
    user friendly computers, 233
Confessions, 164–165
Connecticut v. Barrett, 177
Constables, 20–24, 27
Constitutional protections, U.S. *See* U.S.
    Constitution
Control, immediate, 177
Conviction, 125
Copspeak, 147, 313
Corpus delicti, 142
Corruption. *See* Police corruption
Cosby, Ennis, 120
Counterfeiting, 59
County police, 45–46
County sheriff's department, 30, 45–46
Courtroom demeanor policies, 263
Credentialism, 438–439
Credit cards, unauthorized use of,
    240–243
Crime fighter police style, 331
Crime intervention, 71, 92–93
Crime scene. *See also* Evidence
    blood at, 215–216
    documenting, 203–204
    identification of, 149
    investigation, 203–204
    securing, 73–75, 140, 142–144, 263
Crimes. *See also* Computer crimes
    active criminality of police, 364 (*See also*
        Police corruption)
    by AIDS-infected people, 403–404
    committed *vs.* reported, 72
    definition, 9
    deviance compared, 7–9
    elements of, 149–151
    felony *vs.* misdemeanor, 11
    law and, 9–10
    mala in se, 11–12

Crimes *continued*
  mala prohibita, 11–12
  motivation for, 150–151
  prevention strategies, 35, 102–104
  reducing fear of, 101–102
  reports and report writing, 147–151
  solving of, 120–121, 124–125
  sources of information on,
      145–147
  types of, 10–11
Crimes-against-persons units, 117, 118
Crimes-against-property units, 117, 118
Criminal investigations, 139–152
  complaints and complainants, 145–147,
      174
  of computer crimes, 245–248
  computer programs for, 232–234
  deductive reasoning, 141
  inductive reasoning, 140–141
  information sources (*See* Information)
  modus operandi as factor, 144–145
  preliminary investigation (*See*
      Preliminary investigations)
  primary objectives of, 140
  questions to be answered, 149–151
  reports and report writing, 147–151
  scientific nature of (*See* Scientific
      investigations)
  witnesses (*See* Witnesses)
Criminalistics, 197–198. *See also* Scientific
      investigations
Cultural diversity, 299–302
Cultural diversity training, 302
Culture, 312
  organizational, 350–352
  police subculture (*See* Police
      subculture)
Curtilage, 193
Custody, 154, 159
Customs Service, U. S., 61
Cyberpunks and cyber-criminals,
      238–240
Cynicism of police, 320–322

D
Dade County, Florida
  aircraft use by Sheriff's Department, 89
  civil disturbances, 97
  forensics, computer use for, 234–235
  police corruption, 356
Dallas, Howard E., 383

Dallas, Texas, Police Department
  education of officers, 431
  history, 31
  size, 44
Dangers in police environment, 381–387
DARE (Drug Abuse Resistance
      Education), 132–133
Data diddling (computers), 237
Databases
  large, 231
  limited, 231–235
De facto, 180
Deadly force, use of. *See* Police shootings
Debit cards, unauthorized use of, 243
Deceitful witnesses, 159
Decision-making. *See* Police discretion
Deductive reasoning, 141
Deep cover, 127
Defeminization of policewomen, 294–297
Defenses, legal, 268–269
Denver Police Department alcohol
      counseling program, 392
Deoxyribonucleic acid (DNA)
  Amplified-Fragment Length
      Polymorphism (AMP-FLPS),
      218–219
  double helix, 218
  Polymerase Chain Reaction (PCR), 218
  Restricted Fragment Length
      Polymorphism (RFLP), 218
  typing of biological specimens, 217–219
Department of Justice. *See* U.S.
      Department of Justice
Department of Treasury. *See* U.S.
      Department of Treasury
Deployment of patrol, 75–76
Deputy Chief of Police, 114
Desocialization, 317
Detectives, 115–121
  history of, 115–116
  specializations of, 117–119
  television/movies, 119
Detroit, Michigan
  history of policing, 31
  size of police department, 44
Deviance, 6
  crime compared, 7–9
  police, 355–357, 369
Diddled data (computer), 248
Digital signature (electronic
      authorization), 237

Direct evidence, 202
Discovery, inevitable, 182–183
Discretion. *See* Police discretion
Discrimination by police officers, 367. *See also* Women police officers
  arrests, as factor in, 259, 264–266
  cultural diversity in policing, 299–302
  institutionalized discrimination, 298–299
  police shootings, as factor in, 257–260
Disinterested witnesses, 158
DNA. *See* Deoxyribonucleic acid
Double helix (DNA), 218
Double jeopardy, protection from, 172–173
Double marginality, 302
Drug Enforcement Administration (DEA), 56–57
Drugs
  AIDS and drug users, 402
  aircraft used for drug enforcement, 88
  juveniles, use by, 132–133
  police corruption and, 360
  police officers, abuse by, 367
Duckworth v. Egan, 177

E

Educational levels of police, 415, 418, 430–441. *See also* Training
Egan, Eddie, 360
Electronic bulletin boards, criminal use of, 244
E-mail, criminal use of, 244
Emotional impact of danger to police officers, 385–386. *See also* Stress, effect on police of
Encryption (computer data), 237
Enforcement priorities, 364–366
Enforcers (police style), 332–333
Equal Employment Opportunity Commission, 291
Esprit de corps, police, 325–327, 369
Ethics. *See* Police ethics
Eustress (good stress), 390
Evidence, 200–203. *See also* Blood; Fingerprints
  circumstantial, 202
  collecting, 202–203
  direct, 202
  guns, bullets, and barrels, 222–223
  hair, 219
  indirect, 202–203
  locating and identifying, 204
  microtraces, collection of, 220–221
  non-biological specimens, 219–220
  odontology, 221
  physical, 202–223
  securing computers as, 246–248
  semen, 219, 221
  shoe and tire impressions, 212–214
Excessive force, 266–267, 357. *See also* King, Rodney
Exclusionary rule, 178–183
External stressors, 388
Extortion, 364, 367
Eyewitnesses, 157–158

F

Family disputes
  officer's families, disputes in, 391
  police discretion in, 261–262
Favoritism, 367
Fax systems, 229
Federal Bureau of Investigation (FBI), 53–55, 206
  computer systems, 228–231, 235
  professionalism of, 414
Federal Bureau of Narcotics (FBN), 56
Federal citizenship (Constitutional definition), 173
Federal courts, 268. *See also* U.S. Supreme Court
Federal law enforcement agencies, 52–62
Federal Law Enforcement Training Center (FLETC), 62, 278
Federal Marshals Service, 52–53
Federal postal inspectors, 57–59
Federal witness protection and relocation program, 53
Felonies, 347
  computer, 248
  fleeing felon rule, 274–276
  misdemeanors compared, 11
Fences, 25
Fibers, 220
Field search techniques, 190–191
Field training, 319
Field training officers (FTOs), 319
Fielding, Henry, 26–27
Fingerprint powders, 209

Fingerprints, 204–206. *See also* Automated Fingerprint Identification System (AFIS)
  bulb (finger), 204
  development techniques, 209–210
  files and searches, 210–212
  fuming, 210
  lifting and preserving, 208–210
  live digital fingerprinting, 211–212
  photographing, 208–210
  ten-print card, 206–207
  types of, 206–208
Firearms. *See* Weapons
Firearms Training System (FATS), 277–278
First-responder calls, AIDS-related concerns, 399–401
FIST (Fugitive Investigative Strike Teams), 53
Fixed foot patrol, 83
Fleeing felon rule, 274–276
Florida
  education of police officers, 431
  marine patrols, 90
Florida v. Bostick, 191–192
Foot patrols, 82–83
Force. *See also* Use-of-force policies
  deadly (*See* Police shootings)
  definition, 349
  excessive, 266–267, 357 (*See also* King, Rodney)
  non-deadly, 269–270
  permissible, progressive stages of, 270–273
  reasonable, 266
Forensic imaging
Forensic team, use of, 202–204
Forensics, 121–122, 197–198. *See also* Scientific investigations
  computers and, 234–235
  origins of U.S. forensic laboratories, 198–200
Formal socialization, 328–329
Forward Looking INFRARED device (FLIR), 89
Fraud
  computer, 237
French Connection case, 360
Frightened witnesses, 158
Frisking of suspects, 178, 186–190, 263, 347

Frontiero v. Richardson, 290
Fuhrman, Mark, 344–345, 351
Fuming (fingerprints), 210

G
Gang Offender Comprehensive Action Program (GOCAP), 234
Gangs, juvenile, 131–132
Garden Grove, California, 383
Gary, Indiana, police, 310–311
Gender
  arrests, as factor in, 264–266
  juveniles, effect on treatment of, 257
  women police officers (*See* Women police officers)
General assignment units, 117, 118
Geographic distribution of patrols, 78–82
Glass fragments, 220
Glens Falls, New York, Police Department, 92
Glove compartments, searches of, 186–188
Goddard, Calvin, 199
Good-faith defense, 268
Good-faith exception, 181
Grass eaters, 361
Gratuities, 358–361
Great Britain, history of policing in, 20–29
Greek city states, police in, 19
Griffiths, Sherman C., 382
Grosso, Sonny, 360
Guns, 222–223

H
Hacking (computer), 237, 238, 248
Hair, 219
Handcuffs, 190
Handpicking of evidence, 220
Harrison Act, 56
Heaven's Gate mass suicide (Santa Fe, California), 123–124
Helicopter patrols, 88–89
Henry System of fingerprint identification, 210
Hepatitis-B, 215–216, 396, 398
Hester v. United States, 192–193
Highway patrols, 50–51
Hispanic police officers, 299–300
Historical evolution of policing, 15–40
  Code of Hammurabi, 17–18
  computer applications in policing, 229

cultural diversity in American policing, 299–302
detectives, development of, 115–116
education of police officers, 431, 438
English contributions, 20–29
Greek and Roman era, 19
Industrial Revolution, effect of, 25–26
kin policing, 16–17
Mosaic law, 18–19
origins of U.S. forensic laboratories, 198–200
police strikes, 418
reform movement, 33–36
United States, development of policing in, 29–36
women as police officers, 288–291
HIV contamination, 215–216
Home security surveys, 102–104
Homicide Investigation and Tracking System (HITS), 234
Homicides. *See also* Police shootings; Simpson murder case
clearing of cases, 120–121, 124–125
serial murders, 118–119, 145
Hoover, J. Edgar, 54
Horse patrol, 86–87
Horton v. California, 193
Hostile witnesses, 159
Houston, Texas
size of police department, 44
Hue and cry, 20, 23–24, 30
Human Immunodeficiency Virus (HIV), 397–398
Human nature and social control, 4–7

I

Idealists (police style), 334
Illegal behavior, 342
Immediate control, 177
Immigration and Naturalization Service (INS), 57
Immoral behavior, 342
Impersonation (computer crime), 237
Impressions
casting, procedure for, 212–213
shoe and tire, 212–214
Inadvertent intrusions, 193
Incident to the arrest, 177–178
Indirect evidence, 202–203
Individual stressors, 389
Inductive reasoning, 140–141

Industrial Revolution, effect on policing of, 25–26
Inevitable discovery, 182–183
Informal social controls, 6
Information
gathering, 153–154
interrogations (*See* Interrogations)
interviews (*See* Interviews)
sources of, 145–147, 205–206
witnesses, 147
Information systems, 231. *See also* Databases, large
Injury in line of duty, 383–387
In-service training, 435
Institutionalized discrimination, 298–299
Insulation strategies, 394
Integrity, 355–356
Intentional torts, 268
Interface, 232–233
Intermediate service equipment stage of force use, 271, 272
Internal affairs division (IAD), 114, 129–130
Internal corruption, 362
Internal Revenue Service (IRS), 61–62
Internal stressors, 389
International Association of Chiefs of Police (IACP), 315, 350, 413, 421
Internet, criminal use of, 244, 248
Interrogations, 153–154, 159–166
arranging, 162
confessions and admissions, 164–165
deflating *vs.* inflating ego approaches, 164
emotional approach, 163
indirect *vs.* direct approaches, 163
logical approach to, 162–163
Miranda warnings, 159–161
polygraphs, 165–166
preparation for, 161–162
understating or overstating facts approaches, 164
Interstate Identification Index, 206, 229
Interviews, 153–157
computer crimes, 245
guidelines, 155, 157
preparations, 155–156
of victims, 156
of witnesses, 156–157
Investigations. *See also* Criminal investigations
clearing cases, 124–125
crime scene, 203–204

Investigations *continued*
    policies, discretion in, 260
    preliminary (*See* Preliminary
        investigations)
    sequence of, 121–124
    undercover police work, 126–129
Investigations division, 114, 115
    detectives, role of, 115–121
Invisible prints, 208

J

Jurisdictions, law enforcement agencies,
    41–42
Jury, right of trial by, 172–173
Justice System Improvement Act of 1979,
    291
Justice system teamwork, 345–347
Juvenile division, 130–131
Juveniles
    arrests, police discretion in, 256–257
    drug use by, 132–133
    gangs, 131–132
    rights, police policies on, 263

K

K–9 teams, 90–92, 263
Kansas City Preventive Patrol Project,
    93–95
Kelley, Clarence M., 93
Killing of police officers, 382–387
Kin policing, 16–17
King, Rodney, 97, 98, 171, 351, 356–357
Kiting, 117
Knapp Commission Report, 35, 326, 360,
    362–363
Kneeling position, 190

L

Laboratories, forensic, 198–200
Laboratory Information Management
    System (LIMS), 234–235
Latent prints, 208
Law
    Code of Hammurabi, 17–18
    Mosaic, 18–19
    rational, 18–19
Law enforcement
    AIDS, laws related to, 403–404
    discretion in (*See* Police discretion)
    ethics (*See* Police ethics)
    fair access to, 345, 346

history of (*See* Historical evolution of
        policing)
    myth of full enforcement, 262–266
    priorities, 364–366
    selective, 363
Law enforcement agencies. *See also*
        specific *cities*
    accreditation of, 421–425
    AIDS-related concerns, 399
    corruption of, 366–369
    county, 45–46
    federal, 52–62
    jurisdiction of, 41–42
    municipal police departments, 42–45
    organization of, 41–65 (*See also* Police
        organization)
    state, 46–51
Law Enforcement Assistance Agency
        (LEAA), 419–421
Law Enforcement Assistance Program
        (LEAP), 419
Law enforcement calls, 72
Law Enforcement Education Program
        (LEEP), 431, 440
Law enforcement officers. *See* Police
        officers
Law enforcer police style, 331–332
Laws, 6–7
    case, 10
    common, 10
    crime and, 9–10
    regulatory, 10
    selective enforcement of (*See* Police
        discretion)
    statutory, 10
    uniform application of, 9
Lawson, Edward, 264–266
Lawsuits, 267–269
Lazy-racism, 432
Legal abuse, by police, 267
Leuci, Frank, 368
Lex talionis, 18
Liability of police, 267–269
Light cover, 126–127
List, John, 235
Live digital fingerprinting, 211–212
LoJack, 89
Los Angeles, California. *See also* King,
        Rodney; Simpson murder case
    alcohol counseling program, police
        department, 392

Christopher Commission, 356–357
civil disturbances, 97, 98
history of policing, 31
juvenile gangs, 131
"Night Stalker" case, 211
police shootings, 257
risk of injury or death to police officers, 384
serial murders, 118
size of police department, 44
women hired by police department, 288
Los Angeles County Sheriff's Department, 171
aircraft used by, 89
stolen car pursuit policy, 269

M

Magna Carta, 23
Mala in se crimes, 11–12
Mala prohibita crimes, 11–12
Malfeasance, 364–365
Managing force used by police, 270–273
Manual searches for fingerprints, 210
Mapp v. Ohio, 178, 372
Marine patrols, 90
Maryland v. Buie, 178
Masquerading (computer crime), 237
Massachusetts
    police professionalism, 415
    State Police, 48, 211
Massachusetts v. Sheppard, 181–182
Massey, Bert A., 199
McDuffie riots, 97
Meat eaters, 361
Miami, Florida, Police Department
    aircraft used by, 89
    corruption, 356
Microtraces, collection of, 220–221
Military organization of police, 69–70
Milwaukee, Wisconsin, size of police department, 44
Miranda v. Arizona, 160–161, 176, 372
Miranda warnings, 159–161, 169, 175–177, 183, 365
    police discretion in use of, 260
    policies on, 263
Misconduct, police. *See* Police corruption
Misdemeanors, 11
Misfeasance, 364, 365
Mobile Data Terminals (MDTS), 229–231

Mobile patrol, 84–86
Modus operandi (M.O.), 144–145, 230
Mooching, 367
Moonlighting, 356, 419
Moral behavior, 342
Morris, Adrian, Jr., 404
Mosaic law, 18–19
Motorcycle patrols, 87
Mounted patrols, 86–87
Movies. *See* Television/movies, effect of
Moving foot patrol, 83
Municipal police departments, 42–45. *See also* specific *cities*
Murphy, Patrick, 367–368
Myth of full enforcement, 262–266

N

Narcotics squads, 125–129
National Advisory Commission on Criminal Justice Standards and Goals, 431
National Center for Analysis of Violent Crime (NCAVC), 230–231
National Crime Information Center (NCIC), 55, 206, 229, 231, 234
National Institute of Justice, 443
National Law Enforcement Telecommunications System (NLETS), 230
National Organization of Black Law Enforcement Executives (NOBLE), 421
National Sheriffs Association (NSA), 421
Negligent torts, 268–269
Neighborhood watches. *See* Block watches
New Amsterdam, 30–31
New Mexico Mounted Police, 49
New professionals, 412
New York City
    private security forces in, 441
    serial murders, 118, 145
New York City Police Department (NYPD), 43. *See also* Knapp Commission Report
    aircraft used by, 89
    alcohol counseling program, 392
    Computer-Assisted Terminal Criminal Hunt (CATCH), 232
    history, 30–31, 32
    marine patrols, 90
    police officer killed, 382

NYPD *continued*
  police shootings, 257
  women in, 288, 293
New York v. Class, 186–188
New York v. Quarles, 176
Newark, New Jersey
  history of policing, 31
Night shopping, 367
911 calls, 72
911 enhanced systems, 229
Nix v. Williams, 175, 183
Nixon, Richard, 56
Non-feasance, 364
Norms, 5
North Carolina marine patrols, 90

O

Objective police work, 347–348
Odontology, 221
Off-duty police
  police corruption and, 365–366
  stress and, 391
Officer Friendly programs, 101
Ohio, serial murders, 118
Oliver v. United States, 193
Olmstead v. U.S., 180
Omnibus Crime Control and Safe Street
  Act, 35
On-the-job training, 434–435
Open field doctrine, 192–194
Operation I.D. programs, 35, 102, 103
Optimists (police style), 334
Order maintenance, 72
Organizational culture, 350–352
Organized crime, 371
Overconformity, 8
Oxnard, California, Police Department,
  234

P

Paint chips, 220
Parish constables, 23
Parking the hard drive, 247
Patrol sectors, 80–81
Patrols, police, 114
  activities of, 70–73, 92–93
  allocation of patrol, 75
  corruption and, 371
  deployment of patrol, 75–76
  geographic distribution, 78–82
  Kansas City Preventive Patrol, 93–95

preliminary investigations, 73–75, 121,
  141–144
stress from, 388, 395
team policing, 98–99
temporal distribution (shift structure),
  76–78, 395
types of, 82–92
Pay scot, 30
Peace, maintenance of, 345–347
Peace Officer Standards and Training
  (POST), 317
Peace officers, 169–173. *See also* Police
  officers
Peel, Sir Robert, 27–29, 34, 315
Peelers, 27–29
Penal sanctions, 9
Pennsylvania Crime Commission, 360
Pennsylvania State Police, 48–49, 291
Perjury, 367, 370–371
Personal identification numbers (PINs),
  unauthorized use of, 241–243
Personal weapons used against police
  officers, 383
Persuasion, 349
Philadelphia, Pennsylvania
  alcohol counseling program, police
    department, 392
  block watch program, 95–97
  history of policing, 31
  police corruption, 356
  police shootings, 257
  size of police department, 44
Phoenix, Arizona, size of police
  department, 44
Photographs, 203
  age-enhancement of, 235
  of fingerprints, 208–210
Physical abuse, by police, 266–267
Physical evidence. *See* Evidence
Physical strength or skill stage of force
  use, 270, 271
Picks (computer programs), 237, 244
Plastic prints, 208
Plato, 170
Police. *See also* Community relations;
  Community-oriented policing (COP);
  Patrols, police; Police officers
  future of, 443
  history of (*See* Historical evolution of
    policing)
  organizational culture, 350–352

private, 441–443
proactive *vs.* reactive strategies, 92–97
public protected and served by, 70–73
reform of, 33–36, 424
traffic function, 104–106
Police academies, 315–320, 351, 397, 399
    citizen police academies, 100–101, 373
    dangers, training police for, 385–386
Police Athletic League (PAL), 35
Police behavior. *See* Police subculture
Police brutality, 272, 299
Police cars, use of, 84–86
Police corruption, 355–377. *See also* Civilian review boards; Internal affairs division; Police ethics
    components of, 358–365
    controlling, 372–373
    definition, 365–366
    of departments, 366–369
    enforcement priorities and, 364–366
    external factors in, 369
    of individual officers, 366–368
    internal corruption, 362
    line between deviance and corruption, 355–357
    occupational opportunity and, 369–372
    off-duty, 365–366
    on-duty, 365
    organized crime and, 371
Police department speedups, 417
Police departments. *See* Law enforcement agencies
Police detectives, 115–121
Police discretion, 253–284, 347. *See also* Use-of-force policies
    in arrests, 256–257, 259, 260–263
    decision-making and, 253–254
    firearms policies, 263
    juvenile arrests, 256–257
    misuse of, 363–366
    myth of full enforcement, 262–266
    police corruption and, 371
    police liability and, 267–269
    police shootings, 257–260
    policies for routine police functions, 260, 263
    situational factors, 254–260, 263–266
    traffic citations, 255–256
Police *esprit de corps*, 325–327, 369

Police ethics, 341–354. *See also* Police corruption
    authority *vs.* power, 348–349
    code of ethics, 350, 413
    organizational ethics, 350–352
    social contract of policing, 345–348
    standards, 341–346
Police Executive Research Forum (PERF), 421, 432
Police gratuities, 358–361
Police lock-ups, AIDS-related concerns, 400
Police misbehavior. *See* Police corruption
Police officers. *See also* Discrimination by police officers; Police subculture; Stress, effect on police of
    with AIDS, 402–403
    alcoholism of, 391–392
    careers as, 429–430
    corruption of individual, 366–368
    cultural diversity of, 299–302
    dangers facing, 381–387
    education of, 415, 418, 430–441 (*See also* Training)
    group support, need for, 310–312
    honor of, 311
    individual characteristics and decision-making, 264–266
    individualism of, 312
    injury in line of duty, 383–387
    institutionalized discrimination in hiring, 298–299
    integrity, 355–356
    killing of, 382–387
    loyalty of, 311–312
    occupational role of, 327–329
    as peace officers, 169–173
    police personality, 297–298, 323–325
    role of, 3–4, 92–93 (*See also* Patrols, police)
    styles of, 329–334
    suicides of, 394–395
    training of (*See* Training)
    uniforms, 70
    women as (*See* Women police officers)
Police organization, 69–70. *See also* Investigations division
    divisions of labor in, 113–115
    law enforcement agencies, organization of, 41–65
Police personality, 297–298, 323–325

Police professionalism, 27–29, 33–34, 411–428
  professional police style, 332
  shadow-box professionalism, 413–416
  unions, effect of, 416–421
Police shootings, 272–279
  fleeing felon rule, 274–276
  officer's decision to shoot, discretion in, 257–260
  predicting misuse of deadly force, 278–279
  shoot-don't-shoot activity, 277
  shooting reviews, 274
Police strikes, 417–419
Police subculture, 309–339
  altruism of police, 309–310
  authoritarianism of police, 310, 320–322
  cynicism of police, 320–322
  deviant, 355–357, 369 (*See also* Police corruption)
  esprit de corps, 325–327, 369
  group support, need for, 310–312
  occupation role of police officers, 327–329
  police academies and, 315–320, 351
  police officer styles, 329–334
  police personality, 297–298, 323–325
  public image of police officers, 395
  socialization into, 313–314, 328–329
Police unions, 416–421
Police work slowdowns, 417
Political patronage, 32–33
Polygraphs, 165–166
Polymerase Chain Reaction (PCR), 218
Portland, Oregon, women police officers, 288
Ports (computer), 238
Post factum, 178
Postal inspectors, 57–59
Powders, fingerprint, 209
Power *vs.* authority, 348–349
Praetorian Guard, 19
Precedents, 10
Precincts, 82
Pregnancy Discrimination Act of 1978, 291
Preliminary investigations, 73–75, 121, 141–144
  computer crimes, 245
  procedures, 142–144

President's Commission on Law Enforcement and the Administration of Justice, 129, 419, 431
Press, freedom of, 172
Prisoners, AIDS-related concerns, 400
Private police, 441–443
Private property, 172–173, 192
Proactive police model, 92–97
Probable cause, 177–178, 183, 185
Probable cause defense, 268
Problem-oriented policing (POP), 36
Professionalism. *See* Police professionalism
Program piracy (computer programs), 237
Project DARE, 132–133
Prone position, 190
Prostitution, 25, 404
Providence, Rhode Island, history of policing, 31
Public image of police officers, 395
Public trust, police support of, 345, 346
Punishments, 9
Pursuits, policies on
  fleeing felon rule, 274–276
  stolen cars, 269

R
Race as factor
  in arrests, 257–256, 259, 264–266
  juveniles, treatment of, 256–257
  in police hiring, 298–302, 432
  in police shootings, 257–260
Ramirez, Richard, 211
Rapport, 155–156
Rational law, 18–19
Rattle watch, 31
Reactive police model, 92–97
Reagents (blood), 216
Realists (police style), 334
Reasonable force, 266
Reasonable suspicion, 177
Reciprocators (police style), 333
Records Information Management System (RIMS), 234–235
Reed v. Reed, 290
Reeves, 20–22
Reference group, 328
Reform, U.S. police, 33–36, 424
Regulations, police, 343
Regulatory laws, 10
Religion, freedom of, 172
Reluctant witnesses, 158

Repeat Offender Project (ROP), 95
Reports, crime, 147–151
Resocialization, 317
Restricted Fragment Length
    Polymorphism (RFLP), 218
Revenue Sharing Act of 1972, 291
Review boards. See Civilian review boards
Rh factor, 216, 219, 221
Rhode Island v. Innis, 175–176
Rifling, 223
Riots. See Civil unrest
River patrols, 90
Role conflict of police, 393–394
Role set, 393
Rome, police in, 19
Rotten pockets, 368
Routine cases, 122
Ruby Ridge (Montana), 55, 351

S
Safety, maintenance of, 345–347
Salami slice (computer crime), 237
San Francisco, California, Police
    Department
    diversity in, 402
    history, 31
Scientific investigations, 139–140, 197–
    226. See also Evidence; Fingerprints
    forensic laboratories, origin of, 198–200
    odontology, 221
Search warrants, 178–183, 185, 192
Searches, 347
    AIDS-related concerns, 400
    constitutional limits on, 172, 192–194
    exclusionary rule, 178–183
    field search techniques, 190–191
    police discretion in, 261
    restrictions on, 177–178
    stop and frisk, 186–190
    vehicle, 183–188
    voluntary consent, 191–192
Secret Service, 59
Sectors, patrol, 80–81
Security, maintenance of, 345–347
Security officers, 441–443
Seizures, 177–178
    exclusionary rule, 178–183
Selective enforcement of traffic laws, 106
Self incrimination, protection from,
    172–173
Semen, 219, 221

Serial murders, 118–119, 145
Serpico, Frank, 326, 360
Service baton stage of force use, 270–272
Service calls, 71–72
Service weapon stage of force use, 271,
    272
Shadow-box professionalism, 413–416
Shakedowns, 367
Sheriffs. See County sheriff's department
Shift structure, police, 76–78, 395
Shire-reeves, 21–22
Shoe impressions, 212–214
Shoot-don't-shoot activity, 277
Shooting reviews, 274
Silent witnesses, 158
Simpson murder case, 140, 148, 344–345,
    351
Situational stress, 395
Sketches, drawn, 203
Small vehicles used for patrol, 87–88
Smart cards (electronic i.d. cards), 237
Smugglers, 90
Social agent police style, 331
Social behavior, continuum of, 7
Social contract, policing, 345–348
Social controls, 4–7
Social service referral policies, 263
Socialization into police subculture,
    313–314, 328–329
Special attention cases, 122–124
Special Weapons and Tactics (SWAT)
    teams, 133–134
Speech, freedom of, 172
Spokane, Washington, Police
    Department, 99
St. Louis, Missouri, Police Department,
    229, 230
Staff services unit, 114
Stand-alone programs, 232–234
Standards, 343. See also Police ethics
Standing position, 190
State citizenship (Constitutional division),
    173
State law enforcement agencies, 46–51
State police, 46–51
Status set, 393
Statute of Winchester, 23–25
Statutory law, 10
Stereotypic masculine qualities, 291
Stolen car pursuits, policy on, 269
Stop and frisk, 186–190, 263, 347

Storefront policing, 35, 99–100
Stress, effect on police of, 386–405
   acute or situational stress, 395
   AIDS, effect of, 395–396, 400–401
   alcoholism and, 391–392
   chronic stress, 395
   coping and, 391–392
   eustress (good stress), 390
   external stressors, 388
   family of officer, effect of stress on,
     390–391
   individual stressors, 389
   internal stressors, 389
   role conflict and, 393–394
   suicides, 394–395
   task-related stressors, 389
Stress-reaction training, 317
Style of policing, 329–334
   modern styles, 333–334
   typologies of, 330–333
Subculture. *See* Police subculture
Suicides of police officers, 394–395
Sullivan, Eugene, 356
Super-zapping (computers), 237
Supreme Court, U.S. *See* U.S. Supreme
   Court
Suspect identification, computers used
   for, 231–232
Suspicion, reasonable, 177
SWAT teams, 133–134
Syracuse police, study of, 71

T
Tallahassee, Florida, Police Department,
   415
Tariff Act, 61
Task forces, 117–119
Task-related stressors, 389
Team policing, 98–99
Telecommunications Act of 1996, 245
Telecommunications crimes, 240–243
Television/movies, effect of, 119, 198,
   204, 381–382
   America's Most Wanted, 235
   Dirty Harry, 329–330, 370
   myth of full enforcement and, 262
   on police corruption, 326, 360
Temporal distribution of patrols, 76–78
Tennessee v. Garner, 275–276
Ten-print card, 206–207
Terry v. Ohio, 189–190, 264, 372

Texas Rangers, 46–48
Theft, 367
Time bomb (virus), 237
Timid witnesses, 159
Tire impressions, 212–214
Tithing system, 20–23
Tool programs, 234
Torts, 268–269
Total institutions, 317
Tours of duty, 76–78
Traffic control, 104–106, 114
   accident investigation, 106, 114
   citations, 255–256
   left side *vs.* right side approach to
     stopped vehicle, 105
   selective enforcement of laws, 106, 263
Training. *See also* Educational levels of
   police; Police academies
   AIDS-related, 396–397, 399
   citizen police academies, 100–101, 373
   classroom, 320
   dangers, training police for, 385–386
   entry-level policing, minimum training
     hours required for, 315–317, 434
   experience as teacher, 435–436
   field training, 319
   human relations, 435
   in-service, 435
   on-the-job, 434–435
   police ethics, 351
   stress-reaction, 317
Trap door (computer), 237
Trashing (computer data), 237
Trojan horses (computers), 237
Tuns, 20

U
Unbiased and objective police work,
   347–348
Underconformity, examples of, 7
Undercover police work, 126–129
Uniform Crime Reports (UCR), 55, 93
Uniforms, police, 70
U.S. Constitution, 160–161, 170–173,
   175–177, 192–194, 346
U.S. Customs Service, 61
U.S. Department of Justice, 52–57
U.S. Department of Treasury, 10, 52,
   57–62
U.S. Marshal Service, 52–53
U.S. Secret Service, 59

U.S. Supreme Court, 170, 173
  deadly force, use of, 275–276
  exclusionary rule, 180–183
  open field doctrine, 192–193
  police policy decisions, 372–373
  stop and frisk, 186–190
  suspects, rights of, 160–161, 175–178, 264–266
  vehicle searches, 183–188
  voluntary consent searches, 191–192
  women's rights cases, 290
U.S. v. Leon, 181–182
U.S. v. Ross, 184–186
United States
  development of policing in, 29–36
  federal law enforcement agencies, 52–62 *(See also* specific *agencies)*
Universities, crime at, 79–80
Unreliable witnesses, 158
Unwilling witnesses, 158
Urban cohort, 19
Urban League, 432
Use-of-force policies, 260, 263, 266–279
  deadly force, use of *(See* Police shootings)
  discretion in, 260
  excessive force, 266–267
  firearms training, 277–278
  managing use of force, 270–273
  non-deadly force, 269–270
  permissible force, progressive stages of, 270–273
  reasonable force, 266
  shoot-don't-shoot activity, 277
User friendly computers, 233
Uttering, 117

V

Vacuuming to collect evidence, 220
Valentine's Day Massacre (Chicago, Illinois), 198–199
Vehicle searches, 183–188
Verbal command stage of force use, 270, 271
Verbal-psychological abuse, by police, 267
Vice laws, 125–126
Vice squads, 125–129
Victimization surveys, 72
Victims
  as complainants, 145–147
  interviews of, 156

Videotapes, 203–204
Vigiles, 19
Vignera v. New York, 160
Violent Criminal Apprehension Program (VICAP), 230–231
Viruses. *See* Computer viruses
Visible prints, 208
Voice mailboxes, crimes involving, 241
Vollmer, August, 430–431
Volstead Act, 56
Voluntary consent searches, 191–192
Vulgar language, use of, 8

W

Warrant of arrest, 174
Washing, to collect evidence, 220–221
Washington, D.C.
  Repeat Offender Project (ROP), 95
  size of police department, 44
Washington state Homicide Investigation and Tracking System (HITS), 234
Watches, block. *See* Block watches
Watches (patrol shifts), 76–78, 395
Watchmen
  foot patrols and, 82
  history of American use of, 30–32
  hue and cry, 20, 23–24, 30
  police style, 332
Weapons
  firearms training, 277–278
  personal weapons used against police officers, 383
  police policies, 263
  police use of, 257–260, 271–279
  suicide and police access to, 395
Westover v. United States, 160
Willing witnesses, 157
Winchester, Statute of, 23–25
Witnesses, 145
  information from, 147
  interviews of, 156–157
  types of, 157–159
Women police officers, 287–299
  defeminization of, 294–297
  history of, 288–291
  institutionalized discrimination, 298–299
  male officers compared, 291–293
  as matrons, 288–290
  model career path, 296
  police personality and, 297–298
  promotion of, 293–294